ELIZABETH PROUT
1820–1864

ELIZABETH PROUT
Mother Mary Joseph of Jesus

ELIZABETH PROUT
1820–1864

A Religious Life for
Industrial England

Edna Hamer

GRACEWING

First published in 1994 by Downside Abbey, Bath
this revised edition published 2011

Gracewing
2 Southern Avenue, Leominster
Herefordshire, HR6 0QF

*Doctor Edna Hamer (Sr Dominic Savio CP) is a member of the
Congregation of the Sisters of the Cross and Passion*

Cum permissu superiorum

ISBN 978 0 85244 171 8

CONTENTS

LIST OF ILLUSTRATIONS

The drawings on pages 87 and 212 are by H.E. Tidmarsh

This study of Elizabeth Prout, or Mother Mary Joseph of Jesus, Foundress of the Congregation of the Sisters of the Cross and Passion of Jesus Christ, is based on a doctoral thesis completed in the University of Manchester in 1992. I should like to express my appreciation to the University for an Award from the Harry Thornton Pickles and the Jones Postgraduate Studentship in History Funds and to Professor M.E. Rose, Professor of Modern Social History in the University of Manchester, who supervised my research.

I am indebted to many people and I hope that each will feel assured of my sincere gratitude. In particular, however, I must thank the staff of the Central Library and Chetham's Library, Manchester, the John Rylands University Library of Manchester and the Museum of Science and Industry, Manchester; the Public Record Office, Kew; the County Record Offices in Northampton, Preston, Shrewsbury and Stafford and the Greater Manchester Record Office; the Local Studies Libraries in Northampton, Salford, Shrewsbury, Stafford and St Helens; the Registry Office, Stafford and of the National Library, Dublin. I also thank the librarians and staff of the Catholic Central Library, Westminster; the Catholic Education Office, London; Downside Abbey, Bath; Oscott College, Birmingham; St Joseph's College, Upholland, Wigan; and of Wardley Hall, Manchester and the staff of *Propaganda Fide* and the *Archivio Segreto Vaticano*, Rome. I should also like to thank the Benedictine Nuns, Colwich Abbey; the Dominican Sisters, Stone; the Franciscan Missionaries of St Joseph, Didsbury; the Presentation Sisters in Cork, Fermoy and Manchester; the Sisters of Notre Dame; and the Sisters of the Infant Jesus, Nivelles, Belgium. I owe a special debt to the Passionist archivists in Dublin, Rome and Sutton and in Chicago, Pittsburgh and Union City, USA. I also thank the diocesan archivists of Birmingham, Salford and Westminster; the late Fr J Pinkman, St Dominic's, Stone; and Revd C.A. Harris and T.H. Kaye, St Michael's, Stone.

I should like to record a special word of thanks to Tom Longford, Managing Director, Gracewing Publishing for his care and co-operation in producing this publication. I acknowledge the permission of the Central Library, Manchester, for the reproduction of the panoramic view of Manchester.

Finally I thank the late Mother Margaret Mary Sheehy CP, Superior General and her Council, Sister Anne Cunningham CP, Provincial, and the many Sisters of the Cross and Passion who have helped me to understand the life and charism of our Foundress, Elizabeth Prout, whose Cause for Canonisation was opened by His Grace, Derek Worlock, Archbishop of Liverpool on 18 May 1994.

19 March 2011
Feast of St Joseph

INTRODUCTION

Elizabeth Prout (1820-1864) was the Foundress of the Congregation of the Sisters of the Cross and Passion of Our Lord Jesus Christ, closely associated with the Congregation of the Passion founded by St Paul of the Cross in eighteenth-century Italy and brought to England by Blessed Dominic Barberi in 1841. This book is a study of Elizabeth Prout in the context of the Passionist mission to England and the working classes of the Manchester area, where her apostolate took place. It also seeks to examine how her life was influenced by the social circumstances of her time and how, in turn, it illuminates some issues that currently engage the interest of social historians. In this sense the study offers a new look at 'labour history as the social history of the working class', since Elizabeth Prout was a working-class woman who, in an unusual way, was committed to changing the world in which she lived and worked.[1]

Elizabeth was born in Shrewsbury, Shropshire on Saturday, 2 September 1820, the only child of Edward and Ann Prout. As will be discussed more fully in the first chapter, Edward Prout was a journeyman cooper, living in the industrial suburb of Coleham and probably working at the Coleham Brewery. On Sunday, 17 September 1820 Elizabeth was baptised into the Anglican Communion in St Julian's parish church, Shrewsbury. Nothing is known of her childhood and youth, except that she was sufficiently educated to be able to become a teacher. By 1841 she was living with her parents in New Brewery Yard, Stone, Staffordshire, where her father worked for Joule's Brewery. She was therefore already in Stone in 1842 when Father Dominic founded the first Passionist monastery in England at nearby Aston Hall and was subsequently joined by another Italian Passionist, Father Gaudentius Rossi. Within the next few years Elizabeth Prout became a Catholic. In July 1848 she entered the convent of the Sisters of the Infant Jesus in Northampton, where she subsequently received the religious habit and the name 'Sister Stanislaus'. By January 1849, however, she had contracted tuberculosis in her knee. Declared by the physician a permanent invalid, she had to leave the novitiate. She returned home to Stone, where her mother nursed her so well that she recovered her ability to walk. When she was well enough to go out, however, and wanted to attend Mass, her mother became so abusive that Elizabeth decided to leave home.

In the meantime, while giving a mission in St Chad's, Manchester in January-February 1849, Father Gaudentius had discussed with the parish priest, Father Robert Croskell the need for a religious order specifically for lower-class women, who were debarred from choir membership of the existing orders because they could not pay the requisite dowry.[2] Father Croskell was also looking for a schoolmistress. When, therefore, Elizabeth Prout needed somewhere to go and a means of earning her livelihood, Father Gaudentius arranged for her to teach in St Chad's. Either then or shortly afterwards, she was invited to co-operate with both priests in founding the type of religious order they had discussed. Although her lodgings, and later her convent, were in Stocks Street in the respectable area of Cheetham Hill, between 1849 and 1854 she taught in the poorer quarters of Manchester in Ancoats, Angel Meadow and Deansgate. As will be discussed in Chapter Two, she therefore became familiar with the social and moral condition of the working-class areas of Manchester, including those inhabited by the poorest Irish immigrants.

She founded her order within the same period. As Chapter Three will show, Father Gaudentius' intention was to provide an institute that, like the Passionist Congregation, would be both contemplative and active, forming Martha and Mary in each individual sister. Since the members would pay no dowry, they had to support themselves by continuing to work, a few in the cotton mills, others in teaching and the rest in needlework. They also engaged in parish visitation and instructed converts. On 21 November 1852 the first seven sisters received the religious habit. In 1853, however, with the exception of Elizabeth Prout, they all caught fever and several almost died. While they recuperated, Father William Joseph Daly of St Mary's, Failsworth lent them his house at Newton Heath. There, in Newton House in January 1854, Father Ignatius Spencer entered directly into the affairs of Elizabeth Prout's order, when he came to give the sisters a week's retreat. Since the near fatality of the fever episode had made it clear that the convent in Stocks Street was too small, in April 1854 Bishop William Turner, the first bishop of Salford, gave Elizabeth a new convent at Levenshulme, then a healthy suburb on the outskirts of Manchester. Six of the first sisters professed their religious vows in St Mary's church, Levenshulme on 21 November 1854. From then, Elizabeth Prout was known as Mother Mary Joseph of Jesus.

To try to secure a fixed income, Elizabeth, as well as opening a school for the poorer children of the locality, used part of the Levenshulme house as a boarding school for lower middle-class girls. Thus, as Chapter Four will discuss, having already helped to provide and safeguard Catholic schools for the poor of Manchester, she now joined in contemporary efforts to improve educational opportunities for the lower middle class.

Once the first group of sisters had completed their novitiate, Elizabeth was able to make further foundations, in Ashton-under-Lyne in January 1855 and in Sutton and Blackbrook, near St Helens, the following summer. Chapter Five will examine how this division of the community raised problems of administration, as another sister had to be made superior in Levenshulme. When her lack of ability led the order into debt, she and a number of other sisters left. Elizabeth Prout, faced with determined creditors in the financial crisis of 1857, had to beg in the Lancashire parishes, with Bishop Turner's permission, and then in the south of Ireland. In July 1858, as the result of calumnies spread by ex-sisters, she and her professed sisters had to face a canonical investigation authorised by Bishop Turner. Thus she found herself embroiled in what was arguably the most feminist issue in the mid-nineteenth century: the controversy over the rights and liberties of religious women. Although she was happily exonerated on all charges, the enquiry left its scars both in the immediate and distant future.

From 1849 to 1855 Elizabeth had been guided by frequent letters from Father Gaudentius Rossi. In November 1855, however, his superiors sent him to North America, where the Passionists required an experienced and fluent English-speaking missioner. At his request, Father Ignatius Spencer then became Elizabeth's mentor. In 1857 he took Father Gaudentius' Rule to Rome for the approval of the Holy See. Although he received papal approval of its contents in general, he was told that it was too diffuse and should be based on a Rule written by a founder whose sanctity had been officially recognised by the Catholic Church. Since Paul of the Cross had been beatified in 1853 and Father Gaudentius had given the Passionist spirit to Elizabeth's order, in 1862-3 she and Father Ignatius revised the Rule according to the Passionist *Constitutions*. Before doing so, Ignatius wrote to ask Gaudentius' advice. Although leaving the revision to Ignatius, subject to the approval of Bishop Turner and the Passionist provincial, Gaudentius, as will be discussed in Chapter Six, claimed that neither the nature nor the dress of the institute were as he had originally intended. His claim, coupled with the charges made at the previous canonical enquiry, led Elizabeth Prout and Father Ignatius Spencer to define the primary active apostolate of the order as the provision of homes, or refuges, for factory girls. When Ignatius returned to Rome in 1863 for a Passionist general chapter, he received the first papal approval of this Rule. Bishop Turner was then able to give the institute canonical recognition. While they had been revising the Rule, Elizabeth had also, in 1862, been making a new foundation in Ashton-under-Lyne, where she was invited to conduct sewing classes and night schools for the girls and women who were unemployed on account of the Lancashire Cotton Famine. Elizabeth hoped to open a home for factory girls in Ashton but was unable to acquire the land. Consequently, although she left her blueprint for such homes in the 1863 Rule, she did not live to see even the first one opened, for she died in Sutton on 11 January 1864.

Elizabeth Prout was therefore a Victorian woman, who found herself involved in many of the major issues of her day but whose biography has not yet been written, even within her own congregation. In view of the veneration that religious orders normally have for their foundresses, this biographical lacuna is surprising. Its explanation lies in the 1858 investigation. Although, when placed in its historical context, this canonical enquiry was neither unusual nor scandalous, it marked a watershed in the life of Elizabeth Prout and in the history of her order. The most excruciating of her many sufferings, it was the culmination of a series of difficulties that inevitably arose from the attempt to provide consecrated religious life for women of the poorer classes. Since she was exonerated on every charge, it should have been recalled as a triumph, a vindication of both her virtue and her work. All who participated in it, however, were bound to the strictest secrecy. Not even the founder, Father Gaudentius Rossi was allowed to know its details. The novices who were present in Levenshulme at the time experienced the tension and subsequent relief but never received any explanation for either. The order continued to face opposition, because, although the canons who made the investigation thereafter knew the true state of affairs, others did not and could not be told because of the confidentiality enjoined. It was within the congregation, however, that the silence was most damaging. Three of the participants, Sisters Mary Paul Taylor, Frances Wellard and Catherine Scanlon lived until 1903, 1911 and 1919 respectively. As time passed, they were increasingly questioned about the origins of the congregation and the person of the foundress. Afraid to break the secrecy enforced on them in 1858, they said little about either. Thus the origins became shrouded in the mists of obscurity and a dark shadow was cast over the name of Elizabeth Prout.

Perusals of the congregation's documents did not help. The strong admonitions in Father Gaudentius Rossi's letters, which Elizabeth Prout with profound humility had left for posterity, seemed to portray a foundress who could scarcely be held up for emulation. For her part, Elizabeth had been careful to safeguard Father Gaudentius' reputation for holiness and his primacy as the founder. The sisters did not see his letters until after her death. Even then only the highest superiors had access to the archives. With no-one able to explain their contents, successive mothers general firmly closed their files. To all intents and purposes, it seemed that Elizabeth Prout, as shown in the only photograph then known of her, was dead.

In 1926 Mother Berchmans Livesey attempted to write a history of the congregation to mark seventy-five years from Elizabeth's foundation in Stocks Street.[3] To help her she corresponded with Sister Mary Liguori Maguire in Sutton, who noted down in an exercise book the information she found in the Sutton Convent Records, her own queries and comments and further information she received from elderly members of the order. The survival of this exercise book illustrates the almost total dearth of information about the early days of the congregation. Noting that the sisters had lived in Levenshulme from 1854 to 1864, Sister Mary Liguori made the telling comment, 'It is *of these ten years we know so little*'.[4] She hoped Mother Christina Chambers would be able to enlighten her, but Christina had not entered the congregation until 1867 and even her sister, Mary Margaret Chambers, not until 1860. Although the latter knew Elizabeth Prout, she had not experienced the earliest years. It is significant of the silence about the early period that sisters in 1926 did not realise that five of the first seven sisters had left. They had heard of the fever crisis from Sister Mary Paul Taylor, one of its victims, but they thought it had occurred in Levenshulme. They knew very little about their origins.

In spite of this paucity of information, however, certain strong oral traditions remained, which indicate a constant interest in and even strands of unbroken devotion to Elizabeth Prout. It was common knowledge that she had founded the order with Father Gaudentius Rossi in Manchester; that she was English, delicate and a convert, even converted by Father Dominic Barberi, and that she had incurred her parents' wrath by becoming a Catholic; that she had entered another congregation but had had to leave on account of ill-health; that, as well as teaching, the sisters had always done parish visitation and had homes for factory girls; that there were no laysisters; that Elizabeth Prout had not asked for a dowry for admission; and that the order had always been closely connected with the Passionist Congregation. Sisters Mary Paul Taylor, Frances Wellard, Catherine Scanlon and other early sisters seem to have spoken privately to individual sisters, who in turn imparted their own interest to others.[5] In general, however, with the passage of years Elizabeth Prout was lost, her only photograph that of a corpse, taken the day after her death.

Then, about 1950, Reverend Mother Josephine Murray made a surprising discovery. Chancing to remove a sheet of paper that covered the bottom of the superior general's desk, she found a small brown envelope, containing a photograph of two sisters, one seated, the other standing behind her. It had been taken in St Helens and on the back someone had inscribed in pencil, 'The foundress'. Elizabeth Prout was shown as a beautiful woman of about thirty-five, of fair face yet dark eyes and strong eyebrows suggestive of auburn hair, a foundress composed, confident, even serene, dressed in her religious habit, her modified Passionist Sign over her heart, a crucifix at her side, rosary beads hanging from her waist and in her hands the Holy Rule.[6]

A generation later, in 1973, her remains were exhumed from St Anne's cemetery, Sutton, to be reburied in the adjacent new church, beside those of Blessed Dominic Barberi and Father Ignatius Spencer.

Her bones, nestling in the folds of her well preserved habit, identical with that shown on her photograph, confirmed her small slight physique and confirmed that there had been a destructive disease, particularly in the right leg.[7]

While, however, the photograph fleshed out the skeleton and revived the corpse memorialised in 1864, there was still little documentary information on Elizabeth Prout's life, although various sisters and in particular Sisters Olivia Curran, Wilfrid Daly and Anna Maria Reynolds had made their own contributions to increasing it.[8] It was clear that only full-scale academic research could rescue Elizabeth Prout from obscurity and misinterpretation. This present study is, therefore, an unusual voyage of exploration into the source materials of the nineteenth century to reconstruct the life of Elizabeth Prout and, as a corollary, to examine what further light her life sheds on the great issues in which she was so personally involved. It places her in the double context of the working classes of the Manchester area and the Passionist mission to England. In doing so, it suggests that the Paulacrucian spirituality which was the outstanding characteristic of her congregation a century after her death was the authentic expression of the charism which she and Fathers Gaudentius Rossi and Ignatius Spencer had imparted to it. Although some degree of chronology is logically essential, in order to analyse and highlight her significance the study will follow a thematic approach.

Since Elizabeth Prout's primary apostolate as the foundress of a religious order was fundamentally spiritual, Chapter VII will examine her spirituality in the light of her relationships with Father Gaudentius Rossi and Father Ignatius Spencer. It will also briefly sketch the process by which her institute was aggregated to the Congregation of the Passion, with a final word on the roles played in the history of her order by Fathers Gaudentius Rossi, Robert Croskell and Ignatius Spencer. The concluding chapter will be followed by an Appendix detailing the Catholic struggle for education in Elizabeth Prout's Manchester.

CHAPTER I

THE PASSIONIST MISSION TO ENGLAND

1. THE COOPER'S DAUGHTER

When Elizabeth Prout first encountered Father Dominic Barberi, she was already a woman of at least twenty-one years of age. As a convert, therefore, she brought with her into the Catholic Church the qualities and virtues she had already developed within the Anglican Communion. At the same time she also had a degree of hereditary Catholicism, because her father, Edward Prout was a lapsed Catholic.[1] There is no indication of why he formed part of the general religious 'leakage', other than the difficulty of attending Mass when there was no Catholic church within easy reach.[2] He was born, and presumably baptised, about 1795 in the Middlesex area of London. When he married Ann Yates in the Anglican church of All Saints at Wellington on 5 February 1820 he was described as a resident of the same parish.[3] Between those dates, he had qualified as a journeyman cooper, moved from London to Wellington and lost his Catholic faith.[4] He was therefore typical of the age in being careless of his religion, or fearful in the face of opposition, or simply unable to practise. There was an element of obduracy, however, because he could easily have attended Mass in Shrewsbury; he resisted Father Dominic's approaches in Stone; and when his daughter became a Catholic he did not protect her from his wife's abuse. Even when Ann Prout herself became a Catholic and was buried as one, he did not return to church. He eventually sought Reconciliation on 23 January 1863, took apoplexy and died three days later.[5] Elizabeth Prout, therefore, sprang from a mixed marriage in which her Catholic father was lapsed, while her mother was strongly committed to the Church of England.[6] Since many men considered going to church a women's affair, it was perhaps more typical than might be expected of Victorian England that it was Ann Prout who, from a religious point of view, dominated the home.[7] Delicate from birth, Elizabeth was baptised when only a fortnight old in St Julian's Anglican church, Shrewsbury, by Hugh Owen, its vicar.[8]

Arminian in his views, Owen laid importance on both good works and preaching. Described by a contemporary as 'ever attentive to the sick poor of his flock', he was accustomed to visiting their homes, ready with the 'utmost cheerfulness' to 'relieve the wants of the wretched'.[9] He also played a major role in civic affairs, for in 1820 he was the mayor of Shrewsbury. It was under his leadership that the town introduced gaslighting that year, paved the footpaths in 1821 and laid sewers in 1823. Zealous in both his religious and civic duties and also a pluralist, Owen was typical of one kind of churchman of the time and an urban version of the country 'squarson'.[10] He was obviously a local celebrity, who in one way or another had considerable influence on the early life of Elizabeth Prout. Her childhood pre-dated the Puseyite liturgical reforms but she must have received a sense of the devotional from her early attendance at St Julian's. A medieval church mentioned in Domesday, although mainly rebuilt in red brick in the eighteenth century, it still retained its medieval tower. It also had an organ, six bells and, what would have been particularly attractive to a child, a medieval east window brought from Rouen during the French wars and depicting St James the Apostle in brilliant crimson, the Scriptures held aloft in his hand.[11]

Although Elizabeth was reared as an Anglican, however, with her father even a nominal Catholic she would scarcely have been taught to be anti-Catholic, nor was that the trend in Shrewsbury at that time. Owen was friendly towards the Catholic priests he knew: Father James Corne, from 1776-1817, whom he described as 'very learned and worthy and peaceable'; Father Le Maître, 1817-1822, a Benedictine monk driven from his abbey near Douai by the French Revolution; and Father Samuel Jones, who extended the Catholic chapel in 1826, apparently without any demonstrations from the local people.[12]

Medieval Shrewsbury was part of Elizabeth's culture: the castle built against Welsh invasion, St Mary's with its treasury of stained glass, the Grey Friars' house and the Benedictine abbey, as well as the black and white timbered buildings along the narrow streets. Although she lived in the industrial suburb of Coleham on the outer side of the River Severn, whenever she crossed into the town her surroundings spoke to her of a different civilisation. It accorded with contemporary Romanticism and may even have aroused in her a nascent urge for the cloistered religious life.

Stone was different. Although it had some timbered buildings, Elizabeth Prout's Stone centred on the red brick of Joule's Brewery, where her father worked as a journeyman cooper. She probably attended St Michael's Anglican church, a stately edifice, built about 1770 on the site of an Augustinian priory.[13] With accommodation for 1,400 people in pews, it had two well-attended services each Sunday, prayers on Wednesdays and Fridays and Communion eight times in the year.[14] A Low Church of England establishment, it would have supplemented the religious training she had already received at home, at St Julian's and possibly at school.

As there is no evidence of precisely when the Prout family left Shrewsbury, it is impossible to reconstruct Elizabeth's childhood and education. Since she could already write a good letter when she entered the Northampton convent in 1848, she had obviously received at least a basic English education, either privately or at a school. As a young child, she may have attended the Infant School in Coleham, followed by the National School at Coleham Head. Although intended primarily to educate the poor, it was attended by children of the middle and upper working classes. The boys of wealthy parents could attend Shrewsbury Public School. Poorer children were catered for in John Allatt's Charity School and in Bowdler's Blue School, which provided clothing and apprenticing for the poor children of St Julian's parish. The National School seems to have bridged a gap in providing for children, like Elizabeth Prout, of respectable but fairly low birth. It was popular with parents because it offered a wider curriculum than that of the grammar school and admitted girls as well as boys. It also ensured pupils were instructed in the Anglican catechism and attended the Sunday morning service in the old Benedictine abbey. Children under eight, however, were not admitted to Brown's School, as it was called on account of its uniform and, since the Coleham Brewery was on sale from 1827, it is possible that Elizabeth had already left Shrewsbury before her eighth birthday.[15] The National School in Stone was not opened until 1833, so that if the Prouts moved directly from Shrewsbury to Stone before that date, Elizabeth could have had only private tuition or, possibly, travelled to Stoke or Stafford.[16] Although, therefore, it is clear that she was educated, where and how must remain mere conjecture.

Apart from her religion and education, the most formative influence on Elizabeth Prout was her working-class home. Writing in 1866, Mother Winefride Lynch described her as the only child of a 'respectable tradesman'.[17] Edward Prout belonged to the old, artisan class of skilled craftsmen. He was a man with a trade, bringing home a regular wage. As a journeyman cooper in a brewery, his status distinguished him as superior to the apprentices rather than as inferior to a master cooper.[18] Ann Yates made a respectable match in marrying Edward Prout. His ability to give her the security of an income and a home from the Salopian Brewery immediately after their marriage augured well for their future.[19] Elizabeth's psychologically important first seven years, therefore, were passed with loving parents in a comfortable home in the ancient but progressive town of Shrewsbury, which had responded to the opportunities of the industrial revolution by establishing Hulbert's cotton mill, Hazledine's ironworks and Heathcote's brewery in the Coleham suburb. The cotton mill had had to close in 1817 because Hulbert could not compete with Manchester wages for the right kind of skilled workers.[20] The ironworks, however, was a flourishing concern, as Hazledine provided iron for Thomas Telford.[21] The brewery had been founded in 1806 in a partnership between Sir John Heathcote of Longton Hall and Messrs Bent and Caldwell of Newcastle in Staffordshire.[22] Although it was a comparatively small concern, in the 1820s it was in full business, with a daily output of

120 barrels of porter, which its own barges distributed to places along the River Severn as far as Bristol.[23] It seemed that Edward Prout enjoyed the security of an excellent job, making casks for nine, eighteen and even thirty-six gallons. As an employee, however, he depended on his employers' ability to keep the firm solvent. By the mid 1820s Caldwell had withdrawn from the partnership and Heathcote and Bent had died. Although their successors tried to continue the business, it became clear that the firm of John Heathcote and Company could not survive. In December 1827 the brewery was put up for sale.[24] No other brewer showed interest and finally in 1831 it was bought by Hazledine, 'for a mere bagatelle', for storing timber for his ironworks.[25] The Prouts, therefore, must have left Shrewsbury by 1831 at the latest.

There is no indication of when and how they arrived in Stone. It is unlikely that Edward Prout, as a brewery cooper and a married man, needed to tramp to find a new job.[26] Since coopers were at a premium in an increasingly important industry, they may have had a system of directing information throughout the trade. At any rate, when the census was taken in 1841, Edward Prout was living in New Brewery Yard opposite Joule's cooperage, with his wife and their daughter, Betty, his mother-in-law, Mary Yates and a three-year-old boy, Charles Taft, whom they seem to have adopted.[27] Edward and Ann remained there till their deaths, Ann on 10 August 1862 and Edward on 26 January 1863.[28] Throughout those twenty years his social and economic position constantly improved. The cooper craftsman of 1820 was the labour aristocrat of 1860 and especially so in Stone, where beer was of particular importance.[29]

Developed by Francis Joule from a brewhouse in 1758 to a public brewery in 1780 and expanded by his son, John from 1813, John Joule's Stone Brewery, in the mid-nineteenth century, faced onto the High Street with its premises stretching back extensively to the Trent-Mersey Canal, where it had its own company boats. It was an international enterprise, exporting along the canal and through Liverpool and Hull to Europe, the United States, Australia and New Zealand.[30] Edward Prout had found a secure job. Within Stone itself there was a flourishing market for Joule's Stone Ale. Originally a pilgrim centre beside the priory, by the thirteenth century Stone had become a market town. By the mid-eighteenth century it housed a number of independent and professional people, whose residence lent it an air of gentility.[31] It remained mainly a market town, however, and in the 1840s farmers from the surrounding countryside still sold their produce at the weekly corn markets and their livestock at the fortnightly sheep and cattle sales. There were cheese fairs in April and October and a sheep fair in August.[32] Beef dinners, fortified with Stone ale and lengthened by animated discussions on the condition of England, assured Joule's brewery steady custom.[33] This local market had extended with the coming of the Trent and Mersey Canal in 1772. Apart from the opportunities for export, the resident population increased as new industries clustered along the canal banks: boatbuilding and repair yards, wharves for coal, timber and lime and brassworks and flint grinders. Stone exported the agricultural produce of the area, as well as its associated leather crafts. By 1851, two years after Elizabeth Prout left, it had sixteen wholesale boot and shoe manufacturers.[34] Its population had grown from about 2,000 in the mid-eighteenth century to 8,736, although, compared with Shrewsbury's 23,095 people, it was still a small town.[35]

As well as providing for the local residents, Joule's had another captive market in its numerous visitors, because Stone lay at the heart of England's road system. Since it was on the main London-Chester road, with a branch going directly north to Manchester, Liverpool and Carlisle, one of the busiest routes in England, it had been a posting town since 1660, with its postmaster the third most highly paid in the country after Birmingham and Preston. Industrial changes placed it advantageously between the Potteries and the manufacturing and metalworking districts of Wolverhampton, Walsall and Birmingham. With the arrival of the stagecoach, it became a main staging post.[36] Until the advent of the railway, thirty-eight stagecoaches passed through Stone each day, as well as other coaches, carriers and travellers. Soldiers quartered there, as they moved up and down the country. Irish labourers poured into it as they came looking for work each year in the corn harvest. Providing food and shelter for so many travellers became a second trade, rivalling shoemaking. To cater for so many visitors, Stone had about two dozen inns, many offering stables, all offering Joule's ale and most of them open all night.[37]

The passing of the Beer Act and the repeal of the beer tax in 1830 had also contributed both to Joule's prosperity and Edward Prout's security. Beerhouses multiplied in Stone as elsewhere; beer drinking became more widespread, especially amongst the urban working classes, because ale was cheaper and more nourishing than its alternatives. In the towns it was difficult to find unpolluted drinking water. Milk was double the price of beer and even when fresh might cause tuberculosis. It had little nutritional value, because suppliers diluted it and it was of poor quality anyway, because cattle kept for supplying milk to the towns were frequently pastured in cramped suburban quarters and fed with only poor-quality grain. Beer was also cheaper than tea and coffee. In 1840 Londoners could buy coffee for 1½d. a cup and tea for 2d. a cup but they could purchase a full pint of porter for only 2½d.. The working classes enjoyed drinking places as their recreation centres, where they could enjoy the rest, heat and light, the newspapers and the sanitary conveniences denied them in their homes.[38] Because it was at the heart of England's transport system, Joule's could compete with other firms for this nationwide trade. While the opening of the Grand Junction Railway in 1837 had reduced the volume of road traffic in Stone, it had also opened wider markets, which were again expanded from mid century when Stone gained its own station.[39]

Against this background, skilled coopers like Edward Prout were in a favourable position. Without their casks the ale would remain unsold in the vats. Even journeymen coopers could control their conditions of labour and protect their supremacy from the admission of too many apprentices, especially as they owned their own tools and normally passed their skills only to their own sons or to apprentices chosen by themselves.[40] Although his labour was backbreaking and gave him hands like emery paper and a grip like a vice, Edward Prout could feel pride and satisfaction, both in each cask he engraved with his personal blockmark and in his status as a skilled worker. He was a 'respectable tradesman', a craftsman, whose work called for skill and judgement.[41] Unlike his wife, he was literate, possibly educated.[42] He had a considerable income, security of employment, a comparatively high standard of living and a free issue of beer.[43] His home, rented from Joule's, was a well-built two-up-and-two-down brick house, with toilet, wash-house and ashpit, for common use, beside the row of cottages.[44] His wife added to his respectability, keeping a tidy house, clean curtains at the windows and a well-scrubbed doorstep.[45] She and his daughter attended the services of the Established Church.[46]

Elizabeth Prout therefore continued to enjoy the comfortable home she had known in Shrewsbury. She and her parents were respectable people. She grew up morally strong, with a sense of hard work and thrift, which made her competent in household management. With an elderly granny and a little adopted brother, there must have been a lot of joy and laughter in the Prout household. On 2 September 1841 Miss Prout attained her twenty-first birthday. Tutored by her mother in the arts of housewifery, she had passed through adolescence to become a young lady of the artisan class. As described by Mother Berchmans in 1926, 'Refined, intelligent and gently nurtured, she knew nothing but the love of devoted parents, a comfortable and happy home and bright prospects for the future.'[47] English and Anglican, at her own level Elizabeth Prout, like Victoria, her Queen and close contemporary, could feel the world was at her feet.[48]

She was not, however, unaware of a darker side to life. The ale that made her respectable also caused a major problem of drunkenness in the town. In 1840 a notorious local character, known as 'old tramp shoemaker', was found seriously injured at four o'clock one morning and subsequently died. At the inquest the judge commented on Stone's 'want of an effective police' and of public houses open to a late hour, even all night, with the result that drunken men were 'continually rolling about the streets all hours in the night, and frequently on the Sabbath day, cursing and swearing, to the great annoyance of the peaceable inhabitants'.[49]

Although Elizabeth had a personally sheltered life, she was also aware of even more serious disturbances, especially in 1842, a year of industrial depression and unrest. At Longton in June the butties of a Tory mine owner reduced his colliers' wages without notice from 3/7d. to 3s. a day. The miners went on strike. On 6 July they began a round of all the pits in the Potteries, turning out the men and stopping the engines by raking out the boiler fires and pulling out the plugs. Throughout July and into August there were further marches and strikes in the Midlands and proposals to march to Lancashire to close the mills.[50] In this situation Stone's ready drink supply portended trouble. Elizabeth Prout found herself at the heart of working-class problems. There was so much lawlessness in Stone in August that 700 special constables had to be sworn in to keep order. Since, with the exception of only two or three individuals, every respectable man in the town was sworn in, Edward Prout was presumably one of those who helped to control the lower working classes. The local authorities then forbade public meetings and ordered beerhouses to be closed from ten at night until six in the morning.[51]

Already, however, other events had occurred which were to have more far-reaching effects on the Prout household than the plug plot riots: on 18 February 1842, in Aston Hall, scarcely two miles from their doorstep, Father Dominic Barberi had inaugurated the Passionist mission to England; and on 22 July he had been joined by Father Gaudentius Rossi.[52]

2. PAULACRUCIAN SPIRITUALITY
The nature of the Passionist mission to England, and consequently the ideology which Elizabeth Prout first imbibed and then imparted to her own congregation, cannot be understood without an appreciation of the distinctive spirituality of St Paul of the Cross.[53]

The life of Paul Francis Danei (1694-1775) practically coincided with that of Voltaire, whose rationalism he challenged. Born in Ovada in northern Italy, even as a young man Paul became deeply read in Sacred Scripture and in the mystical writings of Sts Francis de Sales, John of the Cross and Teresa of Avila and, later, in those of John Tauler of the Rhineland school.[54] In his interpretation of these writers he is recognised as the greatest Italian mystic of the eighteenth century.[55] In his own mystical experiences in 1720, Paul understood that he was to found an order in which the members would wear a long, black tunic in mourning for the Passion and Death of Jesus Christ.[56] They would also wear a Sign, consisting of a white cross above the Name 'Jesus', which was also in white to signify 'how pure and spotless that heart should be which must bear the Holy Name of Jesus graven upon it'.[57] Paul bade farewell to his family on 21 November 1720, the feast of the Presentation of the Virgin Mary, a date that was subsequently celebrated as the birthday of the Passionist Congregation and, from 1852, as that also of Elizabeth Prout's order. On 22 November 1720 Paul was clothed by Bishop Gattinara of Alessandria in the long, black tunic. He was not allowed to wear the Sign, however, until 1741, when he received papal approbation of his Rule.[58] By that time he had a clearer understanding that his order's unique charism, its distinctive vocation within the Catholic Church, was to meditate upon and to preach Christ Crucified.[59] Convinced that in the rationalism of the period the world was 'sliding into a profound forgetfulness' of Christ's love in His Passion, the 'memory' of it 'practically extinct', Paul wanted to revive that 'memory' and to keep it alive through his congregation.[60] The Sign that he then gave his followers, therefore, bore the white cross with the inscription, within a white heart: '*JESU XPI PASSIO*', the 'PASSION OF JESUS CHRIST' in Hebrew, Greek and Latin, above three nails. This was the Sign that Elizabeth Prout sought as her own, which she wore in an adapted form from her profession of vows in 1854 and which in 1874-5 was finally given to her order with its aggregation to the Congregation of the Passion.

In 1720 Paul left Bishop Gattinara for a room beside the sacristy of St Charles' church at Castellazzo, where he made a forty days' retreat. During it he wrote the Rule for his proposed congregation and, on the bishop's orders, kept a Spiritual Diary recording his retreat experiences.[61] Both these writings embryonically express the apostolate of his congregation: to keep alive the 'memory' of the Passion.[62] Paul used the word 'memory' in the Scriptural sense of reliving, re-experiencing, actually participating in, in one's 'heart' as also understood in the Scriptural sense of denoting in the depths of one's being.[63] The heart of Paul's spirituality was the Eucharist.[64] He saw the Institution of the Eucharist, set in the context of the Jewish Passover meal, as the commencement of Christ's Sacrifice on Calvary.[65] As the Passover meal was the living memorial of the Exodus, the celebration of the Eucharist, or the Mass, was the living Memorial of Christ's Redemptive Sacrifice.[66] Christ was the Great High Priest, continually present in the Eucharist, offering Himself as the one Sacrifice to God the Father in atonement for the sins of mankind. Paul therefore saw the

Sacrifice of Calvary not merely as an event in the past but as constantly taking place in the present. On the Scriptural testimony that when
the Side of Christ was pierced with a lance there came out Blood and
Water, and following the teaching of the Ancient Fathers that the
Water signified Baptism, the Blood the Eucharist, Paul saw the Church
as born from the Side of Christ. He saw the baptised Christian as
incorporated into Christ through the power of the Holy Spirit. It
therefore followed that the Christian, as baptised into the suffering
Christ, must share with Him in continually offering his own life to the
Father as a living sacrifice in the Eucharist.[67] Hence Paul said his 'sole
desire' was to be 'crucified with Jesus'.[68] In applying this doctrine to
the suffering in the world, Paul saw human suffering as presenting
opportunities to enter existentially into Christ's Passion and thus to
attain with Him to resurrection and glorification.[69] Thus suffering was
the 'most precious gift' God could give.[70] It was an invitation from
Christ to help Him to carry His Cross, as Simon of Cyrene had done
historically.[71] It became a means of reciprocating His love, of
achieving immediate happiness and of enjoying a higher quality of life
in union with Him.[72] Meditation on the Passion was therefore to one's
'advantage'.[73] For Paul suffering was not something to be endured in
this world in order to attain happiness in the next, nor was it an end
in itself. It was not suffering that redeemed the world, but Christ's
love that motivated His Suffering. Suffering without Christ was
meaningless.[74] The Father's love was revealed to mankind through the
Passion of His Son. Human suffering had meaning only as a loving
participation in that Passion.[75] To help the afflicted to bear their
sufferings in this way, Paul emphasised abandonment 'into the hands
of the greatest Good'.[76] He saw reception of the Eucharist as an
encounter with Christ in love and abandonment, because by participating in the Eucharistic feast, the believer shared in both the Death and
Resurrection of Christ. Paul was exceptional at that time in urging
people to receive the Eucharist as often as possible and even daily,
because the Eucharist brought Christ not only into the centre of their
lives but also into their 'hearts'.[77] Although Paul's Passionist movement can be seen as part of the evangelical revival that swept across
Europe and North America in the eighteenth century, it had a different
emphasis from Protestant forms of evangelicalism.[78] Paul kept his eyes
on Christ rather than on man's depravity and he looked at the total
mystery of Redemption: Christ's Nativity, Life, Passion and Death,
and His Ascension and Glorification in the light of the Resurrection.[79]
He focussed his attention on the Cross and Passion, because it was
through His Sufferings that Christ demonstrated the depths of His love
and mercy for mankind. The Passion, however, had efficacy only

because it was followed by the Resurrection, and the fruits of the Resurrection were the Sacraments.[80]

Paul saw the Passionist vocation as an identification with Christ in His Passion, in union with Christ in the Eucharist, the living Memorial of the Passion.[81] Various practical consequences followed from this spirituality. The Passionist lifestyle must be radically evangelical. Paul committed himself and his followers to a community life of 'very deep poverty', more than symbolised in bare feet and modelled on Christ's emptying Himself of His Divinity in His Incarnation, Passion and Death; to a life of solitude and silence as a sharing in Christ's loneliness in Gethsemane, His rejection by His people and His desolation on the Cross; to a life of chastity, obedience and penance as a total oblation in union with the Eucharist; to a life of prayer, so that they lived in union with God; and, in their active apostolate, to a life of awakening and keeping alive the 'memory' of the Passion.[82] Thus a Passionist was committed not merely to devotion to the Passion but to a living 'memory' of it in his own person. The Passionist lifestyle was, therefore, both contemplative and active. It was contemplative in its solitude, silence, prayer and penance; active in its mission to bring others too to a similar union with God through their participation in the Passion.[83] It united the ascetic, contemplative life of the Carthusian or Trappist with the missionary life of the Jesuit.[84] Translated by Father Gaudentius Rossi and Elizabeth Prout into feminine terms, it united Martha and Mary. Its solitude was not a selfish withdrawal from society. It was a deliberate mystical death in an intense life of prayer and penance, a sharing in the Paschal Mystery, so that, having died with Christ, the Passionist could effectively evangelise others.[85]

Such a life invited conflict, as Paul of the Cross, Gaudentius Rossi and Elizabeth Prout all experienced, a conflict between the active and contemplative dimensions, between Martha and Mary.[86] To sustain such a life, Paul found strength in the presence and reception of the Eucharist and in the help of Mary, given to him by Christ on Calvary.[87] Paul's spirituality therefore was scriptural, sacramental, liturgical and devotional.[88] Remaining firmly within the Catholic Church, it depended on the authority of an ordained priesthood and it retained a deep loyalty to the papacy. These three essential elements of Paulacrucian spirituality: the Mass, devotion to Mary and allegiance to the Holy See were identified in England as the most significant tenets of Catholicism. In 1720, when Paul first enunciated his spirituality, English Catholics were being subjected with renewed vigour to laws that penalised precisely those beliefs, which may explain why Paul, an eighteenth-century Italian, was so conscious of England and why he associated it with martyrdom.

It was in this context of martyrdom that Paul committed himself to the conversion of England, by which he meant the restoration of England to Christian Unity under the Holy See in the celebration of the one Eucharist.[89] To Paul the unity of the Church was indispensable. Christ had prayed for it at exactly the time He had instituted the Eucharist. The Church had been born from the Death of Christ, in the Sacraments of Baptism and the Eucharist. As the Eucharist was the Sacramental Body of Christ, so the Church was His Mystical Body and Christ could not be divided. How closely Paul's commitment to England was related to both the Eucharist and martyrdom is demonstrated in his Spiritual Diary, in which all his mystical experiences centred on the Blessed Sacrament.[90] Thus, writing on the feast of the first martyr, St Stephen, Paul explained:

> I experienced a special uplifting of soul especially at Holy Communion. I wanted to go to die a martyr's death in a place where the adorable mystery of the Blessed Sacrament is denied. The infinite Goodness has given me this wish for some time past but today I had it in a special manner, for I desired the conversion of heretics, especially of England with the neighbouring kingdoms and I offered a special prayer for this at Holy Communion.[91]

Again, on the feast of the English martyr, St Thomas of Canterbury, he wrote:

> I had a particular impulse to pray for the conversion of England, especially because I want the standard of the holy Faith to be erected so that there will be an increase of devotion and reverence, of homage and love, with frequent acts of adoration for the Blessed Sacrament... The desire to die as a martyr, especially for the Blessed Sacrament, in some place where people do not believe, does not leave me.[92]

Paul's commitment to 'England with the neighbouring kingdoms' was, therefore, an essential of the total oblation of his life, even to martyrdom.[93] How essential an element it was in Paulacrucian spirituality is evidenced by his claim, after a lifetime of close union with God in prayer, that for fifty years he had never been able to pray without praying for England. This life's work culminated in his mystical vision, shortly before he died, of his 'children' in England.[94] As Father Dominic Barberi, the first Passionist to set foot in England, wrote to the Superior General, Father Anthony Testa in 1844, 'England is our portion, our vineyard, more than any other place in the world. That thought was always dear beyond words, and deeprooted in the mind of our Holy Founder.'[95] As the future Father Ignatius

Spencer had already expressed it while still a secular priest in 1840, the Passionists, 'from the commencement of their existence as a body [had] been sighing to shed their blood for England'.[96] The Passionist mission to England to restore Christian Unity was an intrinsic element of the Passionist vocation as understood by Paul of the Cross, Dominic Barberi and Ignatius Spencer. While not committing his congregation by Rule to work specifically for the conversion of England, for even when he died the country was still in the penal times, Paul bequeathed, as Ignatius said, 'a special injunction to his spiritual children that they should constantly pray for its fulfilment'.[97] As 'children' of Paul of the Cross, Elizabeth Prout and her congregation also inherited that injunction.[98]

For Paul, the conversion of England would be achieved by the 'memory' of the Passion. It was a 'memory' that had particular relevance for the English working classes Father Dominic met in the hungry forties. It was also relevant to the Irish who had teemed into England's towns by his death in 1849; whom Ignatius Spencer looked to for the conversion of England; and whom Elizabeth Prout served in the Manchester area between 1849 and 1864. Paul's message was for everyone but especially for the *anawim* of Sacred Scripture: the marginalised of society, the oppressed, the destitute, the degraded, the sinners, in his case the fisher folk, woodcutters and charcoal burners who dwelt in squalid conditions around the town of Orbetello and the smugglers, bandits and murderers who hid in the marshlands along the coast of Tuscany.[99] Paul would have felt at home among the working classes of Ancoats, Deansgate and Angel Meadow and the Irish hawkers of Elizabeth Prout's Manchester.[100] The message he brought was of the love and mercy of God and the value of suffering.[101] Contemplating the Passion as 'a sea of sorrows', 'an ocean of love', Paul taught the poor to see their suffering as the means to mystical union with God.[102] They should see it as a purification of the soul 'like gold in the furnace', enabling them to share in Christ's Passion and so attain with Him to a glorious resurrection.[103] 'Blessed are they', he wrote, 'who suffer hardship, sickness, persecution, ridicule, contempt for love of God. They are more fortunate than the rich ones of this world, than those who enjoy the delights of earth. Those who suffer for the love of God help Jesus to carry the cross, and if they persevere they will thus share His glory in heaven.'[104]

Paul encouraged the poor to meditate on the Passion in order to attain this prayerful union.[105] Revolutionary in teaching lay people to meditate, he rejected the 'deceit of those who [said] that meditation [was] only for religious and other ecclesiastics'.[106] He wanted to bring mysticism into popular life.[107] He taught people of all states of life to seek God in their hearts, placing themselves in the Heart, the Side of

Christ, which he saw as the gate to union with God in prayer.[108] He suggested families might gather together each day for a quarter or half an hour to meditate in common on the Passion of Christ and the Sorrows of Mary, so that all would become saints, each according to his or her way of life.[109] Paul was a spiritual director rather than a social reformer. If sincerely and generously converted into action, however, his spirituality might unobtrusively effect social revolutions, because Paul preached to the wealthy in the same terms as to the poor. Bosses as well as bandits could understand the graphic scenes of the Passion and by meditating on the divine love that inspired them be moved to a voluntary transformation of their lives. It was only in this sense of meditating on the Passion that Paul appealed to the emotions. He led people into mysticism, not emotionalism. Frenzies were never part of a Passionist mission and Paul never gave passionate harangues.[110] He also forbade his missionaries to use lofty, elegant styles, 'not easily understood by common people and uneducated minds'.[111] His apostolic outreach was mainly to the poor.[112] To instruct them in prayer, he told his priests to meditate 'aloud... on the Most Holy Passion of Jesus Christ'.[113] Their very appearance was to speak of the Passion.[114] Hence, and to show how habitual must be their own 'memory' of the Passion, he wrote in his Rule:

> Beloved, you must know that the main object in wearing black (according to the special inspiration that God gave me) is to be clothed in mourning for the Passion and Death of Jesus. For this purpose let us never forget to have always with us a constant and sorrowful remembrance of Him. And so let each take care to instil in others meditation on the suffering of our Jesus.[115]

This Paulacrucian spirituality was the message that, dressed in the same black habit, Dominic Barberi first began to preach in Aston Hall by Stone in the spring of 1842 and that reached the heart of Elizabeth Prout. Whereas Paul, however, had brought it to people who were at least nominally Catholic, in a Catholic country, Dominic brought it to a Protestant country where most, other than Catholics and Tractarians, derided its ecclesiology and where popular Protestantism saw the Catholic Church as the 'scarlet woman'.[116]

3. APOSTLES OF ENGLAND

Father Dominic Barberi, therefore, came to England to preach the 'memory' of the Passion. When he came first in late November 1840, he came alone. When he came to stay in October 1841, he brought one English-speaking companion, Father Amedeus McBride. That he came at all was largely due to the efforts of Father George Spencer.

Born in 1799, the youngest child of George John, second Earl
Spencer and Lavinia (Bingham), daughter of Lord Lucan, George
Spencer studied at Trinity College, Cambridge before passing into the
Anglican ministry and his charge of St Mary's, Brington on the
family's Althorp estate.[117] In 1830, after a chance encounter with
Father William Foley of Northampton and subsequent discussions,
especially with Ambrose Phillipps in Grace Dieu, he was received into
the Catholic Church by a Belgian Dominican priest, Father Charles
Caestryck.[118] Shortly afterwards, when he was studying for the
priesthood at the English College in Rome, he met Father Dominic,
who was professor of theology at the Passionist retreat of Saints John
and Paul on the Coelian Hill. Ordained on the feast of St Augustine of
Canterbury, 26 May 1832, in the church of St Gregory the Great, also
on the Coelian Hill, George returned to England with the blessing of
Pope Gregory XVI. In August 1832 he was appointed curate in Walsall
and in November parish priest of West Bromwich, with responsibility
also for Dudley, in the South Staffordshire coalfield. He renewed the
evangelical lifestyle he had previously followed at Brington, visiting
his parishioners, using his money to build churches and schools and
for himself desiring no more than 'to be so poor as to be compelled to
lie down and die in a ditch'.[119] How deeply he had imbibed Paulacrucian spirituality, presumably from his discussions with Father
Dominic, was demonstrated in a letter he wrote to the *Catholic
Magazine* in 1840, in which, begging as usual for prayers for the
conversion of England, he asked Catholics 'to consecrate themselves
in a special manner as victims of expiation for their unhappy brethren',
to make themselves 'a holocaust of love', to offer themselves 'in union
with the sacrifice of Calvary' for the salvation of the English.[120]

Father Dominic's departure from Rome en route for England in May
1840 had been preceded by twenty-eight years of personal preparation.[121] With the possible exception of the Superior General, Father
Anthony Testa, Dominic, from any point of view, was the most
high-ranking Passionist of the time. Born near Viterbo in the Papal
States in 1792, his parents farmers of an olive-growing estate, he
received some elementary education before their deaths left him an
orphan at ten years of age. Adopted by an uncle, who, although a
gentleman farmer of independent means, saw little sense in a farmer's
having an academic education, Dominic nevertheless, with an old Latin
dictionary and the Bible as his textbook, became erudite in both Latin
and Sacred Scripture. Later he became familiar with the library of a
group of Passionists, whom Napoleon's suppression of religious orders
had forced to live nearby.[122] Endowed with rare supernatural gifts,
Dominic was advanced in mysticism and had already received a
mystical understanding that he would be both a priest and a missionary

before he entered the Passionist novitiate in 1814, as a laybrother.[123] Shortly after his admission, another mystical experience confirmed the previous promise, assuring him that he would evangelise England and other places in north-west Europe.[124] Thus designated as heir to the promises made about forty years earlier to Paul of the Cross, Dominic too found it impossible to pray without praying for England. He lived his Passionist vocation intensely for Christian Unity in England.[125] Without any endeavours on his part, he was transferred to the clerical status and, in 1818, was ordained a priest.[126] In 1821 he was appointed professor of philosophy and director of students at St Angelo, Vetralla. By 1826 he was professor of theology in Saints John and Paul's, Rome, where he met Dr Wiseman and Ambrose Phillipps, as well as George Spencer.[127] By 1840, in addition to being a 'perfect master of philosophy and theology', Dominic had been professor of Sacred Eloquence.[128] He had produced copious theological, philosophical, mystical, scriptural and religious writings.[129] He had written courses in both philosophy and theology, was a recognised canonist and was conversant with mystical writers and the Fathers of the Church. In his own spiritual life he had received the gift of mystical marriage. He had a prodigious memory, wrote elegant Latin and was well versed in the Latin classics and in ancient and modern Greek. He could read and write English, although he had no-one to teach him its pronounciation. He knew of contemporary religious movements in England and was acquainted with English history.[130] He was a seasoned missioner and a peerless retreat master. He had assisted condemned men at their executions, had administered to the dying in a cholera plague and had several times been at death's door himself.[131] He had proved himself an able administrator, both as rector of a new retreat at Lucca, with novitiate and students, and from 1833-36 as a provincial.[132] He was skilled in clerical discussions, had excellent relations with civil and ecclesiastical authorities and had played a decisive part in reorganising and renewing the Passionist Congregation after the Napoleonic suppression. Between 1832 and 1839 he was always either provincial or provincial consultor. As such he had had a voice at the general chapters of 1833 and 1839.[133] In 1833 he had pleaded for a foundation in England.[134] The chapter decreed that, although it had always been intended to make such a foundation, they must await an invitation from an English bishop. In 1839 Dominic raised the subject again. At Father Spencer's request, Cardinal Acton presented the invitation.[135] The chapter voted unanimously to send missionaries to England when opportune.[136] The election of Father Anthony Testa as superior general guaranteed there would be no delay but obstacles began to appear on the English side. The Catholic Lord Shrewsbury, England's premier earl, who had financed Phillipps' Trappist foundation, was unwilling to help because he wanted to put his money into building churches. He was not impressed either by Dominic's appearance nor by his lack of fluency in spoken English and he thought no English postulants would ever join such a strict order.[137] Phillipps could give a house but nothing more. Father Spencer's cousin, Mrs Spencer Canning, who had promised material help, suddenly found herself financially embarrassed.[138] In 1839 Dominic was re-elected provincial.[139] It seemed that the Passionist mission to England was indefinitely postponed. In January, 1840, however, thanks to the diplomacy of Father Spencer, the Passionists were offered and accepted a house at Ere, near Tournai in Belgium, as a departure point for England.[140] Four missionaries were appointed. Dominic, as a provincial, was not one of them. The ex-general, however, who was chosen as superior, pleaded he could not face so arduous a task.[141] Father Dominic was then asked to take his place. He came, therefore, in circumstances reminiscent of those experienced by St Augustine and with the blessing of Gregory XVI, from the shrine of Paul of the Cross on the Coelian Hill.[142] Leaving Rome on 24 May, he established the first Passionist retreat outside Italy at Ere on 12 June 1840.[143] Father Spencer had helped to pay the travelling expenses.[144] Unfavourably impressed by Dominic's poor appearance, the bishop of Tournai subjected him to an examination in moral theology. The examiners quickly realised they were on the wrong side of the table.[145] Dominic was soon engaged for clergy, seminary and religious retreats, asked to write theological texts and became mentor of both bishop and priests.[146] As Father Gaudentius Rossi testified in 1890, 'Father Dominic's reputation for more than ordinary virtue and learning' preceded him to England, where Bishops Walsh and Wiseman held him in 'very high esteem'.[147] 'A child in the simplicity of his heart', said Wiseman. 'a lion in his intelligence'.[148] He was no peasant with whom Newman had little in common.

Even before Dominic left Rome, Wiseman had been appointed coadjutor to Bishop Walsh of the Midland District. Having made his retreat for his episcopal ordination in Saints John and Paul's, he left for England to take up residence as rector of Oscott College. From there on 28 September 1840 he wrote to Dominic telling him Bishop Walsh intended to offer the Passionists Aston Hall in Staffordshire. He suggested he should ask the superior general's permission to go to England to see it.[149] The permission reached Belgium in November 1840. Dominic had already arrived in Boulogne on 26 November to cross the Channel the next day, when he received a letter from Father Spencer, telling him difficulties had arisen and he had better not cross. In fact, the transaction was being administratively bungled and the incumbent of Aston Hall was refusing to leave. Dominic sought sacramental advice from his friend, the Abbé Haffreingue of Boulogne and was told to cross. He therefore did so, as planned, on 27 November 1840, arriving in London by noon and from there travelling to Oscott to meet Wiseman.[150]

He had intended this preliminary visit to be brief. He extended it to three weeks in the hope of seeing Aston Hall but Wiseman thought a visit would be undiplomatic. Dominic's 'first mission in England' was nevertheless, as Father Spencer remarked, 'most fruitful'.[151] He was esteemed in Oscott; he visited Phillipps in Grace Dieu, where he also met Father Gentili; and he read the Oxford tracts.[152] Having assessed the condition of England, Dominic returned to Belgium to celebrate Christmas with his community. He returned, at Wiseman's request, on 5 October 1841, reaching Oscott two days later.[153] Discovering that Aston Hall was still not available, he was again forced to remain in Oscott.[154] He 'picked up English wonderfully', gave conferences to the students, wrote some theological works, had discussions with some of the Tractarians and, most of all, by day and by night, he prayed.[155] On 17 February 1842 Father Benjamin Hulme at last escorted him to Aston Hall with Father Amedeus McBride and two postulants they had gathered in Oscott.[156] With this community, Father Dominic Barberi inaugurated the Passionist mission to England, with the celebration of the Eucharist on 18 February 1842, the feast, as he noted, of the Lance and the Nails.[157]

4. ELIZABETH PROUT'S CONVERSION TO CATHOLICISM

As pioneer of the Passionist mission to England and superior of a community whose active apostolate depended for its success on its own 'memory' of the Passion, Father Dominic Barberi's first task in Aston Hall was to establish the Passionist lifestyle. Accordingly, from 18 February 1842, he and his companions rose shortly before one o'clock for the Divine Office of Matins, followed by meditation. They returned to bed until shortly before 5.00, when they had Prime and Tierce, followed by Mass. After household chores and study, they met for spiritual reading at 10.15. At 11.30 they each took a solitary walk, followed by Sext and None at noon. Dinner was followed by a siesta, after which they returned to choir for Vespers at 3.00. At 6.00 each took another solitary walk, which was followed by an evening meal. After recreation together, they returned to choir for Compline and the Rosary. Then they retired for rest, at 7.30 in winter and 8.00 in summer.[158]

Although Passionists were not accustomed to taking charge of parishes, Dominic realised that, in view of England's shortage of priests, he must accommodate himself to the situation. He therefore accepted charge of Aston parish, which included Elizabeth Prout's Stone and the neighbouring villages.[159] His first public sermon, given in Aston about two weeks after his arrival, was brief but eloquent of his intent: 'My dearly beloved, love one another because those who love their brothers accomplish perfectly the will of God. Love God, and men for God's sake and you shall be perfectly happy for ever. Amen.'[160] In his first full-length sermon, on Passion Sunday, 13 March 1842, also in Aston Hall, he told his listeners, 'Now I am at the centre of all my desires upon the earth. Now I have nothing to do but dedicate all my soul, my heart, my entire life to the glory of God and to your spiritual advantage.'[161] During the following ten days he gave his parishioners a series of meditations on the Passion. 'Consider frequently the Passion of Our Lord', he told them, 'because there is the will of God and there is also your great advantage.' He suggested they might have forgotten what Christ had suffered for them. 'Let us remember', he said, 'with love, with thanks, with gratitude.'[162] Thus Father Dominic delivered the message of Paul of the Cross in the most solemn way possible: in a parish retreat culminating in the Eucharistic Memorial of Holy Thursday, followed by Good Friday's Memorial of the Passion and the Easter Memorial of the Resurrection. During the next seven years he gave a hundred missions or retreats over the length and breadth of England and also in Dublin.[163] Described by Father Gaudentius Rossi as a 'bright and scorching torch' diffusing the 'light of doctrine and divine fire', he was considered by Catholics and Protestants alike as 'altogether extraordinary'. His 'plain, homely, affectionate and chatty' style and his 'simple and humble ways' surprised everybody and stole 'the hearts of his audience'. While in recreation with his community his English was poor, when he preached it was so correct that 'the dean of one district said he spoke exceedingly well'.[164] He looked like 'an angel from heaven', said a child who attended one of his London missions, possibly his last in June 1849 in Drury Lane, the haunt of 'outlaws of every kind' at the heart of England's capital.[165] In addition to his great missionary labours, he was superior of the Passionist mission to Belgium and England, first rector of each of his foundations at Aston, Woodchester and London, novice-master and lector in theology, philosophy and Sacred Eloquence. He built three new churches, at Stone, Aston and Woodchester, and opened a temporary chapel at the Hyde in London.[166] Historians recognise his importance in finally occasioning Newman's conversion. What is virtually unknown is that there is strong circumstantial evidence that he also converted Elizabeth Prout, the future foundress of a Passionist order for women. No official record has survived for Dominic's conditional Baptism of either Newman or Elizabeth Prout. Newman's reception is well authenticated. Elizabeth Prout's is not. It is based only on a strong oral tradition in her congregation and therefore requires investigation.

It is clear from references to her in contemporary documents that Elizabeth Prout spoke very little of her past. Mother Winefride Lynch, for instance, who knew of her mother's opposition, did not know Elizabeth had lived in Stone. She described her as the daughter of 'a respectable tradesman of the town of Shrewsbury'.[167] It is therefore all the more significant that oral tradition, as recorded by Mother Berchmans in 1926, placed her conversion to Catholicism in the context of the Passionist mission to England:

> In coming to England they [Fathers Domonic Barberi and Gaudentius Rossi] commenced their missionary labours in the large cities and towns. So successful were their labours that innumerable converts were received. One of these Converts, Miss Elizabeth Prout, a refined, intelligent and gently-nurtured lady, was set adrift from her home ... Father Gaudentius made her acquaintance.[168]

Since Mother Berchmans pointed to Father Gaudentius' acquaintance with Elizabeth as after her conversion, her evidence supports the persistent oral tradition that it was Father Dominic Barberi who received her into the Catholic Church. Elizabeth's conversion to Catholicism must therefore be dated after his arrival in Aston Hall in February 1842. On 26 July 1843 Bishop Walsh administered Confirmation at Aston to seventy-two people, forty-three of whom were converts.[169] Father Dominic entered their names in the Aston Confirmation Register.[170] Since Elizabeth Prout's was not among them, she had probably not become a Catholic before July 1843. In July 1848 she entered the convent in Northampton. Her conversion must have occurred before then and probably at least two years earlier.[171] It should therefore probably be dated between late 1843 and 1846.

Mother Berchmans placed Elizabeth Prout's conversion in the context of Dominic's missionary activities. In view of her mother's opposition to Catholicism, she may have been received at a mission outside of Stone. There are three occasions when Dominic commented in his mission accounts and letters that he had received women into the Catholic Church: three, whom he called 'ladies', at Lane End (Longton) in March 1844; two 'women' at Wolverhampton the following November; and two 'ladies', mothers of families, at Rugeley later that month.[172] Elizabeth was clearly not one of the ladies in Rugeley, nor likely to have been one of the women at Wolverhampton. Dominic was particularly excited about the three ladies at Longton, however. He received them at the first public mission he gave in England outside of Aston or Stone and for some reason it surpassed his most optimistic expectations.[173] Dominic mentioned the three ladies in letters to Wiseman, to the Passionist general and to Mrs Canning, as well as in his account of the mission, where he states he administered 'Baptism

sub conditione to three Protestant ladies, one of them of a very
respectable family, and another the mother of Monsignor Ben.
Hulme'.[174] No other record has survived of Mrs Hulme's conditional
Baptism. In an entry for August 1844, Dominic refers to a second of
the three as the 'wife' of a 'gentleman'.[175] She was presumably,
therefore, the lady of a 'very respectable family'. The identity of the
third lady remains a mystery. One of the Passionist Father General's
replies to Father Dominic, however, refers to all three ladies as 'of a
not inferior rank'.[176] As compared with the 'women' received at
Wolverhampton, Elizabeth Prout was 'of a not inferior rank'. Since the
Catholic Beech family of Elmhurst House in Stone had connections in
Longton, she could easily have been escorted there and home again.
Until, therefore, evidence appears to prove otherwise, there remains
the tantalizing possibility that Elizabeth Prout was the third lady
received into the Catholic Church at Lane End, possibly on 25 March
1844, and the real cause of Father Dominic's excitement.[177]

What is of basic importance, however, no matter where, when or by
whom she was received, is that Elizabeth was living in Father
Dominic's Stone. Catholicism as Elizabeth Prout heard it, from no less
a person than Dominic Barberi, was the spirituality of Paul of the
Cross. That was the fact of fundamental importance for herself and her
life's work. Her first attraction to Catholicism, said to have occurred
when she looked at the Eucharist during a Benediction service, and her
early formation in the Catholic faith were intrinsically Passionist
experiences.[178] Her whole devotional orientation was towards the
Passion. Through Father Dominic Barberi, the founder of the
Passionist mission in England and the direct heir to the promises made
to Paul of the Cross, Elizabeth Prout, the future foundress of the
Sisters of the Cross and Passion, entered into her own Passionist
inheritance. The significance of Elizabeth Prout's conversion can,
therefore, be understood only within the context of the type of parish
Father Dominic had in Stone.

The Catholic parish that Elizabeth Prout entered must have been the
most vibrant in England. Father Dominic had quickly realised there
were more Catholics in Stone than in Aston. From 27 November 1842,
therefore, he rented a room in Stone's prestigious Crown Inn.[179] Early
each Sunday morning he and Confrater Austin Edgar tramped the two
miles from Aston into Stone.[180] Until 10 o'clock Dominic heard
Confessions, while Austin gave an instruction to Catholics and
prospective converts. Public prayers followed from 10 - 10.15, after
which Dominic preached for three quarters of an hour. Mass was
celebrated at 11.00, Vespers at 3.00. Dominic then took a children's
catechism class, which many adults also attended. At 6.00 on Sunday
evenings he ran lectures for non-Catholics, at which he explained the

Catholic beliefs and practices that were commonly misunderstood: Transubstantiation; Marian devotions; the Catholic priesthood; indulgences etc. [181] Popular Protestantism made these subjects topical and for the Victorians public lectures were entertainments, especially in a place like the Crown.[182] Dominic's lectures, well attended from the start, were soon packed, with as many as 500 in the room and another 200 listening outside.[183] Many came to scoff but 'his great learning and gentle charity' won 7 converts by June 1842; another 7 by 8 September 1842; 75 by July 1843, with another 20-30 under instruction; and 80 by 15 August 1843. By 22 March 1844 he had 86.[184] As Elizabeth lived within two minutes' walk of the Crown, she must have been aware of these activities. Since Dominic quickly visited every Catholic home in Stone, he would soon have heard that Edward Prout was lapsed.[185] It is more than likely that he visited the Prouts in New Brewery Yard. Edward Prout remained impervious. His daughter did not. She was sufficiently curious to attend a Benediction service.

Local clergymen were alarmed at Father Dominic's success.[186] Services were changed to coincide with his. Two new Protestant churches were built, one in Stone, the other in Aston.[187] The Midlands already had ministers conspicuous for 'petty persecutions and atrocious calumnies'.[188] Now in Stone they took to house-to-house visiting, distributing anti-Catholic tracts.[189] One began a course of lectures, but when threatened with a libel suit for saying Dominic sold Absolution in Confession, he quickly retracted all he had said.[190] Like Father Spencer in South Staffordshire, Dominic was regarded as fair play for attacks from gangs of wastrels, many of whom must have swarmed through alcoholic Stone in that time of industrial unrest. In 1841 Newman had laid down his own conditions on which he would take the Catholic Church seriously. 'If they want to convert England', he had said, 'let them go barefooted into our manufacturing towns - let them preach to the people like St Francis Xavier - let them be pelted and trampled on, and I will own that they can do what we cannot; I will confess they are our betters far.'[191] As Dominic went 'barefooted' into the small 'manufacturing town' of Stone, to 'preach to the people like St Francis Xavier', he was 'pelted and trampled on', even almost killed.[192] This daily memorialising of the Passion in his own person continued for some time, until his persevering goodness finally won him admiration, respect and affection from Catholics and Protestants alike. Although, under Evangelical pressure, in the years after his death many of the Catholics lapsed again, Father Dominic's 'zeal and sanctity' left a 'deep impression on the hearts of the people'.[193]

In his parochial work Dominic paid special attention to catechesis, particularly necessary in view of the general religious ignorance amongst English Catholics, for there could be neither Catholic practice nor ecumenical dialogue at grassroots level unless Catholics knew what they believed and why. He was so anxious that the sermon given at Mass should be accurately expressed that he himself wrote the homily for his Italian confreres to read, until he was sure they knew English well enough to formulate their catechesis clearly.[194] 'Very anxious' that the Catholic children should be 'well-instructed' in Catholic doctrine and practice and 'well-prepared for the reception of the Sacraments', he provided two Sunday schools, taken by the priests, in Aston Hall.[195] From 5-13 April 1843 he preached a parish retreat each morning in the assembly room of the Crown Inn and in the evenings in Aston Hall chapel. Elizabeth Prout had ample opportunity to see and hear him.

She soon had the chance to visit a Catholic church, only two minutes' walk from her home. The increase in Mass attendance in Stone necessitated Dominic's building a church. He asked Pugin to design a church-school on a piece of land donated by Mr James Beech.[196] The church was opened on 22 April 1844, the school the next day, the feast of St George, with twenty-four children and two teachers.[197] In going to and from his church, Father Dominic walked past Elizabeth's house. Once she had become a Catholic, it was in that church that she attended Mass and received the Sacraments.

Dominic encouraged the laity to take an active part in the life of the parish. In 1843 he established a committee of twelve men to take responsibility for the church-school fund.[198] In Stone and Aston he set up a Catholic Society, which held religious discussions on Sunday afternoons, women meeting in his church-school, the men going out to Aston Hall.[199] He allowed previously lapsed Catholics and converts he had himself instructed to assist him in instructing others, so that Elizabeth may have learnt her first teaching skills in this context.[200] Dominic thus strengthened the faith of his assistants, as well as giving them, women included, a ministry in the Church and a solidarity with other Catholics, an important consideration because so many converts, like Elizabeth Prout, had to suffer isolation and even persecution from their families and former friends.[201]

Father Dominic quickly realised there was no possibility of England's conversion to Catholicism *in globo*. There was 'too much prejudice, egoism and indifference.' The Catholics were 'cold, rather egoistic and lovers of their own convenience', even 'downright scandalous, drunkards, blasphemers etc., the greatest obstacle to the conversion of Protestants', while the converts, he discovered, were 'weaker than reeds'.[202] While 'English influence, English energy and might' far surpassed 'that of any other nation', Catholics were extremely ignorant, converts 'cold and careless' and the majority of Protestants 'immersed in a sea of utter indifference to religion'.[203] The spiritual condition of England was poor; Christ's Passion mainly forgotten.

Father Dominic had come to England to live and preach the 'memory' of the Passion. He was seeking the conversion of Catholics as well as of Protestants. After 300 years of persecution, social ostracism and lack of a regular Catholic existence, the English Catholics needed to be strengthened in their faith, their devotions united with Tridentine reforms.[204] As a Passionist, Dominic took especial pleasure in reintroducing into England, privately in the grounds of Aston retreat, the Eucharistic devotion of a Corpus Christi procession. His first, on the feast of Corpus Christi itself, 6 June 1844, was so successful that he repeated it the following Sunday, when 1,000 people attended, half of them Protestant. His next in 1845 attracted at least 2,000.[205] It would be most surprising if Elizabeth Prout had not attended on at least one occasion.

Although on his missions Dominic refrained from introducing either Sacramental or Marian processions, in Stone he liked a splendid liturgy, thus answering the people's need for a devotional religion.[206] He engaged both Pugin and Hansom to design his churches.[207] He made good use of the Stone band in his processions and at the opening of his church-school.[208] He established a choir at Aston and instructed its members in Gregorian Chant.[209] They became so skilled that in 1846 Father Gaudentius invited them to sing at a mission he was giving at Great Haywood.[210] At Woodchester, near Stroud in Gloucestershire, Dominic rejoiced to have an organ. He hoped for a religious who could play it and asked the general to send him priests who could sing.[211] English Catholics were not accustomed to singing hymns, because it would have been too dangerous in penal days. In encouraging congregational hymn singing, therefore, Dominic helped to pull the English Catholic community out of its penal chains. He gave the working classes a Catholic culture. Their religion became something to sing about. Since they had no repertoire, some of the Anglican clergymen converts, notably Father Faber, wrote a number of new hymns, while other priests translated and composed music for Catholic classics, which were introduced at missions.[212]

In Aston and Stone Dominic 'had special affection for the poor and indigent', whom he visited in their homes and whose poverty he shared, for Aston Hall was in such bad condition that Wiseman admitted it needed to be demolished.[213] In January 1847, when the bishop of Kerry established a famine relief fund, Dominic offered to sell a surplus chalice for Irish relief. He and his community reduced their already meagre diet to save money to send to Ireland and when the Irish feverstricken refugees came into Stone, the Passionists were indefatigable in their attendance.[214] Father Dominic took nothing for burials in the grounds of Aston Hall, not even for the grave, and he refused to charge pew rent.[215] He did encourage offertory collections.[216] Even the 'widow's mite' was not only the parishioner's just contribution to the upkeep of the church but also, in Paulacrucian spirituality, the symbol of the donor, in union with Christ, as a sacrificial victim. Dominic's work as a parish priest was so appreciated by the English clergy that they described him as labouring 'with unexampled diligence and success'.[217] As a Passionist, however, he had a wider mission. He inaugurated that evangelical apostolate in Manchester in September 1843 with a sermon in St Mary's, Mulberry Street on Christian Unity.[218] Thus he pioneered the Passionist mission to Manchester, which in her own way Elizabeth Prout was to continue.

After her conversion, she would have met both Fathers Gaudentius Rossi and George Spencer. The latter entered the novitiate in Aston Hall in 1846, was clothed as Father Ignatius on 5 January 1847 and was professed on 6 January 1848.[219] Father Gaudentius was the first Italian priest to join Dominic on the English mission. Born in 1817 at Ospidaletti near Genoa, he entered the novitiate in 1836, was professed in 1837 and ordained a priest on 19 December 1840. He arrived in England on 22 July 1842.[220] At first, however, he had difficulty in learning English and so did not begin his missionary apostolate until 1844.[221] In March 1848 he gave a mission in Northampton, during which he met the Sisters of the Infant Jesus.[222] Founded in Nivelles, Belgium in 1835 by Mother Gertrude Desbille under the guidance of a Jesuit, Father Leblanc for the education of poor children, they had made a foundation in Northampton in 1845.[223] Although they normally required a dowry, they were willing to make exceptions in special circumstances.[224] When Gaudentius returned to Stone in early April, he discussed her vocation and these sisters with Elizabeth Prout. Since, although personally attractive, she had still not married before the age of twenty-seven, it seems that a vocation to consecrated virginity quickly followed her conversion.[225] Her lack of a dowry would have prevented her entering a convent, however, until she heard of these sisters. In July 1848 she joined them.[226]

Although Elizabeth's stay in Northampton was short, it was crucially important. Northampton, like Stone, had a boot and shoe industry. The sisters had a day school, in which they gave a basic education; an evening school for the girls who were working during the day; a Sunday school; and a workroom, where poor girls might 'learn to obtain a decent livelihood by their needle' without having to resort to shops and factories, where they 'would too often meet bad companions, who would corrupt their morals and injure their reputation'.[227] By participating, as even postulants did, in the sisters' apostolic works, instructing converts and teaching Catholic doctrine in the schools, according to the exact catechesis of Father Leblanc, Elizabeth served an apprenticeship for the active apostolate of her own congregation.[228]

She also received her own novitiate training, which she was later to impart to others. She learned how to recite the Little Office of the Virgin Mary in Latin. She experienced religious community life. She learned about structures of government, the horarium, religious customs, how religious poverty was lived, what religious obedience entailed and what types of furniture and fittings were necessary, all of which was basic to her own later establishment of a religious order. Significantly, she discovered that the Paulacrucian spirituality she had imbibed in Stone from Father Dominic and other Passionists was further enriched by her experience of living a Rule which, although specifically directed towards the Infancy of Christ, was actually oriented towards His Passion.[229] Like Paul of the Cross and his Passionists, she was able to link the Nativity, Infancy and Calvary.[230] That was to be of fundamental importance in her application of Passionist spirituality to her own congregation. A fervent novice, Elizabeth was very happy in Northampton, where she received the religious habit and the name 'Sister Stanislaus'.[231] By late January 1849, however, she had swellings in her knees, which the doctor said would make her 'a confirmed invalid'.[232] About early February 1849 she returned home to Stone.[233]

Her mother nursed her so well that Elizabeth did walk again. When she wanted to practise her Catholicism, however, she met with opposition. Thus she found herself deeply involved in three of the main issues of the day: the subjection of an unmarried daughter under her parents' roof; the hostility often experienced by converts to Catholicism; and popular suspicion of conventual life.[234] She had returned from the convent broken in health, thus apparently lending substance to sensational speculations about religious life and the vagaries of Romanism.[235] 'You who have had the happiness of being a Catholic from your birth', wrote Dalgairns to Father Dominic in 1845, 'cannot conceive the pain which Protestant parents feel at the notion of their children becoming Catholics.'[236] Mistress of her Victorian household, Ann Prout refused Elizabeth any breakfast when she returned from Mass and Holy Communion and 'very frequently gave her blows accompanied with abusive language'.[237] Elizabeth realised she must choose between her Catholicism and her home. She chose her Catholicism.

If her position at home was untenable, however, its alternative was stark. In 1844 Father Gaudentius had noted four converts in Cheadle who had had to make 'great sacrifice to flesh and blood'.[238] As well as flouting social convention, Elizabeth, as a well-beloved daughter, was making no small sacrifice in deciding to walk out of her parents' lives.[239] Moreover, she had nowhere to go. 'It was a hard struggle for me who had nothing in a pecuniary sense to lose by the change', said

Captain Charles Pakenham in 1850, referring to his own conversion to Catholicism. 'What then must be the difficulty where Rome means penury or almost starvation?'[240] Elizabeth was taking a real risk, for not only was she remaining a Catholic but she was also seeking readmission to a novitiate, this time in Belgium.[241] If accepted and able to persevere, she might lead a happy and useful life from the security of her home in the convent.[242] If she were refused admission, or if her health broke down again, she would be the scorn of society. In 1850 she would be thirty. Most girls of her class were married by twenty-five.[243] She would be considered to have 'failed in business', a spinster, the butt of popular jokes. From a social point of view, in persisting in her desire for religious life, she was offering herself the possibility of emotional and financial bankruptcy.[244]

Even if later successful in conventual life, her immediate future in 1849 was bleak. She was destitute and must find a way of earning her living. Too respectable to be a domestic servant, shop girl or factory worker, she must become a seamstress or a teacher. Needlework would condemn her to a life of honourable destitution, with ultimate blindness a likelihood and, in her case, consumption a certainty. She could teach in a classroom or perhaps find employment as a private governess. The latter would provide her with a home, although she would be no more than a povertystricken, if genteel, housemaid.[245] She would have difficulty in finding a Catholic home, however, because Catholics who could afford a governess were more likely to send their daughters to convent boarding schools, which had become plentiful in England since the return of the enclosed orders at the French Revolution.[246] She had no choice but to find a classroom.[247] She had become one of the *anawim* for whom Paulacrucian spirituality had a special message. She must now unite her own sufferings with those of Christ in His Passion and Death to transform her life into an identification with His. She discussed her situation with Father Gaudentius Rossi. Having given a mission in St Chad's, Manchester in early 1849, he knew the parish clergy were looking for a schoolmistress.[248] It was arranged that Elizabeth should take the post. Thus, probably shortly after Father Dominic's death, Elizabeth Prout, a woman and alone, left Stone for 'Cottonopolis', then in the throes of cholera.[249]

CHAPTER II

ELIZABETH PROUT'S MANCHESTER

1. A CLASS SOCIETY

Elizabeth Prout came to Manchester in 1849 as a result of the Passionist mission given in St Chad's earlier in the year by Fathers Gaudentius Rossi and Joseph Bunn. Since she came to teach in St Chad's school, it is probable that Father Croskell found her the lodgings she still occupied at 58 Stocks Street when the census was taken in 1851.[1] Stocks Street lay behind St Chad's new church, built in 1847 at Red Bank and thus bridging the affluent area of Cheetham Hill and the working-class district of Angel Meadow.[2]

As described in the 1851 census, 58 Stocks Street was tenanted by a Miss Hannah Rayson, a twenty-six-year-old schoolmistress. In addition to her house servant and Elizabeth Prout, she had another lodger, a William B. Gates, an unmarried man of thirty-five, who was a clerk in the post office.[3] As compared with some of the houses in Stocks Street, number 58 was fairly small and had no garden but in the respectable area of lower Cheetham Hill it was a suitable lodging for a single lady of Elizabeth's breeding. According to the Poor Rate Book of 1852, it had a gross estimated rental of 14 guineas and a rateable value of £12 10s.[4] In August, 1851 Elizabeth Prout rented 69 Stocks Street, at £20 a year.[5] It was a larger house than number 58, with a back yard, toilet and ashpit.[6] In 1851 it had been inhabited by James Conry, an umbrella manufacturer, aged thirty-two and born in Ireland; his wife and daughter, both born in Manchester; and two English servants: a thirty-five-year-old woman and her daughter.[7] A record of its rateable value in 1852 has not survived but, three years earlier, in 1849, it had had a gross estimated rental of £18, with a rateable value of £15.[8]

As illustrated even by these two houses, Stocks Street on windy Cheetham Hill was a respectable and healthy place in which to live. The houses had sanitary amenities and four or five bedrooms. They were also comparatively new in 1849. They had not existed in 1794, when a map of the district showed Stocks House inhabited by R. Ridings, Esquire and the adjacent lands as belonging to the earl of Derby.[9] Like other landowners at the time, the earl was able to rent out his land very profitably for urban development.[10] His ownership was reflected in the names of the streets near Stocks Street in 1851: Derby Street, Stanley Street and Knowsley Street, which had still not been paved in January 1849, when the Passionists gave their mission.[11] Probably, therefore, these houses were some of the 1,600 or so built in Manchester in 1846 or of the additional 500 then under construction.[12] On the Cheetham Hill side, St Chad's was a new church in a newly-developed area. Its priests had still to build up its parish into a worshipping community and that was one reason why they had had a Passionist mission.

Elizabeth's neighbours in Stocks Street were mainly English, tending to be respectable tradesmen, such as cabinet makers, shoemakers, tailors, bookbinders, brewers, artists, master grocers and master wheelwrights. Many of them took in lodgers of a similar class, such as a calico salesman, a clerk, a merchant and a cotton manufacturer. Knowsley Street registered a high bailiff of the County Court, aged twenty; a writing clerk, aged nineteen; and a salesman of woollen goods, aged forty-one.[13] This lower end of Cheetham Hill, therefore, housed a variety of respectable working-class people of all ages and occupations reflecting Manchester's urban and manufacturing society.[14] They were the people who, like the merchants and other middle-class residents of suburban Manchester, might enjoy membership of libraries, attendance at orchestral concerts and the availability of other social amenities.[15] It was a place where Elizabeth Prout, with her artisan background, would have felt at home. It was a place, too, where people of the same social level could feel at home, regardless of race or religion. James Conry, for example, was an Irish Catholic, a significant indication that not all Irish lived in cellars, that some were undoubtedly respectable, even middle class, living in non-ethnic accommodation with their social peers and employing English servants.[16] In neighbouring Park Place there was another Irish Catholic, John Lavery, a wine merchant, whose wife, Amelia was to become one of Elizabeth Prout's most helpful friends.[17]

The other section of St Chad's parish, the large working-class district of Angel Meadow, presented a sharp contrast to the Stocks Street area, for Angel Meadow was Manchester's worst slum. It offered another good reason for the clergy's organising a Passionist mission, for it was in such areas that religious leakage was most widespread. As described in 1850 by Father Sheehan, one of St Chad's clergy, it was 'the most densely populated part of the town... where the poorest, the less educated and the most criminal members of the Community' resided. One and a half miles in length and a mile wide, it had a population of 15,000 Catholics, 'chiefly employed as handloom weavers, hawkers and factory operatives... the poorest members of the community'.[18] Writing to the *Morning Chronicle* in 1849, the journalist A.B. Reach described Angel Meadow as 'the lowest, most filthy, most unhealthy and most wicked locality in Manchester', 'full of cellars', 'the home of prostitutes, their bullies, thieves, cadgers, vagrants, tramps and, in the very worst sties of filth, and darkness,... the unhappy wretches, the low Irish', famine refugees from Westport in County Mayo.[19] Crowded into cellars and lying on rags, shavings or straw, they lived on potatoes, meal and scraps begged on the streets. It was obviously an area that would have appealed to the heart of Paul of the Cross and just the place for a Passionist mission. Elizabeth Prout's first encounter with it, however, set against Manchester's daunting buildings, its smoke, noise, smells and fog, could only have convinced her that Manchester might be the 'most wonderful city of modern times' but it was certainly the 'shock city of the age'.[20] It was also damp and unhealthy, especially for anyone consumptively inclined.[21]

Mid-century Manchester—Angel Meadow in background

Between 1849 and 1854 Elizabeth became familiar with Angel Meadow, as she visited the people in their homes, taught their children in school and walked along their streets on her way to work. She would soon have heard their joys and sorrows. Like Cheetham Hill, Angel Meadow held both English and Irish of the same social level. There were Dales, Stanleys and Browns as well as Cavanaghs, Gallaghers, Regans and O'Briens. As at Cheetham Hill, their occupations reflected Manchester's urban and industrial character, although at a different social level. The men tended to be tailors, chairmakers, glaziers, blacksmiths, painters, bricklayers, navvies and dealers in clothes, fruit, cutlery and delf. Both men and women, especially the English, worked in the silk and cotton industries. Other women were charwomen, bonnetmakers, dressmakers, seamstresses and domestic servants. Angel Street's cellars were enormously congested, and here certainly there was a predominance of Irish hawkers, bricklayers and cotton weavers, at an average of thirteen to fourteen a cellar, generally a family with lodgers, while Angel Street's common lodging houses were the haunts of the 'most depraved and abandoned' and fertile with fever.[22]

In Dyche Street, where Elizabeth probably taught in 1851-2 and where Sister Agnes Lee certainly taught in 1853, the tenants numbered an Irish pig dealer, hawkers, beggars, old clothes dealers, tailors, porters, cotton operatives and cap makers. The Catholic School Court house, as it was described in the 1851 census, was then rented to Philip Goulding, a 49-year-old Irish rag dealer, with a wife and five children. James, the 16-year-old son, was registered as a scholar; John, 15, as a pupil teacher; and Honora and Margaret, aged 9 and 7, also as scholars and so they were probably two of Elizabeth Prout's pupils. There was also a house servant, Mary Lynch, aged 30. In the School Yard House, there were 6 female lodgers, 3 of whom were sisters, all rag sorters and all Irish, their ages ranging from 14 to 32.[23] The two buildings were, therefore, being used for the domestic trade of rag dealing. Since all these occupants were in the same trade, it is possible they were all related, a point not always made in the census returns.[24] In another section of this second house, however, was an 80-year-old English widow from Wigan, a pauper, living with her daughter, aged 39, who worked in a cotton factory. In yet another section was an Irish silk spinner, aged 50, his wife 36, and their 4 Manchester-born children, aged between 13 and 6 months. Since the 13-year-old boy had been born in Manchester, his father could have left Ireland no later than the 1830s, so that these were not refugees from the potato famine. The father was highly skilled but he may have been sick or disabled or have become redundant because he was over 40, another type of detail not supplied by the census returns.[25] Finally, in the same house there was also an English 24-year-old lodger and her 10-year-old son.[26] All these occupants were decent people, forced by circumstances to live in an insalubrious area. Since they were occupying Catholic premises, they were probably all Catholics. Whether English or Irish, they shared the same religion, the same accommodation and the same inconveniences in their neighbourhood.

These nuisances were not far to seek. Round the corner in Simpson Street, where the people were mainly Irish but with a sprinkling of English, someone kept a donkey beside his dwelling, its 'affluvia', as the Manchester and Salford Sanitary Association visitors commented, causing 'the most noxious smell even in the next house'.[27] St Michael's graveyard was also in the vicinity. On 17 October 1849 the *Manchester Guardian* pointed out that it had been full, and therefore closed, since 1842. Its condition was 'indecent' and fraught with 'serious and prejudicial consequences to the health of the neighbourhood... a very poor and populous part of the town.' The corpses, said the paper, were scarcely covered. The coffins were covered with only fourteen inches of soil on top and less than six inches at the side.[28] By 1854 the boundary walls had been pulled down and the cemetery had become a rubbish dump and a rendezvous for gambling and fighting, especially on Sundays.[29] The whole area was so neglected that the streets were not cleansed and the landlords were negligent of even the most basic decencies.[30] In Ludgate Street beside the Dyche Street school, the people had scarcely any water because several of the watercocks had been cut off.[31] The neighbouring courts were even worse.[32] Flag Alley off Ludgate Street had no drainage. Its outdoor common ashpits and privies were in a deplorable condition, with no surface drain and no stench trap.[33] The housesteps were broken down, the pavements destroyed and 'the whole court in a sadly dilapidated state'.[34] According to the current definition of a nuisance as 'any filthy, unwholesome or dilapidated premises', the people's very homes were nuisances.[35]

As these Catholics, and Elizabeth Prout, made their way to and from St Chad's, they had to pass along Ashley Lane beside the 'dirty and crowded pile of dilapidated old buildings, called Gibraltar... peculiarly notorious as a fertile source of fever'.[36] Here twenty pigs were kept in a small open space, scarcely enhancing an area already notorious for its lack of drainage, privy accommodation, cleanliness, light and ventilation.[37] Ashley Lane was a steep hill. Apart from boding ill for Elizabeth's tubercular knee, it was so dangerous that every day and at times even every hour horses fell and were lamed as they struggled past St Michael's Tavern.[38] Then there was the River Irk, one of Manchester's 'natural sewers', that in summer weather sent forth 'a most pestilential affluvia', adding considerably to the 'prospect of contagion', and there was a weir that created stagnant water, which 'in warm weather could not fail to be most noxious'.[39] Gibraltar was considered even worse than Little Ireland.[40]

Such was the first of Manchester's slums with which Elizabeth Prout became familiar. The people who lived around the Catholic school, in Simpson Street, for example, tended to be silk and cotton workers, handloom weavers, labourers, bricklayers, hawkers and washerwomen.[41] They belonged to trades that had been affected by the introduction of machinery, or were seasonal, or brought in little income.[42] Both English and Irish lived here because they could afford no better, not because of their nationality.[43] As in Cheetham Hill, social peers lived together regardless of religious or ethnic differences. As soon as these people, English or Irish, could raise themselves to a better social level, they would move to a more appropriate area, preferably near their work.[44] No slum dweller stayed in the slums longer than was necessary. By 1854 'the name Angel Street and the Neighbourhood of Angel Meadow' had been 'proverbial... for years... to denote something low or mean.'[45] Fever compelled even Elizabeth Prout to leave it that year, first for Newton Heath and then for suburban Levenshulme.

2. THE HEART OF THE CITY

In May 1849 Father Gaudentius returned to Manchester with Father Joseph Bunn to give a mission in St Mary's, Mulberry Street in Deansgate. According to Father Henry Browne in 1854, St Mary's had about 7,000 parishioners over a radius of three miles 'at the very centre of the city'. Very few, if any, were 'of the upper or middle class'. Most were the labouring poor, 'chiefly employed in mills' and living in 'back streets and cellars' and, even 'more unfortunate', in a 'locality noted for wickedness and crime'.[46] He thus corroborated Engels' description of Deansgate as a 'great working men's district' of 'long, narrow lanes... crooked courts and passages', hidden from middle-class view by a facade of shops and inhabited by the 'most demoralized class of all Manchester... people whose occupations were thieving and prostitution'.[47] Like Angel Meadow, it was a place where Paul of the Cross would have felt at home and that needed a Passionist mission. In fact it had several.

St Mary's church, like St Chad's, was a new one, opened in 1848. Whereas St Chad's had been re-built in a different area, however, the new St Mary's had been erected on the site of the old church, built in 1794.[48] Thus St Mary's was, and is, the oldest on-site post-Reformation Catholic church in Manchester. Father Dominic had preached in the old church in 1843 and Fathers Gaudentius and Austin had given a mission in it in 1847.[49] Father Ignatius Spencer attended the opening of the new St Mary's in October 1848.[50] When Fathers Gaudentius and Joseph arrived on 3 May 1849 to give their eighteen-day mission, they were therefore on familiar Passionist ground.

During this mission a Mass was celebrated at 6.30 each morning, after which Father Joseph gave a meditation on the Passion and then said his Mass. At 9.30 there was another Mass, followed by a lecture from Father Gaudentius on the Decalogue. The evening service at 7.00 began with the choir's singing the *Veni Creator*. Father Joseph then gave a lecture on the Sacraments, after which priest and people alternated in singing the Litany of Loreto, a list of invocations to the Virgin Mary. Next, as described by Father Joseph, Father Gaudentius 'preached his accustomed impressive sermons on the Eternal Truths'. Attendance in the mornings was 'as numerous as could be expected' when most of the parishioners were at work. In the evenings, the church was 'crowded to overflowing'. Unfortunately, in contrast to St

Chad's, where there had been about seven priests hearing Confessions, only the parish priest, Father Matthias Formby was able to help in St Mary's, because his curate was transferred to another parish at the very time of the mission. As a result, although the two missioners spent as much time as possible in the confessionals, hundreds, 'I may almost say thousands', wrote Father Joseph, had to be turned away. Amongst those who managed to go to Confession, many received Communion every day. On the last Sunday at least 1,000 did so. On the final Friday, High Mass was followed by the commencement of *Quarante Ore* or the Forty Hours' Exposition of the Blessed Sacrament, which continued until the Sunday. That day the Renewal of Baptismal Vows took place after Mass and before a General Communion during a Solemn Benediction service. The mission was closed as usual with a Papal Blessing and Benediction. During the mission Father Gaudentius had invested 'great numbers' with the red scapular of the Sacred Passion and had enrolled 'many' in the Society of the Sacred Heart of Jesus.[51]

On 3 April 1851 Father Gaudentius again returned to St Mary's, this time with Father Anselm Alcock and for a shorter mission, lasting slightly less than a fortnight. Father Anselm gave the daily instruction on Christian Doctrine; Father Gaudentius the meditations on the Passion after a 9 o'clock Mass and the evening sermons. The church was 'litterally [*sic*] crammed', the confessionals so crowded even from the first day that many had to wait as long as six hours, although there were four priests hearing until 11 o'clock each night. At the end of the mission there were still so many unheard that Father Formby begged the missioners to stay another week. The mission was due to end on Palm Sunday, the beginning of Holy Week, and he wanted as much help as possible to enable the people to make their Easter duties. The missioners were previously committed, however, and so had to leave, as planned, on 16 April, having closed the mission, as Father Gaudentius customarily did, with *Quarante Ore*, the Renewal of Baptismal Vows, Papal Blessing and Benediction. Father Gaudentius noted that at least 200, the vast majority of his penitents, had been away from church for anything between two and seventy years.[52] As Father Dominic had previously told the Passionist general, with rare exceptions that was the pattern wherever the missioners went.[53] Father Gaudentius remarked that in St Mary's they were so anxious to come to Confession that, when they had to be sent away at night, they were there again early the next morning before going to work. He also noted that many adults made their First Communion during the mission.[54]

It was Father Gaudentius' fourth mission in St Mary's in May 1852 that most concerned Elizabeth Prout. This mission was started by

Fathers Joseph Bunn and Bernard O'Loughlin. Father Gaudentius was scheduled to give another in Rochdale, starting a few days later. With the provincial's permission, however, he left his monastery at Cotton, near Cheadle, on 14 May to go to Manchester to see Father Croskell and Elizabeth Prout. Arrived in Manchester, Gaudentius made a friendly call on his brethren in St Mary's. He found himself greeted by Father Formby 'as providentially sent by God'.[55] Father Joseph had had to give so many missions continuously that his health had been impaired. He had struggled on with this one for about five days, when he collapsed with inflammation of the brain and fell into a fever.[56] Since he was very ill when Father Gaudentius arrived, the latter agreed to preach that night. Father Formby, however, had 400 confirmandi, as Bishop Turner was making his first visit to the parish the following Sunday. Many of them were adults and Father Formby had been relying on the missioners to prepare them. He was so anxious that the next day he went down to Cotton to ask the provincial to defer the Rochdale mission, so that Father Gaudentius could stay in St Mary's.[57] Thus he began another mission that was to have momentous results for Elizabeth Prout.

As in 1851, Gaudentius gave the morning meditations on the Passion and the evening sermons on the Eternal Truths. Father Bernard gave the instructions on Christian Doctrine. As 'always' Gaudentius found plenty 'hard and rough work', particularly during the first week when he had the extra burden of preparing the confirmandi. He thought the attendance 'could and should have been better' in the mornings but, 'as usual in the large towns' that at night was very good. At Father Formby's urgent request, the mission was prolonged for a third week.[58] He was obviously deeply indebted to Father Gaudentius. He was even more so when he heard that Elizabeth Prout would take charge of his girls' school. At that time she had been replaced in St Chad's school, a new one in Stocks Street, by the Notre Dame Sisters. She was probably teaching St Chad's infants in Dyche Street but she was also interviewing candidates for her order and one of them, a Sarah Ann Lee from Salford, would be able to take her place with the infants. Father Gaudentius suggested Elizabeth could oblige Father Formby by coming to St Mary's. From September 1852, therefore, she began her daily walk from Stocks Street, Cheetham Hill to St Mary's 'miserable rented rooms' in Royton Street, Deansgate.[59] Thus she became familiar with another working-class area of Manchester.

Royton Street lay in a highly industrialised area, offering labouring jobs in such local trades as a timber yard, a smithy and a coal yard on Hardman Street; another timber yard and sawpit in Gartside Street; and a slaughterhouse and hide and skin yard in Spinningfield. Beyond the immediate vicinity of the school there were plenty of opportunities for employment: in a copper rolling and engraving works, in textile mills, on the Liverpool and Manchester Railway which had its terminus in Liverpool Road, on the quays and on the Bridgewater and Rochdale Canals.[60]

Like Cheetham Hill and Angel Meadow, the district housed both English and Irish. Their occupations reflected their proximity to the shops of Deansgate as well as to the neighbouring industries. Gartside Street, which had mainly English residents, and Cumberland Street and Hardman Street, with their inner courts and passages, including Royton Street, housed clerks, accountants, engravers, booksellers, woodcarvers, tailors and boot and shoemakers; blacksmiths, mechanics and basketmakers; cotton and silk operatives, bricklayers, painters, cutlers; and, amongst the women, shirtmakers, milliners, dressmakers and domestic servants.[61] What would have struck Elizabeth Prout, however, was that there was a gin palace at every corner and the largest palaces were in the poorest streets. She would also have noticed the numbers of children sitting on steps, rolling in the causeway and dashing round the streets, their 'hair long, rough and uncombed', their clothes in rags, their hands and faces filthy and their feet, in most cases, 'presenting a dry coating of dirt, as though they had not been washed from birth'.[62] Through her the Passionist mission to England reached the streets, schools and homes of the urban poor.[63]

Like the poor of Angel Meadow, those in Deansgate were mainly the victims of circumstances. It was the landlord's fault that there were insufficient water closets in the vicinity of Royton Street and therefore that holes in the pavement were filled in with excrement and that passages between the streets were equally soiled. It was his fault that there were open and overflowing middens even beside or below the doors and windows of the houses. The tenants had complained but, as they said, provided he had his rents he cared for nothing else. In Royton Street itself, beside St Mary's School, although the pavements were in fair shape and the drainage good, that end of the street was 'rather dirty', as the people threw their filth onto the street. This was one part of Deansgate that was not cleansed. The common privies were filthy and overflowing, because there were only three for more than twelve houses.[64] Since the 1851 census had shown an average of about nine occupants in each house, these three privies had to serve more than a hundred people.[65] Most of the houses were overcrowded. In one house, for instance, each room was occupied by a separate family, although one couple had three children and another four and the rooms measured only 13ft x 11ft. A married couple with two children lived in the front cellar, which had a chimney and therefore some ventilation. In the back cellar, devoid of fireplace and with its small window blocked with rags, there were two other lodgers. Neither cellar had any furniture. In the back cellar a straw mat was covered with 'some kind of quilt and other clothing'.[66] In Manchester's frequent rains, cellars were invariably damp, as water from the pavement oozed through the side walls and down onto the floor.

In this Anglo-Irish area, Celts and Saxons shared the same house, intermarried and were all equally poor. One house in Austin's Street, adjacent to Royton Street, for example, was occupied in 1851 by an Irish cork cutter, his wife and 3 children and a visitor; an English 60-year-old man with 2 Irish female lodgers and another female visitor; an Irish widow, a shirtmaker, with 2 adult sons and a daughter; an Irish husband with an English wife, 2 children and an Irish lodger; and a young Irish married couple with their infant daughter.[67] They were there, not because they were Celt or Saxon but because they were poor. As in Cheetham Hill and Angel Meadow, English and Irish lived together at their own social level.[68]

Living in such conditions, the children Elizabeth Prout taught must have been unhealthy, dirty, lice-ridden and obstreperous.[69] In 1849, Reach said that in one such district nearly 200 children had died in one year. Over seven years, 13,362 children had been brought up in 'impure streets, left alone long days by their mothers, soothed by opium and when assailed by mortal disease, their stomachs torn, their bodies convulsed, their brains bewildered, left to die without medical aid', a doctor being called only to witness the death and to sanction the funeral.[70] Catholic children from these houses, however, when attired in the white dresses and lace caps supplied by the parish for the annual Whit walks, could process in such splendour, with banners and bands, that the whole of Manchester turned out to admire them.[71]

Like Angel Meadow, Deansgate district usually furnished the doctors with a 'considerable number of fever patients' and not always because of 'dissolute and filthy habits'.[72] When there was a fever epidemic in 1854, in one instance at any rate those who tried to live decently suffered with their neighbours, because of the covetousness of the landlord. The fever, predictably, struck first in a dirty cellar, without lighting or ventilation, occupied and slept in by two widows and their 6 children. All 8 were taken to the fever ward, where they recovered. When they returned to the cellar, however, a boy took the fever again and died. In a nearby house, a family of husband, wife and 4 children all succumbed. The man died. Next the fever struck a woman and her 4 children in a dirty, ground floor room in a court, where the ventilation was deficient. These recovered but in another, very clean house in the court, where a mother and 3 children succumbed, the mother died. When the case was investigated by the Manchester and Salford Sanitary Association, they discovered that below her bedroom and above the living room, 'saturating its walls and floor with the filthy liquid', were two privies, 'depositaries of filth', used by the whole neighbourhood. The 'destructive gases, exhaled from the foul fermenting pits below', they reported, entered the sleeping room 'in ceaseless and comparatively unobstructed streams'. In spite of her efforts to keep her house clean, a wife and mother of three children had died. 'The comfort and happiness of a family' was 'for ever destroyed that the rental of one tenement might be retained.'[73]

Neither Elizabeth Prout nor Father Formby could find a house in this area suitable for a convent, with the result that she limped each day from Stocks Street, twice on Sundays, during the winter of 1852-3.[74] In January 1853 she became very seriously ill and had to leave St Mary's.[75] When she recovered in May 1853, she started a new school in St Joseph's, Goulden Street and thus became familiar with yet another of Manchester's working-class areas.

3. THE WORKING CLASSES

When Elizabeth Prout came to Manchester in 1849, although she lived in Stocks Street she did not work there. Like most of her neighbours she found employment in the grime and noise of more central Manchester, in her case in Ancoats, the heart of the factory system.[76] Here St Chad's girls' school was situated in George Leigh Street in St Chad's former parish.[77] In 1853 Elizabeth opened a new school at St Joseph's church in Goulden Street between the Rochdale and Oldham Roads.[78] This area was later amalgamated into St Michael's parish, centred on George Leigh Street.[79] It is therefore likely that when Father Gaudentius gave a mission in St Joseph's in 1853, it was attended by many of the people from the wider Ancoats area.

In 1849 A.B. Reach described Ancoats as 'entirely an operative colony', with 'some of the most squalid-looking streets, inhabited by swarms of the most squalid-looking people' he had ever seen.[80] Many of the houses were built back to back, so that, like those in Deansgate, they had common privies and middens, instead of yards with private ashpits and toilets.[81] Here, then, were the 'long, straight, hopeless streets of regularly-built houses, all small and of brick', hiding yet more inner courts, alleys and cellars, where the working classes lived.[82] In style they were not dissimilar from Elizabeth's home in Stone but she would have seen little to compare with the size and character of Manchester's streets. 'Fancy', wrote Reach, 'a wide-lying labyrinth of small dingy streets, narrow, unsunned courts terminating in gloomy *culs-de-sac*, and adorned with a central sloppy gutter.'[83] Every twenty yards or so the houses were interspersed with some of the poorer mills, their courtyards paved with cinders and their engine-houses steaming.[84] The doors of the houses generally stood open, with young children clustering on the doorsteps and swarming out onto the pavement. The interiors, 10ft x 8ft, were floored with bricks or flagstones, partially covered with strips of mats or carpeting.[85] They were much superior to the dwellings in Angel Meadow and Deansgate, however. Here the people took pride in their homes. Most of them had a table in the centre of the room and a few chairs, stools and settles placed round it. Some had a large cupboard, displaying 'a shining assortment of plates and dishes'. Some had a 'humble dinner service' arranged on shelves, above a medley of stewpans and cooking utensils. Sometimes the firelight danced on a 'painted and highly-glazed tea tray', while a mirror and a few small pictures in black frames often hung on the walls. A few little stone ornaments adorned the chimneypieces and frequently a pot of geraniums stood on the windowsills, between what Reach described as the 'dingy cotton curtains'. Almost every house had a clock. 'No Manchester operative [would] be without one a moment longer than he [could] help', said Reach, for accurate time keeping was essential for industrial workers.[86]

As in Cheetham Hill, Angel Meadow and Deansgate there were both English and Irish in Ancoats. George Leigh Street was a main road and therefore comparatively wide. In 1851 it was tenanted by poorer craftsmen: tailors, stonemasons, painters, carpenters, shoemakers and handloom weavers. There were also the less skilled: bricklayers' labourers, porters and errand boys. Some of the Irish were dealers in clothes and oilcloth. There was the inevitable pawnbroker, an Irish baker and a few shopkeepers. Many of the people, men and women, were employed in the silk industry, while others were cotton operatives. Some of the women were washerwomen, bonnetmakers, servants and dressmakers and there were also a few paupers. Rents in George Leigh Street were 3s., as they had been in 1838 but, since rents in general had risen by 1851, the tone of the district had deteriorated. It was therefore a poor area. In the neighbouring Swan Court and Bennets Court, many of the people were Irish but some were English. They performed the more menial but necessary tasks of urban life as labourers, hawkers, nightsoilmen, night watchmen and porters, jobs that most people did not want. Some of the women were washerwomen and milliners. The majority, both men and women, were mill workers, people who would have found their entertainments in the Monday night concerts for operatives or in the music saloons of the area. On the whole, Ancoats was a mainly English area, into which Irish workers of the same status had moved and as tenants, not lodgers. Initially they had had to take the poorer houses in the inner courts and alleys with the poorer English. They were moving up the social scale, however, in a largely English district, away from predominantly Irish areas like that around St Joseph's, Goulden Street.[87]

Father Gaudentius Rossi began his sixth and last Manchester mission in St Joseph's, Goulden Street on 20 March, 1853.[88] A new parish, it had previously formed part of St Patrick's under Father Daniel Hearne, a much beloved pastor who had built a Gothic temperance guild hall in Goulden Street.[89] In 1852 Bishop Turner divided the parish, placing a French priest, Father Peter Stephan, in charge of the new St Joseph's, with the guild hall as the church.[90] Father Stephan asked Father Gaudentius several times to give a mission.[91] When in 1853 he also asked Elizabeth Prout to start a school, Gaudentius arranged to come.[92] According to his subsequent account, St Joseph's church was 'at the very centre' of a 'densely populated' part of Manchester, where the majority were 'poor Irish Catholics'. He understood there were about 4,000 parishioners but no more than two or three families could be considered 'respectable' and none 'independent'.[93] He wanted Elizabeth to move her convent into St Joseph's parish. 'The sooner you go there the better', he wrote. 'Take my advice and find a house in St Joseph's district, and if you cannot find a very fine palace learn to be satisfied like the holy family to dwell in a stable or at least to live in a poor house in Nazareth.'[94] Elizabeth began to teach in St Joseph's school on Monday, 23 May 1853. By September she had still not found a house. Mainly back to back, the empty ones she had inspected were either too small for a religious community of ten or were 'full of bugs'.[95] Father Stephan suggested she might rent 'the Rising Sun Inn in the market place'.[96] Although there was a Sun Inn frequently called the 'Rising Sun' in Old Millgate and another 'Sun' in the actual precinct of Smithfield Market, Father Stephan, as quoted by Father Gaudentius, seems to have been referring to the Rising Sun Inn at the corner of Swan Street and Rochdale Road, which by 1906 was transformed into the Rising Sun Music Hall.[97] It faced the entrance to Shudehill, a street Engels described as 'narrow and winding, the houses dirty, old, and tumble-down, and the construction of the side streets utterly horrible'.[98] Since the inn stood across from the Corn Hill at the top of Shude Hill, the Corporation weighing machine and an entrance to Smithfield Market, it was obviously an extremely busy area, hardly a site for contemplative prayer.[99] Elizabeth Prout could only have been relieved when Father Gaudentius objected to it as 'too much exposed to the noise of the people'.[100]

Because the parishioners in this district were so poor and because they had previously had to walk a mile to the nearest Catholic church, they had become negligent about Mass and the Sacraments.[101] They needed a Passionist mission. Father Gaudentius began it alone on Palm Sunday and carried it through the Holy Week services. Father Austin Edgar arrived to help him with Confessions from Easter Monday but 'the indefatigable Father Gaudentius', as a reporter described him, gave all the sermons during the full three weeks, preaching three times each day. A number of Protestants attended, twelve of them being received into the Catholic Church, while others began instructions. As well as the Forty Hours' Exposition, which Father Gaudentius had held in St Chad's and St Mary's, he introduced another innovation: an act of dedication to the Virgin Mary. The mission was most successful. More than 2,000 people received Communion, 600 of whom had not attended church for several years. More than fifty adults were prepared for their First Communion, 'having neglected to receive it before'. Large numbers came to Mass each day and as the mission progressed many became noticeably more devout and recollected in church. The people were griefstricken when Father Gaudentius had to leave. Father Stephan 'expressed his uttermost satisfaction' and afterwards wrote to assure him, 'You have gained for ever the esteem and gratitude of my flock.'[102] Father Gaudentius Rossi had reached the working classes of Manchester.[103]

4. MANCHESTER'S CATHOLIC REVIVAL

Elizabeth Prout came to Manchester as a result of the Passionist mission to England.[104] She therefore found herself not only at the centre of industrialism but at the heart of perhaps the most impressive religious phenomenon of the time: the revival of the Catholic Church in England, a revival that was nowhere more conspicuous than in Manchester, where the Catholic population grew from 287 English Catholic tradesmen, servants and labourers in 1767 to about 80,000 mainly Irish industrial workers in 1852.[105] In 1841, echoing Newman's comments on the Catholic desire to convert England, Dalgairns had written to the French newspaper, *L'Univers*, 'Let them go into our great cities to preach the Gospel to this half-pagan people; let them walk barefoot; let them clothe themselves in sackcloth; let the spirit of mortification be apparent in their looks; in a word, let there be found among them a saint in the measure of the Seraph of Assisi and the heart of England is already won.[106] Father Dominic Barberi had answered him point by point, even to being found a saint in the measure of St Francis. Father Gaudentius Rossi and other Passionists answered the challenge in Manchester. Their mission accounts illustrate both the nature and difficulties of the Catholic revival in such a vast, urban society in the throes of assimilating large numbers of refugees from the Irish potato famine.

The Passionist mission to Manchester was essentially a call to sinners to experience the love and mercy of God in the Sacrament of Reconciliation and to embark on a life of holiness.[107] In all three parishes in which Father Gaudentius gave missions, large numbers returned to practising their faith: 'several hundreds' in St Chad's; about 400 in St Mary's in 1851; and 600 in St Joseph's. The churches were packed, the priests working practically round the clock at great physical cost to themselves. These Passionist missions were obviously reaching the working classes. Moreover, attendance was voluntary. No-one could have forced these working-class men to queue for up to six hours for Confession and to return in the early hours of the morning for either Confession or Mass before going to work. They came because they were convinced it was to their 'advantage' to return to God in memory of Christ's Passion.[108] As exemplified in Manchester, the Passionist mission for the conversion of England was no 'will o' the wisp' but, as Father Gaudentius experienced it in St Mary's, plenty of 'hard, rough work'.[109] As shown particularly in St Chad's, the missions also acted as a unifying force between different social classes. Through the sacramental system, both rich and poor were seen to be equally sinners in need of Absolution and equally potential saints able to receive the Eucharist. They equally constituted the Catholic Church: a community united in faith and Sacraments and in communion, through their priests and bishop, with Peter, the Vicar of Christ. In this context, social status was immaterial, except that the poor were regarded as having been singled out by Christ to represent Him in a special way: 'Whatever you did to the least of My brethren, you did it to Me.'[110] Catholics believed that in assisting the poor they were giving to Christ Himself and even 'a cup of cold water' would not go unrewarded.[111] When they died they could expect to be judged, as they would have heard in Father Gaudentius' 'impressive sermons', on how they had clothed the naked, fed the hungry, visited the sick etc.[112] Catholics were therefore less concerned than contemporary philanthropists about being deceived by the undeserving, because the eternal reward was the same anyway.[113] In his mission programme in the eighteenth century, Paul of the Cross had provided for special sessions for wealthier lay people and for clergy, during which they examined their relations with the poor.[114] Father Dominic held such a meeting for clergy in Dublin in 1849.[115] Although there were some wealthy middle-class Catholics in Manchester, however, they did not necessarily live in the same parish.[116] There is no evidence that such sessions were held there but, in view of this Paulacrucian tradition, all the Passionists would have preached on the rights and duties of both rich and poor and there is ample evidence that Manchester's middle-class Catholics co-operated with the clergy in helping the poor constructively.[117]

Social justice was a subject that was pertinent in Manchester, because so many of the sufferings of the poor were caused by a lack of control over builders, manufacturers and entrepreneurs in general. The basic problem was that the growth of Manchester as England's, even the world's, first industrial city had not been planned. It had developed haphazardly, partly because 'Manchester', an agglomeration of previously independent townships, did not have a centralised local government and partly because of the economic theory of *laissez-faire*. Entrepreneurs were able to locate their various types of workplaces for their own convenience, regardless of what pollution they caused or of what health hazards they presented to the people. Builders had been able to erect poor-quality housing, even on unsuitable sites, with equal thoughtlessness. In 1765 and 1776 the authorities did apply for acts for parliament to enable them to improve at least cleansing and lighting and in 1792 they applied for police commissioners. From then until the 1840s these were responsible for cleansing, lighting, watching and regulating the thoroughfares of Manchester township but there were still many administrative complications. The police commissioners, for example, provided a night but not a day police force; the county of Lancaster had authority in all the townships and made its own administrative divisions; and Manchester township had some limited authority in other townships. Several different authorities were therefore constantly overlapping in their duties. As a result, no single authority could legislate for overall housing, water, refuse clearance and street cleansing or deal with the problems of smoke, pollution, disease and shortage of burial ground.[118] In 1790, Dr Ferriar pointed out that fever epidemics originated in Manchester's small, old houses, particularly in the cellars and overcrowded houses of the working classes. He urged that cellar dwellings should be closed by the authorities and the houses regularly inspected. In 1796 he and Dr Percival tried to warn the wealthy that their own safety depended on adequate housing and sanitary conditions for the working classes but, although a Board of Health had been established, their voices remained mainly unheard.[119] Consequently, as J.P. Kay pointed out in 1832 when cholera had taken its toll, 'a whole mass of cottages filled the insalubrious valley' of the River Irk that passed by Angel Meadow. Its flow was obstructed by weirs, its water blackened with the refuse of dyeworks, sewers, drainage from gasworks and filth from boneworks and tanneries. Near Ducie Bridge stood a large tannery, eight storeys high, dominating 'the crazy labyrinth of pauper dwellings called 'Gibraltar'.[120] Elizabeth Prout knew it well. By the time she arrived in Manchester, its once 'silvery streams' had become 'enormous sewers and cesspools'.[121] It was difficult to improve this system, the town clerk said about 1854, because they were also the sewers for the neighbouring districts, so that they were already polluted before they reached Manchester. It was impossible even to cover them, because they were appropriated by the owners of large mills and works, who saw any bureaucratic intervention as infringements of their rights.[122]

In the few years before Elizabeth Prout's arrival some progress had been made. In 1842 Manchester's municipal borough charter, granted in 1838, was confirmed by parliament; in 1845 the various bodies of township police commissioners finally surrendered their powers to the borough council; and in 1846 the Manchester corporation bought out Sir Oswald Mosley's manorial rights. There was then one single administrative authority, although, with so many systems to amalgamate, it was not until 1851 that the corporation consolidated all the local police acts, administered the highways and controlled the waterworks. Elizabeth Prout was almost two years in Manchester before the new Longdendale Valley reservoirs gave a regular water supply to a wide section of the population. Even then the working-class terraces and courts still lacked a piped supply of pure water, water closets and a main drainage system.[123] In view, however, of the bankruptcies, trade depressions and Irish refugees that had formed the background to its efforts, Manchester's receipt of a royal charter in 1853 was well deserved.[124]

As the authority of Manchester's central government had increased, living standards had been improved. In 1844 the Manchester Police Act had tried to compel the owners of existing houses and future builders to equip each house with an ashpit and with a privy with proper doors and coverings and had forbidden the building of back-to-back houses.[125] Two years later, despite additional expense, the first municipal cleansing department had begun to clear away nightsoil and domestic rubbish. In 1847 the council had cleared all Manchester's privies and ashpits.[126] Hundreds of new houses had been built in the 1840s. Unfortunately, however, there were still so many people looking for accommodation that as one set of people moved into better conditions, another set moved into the poorest. The arrival of famine refugees from the late 1840s ensured that that situation continued for years to come.[127] Houses in Angel Meadow were congested because the alternative was the street, with the workhouse or poor law removal its grim consequences.[128] As Dr Howard had reported in 1842, fever would be prevalent amongst the labouring classes until they were supplied with the common necessaries of life and relieved from their state of extreme wretchedness and destitution.[129] Before the 1849 cholera epidemic subsided, about two months after Elizabeth Prout's arrival, Manchester had had an estimated 814 deaths in two months, as many as in the whole visitation of 1832. Angel Meadow, Ancoats and Deansgate were the worst-affected areas.[130] About 1842 a visitor to Manchester had said he would prefer to face 'the savages of New Zealand... than the worst specimens of humanity to be found in... the Angel-meadows of Manchester.[131] The Irish refugees had no choice.[132]

Reporting on Ludgate Street near the Catholic school in Angel
Meadow in March 1854 the Manchester and Salford Sanitary Association visitors described the dwellings as 'generally in a very dirty state'
and the 'inhabitants of the lowest order, principally Irish.[133] These
houses had not been built for the Irish. The smaller dwellings had been
intended for workers of any nationality; the larger ones for the middle
classes. It was unfortunate that, as the latter fled from the smoke of
their own contriving, the residences they left behind lent themselves to
becoming lodging houses or rented-room accommodation for families
seeking the cheapest rents.[134] Many of the Irish who were squeezed
into them in 1854 were refugees from the potato famine. Some could
not speak English.[135] When they first arrived, they had no money to
pay any rent. They sought refuge with kith and kin in every nook and
cranny they could find.[136] As Father Collingridge of Birmingham had
told the Select Committee on the Irish in 1834, if an Irishman had a
penny, he would give a halfpenny to another Irishman in distress.[137]
Father Hearne had also commented on this Celtic generosity. He told
the commissioners that when Irish people first came over to England,
they were usually destitute. Irish people were always charitable in
helping each other in sickness and want, however, and so, until they
found work, immigrants were often assisted by their relatives or
friends. Nevertheless they generally 'got into debt', which it took them
a long time to clear even when they found work.[138] Sometimes too,
they saved their money to pay for relatives to come to England and
gave them temporary lodgings when they came.[139] The English Father
Crook of St Augustine's, parish priest of both notorious Little Ireland
and middle-class Victoria Park, had reminded the commissioners how
much the Irish contributed to Manchester's civic splendour. Many of
them were bricklayers, he had said, probably the best workers on the
sites, performing the 'most laborious and dangerous part of the work'.
That must also have been true in the 1840s, as many of Manchester's
most prestigious buildings were constructed by Irish labour. Father
Crook said, too, that the Irish all had 'the same desire to better
themselves and to get higher wages, as the English' and would make
'as great exertions to get them'.[140]

The Catholic Church was particularly challenged by the social
condition of Manchester because so many of the poor were Catholics.
Material aid was distributed, to Catholics and Protestants alike, by the
St Vincent de Paul Society and by the Manchester and Salford Catholic
Benevolent Society.[141] Apart from attending to immediate spiritual and
material needs the main concern of the clergy was to provide churches,
where their parishioners could come for Mass and the Sacraments.[142]
When Elizabeth Prout arrived, there were six Catholic churches in
Manchester: St Chad's, the mother church, built in Rook Street about

1773-6 and replaced at Red Bank in 1847; St Mary's, Mulberry Street; St Augustine's, Granby Row, built in 1820; St Patrick's, Livesey Street, erected in 1832; St Wilfrid's, Hulme, built by Pugin in 1842; and St Ann's, Ancoats, opened in 1848. In Salford, St John's, the future cathedral, was built in 1848.[143] The Irish potato famine ensured that these were too few and too small, even as four of them opened their doors for the first time in 1847-48. The Catholic church-building programme would have to continue. In the meantime the souls of about 80,000 Catholics had to be tended and in Manchester itself there were only fourteen priests.[144]

The immediate problem was to reach out to the lapsed, English and Irish.[145] The Passionist missions played a major role in this re-evangelization but even their success was inevitably limited. The 1851 religious census returns illustrate the size of the problem. In general, the figures given for the Catholic population of England and Wales must be treated with caution, because in some places priests counted the attendance at only the 11 o'clock Mass.[146] If two out of three attendances were omitted over a wide area, and especially in a highly populated one, the final figure would differ considerably from the reality. The *Rambler* claimed such was the case, suggesting there were between 1,250,000 and 1,500,000 Catholics rather than Horace Mann's some 200,000.[147] In Manchester there were discrepancies in the returns for St Augustine's, occasioned by the enumerator's having first delivered the Anglican form. When he realised his mistake, he delivered the more appropriate Catholic one, which was filled in differently. Both were forwarded to London.[148] Fortunately, in both St Chad's and St Mary's the priests understood the questions and gave the attendance at all Masses, so that their figures are accurate. In September 1851 Father Sheehan estimated the Catholic population of St Chad's at 15,000.[149] The religious census of the previous March had shown a Mass attendance of 2,060 people, which would have been only moderately improved by allowing exemptions for the very young, the sick and the aged.[150] At the Passionist mission in 1849 Father Croskell had noted 3,700 communicants. In spite of its undoubted success even the Passionist mission had reached only a minority of St Chad's parishioners and general Sunday attendance two years later accounted for even fewer: incidental evidence that the Irish Catholics of Angel Meadow were not subject to an authoritarian priest, Irish or otherwise, any more than they lived in an ethnic ghetto.[151] St Mary's figures show a similar picture. According to Father Gaudentius' 1847 mission account and Father Browne's 1854 figure, St Mary's parishioners increased from 2,000 in 1847 to 7,000 in 1854.[152] Since the increase occurred during the famine immigration, the additional 5,000 were presumably Irish. The census returns in 1851 showed St Mary's with 2,700 Mass attenders.[153] Its attendance was, therefore, considerably better than St Chad's, since allowances for infants, sick and old might have raised it to about 50%. With 50% non-attendance, however, there was still a serious problem of leakage. Although the census figures showed Catholics to be an 8.1 percentage of Manchester's total population and a 23.3 percentage of those who attended church on 30 March 1851, the Catholic clergy would have been more concerned about the large numbers who did not attend.[154]

The problem was not just one of absenteeism. According to the census returns, St Chad's could seat 1,100 and provide standing room for another 150. It could therefore accommodate 1,250 people at one Mass. Since it had three Sunday Masses it could accommodate 3,750 parishioners.[155] Even if the rest came they could not gain admittance. Since many had to walk more than a mile across Angel Meadow's ill-favoured streets, they abandoned the effort, like those in St Joseph's district on the periphery of St Patrick's and equally distant from St Chad's and St Mary's.[156] Again St Mary's picture was similar. It could accommodate 800 sitting and 200 standing, a total of 1,000. At three Sunday Masses, it could accommodate a Mass attendance of 3,000.[157] On census Sunday, it had had almost maximum attendance. Nevertheless about half the parishioners were missing. Manchester needed more priests and more churches.[158]

Another reason for non-attendance, as Gaudentius noted in St Joseph's in 1853, was dire poverty. He had met it before, at Newcastle-under-Lyme in December 1844, where many 'poor Irish... who had neglected their duties... some during their whole life' excused their absenteeism 'under the plea of their poverty'.[159] If they had neglected their duties during their whole lives, many had lapsed before they crossed to England.[160] The same applied in St Joseph's, where Gaudentius found fifty adults who had not made their First Communion. Although Ireland had been able to preserve its diocesan system throughout the penal times and although from 1703 priests had been able to move freely and in some parts had already introduced Tridentine devotions, there were still not enough priests and churches. As a result parishes were extensive. The priests' priority had to be to attend the dying. On Sundays, as in the Manchester area in the eighteenth century, Mass was celebrated on a rota at widely separated mission stations. Since Baptism could be administered by the laity and care was taken to ensure that midwives knew how to baptise, people could be baptised and very quickly were. It was much more difficult to receive other Sacraments or preparatory instructions for them, as Father Gaudentius discovered in St Mary's in 1852 when he had to instruct many adults for Confirmation.[161]

It was in these large parishes of the textile North West that Father Gaudentius, other missioners and Elizabeth Prout met the full force of Anglo-Irish working-class Catholicism: numerous, poor and lapsed. What was significant was that hundreds, even thousands, were seizing the opportunity to return to church. In most cases, leakage was due not so much to indifference, or to a rejection of God, but to lack of opportunity and of religious education occasioned by the extreme length of the penal times.[162] The local clergy saw missions as providing both the opportunity and instructions required. Hence they liked them to coincide with Advent, Lent and preparations for episcopal visitations. The missioners would then help to hear the overwhelming numbers of Confessions and to instruct the confirmandi.[163] In providing opportunities for so many Catholic lapsed to return to their religious duties, the Italian orders, which increasingly, of course, had English and Irish members, played an important role in the Catholic revival.[164] Father Gaudentius in particular was responsible for a great part of it in Manchester. Father Ignatius Spencer also played an important role. Although he did not give many lengthy missions in Manchester, he often preached there. He looked to the working-class Irish in particular to effect the conversion of England. Hence in St John's, Salford, in January 1854, he offered them a complete Christian rule of life, an ideal of Christian lay perfection. He asked them to abandon drunkenness by taking the 'Pledge' and to avoid bad company. He wanted them to replace anger and its consequence, cursing, with a joyful *Deo gratias* for whatever happened and, like Paul of the Cross, he recommended a period of daily meditation on the Passion, vocal prayers such as the Rosary and the frequent reception of the Sacraments. He calculated that the English would be so impressed by such sanctification of the Irish that they would be rapidly converted themselves.[165]

As Father Gaudentius' accounts indicate, the Passionist missions were also useful in assisting the Manchester clergy to graft a large Irish majority onto a fairly small English Catholic minority. It was fortunate in this respect that, before the mass immigration of the famine years, there had been a gradual increase in the Irish community at the same time that more English Catholics had moved into Manchester, notably from the Fylde and Yorkshire.[166] Although, therefore, Manchester's Catholic poor at mid century could not be sustained by a large, wealthier, English Catholic community, as in Preston and Wigan, there had been a gradual assimilation of Irish immigrants into Manchester's Catholic culture. This local English identity was particularly important in Lancashire where, throughout the penal times, the Catholic Church had remained stronger than in any other county in England.[167] Manchester's English Catholic clergy were anxious to preserve and to pass on to posterity this English inheritance. The Irish had St Patrick's church, certainly, but they also had dedications to the early English saints: Chad, Augustine and Wilfrid. Some of the children's Sunday school outings were to Pleasington Priory, a place with penal associations.[168] In this 'living memory' of Lancashire's Catholic martyrs, the Manchester Catholics were well attuned to receive Paulacrucian spirituality. They also offered Irish immigrants a type of Catholicism akin to their own experience of persecution. As a result, the Irish in Manchester could integrate themselves into the local Catholic community. The Catholic clergy, both English and Irish, were anxious to unite 'the sons of St Augustine and St Patrick'.[169] The latter was given his place but, as depicted in St John's Cathedral's east window in 1854, surrounded by English saints.[170] At mid century there were no Irish ghettos in Manchester. The Irish dominated the Catholic Church only by numbers. It did not become an Irish Church.

Moreover, the feverstricken Irish instrumentally introduced another feature into Mancunian Catholicism: the presence of French and Belgian priests who, like Father Stephan of St Joseph's, heroically responded to the English bishops' call for help as their own priests died administering to the sick and dying refugees.[171] Thus Manchester's Catholic community unobtrusively assumed a cosmopolitan and Continental counter-reformation identity, even if the nationality of most of its members was Irish. The Italian missionaries, such as Gentili, added another dimension.[172] The Passionist missioners, whether Italian or British, added the further dimension of Paulacrucian spirituality. In choosing to consolidate the local Catholic Church through the revivalism of the regular missionaries, Manchester's clergy were united with Wiseman in his policy of Tridentine reform. They were deliberately spiritually reuniting the Catholic Church in England with the customs of the wider Catholic Church under the Apostolic See.[173]

Father Gaudentius Rossi's mission accounts are of particular interest in this respect as the only Passionist records of Tridentine, or ultramontane, devotions. While continuing to preach on the Passion, the Commandments, the Sacraments and the Eternal Truths, in 1846 he began to introduce some of the Rosminian practices of Eucharistic and Marian devotions into his missions.[174] Hence in St Chad's, St Mary's and St Joseph's he held the Forty Hours' Exposition in a blaze of candlelight.[175] In St Joseph's he held a service in honour of the Virgin Mary. He also introduced scapulars and devotions to the Sacred Heart.[176] At Woolston, Warrington in 1847 he had held a procession round the church of about forty children, twenty-four girls wearing white dresses and veils 'flowing gracefully down their shoulders with a crown of flowers over their heads' and the boys 'in cassocks and surplices, bearing long wax candles'.[177] Although doctrinally sound, these devotional exercises were controversial at the time, especially amongst some English Catholics who considered they appealed too much to the senses and were therefore unlikely to bear lasting fruit.[178] Father Dominic approved of them in a parochial context but he considered they were not the substance of a Passionist mission.[179] For Dominic it was not a blaze of candles but the memory of the Passion that, by giving meaning to the sufferings of the *anawim*, would raise them up to a higher quality of life in union with God. In Dublin in April 1849 he, Ignatius and Father Vincent Grotti, an even greater preacher than Gaudentius, tested what Italian Passionist techniques were suitable for the British Isles. Some, such as a solemn entry into the church, were already done in England as far as circumstances permitted. Perhaps the most effective in Dublin was the ringing of the great church bell at 10 o'clock every night, when all were asked to kneel down for a short time to pray for the unrepentant. This exercise continued each day until the evening when a meditation was given on Christ's prayer for his executioners. The bell was again rung and all in the church were asked to beg pardon of anyone they had offended. The missioners set the example with Father Ignatius, already garbed in his striking Passionist habit, 'kneeling down with a crown of thorns on his head and a rope round his neck' to beg pardon of the people. Fathers Dominic and Vincent then did the same. Throughout the mission the 'work of Confessions was quite beyond the powers and time of the missionaries.' Every day all the confessionals were 'beset by crowds of penitents, who awaited their turns, many of them from 5 in the morning till 11 at night and this for days in succession never going out for refreshment.' The majority had been years away from the church. 'Those who had not some real difficulty', Ignatius recorded, 'would hardly have endured so long waiting.' On the last Sunday, he preached at the Renewal of Baptismal Vows, when about 3,000 people received Communion. On no score could Gaudentius' methods have improved on this mission.[180]

Father Gaudentius was young, however, and impressed by the Rosminians' success.[181] Moreover, the Sacramental and Marian devotions were certainly sanctioned by Bishop Wiseman, who wanted a popular spirituality that would appeal to the heart.[182] They were highly attractive to working-class Catholics and to Protestants, many of whom attended the missions and saw them as displaying the splendour of the Catholic Church.[183] They became characteristic of English Catholicism until well into the twentieth century.[184] Although, therefore, he was partially straying from strictly Passionist techniques, Father Gaudentius was doing a great deal of good.[185] After 300 years' skulking in garrets and hedges, neither English nor Irish Catholics had ever seen such dazzling religious services as he provided and which elevated them above the drab misery of their social conditions.[186] They had never heard a man who so spoke 'to the heart', even 'captivated the affections' as he did.[187] In 1849 Father Croskell wrote to the *Tablet* of the 'extraordinary excitement' aroused by Father Gaudentius' 'powerful and affecting sermons'. 'Icy, indeed', said a parishioner in Glossop in 1846, 'is the heart which can brave the eloquent appeals of the holy Monk.'[188]

By involving the laity, men, women and children, in the liturgy, Father Gaudentius strengthened parish communities.[189] He introduced them to Catholic Continental practices, thus binding them to the wider Catholic Church. He gave Irish refugees a sense of identity as Catholics in a foreign country. He encouraged the generality of English Catholics to practise their faith more confidently. Helping to transform the Catholic Church in England according to Wiseman's Tridentine policy, Father Gaudentius Rossi made a significant contribution to the development of Catholic devotional practice and working-class culture in the mid-nineteenth century.[190]

Largely through his exertions, the Catholic Church in Manchester in spite of large Irish congregations, became Anglo-Roman, not Irish.[191] The Irish in Manchester were not segregated socially, politically or religiously. They formed an integral part of every section of society. Religiously, as in Ireland itself under the reforming Archbishop Cullen, they were bonded with English Catholics in an upsurge of loyalty to the papacy, all the more ardent for their pontiff's political vicissitudes in Italy and, from 1850, for their own renewed proscription in England.[192] Although his achievement would have been even greater if he had listened to Father Dominic Barberi's wisdom, Father Gaudentius Rossi must be considered one of the great missioners of nineteenth-century England.

This spectacular Catholic revivalism could not go unnoticed. In 1852 it was accompanied in Manchester by the tangible signs of fourteen priests, several schools, an orphanage, religious orders of men and women and thousands of practising working-class Catholics, who packed six churches three or four times each Sunday, while others remained proportionately empty.[193] In the country as a whole it had culminated in September 1850 in Pius IX's restoration of the Catholic hierarchy to England and Wales, with Nicholas Wiseman as resident Cardinal Archbishop of Westminster. That, however, had led *The Times* into a flagrant act of anti-Catholic aggression which had been followed by Russell's appeal to the people of England in order to win himself 'much-needed popularity and political support'.[194] The repercussions were felt in Manchester. It was therefore in a climate of anti-Catholicism as well as within the Catholic revival that in 1851 Elizabeth Prout founded her religious order for lower-class women.

CHAPTER III

A PASSIONIST FOUNDATION IN MANCHESTER

1. POPULAR PROTESTANTISM

Popular Protestantism was not new in 1850. It sprang from the Evangelicals, whom Thomas More had identified in 1531 as being the advocates of the Protestant reformation.[1] The more contemporary Anglican Evangelical Protestant Association had been founded in 1779 in response to the first Catholic Relief Act and had quickly shown its ability to rouse an anti-Catholic rabble in the Gordon riots of 1780.[2] In 1827 the Evangelicals founded the British Society for Promoting the Religious Principles of the Reformation which organized the distribution of anti-Catholic tracts and sent out such lecturers as the Reverend Hugh McNeile of Liverpool and Canon Hugh Stowell of Salford — known to local Catholics as the 'Head Protestant Watchman' and to Dissenters as the 'Pope of Salford'.[3] From 1848 the Evangelicals in Manchester sold a penny weekly, the *Protestant Witness*, 'to advocate uncompromising Protestantism and to maintain and promulgate the Principles of the Reformation'.[4] Constantly reminding its readers of their duty to combat popery, its publications were full of anti-Irish as well as anti-Catholic propaganda.[5] A repository of Protestant mythology, intended for a working-class readership, it circulated articles on purgatory and prayers for the dead, Confession, the Jesuits, Transubstantiation, the Bible, infallibility, the Virgin Mary, Extreme Unction, popish disloyalty, Guy Fawkes, the papacy and nunneries. It gave full coverage to Canon Stowell's frequent anti-Catholic lectures in Manchester and Salford on such topics as 'Roman Catholic institutions of the empire', 'Two great evils of Popery: Mary and the Mass' and 'The Pope as Anti-Christ'. Anything done or advertised by the local Catholic churches was noted and ridiculed. It even, unwittingly, noted Elizabeth Prout's arrival in Manchester, for in October 1849, it commented on St Chad's notices, posted round the walls of Angel Meadow, alerting parishioners to the opportunity for their children to have 'a sound moral and religious education under the superintendence of a master and *a mistress* of their own creed'.[6] It gave similar publicity to the statues adorning the exterior of St Chad's new church, to a notice advertising May devotions in St John's, Salford and to St Mary's new bell, which roused the working classes for a full hour before Sunday's 11 o'clock Mass.[7] Bishop Wiseman was featured on 6 April 1850. Later in the month, great prominence was given to the ex-Dominican Achilli both before and after his address to Manchester's Protestant Reformation Society.[8] Newman was pilloried in May and in October coverage was given to an anti-Catholic lecture in Stockport. It was the news of Pius IX's restoration of the hierarchy, however, that gave the publishers more to think about than a 'Winking Madonna'.[9]

Hardly unaware of this ultra-Protestant reaction to the Catholic revival, Elizabeth Prout had unobtrusively and courageously been founding her religious institute. At twenty-nine years of age in 1849-50, she was the youngest, and the first, Catholic Englishwoman to found a religious order in nineteenth-century England. She was unusual as a Catholic foundress in that the inspiration to found her congregation was not her own. It belonged to Father Gaudentius Rossi. Her personal role in the foundation, however, was of fundamental importance. In co-operating with him and with Father Robert Croskell, she made a deliberate and radical option for the poor: she not only abandoned her chance of a secure religious life in Belgium; she also sacrificed the opportunity to make a respectable marriage, for she had simultaneously received a marriage proposal. From November 1849, on Father Gaudentius' instructions, she had had frequent meetings with 'young friends in Manchester' who wished to join her. She had encouraged them to practise 'solid virtues, prayer, recollection, mortification and retirement from worldly company'.[10] She had written to candidates whose addresses Father Gaudentius had given her, and, despite her general docility to both Fathers Gaudentius and Croskell, she had shown independence, decision and, as Gaudentius agreed, prudence, in rejecting some of them.[11] Between 1849 and 1851 Father Croskell held 'several meetings' of aspirants to explain 'the object and plan' of the proposed institute.[12] He gave them 'a short exhortation or read some spiritual book regarding the religious state'; they 'performed some devotions'; and then they went home. These simple meetings were, as Mother Winefride Lynch later recorded, 'the beginning of the great work' of founding the Sisters of the Cross and Passion.[13] In view of contemporary opinions about the 'viciousness' of factory girls, seamstresses and lower domestic servants, it says much for the virtue of the Catholic working-class girls of Manchester that about thirty young women attended these meetings, seriously considering religious life and continuing their activities as the storm caused by the aggression of *The Times* broke over England.[14]

The restoration of the Catholic hierarchy in England and Wales was Rome's administrative complement to Britain's 1829 Catholic Emancipation Act. Because of the penal laws, it was not possible before 1829 for Catholic bishops in England to function normally under the Holy See. English Catholic affairs had therefore been supervised by the Congregation for the Propagation of the Faith. England had been treated as a missionary country, with its bishops termed 'vicars apostolic'. The 1829 act made that system obsolete. Almost twenty years later, with a massive increase in the Catholic population in England, it was urgently desirable to regularise it.[15] With the knowledge of the British government, Bishops Wiseman and

Ullathorne held negotiations in Rome from 1847. Russell, the prime minister, not only knew of them but, through his father-in-law, Lord Minto, was simultaneously conducting his own, in which he asked for a renewal of diplomatic relations with the Vatican and a voice in the appointment of Catholic bishops.[16] On Lord Eglinton's recommendation, however, parliament stipulated that the pope's ambassador must not be a cleric.[17] Minto was predictably told that, as a head of state, Pius IX would choose his own ambassador and since the appointment of bishops was a spiritual matter internal to the Catholic community, it was not the concern of the British government. Out of courtesy, Pius IX gave him a copy of the plans for restoring the hierarchy, with the titles of the bishops, including Westminster. Russell, therefore, knew everything in advance, as did all interested parties, for the subject was publicly discussed in the *Tablet*, in other newspapers and in parliament. There was open reference to Wiseman's being made a cardinal. Russell had even said he saw no reason why the Catholic bishops could not have the territorial titles of the medieval sees.[18] He had also already referred to the vicars apostolic both as 'bishops' and the 'Catholic hierarchy'.[19]

Pius IX restored the hierarchy on 29 September 1850.[20] Wiseman was nominated a cardinal the next day. He then wrote a letter to *The Times*, as the leading English newspaper, informing it that the expected appointments had been made. On 7 October he sent a pastoral letter to his secretary. *The Times* delayed publishing its letter until 14 October.[21] It then described the restoration as 'one of the grossest acts of folly and impertinence which the court of Rome [had] ventured to commit since the Crown and people of England [had thrown] off its yoke'.[22] Wiseman's pastoral had not provoked this aggression, because it had still not reached England.[23] Other newspapers quickly followed *The Times*' lead. When Wiseman's Flaminian Gate pastoral was published, their excitement knew no bounds.[24]

As a Catholic, Elizabeth Prout found herself at the centre of the greatest religious issue of the day.[25] With her native appraisal of the situation, however, she sensibly ignored the whole furore.[26] On 25 October 1850 she suggested to Father Gaudentius that the new order should be founded on 25 March 1851, a date that may have had special significance for her apart from its being Lady Day.[27] She told him that she and her prospective companions were now calling each other 'Sister' and were reciting the Little Office of Our Lady.[28] Gaudentius was more nervous. Aware of what was happening to religious in Italy and, as a stranger in England, more fearful than she of Protestant antagonism, he warned her on 4 November she must be 'prepared for a difficult undertaking'.[29] A few days later Russell aggravated anti-Catholic hostility by the publication of his 'incendiary letter' to the bishop of Durham.[30] Directed against both Catholics and Tractarians, it was not the 'hasty screed of a compulsive anti-Papist', but 'a pondered missive from the leader of a Liberal government'.[31] 'A good Church cry' could be politically useful.[32] Posing as the champion of English liberty and Protestantism, Russell hoped to use the mirage of papal aggression to win himself 'much-needed popularity and political support'.[33] For that political end, he relied 'with confidence on the people of England', the 'rascal multitude', who had already responded to *The Times*' aggression by covering the country with burning effigies of Pius IX, Cardinal Wiseman and the twelve bishops, by stoning Catholic priests and by attacking Catholic churches.[34] In December 1850 Father Ignatius Spencer was twice attacked in Liverpool.[35]

With such mandates, the Tory *Manchester Courier*, which had already given prominence to anti-Catholic references and lectures in Manchester in 1849-50, covered 'papal aggression' from November 1850 to February 1851 with caustic articles ridiculing Catholic beliefs and practices and with slogans of 'No Popery', 'Church and Queen' and 'No Surrender'.[36] The *Protestant Witness* followed a feature on John Bull and the Papal Bull with an article on 2 November on Guy Fawkes, while at the earliest opportunity Stowell 'preached a most comprehensive and powerful sermon' on the 'Papal Hierarchy' to 'one of the largest congregations ever remembered' in Christ Church, Salford.[37] The *Manchester Guardian* maintained a modicum of restraint, asking for a 'return of common sense and good humour.... There is such a tumult of alarm and indignation as has scarcely been known since the fitting out of the Spanish Armada', it declared. 'We never saw the isle so frighted from its propriety.'[38] It pointed out that most of the hierarchy had already been bishops for some time and that the pope had merely restored a more canonical system of government, which was the internal concern of the Catholic Church. Canon Stowell, however, could not be pacified. Addressing a packed Free Trade Hall on 16 January 1851, he spoke of the 'strong feeling of indignation which the recent appointment of the English Catholic hierarchy had raised throughout the country'. He was persuaded, he said, 'that the great conflict of English freedom, civil and religious - for England's liberty, glory, security and truth - was now being waged.'[39] He appealed to the multitude. It was fortunate he did not know Elizabeth Prout's intentions. His followers had already hounded the Sisters of Charity out of Salford.[40]

Father Gaudentius was anxious: parliament seemed likely to reintroduce anti-Catholic penal laws and there was an increase in popular opposition to convents.[41] In January 1851 he said the congregation could not be started until it was known what parliament would do.[42] Elizabeth Prout, therefore, did not open her convent on 25 March

1851.[43] Canon Stowell's efforts, however, contributed 'in no mean degree' to the Ecclesiastical Titles Bill.[44] At the same time Catholics in Manchester were not idle. In February 1850, by sheer force of numbers, without striking a blow, the Catholic working classes had prevented the holding of an anti-Catholic meeting.[45] In February 1851 a group of seventeen middle-class laity organised a 'great meeting' of 10,000 Catholics in the Free Trade Hall to express 'their grateful acknowledgement for the establishment of the Catholic hierarchy'; to petition parliament 'against any aggression on their civil and religious liberties'; and to deplore the 'ignorance, intolerance and hatred towards Catholics and their institutions', which had been intensified by Russell's having so far forgotten his 'duty to maintain the peace of the kingdom' that he had sounded the tocsin of religious intolerance for his own 'political capital'.[46] Elizabeth Prout was gauging local temper correctly, even though members of parliament were calling for the registration and inspection of convents and the *Protestant Witness* continued its anti-Catholic propaganda. Throughout February and March 1851 it published articles on papal aggression and on Wiseman. It lauded the London lectures of the ex-Barnabite Gavazzi and when he came to Manchester it reported his talks on clerical celibacy; on the horrors of the inquisition, vividly described; and on monastic establishments.[47] A Catholic lecture in St Chad's in July 1851 was quickly followed by a 'powerful address' from an Evangelical in St Thomas's, Red Bank.[48] When Cardinal Wiseman came to Manchester to consecrate William Turner as bishop of Salford on 25 July 1851, Canon Stowell marked the occasion by both preaching and lecturing on Rome's threats to the 'peace and civil liberty of England'.[49] The Ecclesiastical Titles Act was passed on 1 August, forbidding the Catholic bishops to use the titles of English sees.[50] It was thus in a still hostile milieu that, with two companions, Elizabeth Prout founded her religious order at 69 Stocks Street on 15 August, the Assumption of the Virgin Mary, a feast particularly dear to Paul of the Cross.[51] Father Croskell continued to visit them 'to instruct them in the duties of a religious life'.[52] He also presided over the private ceremony they had in St Chad's at Candlemas 1852, when they assumed a uniform black dress as a sign of their religious dedication.[53]

Father Croskell's meetings laid the foundations of the institute. As he himself later insisted, however, he left 'the formation of the spirit and the special direction' of the order to the Passionists, entirely represented in these early stages by Father Gaudentius Rossi.[54] As far as its co-founder, Father Croskell, was concerned, the institute was a Passionist congregation in its 'spirit' and 'special direction' from its beginning. Elizabeth thought the same. Although she was fully cognisant of Father Croskell's position, she regarded Gaudentius as the prime founder and the order as Passionist. As understood by later sisters, Father Croskell in 1849 had 'quite agreed with' Father Gaudentius and 'promised to aid him in his work.... It is necessary to remark', wrote the annalist, after explaining Father Croskell's part in the foundation, 'that all these things were done by the direction and counsel of Father Gaudentius, who on account of his missionary work could seldom visit the Sisters in person, but gave his instructions in writing which were faithfully carried out by the Reverend Mr Croskell.'[55] For his part, Gaudentius eschewed the title 'founder', claiming, like Paul of the Cross, that Jesus Christ was the founder.[56] For a time he carefully deferred to Father Croskell, referring to him in July 1852 as the 'nursing parent of the infant institution', but from the beginning Gaudentius adopted the role of primary founder.[57] Most importantly, in his frequent letters to Elizabeth Prout he inculcated the Paulacrucian spirituality she had already received in Father Dominic Barberi's Stone.

Father Gaudentius had begun his correspondence with Elizabeth Prout on 24 July 1848 in reply to a note telling him of her safe arrival in Northampton and of how happy she already felt amongst the Sisters of the Infant Jesus.[58] Since she treasured his letter so much that she kept it to her dying day, the advice it gave must have formed the basis of her search for holiness. 'You shall always be happy', he told her, 'if you shall always endeavour to become a good and perfect religious. What greater happiness can possibly be enjoyed by a young lady than that of being entirely consecrated to God in religion, and thus to become the true Spouse of Jesus Christ.' It was to rediscover that 'greater happiness' that in 1849 she sought admission to a Belgian convent and then collaborated with Father Gaudentius in founding an order for the poor. What was to become the hallmark of her life, he had already unwittingly laid before her in 1848, 'Humble then yourself before Him and for His sake before every person and particularly your Sisters in religion.'[59] He had encouraged her to consecrate her entire self to God, 'mind and heart, soul and body', to love God as her spouse, to revere Him as her monarch, to obey Him as her master, to respect Him as her Father. He had offered her the 'four wheels of the future carriage' of her perfection: 'profound humility and blind obedience, a most fervent love and habitual recollection of mind.'[60] Sent to such a recipient, it was perhaps the most important letter Father Gaudentius Rossi ever wrote. Although he did not mention the Passion specifically in this letter, its sentiments were Paulacrucian. The same spirituality, which was the only school he knew, was apparent throughout his correspondence from 1849 to his departure for North America in 1855. He urged her to pray 'frequently to Almighty God... to make his will known' and for His 'grace to accomplish it at the appointed time and place.'[61] He encouraged her to try to become 'better and better every day', attending to prayer, daily meditation, humility, charity, meekness and patience. She must not aspire to the honour of being a foundress but she must try to fit herself for the work. Since it was God's work, she should place her confidence in Him. Working as a dead instrument in God's hands, she would be able to work wonders.[62]

A convert to Catholicism, a Victorian unmarried woman of generous nature and embarking on a task about which she knew very little, in 1850 Elizabeth was still diffident and very anxious to please all with whom she worked.[63] Gaudentius told her she was too afraid of giving displeasure. She should try sincerely and earnestly to please God, and then good men could be pleased too and if they were not, since it was impossible to please everyone, it did not matter. She should act, Gaudentius told her, 'purely for God, for God alone'.[64] Then she would receive 'greater lights from heaven, spiritual consolations from God, success in her undertakings and happiness in mind and heart.' At the same time, he told her to practise obedience, self-denial and humility, to attend to prayer, meditation and spiritual reading.[65] As she moved nearer to opening a convent with her first companions, he recommended to all of them fervent prayer, recollection, love of poverty and mortification, humility, self-denial and great esteem, love and respect for each other, while avoiding anything worldly, dissipating, vain or childish, or envy, dislike or antipathy of each other.[66] He admitted in early November 1850, when anti-Catholic aggression was at its height and there was widespread anti-convent propaganda, that she would need 'great confidence in God'. She would have a 'great deal to bear' in every way but if God supported her 'all at last' would 'succeed well'.[67]

In March 1851 Father Gaudentius gave the first clear sign of the Passionist charism he was imparting to the forthcoming institute. Having heard from Elizabeth that one of her prospective companions was ill, he wrote, 'Tell her... to offer all her sufferings to the eternal Father in union with the greater sufferings of our blessed Saviour in atonement for her sins, if she has ever committed any. Tell her to remember this ejaculation *O Suffering Jesus, O Sorrowful Mary, I compassionate You, I love You with my whole heart.*'[68] A traditional Passionist prayer, a hundred years later it was still recited daily at 11 a.m. and 3 p.m. in Elizabeth Prout's congregation to commemorate Christ's Passion and Death.[69] In the summer of 1851, Gaudentius insisted he wanted seven sisters to begin with, in memory of Mary's seven griefs.[70] Then, on 21 December 1851, he wrote to tell Elizabeth he had decided to call the institute the 'Sisters of the Holy Family'.[71]

In view of the distinct Paulacrucian spirituality both he and Elizabeth personally practised and which he had undoubtedly been inculcating as the spirit of the embryonic institute, Father Gaudentius' choice of title might seem surprising. In fact, however, as suggested by a Passionist only a few days before Christmas, the devotion held a specifically Paulacrucian connotation, for Paul of the Cross had had a particular devotion to the Divine Nativity 'amid such lack of comfort and in such poverty'.[72] When Gaudentius made his decision he was giving a mission in St Anthony's, Liverpool, where they would have been erecting the Christmas crib and where the sanctuary walls were adorned with two plaques depicting the Shepherds and the Magi visiting the Holy Family.[73] The Nativity scene would therefore have been uppermost in his mind. It would have been uppermost in that of Elizabeth Prout too when she received his letter, for it would have reached her on Christmas Eve.[74] It was an image that Paul of the Cross frequently dwelt upon. 'I would like you to celebrate the holy feast of Christmas', he wrote in 1761, 'in the poor stable of your own heart, where the dear Jesus will be born in a spiritual way. Offer this poor stable to the holy Mary... and to the holy St Joseph....'[75] For Paul there was no dichotomy between the Incarnation and the Redemption. The crib and the cross were both manifestations of the unfathomable mystery of God's love.[76] The theology of the Incarnation and that of the Redemption were complementary: Christ was born in order to die. The same 'sea of infinite love' was evident in both the Incarnation and the Passion.[77] Mary, Joseph and the Holy Family as such were all important in Paul's spirituality.[78] Although he generally prefixed his letters with the initials 'IXP', for the 'Passion of Jesus Christ' or simply 'Jesus Christ', he also frequently used 'JMJ', for 'Jesus, Mary and Joseph'.[79] Moreover, Paul's particular devotion to the Incarnation stemmed from the teaching of the Dominican mystic, John Tauler of Alsace, who spoke of a divine nativity in the soul. Paul of the Cross, however, while sometimes using Tauler's idea directly, also reversed it, giving it the more Scriptural interpretation of 'the rebirth of the soul in the Divine Word'.[80] Thus Paul associated the Incarnation with the soul's rebirth in Baptism into the Suffering Christ, with the consequent invitation to share in both His Passion and Resurrection. The celebration of Christmas as the Divine Nativity, therefore, held a particular significance in Paulacrucian spirituality. Father Dominic Barberi had shown the same devotion, which was a recognised essential of the Passionist inheritance.[81] In contemporary England it accorded well with the increasing emphasis on family life, which later led in both Anglican and Catholic circles to widespread devotion to the Holy Family.[82] For Father Gaudentius Rossi in 1851 it solved the practical problem of what name he could give his institute. He had no authority to give it the Passionist title. Only the Passionist general could give that, as he later did.[83] In calling the institute the 'Sisters of the Holy Family' in the context of the feast of Christmas, however, Father Gaudentius could and did give it a title that was resonantly Passionist and thus in perfect accord with the Paulacrucian spirituality he was inculcating. In 1852 he gave it a Rule that was also essentially Passionist.

2. MARTHA AND MARY

From June 1852 Elizabeth Prout and her Sisters of the Holy Family lived according to Father Gaudentius Rossi's Rule.[84] In writing it, he faced the same problem as in founding and naming the institute: he had no authority to give it the *Rule* of Paul of the Cross. That Passionist *Rule*, however, was the only Rule he knew.[85] Inevitably, therefore, he took it for his guide. Otherwise he showed the same imagination in prescribing the sisters' lifestyle as he demonstrated in his missionary devotions. As a result, his Rule placed Elizabeth Prout's congregation both in the mainstream of Tridentine Catholicism and in the tradition of Paul of the Cross.

Despite structural differences in the two Rules, Gaudentius followed Paulacrucian thought very closely. Paul's *Rule* was based on his own previous experience, as described in his Preface to his primitive Rule.[86] It was the symbolic structure of those experiences, which his followers were called to share.[87] Paul's *Rule* was therefore based on the heart of the matter: the experience of identification with Christ in His Passion. Gaudentius also began at the heart of the matter, in his case identification with the Holy Family. Because he emphasised the centrality of the devotion, his Rule was a characteristically Passionist Rule of the heart.

Like Paul, Gaudentius emphasised 'memory'. 'The object of the new institute', he said, was 'to honour and to *imitate in a special manner the mode of life*' of the Holy Family at Nazareth, where they were 'all diligently engaged in manual work and continual prayer'.[88] He constantly stressed this reliving, re-experiencing, of the life of the Holy Family in his subsequent correspondence. Thus on 19 March 1855, in words resonant of the earliest Rule of Paul of the Cross and indicating that he gave to the 'memory' of the Holy Family the same profound meaning that Paul had given to the 'memory' of the Passion, Gaudentius wrote to Elizabeth,

> You should *never forget* that the two grand objects of this pious institution is [sic] to *promote a special devotion* to the Holy Family of Nazareth, Jesus, Mary and Joseph and to afford an opportunity to pious and virtuous young females of useful and industrious habits of embracing a state of religious perfection. These two grand objects should *never be out of the mind and heart* of the Sisters...[89]

Thus the purpose of the institute was to provide working-class women with a contemplative lifestyle of manual work and prayer on the pattern of the Holy Family at Nazareth. To promote their contemplative lifestyle, each house was to have a workroom 'provided with all the necessary implements required for the different branches of industry'.[90] They were allowed to have female servants to help with the work and to take out work done for 'some lady or female in the town'.[91] They could also train apprentices.[92] They could sell their work in a saleroom in the convent 'to any female with ready money' but were forbidden to give on credit.[93] Goods were to be labelled with prices, which were to be 'just and moderate'.[94] Only the servants, however, were to do the actual selling and, as a protection of the sisters' vow of chastity, male customers were forbidden.[95] Although based on the Gospel, Gaudentius' ideas reflected those of the time that women should not go out to work.[96] They also reflected Manchester's industry and commercialism. The order, like Manchester society, would be materially sustained by industry and trade. Gaudentius' values, however, were diametrically opposed to those of most manufacturers. Profits, if there were any, would be ploughed back into the congregation but only to enable more working-class women to avail themselves of religious life without a dowry.[97]

In order to inculcate the 'memory' of the Holy Family devotionally, Gaudentius prescribed intentions for every day of the week and novenas for the major feasts of the Church. He wanted a lot of hymn singing, both in the chapel according to the liturgical cycle and at certain times during work to facilitate recollection and, probably, to break the tedium of industry.[98] It was Elizabeth's task to 'give orders and directions to some of the Sisters to teach the proper music' of these hymns.[99] She was also to ensure that the community enjoyed the devotional practices associated with Wiseman's Tridentine reforms, such as Exposition of the Blessed Sacrament, Benediction and Marian devotions during the month of May.[100] Consequently, the sisters had a rich liturgical life and were brought into the mainstream of Catholic devotional culture as increasingly enjoyed by the working classes. They were also to have statues and pictures, particularly of Mary and Joseph and especially in the chapel, and they were to 'keep [them] neat and devoutly decorated'.[101] Thus the convent became devotionally homely and a colourful contrast to Manchester's drab industrial environment.[102]

Their domestic horarium reflected both the traditional monastic observance, in which time, punctuated by bells, had always been important, and the bell-dominated world of Manchester's factory system. To employers time was money.[103] In Paulacrucian spirituality time was a gift from God to be used fruitfully.[104] 'You must be very careful to economise every minute of time and carefully employ it in work', Gaudentius wrote to Elizabeth in 1855.[105] The sisters were to work 'with assiduity and diligence', expecting to receive an eternal reward commensurate with 'the amount of work done for God's sake on earth'.[106] They were to go to their work with a spirit of humility 'reflecting that it was through the sin of the first woman that all mankind had been condemned by God to hard labour....'[107] In spite, however, of thus reflecting the contemporary themes of the basic depravity of human nature and the inferiority of woman, Gaudentius intended that, by living out the 'memory' of the Holy Family, the sisters would express the true Scriptural value of work as a 'blessing' rather than as the 'curse' that was so conspicuous in Manchester.[108] Rosary beads as well as scissors and pincushion hung from their waists.[109] Their sweated labour would be transformed through Nazareth and the Cross into a share in Christ's Resurrection. Industry and prayer, Martha and Mary, were constantly combined.[110] Gaudentius' Rule divided the day into allotted times for spiritual observances, meals and recreation. Their sewing, however, was seldom put away, even during recreation and spiritual reading. Every day, in addition to readings during dinner and supper, they were to have half an hour's common spiritual reading, during which, in practice, the superior read while the others sewed.[111] Father Gaudentius recommended only two spiritual writers in his Rule, the Carmelite St Teresa of Avila, a favourite of Paul of the Cross, and the Jesuit Father Rodriguez, whose *Christian Perfection* was read every day by the Passionists. At Gaudentius' suggestion Elizabeth adopted the same practice of reading it aloud in the refectory during meals.[112]

Gaudentius followed Paulacrucian spirituality and the Passionist *Rule* in giving centrality to the Holy Eucharist, the Memorial of Christ's Passion.[113] The sisters were to attend Mass daily, receive Holy Communion frequently and make both frequent visits to the Blessed Sacrament and frequent acts of Spiritual Communion.[114] To assist them in their life of spiritual perfection and to keep them in a constant state of readiness to receive the Eucharist, they were to make two daily examinations of conscience, one at noon, which was to be a meditation on the pursuit of a particular virtue, and another in the evening, during which each privately reviewed the day and asked God's pardon for any faults or breaches of the Rule.[115] To preserve purity of heart and to receive spiritual guidance, every week each sister was to celebrate the Sacrament of Reconciliation, or Confession as it was then generally called.[116] To facilitate recollection at all times and to cater for sisters who were nineteenth-century working-class women, some illiterate, the Rule prescribed a large number of repetitive vocal prayers to be used even during work and recreation, as well as at times of formal

prayer.[117] Like the Passionists, the sisters were to have outstanding
devotion to Mary, exemplified in numerous ways and in particular in
the daily recitation of the Rosary, a meditation with Mary on the life
of Christ.[118] As Sisters of the Holy Family and like Paul of the Cross,
they were also to have devotion to St Joseph.[119]

Even though he made the Holy Family the central devotion, Father
Gaudentius also gave the institute an unmistakable Passionist identity
in legislating for a distinct devotion to the Passion. 'Like the wounds
of their Divine Spouse', there were five particular virtues they were to
practise: charity, diligence, humility, confidence and prayer. If a sister
felt offended by another's remarks, she was 'to bear it in silence in
imitation of [Christ], Who like an innocent and meek lamb, when He
was reviled He did not revile, but opened not His Mouth.'[120] Friday,
a day of abstinence in honour of the Passion, was to be spent 'in pious
remembrance and honour of the Most Bitter Passion of the Divine
Spouse Jesus Crucified', a phrase Elizabeth Prout made her own in her
deep devotion to her 'Crucified Spouse'.[121] It was also to be offered up
in particular for that traditionally Passionist intention, the conversion
of England.[122] Every Friday, too, the sisters were to say the Stations
of the Cross together. They were to have a particular Lenten devotion
to the Passion. More deeply, they were to follow Christ in their vow
of obedience 'even to the death of the Cross'. They were to practise
a patient endurance of contradictions, humiliations, difficulties and
sufferings. In times of sickness they were to imitate 'their suffering
Redeemer on the Cross'.[123]

It was in his section on the care of the sick and in another inculcating
the respectful, affectionate charity the sisters were to exercise towards
one another that Father Gaudentius most deeply imprinted the heart of
the gentle, kindly spirit of Paul of the Cross.[124] The sisters were to
have great esteem for each other. They were to wear charity as the
livery of their Divine Spouse; to banish from their mind and heart
every uncharitable thought, rash judgement and ill feeling against any
person but especially against any of their religious sisters. Their
convent, like the home at Nazareth, was to be 'the abode of divine
love, concord, harmony, peace and happiness'. To avoid giving
offence to each other, they were never to mention each others' faults,
defects or mistakes. Rather they were to show their love for one
another by praying for each other, patiently bearing each other's short-
comings and imperfections, trying to give each other good example,
helping one another and consoling each other in afflictions.[125] In
particular they were to prove the sincerity of their love towards a sister
who was sick. 'Every attention in their power' was to be paid to her
'as early as possible' and 'every care' was to be taken of her. When
an illness became dangerous, the sister was never to be left alone, day

or night, and the superior 'in her maternal charity and loving watchfulness' was to see she received 'all the sacred rights [*sic*: rites] and
spiritual comforts' of the Catholic Church and 'all care and attention...
to [her] comfort' when she was convalescing.[126] It was this Paulacrucian spirit that the Passionist Father General recognised in the sisters
in 1864 and that led him to claim them as his own.[127]

Father Gaudentius was also careful to transfer into his Rule those
elements in the Passionist lifestyle: prayer, penance, solitude and
poverty that Paul of the Cross had defined as characteristic of the
Passionist Congregation. Reminiscently of Paul's emphasis on the
contemplative nature of his order, Gaudentius devoted the first nine
chapters of his Rule to the sisters' contemplative life of prayer. To
promote their union with God, the sisters were to spend at least one
hour each day in meditation, partly in the morning and partly in the
evening and on Sundays and holidays of obligation one and a half
hours. This meditation was never to be omitted, even at the price of
time prescribed for sleep.[128] Moreover if a sister could not sleep, she
could get up and pray.[129] All the sisters were bound to choir observance, reciting the Little Office of Our Lady, in Latin or English, on
Sundays, holidays of obligation and every day during the annual
spiritual retreat.[130] On weekdays and for sisters who could not read,
the Office could be commuted to vocal prayers but, implicitly,
Gaudentius expected everyone to learn to read.[131] As a support to their
contemplative life, Gaudentius, like Paul of the Cross, laid special
importance on the annual retreat. Made, if possible, under the
guidance of a priest, it was to last eight days, during which the sisters
were to be as free as possible from other duties and were to keep strict
silence.[132] Since penance was an integral part of contemplative life,
Gaudentius provided for a number of penitential exercises, all of them
'acts of penance and mortification' practised by the Passionist Fathers
and Brothers.[133] Since the sisters were committed to exhausting labour,
however, the Passionist fast on Wednesdays, Fridays and Saturdays
was mitigated to abstinence from meat. The sisters were also to take
the discipline three times a week. When this frequency proved
prejudicial to health, however, Gaudentius reduced it in January 1855
to once a week, on Fridays, with additions for suffrages, Advent and
Lent.[134]

At the same time that Gaudentius was legislating for a contemplative
institute, he was aware that, in the absence of dowries, its members
must earn their living. Elizabeth was already engaged in teaching and
parochial work. Her first two companions comprised a domestic
servant and a powerloom weaver. When they joined her at 69 Stocks
Street, the former left domestic service and joined the other in the
factory. All three had to continue to go out to work in order to support

themselves. Gaudentius had also to consider the wishes of his co-founder, Father Croskell, who was looking for parochial help, especially in schools. Although, therefore, Gaudentius envisaged that as far as possible, to preserve their contemplative lifestyle, the sisters would work inside the convent, even in their schools, he followed the Passionist principle of flexibility according to local needs in allowing work outside.[135] In this sense the institute sprang from Manchester's society.[136] Since the precise nature of their work outside the convent would depend on their individual talents, Father Gaudentius told Father Croskell he was not binding them to any particular work. They could 'gain an honest support for the community' in any way 'compatible with the spirit of the institute'. He stressed that he had 'paid every attention' to combining 'the contemplative with the active life'. He had tried 'to form Martha and Mary into one individual person.' He had used every possible means 'to remove dissipation of mind and to nourish an inward spirit of recollection.' While the general principles of his legislation regarding work were again derived from the Passionist *Rule* and *Regulations*, the more specific details arose from the institute's actual membership in 1852 and the needs of the Catholic Church in Manchester at that time. Father Gaudentius Rossi's Rule, therefore, was an application of Paulacrucian spirituality to a female religious order in an urban, industrial and commercial society. It was an extension of the Passionist mission to England. Significantly, this Passionist institute was the first female religious order to be founded in the industrial North West.[137] It was at once an integral component of that society and the antithesis of its values.[138] Although the Passionists were never able to fulfil Father Dominic's desire to have a monastery near Manchester, by founding a Passionist female congregation with Elizabeth Prout, Father Gaudentius created a permanent Passionist presence there, at the heart of England's industrial society.

To correspond to the Passionists' active missionary apostolate, Father Gaudentius envisaged that Elizabeth and her sisters would teach, offer women's retreats and instruct converts, all of which could be done within the confines of the convent, and also that, with the parish priest's permission, they would visit the sick, the spiritually negligent and the homes of the children they taught.[139] Thus, as well as giving them the Passionist apostolate of retreat work, he associated them with the work of parish visitation which Paul of the Cross had seen as part of his missionary activities.[140] Heavily weighted with spiritual duties, as Gaudentius admitted to Father Croskell in June 1852, the Rule, like the Passionist *Rule*, was designed to produce people who would be capable of taking Paulacrucian spirituality into Angel Meadow, Deansgate and Ancoats.[141] The Passionist missioners took it to the parishes in intensive courses concentrated into fairly short missions. The sisters would take it in a much more gradual process of education either through their daily contacts in schools or through parish visitation. In practice, unlike some of the Manchester authorities, they were not dealing with nameless masses, but with the eighty-year-old widow, Mary Little, a pauper who lived in Dyche Street, or the sick lady at Mrs Hanby's in Levenshulme, or the children in their classrooms.[142] As creating a Catholic ethos in schools, or a Catholic culture in society, they might be said to be exercising at least an unconscious form of social control.[143] The Catholic Church, however, was not so much an institution as a caring community. In their classrooms the sisters were giving the children the type of education their parents cherished as an integral part of their Catholic faith. In their parish visitation, like Father Dominic, they 'went amongst their own people'.[144] Theirs was not a proselytising mission. Unlike the Protestant city missions or the Reformation Society's Special Mission to Roman Catholics, they did not seek to attract converts, much less presume to show others the errors of their way.[145] They went only to the Catholic homes to which they were directed by the parish priests and they were forbidden by Rule to go anywhere else.[146]

Their type of visitation was an apostolate that was essentially Passionist and otherwise rare amongst Catholic religious orders.[147] Elizabeth's community was only one of several groups in Manchester, however, that visited the homes of the poor. Nevertheless, although she was not original in doing parish visitation in this sense, her motivation was different. Her aim was solely one of compassion. Carrying neither tracts nor Bibles and unpaid for their endeavours, Elizabeth and her sisters were unlike the paid Bible women and the various types of visitors from the middle classes of society.[148] One of the *anawim* herself, Elizabeth lacked the social influence of the Manchester and Salford Sanitary Association visitors, who tried to ameliorate the living conditions in Deansgate and Angel Meadow in the interests of a healthy environment.[149] Similarly she lacked the prestige and financial resources of the Manchester and Salford District Provident Society. Most importantly, she differed in her approach. Although willing to give 'occasional relief' in times of 'sickness and unavoidable misfortune', the Society's members particularly wanted to encourage 'industry and frugality' and were anxious to suppress mendicity and imposture.[150] In contrast, although her own poverty debarred Elizabeth from giving much material assistance, like the Passionists she was bound by Rule to give food to the poor who came to the convent door.[151] The tradition she imparted to her congregation was reflected in the Golden Jubilee description of her sisters as having 'worldly riches' as neither 'their portion nor inheritance' but as being 'especially loved by the poor to whom they [were] exceedingly kind and generous'.[152] As their work was described about seventy-five years after Father Gaudentius wrote his Rule, they visited the sick and gave them 'all possible help and comfort'. They also visited the homes of the poor and taught them the 'advantages of cleanliness, sobriety and careful housekeeping'. The 'untold good' of such visits, it was said, could not easily be estimated and 'many a hardworking heartbroken man' had 'blessed the Sisters for the happy change in his home'.[153] Thus they demonstrated how women could rise above poverty and privation with dignity. While not primarily expounding doctrines of self-help and improvement, they raised up the poor spiritually, morally, academically and, to some extent, materially.[154] In bringing their particular Paulacrucian spirituality to the working classes, Elizabeth Prout's order also differed from such Catholic ladies' associations as that in St John's Wood, London. As Catholics, these ladies saw visitation as an act of charity incumbent upon them as Christians. Although their motivation differed from that of the Manchester and Salford Provident Society, however, the ladies investigated the merits of respective claims before giving relief and they gave coal, potatoes, blankets etc. rather than money.[155] They were also still ladies. 'Never... allow any person to call [you] ladies', Gaudentius told Elizabeth in 1853.[156] She and her sisters did not give of their largesse. They gave themselves. Unlike the organisers of the settlement houses, they did not need to bridge the social gap between themselves and the poor. They were the poor. They did not offer the working classes 'flights of tea or dinner' and then send them back into the slums.[157] They went into their homes in the slums. Thus, neither evangelical cottage preachers nor middle-class philanthropists, founding neither clothing clubs nor mothers' meetings, but identified by their religious dress and simplicity of manner with a disinterested compassion for the sufferings of others, Elizabeth Prout and her sisters could evangelise the poor in those areas of Angel Meadow, Deansgate and Ancoats not generally reached by formal Christianity.[158] What was particularly Paulacrucian about their active apostolate, however, was that Father Gaudentius saw it as an opportunity to promote the 'memory' of the Holy Family 'in the hearts and minds' of others, in the same way that the Passionist Fathers and Brothers were bound by their fourth vow to promote the 'memory' of the Passion.[159] Thus in this way too he founded a fundamentally Passionist congregation. Their apostolate was no scheme for 'civilising' the poor but an expression of the Paulacrucian spirituality that motivated the Passionist mission to England, of which Elizabeth Prout's contemplative and active religious order formed an integral part.

Since the institute was to be both contemplative and active like his own Passionist Congregation, Gaudentius saw no difficulty in the sisters' exercising a high degree of solitude in spite of an active life in the industrial slums. The horarium he gave them was similar to that delineated in a letter and even headed 'JMJ', written by Paul of the Cross to a lady he was directing in 1733.[160] Within the convent they spent the day in silence, apart from half an hour's recreation after dinner and an hour at night. Since the purpose of solitude was to free the soul for contemplative union with God, they were to reflect on the presence of God throughout the day. To help them, while they worked they recited vocal prayers, such as the Rosary and pious ejaculations, and for two hours, from 10–11.00 a.m. and 3–4.00 p.m., they observed the strictest silence. From night prayers until after Mass the next morning they observed the Great Silence, as in all monastic institutions. Contact with 'the world' was curtailed. They were not to send or receive letters or messages, except through the superior. At recreation they were encouraged to have spiritual conversations and were forbidden to discuss extra-mural affairs. No secular visitors were allowed into recreation, nor into the refectory and certain other parts of the house which were considered within the enclosure. When sisters had to go out, they had to have a companion, as the Passionists normally had, and they had to seek the blessing of the superior both before going out and on their return. While out, they were not to engage in conversation, other than prayers, and were forbidden to enter any public building or private house except as instructed by the superior. Thus they would live totally in the presence of God in a permanent state of spiritual solitude that was enhanced not only by their annual eight-day retreat but by a monthly day of recollection, short, individual, private retreats and eight-day retreats before clothing and profession.[161]

Finally, the Passionist characteristic of poverty lay at the heart of the institute because it was essentially a religious order for the poor. In their practice of poverty the sisters were to be self-supporting, not simply because they were dowerless, but as a means of cherishing the spirit of their vow of poverty. They were required to hand in every farthing of their wages. Poverty was to be observed throughout the house and especially in the refectory and dormitory. There was to be no unnecessary adornment, not even in the chapel. In everything they were to be detached from a love of material goods.[162] Leading a 'perfectly common life', they could possess no personal property, not even their clothing. Everything they had belonged to the community collectively. Nothing could be disposed of by an individual, not even by the superior, who in this respect was a 'steward for the Community'. As a challenge to the 'vain and proud world' in which they lived, the secularist commercialism of Manchester, they were to 'glory to manifest... their spirit of poverty in everything in the house, furniture, clothing, utensils and food'.[163] Thus, like Paul of the Cross, Father Gaudentius Rossi made 'very deep poverty' the essence and standard of his congregation.[164]

3. AN OPTION FOR THE POOR

The characteristic poverty of Elizabeth Prout's order was ensured by the lowly employments of those who joined it, for of the first seven sisters who received the religious habit on 21 November 1852, Elizabeth Prout was a teacher; Catharine Gilday a powerloom weaver; Catharine Toler and Sarah Ann Lee domestic servants; Mary Taylor a lady's companion and Sunday-school teacher; and Mary Johnson a seamstress. The last, Marie Wilson, was, according to repute, 'a living saint' of no stated occupation and seems to have had a middle-class education.

As an uncertificated teacher in St Chad's, Elizabeth Prout was paid £30 per annum from 1849 to about November 1851.[165] She was therefore self-supporting and she was respectable. Her first two companions, Catharine Toler and Catharine Gilday, however, although self-supporting, were not considered respectable.

Catharine Gilday, later Sister Aloysius, was one of the many female Irish immigrants who went into the mills.[166] Twenty years of age in 1851, she lodged in an Irish household at 44 Fairfield Street, the main road to Ashton-under-Lyne and a mainly English shopkeeping and working-class district near Piccadilly.[167] As a powerloom weaver, she had a relatively well-paid job and was fortunate in working in the more moderate temperature of the weaving sheds than in the humid spinning rooms. Nevertheless she faced a formidable array of health hazards, ranging from pains and deformities from having to stand for ten hours a day to sore throats, headaches and deafness because of the din of the machinery.[168] She may also have experienced antagonism from males seeking the same job.[169] There is no evidence for her Irish background but since she had probably had previous experience of weaving, she may have come from the Cavan or Monaghan areas, where there had previously been a flourishing linen industry. There was insufficient food in the area to support the dense population, however, and so in the early 1840s large numbers had emigrated, especially women, and many had come to Manchester. When the potato crop failed, many others followed.[170] If an experienced weaver, Catharine would have easily found a job in Manchester. Mill owners preferred female employees, because they were quick and skilful and more amenable to authority than men, readier to show deference and to accept lower wages. This vulnerability made women particularly attractive to employers in the trade depression of 1847 and in face of the male unions' strike threat in 1848.[171] It also made Catharine Gilday, as an Irish Catholic weaver, more vulnerable to insult, especially in the religious and ethnic prejudice of the time.[172] Unfortunately the heaviest waves of Irish migration to Manchester coincided with industrial depression.[173] From 1847 the refugees from the potato famine came into a Manchester already bearing the brunt of poor relief to its own unemployed handloom weavers and depressed cotton operatives and they brought the additional problems of disease and death.[174] Constant propaganda from the Tory press and the Evangelicals ensured vociferous hostility towards the Irish working classes, which other sources, such as the police returns for 1847, suggest was hardly deserved.[175] Men in the cotton industry resented factory girls anyway. They could be used as strike breakers and, in keeping wages low and men out of work, restricted their ability to support their wives and children.[176] Others despised them. Mill girls were thought inferior to domestic servants and seamstresses and were considered 'cheeky', rough and immoral, although it was generally acknowledged that Irish girls were chaste.[177] Immorality and drunkenness were actually likelier amongst girls in spinning mills, where the intense humidity caused them to wear scanty clothing and to crave for drink, than in Catharine Gilday's weaving shed.[178] Nevertheless, no factory women at that time were considered respectable.

Catharine Toler, later Sister Magdalene, was also Irish and was a house servant.[179] Thirty years old in 1851, she lodged at 4 Nightingale Street, Strangeways, a respectable, working-class area where most of the tenants were English but many of their servants or lodgers Irish.[180] In 1851 domestic servants comprised the largest group of working women in England and Wales, although in Manchester, with a total of 4,246, they were very secondary to the 9,530 mill girls.[181] As a Catholic, Catharine Toler might have been subject to discrimination, although in this respect she was not as vulnerable as resident servants. Even in the 1840s Catholic domestic servants had complained of being refused time to go to Mass or of being offered only meat on Fridays.[182] In 1850 Father Ignatius Spencer indirectly and unintentionally aggravated their position by suggesting that Irish servants, labourers, artisans and others in England should become exemplary in their lives, so that as 'Apostles in the sphere in which they were placed', they would show Catholicism to advantage and thus help to effect the conversion of England.[183] The Evangelicals then took the view that every Irish servant, labourer and artisan was a fifth columnist intent on the downfall of the Establishment. While, therefore, Ignatius asked Catholics to answer Russell's aggression by praying for their persecutors, a 'miracle of charity' that would convince England of their true

Christianity, Catholic servants in Macclesfield, at McNeile's instigation, were losing their jobs.[184] Catharine Toler in Manchester was lucky to have one. Many English girls in Manchester, however, preferred factory work to domestic service because of the latter's low pay and long hours.[185] Service was a relationship between employer and servant rather than a defined set of tasks, so that Catharine Toler did not even have the prestige of job definition enjoyed by Catharine Gilday.[186] Like the factory girls, lower domestic servants were often despised. Upper-class servants might be protected by the supervision of a housekeeper but others could be the victims of a male employer, or of his son, and with no redress because, if they complained, they would lose their jobs without a reference.[187] A testimonial Father Gaudentius sent Father Croskell for a candidate in 1851 demonstrates the type of background Catholic servants might have, the problems they might have to face and the general opinion of what constituted a good domestic servant:

> She is a native of Irland [sic]. But she has been long time in England. She has been several years with the good Sisters of Mercy in Liverpool, first in the house of Mercy as a poor virtuous girl, then as a postulant, and as a novice, but then she left and came as a servant in a family in Stone, where the wife and children are Catholics. She has been there about three years and has gained the most profound respect and esteem of everyone that knows her virtues. She is esteemed and respected by her Master who is a sensual proud infidel.... She is most laborious, diligent, clean, orderly, full of consideration, full of gravity and modesty. She has never been known to have in the least been out of humour, always equal to herself, full of charity, compassion, gentleness....[188]

This particular girl had received some training. Girls who sought domestic employment without passing through some kind of philanthropic system were used mainly as drudges and scarcely paid enough for clothing.[189] Drudgery was also the fate of an older person whose poverty forced her into service.[190] There is no indication of when Catharine Toler arrived in Manchester nor of how long she had been a servant. At thirty years of age, however, she was considerably older than most Lancashire domestic servants, who in general married between fifteen and twenty-four.[191] Like most Irish female immigrants who did not go to the mills, she had taken domestic service as preferable to prostitution or begging.[192] This type of servant found employment with the manufacturers and shopkeepers who, as they moved their homes away from their mill or business into the suburbs, engaged domestic help but not resident servants.[193] Although, therefore, the separation of her workplace from her lodgings gave Catharine

Toler a degree of independence, it also identified her as a socially inferior type of servant.[194] So in fact she proved, for, although she was a likeable person, when she eventually left the order Father Gaudentius commented that 'Poor Magdalene' was 'no loss to the institute'.[195] That opinion, however, did not detract from the courage and perseverance she had shown through great hardships.

Catharine Gilday may have earned about £25 a year, Catharine Toler perhaps between £11 and about £23, until she joined Catharine Gilday in the factory.[196] Since it had been estimated even in 1802 that £50 a year was the minimum on which a semblance of gentility could be maintained, Elizabeth and her companions were poor.[197] As no postulants with means applied for admission and as she became redundant in her school in November 1851, Elizabeth had to face the stark reality of Father Gaudentius' queries about the postulants he had ready to send: 'Whereas almost all of them can work with their needle in dress making and embroidery could you find the necessary work to employ five or six of them? Do you see any other means of maintenance? For scarcely any of them will bring any much quantity of money except few pounds.'[198]

Elizabeth's finances were scarcely enhanced by the arrival of Sarah Ann Lee, the future Sister Agnes, on 3 June 1852, although as a living-in servant she was a grade above Catharine Toler. Born in Brinnington near Manchester, she was possibly English. Aged twenty-four, she was employed at 6 Montague Terrace, Broughton, Salford, by William Fairbairn, a master engineer, probably identifiable as William Andrew Fairbairn, son of Sir William Fairbairn, the prominent Victorian engineer. Aged 26 in 1851, he had been a partner in his father's firm from 1846. His wife, Mariann, aged 23 in 1851, had to conduct a considerable household because, in addition to their 5-year-old son, she also had to cater for her father, a solicitor, and her sister, as well as organising 4 or 5 servants, including a male.[199] In this type of household, Sarah Lee, in contrast to Catharine Toler, was a superior type of servant: resident, literate and probably earning about fourteen guineas a year in addition to her board and lodging.[200] Father Gaudentius certainly considered her of a higher status and thought she had access to influential friends.[201] She was still a servant, however, not the type of person general opinion associated with consecrated religious life. It was this lack of respectability that made some of the Manchester priests oppose Elizabeth Prout's attempt to found her religious order.

This opposition first came to light about July 1852 when Mary Taylor decided to enter. She later became Sister Mary Paul of the Cross. Born in Saddleworth, Yorkshire in 1822 and therefore two years younger than Elizabeth Prout, she also was a convert, but from

Methodism.[202] 'Even during her Protestant life', like most Methodists, 'she was much given to active works of charity.'[203] Forced, like Elizabeth, to leave home, she had been 'adopted' by a Catholic gentleman to be his wife's maid and companion. Already acquainted with teaching from Sunday-school work, she was known to be a steady, reliable person. When priests and her patron heard her decision to enter Elizabeth Prout's order, they tried to dissuade her, wishing her to go to one of the 'fashionable Orders'. Elizabeth's, they said, 'was not a religious Order; it was only a lot of factory girls.' Undeterred, 'for she did not seek grandeur and distinction but humiliation and the cross', Mary Taylor entered the convent at 69 Stocks Street on 4 August 1852, precisely because the sisters were so poor. 'Desiring to become truly poor', she had sought out the 'most despised and poorest order... in Manchester and was attracted by none but the poor convent of the Sisters of the Holy Family', where she found 'a place truly poor, but at the same time', thanks to Elizabeth Prout's respectable housewifery, 'extremely clean, regular and neat'.[204] Like the other postulants who joined the order about this time, she was doubly courageous, because a new wave of anti-Catholic violence was sweeping the Manchester area in the wake of the Stockport riots.[205] Manchester hardly seemed the ideal place to start a new religious order. Elizabeth Prout's, however, was all the more Passionist for being born amidst such opprobrium and in such poverty.[206]

The remaining two of the first seven sisters, Mary Johnson, the future Sister Philomena, and Marie Wilson, later Sister Clare, both lived in London when they encountered Father Gaudentius and decided to enter the order. He therefore sent testimonials for them. 'Mary Johnson', he wrote,

> has been warmly recommended to me by her spiritual director Revd Mr Hunt of Spanish Place, her age about 22. Excellent health. Accustomed to work in different ways, and especially at her needle. She seems to be a very good soul and with very good qualities and dispositions for a religious life. She has cheerful, sweet and pleasing manners, she is very active and industrious, she is calm, considerate, intelligent and prudent. She has firmness of character.[207]

Marie Wilson also had a favourable reference from her parish priest. 'From his own account', wrote Gaudentius to Elizabeth, 'you may see she is a living saint, and that her presence in the house would be a sign of the sanction of heaven upon this important undertaking.'[208] Mary Johnson joined Elizabeth on 5 August 1852, Marie Wilson on the 17th.[209]

Unfortunately the apparent spiritual superiority of these two paragons of virtue did nothing to improve the material prospects of the community, for they both had to be seamstresses. Dressmakers and needle-women could find work in Manchester, because few of the mill girls could make their own dresses but were willing to pay to have them made, as they liked to be well dressed on Sundays.[210] Father Gaudentius, however, ruled that the sisters were not to make any 'low, immodest or too gaudy and vain' dresses.[211] That prohibition possibly reduced them to making shirts but in any case the difficulties of supporting themselves by sewing became increasingly evident after the first seven sisters received the religious habit. 'After their clothing', wrote one of the annalists, 'the sisters were obliged to suffer considerable inconvenience and loss of time', because, thanks to Derby's proclamation forbidding the wearing of Catholic religious dress in public, they had to change into secular dress to go out 'to sew at the houses of those ladies who desired their services'.[212] Perhaps to remedy this inconvenience and because, as contemplatives, they ought to work in the house, as the Rule directed, they began to bring the sewing into the convent.[213] Thus they joined the numerous ranks of slopworkers, the most degraded of all seamstresses.[214] Thereby, as a body, they became identified with a class notorious for prostitution.[215] While by their own lives of chastity they witnessed that, although poor to the point of starvation, it was still possible to live a morally good life, they suffered the real deprivation of that occupation.[216] Their solidarity with the poor was genuine.

As seamstresses they formed part of the reservoir of cheap labour, vulnerable to the fluctuations of an urban market economy and to the unrestricted demands of the affluent.[217] 'Ghosts in the looking glass', victims of the avarice of those who prospered in society, they shared the weakness and misfortune of the needlewomen who lived in Manchester at that time.[218] While any seamstresses were badly paid, at 1s. to 1s.6d. a day for working ten to twelve hours, slopworkers were even more indigent because they were paid for productivity. For striped cotton shirts they might be paid between 10d. and 2s.6d. a dozen; for common white shirts 5s. to 10s. a dozen.[219] Prices were kept down by the glut of needlewomen at the time and by competition from the workhouses, where the women also made shirts.[220] Since it took five hours to make one garment, owing to the intricate sewing of the collars, wristbands, shoulder panels and buttonholes, seven to each shirt, even a conscientious seamstress could reasonably make only two shirts a day.[221] Moreover, the slopworkers had to provide their own thread and needles. Two skeins of cotton, which might cost 1d., would make three to four shirts. The cotton for a dozen shirts, therefore, would cost about 8d., reducing the worker's pay to between 2d. and 1s.10d. for making a dozen of the cheapest shirts.[222] It was not surprising that Elizabeth could not afford fires and that food was meagre.[223]

In Stocks Street they may have had to pay for gaslighting; in Levenshulme for gas or candles, which might cost 10d. to 1s. a week in
wintertime.[224] Working at needlework such long hours a day in such
conditions, the sisters were likely to suffer headaches, indigestion,
heart, spine and pulmonary illnesses, eye affections and ultimately
blindness.[225] If their orders were not completed by the time stipulated,
they would not be paid and might lose their employment. They must
sweat or starve.[226] Since they must be self-supporting, they had to
ensure they did not lose their orders and therefore they often had to
stay up at night to finish them.[227] Elizabeth Prout had not only found
a classroom; she had become a seamstress as well.

Father Gaudentius was aware they were enduring 'extreme poverty,
obloquy, ridicule and scorn', even 'opposition... from quarters where
they might [have expected] kindness.'[228] Sister Mary Paul Taylor later
described how they 'had to suffer the most determined opposition from
all the priests in their neighbourhood, who treated them as persons
devoid of reason for attempting the foundation of a new institute under
what seemed to them such unfavourable circumstances.'[229] Fortunately,
'a great spirit of self-denial and mortification prevailed' among them.
As far as they could, they maintained 'the strictest order and discipline'. Rising at 4 a.m., they made an hour's meditation from 4.15 and
attended Mass at St Chad's. Both in the convent and elsewhere they
tried to keep themselves 'recollected in the presence of God, using
frequent and regular aspirations and ejaculatory prayers'.[230] Their lives
were characterised by the spirit of poverty, prayer, penance and
solitude inherent in their Rule and in the spirituality of Paul of the
Cross. Identified by lifestyle and work, and even by the appearance of
their hands, with the poor working classes, they presented a total
contradiction to the secularist ambitions of Manchester's commercial
elite.[231]

Although he relied on Elizabeth to find employment for postulants,
Gaudentius also envisaged that in each parish where they had a house
they would have patrons, corresponding to the Passionists' benefactors,
who would help them to find work.[232] Most Manchester Catholics were
so poor that it was difficult to find patrons, although Mrs Lavery of St
Chad's parish did fulfil that function.[233] Hence in October 1852
Gaudentius was delighted there was a possibility of the sisters' going
to St John's, Salford. Since Salford had some wealthier parishioners,
such as the calico manufacturer, Daniel Lee JP, Gaudentius hoped they
might assist Elizabeth. 'The good and zealous Missess [sic] Lee', he
said, 'may do a great deal for the establishment of the Institute.'[234] He
also understood a house would be provided, rent free, and there were
excellent new schoolrooms in Cleminson Street. Had the possibility
become a reality it would have been most advantageous, especially as

in June 1852 Elizabeth had already been ill.[235] It would have set her congregation on a firm economic foundation. Instead, however, as at St Chad's, the clergy invited a well-established teaching order to take charge of their school.[236] Elizabeth Prout went to St Joseph's, Goulden Street, not St John's, Salford.

In the sermon he gave during the first clothing ceremony, Father Gaudentius referred to the sisters' poverty, their fervour and to the opposition against them. When their number had reached seven in August 1852, he had exuberantly referred to the foundation of the order as 'a most glorious and most meritorious undertaking', for which Elizabeth had 'the principal responsibility'. At the same time, he had acknowledged that her 'difficulties' would 'be very great'.[237] Nevertheless, since all seven were still persevering in November 1852, it was decided they should receive the habit on Sunday, 21 November, the feast of the Virgin Mary's Presentation. Regarded as the birthday of the Passionist Congregation, it had always been considered a suitable date for Passionist clothings and professions.[238] By holding the first clothings in Elizabeth's order on this date, Gaudentius placed it at the heart of the Passionist tradition. The ceremony was held in the workroom, set out for the occasion as a chapel, at 69 Stocks Street, which, in accordance with the Rule, as the first foundation in the country, was called 'St Joseph's convent'.[239] Although Canon Croskell was present, it was Father Gaudentius who presided and gave the sermon. He praised Elizabeth and her companions for responding to the grace of their vocation to the new congregation, with 'no voice raised to cheer [them] with a consoling friendly word of loving approbation'. On the contrary, 'mistaken friends, secret enemies, open foes' had strongly opposed them. Those who were considered to be the originators and leaders in the new undertaking, he said, had been 'ridiculed and despised for their supposed folly' and the foundation was 'everywhere beset with difficulties'. Exhorting them to be 'strictly exact' in every observance of the Rule, especially as fidelity was 'most particularly required at the beginning of a new Institute', he reminded them that many eyes were fixed upon them, some favourably but others unfavourably. It was their strict observance of the Rule that would multiply their friends by drawing the indifferent and even their enemies to support them. Finally he reminded them why their religious order was being founded: because 'many young Catholic women in the industrious classes' showed 'remarkable virtue' and 'expressed the desire to consecrate themselves to the service of God in a religious state of life' but could not enter the existing orders because they had no 'pecuniary means' and 'insufficient learning'. 'The new Institute of the Catholic Sisters of the Holy Family', he said, was 'intended to remove these obstacles'. While learning would ever be valued and usefully employed in Catholic schools, 'blameless ignorance, when duly accompanied with the more sublime and true practical wisdom of the Saints', would never be 'slighted nor rejected from the Convent of the Holy Family. Christian and virtuous poverty [would] never be a lock but a golden key to the convent gate.' In accordance with the spirit of the Gospel no dowry would be 'demanded from virtuous Postulants as a condition for admission to the Holy Family.'[240] Elizabeth Prout's order was intended for the *anawim*.

4. UNIQUELY PASSIONIST

The congregation that Elizabeth Prout founded with Fathers Gaudentius Rossi and Robert Croskell was different from any other religious institute in England at the time. In asking no dowry for admission, it offered religious life to those who could not afford the dowries required by other orders. It offered a contemplative religious life, with its own type of choir observance, to all members, none of whom were laysisters. Seniority, apart from elected superiors, was based only on order of profession and only superiors held the title 'Mother'. As a Passionist congregation it was different in its nature, end and spirit from any other and there were many, for an inclination to the celibate and religious life was a characteristic of the contemporary religious revival. Thus George Spencer, as an Anglican clergyman in 1827, had decided not to marry, in order to devote himself more fully to his Brington parishioners.[241] Later, as a Catholic, he constantly queried the respective values of the secular and regular priesthood, until he finally entered the Passionist novitiate in 1846.[242] As early as 1826 the Reverend A.R.C. Dallas had founded Protestant Sisters of Charity.[243] For the Tractarians, too, religious celibacy and community were signs of a call to greater sanctity, as well as permitting more effective service to the urbanised poor.[244] Elizabeth Prout's order, however, was not founded for any specific service to the poor, other than that of providing them with consecrated religious life.

Her order was therefore different from the Anglican sisterhoods founded about the same time: by E.B. Pusey and others in 1844 at Park Village West, where the sisters taught poor children, ran an orphanage and visited the homes of the labourers; by W.J. Butler in 1848 at Wantage, where they founded a penitentiary for prostitutes; by Priscilla L. Sellon at Plymouth and Devonport, from where within two years she established no fewer than seventeen charitable institutions; and by J.M. Neale at East Grinstead, where the sisters nursed the sick poor in their own homes.[245] Unlike Elizabeth Prout, all these sisters and, in particular, P.L. Sellon, had ample means and enjoyed the financial and social support of the richer classes in providing their benevolent institutions.[246] Although they worked for the poor, all these

Anglican sisters remained ladies. They did admit women without money or with very little but did not consider them sufficiently educated for the work of helping the destitute and fallen.[247] Poorer women became laysisters, performing the more menial tasks of community life. Only the wealthier aspirants became choirsisters, occasionally even bringing their maids as laysisters.[248] Although these Anglican sisters certainly deprived themselves of their previous riches and entertainments, they did not become so materially poor as Elizabeth Prout. Hers, however, was a Passionist movement: her sisters did not simply work for the poor; they *were* the poor.

Her order was also different from other Protestant sisterhoods, such as Elizabeth Fry's Institute of Nursing Sisters, founded in London in the 1840s and the Anglican St John's Sisterhood, both of which supplied private nursing for fee-paying patients and used their profits to nurse the poor free of charge.[249] It differed from Emily Ayckbown's well-financed Anglican Community of Sisters of the Church, founded in 1870, although both did church needlework and worked for poor girls.[250] It also differed from the evangelical deaconesses, who never took vows, were free to leave at any time and were paid individually for their work of visiting the poor.[251] Elizabeth Prout's ideas were also different from those of Anna Jameson, who in 1855 gave a lecture entitled 'Sisters of Charity', in which she advocated Protestant religious orders to train women in nursing, teaching, social work and other 'womanly' tasks.[252] She was attempting to employ the large number of superfluous single women, as well as to alleviate the distress of the poor. Elizabeth Prout's order, on the other hand, did not exist for social work. It existed to offer consecrated religious life to the poor. It would absorb comparatively few women, because it was so penitential.

It was also unique amongst the Catholic religious orders, of which more were founded in the nineteenth century than at any other time in the history of the Church.[253] It was needed because the medieval, enclosed, contemplative orders, like the Benedictines and Cistercians, required dowries which no female operatives could afford.[254] It differed from them in offering contemplative religious life, with choir observance for all and no dowries for admission, to working-class women. It differed, too, from the modern Catholic congregations doing active work in the mid-nineteenth century. Although Elizabeth owed much to the Sisters of the Infant Jesus in Northampton, both in spirituality and in active apostolate, her order was fundamentally different. They had been founded for the education of the poor.[255] Elizabeth's aim was to give religious life to the poor. In 1852 the Northampton Sisters were assimilated into the Sisters of Notre Dame de Namur, who taught in St Chad's, Manchester, from November 1851.[256] They also had been founded for the education of the poor, as also were the Presentation Sisters in Livesey Street, Manchester; the Sisters of Providence who taught in St Mary's in 1850-51; the Sisters of Loreto who came to St Wilfrid's, Hulme, in 1851; and the Faithful Companions of Jesus who came to teach in St John's, Salford, in 1852. Although the Faithful Companions' foundress wished to unite the contemplative with the active life, she had a division between choir and laysisters, so that her congregation, too, was fundamentally different from that of Elizabeth Prout.[257]

Father Gaudentius and Elizabeth offered religious life for its own sake, not as a means of working for the poor or of stabilising a social work. Their order was therefore different from the two orders in which Pusey showed an interest: the French Sisters of Charity, founded in France in 1633 by St Vincent de Paul and St Louise de Marillac; and the Irish Sisters of Mercy, founded by Catherine McAuley to visit the poor of Dublin's slums and hospitals and who had several houses in England by 1852.[258]

In his anxiety about anti-Catholic aggression, Father Gaudentius thought in January 1851 that his proposed institute could be merged with the Sisters of Charity of St Paul the Apostle, a French order that had made an independent foundation at Banbury in 1847.[259] This idea did not come to fruition, nor did his other idea of assimilation into the Little Sisters of the Poor, another French order that by 1852 had a house in London.[260] Although both these congregations were close enough to his inspiration to make him think they could replace his own order, they were in fact different in that they had both been founded for work amongst the poor rather than to offer religious life to the poor. It is significant that Gaudentius' interest in them preceded his writing the Rule, in which he defined a fundamentally different order.

Apart from Elizabeth Prout's, there were three Catholic congregations founded for women in England about the mid-nineteenth century: the Sisters of Nazareth, the Sisters of the Holy Child Jesus and the Dominican Sisters of Stone. These also were different from hers. The Sisters of Nazareth sprang from a congregation founded in Brittany to care for the poor. One of its members, Victoire Larmenier, received the religious habit on 25 March 1851. A fortnight later she was sent to London with two other novices to open a convent with a home for the aged, the destitute and for destitute children suffering from incurable diseases. They were assisted materially by the St Vincent de Paul Society, who had asked for them, and by a number of the Catholic aristocracy, local parish priests and, from May 1851, by Cardinal Wiseman. They took their vows in December 1856 and Wiseman approved their title 'Sisters of Nazareth', their habit and their constitutions in 1864.[261] Although they were personally poor, they were well supported and had the means to provide institutional welfare services. They were therefore in a different category from Elizabeth Prout and her companions, both in nature and aims. The Sisters of the Holy Child Jesus were also different. They were founded in Derby in 1846 by an American, Cornelia Connelly, supported by Wiseman, specifically for the education of girls, with particular concern for the religious needs of middle-class Catholics.[262] The Dominican Sisters of the Congregation of St Catherine of Siena are particularly interesting, because in 1853 they founded a convent near Elizabeth Prout's home in Stone, on the ground designated for a convent by Father Dominic Barberi. They heard that Elizabeth's father was a lapsed Catholic, immediately began to pray he would return to his religious duties and had the satisfaction of seeing him do so in 1863.[263] They were founded by Mother Margaret Hallahan, who had been born in London of Irish parents, orphaned at nine years of age and put into domestic service, a type of work she continued for the next twenty-seven years. In 1842 she became housekeeper to Bishop Ullathorne in Coventry. She also took charge of a school of 200 girls, worked amongst the factory girls and visited the sick of the parish. In this way she resembled Elizabeth Prout. Already a Dominican tertiary, in 1844, with the approval of the Dominican Provincial and under Dr Ullathorne, she and three companions began a formal religious life as members of the Third Order of St Dominic. Like Elizabeth and her sisters, Margaret Hallahan and her first companions were scorned as 'only a few poor girls' and the 'wenches of Coventry', in contrast to the 'ladies' of the enclosed orders.[264] Margaret differed from Elizabeth, however, in that she always had some material security. Although her first companions were similar to Elizabeth's, one a handloom weaver and another a dressmaker, the latter had a dowry of £25, while a third had an income of £50 a year. Dr Ullathorne also shared his stipend with them. They could therefore leave their trades in order to concentrate on works of charity.[265] Mother Margaret also differed from Elizabeth in requiring a dowry. At first her postulants brought comparatively small amounts but as wealthier candidates came, particularly converts who knew her friend, Father Newman, they brought dowries of £500 and £3,000 and expensive ecclesiastical items.[266] Elizabeth Prout at the same time was worrying about asking her postulants to bring the fare home again in case they were not happy.[267] Like Elizabeth, Mother Margaret did not have laysisters.[268] As a Dominican, she differed in giving her institute an academic orientation. She also wanted the full medieval appurtenances of chanting the Divine Office and conventual architectural structures, as favoured by the Gothic revival, whereas even Elizabeth's largest convents were comparatively small.[269] Most of her foundations started in cottages and all were unadorned.

There were two near-contemporary institutes that bore a closer resemblance to Elizabeth's order.[270] About twenty years after Elizabeth Prout began to found her order, Fanny Taylor, foundress of the Poor Servants of the Mother of God, started a congregation for Irish working-class women in London.[271] The group had been initiated by Elizabeth Twiddy, a seamstress and capmaker, who in 1857, with two other seamstresses, had supported a few orphans they found on the streets, as well as nursing the sick and aged. Lady Georgiana Fullerton and Fanny Taylor became interested and after Elizabeth Twiddy's death Fanny continued her work, adapting a Polish Rule and promoting the spirit of Mary and Joseph at Nazareth. Although she intended her institute to be self-supporting and actually tried to earn a livelihood in sewing before turning to laundry work, she had the patronage of Lady Georgiana and others, as well as her personal prestige as a writer and as an associate of Florence Nightingale in the Crimea. Unlike Elizabeth Prout, therefore, she was able to stabilise her foundation very quickly, although she did not take vows until 1872.[272]

The other order that was similar to Elizabeth Prout's actually sprang from it: the Franciscan Missionaries of St Joseph, founded by Alice Ingham in Rochdale in 1871.[273] Alice met Elizabeth through visiting her friend and former Sunday-school teacher, Sister Mary Paul Taylor, and spoke to Elizabeth about her own desire to enter. Father Gaudentius met her in Rochdale in October 1854. 'I hear great praises in favour of this excellent girl', he wrote to Elizabeth. 'She is 25 years of age, strong constitution and health. She makes women's caps.'[274] Alice had previously worked in a cotton mill from 1846 to 1851.[275] She entered Elizabeth Prout's congregation on 23 January 1855, becoming Sister Veronica.[276] Her 'constitution and health', however, were not 'strong' enough for the sisters' regime. She soon became ill and had to leave before receiving the habit. From about 1865 she received spiritual guidance from Father Gomair Peeters, a Belgian Franciscan at his friary in Gorton, Manchester. In 1871, under his direction, with Sister Mary Paul Taylor's assistance and Bishop Turner's consent, she began to found her own religious order, based on her membership of the Third Order of St Francis. Her Rule, written by Mary Paul Taylor, was an adaptation of Elizabeth Prout's 1863 Rule. Alice Ingham and her sisters wore a close adaptation of Elizabeth's habit and they followed the customs of her order. Alice Ingham differed from Elizabeth, however, in establishing an institute aimed primarily at good works, rather than at the contemplative life. She also had the security, unknown to Elizabeth Prout, of a confectionery and millinery shop and, although her sisters lived a life of poverty, they remained financially secure. After Bishop Turner's death in 1872, Mother Mary Paul Taylor negotiated on Alice's behalf with the second

Angel Meadow with St Chad's in the distance

bishop of Salford, Herbert Vaughan. At his invitation in 1878 Alice and her sisters transferred to the missionary seminary at Mill Hill, London as the Franciscan Missionaries of St Joseph.[277]

Although, therefore, there was considerable apostolic activity amongst Catholic women in this period and these religious were personally materially poor because they put their resources into their apostolates, Elizabeth Prout was the first foundress to provide consecrated religious life for the poor as her first priority. While all congregations spent time in prayer, hers was the first of the modern orders to be founded *for* prayer. She was adamant that the 'active work of Martha' must not interfere or set aside the 'contemplation of Mary'.[278] The extent of her active work was restricted by the nature of her order. Unlike these other religious congregations, she had no material resources. Poverty was a characteristic and a consequence of the nature of her institute. In that charism it was a Passionist congregation from its foundation and in its Rule. As Mother Berchmans wrote in her Annals in 1926, 'It would be difficult to find a more ignoble beginning for a religious Order, but in view of the beautiful name they were to bear later, it was most fitting. They must be simply steeped in the knowledge of the Sufferings of their Divine Saviour.'[279]

CHAPTER IV

POPULAR EDUCATION

1. GOVERNMENT GRANTS FOR CATHOLIC SCHOOLS

The essential poverty of Elizabeth Prout's congregation fittingly reflected the nature of the Catholic Church in Manchester, as shown not only in its mainly working-class membership and shortage of churches but also in its struggle for education. Despite her poverty, Elizabeth Prout played a vital role in Catholic education in the Manchester area.

As Father Dominic had realised in Stone and as the Passionist missions had made abundantly clear in Manchester, after three centuries of less than subsistence-level Catholicism in both England and Ireland, the crying need of most working-class English and immigrant Irish Catholics was for religious education. In the process of evangelisation that was so obviously urgent in Manchester, accurate catechesis in Catholic doctrine was of fundamental importance. Attendance at the Passionist missions demonstrated that Catholics wanted that education, which was their right in virtue of their Baptism. Whilst instruction in secular subjects was considered important, for Catholics the primary purpose of education was to transmit the Catholic faith.[1] It was also a Catholic principle 'that the clergy alone had the sole and exclusive right of teaching in matters of religion'.[2] In practice they delegated their authority to parents, godparents and teachers but it fell to the clergy to supply schools and teachers. In Manchester the old St Chad's in Rook Street had had its schools in George Leigh Street and Mayes Street.[3] The new St Chad's had been built in a district where previously there had been no church and, apart from the property at 19 Dyche Street, the new St Chad's parish had no school.[4] The clergy's next priority, therefore, was to provide one. This was the primary reason why Father Croskell was looking for a schoolmistress in 1849. There were, however, other reasons, which at that time were particular to Manchester, although, as embodied in the 1870 Education Act, they would later affect Catholics throughout the country.

It was only to be expected that, as the pioneers of the industrial revolution and the promoters of free trade, progressive figures in Manchester should turn their attention to education.[5] Having clothed the world cheaply and amassed great wealth for themselves, they had also adorned Manchester with classical centres of culture.[6] While their factories echoed with the 'din and uproar' of the 'clanking of engines' and the 'whirl and rattle of the machinery', they had not forgotten the pursuit of knowledge.[7] What they still lacked, however, was a system of education: for their own children, for those of the shopkeepers and tradesmen and for those of the lower working classes.[8] In 1837 these public-spirited men had already founded the Manchester Society for Promoting National Education as an associated body of the Central Society for Education established in 1836. In 1847 they founded the Lancashire Public Schools Association to promote national, free and secular education.[9] The problem about even the 1846 system of government grants was that aid was still given in proportion to self help. A school had to merit a grant by having already achieved certain minimum standards. As a result, education was still not reaching the poorest working classes, who were either too poor to afford any fees or could pay so little that their schools remained substandard. Throughout 1849 the members of the Association held monthly lectures in Manchester to explain their policy.[10] Arguing that paupers were better educated than the children of the 'industrious operatives', they proposed that local authorities should levy a rate to pay for education.[11] They wanted the instruction given to impart 'useful knowledge' in harmony with their industrialised world. They thought the working classes should understand the 'various qualities and uses of the objects by which they were surrounded' and should be drilled in the need for 'temperance, industry and frugality'.[12] Then they would know how to order their lives correctly.[13] The intention was not to raise the poor above their station but to educate the total working class to the same level so that they would still remain the labouring masses but would work with greater intelligence and skill in harmony with their employers.[14] A boy did not need to read Latin prose but it would help if he could read a notice in the mill.[15] The Association did not want religious teaching, because denominational differences appeared to be destructive of any attempts to produce a national system of education.[16] Religious instruction could be left to Sunday schools.[17] As for those who did not attend them, the study of political economy would teach them the moral truth that if they wanted food and clothing, fuel and shelter, they must show industry, economy, punctuality and honesty, while the study of physiology would teach them to practise temperance and cleanliness.[18] In February 1850, W.J. Fox, on behalf of the Association, presented parliament with a bill for a national system of secular education funded by local rates.[19] It was defeated but in the autumn of 1850 the Lancashire Association became the even stronger National Public School Association and the issues continued to be discussed.[20]

Punch satirised the Manchester scheme as intended 'to imbue ladies and gentlemen with common sense and common information, notwithstanding their calico frocks and corduroy trousers.'[21] For the Catholic Church the proposals posed serious problems, in the light of which both government grants for Catholic schools and Elizabeth Prout's role in Manchester assumed special significance. No-one would have been more grateful for rate-supported education than the Catholic priests of Manchester as they struggled to provide churches and schools for their ever-increasing flocks of labouring poor.[22] From a Catholic point of view, however, it was essential to have Catholic schools for Catholic children in order to teach Catholic doctrine. In a Catholic school the Catholic faith permeated the teaching of every subject and was taught through every subject. The absence of this element would not mean only the lack of Catholic education. It would mean the implantation of another philosophy.[23] If aid were given only to non-denominational schools, however, Catholic schools would be excluded from financial help. Catholic schools would remain deplorably poor, while secular schools flourished on the rates. Moreover, for the sake of educating their children in secular subjects, Catholic parents would be tempted to send their children to the free schools, where they would almost certainly lose their faith. Thus the Catholic Church in Manchester found itself under attack when it was at its weakest, paradoxically, on account of its overwhelming numbers. The clergy were desperate for teachers and money to provide Catholic schools as cheaply as possible. Thus Elizabeth Prout, arriving in Manchester in late 1849, found herself at the heart of a struggle to safeguard Catholic education in the face of secularism and political economy. This was one reason why she was so important to St Chad's in 1849-51.

The new system of government grants was another. The Catholic Church was under a grave disability at mid century, because its schools had been confiscated or destroyed at the Reformation; it had not been allowed to build schools during the penal times; and although the Anglicans and Nonconformists had received government educational grants since 1833, the Catholic Church had received nothing. Its predicament in Manchester was particularly severe because of Irish immigration. In 1847, however, the Catholic Poor School Committee had successfully negotiated for government grants for Catholic schools.[24] The Committee of the Privy Council on Education had agreed to give a support grant of 2s. per pupil, on the average attendance, for desks and apparatus etc. and would supply books and maps at almost 75% cheaper than the normal retail price to a Catholic school that fulfilled its requirements regarding building, equipment and efficiency of teaching. On the same conditions, it would also award a building grant towards a new Catholic school.[25] In 1849, having opened a new church and set off their new parish to a flying start with a Passionist mission, St Chad's clergy wanted a government grant for a new school. They therefore wanted to offer their existing schools for the requisite government inspection. They already had a master, one of the Irish Christian Brothers.[26] They had previously had a mistress but she had left by 1849.[27] The clergy, therefore, wanted Elizabeth

Prout to play the crucial role of reopening the girls' school in George Leigh Street, so that they could apply for government inspection in order to qualify for educational grants. The significance of her role can hardly be overestimated. St Chad's clergy wanted to claim state assistance to reduce their running costs and to provide a new, purpose-built school, on the brink of Manchester's worst slum with a Catholic population of 15,000. Elizabeth Prout's help was vital to their success. On her side, in view of the conditions in which she worked, her physical delicacy and only recent arrival, she showed remarkable availability in agreeing to the inspection.

The Catholic inspector, T.W.M. Marshall arrived to inspect Elizabeth's school on 5 March 1850.[28] Her classroom in George Leigh Street was in an old, long, low-ceilinged warehouse in only 'tolerable' condition.[29] Using the monitorial system of the time, she was teaching a daily average of at least 100 girls, of mixed ability, with an age range of between eight and thirteen.[30] Some were fulltimers; others sleepy but obstreperous halftimers.[31] Some came as it suited them. Some disappeared for weeks at a time because they could not resist the temptation to earn 6d. a week by selling 'chips, periwinkles, or matches', in order to 'add a few loaves to the attenuated store of the starving family at home'.[32] Many appeared in ragged and scanty clothing, with heavy eyes and worn faces, their uncombed hair covered with cotton fluff.[33] They were not necessarily malleable. As Marshall described it, education was 'that great social work... the struggle with ignorance and vice in their strongholds, the masses of an undisciplined and uninstructed population'.[34] Moreover, Elizabeth could work only within her resources and they were meagre. Filling in the Committee of Council's report sheet under the headings provided, Marshall had to say that her desks and furniture were only 'moderate' and her books and apparatus 'rather scanty'. With so little equipment, her methods were 'imperfect' rather than 'excellent' but her organization was 'fair' and her discipline was 'good'. Elizabeth herself, he said, was 'well-disposed, but apparently deficient in energy', which was the normal comment on women teachers.[35] In her case she could hardly have been otherwise, for on that day she had no fewer than 140 girls in her ill-ventilated room, quite apart from having had a recent tubercular illness. In his special remarks on St Chad's schools, Marshall recorded, 'The special difficulty of this school consists in the impossibility of retaining the children long enough either to form their characters or to impart a due amount of solid instruction.' It was therefore 'highly creditable' to Elizabeth, even more than to the managers praised by Marshall, that he considered the results of his inspection so 'satisfactory'.[36] He must surely have included her in his thoughts when he wrote, in his 1850 *Report*, that he had observed with

pleasure that it was precisely in such towns as Manchester, where
hitherto there had been the most conspicuous defect in educational
institutions for Catholic children, that the most earnest efforts were
being made for their maintenance and extension.[37] Moreover, through
her Paulacrucian spirituality, she was bringing the Passionist mission
to England into the hearts and minds of Manchester's working-class
children. As a result of this favourable inspection, on 20 June 1850,
the Committee of Council granted St Chad's £5 8s. 8d. for school
books and maps at reduced prices.[38] Elizabeth Prout had made a first
positive contribution to St Chad's.

A fortnight earlier, on 3 June 1850, Father Sheehan had applied for
a government building grant. He had a site beside the church on a
999-year lease from the earl of Derby. Bounded by streets on two
sides and buildings on the other two, it fulfilled all the government's
health requirements. He wanted to accommodate 350 boys, 350 girls
and 150 infants. Nothing tawdry about it, the new school would
present a complete contrast to Elizabeth's old warehouse. The walls,
a good 18" thick, would be brick with stone dressing, its casement
windowframes red deal, its roofs of the best slate and its spouts of
iron. Its drainage system, composed of sound earthenware pipes,
would lead a healthy 25yds away from the building. Its ceilings would
have two coats of plaster, while the floors would be pine and raised a
healthy 2½ft above the ground.[39] A purpose-built school, it was going
to be the 'finest and most extensive' in the Salford Diocese, with
'suitable light, thorough ventilation, convenient fittings, spacious
playgrounds'.[40] Adorned with Gothic touch and a statue of St Chad, it
would have 'two immense rooms', each three times the size of
Elizabeth's classroom, the boys' on the ground floor, the girls'
upstairs. Each section would have its own entrance, cloakroom and
conveniences.[41] In all, it would be a 'complete establishment'.[42] All
this Elizabeth Prout was helping to make possible.

St Chad's clergy had other plans, however, which affected her very
closely. As Marshall heard when he visited the school on 5 March
1850, they had already negotiated successfully for the well-established
religious teaching order of Notre Dame to take charge of St Chad's
new school when it was built.[43] Whether Elizabeth Prout knew it or
not, she was going to be replaced. 'New school-rooms will shortly be
erected', Marshall reported, 'and the school will enter, in all respects,
upon a new era.'[44] From as early as March 1850, when Elizabeth was
still a laywoman in only the earliest stages of founding her own
religious order, the clergy had decided to replace her as schoolmistress. She remained one of the *anawim*. On 15 August 1851 she
founded her order in deep poverty. Had she had the financial support
and patronage of exalted personages enjoyed by other sisterhoods, her

congregation might have begun with a flourish and quickly attracted potentially competent teachers. That would have rendered it attractive to the Manchester clergy. It would also, however, have changed the whole nature of the institute. It would not have been an order for the poor. It would not have been Passionist. As a fruit of the Passionist mission to England, Elizabeth Prout's congregation could have no other origin than in the degradation and poverty of the 'crucified' poor. When three Notre Dame Sisters arrived in St Chad's on 24 November 1851, both Elizabeth Prout and her old warehouse became redundant.[45]

Father Sheehan had still to meet his expenses of £1,637.[46] He received £200 from the Catholic Poor School Committee; £207 from subscriptions and collections; and he hoped to receive another £150 from further collections and subscriptions.[47] That total of £557 left him with a deficit of £1,080. Because of the testimony of the mayor, John Potter that 'poverty and ignorance' prevailed more in Angel Meadow than in any other part of Manchester, the Committee of Council granted him £620, more than it would normally have given for the size of the school.[48] Largely thanks to the availability and efforts of Elizabeth Prout, St Chad's was the first Catholic school in Manchester and one of the first four in England to receive a government building grant.[49] In her unobtrusive but constructive fashion, she had helped to raise up the working classes of Manchester's worst slum and to foil any attempts at depriving them of Catholic education. That was to remain her role throughout the next few years. A contemplative in action, as others philosophised over the principles of education, Elizabeth Prout stood on the classroom floor, educating Manchester's Catholic poor and preserving intact their Catholic inheritance.

2. EVANGELICALISM IN EDUCATION

Both the eagerness with which St Chad's clergy had welcomed Elizabeth Prout in 1849 and the apparent callousness with which they replaced her in late 1851 were symptomatic of another problem: the shortage of Catholic teachers. Until the Notre Dame Sisters opened Mount Pleasant in Liverpool in 1855-6, England had no training college for Catholic schoolmistresses.[50] In more rural places such as Stone, middle-class women offered their services as voluntary teachers of small classes. In a heavily-populated and working-class town like Manchester it was extremely difficult to find Catholic teachers. The English Catholic Church, however, was part of a wider community, which had a distinct educational superiority in its religious orders of trained teachers. In 1849 most of the Catholic teachers in Manchester were Presentation Sisters or Irish Christian Brothers. The Presentation Sisters were only in St Patrick's but by mid century other religious orders from Ireland or the Continent had moved into England and all the other parishes were negotiating with them to come to Manchester. The advantages were manifest. They were highly trained according to a long tradition of expertise. They would impart an accurate catechesis. They were dedicated in their work because it formed part of their religious as well as their professional vocation.[51] They would not leave to be married or to have children and if a sister were moved she would be immediately replaced by another, so that they would give a school stability for the indefinite future. There would be at least two of them, a headmistress and an assistant and they would teach on a class basis rather than on the increasingly ill-favoured monitorial system. They would also be satisfied with lower salaries than lay teachers might be and their orders might even help to finance parish schools. Because Elizabeth Prout in 1850 could not offer these advantages, she was replaced. That did not mean, however, that she was no longer a valuable educational asset. As still an independent laywoman in 1851, she offered one advantage the religious lacked: she was free to move from school to school as necessity demanded. In the light of the introduction of a second education bill her role in that respect was particularly important.

Manchester's educational debate had continued while Elizabeth taught in George Leigh Street. The Church of England wanted state-supported Anglican schools and religious education based on the Authorised Version of the Bible.[52] Catholics wanted their own schools and the Douai Version of the Bible.[53] Samuel Lucas suggested the Bible issue could be avoided by the adoption of the Irish National System.[54] The secularists eventually agreed that religion could be taught at specific times and Cobden suggested all schools should adopt the Massachusetts system.[55] It was at this stage that Evangelicalism entered the arena. On so religious a topic as education Canon Hugh Stowell could hardly have been expected to remain silent. On 6 January 1851 as a member of the Manchester and Salford Committee on Education led by Canon Charles Richson of Manchester Cathedral, Stowell, two Wesleyan ministers and some Anglican laymen produced their own scheme of local, rate-aided education.[56] Bishop James Prince Lee, first bishop of Manchester, then agreed to restrict religious teaching to particular periods.[57] The Catholics, however, who, represented by Father Turner, the future bishop, and Father George Errington, future bishop of Plymouth, had so far taken part in the discussions, could not accept this marginalisation of religious instruction.[58] They would also have known that the Massachusetts system prohibited Catholic teaching and that in Ireland the National System was unsatisfactory: religious education had been placed at the end of the afternoon and there was a degree of Protestant proselytism.[59] It was the Manchester and Salford

Education Committee's proposals, however, that caused the greatest furore and highlighted the importance of Elizabeth Prout's teaching role in Manchester in the face of anti-Catholic Evangelicalism.

The erection of St Chad's new school coincided with another wave of converts following the Gorham judgement and with Pius IX's restoration of the hierarchy.[60] The worst fears of popular Protestantism seemed to be being realised. In its first number earlier in 1850, a Catholic magazine, the *Lamp*, had unfortunately spoken in triumphalist terms of the Catholic Church's 'resuming... imperial dignity' and affirming 'her power and prerogative throughout the wide domain of proud infidel England.... Her reign must come', it said, 'and it may be nearer than some suspect, for is she not daily exhibiting her increasing influence?'[61] So it seemed as St Chad's 'complete establishment', perfect to the last detail, arose on Cheetham Hill.[62] Canon Stowell and the Manchester Wesleyans had been furious at government grants for Catholic schools.[63] If education was to be the means of effecting a reversal of the Protestant reformation, they were determined Catholics must not be educated, or, at least, not on the rates.[64]

In January 1851, S.N. Stokes, as secretary of the Catholic Poor School Committee, sent two letters to the *Morning Chronicle*, voicing Catholic concern about Richson's scheme.[65] In February, Richson sent Stokes a copy of his committee's report. As formulated by Canon Stowell and two Wesleyans its proposals were predictably aimed at the exclusion of Catholic schools from rate support.[66] Since they knew Catholics were not included in the 1846 Minutes of the Committee of Council, they made eligibility for government grants according to the 1846 Minutes a pre-requisite for rate support in Manchester. Not all non-Catholic schools were covered by the Minutes, however, as the government would not give grants to schools underneath or immediately attached to a church or chapel, nor to those on less than five years' lease. The committee therefore said that such Dissenters' schools in Manchester and Salford would be eligible for rate support but not Catholics', because no Catholic schools were covered by the 1846 Minutes. Similarly, Ragged Schools, which, according to Stokes, were 'generally, perhaps, founded expressly to proselyte poor Irish children', would be rate supported but Catholic Ragged Schools, 'which had the best right to educate the lowest class of Catholics', would not. Stokes reminded Richson that Catholic schools were entitled to government grants by the 1847 agreement. As regarded those not included in it because of their situation or insecurity of tenure, he suggested 'it must be a principle... that similar schools of different religions should be similarly treated'. He also pointed out that, unless clarified, the report's reference to 'Holy Scripture' might be interpreted by 'dishonest persons' as meaning only the Authorised

Version. He pointed out, too, that according to Richson's scheme, 'distinctively and exclusively Protestant' schools would be built in areas where four-fifths of the children would be Catholics. Since loyal Catholics would not use them, he said, they would simply increase the already large amount of 'useless school-accommodation'.[67] Richson did not reply. The Scriptures were defined as the Authorised Version.[68] Thus Catholic schools were definitively excluded.

On 15 March 1851 the Catholic priests of Manchester and Salford submitted their own objections to Richson's draft proposals for a Bill for Local Education in Manchester and Salford. They explained that Catholics could not use the Protestant version of the Bible, nor did they consider 'simple reading of Holy Writ by children a proper, becoming, or legitimate foundation of religious instruction'. They complained that, although Catholics paid rates, their schools would be excluded from rate support. Many Catholic children would be excluded from education because they could not afford even the low fees of the Catholic schools. If they voluntarily attended the free Protestant schools, or were forced to do so by law, they would have to read the Authorised Version and thereby violate their consciences.[69] All Protestant and Dissenting schools in Manchester and Salford would become rate supported but Catholics, in addition to paying rates for the others, would have to continue to finance their own schools. Inevitably these would remain materially poor and numerically insufficient. On this reading, the bill seemed to aim at the impoverishment and proselytism of Manchester's large Catholic community. Having tried unavailingly to persuade the committee to adopt the government's own policy of permitting Catholics in receipt of parliamentary grants to use the Douai Version of the Bible, the Catholic clergy withdrew from the scheme.[70]

The committee remained intransigent. They claimed the proposals involved no violation of justice. Catholic schools were eligible for rate support on the same terms as others: the use of the Authorised Version. There was therefore no inequality. They now asserted, incorrectly, that schools run by 'teachers connected with various confraternities, monastic orders, or religious houses' were excluded from government grants. Such schools in Manchester and Salford would also be excluded from rate support, as grants in their favour would be 'justly obnoxious to the great body of ratepayers, and would prove fatal to the scheme'.[71] Thus they specifically excluded St Augustine's boys' school taught by the Xaverian Brothers, St Patrick's boys' school taught by the Irish Christian Brothers, St Patrick's girls' school taught by the Presentation Sisters and St Mary's girls' school then taught by the Sisters of Providence.[72] Since other sisters were arriving in St Wilfrid's and St Chad's in 1851 they too would be excluded, as would also, in the event, St John's, Salford from 1852. Since Elizabeth Prout had not professed her vows in 1851-2, she was the only 'religious' in Manchester or Salford who could have claimed rate support for a school, except for the basic fact that all Catholic schools were excluded anyway because not one of them would use the Authorised Version.[73]

To the priests' further objection that Protestant children attending Catholic schools could exempt themselves from religious instruction, but that Catholic children attending a Protestant school would be subject to reading the Authorised Version, the committee replied that since, on Catholics' own claims, religious instruction in Catholic schools was not confined to the teaching of 'dogmatic formularies' but permeated the whole curriculum, Protestant children in Catholic schools would not be protected from Catholic instruction. If Catholic parents chose to send their children to Protestant schools, they obviously had no conscientious objections to their children's using the Authorised Version.[74] If Catholic parents were forced to send their children to Protestant schools because there were no Catholic schools available, that was the fault of the Catholic Church for not providing them. The committee confirmed that it proposed to use the rates to build free Protestant schools in the large working-class areas where many people were Catholics.[75] It said Catholic parents would have perfect equality with others in choosing whether or not to send their children to such schools. It did not propose to compel attendance. The only children who would be compelled by law to attend school would be those dealt with by the Poor Law authorities, who would act according to their own guidelines.[76] Catholic pauper children, therefore, would be forced to attend school but others would have a choice of free education at a Protestant school, fee-paying attendance at a Catholic school or continued illiteracy.

Canon Stowell, in the meantime, in March 1851 had given an anti-Catholic lecture in which he had also attacked Milner Gibson, Cobden and Bright for wanting 'to let religion alone' in parliament.[77] In August 1851, as Elizabeth Prout founded her order, the Manchester and Salford Committee on Education offered their bill to parliament, although Cobden had warned them that they could not exclude Catholics without 'downright injustice and negligence' of the 'most necessitous portion of the people'.[78] In October Canon Stowell preached before Queen Victoria in Manchester Cathedral.[79] He was at the height of his career. In November 1851, as Elizabeth Prout was replaced in St Chad's and the new school opened its doors for the first time, the *Protestant Witness* called for the 'withdrawal of all aid from Popish schools'.[80]

3. WORKING-CLASS EDUCATION

While the various educational and religious protagonists were debating the great issue of the Manchester and Salford Bill, Elizabeth Prout was actively engaged in performing a very useful function as a supply teacher in Manchester's Catholic schools. Her role was particularly important precisely because of the background debate and its potential dangers to Catholic education.

Although Father Sheehan had planned a school for girls, boys and infants, the erection of St Chad's infant department had been postponed.[81] At the same time, in the light of the current dangers to Catholic education and as having shown herself a competent teacher in difficult circumstances, Elizabeth Prout was far too useful to become unemployed.[82] In late 1851 she seems to have been asked to open an infant school for St Chad's in a large room at the top of the four-storey building in Dyche Street.[83] There she found herself with about 130 day pupils and 250 on Sundays in accommodation for 140 day pupils and 187 Sunday scholars.[84] The government, the Catholic Poor School Committee and Manchester's secularists and political economists were all encouraging separate schools for infants.[85] Young children, it was recommended, required pictures rather than books and oral instruction instead of reading. They needed singing and articulation and frequent marching to exercise the body and to prevent over-fatigue of the mind. The schools, it was advised, should be on the ground floor; they should be well ventilated; and they should have a playground.[86] Dyche Street school was obviously woefully substandard. In taking charge of it, Elizabeth Prout was once more making an option for the poor, in this case the small children who, 'wild and implike, in dirt and rags', were often left to run and fight in St Michael's graveyard, or to roam the streets to be lost or injured or even drawn into criminal activities.[87] She was extending the Passionist mission to England into the very heart of Angel Meadow. She was also ensuring there was a Catholic infants' school in that very large working-class area.

In July 1852, as further postulants were arriving, Father Croskell asked her if she and some of her sisters would take the girls' night school while the Notre Dame Sisters were away for a time. It had 210 pupils.[88] Elizabeth was just beginning to form her community according to Father Gaudentius' Rule and so at first he refused her permission. He thought she should be with her postulants in the evenings. When pressurised personally by his co-founder, however, he yielded immediately.[89] Night schools were not new at the mid-nineteenth century and there had been one in Manchester in 1794.[90] Most were started by the larger Nonconformist Sunday schools to provide the instruction in writing and arithmetic they were forbidden to give on Sundays.[91] There had also been various types of study groups, especially for men, formed for a variety of reasons, which had promoted adult education among the working classes. There was a veneration for books, a respect for learning, a thirst for knowledge and a considerable amount of self-education amongst the industrialised poor, both male and female.[92] The Irish in particular were avid for education.[93] The vast majority of the working classes, however, and particularly those in the cotton mills, had had little opportunity to attend any classes other than the factory or Sunday schools, until the Ten Hours Act of 1847 had eliminated evening shift work.[94] With free evenings at their disposal, many of the mill girls were glad to attend night schools, if only to learn reading, writing, arithmetic and plain sewing.[95] In the next decade, as Stokes commented in 1860, the night school closed the factory girls' day as naturally as the mill opened it. Provided they had a 'cheerful, warm, well-lighted room' and met the 'pleasant face and kind word of a friendly teacher', they came in large numbers to read, write and sing.[96] The Catholic clergy wanted Catholic night schools to provide instruction in faith and morals as well as in secular education.[97] Moreover, in July 1852 sectarian tension was high in the Manchester area, because of the Stockport riots and other disturbances.[98] 'The struggle with Rome is only begun', Stowell proclaimed that month. 'Spiritually, ecclesiastically, politically she must be withstood.... The battle of the Reformation has to be fought again.'[99] Father Croskell would have been anxious to keep his school open to occupy the Catholic girls and to protect them from insult elsewhere. In co-operating with him, Elizabeth Prout was once again making a valuable contribution to St Chad's parish.

How a Catholic night school functioned at this time was recorded by the Notre Dame Sisters in Blackburn. They began with two classes of 80 and 120 pupils, the first paying 2d. a week, the second 3d. On the first night they were all 'little less than savages, pushing each other on all sides' but they soon settled down. They were so anxious to learn that, within a few months, girls who had not known even their letters were able to read and write 'very nicely'. The last half hour every evening was given to religious instruction. It was revealing that many girls who did not trouble to come for other classes 'never failed to attend this'. Many of the girls were under 14 but the majority were between 20 and 30 and there was also a 'Select Evening School' of 20-30 older women, one of them almost 50, who came to school because they 'felt ashamed of their ignorance'.[100] In Derby in 1847 Cornelia Connelly's 'very crowded night school' ran from 6-9 p.m. It had 100 girls, who came for catechetical instruction, sewing, cutting-out work, reading, writing and simple arithmetic.[101] In taking St Chad's similar night school in 1852, Elizabeth Prout was helping the working-class women for whom she was founding her order. She was also making her own contribution to an educational movement that became particularly popular in industrial Lancashire.[102] She fostered an educational work that within three years was to be described by the Committee of Council on Education as 'most desirable and even indispensable' and as such was to receive special legislation.[103] In 1861 the Newcastle Commission reported the 'civilizing mission' of those who, like Elizabeth Prout, had promoted experiments in adult education.[104] She, however, would not have seen the mill girls as barbarians to be 'civilised' but as the defenceless poor, whose conditions she was able to ameliorate by elevating them out of their educational inferiority.[105] She was unobtrusively but fundamentally and positively helping to make real changes in the unjust structures of the class society.[106] She would not have so expressed it. She was not consciously a social reformer. She did not regard society in that way. Her motivation was spiritual in that she considered that whatever she did for the poor, she did for Christ. She was, however, raising the dignity of working-class girls and women and, through them, as wives and mothers, that of their husbands and children too.[107] She was giving them Catholic morality, numeracy, literacy and a degree of domesticity. With those qualifications they would have a better quality of life. They could climb the social ladder.[108] At the same time, as the foundress of a religious congregation, although she was not founding a specifically teaching order, she was directing her institute towards an apostolate in every form of education.

By July 1852, Elizabeth had already arranged that from September one of her postulants would take the Dyche Street school and she would take St Mary's, in the 'ruined and ill-ventilated rooms' in Royton Street, which the Sisters of Providence had left.[109] As she engaged in the 'almost hopeless struggle... with the poverty-stricken ignorance and semi-barbarism' of Deansgate, Manchester's educational debate moved into its next phase.[110] When the Manchester and Salford Education Bill had come before parliament, a Select Committee had been appointed to enquire into the state of education in the area. The hearings began in Manchester in April 1852 and continued, after an interval, into 1853.[111] Elizabeth Prout, of course, was not cited to appear. She held no directly central part in the proceedings. Her place was in the classroom. Nevertheless, for that very reason, precisely because she was a Catholic teacher in Manchester at the time, she was at the forefront of the attempts to make sufficient educational provision for Catholic children in this crucial period when new legislation might have passed through parliament. By going to teach in St Mary's cottage school in September 1852, she was ensuring that the parish had a girls' school. She was safeguarding the Catholic position in that large working-class area. As long as she held that school open, it could not be said there was no Catholic school in Deansgate. Since she started there in September 1852, it was in St Mary's that she first began to teach according to the educational prescriptions of Father Gaudentius Rossi's Rule.

As a Passionist missioner who preached throughout England and frequently in the large towns, Father Gaudentius was well acquainted with the educational issues of the day. He was also legislating for a religious order that existed specifically for the lower classes and was committed to industry on the pattern of the Holy Family at Nazareth. According to his Rule, the sisters were 'principally' to have schools for the 'daughters of the poor' because, 'being themselves practically acquainted with work', they were particularly suited 'to train up females of the working-classes'. In thus extending the industrial nature of the order to its educational apostolate, Gaudentius stressed the sisters' identification with the poor. They would understand the poor because they *were* the poor. Their educational apostolate arose out of the needs of the poor: the dearth of education for thousands of Catholic children in Manchester. In the classrooms, as in the cloister, the sisters belonged to the poor. In addition to day schools, for older girls who were working during the week, they were also to have Sunday schools, in which they were to teach 'reading, writing and the Catholic catechism'. The Catholic ethos was of paramount importance, as also was the 'memory' of the Holy Family. All the schools were to be dedicated to the Holy Family and, in the equivalent of the Passionists' fourth vow to promote the 'memory' of the Passion, the sisters were 'to study to promote this devotion in the minds and hearts of their pupils'. Like Father Gaudentius' prescriptions for the sisters' domestic industry, his legislation for their teaching reflected general contemporary opinions. Thus they were to 'endeavour to render' their pupils not only 'good practical Catholics' but also 'useful members of society', bearing in mind their future stations in life. The emphasis was on evangelisation, however. 'With all sweetness and dexterity' they were to study to instil into the 'tender minds of their young pupils' the 'maxims... and spirit of the Catholic religion.' They were to use only textbooks that breathed 'a thorough Catholic spirit' even if academically inferior to more secularist types, being 'more anxious to see their pupils solid and virtuous Catholics, than imperfect Christians and more perfect scholars.'[112] Thus Father Gaudentius' Rule expressed the general Catholic opinion that the aim of any Catholic school was to hand on the Catholic faith, devotionally as well as doctrinally, and to prepare the pupils for their future lives by suitable instruction in secular subjects. As an expression of the Catholic principles of education, it was diametrically opposed to the Manchester and Salford Education Bill.

Historians have generally seen Manchester's proposals for a system of national, free and secular education as a movement to educate the working classes. A study of the enquiry held by the Select Committee, however, reveals that while there were intentions to provide rate-supported education for large sections of the working classes, there was also an inner movement to progress towards free education for the lower middle class. As seen in this context, discrimination against Catholics was not necessarily a sign that even all the members of the Manchester and Salford Education Committee shared Stowell's Evangelical views. It was rather, perhaps, a practical formulation of the utilitarian concept of promoting the greatest happiness of the greatest number. At first, however, the investigation continued along the same lines as the previous debate: schools run by religious were specifically excluded and all Catholic schools would in fact be excluded because they would not use the James I Bible. Called to give evidence in April 1852, Canon Richson was well prepared with statistics and maps, purporting to show that Manchester Catholics already had surplus school accommodation, since in their day schools they could provide for 4,660 pupils and had an attendance of only 2,461, while in their Sunday schools they had accommodation for 6,211 and an attendance of 4,590.[113] He admitted, however, that his figures omitted two schools, because, although he had had permission from Bishop Turner to seek information, two priests had refused to co-operate. He had therefore taken the figures he had and those collected by Manchester's Statistical Society in 1834-5 and, apparently without reference to famine immigration, had mathematically deduced his final figures.[114] A comparison with those published in 1852 by the Catholic Poor School Committee, as received from the clergy, reveals his inaccuracy: Manchester Catholics in fact had a day-school attendance of 3,089 in accommodation for 3,860 and a Sunday-school attendance of 7,608 in accommodation for 5,176.[115] Moreover, as the Select Committee suggested to Richson, even had there been overall adequate accommodation, the children seeking education might live miles away from schools with vacancies. St Augustine's day school, for example, had an attendance of 650 in accommodation for 573 and that was in the unhealthy church crypt. In 1849-51, before the new St Chad's school was opened, girls from Red Bank and Angel Meadow had had to walk to Elizabeth Prout's school in George Leigh Street. Further, as Stokes pointed out, even if Richson's figures had been accurate, since the Catholic population of Manchester and Salford was reckoned 'by well-informed persons' to be 80,000, 'of whom one eighth at the lowest admissible computation' should have been in school, the Catholic Church in Manchester and Salford actually required accommodation for 10,000 children. As Stokes saw the situation, even on Richson's figures, Manchester and Salford required additional schools for 5,000 Catholic children and needed to improve attendance.[116]

The Select Committee asked Richson if he thought Catholics faced great difficulties in raising enough money to enable them to take advantage of parliamentary grants. As the factory inspector, Leonard Horner, the Manchester Catholic solicitor, George Richardson and the social reformer, Mary Carpenter all pointed out at different times, the basic weakness of the government's grant system was that it gave most aid where least required and none where most needed.[117] Richson, however, thought the Manchester Catholics had no problem. They appeared to be able to raise 'very splendid buildings', he said, 'far superior, indeed, to those of any other religious body'.[118] He had heard St Chad's school had been built by aid of a parliamentary grant and he thought Catholics were making 'much greater efforts to support their schools and charities than any other body of Christians'.[119] He did not believe Catholics were really poor, because a 'very poor class of people' could not have built St Chad's, where there was 'a complete establishment', nor the cathedral in Salford. When he was reminded there were debts on both buildings, he replied that that problem was not confined to Catholics.[120] Asked if he would pay Catholic teachers, as others, out of the rates, he agreed on condition that their schools submitted to the 'lowest test of teaching religion': the use of the Authorised Version. In fact, therefore, as well as building and maintaining their own schools, Catholics would have to continue to pay their own teachers. Since in many cases Catholic teachers were underpaid, they would be marginalised within what was becoming the teaching profession.[121]

The attitude of another witness, W. Entwistle, was similar. Pressed by Cobden to admit that by making the use of the Authorised Version the criterion on which schools would be given rate support, he was committing 'an act of great injustice' to Manchester's large Catholic population, he finally conceded that Catholics had been deliberately excluded.[122] He said his committee did not intend to 'provide a fund for building schools', although they would build some Protestant schools.[123] He admitted Catholics needed schools but, like Richson, he said they could build their own. Their efforts had been 'very large and extended'. They had built 'new cathedrals, churches and schoolrooms' and were 'extremely active'. There was 'no doubt that they would build sufficient schoolrooms to accommodate their own population.'[124]

Since Entwistle knew Catholics were 'extremely active', he knew they were struggling to raise funds for schools and churches. Another witness, J. Adshead detailed for the Select Committee what a severe struggle it was. Acknowledging that Catholics were making extraordinary efforts to raise funds for educational and other purposes, Adshead showed that under the presidency of Bishop Turner, the vice-presidency of Father Toole of St Wilfrid's, and the leadership of four laymen, the Manchester and Salford Catholic Association collected a halfpenny per week from everyone who could afford it, presumably as they came to church.[125] The takings were divided into six portions, allocated in sixteenths: three for the education of priests for the Salford Diocese; eight, half the fund, for Catholic poor schools; one for the Catholic Poor School Committee; one to a contingency fund; two for the defence of the Catholic faith; and one for the Catholic Defence Association of Ireland, established by Archbishop Cullen in response to the Ecclesiastical Titles Act of August 1851, in order 'to set forth in the press a clear exposition of [Catholic] wrongs and a powerful defence of [Catholic] claims, and to have the interest of [the Catholic] religion properly represented in Parliament.'[126] Thus the Catholic Church in the Salford Diocese was maintained by the halfpennies of the poor. As Bishop Turner said in his *Pastoral Letter* of September 1852, in proportion to the population of Catholics the number of lay contributors to the mission fund for new churches was 'painfully limited', actually to nineteen people from the whole diocese. Bemoaning also the lack of schools for the poor, he diagnosed the contemporary situation. 'Depravity sustained by ignorance sweeps everything before it like a torrent', he said, referring to the condition of many of the working classes. 'A vain sophistry, hardened with scepticism, impious maxims resting upon strange and distinctive opinions, are diffusing a moral desolation around us', he continued, in oblique reference to the educational controversy. 'The time, indeed, would appear to have come', he finished, 'when the direct issue is between religion and infidelity — between the teachings of the Gospel and the suggestions of pride and mammon....'[127]

It was only in the final stages of the first part of the enquiry that the hidden agenda of the Manchester proposals emerged clearly. Questioned by the Select Committee, Richson finally admitted, 'It could not be contemplated to pay for all the children out of the rate.'[128] What he really meant was ultimately and unwillingly explained by Entwistle. 'Is not the main and principal object of this Bill', he was asked, 'to provide education for the people, who are at present so poor as to be unable to pay for admission to the existing schools?' Yes', he replied. 'Therefore', he was questioned, 'the poorer classes are those who are, in fact, most considered by the promoters of this Bill?' Thus pressed, Entwistle had to admit there were other considerations. 'There is a desire to include those more than any others', he said, because we always considered that, however desirable it might be to draw some line of demarcation by which the whole population should not be able to avail themselves of a system so established actually free of all cost to themselves, yet that, speaking generally, they would draw this line for themselves: those that could pay for education of a better character would give it probably to their children; and on the other hand, though some of those who actually paid to the rates would avail themselves of that which may be said generally to be provided for the poor, yet, as they do pay the rates, we cannot pretend to exclude them and admit those who do not pay.[129]

On analysis, therefore, the real aim of the Manchester and Salford Education Committee had been to provide rate support for those lower middle-class parents, who were seeing the children of the labouring classes being better educated than their own. Such parents felt particularly frustrated because they could see that, with the new government grants for buildings, books and maps, certification of teachers and the pupil-teacher system, the working classes would be so well educated that they would compete with middle-class children for superior jobs.[130] Smart working-class pupils who knew how to calculate the poor rate on a property, or the financial differences between various speeds of piecework, and could use cashbooks, daybooks and ledgers, as required by the government's extended curriculum, would be well able to compete successfully with poorly educated, middle--class pupils on their own ground.[131] The Committee of Council, however, would not give parliamentary grants to middle schools.[132] The middle classes must help themselves. They proposed to do so through the Manchester and Salford Education Bill, which was an attempt to finance much needed lower middle-class education out of the rates. The committee had realised it could not afford 'to pay for all the children', especially as that would entail building Catholic schools for the droves of Irish children who had arrived from the potato famine. As Entwistle had said, they did not intend to 'provide a fund for building schools, although they would build some Protestant schools'. In framing its Bill, therefore, the committee had stipulated the use of the Authorised Version in order to draw 'some line of demarcation' that would exclude a large number of children: the Jews and Catholics.[133] It would have been 'fatal to the scheme', as Richson said, to have included them. Having thus eliminated a large part of the population, they next expected that those who 'could pay for education of a better character' would do so. Thus they needed to make provision for only the non-Jewish and non-Catholic working and lower middle classes. Since both the Church of England and Dissenters had been receiving parliamentary grants for education from 1833 and the

Establishment had had an educational drive in Manchester throughout the 1840s, there were enough Protestant schools.[134] The purpose of the Manchester and Salford Education Committee's Bill was to maintain on the rates those existing schools, with, perhaps, a few Protestant additions in the poorest, and largely Catholic, working-class areas and also to aid lower middle-class schools. As John Bright had said in Manchester in 1845, education was needed among those connected with manufacture and commerce. 'I hold it to be quite impossible', he had said, 'that there should be a great raising up of the operative classes unless there be a corresponding improvement among the class next above them in the social world.'[135] The Manchester and Salford Education Bill was intended to help those lower middle classes who were rich enough to pay direct rates but would be glad to avail themselves of rate support for the education of their children. 'As they do pay the rates', Entwistle said, 'we cannot pretend to exclude them and admit those who do not pay.'[136] What he really wanted was parliamentary permission for Manchester's middle classes to levy a rate to provide a sound education for lower middle-class children.[137]

The Lancashire Public School Association had made this intention clear in 1847: 'The Public Schools we propose to establish should not be considered merely as schools for the poor. The education given in a large proportion of the schools established for the middle classes is of a very inferior character.'[138] From 1849 Manchester Grammar School provided a commercial education for mercantile interests and in 1851 Owens College provided a higher education, but for the children of tradesmen and shopkeepers there was little available.[139] In a lecture in Manchester Town Hall in August 1851, W.B. Hodgson, comparing the two schemes for rate-supported schools, commented on the Manchester and Salford Committee's plan, 'There is one feature of it which, introduced casually, as it would seem, has hitherto attracted little attention. Clause xiii provides, "district committees may direct the inspectors of schools within the district to examine the children educated in self-supporting commercial and middle schools, on application of the proprietors or principals thereof."'[140] The district committees could not authorise inspection of self-supporting schools unless they were also offering rate aid. On the pretext of provision for the poor, the Manchester and Salford Education Bill was an attempt to put lower middle-class education on the rates, at the price of excluding the Jewish and Catholic schools.[141] When, therefore, in 1854 Elizabeth Prout opened her own school in Levenshulme for the Catholic lower middle class, she was once more reflecting Manchester's commercial and industrial society and yet again protecting the *anawim* of the Catholic Church.

4. AN APOSTLE OF EDUCATION

Although not a pioneer in education in the generally accepted sense, Elizabeth Prout was a true missionary, an apostle of education. She was totally available, always ready to fill a breach, in the interests of the poor. Consistently unobtrusive, she nevertheless showed single-minded devotion in helping to safeguard Catholic interests in face of the threats inherent in the Manchester schemes for education. By her willingness to act as a bridgehead in one working-class district after another, she played a vital role in the Catholic struggle for schools, even at great cost to herself, as became apparent in St Mary's in the winter of 1852-53.

Although, as compared with her George Leigh Street school, St Mary's was fairly small, Elizabeth still had a class of seventy-five of Deansgate's poor.[142] At the same time, from the first clothing ceremony in November 1852, she was beginning to live community life with her first set of novices. According to one of the annalists,

> Their poverty was extreme. Poor in every sense of the word, there were times when they were even in want of the bare necessaries of life. To the scarcity of food was added the labouring work [they undertook].... From St Chad's they went every Sunday twice to St Mary's to carry on the Sunday school there, and this in all weathers... [while] the distance traversed must have taxed their strength as it was done on foot.[143]

No evidence has survived for the content of Elizabeth Prout's teaching in either St Mary's day school or the Sunday school. When her school in St Anne's, Sutton, near St Helens, was inspected by the Liverpool diocesan religious inspector in 1858, however, he noted her pupils' knowledge of the catechism, the Commandments, the Sacraments, of the meaning of words used in Catholic doctrine and of customary prayers and practices; the children's behaviour in church; and the frequency with which they attended the Sacraments.[144] In Manchester, Sunday schools were important for all Churches and ecclesial communities as perhaps the chief vehicle by which they gave instruction in their particular beliefs, because so many of their working-class adherents could not attend their day schools even if they had them.[145] In the Catholic situation of Elizabeth Prout's Manchester, Sunday schools were particularly important. In view of how many Catholics were too poor to pay even the 2d. or 3d. fees required by St Mary's day school, the free Sunday schools were outstandingly important.[146] In taking charge of St Mary's Sunday school, Elizabeth Prout was again playing a vital role in the process of evangelisation and in Catholic education in general. If her girls did not attend a Catholic day school, the Sunday school was the only place where they would normally receive formal instruction in Catholic faith and practice.[147] This religious education of girls was particularly important, because, as wives, mothers and grandmothers, they would be mainly instrumental in passing on the Catholic faith to future generations.[148] In the Catholic schools, as in some Protestant ones, greater attention was paid to teaching doctrine from a catechism than directly from the Bible.[149] It was more imperative to instruct the children in their living faith and the terse catechism statements lent themselves to the rote learning of the time.[150] Lengthier verbal explanations of either Scripture or theology could be left to the priest's sermon at Mass, which formed an integral part of the Sunday-school day.

In Sutton there was no need to give secular instructions at Sunday school because the 30-40 girls who attended it were probably amongst the 136 who went to St Anne's day school.[151] For the working classes of the heavily industrialised urban areas, however, the Sunday schools frequently presented the only opportunity for acquiring literacy, which was why many who attended a particular church's school did not subsequently attend its services.[152] How a Catholic Sunday school functioned in this situation was explained in a letter from a Christian Brother teaching in Saints Peter and Paul's, Bolton about this time, 'On Sundays, after... breakfast... immediately off to school to lead the boys to Mass. After Mass, Sunday school, in which reading, writing, arithmetic and religious instruction continue until 12.30. Then dinner, after which school again at 2 until 4.30. Then tea, and back to school to lead the boys to church at 6.30 for evening prayers.'[153] In 1846 Cornelia Connelly had written in similar terms to the earl of Shrewsbury about her school in Derby, 'Sunday is a very busy day, with two hundred girls to lead to church for High Mass after an hour's labour in teaching them and from 2 till 4 in the afternoon teaching them to read etc., etc. Much as we deplore the state of things which renders this necessary, we cannot but acknowledge it is the only way to get hold of the working class — the factory girls.'[154] The Notre Dame Sisters in Blackburn told a similar story in 1850:

> They want us to open a Sunday school... this coming Sunday. The church is about 20 minutes' walk from our house and the Sisters should be there at 9 o'clock to take about 200 children to Mass. Then there will be class until half past 3 when they will take the children to Vespers. They will return home about 5. We will be just as busy on Sundays as during the week.... The Sunday school was crowded with young girls, principally those who worked in the factories, and the greatest confusion and disorder reigned among them but they were simple and it was an easy task to subdue them.[155]

Elizabeth Prout was in a similar situation. In 1852 she had 250 girls in the long, low room in Royton Street that was estimated to accommodate 107.[156] According to Adshead's evidence before the 1852 Select Committee, the children in St Augustine's and St Chad's Sunday schools were taught reading from an alphabet and first spelling book, followed by a second, third and fourth reading book and miscellaneous reading.[157] The same practice was probably followed in St Mary's and other Catholic schools. From as early as 1827, the Manchester Catholic Sunday schools had also had lending libraries.[158] After an initial fee of 1s., scholars could take home a book for ½d. a week, with the result that their parents, too, were being introduced to morally good literature, with 'immense benefit' as the 1831 *Catholic Directory* had noted.[159] Adshead also said that arithmetic was taught in the Catholic Sunday schools.[160] The Christian Brother's letter confirms it was certainly taught in boys' schools. It is clear from his letter and from Father Gaudentius' Rule that writing was taught in all Catholic Sunday schools, in contrast to the practice in most others, where neither writing nor arithmetic were taught.[161] Very often, however, other denominations supplemented their Sunday teaching with night classes in secular subjects, whereas there were comparatively few Catholic night schools on account of the shortage of teachers.[162]

From the priests' point of view, the Sunday schools provided the best available means of reaching out to the poorest children to teach them their Catholic faith and to instruct them for their reception of the Sacraments. High attendance indicates their popularity with both parents and pupils.[163] It was through the Sunday schools that the priests, parents and teachers together could build up a practising Catholic community. It was not a matter of social control.[164] Cornelia Connelly was speaking colloquially when she referred to 'getting hold' of the factory girls. The Passionist missions in Manchester, and equally in Derby, demonstrated Catholic working-class devotion to their religion.[165] Catholic children had a right to receive their Catholic inheritance; parents and priests a duty to impart it. Catholic parents were grateful for the Sunday schools. The 1852 attendance figures show a strong desire amongst the working-class Catholics of Manchester to have their children educated and their girls as much as their boys. The Catholic Sunday schools answered working-class religious and educational needs.[166] They did not interfere with their wage-earning activities during the week. They were free, gave the children both religious and secular learning and took them out of the house and off the streets.[167] They were Catholic and working-class expressions of self-help and liberation rather than instruments of ecclesiastical or middle-class social control.[168] In Manchester in 1852 1,550 Catholic boys, 1,211 girls and 328 infants attended Catholic day schools, but

2,955 boys, 3,648 girls and 1,005 infants attended Sunday schools.[169] As a result of such high attendance of girls, Catholic girls, and subsequently women, had a higher degree of literacy than others in the same working classes.[170] Elizabeth Prout's work in the Sunday schools, as in the day schools, made a valuable contribution to the education of the poor, the development of the Catholic Church and the tone of society in nineteenth-century Manchester. In this way too her apostolate was an extension of the Passionist mission to England.

It took its toll of her, however. In January 1853 Elizabeth became seriously ill, either from Deansgate fever or tuberculosis.[171] Thus, although her apostolate in St Mary's was intensive, it was comparatively short. Nevertheless, she was there at that crucial time when the Manchester and Salford Education Committee were constituting such a threat to Catholic education. Because she was there, St Mary's girls had a school. By 10 July 1855 the clergy had received a grant of £460 from the Committee of Council on Education and £100 from the Catholic Poor School Committee towards their new school in Tonman Street.[172] By having ensured St Mary's had a school, Elizabeth Prout had helped to make that possible. In the meantime, she had opened four more schools, all in new parishes: St Joseph's, Goulden Street; the parish day school and a convent boarding school in Levenshulme; and St Ann's girls' day school at Ashton-under-Lyne. In these places, at any rate, she was truly a pioneer in education.

It was while she was ill in the spring of 1853 that Father Stephan of St Joseph's asked Elizabeth Prout to open a school for him in Goulden Street. Bishop Turner, a leading educationalist, wanted to implement the national Catholic policy that wherever there were 'Catholics belonging to the labouring classes, there ought to be a Catholic Poor School' and 'that every mission should have its school'.[173] In a *Pastoral Letter* in September, 1852, having referred to the opening of two new chapels that year, St Joseph's and St Ann's, Ashton-under-Lyne, Bishop Turner continued, 'We are filled with deep concern and are grievously harassed to witness so much spiritual destitution — many wandering like sheep without a shepherd deprived of religious instruction. Alas! we have but too much reason to fear that many of the household of the Faith become lost to us for ever through the absence of religious teaching.'[174] Father Stephan, accordingly, was anxious to open a school. In October 1848 the *Catholic School* had published directives on how to establish a Catholic school. It should be purpose-built, like St Chad's. It should have 'suitable light, thorough ventilation, convenient fittings, spacious playgrounds'. A good site should be selected, preferably a piece of freehold land. An architect's drawing accompanied the advice. The ideal Catholic school, with Gothic touch, was shown as an L-shaped building, with three large rooms, for infants, girls and boys, each section provided with its own entrance, cloakrooms and toilets; two libraries; a house for the teacher; and spacious grounds complete with playground facilities. Not even St Chad's had achieved this degree of finesse. In Goulden Street it was impossible, but, the *Catholic School* had continued, if there were difficulties about obtaining such a site and erecting such a building, the case was by no means hopeless. 'An old warehouse or storeroom... any place capable of containing a sufficient number of children, with facilities for obtaining light and air, [could] at a very moderate expense, be converted into a schoolroom.'[175] Father Stephan was fortunate in that, when Father Hearne had built the temperance guild hall in 1832, he had intended that in the future it should become either a church or a school for that section of St Patrick's parish. He had therefore made it a solid building, even with a Gothic touch.[176] Father Stephan could easily use one storey as a school.

Elizabeth referred the request to Father Gaudentius. He agreed that she could open the school after Easter 1853, provided Father Stephan furnished it 'with what [was] necessary in order to work in it, viz. writing desks, of which there [was] not one..., a stove to warm the room in winter, books, maps, ink, slates etc. and a separate room for the infant school.' In the meantime, he suggested, the children who lived nearest could be sent across the Rochdale Road to Sister Agnes Lee in Dyche Street.[177] Being assured of Elizabeth's co-operation from 23 May 1853, Father Stephan's next problem was financial.[178] He had to maintain the school and he had to pay Elizabeth a salary, although the *Catholic School*, while recommending good salaries for Catholic teachers, admitted that in fact they were regulated by the character and position of the school. Since Elizabeth could not find a decent house in the neighbourhood, her salary was likely to be correspondingly low.[179] According to the *Catholic School*, however, Father Stephan could look to two sources for assistance: the Committee of Council on Education and the Catholic Poor School Committee.

Since a government grant was conditional on successful inspection, Elizabeth Prout once more agreed to an inspection of her teaching. Stokes, by then the second Catholic government inspector, arrived in St Joseph's school on 21 July 1853 to find a mixed class of 179 girls and boys. He regretted the school was too poor to receive a grant. 'This very interesting school', he reported, 'situated in one of the poorest and most populous parts of Manchester, and crowded with children, is not in a condition to claim aid from my Lords. It is imperfectly furnished, and ill supplied with indispensable requisites.' He was favourably impressed, however, by Elizabeth Prout and her companion, probably Sister Mary Paul Taylor, whom he recognised as nuns and accordingly applauded, as was his wont, for he continued,

'Nevertheless the children seem to attend with willingness, and to be much attached to their two amiable teachers, who cannot fail to exercise a moral influence of high value. The instruction', he added, 'is very limited.'[180] Elizabeth was evidently not teaching the government's extended curriculum.[181]

In the knowledge that he had at least a happy school, Father Stephan contributed £1 5s. 0d. to the 1853 collection for the Catholic Poor School Fund and £1 in 1854 but in those years he did not receive anything.[182] Until they had to relinquish the school in autumn 1854, therefore, Elizabeth and her amiable companion had no choice but to limit their instruction according to their ill supply of indispensable requisites. What they were obviously giving was compassion, and in that they were truly Passionist. By opening St Joseph's school for boys and girls in May 1853, Elizabeth Prout had provided Catholic education in that working-class district. She had safeguarded the Catholic situation in that area and had also relieved the educational congestion in the wider St Patrick's mother parish, where another overflow of 165 boys and 55 girls had had to be transferred to the George Leigh Street warehouse.[183] She had once more reached Manchester's working classes. She had again extended the Passionist mission to England into the heart of Manchester's slums.

When her community all succumbed to fever in later 1853, Elizabeth took them to recuperate at Newton House, Father Daly's presbytery at Newton Heath, where they possibly also taught in his school for a time.[184] Since the Stocks Street house was manifestly too small, in April 1854 Bishop Turner provided them with a new convent at Levenshulme, a developing suburb still not part of the city of Manchester.[185] Elizabeth and her companion continued to teach in St Joseph's. Too poor to afford the train fare, they walked the three miles each way from Levenshulme to Goulden Street from April to August 1854. Since they realised they could not do that in winter, they reluctantly decided they would have to leave the city and concentrate all their energies on Levenshulme.[186]

The new convent was a converted farm building, 'beautifully situated' in about two acres of farmland, donated by a Cambridge University convert, Samuel Grimshaw of Errwood Hall in Cheshire, to establish a Catholic mission in the area.[187] Apart from the convent, Grimshaw transformed one building into a church, another into a house for the priest and another into the day school Elizabeth Prout opened.[188] They were all meant to be only temporary. Its condition makeshift, the convent was exceptionally cold on account of its 'bad windows'.[189] In 1857 Bishop Turner finally paid £4 for their repair.[190] In 1853, however, he was thrilled with Grimshaw's generosity. 'We cannot let this occasion pass by', he wrote in his *Pastoral Letter* of

November 1853, 'without adverting, with sentiments of delight and admiration, to the genuine piety of the founder of the new Levenshulme Mission, who, at his own cost, erected both the chapel and the contiguous house for the clergymen.'[191] Named 'Alma Park' in 1857, the area had no address in 1854 and no streetage.[192] The convent, which was adjacent to the church, had extensive gardens, so that 'in this delightful and healthy locality, the sisters were enabled in addition to teaching the poor school in the neighbourhood and St Joseph's in Manchester, to receive as boarders the children of persons of the middle classes'.[193] Thus Elizabeth Prout was able to address herself to the problem that lay behind the discrimination against Catholics inherent in the Manchester and Salford Education Committee's bill: the education of the upper working and lower middle classes.

As described by the Committee of Council, these classes comprised the 'small farmers, small shopkeepers, small tradesmen... above the class of journeymen... foremen and highly skilled artisans', who formed 'the strata of society next above the labourers' and whose resources could so easily disappear in a sudden depression.[194] As Entwistle had admitted to the Select Committee in 1852, these people, paying rates, would have been glad to have had the security of rate support for their schools.[195] Father Gaudentius was aware of the needs of women in this class as he wrote the Rule in 1852. He intended his religious institute to offer them the consecrated religious life they could not afford in congregations that demanded a dowry. Similarly, while he legislated for the sisters' chief educational apostolate amongst the poor, he also permitted them to have day and boarding schools for 'more respectable young females'.[196] Hence Elizabeth Prout was able to open such a school at Levenshulme, which, like Cheetham Hill, was developing as a middle-class residential area.[197]

Elizabeth's school was particularly needed because the education of girls was coming to be seen as even socially necessary 'to fit them not merely to be the companions and helpmates of men of liberal education but to be in the highest degree competent to guide the bringing up of their children'.[198] For the Catholic Church the dearth of middle-class schools posed special problems, as Wiseman had explained to Cornelia Connelly in 1846, when he asked her to come to England precisely to found a religious order to teach Catholic girls of the upper middle class. The English Catholic Church, he told her, must rely on its middle class to provide most of its priests, its charitable confraternities and its 'working religious'. 'To train the future mothers of this class', he said, 'is to sanctify entire families,... to make friends for the poor,... nurses for the sick and dying, catechists for the little ones, most useful auxiliaries in every good work.'[199]

Elizabeth Prout, in the Manchester area, was more concerned about the upper working and lower middle classes. While socially and academically they wanted something better than the mere rudiments of learning provided in the poor schools, they could not afford the fees of the young ladies' academies, nor private tuition fees, and few mothers could teach their daughters themselves.[200] Moreover, Victorian education, like society, was arranged in tiers according to class and, as Wiseman had also explained to Cornelia Connelly, in England it was impossible to mix the classes.[201] For Catholics the problem was two-fold: parents wanted their children to be educated in their Catholic faith and they also wanted them to receive a secular education suitable to their station in life.[202] Without Catholic schools, lower middle-class children must either remain ignorant, which was socially unacceptable, or they must attend the non-Catholic schools available, unsatisfactory, even academically, as many of them were.[203] In attending non-Catholic schools, however, they were not only deprived of instruction in the Catholic faith but exposed to an alien philosophy. The bishops and clergy were so concerned that, on 17 July 1852, at the end of the first Provincial Westminster Synod, they issued a joint letter recommending that, where a sufficient number of Catholics warranted it, 'middle schools' should be established to provide commercial and general education for the children of families 'in a better worldly position'.[204] Manchester was obviously such a place. Engrossed in raising funds for the poor schools and without teachers and government grants for middle-class schools, however, the clergy could only seek help from religious orders. It was because St Chad's clergy 'were grieved to see so many children of the middle class of society attending Protestant schools' that they asked the Notre Dame Sisters in 1852 to open a day 'middle school' in a renovated coach-house at Cheetham Hill.[205]

In opening her middle school at Levenshulme as a boarding school, Elizabeth also hoped to secure a steady income for her community and to provide work within the convent for all her sisters, which was the ideal according to Father Gaudentius' Rule.[206] Thus she could withdraw sisters from the factories.[207] Just as married women who worked in the mills had little time to be houseproud, so it was impossible to combine religious observance in Levenshulme with a long walk to the mills of central Manchester for the 6 a.m. bell. By concentrating on Levenshulme, Elizabeth could strengthen her contemplative community, while employing her teachers in the classroom and her other sisters in looking after the boarders and in needlework.

Father Gaudentius found the first two pupils for the Levenshulme boarding school: Anny Bagnall of Shrewsbury and one of the Whittaker family from Sutton, St Helens. They were both eleven. Since most children left school at eleven, Elizabeth Prout was thus moving her congregation into secondary education.[208] Father Gaudentius had met the Bagnall family when he gave a mission in Shrewsbury in March-April 1854. During it he instructed Anny for Confirmation and First Communion. Always fond of children, he had found this 'dear innocent and most intelligent child... excellent and most promising'. Her parents were respectable but 'reduced in pecuniary circumstances'. He had promised them she could be educated at Levenshulme for £12 a year. Then he had prevailed upon the 'zealous and generous housekeeper' of Sir Edmund Smythe of Acton Burnell to help them with the payment. He hoped that some of the 'respectable farmers' would send their daughters too.[209] Returned to Sutton, he persuaded John Whittaker, a local builder and businessman, to send his daughter to Levenshulme as a companion for Anny.[210] He was willing to pay £14 or £15 a year.[211] The school opened with these two children at least on 25 May 1854, when the Whittakers accompanied Father Gaudentius to Sister Frances Wellard's clothing as a novice.[212]

By October 1855 there were seven boarders and five day scholars.[213] It was therefore the type of girls' boarding school favoured at the time as being homely.[214] The thirty pupils in the parish school would have paid between 2d. and 4d. a week, the usual fee in the Manchester Catholic poor schools.[215] The day girls in the private school paid 1s. a week. Father Gaudentius stipulated this fee, considering it low. 'People cannot pay much and you cannot teach much', he told Elizabeth.[216] Nevertheless, as above the statutory 9d., it identified Levenshulme as a middle school.[217] For £14 a year, the boarders received board, laundry and instructions in English, French, music and needlework, as well as in religion.[218] Thus it compared favourably with the Taunton Commission's *Report* on girls' schools, in which Lord Lyttelton noted that music was not always taught in the cheaper middle schools.[219] Levenshulme prospered so well that Elizabeth thought of building a new wing to provide 'proper accommodation'.[220] Gaudentius, however, was not in favour, 'About building, I do not advise you to build at all at your own expense. The locality is too far from the City and damp, with bad water. If they build for you very well.'[221]

Elizabeth and five companions made their religious vows in St Mary's church, Levenshulme on 21 November 1854.[222] She was then free to divide the community in order to make new foundations. At the request of Father John Quealy, parish priest of St Ann's, Ashton-under-Lyne, she made her first new opening in 'turbulent and fanatical' Ashton in early January 1855.[223] As the foundress, she went there herself.[224] Ashton had a population of about 30,000.[225] There were about 4,000 Catholics, 'exclusively composed of working people, the majority employed in the cotton mills'.[226] Many of them Irish refugees, too poor to pay the rent for better housing, they either stayed in the common lodging houses, which were simply two-bedroomed houses with extra beds pushed in, or rented the worst houses in the town where the walls and even the beds were 'infested with vermin to a fearful extent'.[227] Elizabeth and Sister Mary Paul Taylor 'conducted a school for three hundred children' in St Ann's church-school between Newman Street and Burlington Street. They and two other sisters 'visited the sick [and] sought out and instructed negligent Catholics'.[228] Elizabeth, therefore, knew Ashton's open sewers, its unflagged streets, overflowing middens and the offensive waste from common toilets which polluted the courts between the back-to-back houses. She knew that Ashton in 1855 had no libraries, public baths, parks or recreational facilities. King Cotton reigned supreme.[229] In such conditions, she and her sisters 'had great influence among the people and their work prospered'.[230] Their presence would have been all the more appreciated by the Catholics, because the Ashton area, strongly influenced by Ribbonism, Orangeism and the Protestant Association, was a byword for religious rioting.[231] It was therefore with great sorrow that, when four sisters left the order in November 1857, Elizabeth had to close this foundation. On their side, when the Catholics of Ashton heard the sisters were leaving, there was 'widespread grief and consternation'. They could be pacified only by Elizabeth's promising to send them back again when their numbers increased and the opportunity presented itself.[232]

Even before going to Ashton Elizabeth had contemplated a foundation in Sutton, near St Helens.[233] Fathers Dominic Barberi and Ignatius Spencer had chosen a site there in 1849, at the invitation of the local railway magnate, John Smith, who had then erected a church, a monastery and a school.[234] Father Honorius Mazzini took up residence in late 1850 and was joined in 1851 by a small community. In January 1853, he was succeeded as rector by Father Bernardine Carosi, who remained there until Father Ignatius Spencer became rector in August 1863.[235] The invitation Father Bernardine extended to Elizabeth Prout to take charge of the girls' school signified far more than a further step in her educational apostolate. It represented a recognition on the part of the Passionist Congregation in England that her order had a special affinity with the sons of Paul of the Cross. The difficulty about Sutton, however, was that it was in the Liverpool rather than the Salford Diocese. Bishop Turner had no jurisdiction there and he was anxious to have the sisters in his own diocese. Elizabeth had therefore gone to Ashton.

It was an invitation to take charge of a second boarding school, at Parr Hall, Blackbrook in April 1855 that made Sutton a reality. Parr Hall Seminary, near St Helens, had originally been the manor house of Parr. In 1781 it was purchased by James Orrell of Blackbrook, a notable Catholic coalowner.[236] In 1834 the Orrell family leased it to the Morgans, who opened it as a Catholic ladies' academy. At that time Blackbrook was 'a very healthy part of the country', easily accessible 'with excellent roads, near the St Helens' Railway', which linked with the Liverpool-Manchester line, and with a daily coach passing Parr Hall from Liverpool to Wigan.[237] There were several other expensive boarding schools in the St Helens area, because, as a rich fruit-growing area, it seemed to provide a safe haven from the smoke and noise of the industrial towns.[238] During the 1830s, however, as St Helens' own industry developed, this countryside was destroyed by dense acidic smoke from alkali works. As a result, most of the schools closed. Parr Hall, however, remained open, even in spite of a nearby alkali factory and in 1853 the Morgans continued to describe their school as 'this very healthy establishment'.[239] By 1855 both the Morgans had died and two of their daughters had entered a convent.[240] On Father Bernardine's recommendation, Miss Orrell of Blackbrook then invited Elizabeth Prout to take charge of the school.[241] Elizabeth was not, therefore, opening a new school, as in Levenshulme. She was taking charge of a ladies' academy that was already well established. From 1834 each young lady coming to the school had had to bring two pairs of sheets, three table napkins, three towels and a silver fork and spoon, which were returned to her when she left. The girls had had board and laundry and had been educated in English language, history, geography with the use of the globes, writing, arithmetic and plain and ornamental needlework.[242] At extra cost they had learnt music, dancing and drawing and French from Miss Mary Morgan, who had received five years' education in Paris.[243] By 1855 the curriculum included the use of Chambers' Educational Maps in geography and the newest forms of needlework. Music, French and drawing cost 4 guineas each. Dancing, which also remained an optional extra, was taught by professors 'of the first eminence', who, presumably, dictated their own fees. The boarding fees were 25 guineas a year for girls over ten years of age and 20 for those under, with laundry an extra 2 guineas a year.[244]

It was not the type of school envisaged by Father Gaudentius' Rule but, by taking Parr Hall, Elizabeth could also take the poor school in Sutton and open a new school for the working-class children in Blackbrook. Bishop Turner, her co-founders, Fathers Gaudentius and Croskell, Father Ignatius Spencer and Father Bernardine all wanted her to take Parr. John Smith offered her temporary accommodation in half of his own house, Mount Pleasant, in Sutton and promised he would either build her a convent or build a new house for himself and give her Mount Pleasant.[245] Accordingly about 11 July 1855 Elizabeth and another sister went to live in Sutton.[246] It would be impossible to overestimate the importance of this Sutton foundation. With the blessing of both Bishop Turner of Salford and Bishop Brown of Liverpool and with the approval of her co-founders, Elizabeth Prout was accepting an invitation from two Passionist superiors, Fathers Ignatius Spencer and Bernardine Carosi to collaborate directly in the Passionist mission to England. From the arrival in Sutton of Father Dominic Barberi's incorrupt remains in early November 1855, St Anne's retreat became the heart of that mission.[247] Here in Sutton, for most of the remainder of her life, Elizabeth Prout lived and worked side by side with Fathers Bernardine Carosi, Charles Houben and Ignatius Spencer.[248] Closely identifying her own sisters' apostolate with that of the Passionist Congregation, she ensured that the future spiritual and apostolic progress of her institute would be directed and accompanied by the Passionists of Paul of the Cross.

Elizabeth Prout opened the convent of the Holy Family at Parr Hall on 15 August 1855.[249] As she made out her prospectus for Parr Hall Seminary, now to be called 'Holy Family School', she was conscious it had already flourished for twenty years and she wanted to maintain its good reputation.[250] Accordingly, 'The Sisters of the Holy Family', she published, 'beg to inform the inhabitants of St Helens and its vicinity that they will re-open the School at Parr Hall, assisted by Miss Morgan, on the 3rd of September 1855, and they trust, that by their assiduous care and attention to the pupils placed under their charge, they may deserve the kind patronage which has been shown to the Misses Morgan.' As yet unaware of the smell of rotten eggs that certain winds brought over Parr from the alkali waste, Elizabeth retained the description, 'a very healthy establishment'. Thereafter, however, she substantially changed the nature of the school, making it accessible to the lower middle class. She reduced the fees to 18 guineas a year for weekly boarders over 10 years of age, 16 guineas for children under; 10 guineas a year for day boarders above 10 years old, 9 guineas for those below; 1 guinea per quarter for day pupils above 10; and 15s. for those under. She asked for quarterly payments and required a quarter's notice before the removal of a pupil.[251] Although, on Father Gaudentius' instructions, she had to withdraw French and instrumental music, she arranged for two pupils who wished to learn the pianoforte to go as boarders to Levenshulme.[252] Thus she brought Parr Hall Seminary within the reach of the less affluent middle classes and she made it attractive to even upper working-class pupils living at home.[253] She eliminated class distinctions in dress by introducing a school uniform.[254]

It seems unlikely that Elizabeth herself taught in the private school. Although she had gone to live in Parr, until she opened a convent in

Sutton itself in early September 1855 she and another sister walked each day to Sutton to teach the forty girls in St Anne's poor school.[255] Since Miss Orrell had asked her to establish a poor school in Blackbrook, promising to build both the school and a convent, Elizabeth expected to make a further foundation there. When the school was still not finished in late September 1855, however, and not likely to be before Christmas, Elizabeth herself, on 25 September, opened a poor day school, with twenty-five children, in Parr Hall.[256] When Father Bernardine built 'large and commodious schools' at Peasley Cross in 1857, those girls too were placed 'under the fostering care of the Sisters of the Holy Family', to the immense satisfaction of the parishioners.[257]

Thus, in the seven years from her arrival in Manchester in 1849, having helped to safeguard Catholic education for Manchester's poor in Ancoats, Angel Meadow and Deansgate, Elizabeth Prout had also provided day and boarding schools for the upper working and lower middles classes in Levenshulme and Parr and had staffed further elementary and Sunday schools in Levenshulme, Ashton-under-Lyne, Sutton, Blackbrook and Peasley Cross. She obviously had great organisational ability. In all these areas, the Paulacrucian spirituality she and her sisters had implanted offered a quiet challenge to the secularism of the age. At the same time, she had not only successfully founded her religious order but had extended it beyond the Salford Diocese. As foundress, she had opened the way for future and even broader expansion, particularly in partnership with the Passionist Congregation. In all this unobtrusive enterprise, however, she had encountered numerous difficulties. By 1857 they were approaching their peak.

CHAPTER V

CONVENTUAL DIFFICULTIES

1. AUTHORITY

In view of the contrast between the devotional lifestyle inside Elizabeth Prout's convent and the unavoidably wretched conditions in Manchester's schoolrooms, there was a depth of meaning in Father Gaudentius' admonition, added to his Rule in 1854, that those who had to go out to teach were not to be envious of those who stayed at home.[1] Although she was out most of the day, it was Elizabeth's task, as foundress, superior and novice-mistress, to create that home. As the superior of a community committed to living out the 'memory' of the Holy Family, she had to create a conventual lifestyle that was truly homely. The sisters, Father Gaudentius told her in 1855, had a right to expect in her 'more than a carnal mother, a spiritual mother, all sweetness and kindness'.[2] This spiritual dimension transformed the convent into a home in which the Master was Christ. As His representative, Elizabeth was responsible for the sisters' spiritual as well as their material welfare. 'Much depends on the first training of the novices', Gaudentius told her in December 1852. 'The Superioress ought to be an example to all by her own actions, and strive to go before them.... She must exhort the negligent and lewkwarm [*sic*]. She must with mildness and firmness correct their faults and encourage them to go on with fervour.'[3]

Elizabeth Prout's first task, therefore, as the superior of a religious community that aimed at a combination of Martha and Mary, was to safeguard her sisters' spiritual life of prayer. 'Believe me', Father Gaudentius told her in June 1852,

> the success of your pious labours and wishes must be the effect of continual, sincere and fervent prayers to Him from Whom alone every good and perfect gift has to come. My perpetual cry to the Catholic Sisters of the Holy Family will be *Prayer, prayer, prayer, with prayer you will succeed in every holy undertaking, without prayer you will fail in everything*.[4]

He constantly stressed the need for fidelity to prayer. 'I beg again and again to repeat', he told her in October 1852, 'that the spirit of the institute of the Catholic Sisters of the Holy Family is a spirit of recollection and mental prayer joined with manual labour and other external occupation and that mental prayer or meditation ought to be attended to with all possible care and attention.' He reminded her of her responsibility, 'From the rule you will find that the mother superioress... ought to use great watchfulness and diligence to see this point observed by all the religious Community.... If you all attend to prayer all will be right. If this point is slack all will be slack.'[5] 'The spirit of the new institute of the holy family ought to be a spirit of prayer', he reminded her again in February 1854.[6] 'To you', he wrote in July 1854, 'I recommend above and before all the practice of meditation and continual prayer. Pray with all your heart and soul... pray always without ceasing and tell your Sisters to do the same.'[7] This contemplative life of prayer was the essence of his fusion of Martha and Mary.

At the same time, Elizabeth had to care for her sisters' temporal needs. In September 1852 she had six companions. Her position was comparable with that of the mistress or housekeeper of a middle-class household, as it fell to her to organise her community, in which each had and knew her place as cook, refectorian, sacristan etc.[8] Although a spacious family home, 69 Stocks Street was restrictive as a convent. As the community grew to ten, Elizabeth tried to save space by moving the kitchen to the cellar.[9] Even so the sleeping quarters were very cramped. The sisters slept in a dormitory, with cubicles, or cells as they were called, separated by the blue-and-white-check curtains commonly found in Manchester's working-class homes.[10] Furniture was minimal, even less than in the Northampton convent: a bed, a chair and a small cabinet, which served as a stand for a jug, basin and beaker and as a receptacle for a change of clothing.[11] The beds were made of straw. Gaudentius advised Elizabeth they should be 'sufficiently comfortable for every body... not stitched. The straw should be loose as in a bag' and 'upon canvas'. English straw mattresses, he said, were 'worse than boards'.[12] Apart from a crucifix near the door, there were no pictures or other adornments. The same plainness was apparent everywhere, except for a few statues and devotional pictures and some maxim notices Father Gaudentius suggested should be placed strategically throughout the house. 'Better a little with justice than great revenue with iniquity', he recommended for the workroom. 'Let fraternal charity abide in you', he suggested for the community room, while there was a note of grim reality about his choice for the refectory, 'Better is a dry morsel with joy than a house full of meats with stripes.'[13]

One of Elizabeth's most important duties was to care for her sisters' health. In spite of their poverty, she had to ensure they had sufficient, wholesome food. For breakfast, like the mill workers and as she had had in the Northampton convent, they probably had porridge or bread and dripping, with possibly a slice of bacon.[14] For the other meals, Gaudentius recommended soup, meat four days a week, fish, eggs, puddings or pastry, fruit and cheese.[15] The fish were probably kippers from the Isle of Man.[16] Noticeably, he did not mention bread nor vegetables, which were common amongst the working classes of Manchester.[17] The sisters did have bread and, like most people in the towns, bought it at the shop, at least during the fever episode.[18] How spartan their fare was is indicated by Gaudentius' admonition to Elizabeth in January 1855, 'I know you are poor but... try to give the Sisters some good wholesome ale or beer, or good porter. It is very cold. They have to work and some have been accustomed to some drinks better than water.'[19] 'I hope all the Sisters are well', he wrote in April 1855, 'and going on well. Have great care for their health. Let them have strengthening food, and drink, and fresh air, and exercise out of door.'[20] Elizabeth was only too anxious to 'have great care for their health'. After the fever epidemic of 1853 she wanted to move them to a larger house. In August 1855 she was worried about the ill effects of the chemical industry in Parr.[21] Aware of the dangers from polluted water, she wanted to sink a well in Levenshulme for a fresh water supply. 'I think we should make every effort and any sacrifice to get good water for the Sisters', she told Gaudentius in October 1855.[22] She had already acquired a cow, from the Passionists in Broadway, to ensure a good milk supply.[23]

As the foundress Elizabeth Prout set the tone of her congregation. In spite of their poverty, she established high standards of etiquette. Meals were taken in the refectory, a room separate from the kitchen or community room, and each sister had a linen serviette.[24] Elizabeth maintained her own upper working-class standards, with the added dimension that she and her companions were seeking perfection. Although the order remained 'lowly', it was a measure of the training Elizabeth gave her sisters that the Countess Clementina Stuart found it possible, as Sister Ignatia, to live amongst them for almost thirty years.[25] As one of the annalists wrote,

> Elizabeth Prout was eminently suited for the position in which by the Providence of God she was placed. She was active, intelligent, endowed with great business capacity, but above all her soul was enriched with the highest virtues: her bright example cheered her companions and helped them to surmount the greatest obstacles. On her depended the training of the Sisters, as neither Fr Gaudentius nor Provost Croskell could be always with them owing to missionary labours on the one hand and parish work on the other.[26]

Father Gaudentius also realised her worth. 'I feel more and more convinced', he told her in 1854, 'that God has chosen you as a guide to your Sisters, and as a housekeeper in the Holy Family. Almighty God has given you lights and grace and strength to go through many difficulties.'[27]

According to the Rule the sisters gave Elizabeth Prout considerable deference. 'It is of the highest importance', Gaudentius wrote in July 1854, 'that the religious should be accustomed to respect and obey their superiors.'[28] To instil deference into this first group, however, was no easy task. It probably helped that some had been in service. They practised towards her the customs of social etiquette that a domestic servant followed towards her mistress.[29] They stood when she entered the room. They gave her precedence at all times. Even their seating arrangements demonstrated the order in the community and her superior position in it.[30] It also helped that their deference was different from that of servants or of the working classes towards their employers, which might be evoked more by expediency than by respect.[31] The sisters' subordination was created by their practice and vow of obedience freely undertaken and therefore liberating.[32] It was an expression of their consecration to God and of the harmony in their conventual society. Thus it elevated their lifestyle from social and economic practicalities to a return of Christ's love. It was an expression of their Paulacrucian spirituality. In daily relinquishing their own wills, they were aiming at an eternal resurrection with Him. Their deference was to God, not to Elizabeth Prout *per se*. Nevertheless, by 1854 Sister Philomena Johnson, extolled for her virtues two years earlier, was proving to be deficient 'in charity, humility, diligence at her work, obedience and respect of superiors'. Sister Aloysius Gilday was lacking in 'charity and humility'. Father Gaudentius feared they would have to be dismissed.[33] In September 1854 Father Croskell thought Sister Magdalene Toler should go.[34] While, as Father Gaudentius said, he had 'great compassion' for their 'spiritual weaknesses', he insisted that if they 'habitually neglect[ed] their duties', or were 'habitually haughty, disrespectful, disobedient', they could not 'be admitted to profession'.[35] In the event, Sister Agnes Lee was the only one of the first seven to leave the order before profession, in April 1854, 'having failed', as the annalist said, 'in conforming to the indispensable conditions of a religious life, i.e. submission, respect and obedience'.[36]

From the first professions on 21 November 1854, Elizabeth, as the foundress of a religious order within the Catholic Church, derived her authority from Bishop Turner, the pope's representative in the diocese of Salford.[37] She exercised it according to the Rule, which he sanctioned. During the novitiate it had not been possible for the government of the institute to be determined exactly as prescribed by the Rule, since there were no professed sisters either to vote or to hold office. During those two years, however, Father Gaudentius had appointed those two apparent paragons of virtue, Sisters Clare Wilson and Philomena Johnson as Elizabeth's assistants, the first as monitress and the second as vicaress. Theoretically, therefore, the government of the community had functioned according to the Rule but in fact Elizabeth Prout, as superior and novice-mistress, was the key figure.

The immediate task after the profession ceremony was to establish authority according to the Rule. Consequently, that evening Father Gaudentius presided at the election of the local superior. Elizabeth Prout was elected unanimously.[38] From then she was Mother Mary Joseph of Jesus.

Sister Clare Wilson was elected mistress of novices and reappointed as monitress by Father Gaudentius. This appointment was important, because it gave her spiritual supervision of both novices and professed, including Elizabeth Prout. The latter reappointed Sister Philomena Johnson as vicaress, to help her, as Gaudentius expressed it to Bishop Turner, 'in the management of the more material and temporal affairs of the Community'. These offices were approved by Bishop Turner.[39] After five years' devoted labour, Elizabeth Prout had founded a religious order.

Her continuing role as foundress was based on her authority as the elected superior of that order. 'What shall I say to you', Gaudentius had written to her in February 1854, 'who act not only as Superioress but under the direction of legitimate authority act as a Foundress of the new institute?'[40] According to the Rule, every sister was to accustom herself to consider the person of the Superioress as the person of 'our Blessed Lady or St Joseph or rather as the very person of our divine Redeemer and respect her and obey her orders as if she were to receive them from the mouth of our Lord Himself who says: *He that heareth you heareth Me.*' The spirit of holy obedience was extensive, 'Nobody will ever dare to murmur or detract against the Superioress or contradict, speak against or resist her just orders.'[41] According to the Rule, Elizabeth's authority was virtually unassailable. Because of its provenance, however, it was different from that of the employers in their workplaces or of their wives in their homes. They were not elected and they were owners of their property.[42] Elizabeth had no property. She was merely the administratrix of the community's goods. Her exercise of authority was based on her own vow of obedience to God. She knew that 'before God' she was 'bound in conscience to seek the real spiritual good of the Community and of the whole institute.'[43] Employers represented their own interests; Elizabeth represented God's. Moreover, she had to consult her sisters.[44] After profession she was not allowed 'to transact any business of importance' without the counsel of Sisters Clare and Philomena.[45] On such serious matters as the acceptance or dismissal of a novice, she had to consult the chapter and votes were given by secret ballot.[46] Unlike secular mistresses, therefore, except in the most exceptional circumstances, Elizabeth could not herself dismiss one of her household.[47] A mother to her community, her position was one of service and leadership rather than of power. 'The Sisters have chosen to call you Mother', Gaudentius wrote to her in 1855. 'You should be a Mother, not a proud and haughty mistress.'[48] Finally, she herself had to render obedience and deference to her own superiors, Bishop Turner, Father Croskell and Father Gaudentius Rossi.[49]

Father Gaudentius in particular expected deference from her. It is clear from his letters that he felt a Victorian male ascendancy over her. He did not consult her about the institute's title in 1851 and he imposed the Rule in 1852. He expected the sisters to observe and Elizabeth to enforce a Rule that he had written and he expected it to be received as the will of God. On the other hand, he had adapted the Rule from that of Paul of the Cross, which had already been approved by Rome. The institute was entirely new and the Rule of any religious order was its crucial link with the authority of the Church.[50] If it were not observed at the beginning, it never would be and as Gaudentius rightly said, unless the Rule were kept, no good could be expected of the community.[51] Indeed, unless the bishop of Salford was willing to testify that the Rule was kept, the congregation would never be approved, so that there was much to be said for Gaudentius' strictness in this respect. Since some of the sisters were also, in Victorian terms, 'rough' rather than 'respectable', the Rule had to be rigorously enforced.[52] Sister Mary Paul Taylor later described Gaudentius as 'a faithful friend who never shrank from correcting their faults by salutary reproof' but who was 'at the same time so affectionate that he could thus express himself: "Were I to die, (as Mary of England said of Calais) the 'Sisters of the Holy Family' might be found written on my heart".'[53] As his listeners in Doncaster had observed in 1846, although in denunciation he was 'awfully impressive', in admonition he was 'gentle, kind and courteous'.[54] Nineteenth-century novice-masters, too, often gave acceptably strong rebukes and Gaudentius was understandably anxious about the success of his enterprise, which, as a male, he had had, perforce, to entrust to a foundress. His letters must be read in their context and it is significant that, although he criticised and admonished Elizabeth in his letters to her, in those to other sisters he always upheld her authority, inculcating respect and deference towards her. He did, however, expect his every wish to be accepted as the will of God. 'In regard of the house in St Joseph's district, my wish is that you should take it. This being as I trust the will of God, try therefore to comply with it', he told Elizabeth in May 1853.[55] When faced with such unreasonable demands (for the house was full of bugs), it was fortunate that she owed greater deference to Bishop Turner, whose views invariably coincided with her own.[56] Even in opposing Gaudentius' wishes, however, Bishop Turner was also careful to show him deference. Thus in 1853, when Gaudentius had wanted the sisters to wear a bonnet instead of a veil, Bishop

Turner directed Father Croskell to reply that he had 'come to the conclusion in his own mind, in favour of the veil, but does not wish to declare it, till he has had some conversation with F. Gaudentius, through a becoming deference for the good Father.'[57]

One of Elizabeth's difficulties in co-operating with Father Gaudentius was that, despite his emphasis on her authority, he was a compulsive meddler. 'There is no need to write to me about every trifling thing to be done', he told her in 1853. 'Much must be left to the judgement and discretion of the Superioress. I should not interfere with what arrangements you would please to make.'[58] In fact, however, he could not refrain from interfering with everything she was doing. As Father Ignatius Spencer told him, he had 'eagle's eyes', which saw 'every-thing and more than everything'.[59] In discussing possible superiors in a letter to the Passionist General in 1851, Ignatius had to say that while Gaudentius had shown much ability as the rector of Cotton, he might be better as a consultor but even so he would be difficult. He would meddle in all that the provincial would do, because he was 'always ruled by his own ideas' and was not content unless others followed them.[60] It was therefore not surprising that Gaudentius also wanted to direct Elizabeth and everything and everybody in her order according to his own ideas.

It was unfortunate in this context that he had made Sister Clare Wilson monitress, for if Elizabeth's 'social domination', based on traditional, monastic, legitimate authority, was more stable than the coercive dominance of Manchester's employers, it was also more vulnerable.[61] While some employers' power notoriously pervaded even the homes and religion of their employees, they did not *live* together.[62] While, therefore, deference to Elizabeth's authority was more easily stabilised within the face-to-face social structures of a religious community, like that of a household mistress it could also be more intimately challenged.[63] In 1855, as a result of Clare's reports, Gaudentius accused Elizabeth of levity, which serious Victorians regarded as the bane of religion.[64] 'I must again mention that a certain levity of conduct has been observed not calculated to edify', he wrote.

> I have mentioned to you, what I have seen with my own eyes, your running after the cow and hens, your calling after them in such foolish manner that should not be permitted in public to a postulant. But how unbecoming it must be in a Superioress. For your own excuse you will be ready as usual to say that you did not think any thing about it. But this is the worse for you because it shows that you have no idea of what a religious and a superioress ought to be both in public and in private.[65]

He threatened to replace her with Sister Clare Wilson. Elizabeth was not disturbed. She had often said she was unfit and incapable, 'more injury than profit to the Institute'.[66] As Gaudentius had previously admitted, however, the sisters had 'great confidence' in her.[67] When Elizabeth offered her resignation to Bishop Turner, in June 1855, he confirmed her in her position.[68] In August 1855 Father Gaudentius admitted he had never seriously meant to depose her.[69]

In October 1855, as he prepared to leave for North America, Elizabeth asked his advice on how to guide the sisters, how to govern and how to preserve the spirit of the institute.[70] His reply confirmed both her position of authority and the Passionist charism of the congregation:

> I cannot give any better direction how to govern the Sisters than what you will find expressed in the rules.... The leading spirit of the institute is a union of recollection of mind with work, so much so as to transform Mary and Martha into one person. The characteristic virtue of the Sisters ought to be a special devotion to the Holy Family of Nazareth and a constant aim and effort to imitate their domestic virtues — love of solitude, love of humility, love of humiliations, perfect conformity to God's holy will, full, firm confidence in His Divine Providence.[71]

On that Paulacrucian basis Elizabeth Prout exercised her authority for another eight years.

2. INDUSTRY AND EDUCATION

Another difficulty Elizabeth Prout encountered was in providing religious life for working-class women whilst ensuring that her institute was self-supporting and also responding to the need for Catholic education. In his sermon at the first clothing ceremony on 21 November 1852, Father Gaudentius stated that the order was 'called into existence by the virtue remarkable in many young Catholic females belonging to the industrious classes', many of whom had 'an ardent wish to consecrate themselves to the service of God'. The new institute was intended to open the 'happy gate of religion' to such girls.[72] 'The principal object', he had written to Fr Croskell on 19 January 1852 'is to afford an opportunity to young females of the poorer classes to enter a religious life.'[73] The provision of religious life for the poor was, therefore, the primary apostolate of the congregation.

In its implementation this radical option for the poor raised the economic problem of how such females were to be supported, especially as Father Gaudentius legislated for a contemplative lifestyle in which the sisters would be supported by 'pious industry' within the convent.[74] Similarly, although, in the Passionist tradition of adaptability, he allowed sisters to teach in parish schools, he envisaged they would normally have their own schools, which, although outside the enclosure, would be within the house or at least in an adjacent building.[75] He had therefore seen both industry and education as part of the sisters' contemplative lifestyle.[76]

Basically, both industry and education were the primary means by which the order would support itself. In this economic sense they were equally important. Domestic industry had the added advantage of being more conducive to the contemplative life. Teaching, however, like parish visitation, was an active apostolate akin to the Passionist missions and in Manchester's parish schools it identified the sisters with the working classes. Because of their deep poverty, at the beginning of the order Sisters Magdalene Toler and Aloysius Gilday had to go out to work in the factory, while other sisters went out to sewing houses.[77] Since, however, the Rule stated that the superioress was to 'endeavour to employ the Sisters as much as possible in the religious establishment', Elizabeth speedily withdrew them from the sewing houses to do needlework at home.[78] Thus she established the contemplative lifestyle. As soon as possible, probably in April 1854 when they moved to Levenshulme, she also moved the sisters from the factory to work with the boarders. From early 1853, if not sooner, she had had a workroom for sewing and from early 1854 the sisters made church vestments for Thomas Brown and Son, silk manufacturers of Meal Street, Manchester.[79] Although contemplative in nature, this truly 'pious industry' constituted more of an active apostolate than a mere means of earning a livelihood, because it fulfilled a vital need in providing vestments and altar linens for the ever-increasing number of Catholic churches.[80] Thus both industry and education had a place in the congregation's active apostolate.

Even church needlework, however, was financially unrewarding, so that the community still had difficulty in supporting itself. As Sister Mary Paul Taylor wrote later, 'Apart from the fact that sewing [was] so unproductive as to make it necessary to work almost night and day to make the very poorest living thereby... in teaching, the sisters made a much nearer approach to their primary object' of helping the working classes.[81] Gaudentius, too, had quickly realised in 1852 that the Manchester clergy wanted sisters who could teach and that teaching presented the best available way of earning a living. During the next few years he constantly bent his energies on finding postulants who were teachers, applying for them to the Sisters of Mercy in Derby and even to the North Presentation Convent in Cork.[82] Since learning and study had always been part of the Passionist tradition, he had no difficulty in assimilating an educational apostolate.[83] 'Learning', he had said at the 1852 clothing ceremony, 'will ever be valued and usefully employed in Catholic schools.'[84] He also realised it was impossible to make 'an income from industrial occupation sufficient to support the community.... Every day experience convinces me that you cannot go on without some able and well trained teachers for schools', he wrote to Elizabeth on 1 December 1853, as all her sisters lay ill with fever. 'Had you these you could find support and sympathy and respect everywhere, without these scarcely any body will take notice of you.'[85] 'You have great need of some good and clever school teachers', he told her a week later. 'Try to get some if you can.'[86] Schools had become so important that in July 1854 he expanded that section of his 1852 Rule to prescribe for the election of headmistresses and for daily, private study for the sisters who taught.[87] 'You want persons able to teach schools. You cannot go on well without them', he told Elizabeth again in October 1854.[88]

In May 1855, however, he began to give an industrial slant to the teaching apostolate. 'Again and again', he told Elizabeth as she was preparing to open new schools at Sutton and Parr, 'I must urge the importance of establishing a kind of industrial school. I admit the difficulties but no effort of any kind has been made yet.'[89] Already familiar as Poor Law schools, industrial schools for vagrant children too were becoming 'the great cause of the age'.[90] As spearheaded by such pioneers as the Unitarian, Mary Carpenter, however, they were a cause for concern to Catholics, because they were boarding schools in which no provision was made for instruction in the Catholic faith, although many of the vagrants were Irish Catholics.[91] Manchester Catholics were certainly concerned about 'the present crisis of proselytising, reformatory and educational establishments'.[92] Accordingly in 1854 the Presentation Sisters in Livesey Street opened an industrial school to train girls as domestic servants.[93] Gaudentius, however, probably wanted Elizabeth to have the type of school the Sisters of Mercy had at Kinsale, near Cork, where the girls were taught lace work, knitting, plain work and dressmaking, as well as the three 'Rs'.[94] In 1855 there were already two similar Catholic industrial schools in Liverpool: Mrs D. Powell's Valenciennes-lace school and a laundry and dressmaking school. There was another in Newcastle, where destitute girls were given religious instruction and taught sewing and reading, as well as enjoying a 'hearty meal', paid for from the sale of their articles.[95] To start this type of establishment, however, Elizabeth would have needed capital and even the Kinsale school ran at a loss.[96] Moreover, as Stokes had commented in his *Report* for 1853, industrial schools would be misplaced in Manchester, because there was a brisk demand for juvenile labour.[97] In any case, in 1855 Elizabeth no longer had an opening in the city and there was no demand for an industrial school in Levenshulme.

The opening of a second house at Ashton in January 1855, however, and the consequent necessity of leaving Sister Clare in charge at Levenshulme led the order into real financial difficulties. Father Gaudentius' anxiety led him to suggest in June 1855 that Sisters Magdalene Toler and Aloysius Gilday should return to factory work, this time in Ashton. Gaudentius claimed that that 'was one of the principal objects of the pious Sisterhood'.[98] In fact, according to his own Rule and his 1852 clothing sermon, the principal object was to offer religious life to the class of girls who worked in factories. In order to keep the Rule, however, they could not continue to work in factories. That was why he had legislated for a domestic system of industry in workrooms. His suggestion was therefore surprising. It was even more so in view of increasing public anxiety about women in the mills.[99] Factory work was physically dangerous.[100] It was unhealthy and it frequently led to immorality.[101] Mill girls were likely to lose 'their feelings of modesty and purity, through being obliged to work amongst men and boys or under immoral or irregular masters or foremen'. Some people claimed the situation was so bad that many factory girls scarcely understood the words 'virtue' and 'chastity'.[102] Father Gaudentius was aware of these risks, because in his 1852 Rule he stated that whenever sisters in their workplaces should be 'obliged to speak with their masters or their agents' they were to be as brief as possible. When they had to 'bring in their work or receive orders or their wages' they were to try to have a virtuous companion with them. They were never to 'allow any man to touch them through levity even upon their hands.'[103] His motivation in wanting Sisters Magdalene and Aloysius to return to mill work in 1855 was financial.[104] To have sent two nuns, however, even disguised in secular dress, into a cotton mill in sectarian Ashton in the anti-Catholic and anti-conventual climate of 1855 would have been to court disaster. When Elizabeth, as directed, discussed Gaudentius' proposal with Father Quealy, the parish priest, he immediately forbade it.[105]

Apart from the financial need that had led Gaudentius into suggesting a return to factory work, he also seems to have feared that the order was becoming too highly educational. Although there was no difficulty in having a dual apostolate, there could be a conflict between priorities. A movement towards education was particularly dangerous if it entailed upper-class schools, because it threatened the fundamental 'deep poverty' characteristic of the congregation. It might even endanger an educational apostolate to the poorest classes, to whom the order was committed. It is therefore significant that Father Gaudentius' emphasis on industry coincided with Elizabeth's taking charge of Parr Hall ladies' seminary in 1855.

Father Gaudentius approved of Parr Hall, until he realised Elizabeth would need to engage visiting masters for music and French. Then he was horrified. 'No masters in the house', he said. It could not be allowed. He disapproved 'totally, entirely' and 'absolutely without any appeal'. He then objected to the subjects themselves. 'The Sisters are by rule', he said, 'forbidden to teach the higher branches of education.' They were intended to 'train the children of the poor, of the industrious classes, and at most some respectable children like those of... Mrs Smith.' Had any sisters been qualified to teach French, he continued, he would have allowed it but, 'to hire Masters', he could not understand how it could have entered Elizabeth's 'singular head', except that she was always 'aiming at high great things'. She was to tell Miss Orrell, he told her, that such was the 'nature of the institute'. She was to tell the parents that she was allowed to give only 'a good, practically useful English education'. If they wanted more, they must go elsewhere.[106]

Father Gaudentius was not, therefore, against education. 'I am not against having schools', he told Elizabeth later. 'As far as the sisters can, they ought to teach schools but 1st poor schools, 2, industrial schools, 3, plain, solid, practical English education and not more.'[107] What really concerned him was that the Parr Hall seminary might change the nature of the institute. That kind of adaptability was not acceptable. He feared that his congregation for 'young females of the poorer classes' might become one of the 'fashionable' educational orders, in which it was not unknown for poorer children to be neglected.[108] His order must remain close to the poor. It was at this time that he even thought of replacing Elizabeth with Clare, who was not so keen on schools.[109] He feared Elizabeth had 'never entered heart and soul' into his enterprise, that she was 'determined to conform it' to her 'own personal ideas'.[110] He accused her of not seeking 'entirely and solely... the real good of the institute' but rather her 'personal honour and ambition'.[111] He continued to stress industry. The Holy Family was not a teaching institute, he told her in September 1855. They had to support themselves with 'honest industry'. Moreover, the sisters who were teachers should '*teach religion*'. This would do more good to the children and the sisters, would be 'easier to both and essential to all'.[112] Characteristically inconsistent, however, within a fortnight he was making suggestions that called for teachers of the widest qualifications: 'It would be a great gain', he told Elizabeth, 'if the Sisters could obtain the Catholic Schools at St Helens, and be able to carry them on well.'[113]

From North America he became even more insistent that the order was primarily industrial. In September 1856 he wrote to Sister Philomena Johnson, 'Industry ought to be the first point of consideration, teaching ought to be the second. The Sisters by rule are bound *to honour and imitate* the holy family of Nazareth. Now we cannot find that the principal employment of these holy personages was teaching, but the Gospel shows that it was working.' Although he hastened to add, 'I do not intend to say the Sisters should not teach', he continued, 'I cannot understand why two or three girls from Ashton have not been already received as members of the institute. I knew several of them truly good, and very industrious, very anxious to be received among the Sisters.' He hoped that 'these dear souls for whom principally the institute [had] been established' were not being 'kept back'. He now envisaged only domestic industry, however, urging her as superior in Ashton to use 'greater efforts to obtain employment in the house in needlework and telling her of 'sewing machineries and other machineries for weaving different kinds of stuffs'.[114]

Although he was discovering that in North America, as in England, the clergy and people both wanted nuns who were teachers, he again pursued the same theme with Elizabeth herself in October 1856,

> I have often observed from your letters that you attach great importance to schools, and little about the internal workroom.... This is a great error. Not teaching but work ought to be the first character of the institute. You should be more anxious to have good working Sisters than teachers. I am pained to think that you ever think about teachers of schools.... I must repeat that the principal object of the institute is manual work, and not teaching.

If she had thoroughly entered into these ideas from the beginning, he told her, she would have had fifty or even a hundred 'good and useful Sisters... with plenty of work' and more and better teachers as well. 'I suspect', he said, significantly, 'that both secular and ecclesiastical persons may express to you... different opinions.' He claimed he knew better. 'If God has been pleased... to make use of me... in the establishment of this poor and humble Sisterhood, you should be convinced that He would manifest His views and will rather to me than to any body else, whatever his talents, position, and powers may be.'[115]

There was no possibility of Elizabeth's buying machinery, and certainly not handlooms.[116] Her next letter to Gaudentius was a mere note, carefully hiding from him the havoc Clare Wilson was creating.[117] In 1858 Elizabeth had to face a canonical investigation. Bound to silence, she sent Gaudentius only infrequent and guarded notes. For the same reason, the other sisters were equally reticent. Not understanding the situation in England, because no-one could tell him, Gaudentius felt that someone was trying to pressurise Elizabeth into changing the nature of the institute. 'The fact is', he told her in

February 1859, 'your style of writing made me think *that you had been forbidden or at least advised by some Superior in Manchester* not to write to me about the affairs of the institute.'[118]

Since he knew that Bishop Turner, Father Croskell and Elizabeth had always been in agreement, he seems to have been afraid in 1862 that in the revision of the Rule demanded by Rome the industrial apostolate might disappear. In a letter to Ignatius Spencer in August 1862, therefore, he stressed the industrial nature of the congregation, although, as always, he also made allowance for both day and boarding schools for the lower and middle classes, and he submitted entirely to Bishop Turner's and the provincial's wishes.[119] Out of deference for Father Gaudentius' views, in their revision of the Rule Father Ignatius Spencer and Elizabeth reduced most of his section on education to the Regulations, leaving in the Rule only a short statement on schools, following a lengthy section on homes for factory girls.[120] When he saw a copy of this 1863 Rule, however, Gaudentius indignantly complained to Mother Winefride Lynch, 'Scarcely a word is said about schools, which if not the principal object of the institute yet it has been always considered of great importance.'[121] He therefore wanted a balance between industry and education. Each had a place in his institute. In practice Elizabeth Prout preserved this balance and her congregation continued to do so after her death. When, therefore, he received a copy of the same Rule as approved by Pope Pius IX in 1876, Father Gaudentius wrote with satisfaction to Mother Mary Margaret Chambers:

> The original institute of the Holy Family, mentioned in the brief of the Pope, was gradually developed into existence with the help of Very Rev. Monsignor Croskell, and the encouragement and approbation of the late saintly Bishop Turner. Its object was, 1st, a special devotion and imitation of the Holy Family, Jesus, Mary and Joseph. 2ndly, to afford a more favourable opportunity to many pious intelligent, and industrious young girls of the middle and lower classes to embrace a religious state of life where they could support themselves and help the community by their industry and skill in imitation of the Holy Family. 3dly, that they should manifest their prudent zeal and charity for the children and young women of the industrial class and factory girls. I am glad to find that in the new Rules and Constitutions these three objects are preserved, though the title of the institute has been changed. From different sources of information I have also learned that the Sisters of the Most Holy Cross and Passion work with ability and zeal in schools and other ways for children and young women.[122]

Thus shortly after the congregation celebrated the silver jubilee of Elizabeth Prout's foundation in Stocks Street in 1851, its prime founder, Father Gaudentius Rossi, acknowledged it had maintained its dual apostolate in both industry and education. The essence of his religious order had been the 'memory' of the Holy Family, changed in the 1876 Rule to the 'memory' of the Passion with which it had always been closely linked. For Gaudentius, Elizabeth and her order, as for the Passionists, the 'memory' denoted a lifestyle, not a mere devotion. Industry and education were active apostolates, as well as means of support. Linked by parish visitation and homes for factory girls, they both had a place in the congregation. What was most important, however, was the religious life itself.

3. DOMESTIC ECONOMY

While political economy dictated new values in education, it also urged domestic economy in the home.[123] Although the sisters were poor, up to the first professions in November 1854 Elizabeth budgeted so carefully and practised economy and frugality so well, that even during the fever crisis of 1853-4 she avoided falling into debt. She obviously had a firm grasp of household management.[124] After the professions of November 1854 she opened additional foundations. That growth was necessary to secure approval from Rome and the permanence of the institute but it entailed leaving the administration of one or more houses in hands less capable than her own. Their domestic mismanagement plunged Elizabeth into the 1857 financial crisis and culminated in 1858 in the order's near suppression.

With its type of membership, the order could not have become wealthy but in 1857 it could have been economically viable when supported by incomes from the Levenshulme and Parr boarding schools. Difficulties had been inevitable in 1855: in spite of Miss Eliza Orrell's help at Parr Hall, new houses meant new costs and the departure of three Irish candidates had been an additional expense.[125] Bishop Turner therefore forbade Clare to accept two postulants who were straw-bonnet makers, because 'their business would not answer in Manchester'.[126] Father Gaudentius asked Robert Monteith of Carstairs for 'pecuniary assistance' for the sisters.[127] When Father Ignatius Spencer came to give the community retreat in June-July 1855, he had to arrange his lectures to give them maximum time for sewing, because they could not afford time off.[128] In September, however, Elizabeth was able to assure Gaudentius that money matters were 'going on very well'.[129] The Sutton and Blackbrook bills were paid and, when she had checked a few days earlier, Sister Clare had told her Ashton owed only one bill. Elizabeth expected that by her time of writing it also would have been cleared. The real problem arose two years later.

In 1857 Elizabeth discovered that Clare in Levenshulme had incurred large debts. She was obviously not skilled in domestic economy. Whereas Elizabeth Prout's upper-working-class background had trained her in household management, Clare's education in more elegant accomplishments had not.[130] For the first time in her life Clare had to manage a household. She had to give directions to tradesmen, children, teachers and to her community, both novices and professed.[131] Having to control a budget for a substantial number of people, she needed to plan her expenditure carefully.[132] She would have had no access to the contemporary women's manuals on how to solve the intricacies of making ends meet but she was bound by Rule to keep detailed accounts.[133] Every farthing should have been entered in her columns of expenditure, balanced by income. Thus the mystery would have been taken out of managing finances. Prompt paying of bills was absolutely essential. Irregularity in doing so could bankrupt a convent as much as a family. To keep these rules of domestic economy, however, Clare required some mathematical skill.[134] Her duties evidently outstripped her ability. Already giving 'trouble to higher superiors in many ways', she ran into debt. Sam Grimshaw 'withdrew his support'. Canon Croskell wrote to Elizabeth 'in very urgent terms expressing his apprehension that the sisters would not be able to pay their way but not offering either counsel or assistance'.[135] Father Ignatius heard the full extent of the bad news from Elizabeth when he arrived in Sutton on 1 July from his journey to Rome with Father Gaudentius' Rule. The next day he went to Manchester to see Canon Croskell, who directed him to Bishop Turner. On 3 July the bishop visited Levenshulme convent to examine the accounts. Ignatius stayed in Levenshulme for the next ten days, discussing the problem with Elizabeth and consulting people in Manchester who might help.[136] Elizabeth wrote to Gaudentius but protected Clare's reputation by not telling him why they were in debt. He obviously had his suspicions, however, for he told her to close Parr Hall, leave Sister Zitta Watson in Sutton and return to Levenshulme.[137]

His first three American postulants arrived, unexpectedly, as indigence enveloped the institute. Elizabeth accepted two, Bridget Flanagan, whom Gaudentius had described as 'from Irish parents, but born in America... 27 or 28 years of age, good health.... had a good English education... teaches dressmaking and embroidery'; and Eliza Lang, with whom she had previously corresponded and whom Gaudentius had praised very highly:

...was born in Germany, but came very young in this country with her parents. These were doing very well in business, but her father died six years ago, and her mother about three years ago. I think Eliza is the second among seven or eight living children. She is 25 years of age. She enjoys a very good bodily health. She has had a good German education. She can read, and write English which she speaks perfectly well. She understands dressmaking. She is very handy and clever at every thing.[138]

Two more seamstresses were not going to be financially helpful. In her own circumstances, Elizabeth could not accept the third, Miss Swain, who at almost forty was too old, could not support herself and clearly had no vocation. She had deceived Father Gaudentius about her age and had forced herself into the party.[139]

Facing disrepute if not starvation, Elizabeth braced herself for a begging tour of the Lancashire parishes.[140] On 6 August 1857 Bishop Turner gave her a first donation of £5, with a tactful recommendation:

The Institute of the Sisters of the Holy Family originated in 1850. Its object was to afford pious and industrious young females an opportunity of embracing a state of religious perfection to which many of the humbler classes aspire without having means of obtaining the object of their pious wishes. The purpose for which it was established has realised our expectations. The community number about 20 Sisters who are engaged in teaching poor children at Levenshulme, Ashton-under-Lyne, and at Sutton.

Owing to sickness with which several of the Sisters have been visited, and which entailed considerable expense upon their scanty means, they find themselves in embarrassed circumstances and are compelled to seek aid in their necessities.

Sympathising, as we do, with these poor but most deserving Sisters, we beg to recommend their case to the charity of the Faithful.

Signed William Bishop of Salford.[141]

Before she set out, Elizabeth told Father Gaudentius that she was going to beg.[142] On 2 October 1857 he sent her fifty dollars, which he reckoned as £10, a sum he had previously mentioned as donated to bring sisters over to America.[143] With the donor's permission Gaudentius now sent it to allay their distress. He told her to cash the cheque quickly, because all the banks in North America had suspended payment, even closed down, and 'many manufactories' had stopped.[144] He realised the sum was comparatively little but expected she would 'easily get the money in Manchester'. He supposed the debt was only on Levenshulme. 'I cannot understand why', he said. 'You have house and garden free of rent. You have boarders — the Sisters are able to sew – and work and teach, and my impression is that some help could have been given them from one or two other houses. There must have been mismanagement somewhere...' He trusted the sisters would not 'be abandoned to the scorn and ridicule of the world'.[145] He suggested that Elizabeth should ask for charity sermons in Sutton, Ashton and Levenshulme and organise a little bazaar or raffle during the Christmas holidays.[146]

Elizabeth was once more caught up in wider contemporary issues. The same cotton slump that was closing mills in North America was already being felt in Lancashire.[147] Although she 'travelled over a great part of Lancashire on her difficult and trying mission', she did not collect enough to clear the debts.[148] Bishop Turner suspended the public renewal of their vows.[149] Sisters Magdalene Toler, Clare Wilson, Teresa Hennessy and De Chantal Jones left.[150] Only Elizabeth, Sister Mary Paul Taylor and Sister Philomena Johnson privately renewed their vows on 21 November 1857. Elizabeth had already closed Parr Hall.[151] Now she closed Ashton.[152] On 24 November she and Sister Catherine Scanlon left for Ireland to beg.[153]

With an east-north-east wind, the weather was fine but cold. After a twelve to fourteen-hour crossing, they were met in Dublin by Father Ignatius Spencer, who was in Ireland begging for the new Passionist retreat at Harold's Cross.[154] He escorted them to 43 Dorset Street, where he found them lodgings with a Miss Nolan.[155] In Dublin and in Ireland in general, however, there were already numerous collections for new churches, schools, orphanages and hospitals. For Elizabeth, as she met with 'many repulses, hard words and such like humiliations' there seemed little chance of help in Dublin.[156] As the weather changed first to dull and then to a great gale on 1-2 December, she must have felt it accorded with her despair. After a good chat with Father Ignatius, who wrote to the bishops of the dioceses where she hoped to quest, she set out on 14 December for Borrisokane and then Cork.[157] There is no indication of what success they had in the south, except that they received 'the greatest kindness from priests and people' and especially from the Presentation nuns at Fermoy, where they stayed most of their time, 'visiting the different towns by car and returning at night where as Sr Catherine often said they had a most hearty welcome'.[158] Others, however, were in the same field. Begging was a characteristic of the British, and American, Catholic Church in the nineteenth century, mainly due to the Irish potato famine and subsequent emigration. There were the same problems of poverty and lack of church and school accommodation wherever the Irish went.[159] From November 1857 to 1860 two Oblate Sisters were begging in Ireland for funds for a convent, poor school and orphanage in the Beverley Diocese.[160] Two Passionists from Harold's Cross, Brother Michael Behan and Father Charles Houben were questing, like Father Ignatius, for their new monastery.[161] One of Father Gaudentius' fellow Passionists in North America, Father Albinus Magno with a diocesan priest from Pittsburgh, Pennsylvania had also come to Ireland to collect funds for Bishop O'Connor's new cathedral.[162] Trying to replenish their own resources while still not recovered from the famine, the Irish had little to give.

After two months of 'many rebuffs' but also 'much kindness and sympathy', Elizabeth and Catherine returned to 'dear, kind, Father Osmund' before recrossing to England.[163] They arrived back in Sutton on 27 January 1858, to face 'new and heavy trials'.[164] Philomena 'had proved herself unworthy of the trust.... The sisters in Levenshulme, and especially one of them, whose delicate health rendered her unfit to sustain severe treatment, had suffered much from [her] disorderly government'.[165] Elizabeth discovered that, instead of applying herself to the government of the house, Philomena had negotiated for a transfer to the Cistercians of Stapehill in Dorset and had spent her time making her outfit.[166] She had written to Gaudentius telling him that Elizabeth was begging in Ireland; that the institute was in debt; that some of the sisters had left; that some that remained were 'sickly in body and mind'; that no useful people were joining; and that she was leaving. In an effort to retain her, he invited her to go out to North America with Sister Alban Lang to found the congregation there. Philomena wrote again, telling him she had left.[167]

Gaudentius had been grieved when he heard Elizabeth had gone to beg in Ireland, where, he felt, she 'could not have done much good'. He thought she might have achieved something in Lancashire or should have written to friends. 'What have been the causes of all these failures?' he asked. 'There must have been some fault somewhere.' Philomena had not therefore enlightened him on that score. He did have the impression there had 'been some secret envy between the principal Sisters through motives of ambition', envy of, not by, the foundress, for in 1856 he had stated clearly that Clare was jealous of Elizabeth.[168] Told exactly who had left, he was not surprised, except at Philomena. He did not think she would persevere at Stapehill.[169]

By 28 March 1858 the sick novice, Sister Frances de Sales Brennan, was so ill with tuberculosis that Elizabeth asked Canon Croskell to receive her deathbed vows.[170] Her death on 10 May was the first in the congregation and Elizabeth felt it keenly.[171] During that month 'through the misrepresentations of those Sisters who had left, a rumour went abroad that the institute was going to be broken up.'[172] While it is unclear where Clare and Teresa went after they left, Agnes, Aloysius, Magdalene and De Chantal were all from the Manchester area. Philomena left Stapehill after a few months and so may also have been in Manchester at this time. She had certainly discussed the affairs of the congregation with outsiders.[173] She had also written Gaudentius precisely the type of remark that could have raised such rumours if made in Manchester.[174] The foundress could ignore gossip. She could not ignore Canon Croskell's sudden withdrawal of interest. Alarmed, she wrote to Bishop Turner, asking if it was true he was going to dissolve the institute.[175] He replied on 30 May that he had no intention of breaking up the institute as long as it went on in a satisfactory manner and he was quite certain he had not even hinted such a thing to anyone. He wrote to Canon Croskell for an explanation. 'Mr Croskell may be called the founder of the Institute', he told Elizabeth, 'and you were the person he selected as Superioress.'[176]

Canon Croskell replied, to Elizabeth, on 31 May 1858 that he would be truly sorry if his withdrawal should prove to be any real detriment to the Institute or to any of its members but he was persuaded it was not his province to form and regulate a new religious society in spiritual matters and he felt even less confident about his ability to assist its temporal affairs effectively. 'To speak frankly of my motives in keeping aloof', he added,

> they amount to what I have already stated to you and also to Father Gaudentius, viz. that I consider the attempt to form and establish the Institute a failure. The single fact of its not proving 'self-supporting' is sufficient to determine me to avoid all appearance of being in any way responsible for its success or the liquidation of its debts. I find that people are still under the impression that it is my undertaking and my affair. After advancing money for the commencement of the Institute, I have often said I could not go any further, in outlay or responsibility. This you understand and feel, but the public does not, so long as I am mixed up with its affairs.
>
> I have a great respect for many of the Sisters individually and I wish them every spiritual and temporal blessing. But as to the Institute, I despair of its final success. *This view I keep to myself* and shall be very glad to find that I have been mistaken. Regarding temporal affairs, our good Bishop will be your best adviser and regarding spirituals the exemplary Passionist Fathers coming over from time to time will afford you every necessary aid and direction. You really lose nothing by my absence and you have always my good will and sincere respect.

Adding that he did not really have the time to attend the convent, Canon Croskell suggested that if there were any comments on his absence from professions etc. she should explain that he wished the institute to prosper but he did not wish to be mixed up personally with its affairs. 'I have not a word to say against any member', he ended, 'and I beg that they would pray for me, as a friend and well-wisher.'[177]

While Elizabeth must have been heartbroken at such a letter, she felt reassured the congregation was not on the brink of dissolution. As Father Gaudentius had commented, 'the threshing floor ha[d] been purged'.[178] With so many discordant elements gone, 'everything seemed to promise peace and tranquillity'.[179] From 7 June 1858 the Passionist novice-master, Father Salvian Nardocci gave their clothing retreat to three postulants: the two Americans, Sisters Anne Joachim Flanagan and Alban Lang, and an English girl from Broadway, Sister Mary Vincent White.[180] Next Elizabeth prepared for the annual retreat, to be given by another Passionist, Father Bernard O'Loughlin and at the end of which four novices would make their vows.[181] She therefore wrote to Canon Croskell as vicar general of Salford Diocese for faculties for Father Bernard. At the same time, anxious not to break off their nine years' friendship so abruptly as Canon Croskell's letter threatened, she asked him to return as confessor to Levenshulme.[182]

She had not received his reply when Father Bernard arrived on Friday, 2 July to open the retreat. Bernard therefore left Levenshulme for St Augustine's to ask for faculties. Since Canon Croskell had still not posted his reply to Elizabeth, he gave it to Father Bernard to deliver.[183] It was final: '... I never have and I feel that I never can be the director and regulator of the community. The formation of the spirit and the special direction of the community I have always left to the good Fathers with whom you have been in almost constant communication. As to the appointment of a director, that must be left to the Bishop....'[184] While not encouraging, the letter did not appear ominous. Father Bernard explained, however, that Canon Croskell had invited him to dinner and afterwards had told him privately that the community was about to be dissolved. It was not self supporting. It seemed that the attempt to provide consecrated religious life for lower-class women was an economic failure.

4. THE RIGHTS AND LIBERTIES OF RELIGIOUS WOMEN

Sister Philomena Johnson's remarks to Father Gaudentius about the state of Elizabeth Prout's order were serious even as privately expressed in her letter. Rumoured around Manchester they were dangerous. Having been warned by Father Croskell of the impending dissolution, Father Bernard went to see Bishop Turner on 3 July 1858 and told him he could not give the retreat under such circumstances, nor could he profess novices as intended. As a result, Bishop Turner sent for Father Croskell and it was decided to appoint 'a Commission of enquiry' immediately.[185] Bishop Turner was noted for putting 'things right without much noise'.[186] It was typical of his kindness and prudence that he had a private enquiry. The Anglican Bishop Phillpotts

of Exeter had subjected Priscilla Sellon to a public one in 1848.[187] It
was also characteristic of Bishop Turner that he chose canons who
knew Elizabeth Prout: Canon Formby of St Mary's, Canon Wilding of
St Augustine's and Canon Benoit of St John's.[188] Canon Formby as
parish priest of St Mary's, Mulberry Street, had known her since she
had helped him in 1852-3.[189] Canon Wilding was the canon penitentiary of the Salford Diocese. He had visited the sisters in Stocks Street
and had almost invited them to teach and live in St John's parish,
Salford, where he was parish priest in 1852.[190] He had sent them a
postulant in 1853 and had been invited to a ceremony.[191] Canon
Benoit, a Belgian, was the bishop's secretary and theologian to the
Cathedral Chapter. He had visited Levenshulme convent in June
1854.[192] Since October 1854 he had been one of the patrons for
Levenshulme convent.[193] He had been invited to a clothing ceremony
in 1855.[194] He knew, however, they had had financial difficulties in
1855, because Gaudentius had suggested he be asked to preach a
charity sermon for them.[195] Nevertheless, far from being personally
opposed to Elizabeth, he and the other canons probably had the
greatest admiration for her. She had assumed a well-nigh impossible
task, which had caused her unutterable deprivation, at the same time
that she was performing an arduous and unobtrusively humble service
in helping to safeguard Catholic education for the working classes of
the Manchester area. The canons came, therefore, not necessarily as
enemies but as high-ranking clergy, appointed by Bishop Turner, to
hold an official enquiry. Nevertheless, as Bernard told Elizabeth later,
the situation was 'bad enough'. Although Bishop Turner was for her,
'all the priests' were against her.[196]

It had been clear from 1852 that the Manchester clergy had no
sympathy with the idea of a religious order for lower-class women.
Faced with a large, urban, Catholic population, desperately in need of
churches and schools, they were compelled to calculate even spiritual
priorities in economic and utilitarian terms. They welcomed nuns who
could teach. By 1858 few teachers or even Manchester working girls
had joined Elizabeth Prout's order. Now it was in debt. In view of
women's own lack of interest in it, the order became a luxury, 'a
burden on the Church' they simply could not afford.[197] In 1858,
therefore, 'all the priests of Manchester were roused into opposition
against the sisters and they seemed determined to overthrow the
institute entirely.'[198] Even worse, a number of specific charges were
being made against it. Apart from that of their not being self-supporting, it was said that the dress caused remarks in public; the rules were
not kept; 'the object of its establishment [had] not been obtained, viz.
a refuge for factory girls'; the sisters could not teach; they were
'always travelling in railways and omnibuses'; and that 'great tyranny

[was] employed in the government of the Institute, as *per exemplum, three professed Sisters being locked up in a room for 2 or 3 months etc..*'[199] It was this last sensational charge that identified the rumours for what they really were: an attempt to embroil Elizabeth Prout in the most controversial feminist issue of the mid-nineteenth century, 'the rights and liberties of religious women'.[200] In view of the fanatical popular Protestantism in Manchester, this charge in particular placed Elizabeth Prout in a dangerous position.

Nuns were arguably the most legally persecuted group of women in Britain at mid century. Although some Protestants as well as wealthier Catholics had sent their daughters to be educated in continental convents, in England itself nuns were totally unseen throughout the penal centuries.[201] When they began to return during the French Revolution, they were welcomed as the victims of French aggression. In the light of politico-religious changes taking place in previously Catholic countries and the impossibility of living on alms in Protestant countries, the papacy allowed the enclosed orders to support themselves with boarding schools and they quickly flourished in England.[202] One of the features of the Gothic revival, however, was the publication of a number of 'medieval' romances, depicting monks and nuns as ogres and kidnappers.[203] Transferred from the pages of fiction into the columns of the Reformation Society's newspapers, these weird tales caught the imagination of popular Protestantism. People really believed girls were abducted.[204] In 1841 an attempt was made to 'rescue' a nun in Dublin; in 1850 another in Edinburgh.[205] Misconceptions of celibacy and religious life were popularised in both North America and Britain by Maria Monk's highly sensational *Awful Disclosures of the Hotel Dieu Nunnery, Montreal*, first published in New York in 1836. Confessors were depicted as immoral; mother superiors as tyrants and as murderers of both illegitimate children and rebellious nuns. Convents were portrayed as beehives of secret dungeons and burial holes.[206] Anti-sacerdotalism and anti-virginity joined the fear in the popular Protestant mind of Catholic double allegiance.[207] In Manchester the Catholic revival revealed Passionist monks preaching to packed churches of those dangerous people, the working classes, many of them Irish, while both male and female religious increasingly dominated the schools.[208] On the one hand, the rationalism of the age considered convents anachronistic institutions.[209] On the other, a male-dominated world was terrified of the efficiency of women's teaching orders, or even of religious communities.[210] A society, too, that reduced so many women to prostitution that it was 'the great social evil' found consecrated chastity incomprehensible.[211] Even amongst morally respectable people celibacy seemed unnatural.[212] Many Victorians, with their emphasis on family life and wives and mothers, found the concept of religious life difficult to understand.[213] Nuns appeared to be young women who had given up 'a heart and life capable of love and charity, good works and wifely and motherly affections and duties'.[214] The Puseyites' encouragement of celibacy, convents and confession seemed to threaten the stability of the Church of England.[215] The very fabric of society seemed to be threatened, not, as *Punch* had facetiously remarked in 1844, because so many women were becoming nuns that 'honest men [might] soon want wives', but because popular misconceptions of auricular confession and spiritual guidance saw the confessor as usurping the authority of the father in the Victorian home.[216] Moreover, people delighted in exposing scandals and in the anti-Catholicism of the age priests and nuns were popular targets, especially as they would not retaliate.[217] As displayed in *Punch*, even in 1844 as Father Dominic Barberi began his public missions in England, the ridiculing of nuns' clothing and profession ceremonies had already become a popular mode of theatre entertainment, while the realities were mercilessly lampooned.[218] Even nuns' charitable activities were slandered. When, for example, a convent in London in 1850 sheltered a young unmarried mother in the final stages of pregnancy, the *Morning Advertiser* chose to publish news of a birth at the convent.[219] Newman, planning storage space in his Birmingham Oratory, was accused of building cells 'for the forcible detention of some of Her Majesty's subjects'.[220] Unfortunately, all these fears, misconceptions and scurrilities were inflated not only by papers like Manchester's *Protestant Witness* but by members of parliament like Charles Newdegate.

Although, as Cardinal Wiseman pointed out, propaganda against convents was widespread long before the 1850 restoration of the hierarchy, the wave of anti-Catholicism that swept the country in 1850-52 inevitably increased its intensity.[221] Maria Monk's proven absurdities were reprinted.[222] Popular literature depicted nuns as having been crossed in love.[223] In March 1851, at the time Elizabeth Prout had hoped to found her order, the Evangelical Newdegate, educated at Eton, King's College, London and at Oxford, and member of parliament for North Warwickshire, presented his Religious Houses Bill, ostensibly 'to prevent the forcible detention of females in religious houses'. He proposed that from 15 September 1851, all female religious houses must be registered and no female religious could live in a house that was not registered. Six Justices of the Peace were to be appointed to visit the convents to ensure no-one was being detained. They were to inspect each convent twice each year, at any time, without notice, between 6 a.m. and 8 p.m., with slight variations for winter and summer. They were to interview all the inmates, either privately or collectively, checking their names against the names, addresses and other personal details of their families according to a register which must be kept in each convent. They could transfer anyone at a moment's notice to the workhouse. Anyone who tried to obstruct their entrance by assault was liable to ten years' transportation or two years' hard labour in prison.[224]

Canon Stowell was delighted. On 19 April 1851, referring to 'ecclesiastical rapacity' and 'priestly domination', the *Protestant Witness* called for an official inspection of convents 'as effective as that now exercised over Lunatic Asylums'.[225] Even *Punch*, however, was disgusted. 'People are beginning to ask why lunatic asylums are subjected to so rigorous a system of supervision, whilst conventual institutions are wholly exempt', it said, 'as if there were any similitude or analogy between a madhouse and a monastery.'[226] *Punch* itself was, nevertheless, partly to blame. Even in the 1840s secular relatives, especially of converts to Catholicism, had looked covetously as wealthy young women, even heiresses, disappeared into monastic enclosures taking their fortunes with them.[227] In early 1851, *Punch*, featuring a lengthy article about a girl who had gone into a convent with £80,000, compared conventual life with Sutteeism in India and accused priests of cursing girls into becoming nuns. It had caricatured a friar, coaxing a small girl to take a veil and to hand over a large money bag and it had continued the same type of propaganda in a few lines of doggerel on 'Taking the Veil':

> Here's success to your priests that for fortunes do hunt
> And look out for young damsels with plenty of blunt
> With no laws to forbid them as shown in this tale
> About catching a heiress and taking the veil.[228]

While mocking convents, bishops and priests, however, *Punch* also ridiculed Newdegate and his associates, Lacy, Drummond and Spooner, whose own bills and speeches of 'indelicate and slanderous expressions' continued Newdegate's attempts to legalise the inspection of convents.[229]

The *Protestant Witness* continued its support. Three months after Elizabeth Prout, Catharine Toler and Catharine Gilday had begun their religious life together at 69 Stocks Street, it reported Stowell's recent address to the Operatives' Protestant Association in the Free Trade Hall on nunneries, or 'Romish dens of impurity and female degradation'. Fortunately unaware that Elizabeth Prout was even then founding a religious order in Manchester itself, he 'urged the especial attention of the females' of Manchester and Salford 'to the true position of their own sex', so many of whom, he said, 'breathed the sighs of broken-hearted women... immured within walls where English law had no entrance'. Suggesting the women of Manchester and Salford should present Queen Victoria, on her forthcoming visit, with memorials asking her 'to do justice to her own sex, and to her subjects who were oppressed within the walls of a Nunnery', he questioned why such places had 'high walls, spikes and barred gates' if the people within were happy. 'Let them make their Nunneries like ordinary schools', he said. 'Let the poor Nuns walk abroad. They talked of keeping them pure and secluded... Pitiful, wretched security and seclusion! If it would not stand contact with the ordinary intercourse, and the ordinary scenes and sights of social life, away with it.... It was not fit for the soil of England.'[230]

The Catholic press had not allowed these assaults to pass unchallenged. It was important in the Catholic revival to explain monasticism even to English Catholics of the middle and working classes, because, like possible Protestant readers, they could have known little about it. Accordingly, in response to Lacy's bill, Bishop Ullathorne in 1850 had published *A Plea for the Rights and Liberties of Religious Women,* in which he had explained the Catholic Church's canonical regulations about convents, with respect to authority, admissions, episcopal visitations and chaplaincies.[231] In 1851 the *Catholic School* recorded 'The Nation's Debt To Nuns' in education.[232] In June 1852, Cardinal Wiseman, answering the calumnies of a Hobart Seymour against both Anglican and Catholic convents, pointed out that, while he was not passing any judgements on the Anglican sisterhoods, their conventual system had nothing in common with that of Catholic congregations, which were under episcopal supervision as regulated from Rome. Hence it would be impossible for a Catholic superior to send out a sister at night to travel alone by train, as Seymour had suggested, because, as soon as her bishop heard of it, 'the very next post would carry a letter' suspending her from office. Similarly a Catholic superior could not exact the extraordinary acts of obedience supposed to have been demanded according to Seymour, because the Rule, approved by Rome, protected sisters from any superior's caprice.[233] From about 1840 the Catholic papers had published frequent articles on the type of life practised by the various orders in England and on their clothing and profession ceremonies.[234] These descriptions are invaluable as highlighting the conventual authenticity of Elizabeth Prout's own services. They, in turn, are historically important as exemplifying, against the background of parliamentary debates and Stowell's virulent attacks in Manchester, the care that was taken to guard against the very abuses of which convents were accused.

Because the type of life expressed in the Rule was so different from secular life, the commencement of that lifestyle was marked by a ceremony, significant of what the participants were abandoning and of the obligations they were freely incurring. Since they were assuming a new state of life, distinct from both marriage and spinsterhood, it was also marked by the adoption of a new style of dress, a religious habit, which, although it might be a witness to others of their consecration, was primarily a reminder to themselves of the significance of what they had done.[235] The ceremony was therefore often referred to as a 'clothing' in the habit, or the 'reception' of the habit. Since in donning the religious dress, they were symbolically entering upon a new type of life, they also marked the occasion by assuming a new name. Like the Passionists, Elizabeth and her companions took a devotion to replace their surnames, as well as a new Christian name: they were dead to the world. They had entered upon a new, eschatological life.[236] Father Gaudentius Rossi decided the first clothing ceremony should take place on 21 November 1852, the birthday of the Passionist Congregation. Since it was the first such ceremony in the institute, he also composed the ritual, basing it on that followed by his own Passionist Congregation and on the vestition services of the contemplative Benedictines of Caverswall and the active Sisters of Mercy.[237] As merely an introduction to a period of trial, during which novices were free to leave, the ceremony took place privately at 3.30 p.m. in St Joseph's convent, 69 Stocks Street, in the workroom, converted for the occasion into a simple chapel.[238] While there is no evidence of how the sisters were dressed at the beginning of the first clothing ceremony, at subsequent receptions postulants wore the bridal attire customarily worn in the ceremonies of other congregations.[239] If Elizabeth was offering 'an opportunity to young females of the poorer classes to enter a religious life' such as they were denied on account of their poverty, she ensured their ceremonies were on a par with those in other congregations. Father Gaudentius was careful to question the sisters if they asked of their 'own free will' to receive 'the holy habit of religion'.[240] Between 1852 and November 1854 Elizabeth Prout had to instruct her sisters in the meaning and seriousness of professing religious vows. Significantly, in view of contemporary accusations of abductions, the first profession ceremony on 21 November 1854 was a public service in St Mary's church, Levenshulme. It followed a week's retreat given by Father Gaudentius and took place during Mass celebrated by Bishop Turner at 8 a.m. The sisters, therefore, made a public profession of their vows. Of unique interest as the first profession ceremony in a new religious order, it was attended, as such services normally were, by several priests and a large number of secular laity. Bishop Turner, as the bishop of Salford, represented the authority of the Catholic Church. Without his approval, the ceremony could not have taken place, the vows could not have been made. He publicly queried and the sisters publicly affirmed that they understood their obligations, undertook them freely and intended to persevere until death. It was the Passionist Father Gaudentius, however, who had compiled the service, basing it on the Passionist rituals, and who also preached the sermon.[241] Both the ceremony and habit highlighted the new congregation's position in the Passionist mission to England: each sister was given a black veil; a silver ring bearing a cross and the initials 'JMJ'; and, most significantly, the Passionist Sign, although the words *JESU XPI PASSIO* were changed to the letters 'JMJ'.[242]

In view of these experiences, the ex-sisters who laid the rumours against Elizabeth Prout in 1858 could not claim, nor did they attempt to say they had been abducted or forced to stay against their will. Since they had come without dowries they could not complain of having had their fortunes stolen. Elizabeth Prout had certainly not been crossed in love and there is no evidence that others had been either. The suggestion of captive nuns, however, dying of convulsions after torture, had a special appeal to the popular Protestant mind. Imprisonment was therefore a favourite theme with disgruntled ex-sisters.[243] Priscilla Sellon was supposed to have carried it out in early 1852.[244] In August of the same year, the Catholic sisters at Norwood were put on civil trial for their alleged (and disproved) three months' imprisonment of an orphan.[245] Since those who brought the charge against them had tried to incriminate Cardinal Wiseman and the sisters' confessor, there were good reasons why the Manchester clergy, with Stowell in the vicinity, were anxious in 1858. When Bishop Turner heard the charge against Elizabeth Prout, however, he immediately made it clear he did not believe it, saying that he had only recently made his visitation of the convent and 'was well pleased with what he had seen and heard'.[246] Nevertheless, in view of popular scandalmongering, he had to hold the investigation if only to disprove this charge once and for all, for even the parliamentary attacks on nuns had continued unabated.

Reporting attacks on monks and nuns in Liverpool in May 1853, the *Tablet* described female religious as the 'most cherished objects of vituperation'.[247] Catholics were indignant as Thomas Chambers introduced yet another bill for the inspection of convents, imposing twelve months' hard labour or a fine on any nun who refused to co-operate.[248] Upper-class Catholics were outraged that their daughters and sisters should be forced to endure private, inquisitorial visitations from men like Newdegate and Spooner.[249] In the Catholic outcry, petitions were drawn up and presented to the House of Commons. Protest meetings were held and letters sent to newspapers.[250] Canon Toole of St Wilfrid's wrote to the *Manchester Courier* that the bill would itself be an invasion of the privacy of English homes and would 'dishonour womanhood because it ha[d] the courage and virtue to devote itself with ardour to the service of God, of female youth, and of the poor'.[251] No sooner had this crisis subsided than Cornelia

Connelly was slandered across the country.[252] It was against this background that all Elizabeth Prout's companions caught fever and several almost died.[253] Since Manchester clergy and Catholics thought Elizabeth Prout 'bereft of reason' for trying to found a religious order for the poor, she received neither sympathy nor help from anyone in Manchester save Dr Walsh, who refused to take any fees, and Father Daly, who lent her his house at Newton Heath.[254] As the sisters recovered and moved to Levenshulme in April 1854, yet another bill was introduced into parliament, theoretically 'to secure to persons under religious vows the free exercise of their lawful rights in the disposal of their property'.[255] Again there were widespread Catholic protests.[256] In May 1854 Drummond wanted a Royal Commission on nuns.[257] Catholic Ireland rose in protest. Petitions from all over Ireland, where there were at least 1,500 nuns, flooded into the House of Commons from bishops, priests and people.[258] In the face of this opposition the proposal was muted but although nuns' work in the Crimea brought them a degree of appreciation, it quickly faded.[259] There was a riot in Lewes in 1857 when a young Anglican nun died from fever after bringing the convent a rich dowry.[260] Throughout the fifties and until 1863 newspapers constantly accused Priscilla Sellon of tyranny and cruelty.[261] When a nun died in Northampton in 1857, it was noised abroad that eighty had been murdered.[262] About the same time, Stowell's Manchester Protestant and Reformation Society organised a public rally in the Free Trade Hall to propose the formation of the North of England Protestant Organisation of Anglicans and Dissenters against popery. Amidst the cheers of his listeners one of the speakers proclaimed,

> A man named Ullathorne, who called himself a bishop, had recently taken the duty of visiting the nunneries of England, and he said that he found the young ladies in them all perfectly happy and domiciled. We might ask why then did they want the collateral security of bolts and bars and prison gates? Now Protestants demanded that there should be no institutions in this country at which the law turned pale, and that nunneries should not only be inspected but altogether exterminated and swept away from the nation, nunneries must be unconditionally abolished, as being utterly inconsistent with the British Constitution.[263]

The final 1858 charge against Elizabeth Prout, well-calculated to rouse a mob, was, therefore, very serious in the prevalent climate of credulity and popular Protestantism. More than any other it was a direct, personal attack on Elizabeth Prout. Typical of contemporary tales spread by disgruntled ex-sisters, it suited the public's thirst for convent scandals and their ability to invent what was not there.[264] It

was what they wanted to hear. As a charge it was ludicrous, incompat-
ible with Elizabeth's kindness and physique. Had there been even a
grain of truth in it, Father Gaudentius would have heard.[265] Had he
done so, he would certainly have written to Elizabeth about it, as he
did about milder complaints. Gaudentius never accused Elizabeth of
tyranny. He did accuse her of indulgence in allowing sisters facility to
consult a doctor or to visit the seaside for their health.[266] Nevertheless,
leaked to Manchester's *Protestant Witness*, this last sensational charge
could have created unpleasantness for the Catholic Church and severe
harassment of the sisters themselves. Although it was proved to be
false, it was a cruel recompense to Elizabeth Prout for her unfailing
kindness, her care for the sick, her guidance in both spiritual and
temporal matters and her heroic charity in preserving intact the
reputations of Clare Wilson, Philomena Johnson and the rest. For
Elizabeth, it was a profound sharing in Christ's Passion, a truly
Passionist experience.

After a preliminary meeting of the canons with Father Bernard
O'Loughlin and Father Browne of Levenshulme on Monday, 5 July
1858, Elizabeth received a letter from Canon Croskell informing her
that the enquiry would be held at 11 a.m. the next day. She was to
provide a room in Levenshulme convent and give 'every facility for
the fullest investigation. Let all who are called upon', he added, 'state
the truth to the best of their knowledge, and then a wise and just report
will be made.'[267] He asked Father Bernard to attend the enquiry to
explain any confusing points about religious life. When Bernard said
he felt he could not do so, unless he had the vicar general's authority
in writing, Canon Croskell immediately put his request on paper. The
next day Bernard received the canons at Levenshulme. When he sat
down with them, they politely hinted he should retire. The provost's
written request 'struck them dumb'.[268] They suggested the sisters
would not like him to be present. Elizabeth assured them they would.
Bernard stayed.

For the next three hours the fate of the congregation hung in the
balance. Elizabeth and the other professed sisters were interviewed
individually and interrogated on the seven charges. Since all participants were bound to silence, Bernard was unable to record the actual
examinations, nor could any of the sisters ever mention them.[269] Some
points, however, are self-explanatory. Hitherto Elizabeth had heroically protected Clare Wilson's good name. Bishop Turner knew the
truth about the order's debts. The canons did not. Now they heard how
Clare had involved the institute in debt; how, with her strong sense of
justice, Elizabeth had striven to pay it off; and what it had cost her in
terms of hardship and humiliation. They heard how Clare had given
trouble in a variety of ways and how Philomena had so betrayed the

trust placed in her that a delicate novice had died possibly from lack of care. They must have heard a great deal about the other sisters who had left. From the foundress herself they must have demanded an accurate statement of the financial affairs of the congregation. Ashton, Blackbrook and Sutton had all been self-supporting. Levenshulme should have been, because it had a private school to give it a regular income. Nevertheless, even taking into account Clare's treachery and Philomena's betrayal, it was true that Father Croskell had put money into the institute; Father Gaudentius had, on occasion, asked other priests, including Canon Formby, to give the Sisters money; and, although on the whole, they could manage to eke out an existence when they were well and working, they became destitute if ill and unemployed. Elizabeth could not have felt sure that the institute would survive the day.

The charge that the sisters' dress caused remarks in public could obviously be easily remedied. It was insufficient reason for suppressing the congregation. Like the final charge, it was typical of the period. The Anglican Park Village sisters were accused of being Catholics because they wore a simple black costume.[270] In Elizabeth's case it would appear, from the results of the enquiry, that the mantle trailed along the ground, as was the style of some ladies' dresses at the time.[271] Otherwise, as one of the annalists remarked, when the sisters began their work in Manchester 'the religious instruction of the poorer children was undertaken by Nuns [the Presentation] whose Rules of enclosure obliged them to carry on the work of education within the walls of their convent and school'. To rescue the 'lambs of the Flock of Christ', the 'poor Catholic children whose parents, through poverty and carelessness neglected sending them to school' or sent the 'little ones to the so-called Ragged Schools, where oftentimes they were given food instead of instruction in their religion', Elizabeth and her sisters 'spent much time in hunting them up and persuading their parents to send them to a Catholic School.'[272] Apparently, although they wore a mantle and bonnet to cover the religious habit and veil, in accordance with Derby's 1852 decree, they were still recognisable as nuns. Since nuns were not normally seen on the streets of Manchester, their appearance caused comment. In view of their apostolate, the remarks of Catholics at any rate should not have been derogatory. Such comments were not new in 1858. They had been made from 1854 and, as Father Gaudentius had then commented, they were simply a pretext for opposing Elizabeth's new type of religious order.[273]

The charge that the sisters were 'always travelling in railways and omnibuses' was made in the same vein and was also topical, reminiscent of Seymour's charges about lone night travel in trains. It was frivolous to say Elizabeth Prout's sisters were 'always' travelling in

trains and buses, because they normally walked. They could hardly
have been expected to walk from Levenshulme to Sutton, but they
could have been seen walking from Levenshulme to Goulden Street
between April and August 1854. Gaudentius expected them to walk
part of the way from Levenshulme to Ashton.[274] It was difficult enough
to afford trains and omnibuses when they were necessary; it would
have been impossible to afford private cabs. If they did use public
transport, it could have been only in driving rain or when otherwise
essential. Even in the 1850s, however, to some people trains and
omnibuses were dangerous, new-fangled types of transport, causing
noise and dirt and threatening established social mores. Some ladies
fastidiously refused to use them.[275] *Punch* suggested the pope would
put railways on the Index, a strange proposition in England since, by
facilitating travel, they formed the backbone of the Passionist
mission.[276] Many people considered them ungenteel, however,
unsuitable on any account for nuns. Moreover nuns were not expected
to go out. Stowell might have approved of Elizabeth Prout's 'walk[ing]
abroad', amid the 'ordinary scenes and sights of social life', but some
of the Manchester Catholics did not. Even the city's teaching orders
did not walk the streets. Elizabeth Prout was remarkably courageous
in bearing the brunt of being the foundress of a new kind of religious
order.

The charge that the Rule was not kept was presumably clarified at the
interviews. There is no indication of what it meant but it was certainly
satisfactorily answered. Since it could have been made seriously only
by someone who claimed to know the Rule, it must have come from
sisters who had defected. The charge that the sisters could not teach
reflected the Manchester clergy's need of teaching orders. It was,
however, the surprising charge that the object of the institute's
establishment had not been obtained, viz. a refuge for factory girls,
that proved the most important, because it helped Elizabeth Prout as
foundress to crystallise the aims and nature of her congregation.[277] On
6 July 1858, however, she could not be sure there would be a
congregation much longer.

When the investigation ended at 2 p.m., the canons left to report to
Bishop Turner. On Wednesday 7 July, the novices were in 'great
alarm' about what they had seen the preceding day. They could not
understand why three priests were in the convent for such a long time,
why they were calling in the professed sisters one by one and why
Father Bernard had interrupted the retreat. Convinced they themselves
were going to be 'sent home or where they liked to go', they went to
Elizabeth one by one to 'express their troubles and apprehensions'. She
finally broke under the strain. She 'listened to them as long as she
could, but at last, losing patience, she ran to Father Bernard with tears

in her eyes and words in her *mouth*. She said she really could not stand it any longer; she did not care what the Commissioners did to them; they might dissolve them if they liked.' Bernard asked her to wait patiently. Bishop Turner even then was meeting the canons and he was to go to see him at noon. In the event, Bernard met the bishop outside his house. Manifesting 'the greatest pleasure and satisfaction', Bishop Turner immediately exclaimed, 'Well, Father Bernard, I have good news for you. The Canons are satisfied with the investigation. The Institute is to continue, and now the Canons will in future be in favour of them.' After giving Bernard a detailed report, he sent him back to the convent to tell the sisters and 'in thanksgiving to sing the *Te Deum* and give Solemn Benediction'.[278] At the end of the retreat, on 11 July, Bernard received the vows of the four novices as planned.

Elizabeth communicated her joyous relief to her friend, Father Salvian Nardocci, the Passionist novice-master in Broadway, 'Now we are as firm as any other modern order in the Church.' She told him of her debt to Bernard, 'He has done what no other could have done, not even Father Gaudentius. He would not have been able to have fought (if I may use the term) with the Manchester priests as Father Bernard has done for us.' Anxious to avoid any criticism of Gaudentius, she continued, 'Do not for one moment think we wish to throw the least slight on dear Fr Gaudentius. No, he is our dear Father and Founder, and for ever will be, but next to him we must rank good Father Bernard.'[279] Although, however, the sisters were 'full of thankfulness and joy', they not only remained very poor but became even poorer, for the canons told them to close their flourishing middle school at Levenshulme.[280] On Father Bernard's advice Elizabeth appealed against this verdict.[281] According to Sister Mary Paul Taylor, however, she was not allowed to reopen the Levenshulme boarding school until two years later and so 'the institute struggled on, amidst difficulties and opposition'.[282]

CHAPTER VI

THE FINAL CHARISM

1. RELIGIOUS DRESS

The final charism, or the unique identity that distinguished Elizabeth Prout's institute from any other order in the Catholic Church, was defined in the 1863 Rule, her last will and testament to her congregation. She and Father Ignatius Spencer made this revision of Father Gaudentius Rossi's Rule at the command of the Holy See. Father Gaudentius had realised in 1852 that his first draft of the Rule could not be perfect.[1] There would have to be an experimental period to discover how it worked out in practice. 'It took many years for our B[lessed] Founder to perfect his rule', he told Elizabeth in 1855.[2] Since it was the sisters who were living the Rule, it fell to Elizabeth as foundress to judge what was practicable. She brought to her judgement a full measure of commonsense, which led her to allow necessary dispensations, even at the risk of Gaudentius' accusing her of negligence.[3] She also suggested changes and additions, which he accepted.[4] Experience and Gaudentius' own consultations with Father Ignatius Spencer and other priests dictated other additions, such as a section on schools he inserted in July 1854.[5] By the first professions in November 1854, Gaudentius thought he had completed it. As a preliminary to seeking papal approval he had already begun to translate it into Italian.[6] As he continued that work, he made further adjustments.[7] In September 1855, however, he was convinced it was perfect. 'As far as I can judge', he wrote to Elizabeth, 'I consider the last copy of the rules to be as perfect as we can expect.'[8] Elizabeth loyally replied, 'I agree with you dear Father that the rules are as perfect as they can be. As far as I can judge I think an attempt to improve them would spoil them.'[9] In his final letter on English soil, he wrote, 'These rules ought to be considered as the original and genuine portrait of the pious institute of the Holy Family.'[10] This was the final version of the Holy Family Rule, in Elizabeth Prout's writing, which Father Ignatius Spencer presented to the Holy See in May 1857, with a letter of approbation from Bishop Turner and with the knowledge of Father Gaudentius Rossi.[11]

The point of seeking papal approbation of the Rule was to secure recognition of the institute as a religious order within the Catholic Church. The approved Rule was the canonical link between the sisters who lived it and the magisterium of the Church. It was the nexus of authority within the order, because it legitimised the lifestyle and government of a particular group of people, who were imposing upon themselves stricter moral obligations than were demanded from the main body of Christians.[12] As Cardinal Wiseman and Bishop Ullathorne pointed out in the 1850s, in directing practices within Catholic religious orders their approved Rules prevented excesses and safe-guarded members from the type of misconduct decried by Newdegate, Stowell and their associates.[13] For the members of the order, however, it was much more than a set of legalities. It denoted the way by which they were specially called to serve both their neighbour and God, to live in union with Him and finally to rejoice with Him in heaven for all eternity. It was a manifestation of the will of God, a pledge of eternal life. In Elizabeth Prout's congregation it raised up the poor to a share in the richest blessings of the Catholic Church as bestowed upon religious orders.[14]

Father Ignatius Spencer returned to England in June 1857, however, with Cardinal Barnabò's answer that 'he encouraged the undertaking, the object of which he considered very excellent' but 'he considered the Rule too diffuse'. Ignatius was to 'condense' it, 'make some alterations in its tenor' and base it on 'the Rule of a sainted founder'.[15] Since he did not expect to be in Rome again before the next Passionist general chapter in 1863, approbation of the Rule was thus deferred for six years at least.

In preparation for the revision, Father Ignatius Spencer wrote to Father Gaudentius Rossi in June 1862 to ask his advice on how to alter his Rule in response to Rome's 1857 decree. When Father Gaudentius replied in August 1862, he made a disturbing claim: while he admitted that his co-founder, Father Croskell and also Bishop Turner had wanted the congregation to be as Elizabeth Prout, with his acquies-cence, had made it, he said that as it was it did not represent his original inspiration: 'An institution for good and virtuous young Catholic girls and women of industrious habits to live in a regular religious community, and support themselves through the industry of their minds and hands.' He admitted he had given his 'reluctant consent about the changes that circumstances and Ecclesiastical Persons in high authority seemed to demand' but his original idea had 'always remained in the deepest recesses' of his 'mind and heart'. He had no objection to the sisters' teaching 'ordinary schools both day as well as boarding schools for the lower and middle classes', as he had stated in his Rule, but the 'principal object should have been to receive girls of industrious habits and able to work in any capacity compatible with a Christian and religious mode of life. Hence', he continued, 'I should have preferred an ordinary kind of dress without being obliged to use any religious habit.' Bishop Turner, however, with his vicar general 'and perhaps the Superioress Sr. M. Joseph more than the rest seemed to preffer [sic] the present idea of the institute.' For some time, he said, it had appeared to succeed well and he had acquiesced. It was his opinion, however, that the nearer it approached his original inspiration, the more it would succeed, although he would not hinder the sisters from teaching if they were able to do so. Despite his criticisms, he said he was 'perfectly satisfied' to leave the revision to Father Ignatius Spencer's 'zeal and charity under the advice of the Father Provincial Ignatius and the consent and approval of the good Bishop of Salford.' He repeated, 'I am perfectly satisfied with any arrangement you with Very Rev. Father Provincial Ignatius and the Bishop of Salford may think proper to make about the Sisters of the Holy Family.'[16] He had nevertheless raised two issues, which Elizabeth and her advisers in England would need to consider: the religious dress and the nature of the institute he had founded.

Religious dress was a sensitive issue in England in the mid-nineteenth century. Legal restrictions on its being worn in public, however, were withdrawn in 1848 and thereafter Father Ignatius Spencer happily availed himself of the freedom to wear his habit and sandals wherever he went. His sister, Lady Lyttelton, governess to the royal children, thought his habit 'rather handsome', although she asked him not to visit her in Buckingham Palace when he was 'looking so remarkable'.[17] When Ignatius was twice attacked in Liverpool in November 1850, however, Bishop Brown complained to Rome and the Passionist general asked Ignatius for an explanation. Concern in England had already led him to write an explanatory letter to the *Tablet*, in which he explained that on one occasion he had simply been surrounded by a group of children and on the other accosted by two drunken men who had knocked off his hat. Having described his previous attempts to wear secular, clerical and religious dress, he said he was convinced it was wisest to indicate what he was by openly wearing his habit. He thought the English were 'straightforward people', who liked to be 'dealt with themselves in a sort of straightforward way.' He was sure they were less displeased at a priest or monk who showed himself for what he was than at one who disguised himself 'as if he had a mind to impose upon them', which everybody naturally disliked and particular-ly 'an Englishman'. Reminding his readers that he was a Passionist, he asked, 'Will any one, who reads the history of His Passion in the Gospels, tell me that I, a Passionist, ought not to rejoice at meeting with some insults, and mockery, and even blows from vulgar people and rabble, in the streets of London, or Liverpool, for the sake of my holy habit, after what He suffered for me in the streets of Jerusalem? I hope', he concluded, 'my Catholic Brethren will not be uneasy about me, but let me go on wearing my habit in peace.'[18] When, however, Lord Derby issued his proclamation in the queen's name on 15 June 1852, Father Ignatius Spencer obeyed so promptly that he travelled from Hampshire to London dressed as a sailor rather than break the law.[19]

It was Derby's decree that involved Elizabeth Prout in yet another major issue of the mid-nineteenth century: Catholic religious dress. Occasioned by Father Bernard [Smith?]'s holding a Marian procession from Coton to Weston Hall, a distance of several miles, the proclamation forbade Catholic rites or ceremonies to be held outside churches or houses, the wearing of religious dress in public and processions with religious banners.[20] Thus priests suddenly became liable for a £50 fine for attending a dying man in the street.[21] *The Morning Chronicle* warned Derby he was 'bidding for a few Orange cheers at the perilous price' of 'hinting' to wastrels to 'mob the Papists'.[22] The warning proved correct. The proclamation coincided with pre-election excitement, sectarian rivalry and Sunday-school processions to produce the Stockport riots.

Like all Sunday-school children, the Catholics in Stockport held a procession once a year, normally with banners and flags. Following Derby's proclamation, the parish priest of Saints Philip and James, Father Frith told his people that they would hold the procession as already planned but they would not have banners and he and Father Forster would wear ordinary clerical black. He cautioned them that if they were offered any provocation, they were not to retaliate. He had reason for warning them. Ill feeling had been growing between English and Irish cotton operatives in Stockport for a long time. Mill owners had reduced wages because of slack trade and a plentiful supply of labour. The consequent bitterness had led to public-house brawls, incited to some degree by Tory-supported Orangemen and the Protestant Association. The Tories held one of Stockport's two seats in parliament and had a majority on the local council but their popularity was waning. Like Russell in 1850, they were 'all for a religious cry'.[23] One of their Liberal opponents was already in parliament and had voted against the Ecclesiastical Titles Bill. The Tories therefore associated him with popery. Anti-Catholic and anti-Irish graffiti covered the walls. Orange placards urged Protestants not to elect a 'papist parliament'. The actual procession passed off peaceably on 27 June. That evening, however, some Orangemen arrived from Stalybridge. The next day, Monday, some members of the Stockport Protestant Association, founded in 1850, held a mock procession in derision of Catholic beliefs and burned an effigy of Father Forster. Most of the people ignored them but on Tuesday, 29 June, both English and Irish riff-raff were threatening violence to the other. Father Forster, therefore, warned the police and Stockport's small force of eleven men were stationed round the town. The riots began when two Irishmen were attacked by a troop of boys. An English mob then attacked the Irish in Rock Row and gutted twenty-four houses. More and more boys joined in on both sides 'eager for wanton mischief'.[24] In the street brawls that followed, the windows of St Peter's Protestant school and of some neighbouring houses were broken by stones. The English mob overcame the Irish, leaving about a hundred seriously wounded and one Irishman dead, accidentally killed by another Irishman. By 11.30 p.m., when soldiers arrived, the English had devastated the priest's house at Edgeley, the Catholic school and the church. They had even broken open the tabernacle and scattered the Hosts. In the meantime another English mob had devastated St Michael's Catholic church in Princess Street, again breaking open the tabernacle. Several special constables were seen taking part in the destruction and in the following days Orangemen from Manchester were seen departing with relics from the debris.[25] Two days after the arson in Stockport, a mob assembled round the Catholic church at nearby New Mills, where the priest was a Father Collins. Shouting '£20 for auld Collins' head' (£20 being the sum awarded in penal times for a priest's head), they added that the 'Popish Irish' would have the same fate 'if they would not quit the town'. Father Collins was in Stockport helping to clear up the mess. His housekeeper, who was alone in the house, managed to escape through a volley of stones and ran for the police. The mob were dispersed, promising to return to smash priest and church to pieces the following Friday. They kept their promise to return, 2,000 strong, and burned effigies of Father Collins and the Virgin Mary.[26] Catholics in Manchester were petrified. The civil authorities prepared for disturbances. Bishop Turner, on 1 July, had issued a plea to Catholics not to join or take part in any procession or meeting that might disturb the public peace either then or during the forthcoming elections. He exhorted them to avoid angry religious discussions and, instead, to cultivate and practise charitable feelings towards all and especially those who disagreed with them. In this way, he said, they would demonstrate that Catholicism condemned all resentment and illwill, urged the practice of meekness and forgiveness and supported the strict observance of the law. They would show that while they adhered with firmness and sincerity to their faith, they were also loyal and faithful subjects of the crown.[27] Stones continued to be thrown at convents and presbyteries throughout the country.[28] On 10 July, two days before the 'glorious twelfth', when a skirmish in Hulme between two drunken men turned into an affray between Catholics and Protestants, the Catholics were convinced the Orangemen would burn down St Wilfrid's.[29] As Elizabeth Prout's postulants arrived in Stocks Street, the Stockport saga continued. While Father Frith appealed through the Catholic newspapers for alms for his beggared parishioners, Catholics were outraged by a 'murder ball', as the *Lamp* described it, held near Edgeley itself to raise funds for the defence of the English rioters.[30] It was obvious to all that Catholic lives and property had suffered most of the damage. When, therefore, only three English rioters but eight Irish were sent to prison, the 15,000 Catholics in Stockport felt they had no protection by law. Catholic feeling throughout England was outraged.[31]

Father Gaudentius, who had been finalising his Rule as Derby issued his decree, delivered his manuscript at St Chad's three days before the Stockport procession. In prescribing the dress Elizabeth and her companions would wear, Gaudentius stated that, since they had to mix with secular persons of different religious persuasions, their dress need not be 'very remarkable'. They were all to wear the same, however, and these uniform 'external clothes', as decided by the Mother General, were to be of much the same quality as the 'deep mourning dress of the class of respectable working females', and without any 'sign of vanity or affectation'. The sisters were also to keep their heads covered as convenient and 'proper to their state of life'.[32] They were therefore to wear a simple, modest, black, recognisably religious dress, to which Father Gaudentius frequently referred as a habit and in which they were to be buried.[33]

According to the Rule, then, it was Elizabeth Prout's prerogative to design the uniform religious habit the sisters would wear from the first clothing ceremony on 21 November 1852. She gave them a black dress, possibly with a scapular, certainly with rosary beads, and a head-dress similar to that worn by the Benedictines, the Visitation Nuns and the Sisters of Mercy.[34] To circumvent Derby's 1852 decree, which at first forced the sisters to change into secular dress before going out and therefore caused a waste of time and inconvenience, she provided, for out of doors, a black hood and full-length mantle, which totally concealed the habit, even, apparently, according to the 1858 complaints, to the extent of trailing on the ground.[35]

It was not until May 1853 that Gaudentius criticised this habit. He then complained there was too much material in the sleeves. They smacked of vanity, he said.[36] In June 1853 he objected again, on the grounds that the habit was not 'as little different from other secular persons as possible'. He also criticised the head-dress. He prescribed a new one, like that worn by the Faithful Companions of Jesus in Salford, so that a sister could 'put on her head a black bonnet and black veil, with her cloak, and walk out to any place or to any distance without being remarked.' Then he prescribed a new habit. He suggested a black under-habit with sleeves; a simple, black habit, fastened as already with the Passionist leather girdle; and a simplified rosary. He also wanted to introduce a blue, waist-length cape, bearing a red cross, under which the professed sisters would have, in white, the letters 'JMJ'. This red, white and blue cape would be worn only inside the convents and schools in countries where the majority of people were against religious dress but in Catholic countries it would be worn out of doors as well.[37] At this time, therefore, he certainly wanted a most distinctive religious habit, which he envisaged would be worn publicly if possible. Elizabeth demurred about the red, white and blue cape but, on his instructions, she discussed his ideas with the other sisters at recreation.[38] They shared her views. She also consulted Canon Croskell, who, in turn, consulted Bishop Turner. He wanted to keep the veil and he did not want the colourful cape, although, like Elizabeth, he had no objection to a black one.[39] Elizabeth, therefore, devised a simple, straight underhabit, with sleeves, of a lighter material than the outer habit. She simplified the sleeves of the outer habit and made them detachable. She proposed to adopt the Passionist rosary beads as soon as she could obtain a supply.[40] Finally, she embroidered a black and white Badge, like the Passionist Sign, with a white cross and the letters 'JMJ', as Father Gaudentius had suggested, and on 14 July 1853, with an explanatory letter, posted it to the convent at Loughborough, where he was giving a retreat.[41] Unfortunately the letter was mislaid, so that Gaudentius did not receive it until August. He then expressed pleasure at the Badge and surprise that Bishop Turner did not like the cape. 'However', he wrote, 'I will give you the good example to yield immediately and entirely to his wishes. I am most ready to adopt what changes he may propose. I have no particular choice to this or that dress, but one which is plain, modest, convenient and religious. Moreover this Bishop is the first and true canonical superior of this community.'[42] On 11 August Canon Croskell wrote to Sister Clare Wilson, asking her to tell Elizabeth that Bishop Turner was definitely in favour of a veil.[43] In February 1854, after consulting Father Gaudentius, Elizabeth finally adopted a head-dress, with veil, and a black cape similar to those worn by Mother Seton's Sisters of Charity in North America.[44] Gaudentius was satisfied. In making his own revision of his Rule in 1855, he told Elizabeth categorically he did not wish to change the habit as then worn.[45]

His 1862 letter has to be read in its context and in the knowledge that Gaudentius tended to be a plagiarist. In 1859 and 1860 he gave retreats to the Daughters of the Sacred Heart of Mary who ran a girls' asylum in Cleveland City, Ohio.[46] From there on 3 August 1860 he wrote to Elizabeth, 'This admirable establishment is under the care of a community of ladies who have rules, make temporary vows, but they do not use any religious habit.' Forgetting he had forbidden his sisters ever to be called 'ladies', his carefully prepared clothing and profession ceremonies, the esteem he had inculcated for the 'holy habit', and his own 1852 legislation for perpetual and even solemn vows, he continued, 'I see in them realised the idea that for many years has been in my mind.'[47] This was the first time that Gaudentius had ever suggested he had not wanted a religious habit. As in the 1840s, however, he had copied the missionary techniques of the Rosminians, and in the 1850s had wanted Elizabeth to have an industrial school because he saw one elsewhere, so in the 1860s, faced with an industrial type of religious institute, he decided that that had been his idea all along. Described in his 1859 account in the Pittsburgh Mission and Retreat Book, as 'a pious and religious association', the Daughters of the Sacred Heart of Mary had been founded in France during the Revolution, when all religious orders had been suppressed. The members were intended to work in secular society, living in their own homes. Even after the Revolution, when some began to live in community, others continued to live with their families. Since their Rule had been approved by Rome but they made only private, temporary vows, they bore little resemblance to the institute Gaudentius had invited Elizabeth Prout to co-found in 1849 and had defined in his 1852-5 Rule.[48]

Father Gaudentius told Father Ignatius Spencer in 1862 that at that stage it would be 'more injurious than beneficial' to attempt to change the nature of the institute, which was, in any case, what 'Ecclesiastical Persons in high authority' wanted. Since he left Father Ignatius Spencer, with the approval of Bishop Turner and the Provincial, Father Ignatius Paoli, to do what he thought 'proper' in the revision of the Rule, Ignatius Spencer asked Elizabeth Prout to prescribe the dress she wanted. Mindful of the 1858 criticisms and closely following both Father Gaudentius' earlier strictures and Chapter V of the Passionist *Rule*, she prescribed in meticulous detail a female adaptation of the Passionist habit:

> The dress of the Sisters shall be a habit of coarse black cloth with a cape of the same material used daily on the shoulders reaching to the waist and elbows.... The habit shall be perfectly round at the extremities, and without any train or tail, girded at the waist with a black, leathern girdle with a small modest rosary beads attached at the left side.
>
> In the centre of the breast of the cape a white Cross shall be attached for novices. After the profession of the Sisters the initials of Jesus, Mary and Joseph in white letters on a small figure of a heart, to the top of which shall be added a small cross also white.
>
> The head shall be covered with a plain white undercap with black strings, over this a plain white muslin cap with pleated border, over that a veil pinned one inch from the edge of the border, a plain white veil for the Novices and a black one for the Professed. A small round white linen guimpe not more than two nails deep with a straight band an inch deep fastened behind. A black cloth cloak reaching to the knees with bonnet and veil shall be used when going out of the house.

'This cloak', she added, reminiscently of the practice in women's contemplative religious communities and thus emphasising the contemplative nature of her own order, 'shall also be used when attending Mass in the choir and on other occasions when required.'[49] In endorsing Elizabeth's section on dress, Father Ignatius Spencer inserted that the sisters would wear the Passionist Badge, although with the letters 'JMJ'. Thus he confirmed the Passionist identity of her order in the Rule itself.[50]

Although, however, Elizabeth Prout, as foundress, did not accept Father Gaudentius Rossi's 1862 desire for secular dress, his letter did help her to clarify the nature of her institute and to resolve how she might satisfy him, the Manchester clergy and the factory girls to whose interests she was devoted.

2. SEWING SCHOOLS

Apart from the startling personal attack on Elizabeth herself, the most surprising charge in the 1858 investigation was that 'the object of the institute's establishment had not been obtained, viz. a refuge for factory girls'. It was surprising because Father Gaudentius Rossi had never mentioned a refuge or home for factory girls. In January 1852 he had written to Father Croskell, 'You know that the principal object in view of this institution is to afford the opportunity to young females of the poorer classes to enter a religious life.'[51] Writing to Mother Winefride Lynch in 1866, eight years after the investigation, about which he knew practically nothing, he repeated that aim:

> The idea of the original institute was gradually formed by the frequent requests made to me and to other religious Missioners and Secular Priests by pious young girls from the middle classes of society downward to embrace a religious state of life. Many of these young girls appeared to me to have many good qualities for such [a] state of life.... Moreover I found many young girls very good and virtuous and anxious to consecrate themselves to God in a religious institute, who had not and could not [have] received much education, but were very skillful and very industrious about different kinds of needlework.

The mill girls were the last in his mind, for he continued, 'Among these I should also enumerate those who work[ed] in shops or stores and even in factories.'[52] Thus he had intended Elizabeth Prout to provide consecrated religious life for lower-class women who could not afford the dowries demanded by other orders. His first concern was for the more genteel needlewomen. Then he included shop girls, and only then factory girls. His original idea, therefore, included factory girls

as an extension rather than as a priority and he was offering them
religious life, not simply a refuge.

The first time that Father Gaudentius mentioned homes for factory
girls was in a letter to the third Mother General, Mary Margaret
Chambers in 1868, in reply to her account of the home founded in
Bolton in 1865. 'Your account of the success of the Sisters in Bolton
is very consoling', he wrote. 'The Home for the Factory Girls was one
of the first objects of the institute, which I hope will be carried on.'[53]
As Father Dominic had commented twenty-five years earlier, Gaudentius' memory was never very good.[54] In 1866, as he had acknowledged
to Winefride, it was failing on details. What was significant about his
1868 statement was that it indicated there was sufficient association in
his mind between his initial intention, the provision of religious life for
factory girls, and the home for factory girls mentioned by Mary
Margaret to lead him to give this apostolate the stamp of his approval.
He thus endorsed this particular inspiration of Elizabeth Prout as a
valid expression of the original charism of his congregation.

Elizabeth's inspiration sprang partly from Gaudentius' letter to
Ignatius Spencer in August 1862, in which Gaudentius claimed he had
wanted a mainly industrial institute, and partly from her desire to
answer the needs of the Catholic Church as expressed by the Manchester clergy in 1858. Even before she came to Manchester in 1849, there
was concern about female labour and especially about the factory
operatives.[55] Apart from the general hazards to health, the dangers
from unfenced machinery and the immorality said to be prevalent in
the mills, there was anxiety that, because of the long hours of work,
girls employed in the factories never learned to knit, sew, cook or
wash. Consequently, as wives and mothers they were so unacquainted
with the duties of a housewife that they did not even know how to care
for their children.[56] There was also concern about how factory
operatives spent any free time at their disposal. In 1847 parliament had
passed the Ten Hours Act, restricting adolescents and women in the
cotton mills to ten hours' work a day. Some mill owners, however,
such as the Pendleton firm of Ermen and Engels no less, tried to evade
the inconvenience of having to reduce men's hours too by working the
women and adolescents on shifts at any time between 5.30 a.m. and
8.30 p.m. and even arbitrarily changing the times from day to day.
Thus while nominally working ten hours a day, some women and
young persons between only thirteen and eighteen years of age were
virtually being worked thirteen hours each day. Government inspectors
were concerned not only at the injustice of their being overworked,
and without extra pay, but also at the danger 'to which [their]
morals... were exposed during the hours of forced idleness', when they
had to stay in or near the mill, waiting for their next shift.[57] The

government was also concerned about how the women and young people spent their free time when the act was observed, as, for the most part, it was in Manchester.[58] In 1849 Leonard Horner, factory inspector for the Manchester area, pointed out in his October *Report* that the purpose of the restriction was to give them 'time for their moral and social improvement'.[59] They were intended to have leisure for improving their homes, attending evening schools and enjoying 'healthful and reasonable recreations'.[60] Unfortunately there were few forms of innocent amusement available.[61] In the same year A.B. Reach described the problem in his letters to the *Morning Chronicle*. While it was true that thousands of working men and women attended the Monday night amateur concerts held in the Free Trade Hall, featuring selections from Handel, Rossini and other respectable musicians, others patronised the less prestigious roaring choruses of the music saloons of the London Road area, where boys and girls shouted, laughed and disappeared into taverns together. Even worse were the public houses of the Oldham Road district. Reach had to say that in no city had he ever witnessed a 'scene of more open, brutal, and general intemperance'. On the Sunday night he described, the street 'swarmed with drunken men and women; and with young mill girls and boys shouting, hallooing and romping with each other.' The public houses and gin shops were full. There were rows, fights and scuffles inside and out, while the whole street rang 'with shouting, screaming, and swearing, mingled with the jarring music of half-a-dozen bands'.[62] Elizabeth Prout, arriving in Manchester at the same time, was very prompt in seeing and answering this situation. According to Annals A/E, she and some friends gathered together young Catholic girls from the 'mills and workshops' to give them instructions in their Catholic faith, lessons in needlework and 'means of innocent recreation', thus keeping them away from 'dancing houses, low places of amusement and other dangerous occasions of sin'.[63]

During the next few years the factory girls' conditions did improve. The Factory Act of 1850 restricted the labour of women and young persons in textile factories to between 6 a.m. and 6 p.m. from Monday to Friday and 6 a.m. and 2 p.m. on Saturdays. Horner noted with pleasure that they then had 'at their disposal a reasonable portion of each day for the purposes of rest, domestic duties, mental improvement, and recreation'.[64] Canon Stowell was not so sanguine. In 1852 he asked for better housing and for more recreational facilities and intellectual enjoyments for the working classes, the repeal of the Beer Act and the suppression of dram shops and casinos, which he described as 'nurseries of crime'.[65] Nevertheless, although there were still evasions of the law, outside periods of depression the factory workers had constant employment, good wages and cheap food and clothing.[66] In 1859 Horner's pleasure was reiterated by Robert Baker, another factory inspector, who claimed that the physical condition of the future mothers of the working classes could be challenged to meet that of the mothers of any country. Free Saturday afternoons were an 'immense boon', he said, enabling husbands to carry home their week's wage in time for the market, so that husbands and wives could spend their money together and the women could provide 'every home comfort'.[67] With no-one to teach them domesticity, however, the women could hardly have improved their homes very much. Comparatively few attended evening classes. Only compulsory training in housewifery could really be effective. The opportunity to provide that arose with the Lancashire Cotton Famine, which also enabled Elizabeth Prout to return to Ashton-under-Lyne to help the factory girls.

With two parishes of about 2,000 each, there were still about 4,000 Catholics in Ashton in 1862, 'all poor and simple factory people who worked in the cotton mills of the town'.[68] It now had Turkish baths, a Mechanics' Institute and various recreational facilities, so that it was much improved from the town Elizabeth Prout had known in 1855. Unfortunately, even as early as January 1862 it already had a cotton mill to let, an ominous sign of the distress that would result from the American Civil War. No manufacturing town in Lancashire was so largely dependent on the cotton trade and so exclusively on American cotton as Ashton-under-Lyne.[69] By May 1862 destitution forced almost a quarter of its people to seek relief.[70] They presented a core of utter misery at the heart of the town as wives and children, as well as husbands, were out of work. By June 1862 only eleven of Ashton's thirty mills were working normally. In August a Central Executive Relief Committee, with Lord Derby as chairman and Sir James Kay Shuttleworth as vice-chairman, assumed responsibility for controlling most of the funds pouring into Lancashire from all over the country. Kay Shuttleworth devised a scheme of poor relief, which saved the unemployed from the workhouse and the labour test by providing them with outside payment in money and kind, in return for attending educational classes.[71] It was thus hoped, as far as the women were concerned, to improve the domestic habits of the female operatives.[72] From September, Ashton had several sewing classes, at which the mill girls could learn reading, writing and arithmetic in the mornings and sewing and knitting in the afternoons. At first they were gratuitously instructed by lady volunteers, but within a short time both instructors and pupils were paid.[73] With the weekly increase in distress greater in Ashton than anywhere else in the north of England, by 4 October it had 19,946 people on poor relief. Mill owners were asked to use their premises for adult classes. By 25 October the Borough Relief Committee were making liberal grants to the sewing schools, which then catered for 900 young women.[74] Since many of his parishioners were still looking for help, however, Father Cromblehome, St Ann's parish priest, wanted some Catholic teachers so that he also could provide classes.

Father Cromblehome was known as a 'busy, active little priest, who ran in and out with his cheerful, joyful face, and ready wit and humour to gather the assistance or the sympathy of his friends in the work he engaged in.'[75] He was accustomed to visiting the Passionist retreat in Sutton from time to time and in April 1861 Father Ignatius Spencer had given one of his 'little missions' in Ashton-under-Lyne.[76] Since his parishioners had been asking for Elizabeth Prout's sisters ever since they had left in 1857, Father Cromblehome seems to have raised the question of their helping with sewing classes with Father Ignatius, who immediately saw the possibilities for the future of the order. Ignatius spoke to both Elizabeth and Bishop Turner, who then wrote to tell Father Cromblehome to go to see Elizabeth.[77] Ignatius told Bishop Turner that the difficulty would be to get a man like Father Cromble-home 'full to the brim of energy to run in harness with a little woman like [Elizabeth] also brim full of energy and will, for fear they should both take to kicking and upset the coach'. When he went to see Elizabeth on 6 November, however, Father Cromblehome was 'greatly satisfied'. On the 7th, he, Elizabeth and Ignatius sat down together to make their arrangements. Father Cromblehome said he had a place ready and the relief committee would give 10s. a week to each nun who worked. Ignatius 'never saw two people fall in better with each other's ideas'.[78] As the annalist recorded, it was 'an opening that was hailed with great delight by the Sisters, being in exact accordance with the purpose and spirit of the institute.' Elizabeth could agree without hesitation because the project offered remuneration.[79]

·   Elizabeth had twenty-one sisters at that time but only three professed sisters she could send to Ashton. Since she wanted to send four, she asked Bishop Turner if Sister Mary Margaret Chambers' profession could be advanced six weeks to 21 November, so that she could go. Receiving her vows at the profession ceremony, Father Ignatius took the opportunity to remind the sisters of the work in hand: to form 'the habits and minds of young women... to virtue and industry'. Some, he said, might have religious vocations but most would become mothers. The sisters 'must teach them to be good ones and good wives, to sanctify their families and their homes.' As always he saw 'a bright and beautiful future' opened before them, although he knew there would be difficulties.[80] It was the difficulties rather than the brightness that greeted them on 22 November 1862, when Ignatius arrived in Ashton with two sisters to find Father Cromblehome had nothing ready for them 'but an empty house with beds without any covering'.[81] Noted for not knowing 'good food from bad', Father Cromblehome was 'thoroughly hard in his treatment of himself over food, clothing, shelter and labour' and he had 'no business habits'.[82] He had not thought of providing even the barest necessities. Ignatius' reaction was to remind the sisters to 'thank God, which they did'. When Elizabeth arrived with two more sisters the next day, to find that even then they did not have 'even sufficient clothing to cover them', her reaction was to take them back to Sutton.[83] Ignatius' pleas prevented her but in November's keen winds Elizabeth 'took a serious cold', one that seems to have precipitated the final stages of her tuberculosis in 1863 and finally sent her to the grave in January 1864.[84]

In November 1862 there were 1,200 women in sewing classes in Ashton.[85] The sisters took theirs in St Ann's hall.[86] While Elizabeth was there, she appointed Sister Mary Margaret to teach 200 of the unmarried women over 20 years of age.[87] They might have had some schooling as factory children but, like most mill girls, probably knew nothing about sewing. Many had never even held a needle.[88] They could buy the garments they made, at cost price, or they could sell them to outsiders.[89] Some of the stockings they knitted were distributed amongst the destitute.[90] Elizabeth asked Sister Mary Paul Taylor to take care of 180 married women and Sisters Mary Helen James and Agatha Mann to teach more than 200 girls under 20 years of age.[91] In return for attending these classes, girls between 13 and 15 were paid 2s. a week; women and girls above 15 years of age 3s. a week.[92] There was great competition to attend the sewing schools, so that, by coming to their rescue, Elizabeth Prout performed a very real service for almost 600 Catholic factory girls in Ashton, a substantial proportion of the female operatives in the town's schools.[93]

By the end of November, Father Ignatius could assure his provincial that Elizabeth's prospects in Ashton were 'very bright'. Father Cromblehome was determined to have a convent built. He was 'completely satisfied with the institute' and considered them the 'best type of nuns' for the purpose in hand.[94] In spite of Ignatius' optimism, however, the sisters carried out their apostolate in deep poverty and against a background of riots and popular Protestantism. Distress increased as shopkeepers lost their businesses, householders their rents and few could pay the rates.[95] Ashton was unusual in having two relief organisations: the General Relief Committee and the Borough Relief Committee. The former, however, discriminated against Catholics, so that Father Cromblehome had been forced to dissociate himself from it in October 1862 and had to rely for help on the Borough Relief Committee.[96] As there seemed no hope of the famine's ending, tension mounted in an Ashton still notoriously anti-Catholic, with a very strong Orange and ultra-Tory element, which pervaded the workplaces, churches and social life of the people as well as their politics.[97] In March 1863 Father Cromblehome invited the Redemptorists to give a parish mission. As a result, not a single Ashton Catholic took part that week in the Stalybridge bread riots which the ringleaders tried to extend to Ashton.[98] Father Cromblehome strove to control his flock as disturbances continued. While much had been said about the fortitude of the working classes, he told them, 'an attempt had been made to rob the Irish of their good name'. He knew that Englishmen were 'quite as earnest and active in the recent disturbances as were the Irish, only they had the good fortune to get out of the way.' Warning his parishioners that their distress had still not come to an end, he advised them 'to let the English get into the scrape next time and to keep out themselves'. When making appeals to the south of England for victims of the Cotton Famine, he said, the authorities wanted to portray the Lancashire workers as deserving, law-abiding citizens and so they said it was the Irish who were causing the riots. They forgot, said Father Cromblehome, 'that an English mob had visited St Ann's Catholic school but were sent out by the quiet Irish, without any of them being induced to join the mob.' He knew, he said, that the Irish in Ashton were 'perfectly peaceful'. He felt confident they would 'act up to their sacred principles and maintain their self-respect and manliness.'[99] As 1863 advanced into its winter months, he tried to occupy his par-ishioners in a series of public lectures he gave on Sunday evenings on various points of Catholic belief and with public examinations of St Ann's infants', girls' and boys' schools.[100]

Elizabeth Prout's sisters, in the meantime, 'gave complete satisfaction to all parties, whether Catholic or Protestant'.[101] Father Ignatius brought Bishop Turner to see them in December 1862.[102] The mayor 'visited the schools frequently, and expressed his approval very warmly, saying that the conduct and work of the girls attending them were highly superior to those of any attending the other sewing schools in town'.[103] 'Ladies and gentlemen' and clergymen of other denomina-tions frequently visited them, praising 'very highly the manner in which they were conducted and the conduct of the women and girls'.[104] Sewing classes in general were proving so successful that the Reverend A. Munro, addressing the Manchester Statistical Society in March 1863, recommended that girls and young women should also be sent in groups to public wash-houses and cooking establishments. As most of them could read already, he said, they should be instructed in health and nursing, 'in self government, in the cardinal virtues and minor morals'. Thus they would be better prepared to resume their work, or to become mothers of families, enter domestic service or emigrate. 'Can nothing be done', he asked, 'to raise them out of the state of mere appendages to our mechanisms, up to the proper rank of women?'[105] In Ashton the mayor 'expressed a wish that the Sisters, when their numbers admitted of it, should take charge of a department in the hospital'.[106] In endorsing that wish, Elizabeth Prout enlarged the apostolate of her congregation to embrace nursing and medical care. Her more immediate concern, however, was to open a home for factory girls.

3. HOMES FOR FACTORY GIRLS

Elizabeth Prout had wanted to found a refuge for factory girls since the Manchester clergy had expressed the urgency in 1858. At that time, however, she had had no financial resources, so that she could not hope to answer the need until her own situation improved or an opportunity presented itself. The opportunity seemed to have come in 1862-3, when she sent sisters back to Ashton-under-Lyne. Fortuitously, at exactly the same time she needed to revise Father Gaudentius Rossi's Rule. Although there is no mention of it in the Congregation's records, it seems likely that, when Father Ignatius asked Rome in 1857 for approbation of the Rule, the Holy See requested clarification on why the congregation was founded. Gaudentius had limited its specific object to the 'memory' of the Holy Family. That was significant in defining its contemplative nature but it did not explain its active apostolate. Although his Rule had provided for workrooms, parish visitation, schools, retreats and the instruction of converts, it had not defined any occupation as the distinctive active apostolate of the institute. It therefore fell to Elizabeth and Ignatius to decide on the primary active work of her institute. They defined it as the provision of homes or refuges for female operatives. In the type of home they offered they not only answered the complaint of the Manchester clergy at the 1858 investigation but also responded to Gaudentius' 1862 comments on the nature of the institute.

There was no doubt of the need for homes for factory girls. Wages in the mills made girls of thirteen so independent of their parents that they frequently left home to live in lodgings. It was only too easy for such girls to fall into bad company, especially as some manufacturers' sons made a sport of going into the mills, selecting the prettiest and most modest-looking girls and taking them off to houses they kept for that purpose.[107] In 1839 women in Ashton's Female Political Union had expressed their bitter resentment against the 'haughty and iniquitous capitalists' who thus regarded their daughters 'as only created to satisfy [their] wicked desires'.[108] Conditions inside the over-heated mills, too, made teenage girls and boys crave for drink and excitement with morally disastrous results. Prostitution was so widespread in Ancoats in the 1860s that the area was regarded as a 'wilderness of corruption'.[109] There was concern not only about the fate of such girls themselves but of the peril to future generations if this moral corruption became perpetuated as a hereditary curse.[110]

The need for a home for Catholic mill girls was particularly pressing in the 1850s, because so many were Irish immigrants, forced to live in the ill-reputed common mixed lodging houses and subject to petty persecution on account of both their religion and their race.[111] As Bishop Ullathorne told Russell in 1850, the anti-Catholic hatred he had unleashed had not affected the hierarchy nearly so much as the poor Catholic working classes.[112] As a priest said about this time, 'Every class, order and rank of Catholics in these islands... is brought into situations of difficulty, because into practical relations of some kind or other with the great non-Catholic majority; and is thwarted, or embarrassed, or tempted, or tried, in consequence, according to his characteristic abilities.'[113] As the Manchester clergy pointed out in 1858, the mill girls were particularly vulnerable. In revising Father Gaudentius Rossi's Rule in 1862-3, therefore, Elizabeth Prout and Father Ignatius Spencer defined the provision of homes for factory girls as the institute's 'principal work of active charity'. 'What first inspired the thought of the formation of the institute', they wrote, was 'the deplorable condition of great numbers of Catholic girls employed in the factories in the great towns of England', continually exposed 'to great temptations both against their faith and their virtue, without any persons being particularly devoted to assist their pastors in watching over them.' According to their means and opportunities, therefore, the sisters would open 'houses of refuge or homes for young women of this class in or close upon the outskirts of large factory towns.' They would provide 'lodging and food', on 'moderate terms', for 'such young women as would otherwise have to live in common mixed lodging houses' but who would prefer, 'on condition of complying with some degree of restraint and good discipline', to be 'treated with motherly affection', be provided for 'simply yet with comfort and cleanliness' and be given good instruction in religion, in the 'duties of domestic life' and as far as possible in the first elements of education.[114]

As thus expressed, Elizabeth Prout's homes might not appear any great innovation. There were already homes for milliners, seamstresses, shop assistants, flower sellers and soldiers, as well as children's orphanages, Magdalene homes and reformatories.[115] As early as 1843 the Good Shepherd Sisters had had a Magdalene asylum at Hammersmith and were planning a second one at Much Woolton near Liverpool.[116] In 1851 a Catholic lodging house, or 'Working Man's Institution', as it was called, was opened in Tooley Street, London, while at the same time funds were being raised for a similar institution for fifty poor Catholic families in King William Street.[117] In 1852 a correspondent in the *Manchester Guardian* suggested that District Homes should be established for domestic servants to rescue them from prostitution, the 'crying evil' of the day.[118] About 1858 Louisa Twining established an Industrial Home for Young Women, where she trained girls from workhouses for domestic service and other occupations.[119] Courtauld's silk mills in Essex even had a factory home, a boarding house designed to improve the morals of their young women workers.[120] Elizabeth Prout's homes, however, were different from all of these.

They were different because she was offering the girls not simply a refuge, nor even just a home, valuable as those were. Following Father Gaudentius Rossi's 1862 claim that he had intended his institute 'to receive girls of industrious habits', wearing 'an ordinary kind of dress', Elizabeth offered the factory girls a type of religious life, a modified version of her congregation. They would wear secular dress, continue to work in the mills and retain their wages, while living a religiously orientated community life, in the same house as the sisters, although not within the enclosure and without binding themselves by vows to a lifelong commitment to monastic observance. Thus although she was adopting a form of protection that sundry bodies already offered to people at risk, in her own contemplative fashion she transformed it into something entirely different: a religious association, a type of secular institute, such as Father Gaudentius had described in 1862 but without the obligation of even temporary vows or apostolic responsibilities. At the same time she responded to the Manchester clergy's complaint by offering factory girls a refuge from the common mixed lodging houses and a home that would help them to preserve their virtue.

Elizabeth hoped to found her first home in Ashton-under-Lyne, where the sisters' work was so much appreciated. Father Cromblehome was ready to build them 'a large home that they might carry out the principal work of [the] order to the full extent'.[121] Since there was a tract of land close to the church and school, he and Father Ignatius Spencer agreed that the latter should ask Lord Stamford to donate it for that purpose. Lord Stamford, however, who patronised Ashton's anti-Catholic General Relief Committee, declined.[122] Elizabeth therefore did not achieve her object in Ashton but she continued to hope it would become possible to replace her Levenshulme convent with a home for factory girls in one of Lancashire's industrial towns.

In the event, she did not live to see her ambition realised but, immediately after her death in early 1864, her successor, Mother Winefride Lynch, negotiated for a foundation where she could open a home for factory girls in Bolton.[123] It was a particularly suitable place, because 'some unfortunate females' there, who were 'thrown out of employment' when the cotton famine started, had 'thereby become outcasts of society', so that the town had more 'youthful prostitutes' than it had known for twenty-five years.[124] As usual, 'Father Ignatius Spencer entered into all and... furthered and carried it out.'[125] Appealing to Catholics to support Mother Winefride's raffle to raise the necessary funds, he described the proposed home for factory girls as the most 'thoroughly practical' work of charity currently advanced 'to claim public help' and one 'pregnant with results, present and future.' The sisters, he said, would protect the girls against the dangers of their situation. They would train them in sewing, cooking and all domestic work. They would prepare them for the proper fulfilment of their later duties, whether as servants or wives and mothers. They would be taught what a home should be in cleanliness, order and regularity; how to economise, to be thrifty and to be punctual. They would have companions of approved virtue and recreations and amusements that would elevate rather than demoralise them. The blessing of such a home would spread to society at large and to 'thousands yet unborn' whose lives and future happiness would be influenced by the mothers who had had the sisters' training and care.[126]

Although Ignatius saw the opening of the Bolton convent on 3 August 1864, he did not live to see the first home, as he died on 1 October 1864. It was opened in November 1865. As described by Father Salvian Nardocci, however,

> The way of acting with the poor girls was simple enough. Any honest girl who had no home or was living in lodging houses away from parents etc. would go to the convent where she would have a good supper, and every evening after her day's work in the factory would be taught sewing, knitting, housekeeping, reading, writing, and would have a comfortable bed for the night. The girls, on their part, would, of course, have to pay about 1s. a day to defray the expenses of the food, bed, fire etc.[127]

Spiritually, too, it was a success. 'I found these poor factory girls wonderfully well instructed and extremely good', Father Salvian recorded after visiting them in 1868.[128]

While not excluding factory girls from the order itself, by providing homes Elizabeth had offered them the kind of religious life the majority of them wanted. She had brought a prayerful, devout lifestyle within their reach. Vocations to consecrated religious life, as experience had shown, would be comparatively rare. As Paul of the Cross had always stressed, however, and as Father Ignatius Spencer had said to Bishop Turner in 1854, it was not necessary for women to become nuns in order to aim at Christian perfection.[129] Elizabeth Prout provided a home in which they could have the protection, companion-

ship and devotional life of a religious community, while remaining
independent, wearing secular dress, keeping their wages and leaving
whenever they liked, to become better wives and mothers for having
been there. As described by one of the annalists about seventy-five
years later, young girls and women employed in the cotton mills and
workshops could board in the homes at a nominal cost. Many girls,
saved from 'a life of degradation and peril', were trained to become
'respectable mothers and wives and law-abiding citizens'. The 'Home',
as it was always called, was meant to be a home in its truest sense.
There was no rigid discipline other than what would be expected 'in
a good respectable family'. When the girls came home from work,
they were given a good substantial meal. In the evenings they changed
their working clothes for more suitable wear and could spend the rest
of the time as they liked. They were encouraged to attend evening
classes in 'good plain needlework and also that of a more pleasing
kind'. Thrift was strongly inculcated, neatness in dress insisted upon
and help was given in the choice of material. Any extravagance was
'very strongly discouraged'. The girls were 'gently and kindly
admonished for rudeness, vulgarity and rough behaviour' and it was
'remarkable and gratifying', said the annalist, 'to see the daily
improvement in refinement and womanly conduct', particularly as
these girls had been 'mostly brought up in childhood by indolent and
drunken parents'. Some had even lived in houses of 'evil repute'. After
being received into these homes and 'daily receiving the refined and
careful supervision of the Sisters', they showed plainly what good had
been done for 'these poor girls who otherwise would have been
ruined'. Even when the girls were out of work on account of strikes
and could not pay for their keep, the sisters made no alteration in
either the quality or quantity of food and the girls were saved the
'humiliation of attending soup-kitchens, or begging food tickets etc.,
as so many of their fellow-workers were unfortunately obliged to do'.
All this was done, said the annalist, because the sisters looked upon the
girls as 'beloved daughters entrusted to their care by Jesus Christ
Himself'. In times of stress and hardship, therefore, it was the sisters,
taking the place of mothers, who must bear the burden rather than the
girls themselves.[130] What this particular account omitted to mention,
however, was that Elizabeth Prout's homes also offered the girls a
form of religious life. In thus establishing what was tantamount to a
lay association, she extended to its members her congregation's
spirituality, which in her 1863 revision of the Rule she definitively
identified as Paulacrucian.

4. THE PASSIONIST REVISION OF THE RULE

It was essential that in revising the Rule, Father Ignatius Spencer and Elizabeth Prout should preserve continuity in the congregation. They were not founding a new religious order in 1862-3. They were simply reformulating an existing Rule to satisfy requirements in Rome. The institute they were describing was the congregation founded by Elizabeth Prout in co-operation with Fathers Robert Croskell and Gaudentius Rossi, with Father Ignatius Spencer's permission and Bishop Turner's approval. It was providential that an ulcerous ankle prevented Ignatius from giving missions in October 1862 and incapacitated him in St Anne's Retreat, Sutton.[131] Equally providentially, his role in effecting the second Ashton foundation confirmed the congregation's place in the Passionist mission to England at precisely the time when its final charism had to be defined. Most remarkably, Father Ignatius' response to Father Cromblehome's request for a Passionist priest to go to Ashton until Christmas 1862 to prepare a hundred children for First Communion meant that, as provincial consultor and with the permission of the provincial, he himself took the sisters to Ashton and stayed there, as he noted, at exactly the time of the year that Paul of the Cross had written his *Rule* in 1720. 'It looks like a long time to spend for Ashton only', he wrote to the provincial, 'but if your Paternity is pleased that I should set to work reducing the nuns' rules into form, it is not too long. If I took that in hand, I should make it as near as I could a retreat for that purpose; trying to gain light for it through Blessed Paul, and by the merits of his forty days at Alessandria.'[132] Thus with the permission of the highest Passionist superior in England, Father Ignatius Spencer left Sutton for Ashton on 22 November 1862, the anniversary of Paul's clothing in the Passionist habit and of his retiring into his retreat at Castellazzo, during which he wrote the Passionist *Rule*.[133] Elizabeth Prout arrived in Ashton the following day and stayed five days to make sure her sisters were settled. During that time, she and Ignatius mulled over Gaudentius' Rule together and thoroughly discussed their revision.[134]

In making the revision, Elizabeth Prout knew exactly what she wanted. In view of the Paulacrucian spirituality she had imbibed in Stone and that Gaudentius himself had given to the order, it was unthinkable that the 'sainted founder' mentioned by Rome could be other than Blessed Paul of the Cross, founder of the Passionist Congregation and patron of her own. The foundation of her order had taken place during the final preparations for and the excitement that followed the beatification of Paul of the Cross in 1853. She had already taken as much as she lawfully could of the Passionist habit and as much as she dared of even the Passionist Sign: the white cross above the white heart; the three nails within the heart; and all on a

black background. Even the letters 'JMJ' had been frequently used by
Paul of the Cross.[135] Now, in 1862, she immediately asked for a copy
of the *Rule* he had written for the Passionist enclosed nuns he had
founded in Tarquinia in 1771-2 and which she knew Father Leonard
Fryer was translating into English. Father Ignatius Spencer proposed
to 'draw up a short simple form of a rule, which would embody the
original idea of the institute and suit its present position.' Since he did
not think Father Leonard would have finished his translation in the
time at their disposal, he told the provincial that if he would send him
an Italian copy of the Passionist nuns' *Rule*, he would accommodate
the Passionist spirit to the 'distinct objects' of Elizabeth's institute. He
would send the provincial a copy of his draft for his comments and
corrections and then, if Elizabeth and the sisters accepted it, he would
seek Bishop Turner's approval. He understood he could vouch for
Father Gaudentius, although if time permitted he would send a copy
out to North America for his approval too.[136]

There is no further evidence that Elizabeth used the Passionist nuns'
Rule. She certainly followed that of the Passionist Fathers and
Brothers. Utilising some disused prospectuses of her Parr Hall
boarding school, she scribbled down in pencil more than twenty-nine
pages of sections of the Passionist *Rule* she wished to integrate into the
Holy Family Rule.[137] Thus she deliberately sought to give her institute
a Passionist Rule as clearly as she had already given it a Passionist
spirit; the habit and Sign, as far as she could; and the spiritual
guidance of the Passionist Fathers in Confession, retreats, clothings
and professions and, most recently, in transferring the novitiate to the
Passionist environment of Sutton.[138] Although her sisters did not use
the title until after her death and were not fully aggregated to the
Passionist Congregation until 1874-5, Elizabeth Prout was most truly
the foundress of the Sisters of the Cross and Passion of Jesus Christ.[139]

At the same time, to preserve continuity in the congregation, she
carefully kept its devotion to the Holy Family. Like Father Gaudentius
she placed the contemplative nature of the order first. In a synopsis of
his prescriptions on devotions to Jesus, Mary and Joseph, which he
had culled from the Passionist *Rule*, she emphasised that derivation,
the contemplative charism of the institute and its Tridentine devotions.
In prescribing subjects for meditation, she again preserved continuity
with devotion to the Holy Family, while giving a definite Passionist
orientation to the contemplative life of her congregation. 'Let the
Meditations generally', she wrote, copying the Passionist *Rule*
verbatim, 'be about the Divine attributes and perfections, also about
the mysteries of the Life, Passion and Death of Our Lord Jesus Christ,
from which all religious perfection and sanctity takes its rule and
increase and also', she added, 'about the hidden and laborious life of

the Holy Family in the Cottage of Nazareth."[140] Like Father Gaudentius and in keeping with her institute's Paulacrucian spirituality she
emphasised devotion to the Holy Eucharist and to the Virgin Mary.[141]
To ensure perfect continuity in the future congregation with the spirit
and practice of the Rule the sisters had observed during the previous
ten years, she made some of Gaudentius' more detailed prescriptions
into a chapter on the training of novices. At the same time, to ensure
her novices had a Passionist training, *mutatis mutandis* she took
directly from the *Rule* of Paul of the Cross:

> Let her... be proved in the practice of acts of humiliation. Let her
> wash the dishes, serve in the kitchen, sweep the house, and give
> other proofs of Christian submission and patience. For this end she
> shall be publicly reprehended, particularly in the refectory, and shall
> sometimes eat upon the ground and perform other humiliating and
> mortifying works ordered by superiors, from which it may be clearly
> known whether she has a real love of being despised; whether she be
> dead to herself and the world, in order to live only to God, in God,
> and through God, willingly hiding her life in Jesus Christ, Who, for
> our sakes, chose to become the reproach of men, and the outcast of
> the people, giving the most faultless example of all virtues. Let no
> regard be had of any person, whatever may be her condition. Let one
> of noble family be proved by a more strict trial; in such manner,
> however, that humble charity and impartial prudence be never
> wanting.[142]

Similarly, combining the 'memory' of the Holy Family with the
Passionist *Rule* on professions, she again gave both her Rule and the
profession ceremony a very distinct Passionist orientation:

> According to the distinguishing custom of the Institute, the cross is
> placed on her shoulders, a crown of thorns on her head, and the Sign
> displaying the venerable names of Jesus, Mary and Joseph is attached
> to her breast, after which the Blessed Sacrament shall be held by the
> priest whilst the novice shall make her vows of Obedience, Voluntary
> Poverty and Chastity; she shall also promise that to the utmost of her
> power, she will promote among the faithful a grateful remembrance
> of and a devotion to the Holy Family in the Cottage at Nazareth.[143]

An unfinished sentence indicates that not all Elizabeth's notes have
survived. There are sufficient, however, to show in what direction she
was pointing her infant congregation. The aggregation of the institute
to the Passionist Congregation, initiated by the Passionist general on
his first visit to England shortly after her death in 1864 and completed
in 1875, when each sister received the full Passionist Sign, was simply
the fulfilment of the work she had deliberately begun, with the

approval and co-operation of Father Ignatius Spencer, of the Passionist Provincial, Father Ignatius Paoli and of Bishop William Turner of Salford. Ultimately it was that Passionist identity that made Elizabeth's order acceptable to the Manchester clergy and gave it its unique position amongst the religious congregations of the Catholic Church. In 1862-3, however, she could not be allowed to take the Passionist *Rule* as directly as she wished, because, like Father Gaudentius in 1852, she would have needed the permission of the Passionist general. In 1874 the Passionist general chapter gave her congregation the *Rule* she had wanted in 1862, but at that time it was mainly Father Ignatius Spencer's 'short simple form of a rule', influenced by Elizabeth's contributions, that comprised the version presented to Rome.

Ignatius did not make the progress he had anticipated when he went to Ashton in November 1862, supposedly to rest his ulcerous ankle, instruct the children and revise the Rule. In arranging that schedule with his provincial, he had referred to the austerities Paul of the Cross had practised as he wrote his *Rule* in his solitary cell in 1720. Ignatius' sojourn in Ashton was no less penitential, although his penances sprang more from the Cotton Famine than from elected fasting. No sooner had Elizabeth returned to Sutton than his ulcer closed. Realising that Father Cromblehome was kept so occupied with famine relief that he had no time to visit the sick, throughout November and December Father Ignatius, at sixty-two years of age, went out early each morning to take the Sacraments to the sick and dying. Every evening, except Sundays, he sat in the cold church, from 5.00 to 11.00, 'hearing the Confessions of a great lot of men and women who [had] been very careless'.[144] 'I never had such work in this way in all my thirty years', he told the provincial. 'The sickness is just what might have been expected from the people having all been short of food and still more short of clothing and bedding. Feverish cold. I read the burial service one afternoon last week over three children in succession.'[145] He obviously had little time to continue the revision of the Rule. At the end of December, he went to Leicestershire to try to ask Lord Stamford for land for a convent and a home for factory girls.[146] From January 1863 he returned to giving missions. It was therefore not until April 1863 that, returned to Sutton, he was able to finalise his revision. After discussing it with Elizabeth, on Easter Monday, 6 April 1863 he spent 'all day at the convent making a new copy of the rules'.[147] 'I am much pleased at the way in which we have got on together in the revision of the rule', he wrote to Elizabeth on 11 April, as he waited for a train en route for Rome.[148]

Their final revision followed the Paulacrucian spirituality of Father Gaudentius Rossi's Rule in inculcating the 'memory' of the Holy Family and in balancing the active and contemplative characteristics of the order. Their emphasis on the Holy Family was not restricted to the Childhood of Christ. Like Paul of the Cross and as already emphasised by Gaudentius in his Rule, they directed the devotion to Christ the Redeemer, Christ on the Cross, aided towards that salvific mission by Mary and Joseph. They stressed the importance of mental prayer, as Father Gaudentius had done unceasingly. They also confirmed all the spiritual exercises already practised by the sisters, which Gaudentius himself owed mainly to the Passionist Rule: silence; an hour's mental prayer; daily attendance at Mass; frequent reception of the Eucharist; recitation of the Little Office of the Blessed Virgin Mary; two daily examinations of conscience; weekly Confession; the Rosary, the Way of the Cross; annual eight-day retreats; and other devotions and practices. Acting on Gaudentius' instructions in his letter of 6 August 1862 and on his emphasis in previous letters to Elizabeth that the principal object of the institute was manual work, not teaching, they finally gave such prominence to the industrial nature of the order that they scarcely mentioned schools. Education was nevertheless given its place in the apostolate: 'They shall take charge of schools, provided they have subjects qualified for it.' Out of deference for Gaudentius' repeated opinions, they added: 'Let it be remembered on this point that they should rather choose to be employed among the poorest and most neglected class of children in day schools and in what are termed industrial schools.' Equally consistently with Gaudentius' expressed views, they also added: 'The sisters however are not forbidden by virtue of this rule to receive children of a higher class as boarders, if specially authorised to do so by the Bishop.'[149] Thus, like Gaudentius' Rule, the revision emphasised the order's particular mission to the poorest but left an opening for an apostolate amongst the materially better endowed if circumstances demanded it. As well as continuing parish visitation and other parochial work, in an extension of Gaudentius' legislation that secular ladies could be admitted to the sisters' retreats, Ignatius and Elizabeth, with another Paulacrucian touch, widened this apostolate to providing retreats in the convent specifically for women who might wish to avail of them. They carefully safeguarded those characteristics of the congregation that offered religious life to the lower classes. Postulants would not require a dowry, not even, if the financial state of the order permitted it, an admission fee. There would be no distinction of choir and laysisters. Members must work, for the order must be self-supporting, but they could do any kind of work compatible with the spirit of the institute, according to their health and constitution, their previous habits and their education. Postulants possessed of fortunes could be received only on condition that they were willing to apply themselves to remunerative manual work or teaching, in order to enable others to enter without any fees.

Thus the revision constantly emphasised that the order existed for the benefit of the poor, not merely in the sense of going out to work amongst the poor but in providing consecrated religious life for them. Following Gaudentius' Rule, too, the revised Rule stressed that sisters who did not go out to work would be engaged in the contemplative type of industry in the workroom. The revision retained Gaudentius' Passionist customs on their conduct outside the convent. His penitential prescriptions, however, were slightly modified. The government of the institute followed that of the Passionist Congregation. What finally emerged, therefore, was a refined edition of the Gaudentian Rule, which, stripped of its devotional extravaganza, revealed a conspicuous similarity to the Paulacrucian *Rule* that Father Gaudentius, as a Passionist, had himself followed and by which he had been inspired. In its revised, as in its original form, his Rule was an adaptation of the Passionist *Rule*, suited to lower-class women in nineteenth-century industrial England. It offered them contemplative religious life while simultaneously providing them with an active apostolate suited to their feminine gifts and the exigencies of the time.

On 10 April 1863 Father Ignatius Spencer took the revised Rule to Bishop Turner. He found Canon Benoit with him and they all spent about three hours examining it. Both Bishop Turner and Canon Benoit were enthusiastic, except that Canon Benoit, as in 1858, objected to its provision for boarding schools. Both he and the bishop wanted the institute to 'take up the poorest classes and cultivate and improve them'. Canon Benoit was afraid that if an order catered for rich and poor, the poor might be neglected for the rich. Bishop Turner 'wanted everything like formality and dignity to be got rid of'. Both, however, said Ignatius, were 'most interested in everything'. Next he took the Rule to Levenshulme and to Ashton to read it to the sisters. In both places they 'were well satisfied' with it. 'I must leave you to go on with your work about them all, meeting difficulties gallantly, as indeed you have done', he wrote to Elizabeth as he left for London, Rome and the general chapter.[150] When he arrived there he received a 'most handsome testimonial for the Institute' from Bishop Turner.[151]

By then Elizabeth's tuberculosis was reaching full development, as the 'serious cold' she had caught in Ashton-under-Lyne kept its grip on her frail constitution. She had little chance to recover, for Sutton too lay in the throes of the poverty that emanated from the Cotton Famine. At the beginning of November 1862 about 600 paupers had been relieved in the Prescot poor law union, which included Sutton, and more than 1,100 in the St Helens union.[152] In April 1863 about 625 were relieved in the Prescot union and more than 1,400 in the St Helens union.[153] Since the Passionists themselves normally subsisted principally on the alms of Catholics, they could not meet both their daily current expenses and 'the increasing number of poor' that daily thronged to their doors. 'Amongst the thousands of poor suffering people in this impoverished population,' one of them wrote at this time, 'are to be found an almost incredible number of our former constant and devoted benefactors and we now relieve at the door, those very persons who in 1860 and 1861 were contributors to our support.'[154] Sutton did not have a cotton industry, nor did St Helens, and the impoverishment mentioned was not sufficiently widespread to make headlines in the local papers. There was, however, mention of poverty in the area and of financial difficulties on account of the trade depression resulting from the American Civil War.[155] An Irishwoman in Widnes was charged with stealing a loaf and an eleven-year-old girl with stealing clothing from a pawnshop and pawning it in another shop.[156] A number of farmers were selling out because of chemical destruction.[157] There were bankruptcies in the area, as all over the country.[158] There were collections for the cotton operatives in the neighbouring towns, especially in nearby Wigan, and in 1863 a rate-in-aid was introduced which, by raising local rates, may have induced lower wages and redundancies, especially in the watchmaking domestic industry, which was already suffering from foreign competition.[159] Possibly many of the poor who clamoured round the monastery door, and undoubtedly at the convent door too, were paupers from the distressed cotton towns who had left the Sutton area for the good wages in the textile industry but had now returned. No matter what the reasons for the dire poverty in Sutton, however, in such circumstances there could have been few fees' being paid in school, so that the sisters, like the Passionists, would have found themselves in dire necessity. Elizabeth Prout would have made every sacrifice to succour the poor. As Father Ignatius Spencer's ulcer reopened as a result of his exertions in Ashton, so her health deteriorated in Sutton.[160] In April 1863 the doctor said that only a change of climate, that Victorian panacea, could save her.[161] Like a number of Passionists who had been in the same position, she was offered a visit to France, possibly by Mr and Mrs Smith of Sutton.[162] When Ignatius asked Bishop Turner's permission, he readily gave it.[163] Elizabeth left England for Paris on 20 May 1863.[164] On her return on 3 June, she discovered John Smith was seriously ill. Despite her own serious condition, she nursed him until his death on 10 June. Then she nursed Mrs Smith for another ten days, after which she took her to Levenshulme, where the air was fresher than in polluted Sutton.[165] She was therefore in Levenshulme when she received a message from Father Ignatius Spencer, delivered through a letter to his friend, Mrs Mackay, that their affairs were going on well in Rome.[166]

Arrived in Rome on 22 April 1863, Father Ignatius Spencer had had the Rule translated into Italian and then, on 28 April, had presented it to Cardinal Barnabò, Secretary of *Propaganda Fide*. On 15 May the cardinal had returned it 'with great approbation'.[167] He told Ignatius he had read it carefully and thought the object of the institute excellent. He asked for two corrections, which Ignatius made to his satisfaction. The cardinal also told him that the institute must work well for a few years and then, when it had four or six houses, it would have no difficulty in securing papal approbation. It could apply to the pope immediately for indulgences on certain feastdays and could be canonically established by a bishop. Ignatius therefore made out a petition for indulgences and presented it to Pius IX when he and Father Ignatius Paoli had an audience with him on 27 May. Elizabeth Prout's petition was thus presented to the pope himself by the highest Passionist authorities in England, Father Ignatius Paoli, the provincial and Father Ignatius Spencer, provincial consultor. The Passionist Congregation owned Elizabeth Prout as its protege. Pius IX kept the petition to consult Cardinal Barnabò about it. Significantly for their place as an integral part of Elizabeth's congregation, Ignatius included the factory girls in the petition, for translated it read:

> Most Holy Father, Sister Mary Joseph of Jesus (Prout) Superior of the new Institute of the Sisters of the Holy Family destined especially for the care of the girls employed in the factories, already approved with simple vows and suitable rules by their Bishop of the Diocese of Salford, in England, My Lord Turner, prostrate at the feet of Your Holiness, humbly implores You with her daughters to deign to grant the indulgences on the days here below mentioned, and that they may be obtained, if Your Holiness approves, also by the girls and women, who will have been at least six months under the care of the sisters, observing in a praiseworthy manner, the rules approved for their conduct by the Bishop, Superior of the house.[168]

On Saturday, 13 June 1863 when Cardinal Barnabò went, as usual on Saturdays, to Saints John and Paul's Passionist retreat, he returned the approved petition directly to Father Ignatius Spencer. Thus Ignatius, doyen of the English sons of Paul of the Cross and representing Elizabeth Prout, received the first papal approval of her congregation in the very place where Paul of the Cross had lived, had had his vision of his children in England, had died and was enshrined. Ignatius wrote to tell Elizabeth the good news. He told her the petition had been made in her name, and 'so', he wrote, 'you may consider yourself as having been prostrate at the feet of His Holiness and having got all you asked for'. He told her to show his letter to Bishop Turner.[169]

When Elizabeth received this letter on 21 June 1863, she 'was completely beside herself with joy'. After reading it to the Levenshulme community, who were also 'greatly rejoiced', she sent it to Bishop Turner.[170] He replied, with his congratulations, that as soon as he was 'officially informed by Rome' he would have 'much pleasure in granting the Indulgences etc.'[171]

The revised Rule, approved by Rome, was Elizabeth Prout's definition of the charism of her congregation. Like the *Rule* of Paul of the Cross, it was the fruit and the expression of her own 'memory' of the Holy Family, lived in close association with her 'memory' of the Passion of her 'Crucified Spouse'.[172] It was both a statement of what she bequeathed to her congregation as its special heritage and a programme for the future. It was truly her last will and testament. As an expression of her own experiences as foundress, which she invited her daughters to share in the circumstances of their own lives, it described the type of order she presented to lower-class women in particular and the Paulacrucian spirituality she offered to all. Elizabeth Prout's special charism as foundress lay in her ability to synthesise Father Gaudentius Rossi's 1862 claims with the wishes of the Manchester clergy in answering the needs of the factory girls and, at the same time, to preserve the nature of her religious order according to the wishes of her sisters, Bishop Turner, Father Gaudentius himself as she had previously understood him, Father Ignatius Spencer, his 'partner founder' and 'plenipotentiary' as he called himself, and the Passionist Provincial, Father Ignatius Paoli, who then and to the end of his life took a very deep interest in her congregation.[173]

At the beginning of July 1863, Elizabeth returned to Sutton for the annual retreat, to be given by her friend, Father Salvian Nardocci.[174] Her last retreat, it was a period of intense physical suffering as the Sutton annalist recorded. 'I must remark', she wrote, 'that the health of our dearly beloved and Rev. Mother was at this time very weak. The shock occasioned by the great joy on receiving Father Ignatius' letter worked considerably upon her. She told me frequently, but particularly during the retreat, that she felt sure her mission was ended and that she was making the retreat as a preparation for death....'[175] It was appropriate that, as a woman who had been deeply involved in so many of the major issues of her time, Elizabeth Prout should also suffer nineteenth-century woman's most common illness.[176] On 12 July, the last morning of the retreat, she awoke with a violent pain in her side. She went down to the chapel to attend Mass, during which she formally renewed her vows but afterwards the pain became so great that the doctor was called. He diagnosed inflammation and feared it would be fatal. In the remaining six months of her life, Elizabeth experienced and demonstrated the depths of her Paulacrucian spirituality. As foundress she set the standard by which her daughters would approach death. Delicate, in a hurry from her birth and always having had to struggle against both time and ill-health, she continued her work with characteristic singlemindedness.[177] Warned by Sister Winefride that Elizabeth was ill, Father Ignatius Spencer went north to Sutton as soon as possible after returning from Rome at the beginning of August.[178] On 17 August 1863, practically twelve years to the date from her foundation in Stocks Street, Bishop Turner, with Rome's approbation, canonically established her congregation.[179]

On 23 August, at the provincial chapter held in Broadway, Father Ignatius Spencer was appointed rector of St Anne's, Sutton.[180] 'This was very joyful news for the Sisters of the Holy Family', wrote the Sutton annalist. Arriving in Sutton on 27 August, the anniversary of Father Dominic's death in 1849, Ignatius, now the custodian of Dominic's incorrupt remains, 'came as... the father of both religious houses', sparing 'no labour in instructing the Sisters in the path of perfection'.[181] Thus Father Ignatius Spencer was in a position to help Elizabeth Prout to complete the course on which Fathers Dominic Barberi and Gaudentius Rossi had set her in the 1840s. Her inflammation was abated by October but was followed by consumption. Informed immediately, Ignatius, who was in Levenshulme at the time, returned to Sutton at once to tell her she was dying.[182] Together they prepared for the first general chapter of the congregation.

Bishop Turner appointed 23 October, feast of the Holy Redeemer, for the election of the first superioress general. 'It is very consoling', he wrote to Father Ignatius, sending Elizabeth his blessing, 'to learn that the Rev. Mother is in such happy dispositions, and I hope she may live some time to direct the Institute'.[183] Ignatius shared his confidence. Writing to Father Eugene Martorelli, provincial consultor, he told him the chapter would probably not have been called so soon, had it not been for the 'dangerous state of the Rev. Mother'. 'The Bishop and all', he said, 'desire that she may be elected the first superior general, on the newly framed constitution of the body, as no doubt she will be unanimously.' His confidence was all the more remarkable because he continued, 'She will not be able to be present at it, as it must be held at Levenshulme, near Manchester, and she will perhaps never leave the house here again alive.'[184] Her sisters felt the same confidence. With the exception of the foundress herself and of Sister Catherine Scanlon, who had scalded her leg with boiling water, all the professed sisters gathered in St Joseph's convent, Levenshulme on 22 October 1863.[185] The next morning, after Father Ignatius Spencer had offered Mass 'to beg light from God' on their work, Bishop Turner arrived to preside at the chapter. All the sisters assembled in the chapter room. Forming a procession, they went to the chapel, sang the *Veni Creator* and, after other prayers, processed back to the chapter room to begin their work. Ten in number, they unanimously elected their foundress, Elizabeth Prout as their first Superioress General.[186] Bishop Turner promptly issued his certificate confirming her in office.[187] Sister Winefride Lynch was elected as first consultor, with right of succession; Sister Gertrude Blount as second consultor; and Sister Benedicta Hynes as novice-mistress. Elizabeth was also superior of Sutton. Ashton was to be given an interim superior, appointed by Elizabeth, because, with the sewing schools coming to an end, she and Bishop Turner had already decided to close it.[188] Ignatius wrote to his provincial, 'This is rather a great despatch for me and the nuns.... The Rev. Mother was elected General with all honour....' In an enlightening comment on Elizabeth's mental and spiritual condition, in spite of her physical debility, he continued, 'The *Mother General* keeps up in a better way, though not materially improved, and is in full vigour for her office....'[189] On the anniversary of the first professions, 21 November 1863, in Levens-hulme, on the instructions of Bishop Turner, Father Ignatius Spencer received the perpetual vows of Mothers Winefride, Gertrude and Benedicta. At the same time, with the permission of Bishop Goss of Liverpool, Elizabeth Prout, confined in Sutton, made her perpetual vows in the presence of Father Joseph Gasparini, vice-rector in Sutton. The Sutton annalist commented on Father Ignatius Spencer's joy, 'I need not say how great was his joy and exultation on this occasion, its being the finishing of the great work and setting in order the govern-ment of the Institute.'[190]

Father Ignatius described the character of Elizabeth Prout's institute in a letter he wrote at that time to a Scottish friend, Mrs Hutchison of Edinburgh, who was loth to part with her friend, Jane Mary Durie, just about to enter the novitiate in Sutton:

> As far as I can judge from what I have seen of her, I do sincerely think that the career opening to her here is one promising her not only great merit but most abundant fruits of salvation and great happiness, to be purchased however at the sacrifice of some of her feelings, since the members of the institute thus far are not of the superior classes in society of which religious communities have usually been principally composed; and I wish the body may not lose this, its lowly character, which however will not be against its drawing to it some of the brightest, most cultivated minds, who like Mrs Durie will rejoice in thus following Him Who chose for us the way of poverty and abjection, when He was Lord of all.[191]

From late November 1863, Elizabeth was sinking.[192] When she became decidedly worse about the second week in December, Father Joseph Gasparini gave her the Last Rites of the Catholic Church. The annalist noted she 'evinced wonderful calm and recollection during the whole.... [Previously] troubled and perplexed about the infant Institute', she was now full of 'a wonderful confidence and peace', like 'the peace and confidence of a child reposing on its mother's bosom in a soft slumber'.[193] Elizabeth Prout had scaled the heights of Paulacrucian spirituality. She had courageously accepted as God's will 'inner and outer fears, desolation and bodily pain'. Now she had reached the goal of resting 'in the bosom of the heavenly Father', ready for her exaltation with the Risen Christ.[194] In this sense, her deathbed experience was her most final definition of the charism of her order. It was the completion of the Passionist lifestyle she was bequeathing to her congregation. As usual in tubercular cases, her mind remained 'most clear and strong to the very end'. On Christmas Day she called all the community to her room. She spoke individually to each one of them. Then, as they stood around her, conscious that this was the last time that, as a group, they would listen to their foundress, 'she gave a parting exhortation', reminiscent of that given by Paul of the Cross in 1775.[195] Encouraging them 'to perseverance and fidelity in their vocation', she assured them that 'God would bring out the Institute victorious over all its enemies if they were only faithful to Him'. According to religious custom in the congregation, before they left they knelt to ask a blessing. 'God bless you, Sisters' would therefore have been her last words to her community. Then they all departed in tears and silence.[196]

On 3 January 1864, the birthday of Paul of the Cross, all the professed sisters who had not already done so made their final vows. The congregation was now secure. On 4 January Elizabeth sent Mother Winefride to close her Ashton convent. The trauma of closing this work for the mill girls took its toll, for when Winefride returned on 6 January, she found her worse in health although calm and resigned. On 9 January Father Ignatius Spencer heard her last Confession, a final step in her conversion process according to Paulacrucian spirituality.[197] There still remained one important task she must perform as foundress. Like Father Gaudentius, she had legislated for both industry and education. She had established workrooms and had set on foot the final arrangements for homes for factory girls. Now, at the beginning of January 1864, she appointed Jane Durie, who had arrived in Sutton on 28 December, to take charge of the school at Peasley Cross, with Winefride's young sister, Jane, as an apprentice teacher.[198] Thus Elizabeth Prout established education, including teacher training, as part of the active apostolate of her congregation.

Very early in the morning on 11 January 1864, Elizabeth was seized with violent pains. At 4 a.m. the sister who was looking after her called Mother Winefride. 'Every kind of hot application was tried' but to no avail.[199] The pains continued until four o'clock in the afternoon. During the whole day, she remained 'resigned and patient'. Amongst her own community, as amongst the Passionists, Elizabeth already had a reputation for sanctity. 'It would seem from this last but severe pain', wrote the Sutton annalist, 'that some dross still remained to be atoned for and that our dear Lord sent this as an atonement.' From about 5 p.m. her breathing became short but she remained perfectly conscious. When told she was dying, she gave a grateful and affectionate glance to the Sisters attending her and then collected herself in prayer. 'The community were at once brought in to say the prayers for the departing and Father Ignatius sent for.' As he entered her room, she 'turned and recognized him with a grateful glance, which was not more than five minutes before her death.' As she died, he raised his hand in a final Absolution. 'So peacefully and calmly', wrote the Sutton annalist, 'did her soul separate from her body that we scarcely knew she was dead and her spirit had passed to her dear Lord and Spouse. "May she rest in peace."'[200]

Sister Helen James closed the foundress' eyes.[201] Father Ignatius Spencer wrote in his diary for Monday, 11 January 1864, 'Saw Rev. Mother die at 6', his terseness hiding his grief.[202] He wrote immediately to inform Bishop Turner. The bishop's reply on 12 January was typical of the unwavering trust he had always had in her: 'I received your favour informing me of the death of the Rev. Mother. Well, she did a good thing in her life by establishing the Institute of the Holy Family, and I trust she is now enjoying the rewards of her labours. The Order will I think go on well but it is a work of time.... Great progress has been made of late and I have confidence in the future.'[203]

On Tuesday, 12 January, thinking perhaps that they had no photograph of the foundress, Mother Winefride had a photograph taken of her corpse.[204] Elizabeth's remains were laid out in the convent chapel according to the Rule, her feet bare, her body clothed in the habit, her modified Passionist Sign over her heart, the scroll of her vows and her crucifix in her hands. Her physician, Dr Thomas Chisnall registered her death in the registry office in Prescot, St Helens.[205] Word of her death was passed immediately round the Passionist houses, a clear indication of her recognised position in the Passionist mission to England. Father Salvian in Broadway received the news on 12 January.[206] He entered in his diary:

> Memorandum. On Tuesday morning we received the news of the death of the Revd. Mother Mary Joseph, the Foundress of the Congregation of the Sisters of the Holy Family, which took place in H. Cross Convent Sutton near St Helen's [sic] Lancashire, on the 11th of this month.... The death of this Holy Sister will be felt very

much by the Sisters of the Holy Family. In the Revd Mother Mary Joseph they have lost their Founderess [*sic*] and guide. R.I.P.[207]

Elizabeth's funeral took place on Thursday, 14 January 1864. A son of obedience, Father Ignatius had left for a mission in Wolverhampton, as previously planned.[208] The coffin was carried from the convent by eight of the professed sisters, 'the rest walking in solemn procession after the corpse'. They were met by the Passionists in surplices, the celebrant, Father Leonard, and the acolytes, 'who joined in the procession chanting the Office for the Dead in a most solemn manner'. 'When we reached the church', the Sutton annalist wrote, 'the coffin was placed on the bier in front of the sanctuary and a solemn Requiem sung, at the end of which she was interred in the churchyard and the Sisters returned home sorrowful and in silence', a group of respectable but lowly women, whose task was to continue the apostolate of Elizabeth Prout.[209]

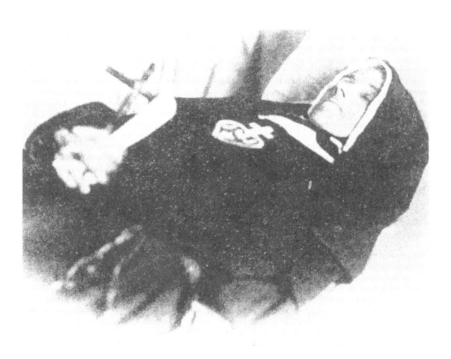

Elizabeth Prout—Mother Mary Joseph
12 January 1864

CHAPTER VII

THE ROYAL ROAD OF THE HOLY CROSS

1. ELIZABETH PROUT'S PAULACRUCIAN SPIRITUALITY

Throughout the period from 1849 to 1855, Father Gaudentius Rossi's occasional comments on Elizabeth Prout's virtues indicate her personal Paulacrucian spirituality, which she had received from Father Dominic Barberi in Stone and which Father Gaudentius had subsequently inculcated as the spirituality of the congregation. Hence on 23 January 1849, when she was still in the Northampton convent, he admired her 'peace and calm of mind with a perfect resignation to God's holy will' about her illness and its consequence that she would have to leave the novitiate.[1] By 1852 he had an extremely high opinion of her virtues and of her ability to instruct others, for he expected her to lead Sister Clare Wilson to 'a more than ordinary state of perfection'.[2] Her care of her feverstricken sisters in later 1853 led him to comment that her dispositions of mind were such that they gave him 'great edification' and 'great joy to the very angels and saints of heaven'.[3] As Sister Agnes Lee again took ill in February 1854, he wrote to Elizabeth, 'I most sincerely sympathise with you, my dear Sister Mary Joseph, for the large share of the Cross which our B. Redeemer gives to you in different ways. Try to bear all well and you shall be rewarded both in the present and future life.'[4] He acknowledged her humility and her meekness and patience in receiving hard corrections, even feeling he must praise her in this respect.[5]

Apart from such glimpses afforded through Father Gaudentius Rossi's letters, Elizabeth Prout's personal spirituality has remained as well hidden as other details of her life. She wrote no learned treatises on the spiritual life. She left no diaries recording graces she had received. References in Father Gaudentius' replies to her letters, however, supported in one instance by an incident recorded in Annals C, indicate she received singular practical favours through St Joseph's intercession and in June 1853 she did reveal something to Father Gaudentius that led him to reply, 'You state that you have done very little to deserve such inward spiritual consolations.... You should receive these spiritual favours with a truly humble and grateful heart....'[6] Such experiences, however, were rare. For most of her life as foundress she epitomised in her own spiritual struggle the inherent conflict between Martha and Mary that was essential to the institute's Paulacrucian identity. Thus in February 1854 she told Gaudentius of her 'dryness in prayer and spiritual desolation'.[7] One would suspect that spiritually she had already outstretched him, for he was unable to direct her. He accused her of neglecting prayer as laid down in the Rule, recommending her to read again the sermon he had given at the first clothing ceremony and Rodriguez' treatise on the observance of the Rule.[8]

He gave her similar advice in 1855. On 18 February she had written to him about something that had happened at Levenshulme and had upset her so much that she felt she could never feel happy there again.[9] Later in the month, hearing he was going to give a mission in Stockport and would call at Levenshulme convent, she went from Ashton to see him, desperate to seek his advice. She was unable to do so, because he spent most of his time with Sister Clare Wilson. Elizabeth was suffering intense spiritual desolation. Overwhelmed by this, by ill-health, by worry about Sister Clare and the institute and unable to seek advice from the only person able to give it, she felt rejected by both God and men and, in a fit of utter depression, she wrote to Father Gaudentius asking him to ask Bishop Turner for a dispensation from her vows.[10] In similar circumstances Paul of the Cross had written to a nun he directed, in a passage with which Elizabeth Prout appears to have been familiar:

> Whoever loves Jesus seeks nothing else but suffering. I am consoled to know that you are one of these very happy souls who walk the path of Calvary following our Redeemer. Happy are you if you follow this precious path, for one day in the company of other lovers of the cross you will sing: 'Dear God, your crosses are the joys of my heart.' How beautiful it is to suffer with Jesus! Would that I had a seraph's heart to unfold the loving desire to suffer sought by the good friends of the Crucified. If here below there are crosses, above in paradise there are crowns! With all our hearts let us seek to attain perfection, humility, obedience and above all continued resignation to the divine Will. Do you think that those things that happen to you are really contradictions? Realise instead that they are designs of our kind Spouse for your greater good; so constantly call out to the Sacred Heart of the divine Lover saying, 'Thy will be done!'... The more you suffer, the more you will resemble our dear spouse Jesus.[11]

In 1855, however, Father Gaudentius told Elizabeth Prout:

> More humility would have freed you from much trouble. Neither I nor God has abandoned you as the devil makes you imagine. You have been brought into this trouble because I fear you have neglected prayer and the exact observance of the rules. Begin now to do both and all will be right again. I cannot and will not write to the Bishop for what you ask. It is your duty to keep your vows and promises to God. By ourselves we can do nothing, but can do everything by the power of Him Who strengthens us. Prayer, prayer, prayer and a thousand times prayer.'[12]

In emphasising prayer he was right. As Paul of the Cross had recognised, it was only prayer, the living prayer of the 'memory', that could unite Martha and Mary, that could hold the balance between the active and contemplative lives. Gaudentius was wrong, however, in suggesting Elizabeth Prout had neglected either prayer or the exact observance of the Rule. She quickly wrote him an apology, assuring him that, of course, she had not really meant to leave religious life and, as one of the annalists wrote:

> She would not allow the slightest deviation in the Rule or in regular observance. She showed by her own example and also by those who persevered with her that to those who really loved God, there was nothing impossible in the Rule and Customs. She would not allow on any account the active work of the Sisters to interfere with the spiritual observances. The 'active work of Martha' must in no way interfere or set aside the 'contemplation of Mary'.[13]

Her estrangement from Father Gaudentius was one of Elizabeth's most acute sufferings. She constantly asked his forgiveness, expressing her regret that they had lost their former happy relationship. It was to no avail. 'Change your ideas, change your conduct', he wrote in 1855, 'act as a true Sister of the Holy Family, and you will find me always the same as before.'[14] In spite of his almost harsh treatment, she never lost her affection, respect and admiration for him. Thus on 12 September 1855 with reference to his possible departure for America, she warmly wrote, 'I hope and still hope that Almighty God will not allow you to leave England. I do feel your going very keenly, but', she continued, her submission to the will of God as always paramount, 'if God wills that you must go, we must pray for generosity and courage.'[15] She still displayed that calm resignation to God's will that Gaudentius had applauded in January 1849 and that lay at the heart of Paulacrucian mysticism.[16]

Vigilant in her concern for the institute, she was also careful to accord Gaudentius his place as founder. Noting the need for sisters who were teaching religious doctrine to be accurately informed themselves and aware of the possible dangers, in practice, of visits to the parlour and parish visitation, she prudently asked him 'to leave a command for the Catechism to be studied ... at least once a week'.[17] She asked him to state that no Sister should be allowed to stay longer than a quarter of an hour in the parlour, except to take orders for work. She suggested he make it mandatory that the sisters who visited the sick should be frequently changed and that none should visit seculars except to exhort them to come to Mass or to send their children to school.[18]

She again told him of her spiritual desolation, which seems to have been accentuated by his persistent allegations that she was neither keeping nor upholding the Rule. She was conscious of her 'sins and wretchedness'.[19] 'I sincerely regret my past negligent life', she told him. 'With the assistance of divine grace' she resolved and hoped to correct herself. She made the resolution to do so every day but she felt she broke it every day too. She felt she would have to fight against her 'wicked passions and bad temper' as long as she lived and she often feared she would never conquer one of them. Like many Victorian evangelicals, and also like Paul of the Cross, she had a strong sense of hell. She feared she would spend her whole life in making resolutions and breaking them and that in her last moments the 'enemy' would take advantage of all her broken resolutions, putting them before her in their true light, would then throw her into despair and that in the end she would be eternally lost. 'I often fear', she told Gaudentius, 'that I shall be condemned to hell for the abuse of the great graces I have received.' It was her 'earnest desire to begin to live for God alone' and yet she felt she could not claim 'one single good action' she had ever done or a thought she had ever had that she had not tainted in some way 'by some bad thought, words or works'. She begged his help, feeling she had 'lived such an unhappy life' for such a long time that she felt she could continue it no longer. 'I feel that I must now begin in earnest', she wrote, 'and not pretend any longer but I seem not to know how to begin. If you have time to answer this will you please do so.'[20]

Gaudentius answered the disciplinary points of Elizabeth's letter in his own of 14 September 1855, but to her humble, even piteous cry for spiritual help, he made no reply either then or later. Alone, she continued to climb that ladder described by Paul of the Cross, where souls 'find pure suffering, devoid of consolation either in heaven or on earth'.[21] She was truly living by faith. She claimed neither visions nor ecstasies. Trying to help with a Levenshulme bazaar at the same time that she was checking Gaudentius' final version of his Rule and opening the poor school for the Blackbrook children, she was utterly distracted, torn between Martha and Mary. 'I never could pray much', she wrote to him on 25 September 1855,

> but now I can do nothing.... If I try to reflect on some part of Our Lord's Passion I am sure to begin to think of something worldly in a minute or two and yet during the day when thinking over my duties and I see difficulties I feel that with prayer I can overcome them, and I feel such a desire to be praying continually, but still at the same time I know if I was to go to pray or even to try where I was that in five minutes I should have my thoughts wandering all over the world.[22]

Well they might be as she thought of Gaudentius' departure for North America. The news that he was definitely going came upon her 'like a thunder clap'.[23] Disturbed by her disagreements with him, she again asked his pardon for her 'repeated oppositions' to his wishes. She assured him she would never have opposed him had she 'not felt in conscience bound to do so, for the welfare of the community and institute'.[24] She was still suffering spiritual desolation. She felt that if she could live her life over again, she would try to live so differently. Sometimes she thought she would try to begin again and 'try to live for God alone', and yet she never seemed to begin. There was always something keeping her back.[25] She craved for solitude, thinking a strict retreat would cure what she considered her tepidity, because whenever they had retreats in the convent there was always so much to distract her that she could not concentrate.[26] She longed to live in the presence of God, yearned to pray and was faithful to her times of prayer but she felt she never prayed. Although she made countless resolutions to the contrary, she always found that when the time came 'for prayers, Mass, reading or any of the exercises', she felt 'quite weary and disgusted'. She had to spend the whole time of prayer in driving away distractions, so that, instead of coming from prayer refreshed with lights and inspirations, she felt instead 'quite discouraged and disgusted'.[27] Through this dark night, however, she had become a woman of acute spiritual perception. She was so sensitive to the value of suffering, so afraid of falling into spiritual pride, that when she received any consolation in prayer she almost rejected it. She was ever forgetful of self. Warmly assuring Gaudentius , 'We do pray for you my dear Father and ever shall', she invited him to Sutton and Blackbrook for a day or two before he left.[28]

Her deep self-knowledge was illustrated in her next letter, of 7 October 1855, in which, having asked, with profound humility, for permission to ask Sister Philomena to tell her her faults, she wrote, 'You know my dear Father how weak I am in virtue and how necessary it is for me to have someone that knows me and will make me keep up to the point.' She would have preferred to ask Sister Clare Wilson 'but', wrote Elizabeth, 'she has not courage to tell me of my faults and therefore passes them over. I suppose', she added, 'it is because she has seen me bear things so ill, I mean humiliations and corrections and therefore she shrinks from the task.' Philomena Johnson would be ready to tell her of her faults. Elizabeth chose her because she would be a hard taskmistress, for already Philomena gave her 'plenty of opportunities of practising humility and patience'.[29] This was, indeed, total abandonment to God's protection.

Father Gaudentius' departure for America practically coincided with the anniversary of the first sisters' profession. Accordingly, on 20 November, Elizabeth went from Sutton to Levenshulme and there, at Mass on Wednesday, 21 November 1855, the sisters renewed their vows before 'their Father and Founder', who gave them his last sermon in England, on the Virgin Mary.[30] On Friday, 23 November Elizabeth Prout and her companions in Sutton attended his Mass in Blessed Paul's chapel in St Anne's monastery church, during which they received Holy Communion from him for the last time.[31] As the Memorial of the Passion, the central feature of Paulacrucian spirituality, this celebration had a very special significance for Father Gaudentius and the sisters. He and Father Ignatius then took the train to Liverpool, where Gaudentius stayed that night at St Augustine's presbytery.[32] With time on his hands, he wrote his parting letter to Elizabeth Prout.

Sincerely convinced of her utter sinfulness, Elizabeth had always received his rebukes with docility and gratitude. Perhaps, therefore, she was more conscious of his affection than his harshness as she read his last rebuke delivered on English soil:

> Last Tuesday and especially on Wednesday at Levenshulme during recreation there was greater noise and confusion of talk than could be allowed in a religious Community. Some Sisters spoke and laughed very loud, and several strove to speak at the same time and because all could not be heard at once, hence like persons without education and without virtue they strove to drown the voice of the other speaking sister. If I am not mistaken I could hear your voice more boisterous than the rest.... Eh! my dear Sister there were too many and too strong reasons on that memorable day, why the Sisters should have been more recollected and devout, and rather serious during that solemnity....[33]

Elizabeth had just renewed her vows and therefore, in spite of all her sufferings, spiritual, physical and mental, and Gaudentius' imminent departure, she laughed joyfully. That, as well as the photograph of a serene and solemn foundress, was the image of her that willy-nilly Father Gaudentius Rossi carried to North America, as he sailed from Liverpool to Boston on the steam packet, 'America', on 24 November 1855.[34]

He left Father Ignatius Spencer as his representative and substitute. 'I have great confidence in him', he had written to Elizabeth in October 1855, 'and full confidence in his personal virtue or rather extraordinary sanctity.'[35] During the next few days Father Ignatius visited the sisters in each convent, had several consultations with Elizabeth and visited Bishop Turner and Father Croskell on her behalf.[36] In late December and early January he again went to each convent, holding long conferences with the sisters, hearing Confessions and celebrating Mass. On 5 January 1856 he read a paper on perfection to Elizabeth and her community in Sutton. On 8 January he visited Sister Veronica Petrolini, who had broken a blood vessel, and the next day he accompanied Father Bernardine when he gave her the Last Rites.[37] From February to November 1856 Father Ignatius was on the Continent preaching his crusade of prayer for the conversion of England and begging for financial support for the Passionist retreat in London.[38] In Sutton for Christmas 1856, he spent 26 December having conferences with the sisters in Parr Hall and Sutton and 29 December with those in Ashton and Levenshulme. Sent to Dublin to beg for funds for the new retreat at Mount Argus, before leaving on 2 January 1857 he had another conference with Elizabeth Prout in Sutton.[39] They discussed the desirability of papal approval of the Rule; the possibility that Father Ignatius might take it to Rome when he went later in the year for the Passionist general chapter; the need for some good postulants; and Elizabeth Prout's own spiritual welfare. Arrived in Dublin, he continued these discussions in a letter to her dated 11 January 1857. Having discussed the qualifications of two prospective Irish postulants, he continued, 'I seem to see all the brightest prospects to be opening for your body, depending however mainly on the one resolution to become perfect, in yourself first, then in others who would soon follow.' He encouraged her to seek sanctity. 'Do not', he said, 'by your own choice, disappoint the expectation of our Lord, the B. Virgin, S. Joseph, of the Church, of the Institute, of Fr. Gaudentius, and, let me add, of poor myself.' He was convinced, he said, that what was most important for the complete success of the order was that she, who was 'the leader, and the mother of all the rest', would make the 'good resolution' to seek perfection and thus be 'their mother indeed.'[40]

Elizabeth candidly replied that it was her 'sincere wish and desire to become perfect', that she loved her 'dear Lord' and yet everything she did she found 'loathsome and disgusting'.[41] Since she already broke her resolutions every day, she said, she saw no point in making yet another one. Ignatius' own spirituality, which was epitomised in his reply of 1 February 1857, was essentially simple: he thanked God for everything. That was the only way, he had once told Louisa Canning, he could manage to survive his own problems.[42] With his own Paulacrucian spirituality, he assured Elizabeth she must distinguish between what was her own will and what was not. She must correct the former and thank God for the latter. Everything she did being loathsome and disgusting was manifestly not her own will, because when she did her own will she inevitably sought her own pleasure. Since it could not be pleasurable to find everything loathsome and disgusting, that was clearly not her own will. That was something to thank God for. In thanking Him, she would achieve 'humility, purity of intention, detachment from the world, pure love of God etc.' Next he examined her refusal to make a resolution to become perfect. In virtue even of her Baptism, he said, quite apart from her religious profession, she was already committed to love God with all her 'heart and consequently to strive in all things to please Him'. She was already obliged to seek perfection. A resolution to seek it was not giving herself a new obligation but fulfilling an existing one. Refusal to fulfil it was wilful opposition to God's will and an injustice to Him.[43] So courteously expressed, his letter could not have offended her, accustomed as she was to Gaudentius' heavy beratings. Probably delayed by needing to ask Bishop Turner about accepting the Irish postulants, she had not replied by 25 February 1857 when Ignatius wrote again. He was disappointed at not having heard from her. Unaware of the type of letter she sometimes received from Father Gaudentius, Father Ignatius thought she must have been angry with him. 'This however should not keep you silent with me', he chided. His letter, in which he accorded her her full position as foundress, incidentally provides a valuable portrait of Elizabeth Prout as appreciated by Father Ignatius Spencer:

> If you thought me in the wrong for writing as I did, you should tell me so and try to make me see it as you do. I would with God's grace take that well and thankfully from anyone, but especially from one like you, who are in authority to guide others to perfection. You cannot divest yourself of that character and responsibility. It has been laid upon you and accepted. There is nothing for it but to bear it worthily; for which it is not knowledge and abilities which are wanted, and you have enough of them, but humility to receive admonitions and diligence in correcting and improving yourself. The best conclusion would be for you to write to me just your real feelings on it, and explaining if you see me to have mistaken you at all.... Now write to me a candid gentle letter about it all, and, please God, you will find yourself quickly all right, that is, on the way to being all right, for we can be nothing better than this here below.[44]

Under this gentle, encouraging and firm direction, Elizabeth continued her pursuit of spiritual perfection. Ignatius was on his return journey from Rome when he received word that Sister Clare in Levenshulme had led the order into debt and that she and several others were threatening to leave. 'Take courage', he wrote to Elizabeth, 'do you not see that this is the time of trial?   I will come and see what these

Sisters have to say, and if they wish to kick, bite and run, let them. The children of Blessed Paul did the same, so did the children of St Francis but God gave them others more faithful and worthy, and so He will give you. If they all go, "God speed them"; we can begin again with God's blessing.'[45]

As described by the Sutton annalist, Elizabeth's trials continued throughout the next few years, 'During this year [1859] there were many and great difficulties in the Institute. Many members had left and the Superiors... were almost crushed to the very earth, for it seemed almost impossible for the dear Institute of the Holy Family, for which they had laboured so much to succeed, for all the powers of hell seemed to be combined against it.'[46] It was in this period, however, that Father Ignatius' 'confidence in the order was so great that he sent postulants' to it 'when to all human appearances' it would be 'broken up in a few weeks'. He sent Teresa Mary Hynes in 1857 and Honora Chambers in 1860. Both became superiors general. At the time of their admissions, however, Elizabeth's sufferings were acute. In May 1860 Sister Zitta Watson, superior in Sutton, became so ill that Elizabeth had to leave Levenshulme again to take charge of Sutton. In February 1861 Sister Mary Cecilia Reddan dropped dead in Sutton of a heart attack. Sister Juliana Rawlins had to be dismissed in June 1861. Sister Veronica Petrolini died of tuberculosis on 14 August 1861, Sister Zitta Watson on 9 November. Ann Prout died of hydrothorax on 10 August 1862 and Edward Prout of a sudden stroke on 26 January 1863. Even Elizabeth's virtue was assailed. While she and Father Ignatius Spencer were revising the Rule together in 1862-3, he had to visit the convent more frequently than usual. A priest, whose identity was never revealed, 'through mistaken zeal, gave out the most injurious insinuations' about Father Ignatius and the foundress.[47]

> When Father Ignatius heard of it, he sent for the reverend mother to exhort her to bear the calumny with love and resignation. In speaking to her he said that God had asked all of him, and he had freely given all but his good name, and that he was ready now to offer as it had pleased God to ask for it, for all belonged to Him and he thanked Him for leaving him nothing. 'Will you not', he continued, 'do the same? Do you not see that God is asking you for the dearest thing you can give Him? Give it, then, freely and thank Him for taking it, for don't you see that by this you are resembling Him more closely? Besides, He has permitted this to happen, and if we do not give up our good name, which already belongs to Him, cheerfully and willingly, He will take it, in spite of us, and we shall lose the merit of our offering. How foolish, therefore, is it to go against God! Let us resign ourselves unreservedly into His Hands. However to remove any scandal that might follow, and to show this good priest that I

have no ill-feeling against him, I will go and visit him in friendly terms.' And so he did.[48]

Undoubtedly Elizabeth Prout would have borne this latest calumny 'with love and resignation', as Father Ignatius suggested. She had been tried in the crucible of suffering. Bowed down with humiliations, ill-health, defections, deaths and always the constant, harsh, daily grind of hard work and deep poverty, she had learnt to love the Cross.[49] Her Paulacrucian spirituality was well expressed in a verse she had written on a feastday card for Sister Mary Patrick O'Neal in March 1862:

> A cross no cross where Jesus is;
> With Jesus crosses are my bliss;
> Why should the cross so frighten me
> When on the Cross my God I see?[50]

While, however, Elizabeth constantly meditated on the Passion, clung to her 'Crucified Spouse' and directed her order towards a more obvious Passionist identity, she retained a kindred devotion to the Holy Family.[51] As the foundress of the Institute of the Sisters of the Holy Family, she both practised that devotion and inculcated it in others.[52] By Rule every quarter of an hour during recreation and every half hour at other times, except those of strict silence, she and all her sisters prayed that 'Jesus, Mary and Joseph' would 'be for ever praised, honoured and glorified'.[53] Her few remaining letters, as well as references in Father Gaudentius Rossi's replies to others, indicate her deep devotion to Mary, to Joseph and to the Holy Family as such.[54] As early as 1850 Elizabeth herself had demonstrated her 'sincere and solid devotion to the... Holy Mother of our Divine Redeemer' by initiating the common recitation of the Little Office of Our Lady.[55] On 25 April 1858 she told Gaudentius she was convinced St Joseph was protecting them.[56] In her 1858 letter to Father Salvian she attributed Father Bernard's successful work on her behalf to the intervention of the Holy Family.[57] Finally, in her Passionist revision of Father Gaudentius Rossi's Rule in 1863, she was very careful to preserve the customs of his institute. Its spirituality, like hers, was already Paulacrucian.

2. THE FINAL CROSS

Probably the most outstanding lacuna in the archives of Elizabeth Prout's congregation is a letter from Father Gaudentius Rossi in 1864 replying to the news of her death. Although he wrote to her successor, Mother Winefride Lynch in both June and November 1864, he made no reference to the deceased foundress. His first extant mention of her is in a letter dated 11 April 1866, more than two years after her death.

In this letter, he made two complaints: about the conduct of Sister Anne Joachim Flanagan, whom Winefride, on Elizabeth's dying wishes, had sent to North America to make a foundation there as Father Gaudentius had so often requested; and about the revised Rule, of which Anne Joachim had brought him a copy. In particular he criticised its section on the government of the order and then he wrote:

> Finally I may state here that for some years I could not be entirely satisfied with the way in which the late Superioress Mother Mary Joseph conducted the affairs of the institute. She may have had the best intentions, but under her authority the Sisters in general were not happy, and the institute did not prosper. I know however that she had severe trials and great deal to suffer both in mind and body. She had many good qualities and great virtues, and I hope she is now enjoying a full reward of them in heaven.[58]

Father Gaudentius' complaint bears sufficient affinity with the last 1858 charge to require examination.

Between 1849 and 1854 Father Gaudentius was increasingly aware of Elizabeth's competence in government. 'I am fully convinced both of your purity of intention, and of your sincere and earnest desire to advance the spiritual and temporal interests of the Holy Family', he told her in July 1854.[59] He had no reason at that time for wishing to replace her government. Her unanimous election as superior in November 1854 indicated her sisters were happy with her 'conduct of affairs'. Father Gaudentius Rossi's claim in 1866, therefore, cannot be sustained up to November 1854 by the evidence of either his own letters or the sisters' election.

From the first professions, however, as Sister Clare Wilson increasingly challenged Elizabeth's authority, his criticisms also increased. In June-July 1855 he was resident in the Passionist retreat in London as vice-rector, which meant he was not so free as previously to give missions. Apparently chafing at his missionary inactivity and told to let Elizabeth manage her own affairs, he was at his most critical towards her. Although he had told her to consult Father Bernardine in Sutton about the schools there, he disagreed with their decisions. It was her 'habitual conduct', he told her in July 1855, to ask his advice 'upon trifles' and to do as she pleased 'upon matters of most serious importance, so much so that [she had] made some members of the institute think and say that [she acted] as if [she had] founded an order of [her] own.'[60] Circumstances had pointed to her, he told her in August 1855, 'as the first and the leader of the Sisters of the Holy Family'. He had firmly believed that God had chosen her 'for this important and responsible position'. It should have been a 'source of consolation and satisfaction' to him, he said, to find her 'corresponding with the designs of God'. For some time she had given 'some satisfaction but never a full satisfaction'. At Stocks Street, he now claimed, she treated the sisters with 'too much authority and haughtiness'. She had been indifferent about the rules, although she had made him believe they were observed. She had granted dispensations from some rules and had suspended the observance of others. She was disposed to 'show and finery'. She had neglected 'to make the institute a self-supporting industrial institution', preferring 'fine things, high aspirations, grand schools', which, he claimed, had completely failed 'in every way' because of her 'bad management'. Since her profession, he said, she had been 'getting worse', so that his 'former confidence' in her was 'very much shaken'. 'My fear is', he told her, 'that you have never entered heart and soul into this important undertaking, that you have never seriously studied to understand the real spirit, nature and object of the pious Sisterhood of the Holy Family, or what is worse if you have understood it, you did not like the humility, the self denial, which it requires, and the care, vigilance, exertions, necessary....'[61]

Although his next letter expressed his 'pleasure and edification at the meek and patient manner' in which she received his corrections, within a fortnight he criticised her again. His letters indicate how much he was influenced by Clare Wilson.[62] On her complaints he forced Elizabeth to depose Sister Mary Paul Taylor as superior in Ashton, while he told Elizabeth herself that whatever she 'undertook to manage' did 'not seem to prosper' under her 'care and superintendence'.[63] He even broke the news of his going to North America in the context of upbraiding her as an unworthy superior, practically inviting her to resign in Clare's favour:

> I have repeatedly found that you do not seem willing to enter into the real spirit of the institute, and you seem determined to conform it to your own personal ideas and feelings.... Your mode of acting makes me fear that you do not entirely and solely seek the honour and glory of God and the real good of the institute, but rather your personal honour and ambition.... Perhaps I may go to America and soon. Before I go I should like to hear more from you, and give me satisfaction upon these points mentioned above. You may easily imagine how uneasy I should feel to leave things as they appear to me at present in your regard.[64]

He was wrong. On that score, as he had suggested, she could 'console' herself 'before God', Who was 'the sole witness' of her intentions. She was in fact already seeking 'in earnest God's greater glory, ... the welfare of the institute, and the real spiritual advancement of every member of it'. The true state of affairs must have been plain to all save Gaudentius, when Clare became 'upset in her mind' at the news of his possible departure.[65] It was she who, in her capacity as monitress, had constantly insinuated to him that Elizabeth was not fit for her office. 'I am only a subject and Sr. and not one in Authority', she wrote to Gaudentius in 1855, implying she was thus hampered in her task as novice-mistress.[66] Even when he knew she acted independently of Elizabeth, had disobeyed both her and Bishop Turner and had deceived Father Croskell, Gaudentius still upheld Clare against them.[67] With the news that Gaudentius was likely to depart, she asked to leave the order. He persuaded her to stay.[68] Gaudentius believed all Clare said or insinuated against Elizabeth. Reassured by Bishop Turner's confidence in her, however, in September 1855 he wrote in a more mollified tone, 'I believe that you mean well, and with the assistance of God you will do well and good.'[69] Nevertheless he maintained his predilection for Clare, even from North America. In June 1856 he suggested she should pioneer an American foundation. It would be agreeable to her dispositions, he said. She liked 'to do, to act and to direct. Perhaps she has a little envy against you', he admitted. 'This is wrong, but this envy would be extinguished in crossing the ocean, and she might have a new world as a field for her zeal, and holy ambition in behalf of the institute.'[70] In July 1856, however, he had to admit he was 'pained and disappointed' in her. 'What is become of all your grand expressions, of all your great promises, of all your long letters, of all your long spiritual conferences made, and instructions received?', he asked her. He assured her she was wrong in suggesting Elizabeth had written to him about her.[71] He knew she did not like Elizabeth, nor Father Ignatius Spencer, nor Father Croskell.[72] He feared that a 'spirit of secret spiritual pride and want of sincerity and prayer' were 'at the bottom of all her troubles'.[73] In October 1856 he told Elizabeth to replace her in Levenshulme with Sister Philomena Johnson, to return to Levenshulme herself and to make a number of other changes.[74] Bishop Turner, however, intervened. 'I think it will be better to defer all changes until the next election', he told Elizabeth. 'I do not think that the suggestions of Fr. Gaudentius can be carried out. He does not fully understand all matters connected with the Institute.'[75]

In June 1857 Gaudentius complained that Elizabeth was too indulgent. She had sent a sister to the seaside for her health. 'I could never approve,' he wrote. 'This may be very well for rich worldlings, but a poor religious person, that ought to be crucified to the world, and to self love, could not look very well in company with worldlings at the seaside. You know', he continued, 'that more than once I have been obliged to disapprove the facility with which the Sisters were allowed to go to the doctor.' He had also heard that Elizabeth had given dispensations from the Rule and he had received complaints about her from Sisters Clare and De Chantal, although the latter was the sister she had sent to the seaside. On Clare's account of De Chantal, he told Elizabeth to dismiss her.[76] In early November 1857 he told her to dismiss Sister Magdalene Toler and even Clare Wilson.[77] They had probably already gone of their own accord before Elizabeth received his letter. Sister Philomena followed about February 1858. Father Gaudentius sent Elizabeth a rare word of sympathy, 'The same trials have befallen almost every institute at the beginning', he wrote. 'Such was the case with our B[lessed] Founder Paul of the Cross.... I firmly believe that after this trial every thing will go on much better.'[78] By August 1858, however, forgetting he had told Elizabeth to dismiss them, Father Gaudentius began to blame her for their leaving. 'I have reasons to believe that Sr. Frances' conduct has been the principal occasion of the departure of the three London Sisters, but certainly of Sr. Philomena and Clare', he wrote.

> With a mistaken charity you took too much the side of Sr. F. The others felt unjustly aggrieved, found no redress, and thus lost first their confidence in you, then their peace of mind, lastly their vocation.... In whatever point of view the departure of Sr. Clare, Philomena, and Teresa may be considered, it is after all a serious loss to the poor infant institute.... I have long been observing that you cannot succeed to keep almost any of the more solid and intelligent novices or even professed Sisters. The three London Sisters, Sr. de Chantal, and some others, are my proof. What is the cause of this? I must confess that a suspicion some times comes to my mind - is it envy? Is it any fear for their higher abilities? I cannot believe it.'[79]

The ex-sisters were, therefore, writing to Gaudentius throughout 1858, while Elizabeth sent him no more than 'little notes' and Father Croskell did not answer his letters.[80] Gaudentius heard from the ex-sisters that the Manchester clergy were against the order and that there was an investigation.[81] He did not hear the charges. Since Elizabeth and all the sisters were bound to silence, none of them could tell him. Even when he asked directly, and twice, Elizabeth could only refer him, to his anger, to Fathers Bernard O'Loughlin and Ignatius Spencer.[82] Since Elizabeth had never told him of Clare's debts, nor of Philomena's misconduct, any information he had received had come from those who had left. He therefore had an unbalanced picture.

From June 1859, however, his letters to Elizabeth were friendly.[83] His criticism of her promotion of education in his letter of 6 August 1862 to Father Ignatius Spencer must, therefore, have been particularly hurtful.[84] He sent her no greetings, nor did he write to her again until

24 April 1863. He then admitted she had reason to complain of his long silence. He gave her the reason. 'The principal cause of my long silence', he told her, 'was the unfavourable impressions I had received partly from your own letters, and more from others, about the unsatisfactory condition of the new institute.' He was therefore still receiving letters from ex-sisters. He said he did not mind the sisters' teaching, but they had 'lost too much sight of the original idea.... Another cause' that had 'contributed to the temporary failure of the institute', he said, was 'the mode of governing it. I fear', he told her, 'you have not in every thing sought the honour of the Holy Family, the real spiritual improvement of the Sisters, and welfare of the institute. A Superior should not seek herself, but God alone.'[85] He continued the same theme in his next letter on 28 August 1863, the last she received from him. Even knowing she was seriously ill and hurt by his previous remarks, he wrote, 'No doubt I have heard several complaints from different parties and at different times made against your conduct in relation to the institute and to the Sisters.'[86] Heroically maintaining her silence about those same ex-sisters, Elizabeth Prout died in Father Gaudentius Rossi's disfavour. It was her final cross.

Gaudentius, however, was not being honest. As soon as he had heard, in September 1855, that he was likely to go to North America, he had determined to take the sisters there too.[87] From 7 June 1856 he constantly asked Elizabeth to send out some sisters.[88] He quickly realised, however, that Canon Croskell and Bishop Turner, having founded an institute they hoped would benefit the poor of Manchester, were not yet prepared to send its members abroad.[89] Gaudentius therefore sent three postulants to England, two of whom Elizabeth accepted.[90] He intended they should return to found the institute in Pittsburgh.[91] In the crisis of 1857-8, he proposed Elizabeth should remove the congregation entirely to North America.[92] She did not do so, because Father Bernard O'Loughlin advised her against it.[93]

Unknown to her, however, Father Gaudentius was simultaneously pressing his superior, Father John Dominic Tarlattini, for the foundation of a new American sisterhood of teachers. Typically not sure of what he wanted, Gaudentius seems to have been proposing his own sisters from England; a completely new American sisterhood; and a convent of the Passionist nuns from Italy.[94] Father John Dominic approached the Passionist general for permission to make a foundation of Passionist nuns and 'for a few pious women, under his supervision, to begin instructing children who were indirectly his responsibility both at St Michael's [Pittsburgh] and at the recently-formed foundation at Dunkirk'.[95] There is no indication that he specifically mentioned the sisters from England, although he certainly knew about them.[96] He did mention Father Gaudentius Rossi.

The Passionist Father General, Anthony Testa, knew Gaudentius very well from correspondence about wearing the habit and sandals in the 1840s and from the numerous reports he had received from Fathers Dominic Barberi and Ignatius Spencer, from his visitator general and from other Passionists in England.[97] He must have heard of the 'Gaudentian nuns', as the Passionists in England called Elizabeth's sisters.[98] It is likely that he had heard of Gaudentius' cavalier treatment of Elizabeth Prout. He was also receiving adverse reports from North America, both about Gaudentius' missionary methods and his proposed convents.[99]

On 25 November 1859 Father Gaudentius told Elizabeth he was praying 'for a very important object', which, if granted, he would consider 'one of the best sanctions' of her 'pious institute'. He hoped that in 1860 she would be able to send two or three sisters to establish the institute in North America. He reminded her he had always intended the Americans to return. 'I trust', he wrote, 'the time will soon arrive for the final accomplishment of my long and ardent desires. Next year we hope to open a new monastery in some other part of the United States.... This will also be a good opportunity for the Sisters.'[100] He was therefore planning to make her foundation in Dunkirk, not in Pittsburgh as he had previously promised.[101] He also proposed to Father Ignatius Spencer that he should go out to North America to preach his crusade for the conversion of England and to establish the sisters there.[102]

Within a month of his letter to Elizabeth, Gaudentius wrote to the mother president of the Passionist nuns in Italy. He offered her two postulants, Isabelle Lynch, who apparently had extraordinary graces and visions, and Rose McCabe, also said to be remarkably endowed. Since Italy was in the throes of war, Gaudentius suggested the Passionist nuns should make a foundation in either England or North America. He asked the mother president if, provided she were invited by an American bishop, she would send over two or three of her best sisters. In words reminiscent of his letter to Father Croskell on 31 January 1851, he wrote, 'I already have eight or ten prepared to begin.'[103]

In his next letter to Elizabeth on 3 August 1860, Gaudentius told her that, in regard to her foundation in North America, he was still waiting for 'a more clear manifestation of God's Will'. At the same time, however, he was stressing the industrial nature of the institute to the extent of claiming he had never wanted the religious habit and that he saw realized in the Daughters of the Sacred Heart of Mary in Cleveland 'the idea that for many years' had been in his mind.[104] He therefore seems to have been proposing to found three orders: Elizabeth Prout's sisters from England as an industrial, almost secular institute; a new American order of teachers; and the contemplative

Passionist nuns. There was no indication in his letter that he wished to bring out Elizabeth's order to teach, although he had previously asked her to send teachers and in general he still saw teaching as part of its apostolate.[105]

Father Anthony Testa's reply, written on 27 October 1860, contained an almost carbon copy of Elizabeth Prout's process of founding her congregation. Giving permission for Father John Dominic to found a Passionist active-contemplative order of women in North America, Anthony said that, with the approval of the bishop they were first to be brought together in one house (as Elizabeth and her companions had come together in Stocks Street); a superior with 'both the proper spirit and administrative ability' was to be appointed (whereas Elizabeth had been elected); the habit was to be 'simple, modest, long' (as hers was); the sisters were to be active but 'at the same time blend in as many of the elements of the Rule of the Passionist Nuns as possible' (which was what Elizabeth was even then, in her revision of the Rule, planning to do); through their work of education they were to be self-supporting (as Elizabeth's congregation was); when the group had grown, a proper community could be considered (as had been effected in Elizabeth's case in 1852-1854); and they could also have boarding schools (as Elizabeth had) and houses of retreat (as Elizabeth inserted into her 1863 Rule).[106] Elizabeth Prout's congregation therefore actually surpassed the general's expectations in also providing for parish visitation, sewing workrooms and, from 1863, homes for factory girls. But, said Father Anthony Testa, laying the full responsibilty for this order, as for the Passionist nuns, on Father John Dominic, 'No one else is to get mixed up in it.'[107] Father Gaudentius Rossi was specifically excluded. '*Gaudenzio e storto ed in materia di governo farebbe rovine*', the general commented at this time.[108] 'Father Gaudentius does not have either the gifts or the virtues to govern', Anthony told John Dominic. 'I fear he would be much too quick to believe in and to approve extraordinary things.'[109] Finally, Anthony reminded John Dominic, he needed a foundress, 'a good, holy and virtuous woman, who had a talent to govern'.[110] He needed an Elizabeth Prout. As far as the general could judge, John Dominic did not have one. In 1861, after receiving more information from Father Albinus Magno, sent to Rome by Father John Dominic, the general prohibited all Father Gaudentius Rossi's proposed foundations.[111]

Thus, although Gaudentius never told Elizabeth, from late 1860 he knew he could not bring her sisters to North America. It was from then that he lost much of his interest in them, as indicated by his lack of correspondence, his delay in writing, even to Ignatius Spencer, about the revision of his Rule and by his peevish criticism of Elizabeth's government. Then in 1864 Sister Anne Joachim arrived in North

America, sent out, as she told Father Anthony Calandri and other Passionists in America, on Elizabeth's instructions to fulfil Father Gaudentius' expressed insistence that she was to return to found the order in the States, her fare paid by the American donation made for that purpose in 1857 and which Elizabeth had carefully set aside in spite of the order's debts. Embarrassed beyond measure, even two years later a letter from Mother Winefride led Father Gaudentius Rossi into repeated complaints against Anne Joachim and a final invective against Elizabeth Prout, although at the same time he had to acknowledge her great virtue.[112]

3. THE TRIUMPH OF THE CROSS

Although the revised Rule was Elizabeth Prout's definition of the charism of her congregation, in the form in which it was presented to Rome in 1863 it did not contain all the passages she had earmarked from the Passionist Rule. Within only six months of her death, however, at the suggestion of no less a person than the Passionist Father General, negotiations were opened that led in 1876 to the incorporation of her excerpts into her Rule or Regulations.

Without the general's direct intervention, the sisters would not have thought of applying to Rome for further approbation until, as directed by Cardinal Barnabò, they had lived the 1863 Rule for a few years and had four or six houses. On 24 June 1864, however, during a visit to Sutton, Father Peter Paul Cayro, the first Passionist general to visit England, was introduced by Father Ignatius Spencer to Elizabeth Prout's sisters. Pleased with both the sisters and the convent, he immediately expressed a desire that the order should be aggregated to the Passionist Congregation.[113] He said it was already Passionist in everything but name. It had been founded by a Passionist, Father Gaudentius Rossi and, since his departure for North America, another Passionist, Father Ignatius Spencer had looked after its affairs. He had been responsible for the revision of the Rule, much of which had been taken from the Passionist *Rule*, and for its first approbation in Rome. The sisters taught in Passionist schools in Sutton and Peasley Cross and they already received spiritual direction from the Passionist Fathers. Aggregation would give them that as a right. In March 1865 he went further: he proposed they should change their title to 'Sisters of the Cross and Passion of Jesus Christ'.[114]

Father Ignatius Spencer had died on 1 October 1864.[115] The Passionist Provincial, Father Ignatius Paoli, who was as keen as the general on the aggregation, had then appointed his consultor, Father Eugene Martorelli, previously visitator general and then provincial, as the sisters' director. On 21 March 1865 Ignatius Paoli assured Mother Winefride Lynch she could have the full Passionist Badge 'with all the letters or inscription exactly like ours'.[116] Since the Passionist general needed a copy of the Rule, Eugene translated it into Italian, making a few minor changes as he did so. On 22 January 1866 he told Wine-fride he thought the Rule 'such as ought or can be, for *Passionist Nuns, in England*'.[117] Informed by Winefride of the proposals, Father Gaudentius Rossi was delighted. He 'truly rejoiced', seeing the interest the general, the provincial and his consultor, Father Eugene, were taking in his institute as 'the best guarantee of its future success and general usefulness'.[118]

When the general opened negotiations in Rome, however, he discovered it was not possible to grant aggregation without applying to the Holy See for 'an *authoritative* approbation of the Rules' and that he required an account of the beginning and progress of the Institute; a statement of the good it had done and was doing; and evidence of the sentiments of the bishops in its regard, their approbation and their recommendation.[119] Eugene was ready to write the required history if Winefride furnished him with the material. He left it to her to ask for Bishop Turner's testimony. She had already asked Father Gaudentius for information on how the order had originated.[120] With his reply and remembering all she could of what Elizabeth Prout had told her, Winefride now wrote her 'Records of the Institute of the Holy Family', covering the period from 1849 to 10 August 1852.[121] Sister Mary Paul Taylor wrote her 'Notes of the Institute' from the foundation of the congregation on 15 August 1851 to the results of the first general chapter in 1863.[122] In Eugene's hands by 12 June 1866, by 12 July these papers, with Bishop Turner's testimonial, had reached Cardinal Barnabò.[123] It seemed as though aggregation to the Passionist Congre-gation might coincide with the canonisation of Paul of the Cross in 1867. When the Rule was scrutinised by *Propaganda*, however, Father Ignatius Paoli, by then a general consultor resident in Rome and looking after the sisters' affairs there, was told it required 'several alterations' on points taken from the Passionist *Rule*. Even there, he was told, they were irregularities, which must have been granted as 'privileges or concessions'. They could not be allowed 'according to the present system of the Church in approving Religious Orders in the 1860s'.[124] Posthumously Elizabeth Prout was meeting the same difficulties as Paul of the Cross had encountered, on account of the combination of the Trappist and the Jesuit, or of Martha and Mary, which defied a legalistic definition.

At the sisters' second chapter, held in the new convent of the Infant Jesus, Bolton in 1867, Sister Mary Margaret Chambers was elected third Mother General, so that it then fell to her to pursue both the aggregation and approbation. With her co-operation, Father Eugene then made the required alterations in the Rule. The sisters observed the slightly altered Rule for a year and in 1869 Eugene took it back to Rome when he went out for the Passionist general chapter.[125] Since he was re-presenting the Rule for approbation, he once more had to submit 'a short history of the origin and development' of the institute; the number of houses, schools and homes in 1869; the number of professed sisters and novices; and the means of supporting the various communities. The Holy See also required to know if the congregation had any debts or any money in reserve. Bishop Turner had to give another indispensable petition and commendatory letter.[126] Going to the 1869 chapter with all these documents, both Ignatius Paoli and Eugene expected the matter to be settled while they were there. Instead the Passionist general chapter itself remodelled the Rule to bring it 'as far as possible into harmony' with the Passionist *Rule*. In doing so, they inserted most of the sections Elizabeth Prout had wanted to take in 1863. Ignatius told Mary Margaret in June 1870, it had 'undergone a thorough demolishing and reconstruction', with the final result, however, that 'nothing that was substantial' had been omitted from the 1863 version nor had anything substantial been added. Only 'some passages' which had seemed 'dry and stiff' had been made 'richer', while others that were considered 'too bulky and verbose' had been made 'thinner'.[127] The highest legislative body in the Passionist Congregation had given Elizabeth Prout's congregation the Rule she had wanted in 1863. It was more than ever her last will and testament. By 25 June 1870 it was ready for presentation to *Propaganda*.

Approbation, and therefore aggregation, was again delayed, however, because the appropriate consultor from the Sacred Congregation of Religious was absent from Rome until October 1870. Before he returned, Father Ignatius Paoli was appointed bishop of Nicopolis. He assured Mary Margaret his episcopal rank would expedite rather than impede the Rule's progress. He would present his own petition, in which he would express his desire and intention to introduce the congregation into Bulgaria. Father Gaudentius' hopes for extension to 'the eastern hemisphere' were about to be realised and, in the event, one of his American postulants, Sister Anne Joachim Flanagan was one of the pioneers.[128] Bishop Ignatius Paoli, having appointed a general consultor to act in his name, left for his diocese in early September 1870.[129] Before anything further could be done about the Rule, however, Victor Emmanuel II marched into Rome. None of the papal offices could have continued to function normally. Thus even after her death Elizabeth Prout's affairs managed to become involved in the great issues of the day.

By 1872 papal machinery was moving again but the papers Ignatius Paoli had had ready for presentation in 1870 needed to be updated. By then also Father Eugene had left England. Father Bernard O'Loughlin had become provincial and had appointed Father Alphonsus O'Neill, rector in Sutton, as the sisters' director.[130] In July 1872 the Passionist general came to England. While in London, he visited Archbishop Manning, who had already invited the sisters into his diocese, and asked him to send a petition to Rome in favour of their approval by the Holy See. Mother Mary Margaret was requested to approach Bishop Turner yet again, this time for a supportive letter to Manning. Bishop Turner's subsequent petition, on 8 July 1872, only a few days before his sudden death, was the last of his many services to Elizabeth Prout's congregation.[131] The aggregation had become urgent, because in 1873 the sisters were going out to Bulgaria as the Sisters of the Cross and Passion. Mary Margaret asked permission for them to wear the full Passionist Sign. Father Bernard added his voice to hers, as did Alphonsus, who asked the Passionist general to complete 'the good work', which would give satisfaction to the Passionists and joy to the sisters. It would enable them, as Passionists, to 'leaven the classes of poor', so many of whom the Passionist Fathers could not reach, 'with this holiest devotion' of 'Our Lord's Sacred Passion'.[132] Thus he confirmed that Elizabeth Prout's order was an authentic extension of the Passionist mission to England. It was a vital means of reaching the working classes. In reply, the Passionist procurator general, who was also a consultor at *Propaganda* and appointed by both the Passionist general and *Propaganda* to supervise the Rule's scrutiny, wrote to Father Alphonsus:

> The nuns are going on *magnificently*. I must say even now that I am delighted with their 'Holy Rules and Constitutions'. I have read many others but I know of none better suited for the wants of the times and which more beautifully and practically combine the two lives — the Active and the Contemplative and I believe that if the Holy See will approve of them soon the Sisters of the Cross and Passion will grow into '*the* greatest of all Conventual Communities' in these northern countries.[133]

The negotiations for approbation and aggregation were clearly in their final stages. On 5 September 1874 Mother Mary Margaret Chambers asked the Passionist general to confer the privilege of 'bless[ing] and send[ing] the first Badge'.[134] On 9 November the Passionist general curia granted the use of the full Passionist Sign to Elizabeth Prout's congregation and on the 15th the new Father General, Dominic Giacchini wrote to Mother Mary Margaret:

> ... I have come to understand that among the pious practices and holy exercises prescribed by the Rule for the Sisters, there is

assigned a distinct place for salutary meditation on the sorrowful mysteries of the Passion of our Divine Redeemer, joined to a special study to awaken in the hearts of others also a pious and grateful memory of the same. Because of this my heart experiences an unspeakable consolation, and with a sweet violence it opens my heart to love with a special affection a Congregation whose spirit so well accords with that of the Institute of St Paul of the Cross.... The... Congregation of the Sisters of the Most Holy Cross and Passion of Our Lord Jesus Christ is already in possession of the first place in my heart after that which is due to the Sons and Daughters of St Paul of the Cross....

It was more fitting than he realised that he sent her 'the SIGN' through 'Very Rev. Fr Provincial, Fr Bernard of the Virgin Mary', the 'good Father Bernard' of Elizabeth Prout's 1858 crisis.[135] She would have approved of Mother Mary Margaret's reply:

No words can express the joy which your Paternity's letter and the beautiful and Holy Badge of the Passion which it accompanied has brought to my heart and the hearts of all the Sisters of the Most Holy Cross and Passion.... We can only offer the feeble expression simple words can convey of the imperishable gratitude in which we shall ever hold in memory the favour you have done us in assigning us our place as children of St Paul of the Cross. We shall strive daily with the Divine Aid to become more worthy of the distinctive favour conferred by increased devotion to the Holy Passion of Our Lord and to our Father and Protector St Paul of the Cross.[136]

In 1875 the sisters joined with the full Passionist Congregation in celebrating the centenary of the death of St Paul of the Cross. When, on 9 April, Father Alphonsus O'Neill, appropriately beginning in Manchester, visited each convent to present each sister with the full Passionist Sign, Elizabeth Prout's own Passionist congregation attained its true identity.[137] On 2 July 1876 the Holy See granted the order ten years' approbation.[138] On 15 August the sisters celebrated the silver jubilee of its foundation at 69 Stocks Street. It was Elizabeth Prout's Rule that was approved, her founding of the order that was celebrated. As Bishop Vaughan said, 'the Seal of Peter' had been set upon her Rule and her congregation 'belonged to St Paul of the Cross'.[139]

Mother Mary Margaret Chambers had the approved *Rule* printed. She then sent a copy to Father Gaudentius Rossi. He noted the title, 'The Congregation of the Holy Cross and Passion'. He took out the copy of his own 1852-5 Rule that Elizabeth Prout had written out for him in 1855. He carefully compared the two. Then, on 21 October 1877, he replied, 'Though the original Rules and Constitutions have been almost entirely changed, yet the object of the original institute has been preserved.... Devotion to the Passion of Our Divine Saviour is now also a special characteristic of the Sisters, and I am very much pleased with this new improvement.'[140]

Thus Father Gaudentius Rossi finally sanctioned Elizabeth Prout's 1863 revision of his Rule and recognised the Sisters of the Cross and Passion as his own. He was now engaged in parish work in West Hoboken and busily writing books, after a long missionary career, during which he had travelled the length and breadth of England and thousands of miles in North America, a devoted, unwearying preacher and missioner, constantly in demand for parish, clergy and nuns' retreats and keeping his 'audiences spellbound for hours'.[141] A provincial consultor from 1863 to 1866, he was novice-master from 1866-69.[142] In 1878 he was appointed lector in Sacred Eloquence in Dunkirk.[143] He continued to give a few retreats, and even an occasional mission, until 1883.[144] In 1885, aged sixty-eight, he became resident chaplain to the Christian Brothers' school at Louisville, where he was much beloved for his kindness.[145] It was appropriate that Rome's final approbation of the institute in 1887 should coincide with the golden jubilee year of his religious profession.[146] After four years as school chaplain he was suddenly taken ill in 1889 and almost died.[147] He recovered, however, and in January 1890 was required to give a written statement, under oath, on the virtue and holiness of life of Father Dominic Barberi.[148] In August 1890 he returned to live in West Hoboken.[149] There, in April 1891, he was again cited as a witness to Father Dominic Barberi's virtue.[150] Father Gaudentius continued to lead an active community life and to say Mass each day until he was suddenly taken ill, 'with a grave internal disorder', in July 1891.[151] He died on 12 August 1891, aged seventy-four, and was buried the next day.[152] Two days later, on 15 August 1891, the sisters celebrated the ruby jubilee of Elizabeth Prout's foundation at 69 Stocks Street.[153] Amongst them was an American, Sister Gaudentia McClowry, whom he had sent to England in 1888, the final mark of his approval.[154]

Provost Robert Croskell had also renewed his friendship with Elizabeth Prout's congregation. In 1875 he expressed his approval of its homes for factory girls.[155] He presided at a profession ceremony in 1878.[156] In 1887 he joined in the congratulations and celebrations on its final recognition as a religious order within the Catholic Church.[157] Told of Father Gaudentius' death in 1891, he expressed the wish to hear more particulars 'of his last days upon earth and his death' after his 'long and meritorious life'.[158] He was pleased in 1893 to visit Bolton and to meet an 'imposing number of novices'.[159] He was pleased, too, in his last years, to exchange Christmas and Easter greetings with Sister Mary Paul Taylor and to receive the sisters' frequent visits in Levenshulme until his own death in 1903.[160] When

St Robert's church, Longsight was opened in his memory in 1915, Elizabeth Prout's sisters sent the vestments for the opening Mass as a recognition of his help in times past.[161]

It was Father Ignatius Spencer, however, who had the most enduring influence on the congregation, in furthering its apostolate amongst factory girls, the approbation of its Rule in Rome, its educational work, its growth in numbers through Irish postulants and its part in his crusade for the conversion of England, or, as he expressed it, for 'unity in the truth'. The sisters were first committed to praying for the conversion of England by Father Gaudentius Rossi in his 1852 Rule, in which he legislated that they were to spend every Friday 'in pious remembrance' of the 'most bitter Passion of their divine spouse Jesus Crucified', offering up to God 'all their good works, devout prayers and sufferings' in union with the Passion, first for the 'conversion of poor sinners' and secondly 'for the conversion of pagans, infidels and heretics, and especially for the Conversion of England....'[162] Father Gaudentius, therefore, deliberately linked their commitment to pray for the conversion of England to devotion to the Passion, even echoing the diary entries of Paul of the Cross, 'I desired the conversion of heretics, especially of England with the neighbouring kingdoms ...' and 'I had special recollection in offering His most holy Life, Death and Passion ... especially for heretics. I had a particular impulse to pray for the conversion of England....'[163] Father Gaudentius' terminology also linked the sisters' commitment to Father Ignatius Spencer's crusade of prayer for England.[164] It was therefore part of the charism of Elizabeth Prout's congregation to share the Passionist perennial apostolate for the conversion of England and to be part of Father Ignatius Spencer's nineteenth-century movement.[165] In his contacts with the order, that commitment was constantly emphasised. Thus at the first retreat he gave them in January 1854 he preached at least one sermon on the conversion of England and enrolled six of them in his association of prayer, by which, in return for their daily prayers for England, they could be assured of the reciprocal prayers of the Passionist Congregation and of certain indulgences granted by the Holy See.[166] From 1853 he was pursuing his objective with ever increased fervour, because he saw the forthcoming beatification of Paul of the Cross as closely connected with the conversion of England.[167] In view of her close contacts with Father Ignatius, Elizabeth Prout's own request to Father Gaudentius in 1853 to have Paul of the Cross as a patron of the institute suggests that, in deliberately strengthening its Passionist links, she was also intentionally committing it more deeply to that sacrificial 'holocaust of love ... in union with the Sacrifice of Calvary' for which Father Ignatius asked and which linked his crusade for England to his Paulacrucian 'memory' of the Passion.[168] Indeed, like Ignatius, she and other sisters had a vested interest on behalf of their own families. Ever inventive of new modes of appeal, by September 1855 Ignatius had introduced a new approach to induce the Irish to pray for England: he asked them to pray for the conversion of England and the sanctification of Ireland. From June 1858 his crusade was linked to his new apostolate of 'little missions', primarily in Ireland and Scotland but also in England, whereby he preached in a place for only three days, instead of the customary two or three weeks.[169] As a result he covered a much wider area. It was in this context that he attracted Irish girls to Elizabeth Prout's order. Frequently resident in Sutton from 1862 he gave her and her sisters 'many treats of spiritual conferences upon his favourite topic of the conversion of England and the sanctification of Ireland'. Addressing them at the profession of Sister Mary Margaret Chambers on 21 November 1862, preparatory to their taking the sewing classes in Ashton, he said he saw their apostolate amongst the mill girls as a sign to English Protestants of 'what the Catholic religion [would] do for her children'. Likewise, at the clothing of Sister Frances de Sales Durie in July 1864, the last ceremony he attended before his death, he preached on the 'great topic, the great cause of which [he had] so often spoken... the conversion of England and the sanctification of Ireland. This I am sure', he said, 'you will not forget to pray for now and always. I don't know,' he added wistfully, 'that God will permit me to see this great work accomplished but... when I am no more I leave it to you to carry on.'[170] It was no coincidence that in 1926 Mother Berchmans called the introduction to her proposed history of the congregation, 'England's Conversion'.

Father Ignatius Spencer's contribution to the educational development of Elizabeth Prout's order lay principally in his attracting Jane Mary Durie to join it. Born at Stobo in Peebleshire on 18 October 1816, she was left a widow with a little daughter. Having then to earn her own livelihood, like Elizabeth she became a teacher and later she became a Catholic. She possibly met Elizabeth in Sunderland on 18 June 1850, when she went to sit the government's examinations for teacher certification. Changes were made in the arrangements without due notice, however, and so Elizabeth, like most other prospective candidates, may not have been there.[171] Only five women sat the examinations. Only three, including Jane Durie, passed.[172] Inspecting her school at St Mary's, Edinburgh, S.N. Stokes was always expansive in his praises. His reports refer to 'her ability and professional order'; her well-used circulating library; her 'conscientious and capable skill' in training pupil teachers; and the 'comprehensive and minute detail' and the 'beautiful calligraphy' of her registers, which he ranked amongst 'the excellences' of her school as deserving the 'highest commendation'.[173] Jane Durie received the religious habit from her

Factory Girls and Mills, Ancoats

friend, Father Ignatius on 6 July 1864 and took her vows on 2 July 1866. Considered the 'cleverest teacher in England', with Stokes' help she then established a teacher training college for the order. From then until her death on 12 May 1883 she used her skills to forge a highly-trained generation of Passionist teachers, who conducted many of the Catholic primary schools in the industrial towns of Lancashire and Yorkshire.[174]

Father Ignatius Spencer had appreciated Elizabeth Prout's 'knowledge and abilities' and her spiritual heroism as she saw her infant institute 'tossed to and fro and beaten about till it seemed impossible, except by divine aid, to keep it together'.[175] Father Salvian Nardocci, no easy taskmaster, had seen her as 'an excellent Religious', who had 'a great desire of doing good especially to poor Factory Girls'. She governed her congregation for thirteen years, he said, 'with great skill and prudence' in spite of the many 'trials and contradictions she had to endure the whole of that time'.[176] In Father Gaudentius Rossi's poetic phraseology, starting 'in a low, poor, simple way', she had guided her congregation from its 'small beginnings' at Stocks Street, through 'the blasting colds and storms of winter', of fever, debt, defections and investigation, to 'the smiles of spring and summer' in Rome's approbation and the first general chapter.[177] She had established the Institute of the Holy Family; she had founded the Congregation of the Sisters of the Cross and Passion. In so doing, she preserved intact the full Paulacrucian heritage of the 'memory' of both the Holy Family and the Passion.

CHAPTER VIII

CONCLUSION

A woman of her time, Elizabeth Prout puts a human and feminine face on the social history of the Manchester area in the mid-nineteenth century. Her life illuminates a number of issues currently debated by historians: the place of religion in society; the consequences of Manchester's swift industrial urbanisation and the position in that society of the immigrant Irish; the means by which respectable but impoverished women could earn a livelihood in the industrial city; the different types of female religious orders and the class society within them; the history of education; the role of philanthropic organisations and their attitudes towards those whose poverty they alleviated; contemporary ideas of self-help and political and domestic economy; and concern for the domesticity and moral improvement of working-class women.

In every sense Elizabeth Prout belonged to the working classes. In adding an intimate touch to more general publications on coopers and the brewing industry, her home life helps to illuminate what P. Mathias has called 'an unexplored tract of English industrial history'.[1] It provides an insight into how a cooper's family in the mid-nineteenth century fitted into the social life of their environment and were influenced by the events and ideas of their time. This particular type of independent and respectable working-class home was, in turn, of fundamental importance in shaping Elizabeth's character and attitudes and in enabling her to fulfil her administrative tasks as the foundress of a religious order. With her Paulacrucian spirituality, it gave her the courage and integrity to withstand even Father Gaudentius Rossi on those rare occasions when the good of the congregation demanded it. It also made her put on one side for its originally intended purpose the money he had received to bring sisters to North America but which in 1857, with the donor's permission, he sent to alleviate her distress. Similarly, it kept her from using a legacy Sister Gertrude Blount brought to the congregation at the height of the 1858 crisis.[2] This moral rectitude was accompanied by an irrepressible sense of fun that must have sprung from her happy family background and which, developed by her spiritual life into a holy joy, radiated the affectionate joyfulness she imparted to her congregation. Close enough to the poor to understand them, she was also sufficiently above them to be able to assist them at the different levels of providing religious life, conducting schools and inculcating domesticity, with a practical common sense that lent competence to her endeavours.

Elizabeth Prout's foundation of her order was truly Passionist. Describing her abandonment of both established religious life in

Belgium and a marriage proposal, Mother Winifride Lynch said, 'The latter she would not hear of and the former she declined to enter herself amongst the list of the poor.'[3] It is significant that Winefride did not say Elizabeth dedicated herself to the service of the poor. She did something much more radical: she entered herself 'amongst the list of the poor'. She actually became one of the poor. Winefride stressed the point, for she had already said that Elizabeth's motivation was 'a love of poverty'. She abandoned herself to God in real poverty. She made these choices out of obedience to what, as an 'external call', manifested for her the will of God.[4] In 1851 she gave a practical demonstration of her sincerity, for, whereas in joining her in Stocks Street, Catharine Toler and Catharine Gilday raised their social standing, in joining a domestic servant and a factory worker, even in Stocks Street, Elizabeth lowered hers. Her religious order belonged by foundation to the *anawim*. At great personal risk, she embraced a religious life aimed at offering the poor religious life itself. That was her primary apostolate, her radical option for the poor. It was an authentic expression of the Paulacrucian spirituality she had received from Father Dominic Barberi. Her order was an extension of the Passionist mission to England. Moreover, in that first crucial period of almost three years from November 1849 to late June 1852, before Father Gaudentius wrote the Rule, it was Elizabeth Prout who indelibly printed upon her embryonic congregation the features of her own spirituality and education. At that early stage, neither Fathers Gaudentius nor Croskell proposed either central devotion or title. They offered neither rule of life nor active apostolate. All they had was a foundress who supported herself by teaching in the parish school. That was the position in November 1849 when Elizabeth exchanged letters with Gaudentius, in which she took the initiative in speaking of taking a house suitable as a convent. If the inspiration to found an order for lower-class women belonged to Father Gaudentius Rossi, its implementation depended on Elizabeth Prout. She was truly the foundress.

From August 1851 it was Elizabeth Prout who had the difficult task of realising Father Gaudentius Rossi's revolutionary inspiration for a religious order for the poor in the harsh conditions of nineteenth-century Manchester. It was she who first made consecrated religious life, with choir observance, available to working-class women. In religious terms, she put them socially on a par with the endowed orders. In spiritual terms, she enabled them to reach heights of sanctity. She gave them a truly contemplative life. Her order's lifestyle was not shaped by apostolic activity but by its essential 'memory'. In his parting letter on English soil, Father Gaudentius did not tell Elizabeth to strive to reduce social grievances. He told her, in the language of both Saints Paul and John of the Cross, to go before her sisters as a 'burning and bright lamp of good example'.[5] She gave her sisters a way of life, a mysticism of the heart, not an intellectual or apostolic spirituality based on the will. She did not begin with concern for the poor but with the 'memory' of the Holy Family and the Passion. It was that 'memory', always in her heart and mind, that motivated her lifestyle and produced the kind of person who would be concerned for the distress of the poor and who would also be capable of facing the realities of Manchester's worst slum. Her homes for factory girls were significantly an extension of her religious order. She sought to incarnate the 'memory' of the Holy Family in the refuge. Hence it was properly called the 'Home'. Similarly, she brought that 'memory' into the homes of the working classes through her visitation and the children she taught. It was that emphasis on the contemplative nature of the institute that permitted its diversity of active apostolate. The success of the sisters' active ministry, however, depended on the quality of their contemplative life, for, while other women could teach or visit the poor, only Passionists could impart their particular brand of spirituality. Hence in contrast to the increasing permissiveness of her time, she moved towards greater austerity. Although in her active apostolate she mirrored the industrial society in which she lived, she maintained a strong contemplative, all-pervading ethos against its materialistic standards. She consistently maintained the balance in the dual identity of her congregation, so that, like the Passionist Fathers and Brothers, she and her sisters were truly contemplatives in action. Their union with God was the dynamic force behind their rigorous active apostolate and the source in which they constantly renewed their apostolic strength. From June 1852 she lived according to Father Gaudentius Rossi's Rule, which expressed for her the will of God. It was only her willingness to sublimate it in that way that gave any substance to his writ or offered it any chance of success. It was her task as foundress to live the Rule, to interpret it and to enforce it. Occasionally Father Gaudentius accused her of being too ready to give dispensations but, as previously mentioned, according to the lasting tradition recorded by Mother Berchmans, 'She would not allow the slightest deviation in the Rule or in regular observance. She showed by her own example and also by those who persevered with her that to those who really loved God, there was nothing impossible in the Rule and Customs.'[6] It is interesting in this context that of the first seven sisters, the two who persevered finally, Elizabeth Prout herself and Mary Paul Taylor, had both been English Protestants. As such, they highlight the social and spiritual debt the English Catholic Church owed to its converts in the mid-nineteenth century. Their achievements demonstrate how much Catholic women could accomplish within what Evangelicals liked to say was an authoritarian and male-dominated organisation.

As a woman, Elizabeth Prout certainly relied on males for the existence and approval of her religious order within the Catholic Church, an organisation that, by reason of its sacramental nature, depended on an ordained, male priesthood. Nevertheless, her feminine contribution to the development of Passionist spirituality was outstanding. By founding a Passionist religious order specifically for lower-class women, she fulfilled to an eminent degree the teaching of St Paul of the Cross that holiness was within the reach of every human person of any class. She demonstrated that women from any class of society could receive a call from God to serve Him in consecrated religious life. Choir observance was not the preserve of the upper and middle classes. It was open to the uneducated and even illiterate. Paul of the Cross himself had founded the totally contemplative Passionist nuns. Elizabeth Prout extended his apostolate by founding a female institute that accurately reflected his male congregation in combining the contemplative and active lives. While he united the apparently contradictory Trappist and Jesuit lifestyles, she, as Father Gaudentius expressed it, united Mary and Martha into one person.

As a nun Elizabeth Prout excluded herself from social life and yet, as the foundress of a new type of religious order, she had a wider field of social activity than that enjoyed by most women. Her experiences in Manchester demonstrate the dehumanizing conditions into which swift and uncontrolled industrialisation pitched the very employees whose labour produced the capitalists' profits. These industrial workers were in a very different position from Edward Prout, although their toil was equally essential to entrepreneurial success. They were more vulnerable because they worked in a free market in which a glut of labour prevented their controlling their employers. Whenever they could escape from the direst poverty trap, however, all of them, English and Irish, were as houseproud and as anxious to enjoy their comforts as any other class in society. Furthermore, they enjoyed them together. English and Irish could live happily together both in Elizabeth Prout's order and in the slums of Manchester.

Her experiences in Manchester also confirm recent writings on class society in the industrial towns and on Irish assimilation into the host community. The Irish in Elizabeth Prout's Manchester were neither ethnically nor religiously segregated. They formed part of the general community, each individual or family finding a niche at the appropriate social level. Traditional histories of Irish immigrants have emphasised the alcoholic and disorderly delinquencies of the conspicuous few rather than the sober and law-abiding behaviour of the majority. Attendance at Passionist missions and a presence in every class of society and type of housing confirm more recent historians' conclusions that such historiography has been distorted. The Irish were so

well assimilated that their positive contribution to the city's development has been overlooked.

Elizabeth Prout's life suggests that the hostility shown by English
workmen towards Irish immigrants was intrinsically economic, rather
than ethnic or religious, even in the Stockport riots. Male English
workers showed similar opposition towards female counterparts and
would have shown comparable hostility towards any non-local English
male workers whose presence caused wage reductions or redundancies.
Nor was there necessarily conflict between Catholic and Protestant.
One of the remarkable features of Elizabeth Prout's life was that she
founded her order at the height of anti-Irish and anti-Catholic hostility
and in an area influenced by the staunch Evangelical, Canon Hugh
Stowell. The Stockport riots indicate how accurately Paul of the Cross
had associated his own desires for England with possible martyrdom.
They also underline the widespread Evangelical campaigning against
Catholicism illustrated in Manchester's *Protestant Witness* and
experienced by both Fathers Dominic Barberi and Ignatius Spencer.
What is significant, however, is that from the mid-eighteenth century
there had been no sign of popular anti-Catholicism until it was
fomented by the Evangelicals. Traditional suspicion of Rome does not
seem to have been a characteristic of English lower-class society. It
became a reality in Elizabeth Prout's experience when deliberately
contrived by a Tory press; by Tory employers anxious to keep their
workmen divided and thus controlled; and by Evangelical preachers
and their henchmen. What is also significant, however, is that although
there was sectarian conflict in Ashton-under-Lyne and Stockport, the
Catholic Church in Manchester itself was sufficiently prestigious and
powerful to be able to contain it.

Elizabeth carried out her educational apostolate at a time of conflict
and development, especially as the issues that found expression in the
1870 Education Act were then being debated in Manchester. Her initial
work in St Chad's demonstrates the significant role a dedicated secular
laywoman could play in the Catholic Church in such an urban
situation. At the same time, the clergy's preference for the professional
religious teaching orders points to the vast contribution both male and
female religious were to make to education in Manchester and thus to
the social history of its working classes. Elizabeth Prout's immediate
contribution to education lay in her selfless adaptability. In the long
term, her contribution lay in the fruit of that availability: while
consistently opting for the poor, her sisters have filled positions in the
whole range of education from nursery schools to training college in
England, from sewing classes to university in Botswana.

Her life sheds valuable light on the Catholic revival as experienced
by Manchester's working classes. If Manchester was the frontier town

of the industrial revolution, it also pioneered the new Catholic Church of the urban workforce and both Elizabeth Prout and the Passionist missioners played a fundamental role in its formation. Manchester was a fitting cradle for Elizabeth Prout's order. To her the working classes were not dissolute ne'er-do-wells. The Irish were not superstitious savages. The value of human beings could not be calculated in terms of utility. Through her parish visitation the poor knew they were not forgotten. She brought a personal touch, which the priests, on account of overwork, could bring only to the sick and dying. Hers was an inconspicuous form of religious life, which deterred even some clergy from considering her sisters 'proper nuns' but it identified them as close to the people they helped.

Since they, like others in an urban situation, had to support themselves by the work they could find there, her life provides an insight into women's labour in such a society and into poverty in an urban environment. She and her sisters formed an integral part of urban life in going out to work, at first in factories and sewing houses and always in parochial schools; in travelling on trains and omnibuses; in living in comparatively small convents; and in visiting the working classes in their own homes. Having to struggle to eke out an existence mainly by needlework, like other seamstresses they had to work every available minute. Their lives thus reflected their materialistic environment in which labour was seen as merchandise which the employee sold to the capitalist. Forced by the economy to sell their time and talents at the lowest price, their hours of work had to be stretched to the limit consonant with contemplative religious life. It was only Elizabeth's rigorous insistence on that dimension that protected them from total drudgery. At the same time, however, it was that very real poverty, coupled with her Paulacrucian spirituality, that marked her order as essentially Passionist.

Like St Paul of the Cross, Elizabeth Prout received her strength from her reception of the Sacraments and from the Presence of the Blessed Sacrament, the Memorial of the Passion. The privilege that, as a religious, she sought above all others was to have the Blessed Sacrament in the convent chapel.[7] Of central importance in Paulacrucian spirituality, its significance in the sisters' active-contemplative life was expressed by a later annalist as she explained how they 'felt they were truly His Spouses, living under the same roof with Him. Now, when the day's toil was over they could visit Him, and when weary and discouraged, often seeing little fruit in their work for souls, they could lay the burden at His Feet, and always receive comfort, and strength to take up His Cross and follow Him once more.'[8]

Like St Paul of the Cross, too, Elizabeth Prout did not want anything of herself to remain in her institute. She lived on in her congregation,

however, through the Paulacrucian spirituality which she and Father
Gaudentius Rossi imparted to it; which she developed into a clearer
Passionist charism in her 1863 Rule; and in which, through that Rule,
every sister was invited to share. It was precisely because she was
immersed in the contemplation of the Passion that she was not closed
in on herself in an egoistic or sterile introspection but was called to
offer herself for the service of those around her. In practical terms
there was a conflict between the active and contemplative dimensions
of her lifestyle and for most of her life as foundress she epitomised in
her own spiritual struggle the inherent conflict between Martha and
Mary. It was this Paulacrucian spirituality, with its attendant attitude
towards the poor, that makes it inappropriate to present Elizabeth Prout
as either a philanthropist or a social reformer. She made her own the
poverty, prayer and solitude of the Passionist Congregation. This
austerity led her into intimate union with her 'Crucified Spouse', while
also enabling her to find Him in the 'crucified' poor in Manchester's
sordid slums. Her aim was a radical identification with Christ in His
Passion, partly through a life of personal austerity and partly through
a commitment to serve Him in the poor. The rationalism of the age
would have seen her philosophy as an affront to civilisation, an
expression of popish superstition and anachronism in the face of
progress. Secularists would have pointed to her poverty as the proof
of her irrationalism. Even more incomprehensibly to contemporary
mentalities, she was poor because she had chosen to be, in order to
raise up the poor both spiritually and materially. Although, therefore,
she was ready to embrace poverty in order to help the poor, she was
also committed to its destruction. She remained singularly respectable,
even to the extent, as Father Gaudentius told her, of always aiming 'at
high great things'. Ironically, it was her radical option for the poor
that made her incomprehensible even to most of Manchester's Catholic
clergy, because it prevented her from offering the institutional welfare
services they were seeking for the poor. In offering the poor religious
life itself, however, and in visiting the working classes in their own
homes, she was spreading a much wider leaven amongst them than was
possible through a restricted institutional service. She and her
companions were parish sisters from the start. In 1964, a hundred
years after her death, although her order was still a comparatively
small congregation with fewer than 800 members, it had 63 houses
scattered over 5 provinces in the British Isles, North and South
America and Africa, carrying out her apostolate of parish visitation,
education, vestment making, religious confraternities, homes for
working girls, retreats and nursing. Energising this active apostolate
was the Paulacrucian spirituality that she, Father Gaudentius Rossi and
Father Ignatius Spencer had all inculcated and which they had received

from Father Dominic Barberi, the pioneer of the Passionist mission to England.

Elizabeth Prout was part of that 'extensive missionary work' of the Catholic Church and in particular of the Passionist Congregation that, as G. Kitson Clark suggested in 1962, had 'an important bearing on the history of a considerable section of the British working class'.[9] As the foundress of the Sisters of the Cross and Passion, she shines as the sole woman in a galaxy of eminent Passionists: Blessed Dominic Barberi, Saint Charles Houben of Mount Argus, the 'saintly' Father Ignatius Spencer, Father Paul Mary Pakenham, Father Bernard O'Loughlin, the 'saint of Broadway' and, of course, Father Gaudentius Rossi. A study of Elizabeth Prout adds a new, previously unexplored, feminine dimension to the Passionist mission to England. It casts light on Father Gaudentius Rossi, not simply as a Passionist founder of a religious order but as a missioner in the Catholic revival in both England and North America. It opens a new file on the historical significance of Father Ignatius Spencer. It extends the influence of Blessed Dominic Barberi to hitherto almost inconceivable horizons. A true mystic of the Passion, Elizabeth Prout is deservedly interred with those 'heroic figures the Passionists, Blessed Dominic Barberi and Father Ignatius Spencer'.[10]

APPENDIX

THE CATHOLIC STRUGGLE FOR EDUCATION

a) Catholic Parochial Collections for Schools and Churches in Manchester, Feb.-Aug. 1852 [Source: *Tablet*, 21 Aug. 1852]

St Augustine	Feb.	to Aug.	£73	7s.	3½d.
St Wilfrid	Feb.	to Aug.	£38	3s.	6½d.
St Patrick	Apr.	to Aug.	£ 5	7s.	9½d.
St Chad	May	to Aug.	£22	5s.	8½d.
St Mary	late May	to Aug.	£13	7s.	4½d.
St Ann	late May	to Aug.	£10	0s.	10½d.

Total: £162 12s. 7d. *Catholic population:* c.80,000

b) Parish Collections for the Catholic Poor School Committee 1852
     [Source: *Catholic Poor School Committee Report*, 1852, pp.21-22]

St Augustine	£23	2s.	1d.
St Chad	£ 8	12s.	0d.
St Mary	£ 6	4s.	0d.
St Wilfrid	£ 4	17s.	0d.
St Ann	£ 4	10s.	0d.
St Patrick	£ 2	4s.	0d.
St Joseph	£ 1	0s.	0d.

Total: £50 9s. 1d. *Grand Total:* £213 1s. 8d.

c) Catholic Schools in Manchester in 1852 [Source: ibid., p.85]

St Augustine	church crypt	6 Xaverian Brothers
		6 Notre Dame Sisters
Annexe (Ardwick)	chapel crypt	1 male
Annexe (Rusholme)	cottage	
St Chad	schools, Stocks St	1 master
		6 Notre Dame Sisters
Dyche St	over cottages	
St Mary	cottages	1 female
		1 female
St Wilfrid	school, Hulme	1 master
Annexe (Sun.)	Christ Church Sq.	6 Loreto Sisters
Annexe (Sun.)	Poplar Street	
St Ann	over cottages	1 male
St Patrick	schools, Livesey St	6 Christian Brothers
		9 Presentation Nuns
		7 Pupil Teachers
Annexe	George Leigh St	1 male
	warehouse	1 female

d) Attendance at Day Schools and Sunday Schools [Source: *CPSC Report*, 1852, p.85]						
	Day Schools			Sunday Schools		
	Boys	Girls	Infants	Boys	Girls	Infants
St Patrick	725	324	198	1,345	940	395
St Augustine	350	300		420	500	
Ardwick	100[†]			150	150	
Rusholme				10	18	
St Chad	180	292[*]	130	580	1,200	250
St Wilfrid	95	170		200	440	
St Mary	80	75		150	250	360
St Ann	70			100	150	

Notes: † Mixed.   * St Chad's also had a girls' High School
with 40 pupils and a girl's Middle School with 44 pupils.

Saint Paul of the Cross

Blessed Dominic Barberi

Father Gaudentius Rossi and (below) his letter to Elizabeth Prout of 25 February 1854

I most sincerely sympatize with you, my dear Sister mary Joseph, for the large share of the Cross which our B. Redeemer gives to you in different ways. try to bear all well and you shall be rewarded both in the present and future life.

Please to write to me again for many Morning before I start. with my kind respects to all, I am

Gaudentius Passionist

*Father Ignatius Spencer
and the end of his letter
to Elizabeth Prout
from Rome,
14 June 1863*

Monsignor Robert Croskell

Bishop William Turner

day & Instruct & Guide mine so that I might fulfil my duty, & at the same time, that it might be pleasing to God, if it is not presumption on my part, would you agree to this contract. You know my dear Father how weak I am in Virtue & how necessary it is for me to have some one that knows me & will make me keep up to the point & I do not expect any one else to have the patience with me that you have had.

When do you set out; when must you leave England.

I remain my dear Father your in

Mary Joseph & Jesus

I hope I may be allowed to write to you some times in the New World if God grant you may you arrive safe

*From a letter of Elizabeth Prout to
Father Gaudentius Rossi, 7 October 1855*

AAB	Archives of the Archdiocese of Birmingham
AAW	Archives of the Archdiocese of Westminster
ACCM	Archives of the Corporation of the City of Manchester
ACEC	Archives of the Catholic Education Council
ADS	Archives of the Diocese of Salford
AMR	Aston Missions and Retreats
CAC	Colwich Abbey Collection
DAS	Dominican Archives, Stone
DBPLR	Dominic Barberi: Postulation Letters, Rome
DFGR	Deposition of Fr Gaudentius Rossi
GA	General Archives
HMR	Hyde Missions and Retreats
LAO'N	Letters, Alphonsus O'Neill
LBO'L	Letters, Bernard O'Loughlin
LCW	Letters, Clare Wilson
LDB	Letters, Dominic Barberi
LDBCAC	Letters, Dominic Barberi, Colwich Abbey Collection
LEM	Letters, Eugene Martorelli
LEP	Letters, Elizabeth Prout
LGR	Letters, Gaudentius Rossi
LIP	Letters, Ignatius Paoli
LIS	Letters, Ignatius Spencer
LISCAC	Letters, Ignatius Spencer, Colwich Abbey Collection
LISN	Letters, Ignatius Spencer, Northampton
LISR	Letters, Ignatius Spencer, Rome
LRC	Letters, Robert Croskell
LRO	Lancashire Record Office
LWT	Letters, William Turner
MCL	Manchester Central Library
PGAR	Passionist General Archives, Rome
PPA	Passionist Pittsburgh Archives
PPAC	Passionist Provincial Archives, Chicago
PPAD	Passionist Provincial Archives, Dublin
PPAS	Passionist Provincial Archives, Sutton
PPAUC	Passionist Provincial Archives, Union City
PRO	Public Record Office
Sh.RO	Shropshire Record Office
SMR	Sutton Missions and Retreats
St.RO	Staffordshire Record Office

NOTES TO THE INTRODUCTION

1.   J. Winter (ed.), *The Working Class in Modern British History* (Cambridge, 1983), p.vii. Will be cited as Winter.

2.   Strictly, 'order', like 'nuns', refers to women with solemn vows, who normally live in enclosed communities. 'Sister', like 'congregation' and 'institute', refers to those in active apostolates. The Passionists, however, although exercising an active apostolate and not having solemn vows, refer to themselves and are referred to as 'monks', the male equivalent of 'nuns'. Fr Gaudentius Rossi in his 1852-5 Rule and Fr Ignatius Spencer and Elizabeth Prout in their 1863 revision all legislated for solemn vows. Although Fr Gaudentius normally referred to Elizabeth and her companions as 'Sisters', other Passionists, including authorities in Rome, referred to them as 'Nuns'. Although, therefore, solemn vows were not ultimately permitted, the originators of the institute intended it to be an 'order' and its members 'nuns' in the Passionist sense. In common practice, 'sister', 'nun', 'congregation', 'institute' and 'order' tend to be used loosely. In this study they will have the connotation given by the primary sources. The term 'parish', meaning the area spiritually cared for by a priest, is also used loosely. The contemporary term was 'mission' and 'parish priests' were 'missionary rectors'. Parishes as understood by Canon Law were not established in the Catholic Church in England and Wales until 1918. See E. Norman, *The English Catholic Church in the Nineteenth Century* (Oxford, 1984), p.1 (will be cited as Norman, *English Catholic Church*).

3.   Annals A/E, no title, 1926, [G]eneral [A]rchives of the Sisters of the Cross and Passion, Northampton, I/B/3/a and e.

4.   Annals G, no title, 1926, GA I/B/3/g.

5.   Results of a questionnaire the present writer conducted throughout the Congregation of the Sisters of the Cross and Passion in April 1980 on behalf of the Mother Mary Joseph Commission set up by M. Wilfrida McHale CP, Superior General.

6.   GA I/B/1/h.

7.   Dr F. S. Mooney, M.D., M.B., Ch.B, B.Sc., M.R.C.S., L.R.C.P., F. C. Path.; Sr Martin Joseph Taylor CP, M.B., B.Sc., M.R.C.S., L.R.C.P., Dip. Obst., R.C.O.G., F.R.C.S.; and Dr M. M. Walker, M.B., Ch.B., An Account of the Exhumation, Recognition and Re-Interment of the remains of Mother Mary Joseph Prout CP, performed on 20 June 1973 in the graveyard attached to the Monastery, Sutton: Medical Report A, GA I/C/1/ f, h, i and j.

8.   Sr O. Curran CP, *Sisters of the Cross and Passion* [published anonymously] (Dublin, 1960); and *Unless the Grain of Wheat Die... — Life of Mother Mary Joseph, Foundress of the Sisters of the Cross and Passion* (Bolton, 1973), a pamphlet; Sr W. Daly CP, *Compassion, A Biographical Sketch of Mother Mary Joseph Prout, Foundress of the Sisters of the Cross and Passion* (privately printed, Ballycastle, Co. Antrim, N. Ireland, 1963), limp; Sr A.M. Reynolds CP, 'Born out of Love', *The Cross*, 67 (1976), 19-20; and 'Loss and Gain: A Tale of Two Converts', *Clergy Review*, 62 (1977), 308-317.

1.   Records of St Dominic's Priory, Stone, 1859-1863, T 865, p.26, 24 Jan. 1863, written by Sr Francis Raphael Drane OP, Archives of the Congregation of St Catherine of Siena, Stone. Will be cited as Records, [D]ominican [A]rchives, [S]tone.
2.   Until 1834 there was no Catholic church in Wellington, Shropshire, where Edward Prout lived in early 1820. He could, however, have made the effort to go to Madeley, where there had been a church since 1760 (*Catholic Directory of England and Wales*, 1990, p.383, which will be cited as *Catholic Directory*).
3.   According to his Death Certificate (Register of Deaths, 1863, entry 68, Certificate HB 955360, Registry Office, Stafford), Edward Prout was 71 when he died and therefore should have been born in 1791-2. In the 1851 census, however, his age was given as 56, which would date his birth in 1794-5 (MF 51/3, entry 8, [St]affordshire [R]ecord [O]ffice, Stafford). For his marriage, see Register of Marriages, 1820, All Saints, Wellington, Shropshire, entry 291. See also the All Saints Register of Baptisms for Ann Yates' Baptism on 5 Nov. 1797, her brother Richard's, 10 Mar. 1799 and her sister Elizabeth's, 21 May 1800. I am grateful to Mrs D. Randall, St.RO for helping me to locate the Prout family in Stone.
4.   He may have left London c.1816 when coopers' wages were cut in the dock areas. See I. Prothero, *Artisans and Politics in Early Nineteenth Century London: John Gast and His Times* (Chatham, 1979), p.64. Will be cited as Prothero.
5.   Death Certificate; Register of Deaths and Burials 1856-1957, St Dominic's church, Stone: death, 26 Jan.; burial, 28 Jan. 1863; Register of Burials, St Michael's, Stone, entry 1339, 28 Jan. 1863; Records, T 865, p.26, DAS.
6.   Cf. Records of Missions and Retreats, St Joseph's Retreat, The Hyde [HMR], entry 103, [P]assionist [P]rovincial [A]rchives, [S]utton, for mixed marriages in Ashton-under-Lyne in 1860.
7.   Cf. D.W. Bebbington, *Evangelicalism in Modern Britain, A History from the 1730s to the 1980s*, 1989, p.128 (will be cited as Bebbington); H. McLeod, *Class and Religion in the Late Victorian City*, 1974, pp.30 and 220 (will be cited as McLeod).
8.   St Julian's Register of Baptisms 1813-1833, p.68, entry 543, 2711/Rg/6, [Sh]ropshire [R]ecord [O]ffice, Shrewsbury.
9.   *Salopian Shreds and Patches*, 20 Mar. 1878, article: 'Distinguished Salopians', Local Studies Library, Shrewsbury.
10.   *Shrewsbury Chronicle and North Wales Advertiser*, 7 and 14 Jan. 1820 (will be cited as *Shrewsbury Chronicle*); H. Owen and J.B. Blakeway, *A History of Shrewsbury*, 2 vols (Shrewsbury, 1825), 1, 521. Cf. R.W. Church, *The Oxford Movement: Twelve Years 1833-1845* (written c.1890; ed. and introd. G. Best, Chicago, 1970), p.11.
11.   H.E. Forrest, *The Old Churches of Shrewsbury* (Shrewsbury, 1922), p.124; C. Hulbert, *The History and Antiquities of Shrewsbury by Thomas Phillips, the Second Edition with a Continuation of the History including the History and Description of the County of Salop*, 2 vols (Shrewsbury, 1837), 2, 306 (will be cited as Hulbert); H. Owen, *Some Account of the Ancient and Present State of Shrewsbury* (Shrewsbury, 1808), pp.292-294 (will be cited as Owen); T. Phillips, *The History and Antiquities of Shrewsbury* (Shrewsbury, 1779), pp.106-107 (will be cited as Phillips, *Antiquities*); H. Pidgeon, *Memorials of Shrewsbury*, n.d.: c.1854?, p.98 (will be cited as Pidgeon).
12.   Owen, p.317. For a later growth of anti-Catholicism, however, see Missions, Retreats and Triduums Given by Our Religious of St Michael's Retreat, Aston, Staffordshire, 1842-1852 [AMR], 25 Oct. 1849, PPAS; P. Phillips, 'A Catholic Community: Shrewsbury Part I: 1750-1850', *Recusant History* [RH], 20 (1990), 239-61; 'Part II: 1850-1920', 20 (1991), 380-81; P. Richards, 'R.A. Slaney, The Industrial Town & Early Victorian Social Policy', *Social History* [SH], 4 (1979), 85-101.
13.   M. Allbut and S.R. Broadbridge, 'The Origins of Stone' in *The Stone Survey*,

Journal of the Staffordshire Industrial Archaeological Society [*JSIAS*], 4 (1973), 1; W.H. Bowers and J.W. Clough (compiled), *Researches into the History of the Parish and the Parish Church of Stone* (Birmingham, 1929), pp.1, 19, 31-32 and 37; pictures of St Michael's church in 1841 between pp.114 and 115, 122 and 123 and 124 and 125 (will be cited as Bowers and Clough); C. Masefield, *Staffordshire*, 1910, third edition 1923, pp.221-222; *Life of Mother Margaret Mary Hallahan*, 'written by her religious children', 1869, p.235, DAS (will be cited as *Hallahan*).

14.   Archdeacon's Visitation Report, 1830, St.RO.

15.   *Shrewsbury Chronicle*, 14 Jan. 1820 and 14 Aug. 1835; Hulbert, 2, 306-307; Owen, p.402; Phillips, *Antiquities*, pp.120-121; Pidgeon, p.193. No log books or registers have survived for these Shrewsbury schools from the 1820s and 1830s. E. Prout is not listed in a Bowdler's Trustees' Minute Book that has survived and is now preserved in the Shrewsbury Local Studies Library but it is unlikely that a cooper's daughter would have attended a charity school. The sale of the brewery was first advertised in the *Shrewsbury Chronicle* on 21 Dec. 1827.

16.   Bowers and Clough, p.169; W. White, *History, Gazetteer and Directory of Staffordshire* (Sheffield, 1834), pp.673 and 678 (will be cited as White, *Directory*); Pigot and Co., *National Commercial Directory, Midland*, 1835, pp.427, 444 and 447. No Stone school log books or admission registers have survived for the 1820s and 1830s.

17.   Records of the Institute of the Holy Family, 1849-1852, GA I/B/4/c. A small, red, hard-backed excercise book, it will be cited as Red Bk. Cf. Prothero, p.26; R. Gray, *The Aristocracy of Labour in Nineteenth-Century Britain, c.1850-1914*, 1981, p.37 (will be cited as Gray, *Aristocracy of Labour*); P. Bailey, '"Will The Real Bill Banks Please Stand Up?" Towards a Role Analysis of Mid-Victorian Working-Class Respectability', *Journal of Social History* [*JSH*], 12 (1979), 338; E.J. Hobsbawm, 'Artisan or Labour Aristocrat?', *Economic History Review* [*Econ.HR*], 37 (1984), 357 (will be cited as Hobsbawm, 'Artisan or Labour Aristocrat?'); H.F. Moorhouse, 'The Significance of the Labour Aristocracy', *SH*, 6 (1981), 233 (will be cited as Moorhouse).

18.   Hobsbawm, 'Artisan or Labour Aristocrat?', pp.355-357; and *Labouring Men: Studies in the History of Labour* (reprint of second edition, with minor corrections, 1968), pp.273 and 275 (will be cited as Hobsbawm, *Labouring Men*).

19.   There is no definitive proof that Edward Prout worked at the Coleham Brewery but since he was a journeyman cooper, rather than a master, and lived in Coleham where there was a brewery, it is a reasonable guess that he did work there and that he lived, at a nominal rent of 1s., in one of the adjacent brewery cottages. Until 1980 there were 5 houses adjacent to the brewery yard and opposite the coopers' shed, which still exists. No records survive to prove the Prouts did inhabit one of them but since, when the family moved to Stone, they lived in a brewery house opposite the cooperage, it seems likely that they lived in a similar position in Coleham, and, if not in one of these 5 houses, in another of the same style. See *Old Brewery, Coleham, Sale Catalogue*, 16 July 1959, 2118/115, Sh.RO. There is no evidence of where Edward Prout worked before his marriage, although I am indebted to the following for checking their records of employees: The Shrewsbury and Wem Brewery Co. Ltd; Allied Breweries (UK) Ltd, Burton-on-Trent; The Brewers' Society, London; The Worshipful Company of Coopers, London; and Greenall Whitley and Co. Ltd. The Shropshire Brewery at Wellington did not open until 1851 (Noted Breweries of Great Britain, Wellington Papers, Shropshire Brewery, 3022/2, Sh.RO).

20.   Hulbert, 2, 307-308. Cf. S.D. Chapman, 'The Cotton Industry in the Industrial Revolution' second edition in L. Clarkson (ed.), *The Industrial Revolution: A Compendium*, 1990, p.37.

21. Sale of William Hazledine's Property, Coleham, 1841, Shrewsbury Papers, 901/1, 1709/16/II 4, Sh.RO.

22. Hulbert, 2, 308.

23. According to the notice which appeared in every copy of the *Shrewsbury Chronicle* from Dec. 1827 to Aug. 1828 advertising the sale of the brewery. Brewing about 50,000 barrels a year, it was a considerably smaller concern than firms like Whitbread and Barclay Perkins, which by 1800 were producing annually 100,000-200,000 barrels (36 gallon casks). See K.H. Hawkins and C.L. Pass, *The Brewing Industry*, 1979, limp, p.14. Will be cited as Hawkins and Pass.

24. *Shrewsbury Chronicle*, 21 Dec. 1827.

25. Hulbert, 2, 308. I am indebted to Mr and Mrs P. Rowlands of Rowlands and Co., Shrewsbury, the present owners, for information from their deeds on the 1831 sale.

26. Hobsbawm, *Labouring Men*, pp.34-63 and 77-78; B. Harrison, *Drink and the Victorians*, 1971, p.51 (will be cited as Harrison); H.R. Southall, 'The Tramping Artisan Revisits: Labour Mobility and Economic Distress in Early Victorian England', *Econ.HR*, 44 (1991), 274; R. Vorspan, 'Vagrancy and the New Poor Law in Late-Victorian and Edwardian England', *English Historical Review* [*EHR*], 92 (1977), 59-60.

27. Census 1841, MF 41/9, St.RO. Charles was still with them, described as a scholar, aged 13, in the 1851 census, MF 51/3, St.RO. There is an interesting entry in the Register of Confirmations, St Chad's, Birmingham, vol.1, 1850-1863, 30 May 1858, [A]rchives of the [A]rchdiocese of [B]irmingham, of a Mary Yates, who took the Confirmation name 'Mary Joseph'. If she was E. Prout's grandmother, she was then about 82. The Stone cooperage has been demolished only in recent years. I understand from Sr Cyprian Connolly CP that the tradition that Elizabeth was familiarly known as 'Betty' was handed down in the Congregation by Sr Frances Wellard CP.

28. Death Certificates. Ann Prout: Register of Deaths, 1862, entry 489, Certificate HB 955359, Registry Office, Stafford. Both had two funeral services: the Catholic Requiem Mass in St Dominic's church, noted on 14 Aug. 1862 and 28 Jan. 1863 (Register of Deaths and Burials); and the burial in St Michael's graveyard, the town's cemetery, on the same dates (Register of Burials, St Michael's, Stone). The Prout headstone, with comparatively very fine engravings, can still be seen near the boundary wall to the south east of the church. Apparently it was inscribed after Edward's death, because his name appears first and Ann's death is dated as after his.

29. See Gray, *Aristocracy of Labour*, p.8 and *Labour Aristocracy in Victorian Edinburgh* (Oxford, 1976), pp.2, 4 and 92-93 (will be cited as Gray, *Victorian Edinburgh*); Hobsbawm, 'Artisan or Labour Aristocrat?', pp.355-356; Moorhouse, pp.229-233; A. Reid, 'Intelligent Artisans and Aristocrats of Labour: the Essays of Thomas Wright' in Winter, p.171.

30. J. Rhodes and C. Ecclestone, *And By Joule's It's Good - Joule's Brewery Bi-Centenary 1780-1980*, Stafford, 1980, a pamphlet, n.p. Cf. R. Sherlock, *The Industrial Archaeology of Staffordshire* (Newton Abbot, 1976), p.194 (will be cited as Sherlock); K. Kilby, *The Cooper and His Trade*, 1971, p.163; W.J. Thompson, *Industrial Archaeology of North Staffordshire* (Buxton, 1978), p.108 (will be cited as Thompson, *Staffs.*); A.F. Denholm, 'The Impact of the Canal System on Three Staffordshire Market Towns 1760-1850,' *Midland History* [*MH*], 13 (1988), 68 (will be cited as Denholm); C.H. Underhill and J.G. Jenkins, 'Beer' in M.W. Greenslade and J.G. Jenkins, *A History of the County of Stafford, Victoria County History*, II (Oxford, 1967), p.246 (will be cited as *VCH, Staffs.*).

31. Denholm, pp.61-62.

32.   White, *Directory*, 1851, p.358; Denholm, p.63.

33.   Beer and beef were considered inseparable. Cf. G. Eliot, *Middlemarch,* 1871-2 (Penguin 1985), pp.429-430 (will be cited as Eliot, *Middlemarch*); P. Mathias, *The Brewing Industry in England 1700-1830* (Cambridge, 1959), p.xi (will be cited as Mathias, *Brewing Industry*).

34.   Denholm, pp.68-69; Sherlock, p.45; Thompson, *Staffs.*, pp.24-25 and 109; M. Allbut, 'The Directories of Trade', pp.4-6; E. Broadbridge, 'Occupations in Stone from the Census of 1851', pp.7-8; 'The Trent and Mersey Canal', pp.15-17; and 'The Boot and Shoe Industry', pp.21-22, all in *JSIAS*, 4 (1973); J.G. Jenkins, 'Footwear', *VCH, Staffs.*, II, 233.

35.   Pidgeon, p.xi; W. Page (ed.), *VCH Staffs.*, I (1908), 326.

36.   Denholm, pp.63-64; Thompson, *Staffs.*, pp.16-17; F. Brook, 'The Trunk Roads', *JSIAS*, 4 (1973), 11-15; A.D.M. Phillips and B.J. Turton, 'Staffordshire Turnpike Trusts and Traffic in the Early Nineteenth Century', *Journal of Transport History*, 8 (1987), 137 (will be cited as Phillips and Turton).

37.   White, *Directory*, 1851, pp.358 and 367.

38.   Mathias, *Brewing Industry*, p.xii; Harrison, pp.19, 37-39 and 46-47; Hawkins and Pass, pp.16 and 18; J.L. Hammond and B. Hammond, *The Age of the Chartists 1832-1854, A Study of Discontent*, 1930, pp.149, 152 and 155-156 (will be cited as Hammonds, *Chartists*); P.J. Atkins, 'Sophistication Detected: Or the Adulteration of the Milk Supply 1850-1914', *SH*, 16 (1991), 320. Cf. Letters of Fr Gaudentius Rossi [LGR], 12 Feb. 1855, GA I/B/1/b-d; Pius Devine CP, *Life of the Very Rev. Father Dominic of the Mother of God (Barberi), Passionist, Founder of the Congregation of the Passion, or Passionists, in Belgium and England*, 1898, pp.200 and 210 (will be cited as Devine, *Dominic*).

39.   White, *Directory*, 1851, p.358.

40.   Gray, *Victorian Edinburgh*, pp.2 and 144-145; *Aristocracy of Labour*, pp.31-32; Hobsbawm, 'Artisan or Labour Aristocrat?', pp.361, 363-364 and 366; Mathias, *Brewing Industry*, pp.53-54; Prothero, pp.24 and 26; G. Elkington, *The Coopers: Company and Craft*, 1933, pp.158-159; B. Gilding, *The Journeymen Coopers of East London*, 1971, pp.I-III, 2, 13-14, 50-52, 60-61 and 75-82 (will be cited as Gilding); K. Kilby, *The Village Cooper* (Aylesbury, 1977); E.P. Thompson and E. Yeo (ed. and introd.), *The Unknown Mayhew, Selections from the 'Morning Chronicle' 1849-1850*, 1971, p.420 (will be cited as Thompson and Yeo).

41.   Gilding, p.2; Gray, *Victorian Edinburgh*, p.139; Hobsbawm, 'Artisan or Labour Aristocrat?', pp.357-358; Prothero, p.27.

42.   Ann Prout put a cross for her name in the Marriage Register, 1820, All Saints, Wellington, entry 291. Cf. Thompson and Yeo, p.422.

43.   I am indebted for this last information to Mr C.W. Gaskin of Burton-upon-Trent, previously of Stone, who, like his father and grandfather before him, was a cooper in Joule's Stone Brewery and who assured me that free beer was traditional practice. See also Gray, *Aristocracy of Labour*, pp.37-38; Hobsbawm, *Labouring Men*, p.273; N. Tomes, 'A Torrent of Abuse: Crimes of Violence Between Working-Class Men and Women in London 1840-1875', *JSH*, 11 (1978), 341.

44.   I owe this information also to Mr Gaskin, who, like his father and grandfather, lived in one of these houses until Joule's closed in 1976. They were demolished shortly afterwards. What may have been the quality and nature of the houses in New Brewery Yard can, however, still be seen in the practically adjacent Globe Court, where the houses have been converted into small business premises and where the common toilet, ashpit and wash-house still exist. Cf. Gray, *Victorian Edinburgh*, p.92; G. Crossick, *An Artisan Elite in Victorian Society, Kentish London 1840-1880*, 1978, pp.106-108.

45.   Moorhouse, p.233; P. Branca, *Silent Sisterhood: Middle-Class Women in the Victorian Home*, 1977, p.7 (will be cited as Branca, *Silent Sisterhood*).
46.   Cf. McLeod, p.30.
47.   Annals A/E.
48.   Both her parents were English. For the etymology of 'Prout' and 'Yates' see P.H. Reaney, *A Dictionary of British Surnames*, second edition 1976, pp.283 and 396.
49.   N.A. Cope, *Stone in Staffordshire: The History of a Market Town* (Hanley, 1972), p.96.
50.   A.G. Rose, 'The Plug Riots of 1842 in Lancashire and Cheshire', *Transactions of the Lancashire and Cheshire Antiquarian Society [TLCAS]*, 67 (1957), 84-85 and 99. Cf. E. Hopkins, *A Social History of the English Working Classes 1815-1945*, 1975, p.46; R.F. Wearmouth, *Methodism and the Working-Class Movements of England 1800-1850*, 1937, p.134 (will be cited as Wearmouth, *Working-Class Movements*).
51.   *Staffordshire Advertiser*, 27 Aug. 1842.
52.   Arrivals and Departures, St Michael's Retreat, Aston, 1842-1851, entries 1 and 4, PPAS; Salvian Nardocci CP, Annals of the Anglo-Hibernian Province, 1842-1872, 3 vols, 1, 16-17 and Annals of the Anglo-Hibernian Province 1842-1890, 3 vols, 1, 19 and 24-25, which will be cited as Salvian, Annals, 1872 and Annals, 1890 respectively, [P]assionist [P]rovincial [A]rchives, St Paul's Retreat, Mt Argus, [D]ublin, Eire; Devine, *Dominic*, p.153; C. Charles CP, 'The Foundation of the Passionists in England 1840-1851', 2 vols, a doctoral thesis in Ecclesiastical History, Gregorian University, Rome, 1961, 2, 239 and 249, copy, GA V/F/2 and 3 (will be cited as Charles, thesis).
53.   See Martin Bialas CP, *The Mysticism of the Passion in St Paul of the Cross (1694-1775): An Investigation of Passioncentrism in the Spiritual Doctrine of the Founder of the Passionist Congregation* (San Francisco, 1990), which will be cited as Bialas, *Mysticism*.
54.   Bialas, *Mysticism*, pp.28-42 and 97-146; D. Barsotti, *The Eucharist in St Paul of the Cross, Studies in Passionist History and Spirituality [SPHS]*, 21 (Rome, 1988), p.3 (will be cited as Barsotti); Edmund [Burke] CP, *Hunter of Souls, A Study of the Life and Spirit of Saint Paul of the Cross* (Dublin, 1946), which will be cited as [Burke], *Paul*; and with Roger Mercurio and Silvan Rouse CP (eds.), *Words from the Heart, A Selection from the Personal Letters of St Paul of the Cross* (Dublin, 1976), pp.1-4 (will be cited as *Words from the Heart*); Felix Ward CP, *The Passionists* (New York, 1923), pp.25-57 (cited as Ward, *Passionists*). For the life of Paul of the Cross see Rt Revd, later St, Vincent Strambi CP, *The Life of Blessed Paul of the Cross, Founder of the Congregation of the Barefooted Clerks of the Most Holy Cross and Passion of Jesus Christ*, 3 vols, transl. Oratorian Series, 1853, (will be cited as Strambi); Fr Ignatius Spencer CP, *The Life of Blessed Paul of the Cross, Founder of the Congregation of Discalced Clerks of the Most Holy Cross and Passion of Jesus Christ*, 1860 (a transl. of a life by an Italian Passionist and now preserved in PPAS); Pius Devine CP, *The Life of St Paul of the Cross*, 1867, revised 1924 (will be cited as Devine, *Paul*); Fabiano Giorgini CP, *The Congregation of the Passion of Jesus* (ed. Dominic Papa CP, Rome, 1988); and *St Paul of the Cross, Founder of the Passionists, 1694-1775*, *SPHS*, 4 (Rome, 1984), which will be cited as Giorgini, *Paul*; and, with Carmelo Amedeo Naselli CP and ed. Dominic Papa CP, *History of the Passionists*, 2 vols (Rome, 1987), vol.1 of which will be cited as Giorgini and Papa, *Passionists*; BennetKelleyCP, *Listen To His Love: A Life of St Paul of the Cross* (Union City, New Jersey, 1985); Jude Mead CP (ed.), *St Paul of the Cross: A Source/Workbook for Paulacrucian Studies* (New York, 1983), which will be cited as Mead, *Sourcebook*;

Cajetan Reynders CP, *St Paul of the Cross: His Spirit and Virtues* (New York, 1960); Paul Francis Spencer CP, *As a Seal upon your Heart — The Life of St Paul of the Cross, Founder of the Passionists,* (St Paul's Publications, Middlegreen, Slough, 1994); Alfred Wilson CP, *St Paul of the Cross, Passionist* (Consett, n.d.), a pamphlet.

55.   Bialas, *Mysticism,* p.22; C.J. Yuhaus CP, *Compelled To Speak: The Passionists in America, Origin and Apostolate* (New York, 1967), p.13 (will be cited as Yuhaus).

56.   *Words from the Heart,* pp.2, 12 and 14. See also [Burke], *Paul,* p.13; Giorgini, *Paul,* p.25.

57.   *Words from the Heart,* p.12.

58.   [Burke], *Paul,* p.50; Strambi, 2, 204.

59.   Bialas, *Mysticism,* p.151.

60.   Mead, *Sourcebook,* pp.279-283; Antonio M. Artola CP, *The Presence of the Passion of Jesus in the Structure and Apostolate of the Passionist Congregation, SPHS,* 3 (1982), pp.16 and 34 (will be cited as Artola); F. Giorgini CP (ed. and introd.) and S. Rouse CP (transl.), *St Paul of the Cross: The Congregation of the Passion of Jesus - What It Is and What It Wants To Do, 1747-1768, SPHS,* 1 (Rome, 1982), 3-4, 9, 10, 16 and 21.

61.   Mead, *Sourcebook,* pp.21-52; *Words from the Heart,* pp.17-39; Martin Bialas CP, *In This Sign: The Spirituality of St Paul of the Cross,* [extracts from texts of St Paul of the Cross with introductions], (ed. and transl. Anthony O'Leary CP and Others, Dublin, 1984), pp.37-55 (will be cited as Bialas, texts).

62.   Cf. Artola, pp.10 and 12.

63.   Artola, pp.15, 20 and 29-31; Carroll Stuhlmueller CP, *Remembrance in the Old Testament, SPHS,* 21 (Rome, 1988), 32-33.

64.   Bialas, *Mysticism,* pp.189 and 294-295.

65.   Artola, p.33; Barnabas Ahern CP, 'Remembering the Passion of Christ' in *The 'Memoria Passionis' in the Constitutions, SPHS,* 20 (Rome, 1986), 3 (will be cited as Ahern).

66.   Bialas, *Mysticism,* p.189.

67.   Ahern, p.5. For the fundamental Trinitarian structure of Paul's spiritual doctrine, see Bialas, *Mysticism,* p.215.

68.   *Words from the Heart,* p.17. Cf. Bialas, *Mysticism,* p.122.

69.   Bialas, *Mysticism,* pp.39 and 234-241.

70.   Bialas, *Mysticism,* p.115.

71.   Bialas, *Mysticism,* p.245.

72.   Bialas, *Mysticism,* pp.187, 287 and 329.

73.   See above, Ch.I, section 4, p.24

74.   Bialas, *Mysticism,* pp.121-122; Flavio di Bernardo CP, *The Mystique of the Passion, SPHS,* 5 (Rome, 1984), p.7 (will be cited as Di Bernardo).

75.   Bialas, *Mysticism,* pp.140-142.

76.   Bialas, *Mysticism,* pp.154, 159, 202-204 and 284; Di Bernardo, p.10.

77.   Bialas, *Mysticism,* pp.190, 294-297 and 299-300.

78.   Cf. and contrast Bebbington, pp.48-53 and 74; I. Bradley, *The Call to Seriousness: The Evangelical Impact on the Victorians,* 1976, pp.16 and 157 (will be cited as Bradley); R.E. Davies, *Methodism,* 1963, pp.35-56; D. Hempton, *Methodism and Politics in British Society 1750-1850,* 1984, p.31 (will be cited as Hempton); B. Hilton, *The Age of Atonement: The Influence of Evangelicalism on Social and Economic Thought, 1795-1865* (Oxford, 1988), p.8 (will be cited as Hilton); M. Hurley SJ (ed.), *John Wesley's Letter to a Roman Catholic,* 1968, passim (will be cited as Hurley); K. Hylson-Smith, *Evangelicals in the Church of England 1734-1984* (Edinburgh, 1988), p.53 (will be cited as Hylson-Smith); E. Jay, *The Evangelical and Oxford Movements,* (Cambridge, 1983), p.10 (will be cited as Jay, *Movements*); and

Faith and Doubt in Victorian Britain, 1986, p.1 (will be cited as Jay, *Faith and Doubt*); E. Royle, *Victorian Infidels: The Origins of the British Secularist Movement 1791-1866* (Manchester, 1974), p.13; P. Thureau-Dangin (revised and re-ed. from a transl. by the late W. Wilberforce), *The English Catholic Revival in the Nineteenth Century*, 2 vols, 1914, 1, xxxix-xli (will be cited as Thureau-Dangin); J. Wolffe, *The Protestant Crusade in Great Britain 1829-1860* (Oxford, 1991), p.11 (will be cited as Wolffe); H.D. Rack, 'Survival and Revival: John Bennet, Methodism and Old Dissent', in K. Robbins (ed.), *Protestant Evangelicalism: Britain, Ireland, Germany and America c.1750-c.1950* (Oxford, 1990), p.1 (will be cited as Robbins, *Evangelicalism*).

79. Artola, p.29; Bialas, *Mysticism*, pp.271-272, 284 and 329; Bradley, p.20.
80. Bialas, *Mysticism*, p.198.
81. Ahern, pp.3-6; Barsotti, p.22.
82. *Words from the Heart*, p.11; Mead, *Sourcebook*, pp.120-124; Di Bernardo, pp.9-10; Giorgini, *Paul*, p.24; and (ed. and introd.), *St Paul of the Cross: Guide for the Spiritual Animation of Passionist Life: "The Common Regulations of 1775"*, SPHS, 2 (Rome, 1984), 5-8; Bernard Lowe CP, 'Poverty as a Characteristic of our Congregation', pp.5-11 (will be cited as Lowe, 'Poverty'); and Harry Gielen CP, 'Solitude: In Search of a Value', pp.23-36, both in *Reflections on Some Traditional Characteristics of Passionist Christian Spirituality - Part II, SPHS*, 9 (Rome, 1982); Silvan Rouse CP, 'Solitude in the Christian Mystery and in St Paul of the Cross' in *Reflections on Some Traditional Characteristics of Passionist Christian Spirituality - Part III, SPHS*, 10 (Rome, 1982), 11-19 (will be cited as Rouse, 'Solitude'); M. Villers SJ, *The Will of God in the Spiritual Doctrine of St Paul of the Cross, SPHS*, 25 (Rome, 1990).
83. [Burke], *Paul*, p.110; Giorgini, *Paul*, pp.23-25.
84. Dominic Barberi in Strambi, 1, 'Introduction', p.1, written in 1847, when it was arranged Faber should make the translation. See also [Burke], *Paul*, p.110.
85. Barsotti, pp.17 and 20; Bialas, *Mysticism*, p.169; and 'Fundamentals of Our Life' in *Commentaries on the General Constitutions C.P.*, SPHS, 16 (Rome, 1987), p.3 (will be cited as Bialas, 'Fundamentals'); Rouse, 'Solitude', p.11. For the treatise on mystical death Paul recommended, see Mead, *Sourcebook*, pp.160-177 and p.123 for a list of references to this teaching in Paul's other writings.
86. Bialas, *Mysticism*, p.39.
87. *Words from the Heart*, pp.11, 19, 21, 26, 27, 31 and 33; Mead, *Sourcebook*, pp.38, 189 and 199; Barsotti, pp.8-13, 21 and 25; Giorgini, *Paul*, p.25.
88. Barsotti, p.2; Simon Paul Wood CP, 'The Liturgical Spirit of St Paul of the Cross' in Mead, *Sourcebook*, pp.246-250.
89. I am grateful to Fr Paul Francis Spencer CP for drawing my attention to the context of martyrdom.
90. Barsotti, pp.3-4; J. [Paulinus] Vanden Bussche CP, *Ignatius (George) Spencer, Passionist (1799-1864), Crusader of Prayer for England and Pioneer of Ecumenical Prayer* (Louvain, 1991), pp.128-129. Will be cited as Vanden Bussche.
91. *Words from the Heart*, p.30.
92. *Words from the Heart*, p.32; Vanden Bussche, pp.128-129.
93. Barsotti, p.6.
94. Devine, *Paul*, p.413.
95. Urban Young CP (transl. and ed.), *Dominic Barberi in England, A New Series of Letters*, 1935, p.121. Will be cited as Young, *Dominic in England*. Cf. also Fr Dominic's 'Introduction', Strambi, 1, 1, 5 and 8.
96. *Catholic Magazine*, 4 (1840), 155 and cf. 6 (1842), 287-288, Catholic Central Library, Westminster. See also Vanden Bussche, pp.127-130.

97. Vanden Bussche, p.34. Cf. Salvian, Annals, 1872, 1, 20; Yuhaus, p.29.
98. Annals A/E.
99. Bialas, *Mysticism*, pp.80-87; [Burke], *Paul*, pp.35-36; Lowe, 'Poverty', pp.7-8.
'*Anawim*' is a term used in Scripture to denote poor with a moral shade of meaning.
Because they are destitute and oppressed, the poor or the lowly are especially suitable
for the Kingdom of God. Although it is possible for the materially wealthy to have a
spirit of poverty, the term usually implies actual poverty, deprivation or
marginalisation. Cf. Matthew, 5:3; Luke, 1:46-55.
100. See above, Ch.II.
101. Strambi, 2, 17; Bialas, *Mysticism*, p.96.
102. Bialas, texts, p.75 and *Mysticism*, p.122; Strambi, 2, 76.
103. *Words from the Heart*, p.28 discussed by Costante Brovetto CP, *The Spirituality
of St Paul of the Cross and Our Passionist Spirituality as Symbolized in the Fourth
Vow*, *SPHS*, 7 (Rome, 1982), p.20 (will be cited as Brovetto); Bialas, texts, pp.28,
72 and 84; Barsotti, pp.22-23.
104. *Words from the Heart*, p.92.
105. Bialas, texts, p.80; *Words from the Heart*, p.33.
106. Mead, *Sourcebook*, p.292, 1741 Rule, norm 64.
107. Bernard Lowe CP, 'St Paul of the Cross and Prayer as a Characteristic of our
Congregation' in *Reflections on Some Traditional Characteristics of Passionist
Christian Spirituality - Part I*, *SPHS*, 8 (Rome, 1982), 3-4 (will be cited as Lowe,
'Prayer').
108. *Words from the Heart*, pp.81-3 and 162-4; Barsotti, p.22.
109. *Words from the Heart*, p.93; Bialas, texts, p.80 and *Mysticism*, p.211.
110. [Burke], *Paul*, p.166; Lowe, 'Poverty', pp.8 and 10 and 'Prayer', p.4. Cf. Jose
Ramon Zubizarreta CP, *Passionists and the Present Day Theology of the Cross*, *SPHS*,
11 (Rome, 1982), 14-15. Although Paul was an evangelical, neither his teaching on
suffering nor his missions would have had anything in common with the
indoctrination, camp meetings or lovefeasts as described by E.P. Thompson, *The
Making of the English Working Class*, 1963 (Pelican 1980), pp.402-410 (will be cited
as Thompson, *English Working Class*); nor with the lovefeast as described by W.J.
Johnson, 'Piety Among 'The Society of the People': The Witness of Primitive
Methodist Local Preachers in the North Midlands 1812-1862' in *Studies in Church
History*, 26 (1989), 350.
111. Mead, *Sourcebook*, p.292, 1741 Rule, norm 62.
112. Bialas, 'Fundamentals', p.5; Lowe, 'Poverty', pp.7-8 and 10.
113. Mead, *Sourcebook*, p.290, 1741 Rule, norm 46.
114. Antonio M. Artola CP, 'The Memory of the Passion in the Constitutions' in *The
'Memoria Passionis'*, *SPHS*, 20 (Rome, 1986), 20-21.
115. *Words from the Heart*, p.14, the 1720 Rule, discussed by Brovetto, p.18.
116. J.L. Hammond and B. Hammond, *The Bleak Age*, 1934, p.102; H.F. Mathews,
Methodism and the Education of the People 1791-1851, 1949, p.132; S. Gilley,
'Protestant London, No-Popery and the Irish Poor (1830-1860), Part I', *RH*, 10 (1969-
70), 214 (will be cited as Gilley, 'Protestant London', Part I').
117. For the life of Fr Ignatius Spencer CP, see Vanden Bussche; Pius Devine CP,
*Life of Father Ignatius of St Paul, Passionist (The Hon. and Rev. George Spencer),
Compiled Chiefly From His Autobiography, Journal and Letters* (Dublin, 1866), which
will be cited as Devine, *Ignatius*; Urban Young CP, *Life of Father Ignatius Spencer*,
1933 (will be cited as Young, *Ignatius*); Jerome Vereb CP, *Ignatius Spencer,
Passionist, Apostle of Christian Unity*, second edit. 1992, a pamphlet; B. Walsh,
Father Spencer, a pamphlet, 1981. See also Devine, *Dominic*, pp.192-194; A. Lister,
'The Althorp Library of Second Earl Spencer, now in the John Rylands University

Library of Manchester: Its Formation and Growth', *Bulletin of the John Rylands University Library of Manchester [BJR[U]L[M]]*, 71 (1989), pp.67-86.

118. See Vanden Bussche, pp.25-29. Cf. K.L. Morris, 'The Cambridge Converts and the Oxford Movement', *RH*, 17 (1985), p.390 (will be cited as Morris, 'Cambridge Converts').

119. Salvian, Annals, 1890, 1, 66; Devine, *Ignatius*, pp.221-223 and 242; Young, *Ignatius*, pp.71, 73-74 and 86; O. Chadwick, *The Victorian Church*, 2 vols, 1966, 1, 167 (will be cited as Chadwick, *Victorian Church*); G.C. Baugh, M.W. Greenslade and D.A. Johnson, 'West Bromwich' p.61 and C.R.J. Currie, M.W. Greenslade and D.A. Johnson, 'Walsall', p.240, both in M.W. Greenslade (ed.), *VCH, Staffs.*, XVII (Oxford, 1976);   R.H. Trainor, 'Anti-Catholicism and the Priesthood in the Nineteenth-Century Black Country', *Staffordshire Catholic History*, 16 (1976), 19-20. Fr Spencer achieved his ambition to die in a ditch when he dropped dead in the drive of Carstairs House, near Lanark, Scotland on 1 Oct. 1864. See above, Ch.VII, n.115.

120. *Catholic Magazine*, 4 (1840), 154-155.

121. For the life of Blessed Dominic Barberi CP, beatified by Pope Paul VI on 27 Oct. 1963 during the Second Vatican Council, see Charles, thesis; and 'The Origins of the Parish Mission in England and the Early Passionist Apostolate, 1840-1850', *Journal of Ecclesiastical History [JEH]*, 15 (1964) (cited as Charles, 'Origins'); and *Il B. Domenico della Madre di Dio* (a pamphlet in 5 languages, Rome, 1963); Devine, *Dominic*; D. Gwynn, *Father Dominic Barberi*, 1947 (will be cited as Gwynn, *Dominic*); J. Mead CP, *Shepherd of the Second Spring, The Life of Blessed Dominic Barberi CP, 1792-1849* (Paterson, New Jersey, 1968) which will be cited as Mead, *Dominic*; A. Wilson CP, *Blessed Dominic Barberi*, 1967 (will be cited as Wilson); U. Young CP, *Dominic in England* and *Life and Letters of the Venerable Father Dominic (Barberi) CP, Founder of the Passionists in Belgium and England*, 1926 (will be cited as Young, *Life and Letters*).

122. Gwynn, *Dominic*, pp.11-12; Wilson, pp.28 and 41-42; Young, *Life and Letters*, pp.13-14.

123. Fr D. Barberi CP, *Arcana Verbi*, written 31 May 1844, found, sealed, after his death in 1849 and published in Young, *Dominic in England*, pp.3-8. See Gwynn, *Dominic*, pp.13-14; Wilson, pp.26-32; Young, *Life and Letters*, pp.17-18. Dominic's mystical experience was considerably more than a farm lad's dream, as S. Gilley has termed it, *Newman and His Age*, 1990, p.224. Will be cited as Gilley, *Newman*.

124. Gwynn, *Dominic*, p.15; Wilson, pp.35-36; Young, *Life and Letters*, p.20.

125. Wilson, pp.36, 47, 59, 66-67, 87, 122 and 161.

126. Devine, *Dominic*, p.32; Wilson, pp.39-42 and 60; Young, *Life and Letters*, pp.21-22 and 27.

127. Devine, *Dominic*, pp.41, 51-52 and 58-59; Gwynn, *Dominic*, p.23; Mead, *Dominic*, p.78; Wilson, pp.74, 97 and 123-125; Young, *Life and Letters*, pp.30, 34 and 43-48; and *Dominic in England*, p.9. Cf. Morris, 'Cambridge Converts', p.390; B. Fothergill, *Nicholas Wiseman*, 1963, pp.58-60, 63 and 91-92; J.D. Holmes, *More Roman Than Rome: English Catholicism in the Nineteenth Century*, 1978, p.56 (will be cited as Holmes).

128. Deposition of Fr Gaudentius Rossi CP, Apr. 1891. Will be cited as DFGR, 1891. I am indebted to Sr Wilfrid Daly CP for a copy of this document. See also Wilson, pp.34 and 130.

129. Gwynn, *Dominic*, p.20; Mead, *Dominic*, p.61; Wilson, pp.88-89, 99, 114-116, 130-133, 136-141, 151, 158, 164, 178-195, 198-199, 229 and 235; Young, *Life and Letters*, pp.32-33, 35 and 247.

130. Gwynn, *Dominic*, p.19; Wilson, pp.77-78 and 94; Young, *Life and Letters*, p.31.

131. Devine, *Dominic*, pp.88-90 and 92-93; Wilson, pp.151, 156-157 and 166; Young, *Life and Letters*, pp.69-70, 92 and 118-120.

132. Devine, *Dominic*, p.76; Mead, *Dominic*, p.63; Wilson, pp.127, 130 and 143; Young, *Life and Letters*, pp.53-55 and 89-91.

133. Devine, *Dominic*, pp.69-70; Gwynn, *Dominic*, pp.44-45; Mead, *Dominic*, pp.63-64; Wilson, pp.130, 133, 198 and 203; Young, *Life and Letters*, pp.67 and 97.

134. Wilson, p.151; Young, *Life and Letters*, p.87.

135. Strambi, 3 (Supplement), pp.327-328; Devine, *Dominic*, pp.105-111; Young, *Life and Letters*, pp.123 and 127-129; Vanden Bussche, p.67. Chadwick, *Victorian Church*, 1, 276 and D. Gwynn, *Lord Shrewsbury, Pugin and the Catholic Revival*, 1946, pp.85-86 (which will be cited as Gwynn, *Shrewsbury*) are inaccurate in saying Ambrose Phillipps brought Fr Dominic to England.

136. Mead, *Dominic* p.70; Wilson, pp.201-202; Young, *Life and Letters*, p.129.

137. Gwynn, *Shrewsbury*, p.66; Wilson, p.202; Young, *Life and Letters*, pp.127-128.

138. Letter of Fr G. Spencer to C. Acton, 10 May 1839, Letters of Fr I. Spencer CP, File: St Joseph's Province, General Archives of the Congregation of the Passion, Saints John and Paul's, Rome. Will be cited as LISR and [P]assionist [G]eneral [A]rchives, [R]ome. See also Wilson, p.202. For Mrs Louisa Spencer Canning, see Young, *Life and Letters*, p.114; and J. Gillow, *A Bibliographical Dictionary of the English Catholics from 1534 - The Present Time*, 5 vols, 1885, 1, 395, which will be cited as Gillow.

139. Gwynn, *Dominic*, p.71; Wilson, p.203; Young, *Life and Letters*, p.131.

140. Salvian, Annals, 1872, 1, 21; Gwynn, *Dominic*, p.72; Vanden Bussche, p.69; Young, *Life and Letters*, pp.131-132.

141. Devine, *Dominic*, p.113; Gwynn, *Dominic*, pp.72-73; Wilson, pp.204-206; Young, *Life and Letters*, pp.132-133.

142. Devine, *Dominic*, p.114; Gwynn, *Dominic*, p.74; Mead, *Dominic*, pp.91-92; Wilson, pp.208-209; Young, *Life and Letters*, p.134.

143. Mead, *Dominic*, pp.91-92; Wilson, pp.209-210; Young, *Life and Letters*, pp.141-145.

144. Young, *Dominic in England*, p.32. See also Wilson, p.209.

145. Mead, *Dominic*, p.97; Wilson, pp.211-212.

146. Devine, *Dominic*, p.120; Gwynn, *Dominic*, pp.102 and 123; Mead, *Dominic*, p.102; Wilson, pp.215 and 229-30; Young, *Life and Letters*, pp.181-182 and 186; and *Dominic in England*, pp.25-26 and 56.

147. A Written Statement of the Virtue and Holiness of Life of the Deceased Father Dominic of the Mother of God, a Religious Priest of the Congregation of the Most Holy Cross and Passion, Made in the City of St Louis, State of Missouri, North America by Father Gaudentius of St Stephen, in the world Stephen Rossi, a Member of the Same Religious Congregation, St Louis, Missouri, 25 January 1890. I am indebted to Fr Cassian Yuhaus CP, St Paul's Passionist Monastery, Pittsburgh, Pennsylvania, USA for access to a copy of this document, which will be cited as DFGR, 1890.

148. Young, *Life and Letters*, p.277.

149. Devine, *Dominic*, pp.134-135; Wilson, pp.217-218; Young, *Life and Letters*, pp.150-151 and 171. Chadwick, *Victorian Church*, 1, 276 is inaccurate in saying Fr Dominic went to Oscott to teach.

150. See Charles, thesis, 2, 204; Wilson, p.220; Federico Menegazzo CP, *Life of Venerable Dominic of the Mother of God*, typescript transl. Bede O'Brien CP (Rome, 1962), pp.119 and 121, PPAS (will be cited as Menegazzo/O'Brien). See also Devine, *Dominic*, pp.136-137; Young, *Life and Letters*, pp.152-153 and 173; and *Dominic in England*, pp.29-30. A colourful story of Fr Dominic's arriving in England on 5 Nov.,

which has been used to his discredit (Chadwick, *Victorian Church*, 1, 276), probably stemmed from confusion about his having arrived twice: in Nov. 1840 and on 5 Oct. 1841. Unfortunately this imaginary drama of Dominic's entering England in a hail of anti-Catholic demonstrations was committed to writing by Devine, *Dominic*, p.137 in 1898, followed by the Passionist historians, Young, *Life and Letters*, pp.151 and 174 and Mead, *Dominic*, p.99 and has been repeated by Chadwick, by Gwynn, *Dominic*, p.87, Norman, *English Catholic Church*, p.21, B. Ward, *The Sequel to Catholic Emancipation*, 2 vols, 1915, 2, 22 (which will be cited as Ward, *Sequel*) and G.I.T. Machin, *Politics and the Churches in Great Britain 1832-1868* (Oxford, 1977), p.90 (which will be cited as Machin, *Politics*).

151. Young, *Dominic in England*, p.33.

152. Gwynn, *Dominic*, pp.93 and 100-101; Wilson, pp.221-222; Young, *Life and Letters*, pp.175-179; and *Dominic in England*, pp.30-33 and 42-43.

153. *Ven. Domenico della Madre di Dio Passionista: Lettere Postulazione dei PP. Passionisti - SS Giovanni e Paolo*, Rome (DB[P]ostulation [L]etters, [R]ome), p.94, XLVIII, Fr Dominic, Oscott, 8 Oct. 1841, to Phillipps, saying he had arrived 'yesterday evening'. See Strambi, 3 (Supplement), pp.359-360; Charles, thesis, 2, 230; Devine, *Dominic*, p.144; Menegazzo/O'Brien, p.127; Young, *Life and Letters*, pp.191 and 193.

154. Gwynn, *Dominic*, p.131; Ward, *Sequel*, 2, 23; Wilson, p.233; Young, *Life and Letters*, pp.194 and 199. For the incument of Aston Hall, Fr Benjamin Hulme, see Letters of Fr G. (Ignatius) Spencer, 1841-1856, Colwich Abbey Collection [LISCAC], 24 Feb. and 5 Dec. 1841; AMR, entry 1, Lent 1842; Salvian, Annals, 1872, 1, 16 and Annals, 1890, 1, 22; Records of St Dominic's Priory, Stone, 1850-1859, T 864, p.36 and Records of Bristol Convent, T 862, pp.38-39, DAS; Charles, thesis, 2, 241; Gillow, 3, 470; A.G. Wall, *The Glory of Aston Hall*, 1963, limp, pp.14-15.

155. Devine, *Dominic*, pp.150-151; Wilson, pp.234-236. See also Colwich Abbey Collection [LDBCAC], VI for Fr Dominic's first letter in English, to Mrs Canning, 9 Jan. 1842, in which he refers to praying for the 'conversion of England'.

156. Young, *Dominic in England*, pp.71-72.

157. The Lance that pierced the Heart of Christ; the Nails used in His Crucifixion. See Salvian, Annals, 1872, 1, 16; Annals, 1890, 1, 22; and his Early Novices, 1842-1859, entry 8, PPAD; Wilson, p.241; Young, *Life and Letters*, p.203.

158. Salvian Nardocci CP, Small Chronicle, Annals of the Anglo-Hibernian Province 1842-1883, 3 vols, 2, 1858, PPAD. Will be cited as Salvian, Small Chronicle.

159. Fr D. Barberi, Strambi, 'Introduction', cited and amplified in Herbert [Greenan] CP, *The Preachers of the Passion; or, The Passionists of the Anglo-Hibernian Province*, 1924, pp.11-14. Will be cited as [Greenan]. Fr Dominic also accepted parishes in Woodchester, London and Sutton. See DBPLR, p.130 for his instruction, 7 July 1849, that there must always be a priest at Aston 'to mind the people of our congregation'; and also PGAR, File: Letters of Fr A. Testa, St Joseph's Province, A. Testa to W. Leigh of Woodchester, 3 Aug. 1850, explaining the circumstances in which Passionists could hold parishes. See also Devine, *Dominic*, pp.157-158, 204 and 213; Gwynn, *Dominic*, p.91; Young, *Life and Letters*, pp.250 and 306.

160. Wilson, p.242; Young, *Life and Letters*, p.204. English slightly modified grammatically.

161. Charles, thesis, 2, 239; Wilson, pp.242-243. Cf. above, Ch.I, section 2. p.15.

162. For the full text of Fr Dominic's sermons see Paul Francis Spencer CP, *Elements of Passionist Spirituality*, SPHS, 29 (Rome, 1992), Appendix, pp.i-xiii. Will be cited as Spencer, *Passionist Spirituality*.

163. Young, *Dominic in England*, p.207. Wilson, pp.265-266 thinks Dominic's own

figure of 100 is correct. Charles, 'Origins', p.73 gives a total of 47 but admits some records have been lost. Cf. AMR; Salvian, Annals, 1872, 1, 16-42; and his List of Missions and Retreats given by the Passionists of the Anglo-Hibernian Province, 1842-1883, pp.1-13, PPAD. For contemporary assessments of Father Dominic, see his Obituary in Suffrages for Our Benefactors and Religious Dead 1848-1850, Woodchester, 29 Aug. 1849, PPAS; Letter, Fr G. Rossi to abbess of Colwich, 29 Aug 1849, CAC; DFGR, 1890 and 1891; Salvian, Annals, 1872, 1, 43-44; Annals, 1890, 1, 86-87; and Autobiography, 2 vols, PPAD; *Tablet* and *Staffordshire Advertiser*, both 1 Sept. 1849.

164. Wilson, p.264.

165. Young, *Life and Letters*, p.317. Cf. Chadwick, *Victorian Church*, 1, 272-273.

166. Salvian, Annals, 1872, 1, 16, 29-30, 32, 34-35, 39, 41 and 43-44; Annals, 1890, 1, 26 and 48-51, 55, 58, 59-61, 64, 67-72, 74-84 and 88; *Tablet*, 5 Dec. 1846; Devine, *Dominic*, p.199; Gwynn, *Dominic*, p.195; Wilson, p.324; Young, *Life and Letters*, pp.287, 296-297 and 301-306; *Dominic in England*, pp.131-132, 141-142, 150-156, 158, 160, 173-176, 178, 182-183, 187, 195-199 and 206. Norman, *English Catholic Church*, p.130, following Ward, *Sequel*, 2, 178, is inaccurate in saying Wiseman 'set up Father Dominic Barberi and the Passionists at Highgate'. Wiseman gave Fr Dominic the very old Poplar House, Hampstead in 1848. After it was condemned by a surveyor, the Passionists moved to the Hyde in 1850. In 1858 they moved to Highgate. Dominic lived only at Poplar, amongst the Irish poor, from 1848-9. See Devine, *Dominic*, pp.204-205.

167. Red Bk.

168. Annals A/E.

169. *Tablet*, 9 Sept. 1843.

170. Register of Confirmations, Aston-by-Stone, Aston Box, vol. 4, AAB.

171. See LGR 7 May 1853 for the comment that it was imprudent to accept a recent convert into the novitiate.

172. AMR, entries 4, 20 and 21: 24 Mar. and 3 and 17 Nov. 1844 respectively.

173. LDBCAC, XIII, Apr. 1844, to Mrs Canning; Devine, *Dominic*, pp.159-160; Wilson, pp.262-263.

174. AMR, entry 4; DBPLR, 1 Apr. 1844, to Wiseman, p.97, no.29; Wilson, p.263; Young, *Life and Letters*, p.240; and *Dominic in England*, p.97.

175. AMR, entry 16, 22 Aug. 1844.

176. Letter A. Testa to D. Barberi, 26 May 1844, PGAR, File: *A Testa a P. Domenico, B. Domenico d. Madre di Dio, Testimonianze, lettere... a Lettere Antonio di S. Giacomo*. I am indebted to Fr Fabiano Giorgini for this translation. See Young, *Life and Letters*, pp.241-242 for an edited version of the letter.

177. Extensive and repeated enquiries, including two *Ad clerums* from Archbishop O'Dwyer of Birmingham, have failed to discover any trace of Elizabeth's reception in any Catholic church in England in the 1840s, or of her Confirmation. Possibly Fr Dominic kept his own notebook, as Fr G. Rossi did in N. America. See Fr G. Rossi CP, A Register of Baptised Protestants 1856-1862, Archives of the Eastern Province, Passionist Missionaries, Union City, New Jersey, USA [PPAUC].

178. Cf. J.E. Bowden, *The Life and Letters of Frederick William Faber, D.D.*, 1869, p.206. Will be cited as Bowden.

179. *Platea*, St Michael's Retreat, Aston, 1842-1853 [Aston *Platea*], PPAS; Salvian, Annals, 1872, 1, 17; Annals, 1890, 1, 25; Charles, thesis, 2, 253-254; Devine, *Dominic*, p.154; Gwynn, *Dominic*, p.147; Wilson, p.247; Young, *Life and Letters*, p.208.

180. Wilson, p.248. 'Confrater' is the Passionist title for a professed but unordained cleric, to distinguish him from a laybrother.

181. Wilson, p.248. Compare R. Whately, *Essays on the Errors of Romanism*, 1850; N. Wiseman, *Lectures on the Principal Doctrines and Practices of the Catholic Church*, 2 vols, 1836.

182. Charles, 'Origins', p.60; E.R. Norman, *Anti-Catholicism in Victorian England*, 1968, p.19 (will be cited as Norman, *Anti-Catholicism*).

183. Wilson, p.248; Young, *Dominic in England*, pp.82-83.

184. LDBCAC, II, 13 Feb. 1843; XI, 27 Apr. 1843, both to Mrs Canning; DFGR, 1890. Cf. Charles, thesis, 2, 243, 248 and 252; Wilson, p.254; Young, *Dominic in England*, pp.89 and 95; *Life and Letters*, p.206.

185. Records of St Dominic's Priory, Stone, 1853-1855, T 863, p.13, DAS.

186. Wilson, p.250; Young, *Life and Letters*, p.219; *Dominic in England*, pp.83, 89, 91 and 93.

187. Salvian, Annals, 1890, 1, 28-29; White, *Directory*, 1851, p.363; Gwynn, *Dominic*, p.148; Wilson, pp.250 and 257; Young, *Life and Letters*, pp.222 and 240; *Dominic in England*, pp.83 and 95-96.

188. Charles, 'Origins', p.62.

189. Salvian, Annals, 1890, 1, 28; Gwynn, *Dominic*, pp.148-149.

190. Wilson, p.255; Young, *Life and Letters*, p.222.

191. Gwynn, *Dominic*, p.110; Wilson, p.296; Ignatius McElligot CP, 'Blessed Dominic Barberi and the Tractarians — an Exercise in Ecumenical Dialogue', *RH*, 21 (1992), 51-85 (will be cited as McElligot).

192. Salvian, Annals, 1890, 1, 23 and 25-26; Devine, *Dominic*, pp.162-163; Gwynn, *Dominic*, pp.150-151; Mead, *Dominic*, pp.128-130; Wilson, pp.250-253; Young, *Life and Letters*, pp.209-213.

193. Records, T 863, p.13.

194. Wilson, p.245; Young, *Dominic in England*, p.90.

195. DFGR, 1890. Cf. DBPLR, p.68, IV-A, 18 Mar. 1843, to l'abbé Haffreingue, Boulogne and pp.110, 115 and 118, to W. Leigh in Mar. and May 1846 about a school and library in Woodchester. See also Wilson, p.249.

196. LDBCAC, XI, 27 Apr. and XII, 9 Nov. 1843, to Mrs Canning.

197. Aston *Platea*; LDBCAC, XII, 9 Nov. 1843, to Mrs Canning; Salvian, Annals, 1872, 1, 19; Annals, 1890, 1, 27-28 and 30-31; *Tablet*, 9 Sept. 1843; Charles, thesis, 2, 270; Wilson, p.256; Young, *Life and Letters*, pp.220-222, 227 and 237; and *Dominic in England*, p.95.

198. *Tablet*, 16 Dec. 1843. Cf. *Tablet*, 15 Feb. and 8 Mar. 1845 and 30 Dec. 1848; Letters, Bp Walsh to Dr Errington, 12 Dec. 1844 (B.797) and 3 Jan. 1845 (B.817), AAB.

199. Salvian, Annals, 1890, 1, 31; Charles, thesis, 2, 271.

200. DBPLR, pp.68-69, IV-A-B, 18 Mar. 1843, to l'abbé Haffreingue, Boulogne.

201. Aston *Platea*; Salvian, Annals, 1890, 1, 25-26. Cf. W.E. Houghton, *The Victorian Frame of Mind 1830-1870*, 1957, pp.83-84. Will be cited as Houghton.

202. Charles, thesis, 2, 266; Gwynn, *Dominic*, p.214.

203. Gwynn, *Dominic*, pp.197 and 214; Wilson, p.276; Young, *Dominic in England*, p.147. Cf. Young, *Life and Letters*, pp.107-109 for Fr G. Spencer's similar views expressed in 1836. See also F. Engels, *The Condition of the Working Class in England* (Germany, 1845; Penguin 1987), p.151 (will be cited as Engels); J.M. Golby (ed.), *Culture and Society in Britain 1850-1890* (Oxford, 1986), pp.40-44 (will be cited as Golby).

204. DFGR, 1890; Gwynn, p.152. Cf. Records Relative to Our Missions and Retreats, 1851-1855, St Anne's, Sutton [SMR], 19 Mar. 1855, PPAS.

205. Aston *Platea*; Salvian, Annals, 1872, 1, 25; *Tablet*, 15 June, 1844; Charles, thesis, 2, 274; Wilson, pp.259-260; Young, *Dominic in England*, pp.99 and 130; *Life*

and Letters, pp.252-253.

206. E. Norman's remarks associating Fr Dominic with Fr Gentili in this context are misleading: *Roman Catholicism in England* (Oxford, 1985), p.74. Will be cited as Norman, *Roman Catholicism*.

207. *Tablet*, 1 July 1848; Young, *Dominic in England*, p.143.

208. Charles, thesis, 2, 262; Devine, *Dominic*, p.184. Cf. Chadwick, *Victorian Church*, 1, 518-519.

209. Cf. H. Formby, *The Catholic Christian's Guide to the Right Use of the Christian Psalmody and of the Psalter*, 1846. See also Gwynn, *Shrewsbury*, p.125; Norman, *English Catholic Church*, pp.230 and 237.

210. AMR, entry 55, 14 June 1846.

211. Gwynn, *Dominic*, pp.191 and 242; Young, *Dominic in England*, pp.121 and 205.

212. As in St Chad's, Manchester. See AMR, entry 103, 25 Jan. 1849. Cf. Salvian, Annals, 1890, 1, 80; Devine, *Dominic*, p.185.

213. DFGR, 1890.

214. *Tablet*, 16 Jan. 1847; *Staffordshire Advertiser*, 6 Feb. 1847 and 15 May 1847; Aston *Platea*; Salvian, Annals, 1890, 1, 63-64; Charles, 'Origins', p.70; Devine, *Dominic*, pp.195-197; Gwynn, *Dominic*, pp.225-231 and 233; Young, *Life and Letters*, pp.285-287; *Dominic in England*, pp.178-180, 182 and 185-187.

215. DFGR, 1890.

216. Aston *Platea*.

217. Young, *Life and Letters*, p.225.

218. Young, *Life and Letters*, pp.224-225 and 241; *Dominic in England*, p.93.

219. LISCAC, 14 Oct. 1846 and LDBCAC, V, 30 Oct, [1846], both to Mrs Canning; Aston *Platea*; Salvian, Annals, 1890, 1, 56; Devine, *Ignatius*, pp.348-360; Vanden Bussche, p.130; Young, *Life and Letters*, pp.278-282; and *Ignatius*, pp.137-153.

220. DFGR, 1890; Aston *Platea*; Hugh K. Barr CP, X, Biographical Sketches of the Passionist Priests, Students and Brothers in the Province of St Paul of the Cross in America, p.79, PPAUC (will be cited as H.K.B., X, Biography CP).

221. Young, *Dominic in England*, p.78.

222. AMR, entry 89, 8 Mar. 1848; *Tablet*, 18 Mar. 1848.

223. Sr M.E. Hanoteau IEJ, *Mère Gertrude (Justine Desbille), Fondatrice Des Soeurs De L'Enfant-Jésus de Nivelles 1801-1866* (Nivelles, Belgium, 1985), pp.31-44, 83-92.

224. I owe this information to the late Mère Marie-Emilie Hanoteau IEJ.

225. Cf. Branca, *Silent Sisterhood*, pp.4-5.

226. LGR 24 July 1848.

227. Rt. Revd W. Wareing, Vicar Apostolic of the Eastern District, *Letter to the Clergy*, 4 Nov. 1845, Archives of the Diocese of Northampton, Northampton; *Tablet*, 22 Nov. 1845.

228. *Tablet*, 24 June 1848 and 3 Nov. 1849; GA I/C/5/a-k for copies of:- an English translation of a commentary on the Rule observed by the Community of the Infant Jesus, Northampton; An Anonymous Manuscript found in the Notre Dame Archives, Northampton; and An Account of the Community of the Infant Jesus, Northampton 1849-1854 written by Sister Ethelreda Bocock (will be cited as Sr E. Bocock's Account), all now preserved in the Provincial Archives of the Sisters of Notre Dame de Namur, Liverpool. See also copies of:- Affiliation to our Institute of the Community of the Infant Jesus, Northampton, Oct. 1852; and Present Occupations of the Sisters of the Infant Jesus, Northampton, originals of both documents in the General Archives of the Sisters of Notre Dame de Namur, Namur, Belgium. In 1852, after four sisters had died of fever, the Sisters of the Infant Jesus joined the Notre Dame Sisters, who then took over their property and apostolate in Northampton. I am

grateful to Sr Marie-Chantal Schweitzer SND, Namur for a copy of Annals and Other Matters Relating to the Sisters of the Infant Jesus, Northampton.

229. See a Commentary on the Rule of the Sisters of the Infant Jesus, Northampton: 'In order to imitate the suffering life of Our Lord let us go to the Cross... let us look at the Cross... consider the Cross... study the Cross... and carry the Cross... by self-abnegation, sacrifice, interior mortification... by supporting with resignation and generosity sufferings, contradictions, trials and ennui in union with those of Jesus Christ upon the Cross'; and also GA I/C/5/a-k for a copy of An Account of the Memories of Sister Mary Joseph, a Sister of the Infant Jesus and later a Sister of Notre Dame, 1894, original in Notre Dame Archives, Liverpool.

230. For Paul's devotion to the Nativity and Infancy, see Bialas, *Mysticism*, pp.291-292 and 312-315; Mead, *Sourcebook*, p.160. Cf. Wilson, p.107. See also above, Ch.III, pp.64-65.

231. LGR 23 Jan. 1849, letter dated only '23.' 1849'. Can be dated 'January' by its reference to his forthcoming mission in St Chad's, 25 Jan.-11 Feb. 1849. See also GA I/A/3/a, a copy of *Office of the Blessed Virgin Mary* (Mechlin, 1844), inscribed '+J.M.J., Mary Joseph of Jesus' and holding a card addressed to 'Sr Stanislaus'.

232. Red Bk. According to J. Foster, *Class Struggle and the Industrial Revolution*, 1974, p.94, TB was rife in Northampton.

233. On the basis of LGR 23 Jan. 1849 and the Red Bk.

234. Cf. M. Forster, *Significant Sisters: The Grassroots of Active Feminism 1839-1939*, 1984, p.105 (will be cited as Forster); L. Strachey, *Eminent Victorians*, 1922, pp.117-120.

235. Cf. *Staffordshire Advertiser*, 1 Jan. 1848; *Punch*, 6-7 (1844), p.93. See above, Ch.V, section 4.

236. Gwynn, *Dominic*, p.199.

237. Red Bk. At that time a Catholic had to fast from midnight before receiving Holy Communion.

238. AMR, entry 22, 24 Nov. 1844.

239. M. Vicinus, *Independent Women: Work and Community for Single Women 1850-1920*, 1985, p.10. Will be cited as Vicinus, *Independent Women*.

240. Joseph Smith CP, *Paul Mary Pakenham, Passionist* (Dublin, 1930), p.24 (will be cited as Smith, *Pakenham*).

241. Red Bk.

242. Cf. Vicinus, *Independent Women*, p.31.

243. Branca, *Silent Sisterhood*, pp.4-5; and 'Image and Reality: The Myth of the Idle Victorian Woman' in M.S. Hartmann and L. Banner (eds), *Clio's Consciousness Raised: New Perspectives on the History of Women*, 1974, p.185. Will be cited as Branca, 'Image and Reality'.

244. M. Vicinus (ed.), *Suffer and Be Still: Women in the Victorian Age*, 1980, p.xii. Will be cited as Vicinus, *Suffer and Be Still*. Cf. M. Hill, *The Religious Order: A Study of Virtuoso Religion and Its Legitimation in the Nineteenth-Century Church of England*, 1973, p.274 (will be cited as Hill); J.H. Murray, *Strong-Minded Women*, 1982 (Penguin 1984), pp.49-50 (will be cited as Murray).

245. *Punch*, 12-13 (1847), 117 and 131; 16-17 (1849), 240-241; 18-19 (1850), 129; J. Burnett (ed.), *Useful Toil: Autobiographies of Working People from the 1820s to the 1920s*, 1974, p.153 (will be cited as Burnett, *Useful Toil*); L. Davidoff and C. Hall, *Family Fortunes: Men and Women of the English Middle Class 1780-1850*, 1987, p.293 (will be cited as Davidoff and Hall); E.O. Hellerstein and Others (eds.) *Victorian Women* (Brighton, 1981), pp.341-346 (will be cited as Hellerstein and Others); L. Holcombe, *Victorian Ladies At Work* (Newton Abbot, 1973), pp.12 and 14 (will be cited as Holcombe); P. Hollis, *Women in Public 1850-1900: Documents*

of the Victorian Women's Movement, 1979, p.90; W.F. Neff, *Victorian Working Women* (Holland, 1966), pp.122-123 (will be cited as Neff); F.K. Prochaska, *Women and Philanthropy in Nineteenth-Century England* (Oxford, 1980), p.14 (will be cited as Prochaska, *Women and Philanthropy*); M.J. Peterson, 'The Victorian Governess' in Vicinus, *Suffer and Be Still*, pp.4-8.

246. W.J. Battersby, 'Educational Work of the Religious Orders of Women 1850-1950' in Rt Revd G.A. Beck AA (ed.), *The English Catholics 1850-1950*, 1950, pp.338-339. Will be cited as Battersby and Beck respectively.

247. Compare Eliot, *Middlemarch*, p.435.

248. AMR, entry 103, 25 Jan. 1849; *Tablet*, 24 Feb. 1849.

249. There was cholera over the country. See Salvian, Annals, 1872, 1; *Northampton Mercury*, 12 Aug. 1848; *Northampton Herald*, 19 Aug., 1848, both in Northamptonshire Record Office, Northampton; R.A. Smith, 'Some Ancient and Modern Ideas of Sanitary Economy', *Memoirs of the Literary and Philosophical Society of Manchester*, 11 (1854), 63 (will be cited as Smith, 'Sanitary Economy'). See also A.S. Wohl, *Endangered Lives: Public Health in Victorian Britain*, 1983, p.118 (will be cited as Wohl); A. Briggs, 'Cholera and Society in the Nineteenth Century', Past and Present [*PP*], no.19 (1961), 79 (will be cited as Briggs, 'Cholera'); G. Davis, 'Little Irelands' in R. Swift and S. Gilley (eds), *The Irish in Britain, 1815-1939*, 1989, p.118 (will be cited as Davis and Swift and Gilley, *Irish in Britain* respectively); M.E. and C.G. Pooley, 'Health, Society and Environment in Victorian Manchester' in R. Woods and J. Woodward, *Urban Disease and Mortality in Nineteenth-Century England*, 1984, p.155 (will be cited as Pooleys, 'Victorian Manchester' and Woods and Woodward respectively).

NOTES TO CHAPTER II

1. For Fr R. Croskell, see Gillow, 1, 599-600; *Harvest*, 11 (1898), 118-120; 16 (1903), 19-21; and 29 (1916), 8-9, 207 and 237; C.A. Bolton, *Salford Diocese and Its Catholic Past* (Manchester, 1950), p.89 (will be cited as Bolton).

2. Cf. Engels, p.86; W. Cooke Taylor, *Notes of a Tour in the Manufacturing Districts of Lancashire*, 1842, p.12 (will be cited as Cooke Taylor); H.B. Rodgers, 'The Suburban Growth of Victorian Manchester', *Journal of the Manchester Geographical Society*, 58 (1961-2), 6 (will be cited as Rodgers). For the opening of the new St Chad's, see *Tablet*, 2 Aug. 1845; 7 Feb. and 7 Mar. 1846; 31 July and 21 Aug. 1847.

3. Census, 1851, MF 2900, Market St District, entry 72, Microfilm Unit, [M]anchester [C]entral [L]ibrary. Will be cited as Census, 1851, MF 2900.

4. Rate Books for Relief of the Poor, vol. 1: Cheetham Overseers, Township of Cheetham 1848-1852, entry 928, levy of 1s. 9d. in the £, annual poor rate £1 1s. 10½d., M 10/16, [A]rchives of the [C]orporation of the [C]ity of [M]anchester, Local Studies Unit, MCL.

5. Annals B and C, GA I/B/3/b and c; LGR 12 Sept. 1853; Book of Agreements of Postulants joining the Sisters of the Holy Family, GA IV/C/15 (will be cited as Postulants' Agreements).

6. *Ordnance Survey Map of Manchester*, 1849, sheet 104/6, Geography Department, University of Manchester. According to a memorandum submitted by the Chief Constable to the Watch Committee on 2 Aug. 1849 (M9/62/1/20, ACCM, Local Studies Unit, MCL), 2,397 houses, shops etc. in the Cheetham area had private privies; only 28 common ones. There were, however, problems of refuse removal. See also M9/62/1/20 for a letter of complaint from the occupier of 53 Stocks St to the

Lamp and Scavenging Committee, 7 June 1848 and for a direction from the Town Council, 18 Sept. 1853, to the nuisance officers to co-operate with the scavenging department in cleansing ashpits, privies etc.

7.   Census, 1851, MF 2900, entry 73. This James Conry was probably related to John Conery of Joiner St, umbrella manufacturer and shipper, 'one of the biggest in the country', who was on the Council of the Catholic Salford Protection and Rescue Society and who died in Manchester in 1911 (*Harvest*, 24 (1911), 206).

8.   Rate Books for Relief of the Poor, vol. 2: Districts 3, 4, 6, 7 and 12, 1849, entry 2077, levy of 4s. in the £, annual poor rate £3, M 10/16, ACCM, Local Studies Unit, MCL.

9.   W. Green, *A Plan of Manchester and Salford 1787-1794* (Manchester, 1794). Will be cited as Green's *Map*, 1794.

10.   Cf. D. Cannadine, *Lords and Landlords: The Aristocracy and the Towns 1774-1967* (Leicester, 1980), pp.391-394.

11.   AMR, entry 103, 25 Jan. 1849.

12.   C. Makepeace, *Manchester As It Was*, 3 vols (Manchester, 1973), 3, 20. Will be cited as Makepeace.

13.   Census, 1851, MF 2900.

14.   Cf. Rodgers, p.5; D. and A. Shelston, *The Industrial City 1820-1870*, 1990, p.40 (will be cited as Shelstons).

15.   See the *Manchester Guardian*, for example in 1852 (MF G27, Microfilm Unit, MCL) for references to the Manchester Free Library and advertisements of concerts of orchestral and classical chamber music, led by such musicians as Hallé, Jullien, Seymour and Harris.

16.   Cf. M.A.G. O'Tuathaigh, 'The Irish in Nineteenth-Century Britain: Problems of Integration', *Transactions of the Royal Historical Society*, 31 (1981), 155 (will be cited as O'Tuathaigh); Swift and Gilley, 'Introduction', p.4; and C.G. Pooley, 'Segregation or Integration? The Residential Experience of the Irish in Mid-Victorian Britain', pp.70-72 (which will be cited as Pooley, 'Segregation or Integration?'), both in Swift and Gilley, *Irish in Britain*.

17.   St Mary's Register of Baptisms 1832-1841, 26 Dec. 1837, RCMm/4(1), [L]ancashire [R]ecord [O]ffice, Preston; LGR undated (post 19 July 1850 according to its reference to his having given 2 clergy retreats, as occurred in 1850: one in Oscott from 8-12 July and another from 15-19 July in St Edmund's); *Tablet*, 21 Sept. 1850; Lavery headstone, 1862, St Chad's graveyard, Cheetham Hill; H.G. Duffield, *The Stranger's Guide to Manchester*, 1850 (reprint Manchester, 1984), paper, p.34 (will be cited as Duffield); W. Whellan and Co. Ltd, *Directory of Manchester and Salford* (Manchester, 1852), p.192 (will be cited as Whellan, *Directory*). John Lavery was possibly related to Patrick Lavery, silk merchant of 2 Angel St, 1820, who donated £2,000 for the convent and school of the Navan Presentation Srs in Livesey St. See Annals of the Presentation Convent, Livesey St, 1836-1957, p.1 (will be cited as Presentation Convent Annals). See also G.P. Connolly, 'Catholicism in Manchester and Salford 1770-1850: The Quest for 'Le Chrétien Quelconque'', Ph.D. thesis, University of Manchester, 1980, 3 vols, 1/2, 264. Will be cited as Connolly, thesis.

18.   *Treasury and Committee of Council on Education: Building Grant Applications* (ED. 103), [P]ublic [R]ecord [O]ffice, London, no.54, p.829. Will be cited as PRO ED. 103/54. Cf. *[Brit]ish [Parl]iamentary Papers, House of Lords Papers, Local Reports on the Sanitary Condition of the Labouring Population of England*, 1842, Report 20: Dr R.B. Howard, *Report on the Prevalence of Diseases Arising from Contagion and Certain Other Physical Causes Amongst the Labouring Classes in Manchester*, pp.313-314, P 1173, [S]ocial [S]ciences Library, MCL. Will be cited as *Manchester Sanitary Report*, 1842. For a picture of Angel Meadow with St Chad's in

the background, see W.A. Shaw, *Manchester Old and New*, 3 vols, 1894, 2, 121 (will be cited as Shaw). For the derivation of the name, from an inn, 'The Sign of the Angel', see J. Stanhope, 'Noticeboard', *Manchester Region History Review [MRHR]*, 4 (1990-91), 60. Fr William Sheehan, an Irish Gaelic-speaking priest, became rector of St Chad's in 1852 and remained there until his death in 1891. He was particularly loved by his parishioners in Angel Meadow for transforming 19 Dyche St into St William's school in 1865. From 1876 he was joint vicar general of Salford Diocese with Provost Croskell. See PRO ED. 7, *Public Elementary Schools: Preliminary Statements, St Chad's* (will be cited as PRO ED. 7/64/12); *Harvest*, 3 (1889), 28-29; and 6 (1893), 139-140, 163-164 and 192-194; Bolton, p.89; R. Bracken, *Irish Born Secular Priests in the Diocese of Salford* (Manchester, 1984), a pamphlet, n.p. (will be cited as Bracken); P. Hughes, *A Historical Record of St Chad's Parish, 1773-1966* (Manchester, 1966), a brochure, n.p. (will be cited as Hughes, *St Chad's*).

19.   A.B. Reach (ed. C. Aspin), *Manchester and the Textile Districts in 1849* (Helmshore, 1972), p.53. Will be cited as Reach.

20.   B. Disraeli, *Coningsby or The New Generation*, 1844, World's Classics paperback (Oxford, 1982), p.138 (will be cited as Disraeli, *Coningsby*); A. Briggs, *Victorian Cities*, 1963 (Penguin 1968), p.96 (will be cited as Briggs, *Victorian Cities*). Cf. E. Gaskell's Margaret Hale's reactions, *North and South*, 1854-5 (Penguin 1988), pp.96-97 and 104-105 (will be cited as Gaskell, *North and South*). See also Cooke Taylor, p.1; Reach, p.1; L. Faucher, *Manchester in 1844*, 1844, pp.15-17 (will be cited as Faucher); Shelstons, p.9 for H. Ainsworth's description of Manchester, 1851-8; M. Kennedy, *Portrait of Manchester*, 1970 (cited as Kennedy), pp.49 and 77 for H.S. Gibbs' comments on his arrival by train in Feb. 1850 [E. Prout would have travelled to the same London Rd station, now Piccadilly, by the North Staffordshire and London and North West Railways (Whellan, *Directory*, pp.636-637)]; W.H. Thomson, *History of Manchester to 1852* (Altrincham, 1966) (cited as Thomson, *Manchester*), p.360 for Hugh Miller's impressions in 1845.

21.   According to *Manchester Guardian*, 15 Sept. 1849, MF G21, Microfilm Unit, MCL, the town had recently had a lot of rain and gloomy skies. See also *Manchester Guardian*, 21 Aug. 1852 for comments on bronchial and pulmonary diseases' being occasioned by Manchester's atmosphere. Cf. Gaskell, *North and South*, p.104.

22.   Census, 1851, MF 2904 and MF 2905, St George's District, Microfilm Unit, MCL. Will be cited as Census, 1851, MF 2904 and MF 2905. Cf. *Manchester Sanitary Report*, 1842, pp.320-322. For a photograph of Angel St, see Makepeace, 3, 11.

23.   Census, 1851, MF 2904; LGR 7 Feb. 1853; *London and Dublin Orthodox Journal of Useful Knowledge*, 18 (1843-4), 127 (will be cited as *Orthodox Journal*); Deeds of St William's Catholic School, Angel Meadow, Manchester, Salford Diocesan Deeds Index, pp.187-188, [A]rchives of the [D]iocese of [S]alford (will be cited as Deeds Index). For the rag trade cf. Thomson, *Manchester*, p.365.

24.   Cf. P. Rushton, 'Anomalies as Evidence in Nineteenth Century Censuses', *Local Historian [LH]*, 13 (1979), 482.

25.   Cf. M. Rose and Others, 'The Economic Origins of Paternalism: Some Objections', *SH*, 14 (1989), 94-95.

26.   Census, 1851, MF 2904.

27.   Manchester and Salford Sanitary Association Reports, M126/2-6/2, Rochdale Rd District, 1 Dec. 1852, Local Studies Unit, MCL. Will be cited as MSSAR. Cf. J. Bembridge, Journal, 1841-1853, 13 vols, 27 May 1850, B. R. MS 259 B1, Nineteenth-Century Diaries, Local Studies Unit, MCL (will be cited as Bembridge); A. Ransome and W. Royston, 'Report upon the Health of Manchester and Salford during the Last Fifteen Years' in G.W. Hastings (ed.), *Transactions of the National*

Association for the Promotion of Social Science [*TNAPSS*], 1866-7, pp.459-460, Manchester and Salford Education Aid Society Papers, Local Studies Unit, MCL (will be cited as Ransome and Royston).

28.   *Manchester Guardian*, 17 Oct. 1849.

29.   MSSAR, M126/2-6/7, 16 Mar. 1854.

30.   MSSAR, M126/2-6/4, 1 Apr. 1853 and M126/2-6/6, 16 Mar. 1854.

31.   MSSAR, M126/2-6/6. Cf. Reach, p.9.

32.   Cf. G. Best, *Mid-Victorian Britain 1851-1875*, 1971 Fontana,1979, p.38. Will be cited as Best, *Mid-Victorian Britain*.

33.   MSSAR, M126/2-6/9. Cf. M126/2-6/7, 16 Mar. 1854; *Brit. Parl. Papers, House of Lords Papers, Report to Her Majesty's Principal Secretary of State for the Home Department from the Poor Law Commissioners on an Inquiry into the Sanitary Condition of the Labouring Population of Great Britain*, 1842, pp.38 and 64-65, P 1172, SS Library, MCL (will be cited as *Sanitary Reports*, 1842).

34.   MSSAR, M126/2-6/6, 6/9 and 6/10, 16 Mar. 1854.

35.   *Brit. Parl. Papers, Reports from Committees*, vol.7, part 2, *Public Health Bill and Nuisances Removal Amendment Bill, Select Committee Report on Public Health: Manchester*, 1854-5[244], XIII, pt 2, 43, p.185. Will be cited as *Manchester Public Health Report*, 1854-5.

36.   *Manchester Sanitary Report*, 1842, p.313.

37.   MSSAR, M126/2-6/4, 1 Apr. 1853; 6/5, 11 and 13 Mar.; 6/6 and 6/10, 16 Mar. 1854. Cf. J.P. Kay Shuttleworth, *The Moral and Physical Condition of the Working Classes Employed in the Cotton Manufacture of Manchester*, 1832 (ed. W.H. Chaloner, 1970), pp.38 and 40-41. Will be cited as Kay Shuttleworth, *Condition of the Working Classes*.

38.   Letter, 30 Jan. 1854, from the ratepayers of St Michael's Ward to the Manchester Improvements Committee, M9/63/3/16, Local Studies Unit, MCL.

39.   MSSAR, M126/2-6/5, 23 Mar. 1854 and 6/10, 1854.

40.   See *Brit. Parl. Papers, Accounts and Papers, Reports from Commissioners*, 13, 1836, XXXIV, *Report on the State of the Irish Poor in Great Britain*, p.56. Will be cited as *Irish Report*. Cf. A.D. George and S. Clark, 'Little Ireland, Manchester', *Industrial Archaeology*, 14 (1979), 36-40.

41.   Census, 1851, MF 2905.

42.   Cf. Kay Shuttleworth, *Condition of the Working Classes*, p.44; Hammonds, *Chartists* p.25; Swift and Gilley, *Irish in Britain*, p.4; M. Anderson, *Family Structures in Nineteenth-Century Lancashire* (Cambridge, 1971), p.22; P.E. Malcolmson, *English Laundresses, A Social History, 1850-1930* (Illinois, 1986), pp.11-12 and 16-17.

43.   Cf. Swift and Gilley, *Irish in Britain*, p.4; R. Dennis, *English Industrial Cities of the Nineteenth Century, A Social Geography* (Cambridge, 1984), p.72 (will be cited as Dennis); W.J. Lowe, *The Irish in Mid-Victorian Lancashire: The Shaping of a Working-Class Community* (New York, 1989), pp.68-69 (will be cited as Lowe, *Irish in Lancashire*); A. Chiswell, 'The Nature of Urban Overcrowding', *LH*, 16 (1984), 156; H.J. Dyos, 'The Slums of Victorian London', *Victorian Studies* [*VS*], 11 (1967), 17-18 (will be cited as Dyos, 'Slums of London').

44.   Cf. Best, *Mid-Victorian Britain*, p.77; Davis, p.114; Dyos, 'Slums of London', p.34; F.M.L. Thompson, 'Social Control in Victorian Britain', *Econ.HR*, 34 (1981), 196.

45.   Letter, 1 July 1854, from the clergyman, churchwardens and others of St Michael's church, M9/62/1/21, a Letter Book, Local Studies Unit, MCL. Addressee obliterated by the letter's having been stuck into the book.

46.   PRO ED. 103/32.

47.   Engels, p.99. Cf. Kay Shuttleworth, *Condition of the Working Classes*, p.36.

48.   See Green's *Map*, 1794; A. Godfrey, *Old Ordnance Survey Maps*, Sheet 28, *Manchester City Centre 1849* (Gateshead, 1988) (will be cited as Godfrey, *Manchester City Centre 1849*); N. Paxton, 'M.E. Hadfield and the Rebuilding of St Mary's, Manchester, 1844', *North West Catholic History* [*NWCH*], 17 (1990), 29-36 (will be cited as Paxton).

49.   AMR, entry 66, 3 Jan. 1847. Fr Amedeus McBride CP gave 5 sermons in Manchester on the Passion and one on the Resurrection during Holy Week and on Easter Sunday 1844. His account, however, AMR, entry 6, does not state in which church.

50.   *Tablet*, 28 Oct. 1848.

51.   AMR, entry 110, 3 May 1849.

52.   AMR, entry 135, 3 Apr. 1851; SMR, pp.2-4.

53.   Young, *Dominic in England*, p.129 and cf. p.117.

54.   SMR, pp.2-4.

55.   SMR, pp.26-27.

56.   HMR, pp.42-43.

57.   SMR, pp.26-27. For Bp Turner see *Harvest*, 14 (1901), 159-161, 207-210, 258-260; F.O. Blundell OSB, *Old Catholic Lancashire*, 3 vols, 1925-38, 1, 111-112 (will be cited as Blundell).

58.   SMR, pp.26-27.

59.   PRO ED. 103/32. Cf. Godfrey, *Manchester City Centre 1849*. The Sisters of Providence, who taught in St Mary's from 1850-51, left on 12 Apr. 1851 'on account of bad school accommodation and other serious inconveniences' (*Harvest*, 19 (1906), 206).

60.   Godfrey, *Manchester City Centre 1849*; J.H. Smith, 'Ten Acres of Deansgate in 1851', *Transactions of the Lancashire and Cheshire Antiquarian Society* [*TLCAS*], 80 (1979), 43-44 (will be cited as Smith, 'Deansgate').

61.   Census, 1851, MF 2897, Deansgate, Microfilm Unit, MCL. Will be cited as Census, 1851, MF 2897.

62.   J. Robertson, 'The Duty of England to Provide a Gratuitous Compulsory Education for the Children of Her Poorer Classes', *Transactions of the Manchester Statistical Society* [*TMSS*], 1865, p.83. Cf. P. Gaskell, *The Manufacturing Population of England, Its Moral, Social and Physical Conditions, and the Changes which have Arisen from the Use of Steam Machinery*, 1833, p.117. Will be cited as P. Gaskell.

63.   Cf. Shelstons, p.89; S. Meacham, 'The Church in the Victorian City', [*VS*], 11 (1968), 360 (will be cited as Meacham).

64.   MSSAR, M126/3-3/6, 23 June 1853; *Manchester Sanitary Report*, 1842, p.314; *Sanitary Reports*, 1842, p.38; Smith, 'Sanitary Economy', p.70. Cf. A. Sharratt and K.R. Farrar, 'Sanitation and Public Health in Nineteenth-Century Manchester', *Memoirs and Proceedings of Manchester Literary and Philosophical Society*, 114 (1971-2), 55.

65.   Census, 1851, MF 2897.

66.   MSSAR, M126/2-3/6. Cf. P. Gaskell, p.133; Kay Shuttleworth, *Condition of the Working Classes*, p.32; *Manchester Sanitary Report*, 1842, pp.306 and 311-312. See also *The Builder*, 20 (1862), 840, 856 & 858-860 for 'Sanitary State of the Cotton Districts', with reference to Manchester and Ashton-under-Lyne.

67.   Census, 1851, MF 2897. Cf. *Sanitary Reports*, 1842, p.125.

68.   Dennis, p.72; Smith, 'Deansgate', p.49.

69.   Cf. Records of St Mary's Convent, Manchester, vol. 1, 1873-1900, 21 Apr. 1873, Cross and Passion Convent, Parkmount, Salford for a reference to the children in St Mary's school, Tonman St as 'rough and undisciplined'. Will be cited as Parkmount Records.

70. Reach, p.32. Cf. Faucher, p.76; P. Gaskell, p.100; B. Disraeli, *Sybil or the Two Nations*, 1845 (Penguin 1985), pp.131-132.

71. Cf. *Manchester Guardian*, 14 June 1851, MF G24, Microfilm Unit, MCL. St Mary's led the procession with a guild band, comprising 180 boys and 170 girls, 'wearing their peculiar costume', both girls and boys wearing a small crucifix round their necks. In that procession E. Prout would have walked with the St Chad's children. Cf. W.E.A. Axon, *The Annals of Manchester*, 1886, p.258 (will be cited as Axon); *Catholic Times and Catholic Opinion*, 25 May 1894 [an account of the Catholic Golden Jubilee Whit Walk]; *Harvest*, 21 (1908), 172.

72. *Manchester Sanitary Report*, 1842, p.314. Cf. D. Noble, 'Popular Fallacies Concerning the Production of Epidemic Disease', *TMSS*, 1859, p.9. Will be cited as Noble.

73. MSSAR, M126/2-3/26, 1854. Cf. Kay Shuttleworth, *Condition of the Working Classes*, p.28; Smith, 'Sanitary Economy', pp.57-63.

74. Annals A/E. The Providence Srs' convent in Brazennose St was evidently no longer available (*Harvest*, 19 (1906), 206).

75. LGR Feast of the Purification [2 Feb.] and 7 Feb. 1853.

76. Cf. R. Lloyd-Jones and M.J. Lewis, *Manchester and the Age of the Factory*, 1988, p.6. Will be cited as Lloyd-Jones and Lewis.

77. *Tablet*, 7 Nov. 1846; A. Godfrey, *Old Ordnance Survey Maps*, Sheet 24, *Manchester (New Cross) 1849* (Gateshead, 1988), which will be cited as Godfrey, *Manchester (New Cross), 1849.*

78. St George's Rd was renamed Rochdale Rd in the 1850s (Makepeace, 3, 36).

79. St Joseph's school was closed in 1872, when St Michael's was opened on the site of E. Prout's school. The parishes were amalgamated in 1887. See PRO ED. 7/64/10, /12 and /107; ED. 7/65; Bolton, p.212.

80. Reach, p.3.

81. Godfrey, *Manchester (New Cross) 1849*. Cf. Engels, pp.93-97. See also Hammonds, *Chartists*, p.81; T. Gansden, 'Manchester Early Dwellings Research Group', *Manchester Region History Review* [*MRHR*], 2 (1988), 39; and *MRHR*, 7 (1993) for a special issue on Ancoats.

82. Gaskell, *North and South*, p.96.

83. Reach, p.6.

84. Reach, p.6. Cf. Cooke Taylor, p.12.

85. Reach, p.6. Cf. Gaskell, *North and South*, p.143.

86. Reach, pp.6-7.

87. Census, 1851, MF 2891, Ancoats, Microfilm Unit, MCL; Godfrey, *Manchester (New Cross) 1849*; P. Rushton, 'Housing Conditions and the Family Economy in the Victorian Slum: A Study of a Manchester District, 1790-1871', an unpublished Ph.D. thesis, University of Manchester, 1977, pp.91 and 95 (will be cited as Rushton, thesis). Cf. Cooke Taylor, pp.11 and 131-132; Gaskell, *North and South*, p.132; Reach, pp.8 and 57-62. See also J.G. Williamson, 'The Impact of the Irish on British Labor Markets During the Industrial Revolution' in Swift and Gilley, *The Irish in Britain*, pp.139-157.

88. SMR, pp.45-47.

89. See Presentation Convent Annals, pp.56-59; *Tablet*, 4 July and 7, 14 and 21 Nov. 1846; *Orthodox Journal*, 18 (1843-44), 126-128 and 19 (1844-45), 127. For Fr D. Hearne see also Bracken; J.B. Marsden, *Memoirs of the Life and Labours of the Reverend Hugh Stowell, M.A.*, 1868, pp.61-105 (will be cited as Marsden); J. Reilly, *History of Manchester* (Manchester, 1861), pp.339-341 and 379 (will be cited as Reilly); J.T. Slugg, *Reminiscences of Manchester Fifty Years Ago* (Manchester, 1881), p.190 (will be cited as Slugg); G.P. Connolly, 'Little Brother, Be At Peace: The Priest

as Holy Man in the Nineteenth-Century Ghetto', *Studies in Church History*, 19 (1982), 191-206; P. Hughes, 'The Bishops of the Century' in Beck, p.195; J.T. Ward, 'The Factory Movement in Lancashire 1830-1855', *TLCAS*, 75-76 (1965-66), 191 (will be cited as Ward, 'Factory Movement in Lancashire'); W.R. Ward, 'The Cost of Establishment: Some Reflections on Church Building in Manchester', *Studies in Church History*, 3 (1966), 280 (will be cited as Ward, 'Establishment').

90.   *Acta Primi Episcopi Salfordensis, Printed Documents of Bishop W. Turner 1851-1872 [Pastoral Letters* and *Ad Clerums]* with a brief summary of their contents prepared by Fr D. Lannon, 1987, *Pastoral Letter*, 24 Sept. 1852, ADS (will be cited as Turner, *Pastoral Letters*). Father Peter Noel Mary Stephan was born at Plouhinec in France on 16 July 1807 and was ordained at Quimper on 21 Dec. 1839. Hoping that his Breton language would assist his evangelising Wales, he subsequently came to England. In view of Irish immigration, he was sent, not to Wales, but to St Anthony's, Liverpool in Mar. 1848 and to St Patrick's, Manchester on 3 June 1848. Receiving charge of St Joseph's in Mar. 1852, he remained there for 25 years, until in 1877, worn out by age and ill-health, he returned to France, where he died on 26 Nov. 1878. I am indebted to Fr Lannon for this reference, taken from the *Catholic Almanac*, 1880, p.46. According to PRO ED. 7/64/107, in 1871, and probably therefore in 1853, Fr Stephan lived at 43 Mason St/Swan St.

91.   SMR, pp.45-47.

92.   LGR 21 Apr. 1853.

93.   SMR, pp.45-47.

94.   LGR 21 Apr. 1853.

95.   LGR 4 May 1853; Godrey, *Manchester (New Cross), 1849.*

96.   LGR 7 Sept. 1853.

97.   R.W. Procter, *Memorials of Manchester Streets* (Manchester, 1874), p.28; T. Swindells, *Manchester Streets and Manchester Men*, fourth series (Manchester, 1908), p.74; Godfrey, *Manchester (New Cross) 1849* and Sheet 23, *Manchester Victoria 1849* (Gateshead, 1987); *Harvest*, 10 (1897), 35-37; Collection of Photographs, no.792, Acc.4746, Local Studies Unit, MCL.

98.   Engels, p.87.

99.   Godfrey, *Manchester (New Cross) 1849.*

100. LGR 7 Sept. 1853.

101. SMR, pp.45-47. Cf. R.W. Ambler, 'The 1851 Census for Religious Worship', *LH*, 11 (1975), 379.

102. SMR, pp.45-47.

103. Cf. Meacham, p.294; Shelstons, p.89.

104. Cf. Norman, *English Catholic Church*, p.223.

105. E.S. Worrall (transcribed), *Returns of Papists, 1767, Diocese of Chester* (Catholic Record Society, 1980), pp.34-36.

106. Wilson, p.297. For the full text of Dalgairns' letter see *Catholic Magazine*, 5 (1841), 310-313; and also McElligot, pp.51-85.

107. Cf. B.M.G. Reardan, *Religious Thought in the Victorian Age*, 1971, paperback 1980, p.27.

108. See above, Ch.I. pp.15 and 24.

109. See S. Gilley, 'Evangelical and Roman Catholic Missions to the Irish in London 1830-1870', a Ph.D. thesis, University of Cambridge, 1970, p.6 (will be cited as Gilley, thesis).

110. Matthew, 5:3; 25:40. Cf. *Letter of the St John's Wood Catholic Ladies' Association*, 18 Nov. 1847, 2/4/42b, [A]rchives of the [A]rchdiocese of [W]estminster (will be cited as *St John's Wood Letter*); S. Gilley, 'Papists, Protestants and the Irish in London 1835-1870', *Studies in Church History*, 8 (1972), 260.

111. Matthew, 10:42.
112. Matthew, 25:31-46.
113. Gilley, thesis, p.127. Cf. *Manchester and Salford Provident Society Reports 1833-1858*, 1849 *Report*, p.3, 361 M20, Local Studies Unit, MCL.
114. [Burke], *Paul*, p.166. For a description of how Passionist missions were conducted in Italy, see [Burke], *Paul*, pp.168-172; Yuhaus, pp.224-232.
115. AMR, entry 109, 27 Apr. 1849.
116. Cf. P. Hughes, 'The Coming Century' in Beck, p.19; G. Connolly, 'The Transubstantiation of Myth: Towards a New Popular History of Nineteenth-Century Catholicism in England', *JEH*, 35 (1984), 82-84 (will be cited as Connolly, 'Transubstantiation of Myth').
117. See PRO ED. 103/54, for example, for James Conry and John Lavery as signatories to St Chad's application for a government school building grant in 1851.
118. Cf. Reach, p.11; Briggs, *Victorian Cities*, p.56; Davis, pp.104-105; Hammonds, *Chartists*, pp.80-81; Lloyd-Jones and Lewis, pp.5-6; J. Aikin, *A Description of the Country from Thirty to Forty Miles Round Manchester*, 1795, pp.192-193; T.S. Ashton, *Economic and Social Investigations in Manchester 1833-1933: A Centenary History of the Manchester Statistical Society*, 1934, pp.1-2 (will be cited as Ashton); W.H. Brindley (ed.), *The Soul of Manchester* (Manchester, 1929; reprint Yorkshire, 1974), p.43 (will be cited as Brindley); N.J. Frangopulo (ed.), *Rich Inheritance: A Guide to the History of Manchester* (Manchester, 1962), p.40 (will be cited as Frangopulo); W.M. Frazer, *A History of English Public Health 1834-1939*, 1950, pp.2 and 9 (will be cited as Frazer); E. Gauldie, *Cruel Habitations, A History of Working-Class Housing 1780-1918*, 1974, pp.92-93, 114 and 119 (will be cited as Gauldie); E. Halévy (transl. E.I. Watkin), *A History of the English People in 1815*, 1924, paperback 1987, p.243; R.M. Hartwell, *The Industrial Revolution and Economic Growth*, 1971, pp.319-320; P. Mathias, *The First Industrial Nation, An Economic History of Britain 1700-1914*, 1969, p.207. (will be cited as Mathias, *First Industrial Nation*); A. Redford, *Labour Migration in England 1800-1850*, 1926 (revised Manchester, 1964), pp.13-17 and 69 (will be cited as Redford, *Labour Migration*) and 'The Emergence of Manchester', *History*, 24 (1939-40), 32-34, 37, 39 and 43-44 (will be cited as Redford, 'Manchester'); J.N. Tarn, *Five Per Cent Philanthropy, An Account of Housing in Urban Areas between 1840 and 1914* (Cambridge, 1973), p.xiii; D. Chadwick, 'On the Social and Educational Statistics of Manchester and Salford', *TMSS*, 1861, p.1; H.J. Dyos, 'The Growth of Cities in the Nineteenth Century: A Review of Some Recent Writing', *VS*, 9 (1966), 227; R. Lawton, 'Population Trends in Lancashire and Cheshire from 1801', *Transactions of the Historic Society of Lancashire and Cheshire [THSLC]*, 114 (1962), 193.
119. Brindley, pp.45-47; Frazer, pp.2 and 23; Kennedy, p.51; Smith, 'Sanitary Economy', pp.75-76; Thomson, *Manchester*, pp.238 and 254; C. Aspin, *Lancashire, The First Industrial Society* (Helmshore, 1969), pp.94-95 (will be cited as Aspin, *Lancashire*); E.P. Hennock, 'Urban Sanitary Reform A Generation Before Chadwick?', *Econ.HR*, 10 (1957-8), 113-116; C.H. Hume, 'The Public Health Movement' in J.T. Ward (ed.), *Popular Movements c.1830-1850*, 1970, paperback 1983, pp.183-186; B. Keith Lucas, 'Some Influences Affecting the Development of Sanitary Legislation in England', *Econ.HR*, 6 (1953-4), 291-292.
120. Kay Shuttleworth, *Condition of the Working Classes*, pp.37-38. Cf. Engels, pp.88-89.
121. Whellan, *Directory*, p.xviii. Cf. *Sanitary Reports*, 1842, p.64. See also Thomson, *Manchester*, p.362; B. Love, *Manchester As It Is* (Manchester, 1839; second edition 1842; reprint 1971), p.9 (will be cited as Love).
122. *Manchester Public Health Report*, 1854-5, p.131.

123. See M9/62/1/20, ACCM, Local Studies Unit, MCL for a resolution, 24 Jan. 1849, of the Building and Sanitary Regulations Committee, to permit the construction of water closets, on condition that the Lamp and Scavenging Committee would remove the ashes, at a charge equal to half the estimated expense of removing ashes, and provided the parties interested would undertake to obtain the requisite supply of water for cleansing from the Water Works Company, a provision outside the scope of the poor. Cf. Pooleys, 'Victorian Manchester', p.174.

124. Redford, 'Manchester', pp.43-46. Cf. Best, *Mid-Victorian Britain*, p.62; Briggs, *Victorian Cities*, p.111; Davis, p.104; Frangopulo, pp.56-57; Thomson, *Manchester*, p.363; S.D. Chapman, 'Financial Restraints on the Growth of Firms in the Cotton Industry 1790-1850', *Econ.HR*, 32 (1979), 60-61 (will be cited as Chapman, 'Financial Restraints'). For the immigration of Irish refugees from the potato famine and the consequent problems of poor relief and removal see Chapman, 'Financial Restraints', pp.60-65; Lowe, *Irish in Lancashire*, pp.35 and 41; Redford, *Labour Migration*, pp.131, 156-158 and 189; and *Manchester Merchants and Foreign Trade 1794-1858* (Manchester, 1934), pp.81 and 83 (will be cited as Redford, *Manchester Merchants*); Reilly, p.442; C. Woodham-Smith, *The Great Hunger: Ireland 1845-1849*, 1962, pp.183, 188-189, 216 and 281 (will be cited as Woodham-Smith); D.A. Kerr, 'England, Ireland and Rome 1847-1848', *Studies in Church History*, 25 (1989), 262 (will be cited as Kerr, 'England, Ireland and Rome'); F. Neal, 'Liverpool, the Irish Steamship Companies and the Famine Irish', *Immigrants and Minorities*, 5 (1986), pp.29-46 and 51-53; M.E. Rose, 'Settlement, Removal and the New Poor Law' in D. Fraser (ed.), *The New Poor Law in the Nineteenth Century*, 1976, pp.26, 29 and 38-39 (will be cited as Rose, 'Settlement'); R. Scally, 'Liverpool Ships and Irish Emigrants in the Age of Sail', *JSH*, 17 (1983), 7 (will be cited as Scally); J. Werly, 'The Irish in Manchester 1832-1849', *Irish Historical Studies [IHS]*, 18 (1973), 354 (will be cited as Werly).

125. Best, *Mid-Victorian Britain*, p.38; Briggs, *Victorian Cities*, p.111; Frangopulo, p.56.

126. Thomson, *Manchester*, p.362. Cf. *Sanitary Reports*, 1842, pp.53-54.

127. Pooleys, 'Victorian Manchester', p.152. Cf. H.C. Oats, 'Report of the Committee set up by the Manchester Statistical Society to Inquire into the Educational and Other Conditions of a District in Deansgate', *TMSS*, 1864, pp.1-5.

128. Cf. Reach, p.56.

129. *Manchester Sanitary Report*, 1842, p.330.

130. *Manchester Guardian*, 17 Oct. 1849; Reilly, p.447. Acc. to Bracken, Canon E. Cantwell, an Irish priest in Manchester in 1848, gave the Last Sacraments to 17 fever victims in one house in Angel Meadow.

131. Cooke Taylor, p.124.

132. J.A. Jackson, *The Irish in Britain*, 1963, p.40 (will be cited as Jackson).

133. MSSAR, M126/2-6/6.

134. J.E. Mercer, 'The Conditions of Life in Angel Meadow', *TMSS*, 1897, p.161.

135. Cf. SMR, 1 and 22 Mar. 1854; S. Gilley, 'The Roman Catholic Mission to the Irish in London, 1840-1860', *RH*, 10 (1969-70), 141. Will be cited as Gilley, 'Roman Catholic Mission'.

136. L.H. Lees, 'Patterns of Lower-Class Life: Irish Slum Communities in Nineteenth Century London' in S. Thernstrom and R. Sennett, *Nineteenth-Century Cities*, 1969, fourth printing (Yale, 1974), p.380 (will be cited as Lees, 'Patterns').

137. *Irish Report*, Appendix III, p.xxv.

138. *Irish Report*, p.62. Cf. S. Bamford, *Passages in the Life of a Radical*, 1844, ed. T. Hilton, 1967, p.122.

139. *Irish Report*, p.62.

140. *Irish Report*, p.61. Cf. Duffield, pp.4-16; Everett's *Manchester Guide* (Manchester, 1840), pp.212-227 (will be cited as Everett).

141. The SVP was introduced into England as the result of an appeal made by Fr George (Ignatius) Spencer. See *Tablet*, 4 Feb. 1843. In 1849-50, 1,029 indigent sick were relieved by the Benevolent Society (*Tablet*, 21 Sept. 1850). See also the *Manchester St Vincent de Paul Society Manual*, 1854-1929 (Manchester, 1929), pp.7 and 13. I am indebted to the late Sr St Pius Dalton CP, St Gabriel's Hall, Manchester for drawing my attention to this source. Cf. F.J. Doyle, *The Society of St Vincent de Paul in Manchester: The First Hundred Years 1845-1945* (Manchester, 1945), pp.7-8; A.J. Dunn, *Frederic Ozanam and the Establishment of the Society of St Vincent De Paul*, 1913, pp.68-70; A.R. Vidler, *A Century of Social Catholicism 1820-1920*, 1964, paperback 1969, pp.24-25.

142. Cf. Hughes in Beck, p.3.

143. See Building Fund Account Book, St Mary's, Manchester, 1835-1861, LRO RCLy/7/4; *Census of Great Britain, 1851, Ecclesiastical Returns*, PRO HO 129/473-4-19 (St Chad's); 473-4-18 (St Mary's); 473-3-12 (St Augustine's); 473-5-13 (St Patrick's); 473-1-1 (St Ann's); 472-3-1-7 (St John's) (will be cited as PRO HO 129); *Catholic Magazine*, 2 (1832), 216-219; Duffield, pp.31-34; *Tablet*, 7 Feb. and 7 Mar. 1846, 31 July and 21 Aug. 1847 and 28 Oct. 1848; Canon L. Toole, *Catholic Tradition of Manchester and Salford*, a newspaper account of a lecture he gave in St John's, Salford, May 1867, Owen MSS, MF 572, ff.95-96, Microfilm Unit, MCL. See also Axon, pp.102, 121, 159, 240 and 246; Blundell, 2, 34, 38 and 44; Bolton, pp.69-70, 87-92, 104, 109-110, 113, 115 and facing 145 for a photograph of the interior of St Augustine's, Granby Row; Connolly, thesis, passim; Hughes, *St Chad's*; Paxton, pp.29-36; Slugg, pp.38 and 189-190; Thomson, *Manchester*, pp.252 and 309; D. Clinch, *Manchester's Hidden Gem* (Manchester, 1992); C. Stewart, *The Stones of Manchester*, 1956, pp.47-50; D. Lannon, 'Rook St Chapel, Manchester', *NWCH*, 16 (1989), 13; *Harvest*, 21 (1908), 172; *St Mary's, Failsworth 1845-1964*, a brochure, P53, ADS.

144. *Catholic Directory*, 1849, p.57; *Tablet*, 21 Aug. 1852.

145. Cf. Best, *Mid-Victorian Britain*, p.207; Houghton, p.59; McLeod, p.x; K.S. Inglis, *Churches and the Working Classes in Victorian England*, 1963, reprint 1964, pp.1-2, 4, 16 and 18 (will be cited as Inglis); D. Gwynn, 'The Irish Immigration' in Beck, pp.266-270 and 'Growth of the Catholic Community' also in Beck, pp.410, 412-413 and 417.

146. *Tablet*, 21 Jan. 1854. Cf. K.S. Inglis, 'Patterns of Religious Worship in 1851', *JEH*, 11 (1960), 74-86; W.S.F. Pickering, 'The 1851 Religious Census - A Useless Experiment?', *British Journal of Sociology*, 18 (1967), 390; D.M. Thompson, 'The 1851 Religious Census: Problems and Possibilities', *VS*, 11 (1967-8), 87-97.

147. 252,783. See *Rambler*, 1 (1854), 183-190 and 257-280; Norman, *English Catholic Church*, p.205.

148. PRO HO 129/473-3-12.

149. PRO ED 103/54.

150. PRO HO 129/473-4-19.

151. *Pace* Werly, p.351. Cf. Lowe, *Irish in Lancashire*, pp.112 and 115-116; and 'The Lancashire Irish and the Catholic Church 1846-71: the Social Dimension', *IHS*, 20 (1976), 139 (will be cited as 'Lancashire Irish').

152. PRO ED 103/32; AMR, entry 66, 3 Jan. 1847.

153. PRO HO 129/473-4-18.

154. B.I. Coleman, *The Church of England in the Mid-Nineteenth Century*, [Hist]orical [Assoc]iation [Pamphl]et, 1980, p.41 (will be cited as Coleman). Cf. P. Joyce, *Work, Society and Politics, The Culture of the Factory in Later Victorian*

England (Brighton, 1980), p.244. Will be cited as Joyce, *Work, Society and Politics*.
155. *Catholic Directory*, 1851, p.58. Cf. A. Hume, 'Remarks on the Census of Religious Worship for England and Wales', *THSLC*, 12 (1859-60), 4.
156. SMR, pp.45-47.
157. *Catholic Directory*, 1851, p.58.
158. Cf. Connolly, 'Transubstantiation of Myth', pp.88-93; Gilley, 'Roman Catholic Mission', p.124; O'Tuathaigh, pp.165-166; J.L. Altholz, *The Liberal Catholic Movement in England: 'The Rambler' and Its Contributors 1848-1864*, 1960-62, p.4; R. Swift, 'Anti-Catholicism and Irish Disturbances: Public Order in Mid-Victorian Wolverhampton', *MH*, 9 (1984), 89 (will be cited as Swift, 'Wolverhampton').
159. AMR, entry 23. Cf. Bembridge, 13 Aug. 1841; *Rambler*, 1 (1854), 188-190.
160. Cf. AMR, entry 109, 27 Apr. 1849. See also P. Corish, *The Irish Catholic Experience, A Historical Survey* (Dublin, 1985), pp.164-166 (will be cited as Corish); L.H. Lees, *Exiles of Erin: Irish Migrants in Victorian London* (Manchester, 1979), p.166 (will be cited as Lees, *Exiles of Erin*); C. O'Gráda, *Ireland Before and After the Famine: Explorations in Economic History, 1800-1925*, (Manchester, 1988), p.15 (will be cited as O'Gráda); G.P. Connolly, '"With More than Ordinary Devotion to God": The Secular Missioner of the North in the Evangelical Age of the English Mission', *NWCH*, 10 (1983), 9-10, 13 and 18-19; and 'Irish and Catholic: Myth or Reality? Another Sort of Irish and the Renewal of the Clerical Profession Among Catholics in England 1791-1918' in R. Swift and S. Gilley, *The Irish in the Victorian City*, 1985, p.230 (will be cited as Swift and Gilley, *Victorian City*); E. Larkin, 'The Devotional Revolution in Ireland 1850-1875', *American Historical Review*, 77 (1972), 638 (will be cited as Larkin); T.G. McGrath, 'The Tridentine Evolution of Modern Irish Catholicism, 1563-1962: A Re-examination of the 'Devotional Revolution' Thesis', *RH*, 20 (1991), 515-516 (will be cited as McGrath); D.W. Miller, 'Irish Catholicism and the Great Famine', *JSH*, 9 (1975), 83-87 (will be cited as Miller); J.F. Supple, 'The Catholic Clergy of Yorkshire, 1850-1900: A Profile', *Northern History [NH]*, 21 (1985), 232-233 (will be cited as Supple).
161. *Catholic Magazine*, 2 (1832), 216; Bolton, pp.87-88; Larkin, pp.627, 636 and 638; McGrath, pp.516-522; Miller, pp.82-87 and 90; D.J. Keenan, *The Catholic Church in Nineteenth-Century Ireland* (Dublin, 1983), p.1.
162. Cf. McGrath, pp.516 and 518.
163. Cf. R.J. Schiefen, *Nicholas Wiseman and the Transformation of English Catholicism* (Shepherdstown, USA, 1984), pp.101-102 and 135. Will be cited as Schiefen, *Wiseman*.
164. Cf. Norman, *English Catholic Church*, pp.230 and 232.
165. Letter, 11 Mar. 1850 to the *Rambler*, 5 (1850), 388-390. Cf. Vanden Bussche, pp.199, 203-204, 213-215, 223-225 and 228-229. Cf. Bowden, p.336 for Fr Faber in 1852: 'If we could only make our Celts saints, we would do something to our Saxons'; and Inglis, p.122 for Cardinal Manning's expressing similar sentiments. For the possible origin of Fr Ignatius Spencer's rule of life, see the request made to him by *Unus* in the *Catholic Magazine*, 12 (1850) 60-61 to institute such a rule of life as a Passionist lay association.
166. *Brit. Parl. Papers, Report from Committees*, vol.7, pt 1, 1854-55[308], XIII, pt 1, *Report on Poor Removal*, p.245 estimated, according to information received from the priests, '46,000 Irish labouring Catholics' in Manchester, Chorlton and Salford. 'Other Catholics are Lancashire and Yorkshire families who cannot be classed with the Irish population.' See also St Augustine's Baptism Register, 1820-1826 (RCMa/1) and Marriage Register 1837-1850 (RCMa/2), 1850-1855 (RCMa/3); St Chad's Baptism Register 1810-1820 (RCMc/3), 1828-1837 (RCMc/4), 1838-1847 (RCMc/5) and Marriage Register 1828-1840 (RCMc/6), 1828-1850 (RCMc/7); St Mary's

Baptismal Register 1794-1812 (RCMm/1), 1812-1819 (RCMm/2), 1820-1826 (RCMm/3), 1832-1841 (RCMm/4(1), 1842-1844 (RCMm/4(2) and Marriage Register 1837-1855 (RCMm/5); St Patrick's Baptismal Register 1832-1842 (RCMp/1), Marriage Register 1833-1856 (RCMp/2) and Burial Register 1845-46, continued into the 1850s (RCMp/3); St Wilfrid's Baptism Register 1842-1855 (RCMw/1/1), all in LRO; *Catholic Magazine*, 2 (1832), 216-219 and 3 (1833), 170-171; Coleman, pp.29-30; Connolly, 'The Transubstantiation of Myth', pp.78-104; and 'Shifting Congregations: Catholic Rural Migration in Late Eighteenth-Century Lancashire' in J.A. Hilton (ed.), *Catholic Englishmen* (Wigan, 1984), p.16; Shaw, 2, 133; J. Bossy, *The English Catholic Community 1570-1850*, 1975, pp.298-299 and 302-309 (will be cited as Bossy); J.H. Clapham, *An Economic History of Modern Britain*, 2 vols (Cambridge, 1926-32), 1, 56-59 and 61 (will be cited as Clapham); B.G. Blackwood, 'Plebeian Catholics in Later Stuart Lancashire', *NH*, 25 (1989), 153-173. For Irish immigration before the potato famine, see Lees, *Exiles of Erin*, p.33; Mathias, *First Industrial Nation*, p.199; O'Tuathaigh, p.151; Pooley, 'Segregation or Integration?', p.67; Redford, *Labour Migration*, p.41; D. Mathew, *Catholicism in England 1535-1935, Portrait of a Minority: Its Culture and Tradition*, 1936, pp.182-184 (will be cited as Mathew); B. Collins, 'Proto-Industrialisation, a Pre-Famine Emigration', *SH*, 7 (1982), 127-146 (will be cited as Collins); B.M. Kerr, 'Irish Seasonal Migration to Great Britain, 1800-1838', *IHS*, 3 (1942-3), 365-380; R. Lawton, Irish Immigration to England & Wales in the Mid-Nineteenth Century', *Irish Geography*, 4 (1959), 35-54.

167. Blundell, 1, 76-145; 2, 27 and 34; 3, 27-76; J. Bossy, 'Catholic Lancashire in the Eighteenth Century' in J. Bossy and P. Jupp (eds), *Essays Presented to Michael Roberts* (Belfast, 1976), pp.54-69; G. Scott OSB, *Gothic Rage Undone: English Monks in the Age of Enlightenment* (Downside Abbey, Bath, 1992), pp.86-89, 97, 99, 102, 117 and 126 (will be cited as Scott, *Gothic Rage Undone*); and 'Fighting Old Battles: The English Benedictine Mission 1689-1715', *Downside Review* [*DR*], 98 (1980), 11; E.D. Steele, 'The Irish Presence in the North of England 1850-1914', *NH*, 12 (1976), 221 (will be cited as Steele, 'Irish Presence').

168. *Manchester Guardian*, 14 June 1851; Blundell, 1, 162-166; J.A. Myerscough SJ, *A Procession of Lancashire Martyrs and Confessors* (Glasgow, 1958), pp.228-231.

169. The Irish Fr Sheehan at the Jubilee Dinner of the Benevolent Society (*Tablet*, 21 Sept. 1850).

170. *Harvest*, 21 (1908), 195; *The Cathedral Church of St John the Evangelist, Salford 1890-1990* (Salford, 1990), a brochure. Cf. Bolton, p.117; P. Doyle, 'Bishop Goss of Liverpool (1856-1872) and the Importance of Being English', *Studies in Church History*, 18 (1982), 433-447.

171. See the *Tablet*, 21 Sept. 1850 for Fr Sheehan in Manchester on 10 Sept.: 'Look at the number of priests carried off in the flower of youth in Liverpool and Manchester during the great fever year.' Cf. *Harvest*, 12 (1899), 37; Connolly, 'Transubstantiation of Myth', pp.99-101; Lowe, *Irish in Lancashire*, p.27; and 'Lancashire Irish', pp.139 and 142.

172. See Norman, *English Catholic Church*, pp.224 and 230.

173. Cf. McGrath, p.519.

174. See Gilley, 'Roman Catholic Mission', pp.132-133. The continental devotions played a conspicuous role in Redemptorist missions too but, apart from a mission in St Wilfrid's, Hulme in 1850, the Redemptorists did not give parish missions in England until c.1858. See J. Sharp, *Reapers of the Harvest: The Redemptorists in Great Britain and Ireland 1843-1898* (Dublin, 1989), pp.4, 9, 12-13, 18, 93, 95-96, 124-125, 171 and 173. Will be cited as Sharp.

175. Cf. C.R. Leetham, *Luigi Gentili, A Sower for the Second Spring*, 1965, p.243

for Gentili's having 3,000 candles for the Forty Hours' devotion in St Augustine's, Manchester c.1846 (will be cited as Leetham).

176. Cf. Bowden, p.180.

177. AMR, entry 76, 10-23 June 1847.

178. Cf. Holmes, p.49; Mathew, p.195; Norman, *Roman Catholicism*, p.75; Schiefen, *Wiseman*, pp.38 and 135; Sharp, p.94; Thureau-Dangin, 2, 63-65; B. Martin, *John Henry Newman: His Life and Work*, 1982, second edition 1990, p.154. According to Norman, *English Catholic Church*, p.10, Bishop Milner had introduced devotions to the Sacred Heart in 1814.

179. AMR, on the page facing entries 72 and 73 and at the end of entry 110; and also in Fr Dominic Barberi CP, Recollections Left to our Young Missionaries in England, 1849, transl. Fr Conrad Charles CP, PGAR. I am indebted to Fr Charles for his translation and to Fr Paulinus Vanden Bussche CP for a copy of it. Ward, *Sequel*, 2, 26 is inaccurate in saying Fr Gaudentius Rossi was Fr Dominic's 'usual companion'. According to AMR he was with Dominic only three times: at Derby in Mar. 1845; and on two missions in London in Feb. 1847. Ward is also incorrect in stating that Gaudentius learned 'English with great rapidity though by no means accurately'. He learned it slowly but, in the main, accurately (Young, *Dominic in England*, p.78). Ward, *Sequel*, 1, 68, 139-140 and 208 also inaccurately associates Dominic with Gentili's 'over-enthusiasm'. Norman's remarks, *English Catholic Church*, p.230, equating Dominic's practices with those of Gentili must also be treated with caution, especially in view of his comments on p.228 that Gentili 'combined the Italian-style emotional preaching with the mass-meeting techniques of Methodist traditions'. That was not Passionist style.

180. AMR, entry 109, 27 Apr. 1849; Charles, 'Origins', pp.72-73.

181. Cf. Norman, *English Catholic Church*, pp.226-228.

182. Cf. Holmes, p.50; Norman, *English Catholic Church*, pp.110-111, 118 and 142-143; Ward, *Sequel*, 1, 208.

183. Cf. McLeod, pp.248-249.

184. Norman, *Roman Catholicism*, p.74.

185. Letter, Fr Ignatius Spencer CP to the Passionist General, Fr Anthony of St James (Testa) CP, 21 Feb. 1851, LISR. I am indebted to Sr Cyprian Connolly CP for her translation.

186. Cf. Gilley, thesis, p.242.

187. *Tablet*, 16 Mar. 1850.

188. *Tablet*, 4 Apr. 1846.

189. Cf. Sharp, pp.95 and 124-125.

190. Cf. Gilley, thesis, pp.200 and 218-219; and 'Protestant London, No Popery and the Irish Poor: II (1850-1860)', *RH*, 11 (1971-2), 37; Lees, *Exiles of Erin*, p.164; Mathew, p.213; Norman, *English Catholic Church*, p.232; Sharp, p.125.

191. Cf. E.I. Watkin, *Roman Catholicism in England from the Reformation to 1950*, 1957, p.181.

192. Cf. Faber's hymn, 'Faith of Our Fathers' and Wiseman's 'Full in the Panting Heart of Rome', *The Westminster Hymnal*, 1949, nos 210 and 226 respectively.

193. *Catholic Directory*, 1852, p.57.

194. Machin, *Politics*, p.210.

1.   Bebbington, p.1. Cf. Hylson-Smith, p.vii.
2.   *Dolman's Magazine*, 5 (1847), 471, Oscott College Library. See also the *Lamp*, no.4 (1852), 365. Cf. Hempton, pp.38-39; Mathew, pp.142-143; Thompson, *English Working Class*, p.77; Wolffe, p.13; E. Duffy (ed.) *Challoner and His Church, A Catholic Bishop in Georgian England*, 1981, p.23; D. Gwynn, *Bishop Challoner*, 1946, p.235 (will be cited as Gwynn, *Challoner*); J. Hickey, *Urban Catholics: Urban Catholicism in England and Wales from 1829 to the Present Day*, 1967, p.23; C. Haydon, 'The Gordon Riots in the English Provinces', *Historical Research [B]ulletin of the [I]nstitute of HR]*, 63 (1990), 354-355 and 358.
3.   The Wesleyan newspaper was called the *Watchman* (Hempton, p.124; J.L. Altholz, *The Religious Press in Britain, 1760-1900* (Westport, Connecticut, 1989), p.81). See also *Northampton Herald*, 8 July, 5 Aug. and 4 Sept. 1848; Altholz, *Religious Press*, pp.51-52; Bracken; Chadwick, *Victorian Church*, 1, 167; Coleman, p.33; Gilley, *Newman*, p.270; and 'Protestant London, Part I', pp.213-218; Hempton, pp.122, 158 and 163; Hylson-Smith, pp.95-96, 115 and 147-150; Joyce, *Work, Society and Politics*, pp.248 and 265, ftnote 67; Machin, *Politics*, pp.65 and 98; Marsden, passim; Norman, *Anti-Catholicism*, pp.14-15, 33 and 70; Wolffe, pp.31-32, 36-37, 54, 109-110, 112-113, 119, 123-126, 136, 150, 152-153, 172, 174, 194 and 265; W.L. Arnstein, *Protestant versus Catholic in Mid-Victorian England: Mr Newdegate and the Nuns*, 1982, p.5 (will be cited as Arnstein); C. Hulbert, *Memoirs of Seventy Years of an Eventful Life* (Shrewsbury, 1852), p.153; G. Kitson Clark, *Churchmen and the Condition of England 1832-1885*, 1973, p.71 (will be cited as Kitson Clark, *Churchmen*); D.M. Lewis, *Lighten Their Darkness: The Evangelical Mission to Working-Class London, 1828-1860* (Westport, Connecticut, 1986), pp.190, 193 and 204 (will be cited as Lewis, *Evangelical Mission*); C.T. McIntire, *England against the Papacy 1858-1861* (Cambridge, 1983), p.33; S.E. Maltby, *Manchester and the Movement for National Elementary Education 1800-1870* (Manchester, 1918), pp.53 and 62 (will be cited as Maltby); J. Murphy, *The Religious Problem in English Education: The Crucial Experiment* (Liverpool, 1959), p.246 (will be cited as Murphy, *Religious Problem*); D.G. Paz, *The Priesthoods and Apostasies of Pierce Connelly* (New York, 1986), p.177 (will be cited as Paz, *Connelly*); B. Williams, *The Making of Manchester Jewry 1740-1875* (Manchester, 1976), pp.46-47 (will be cited as Williams, *Jewry*); A.F. Young and E.T. Ashton, *British Social Work in the Nineteenth Century*, 1956, p.32 (will be cited as Young and Ashton); R.L. Greenall, 'Popular Conservatism in Salford 1868-1886', *NH*, 9 (1974), 133; J. Kent, 'Anglican Evangelicalism in the West of England 1858-1900' in Robbins, *Evangelicalism*, p.179; N. Kirk, 'Ethnicity, Class and Popular Toryism 1850-1870' in K. Lunn (ed.), *Hosts, Immigrants and Minorities: Historical Responses to Newcomers in British Society 1870-1914* (Folkstone, 1980), pp.73-74 (will be cited as Kirk, 'Ethnicity'); V.A. McClelland, 'The Protestant Alliance and Roman Catholic Schools, 1872-1874', *VS*, 8 (1964-5), 174-175 (will be cited as McClelland, 'Schools').
4.   *Protestant Witness* (Manchester, 1849-1851), title-page.
5.   Cf. Joyce, *Work, Society and Politics*, p.251; Kirk, 'Ethnicity', pp.73-74; L.P. Curtis, *Anglo-Saxons and Celts* (Connecticut, 1968), pp.3, 19 and 26.
6.   *Protestant Witness*, 20 Oct. 1849, p.233. Italics mine.
7.   *Protestant Witness*, pp.143, 147 and 157.
8.   *Protestant Witness*, pp.346-350.
9.   *Protestant Witness*, pp.431 and 446-448. Cf. J. Markus, 'Bishop Blougram and the Literary Men', *VS*, 21 (1977-8), 177-179.
10.   LGR 17 and 30 Nov. 1849; Red Bk.
11.   LGR 30 Nov. 1849 and [post 19 July 1850].
12.   LGR 11 Apr. 1866.

13. Red Bk; LGR 11 Apr. 1866.

14. Manchester and Salford Education Aid Society, Folio of Newspaper Cuttings collected by E. Brotherton, pp.16-17, Local Studies Unit, MCL. Will be cited as Brotherton.

15. *Dolman's Magazine*, 2 (1845), 187.

16. Machin, *Politics*, pp.211 and 214; Norman, *Anti-Catholicism*, pp.53-54; Schiefen, *Wiseman*, pp.253-254; and 'The Crusade of Nicholas Wiseman' in P.T. Phillips (ed. and introd.), *The View from the Pulpit: Victorian Ministers and Society* (Canada, 1978), p.250 (will be cited as Schiefen, 'Crusade'); Kerr, 'England, Ireland and Rome', p.261; D.A. Gowland, 'Methodist Secessions and Social Conflict in South Lancashire 1830-1857', an unpublished Ph.D. thesis, University of Manchester, 1966, pp.170 and 197 (will be cited as Gowland, thesis).

17. *Rambler* 1 (1848), 178-179; Kerr, 'England, Ireland and Rome', p.273; Schiefen, 'Crusade', p.250; G.I.T. Machin, 'Lord John Russell and the Prelude to the Ecclesiastical Titles Bill, 1846-1851', *JEH*, 25 (1974), p.287 (will be cited as Machin, 'Russell').

18. Chadwick, *Victorian Church*, 1, 286; Machin, *Politics*, pp.213-214 and 'Russell', pp.284 and 287; Norman, *Anti-Catholicism*, pp.53-54; W. Ward, *The Life and Times of Cardinal Wiseman*, 2 vols, 1897, 1, 521-525 (will be cited as Ward, *Wiseman*); G. Albion, 'The Restoration of the Hierarchy, 1850' in Beck, pp.89 and 99 (will be cited as Albion); A.O.J. Cockshut, 'The Literary and Historical Significance of the *Present Position of Catholics*' in I. Ker and A.G. Hill (eds), *Newman After A Hundred Years* (Oxford, 1990), p.113 (will be cited as Cockshut, 'Newman').

19. *Dolman's Magazine*, 5 (1847), 419.

20. Albion, pp.107-115.

21. Ward, *Wiseman*, 1, 539-540; Machin, 'Russell', p.278; Norman, *English Catholic Church*, p.104.

22. Gilley, *Newman*, p.264; Holmes, p.75; Machin, *Politics*, p.209; Norman, *Roman Catholicism*, p.68; and *English Catholic Church*, pp.103-104; Ward, *Wiseman*, 1, 532-533 and 540.

23. Ward, *Wiseman*, 1, 534 and 540.

24. *Tablet*, 26 Oct. 1850. A letter on the same page pointedly referred to Q. Victoria's having erected a see in Jerusalem. See also *Punch*, 18-19 (1850), 192-193, 197, 207, 225, 243 and 256; Ward, *Wiseman*, 1, 542-543. Cf. Chadwick, *Victorian Church*, 1, 291; Cockshut, 'Newman', p.114; Inglis, p.122; Mathew, p.197; Norman, *Anti-Catholicism*, p.56; *English Catholic Church*, p.106; F. Neal, *Sectarian Violence: The Liverpool Experience, 1819-1914, An Aspect of Anglo-Irish History* (Manchester, 1988), p.131; D.G. Paz, 'Popular Anti-Catholicism in England 1850-1851', *Albion*, 11 (1979), 331-359.

25. Ward, *Wiseman*, p.534.

26. Newman called the anti-Catholic 'fulminations a clamour of bells' (Gilley, *Newman*, p.268).

27. Letter known only from his reply, LGR 4 Nov. 1850. See above, Ch.1.

28. Cf. above, Ch.I, p.31 and note 231.

29. LGR 4 Nov. 1850.

30. *Rambler*, 1 (1854), 267.

31. Machin, *Politics*, p.210.

32. Cf. Disraeli, *Coningsby*, p.76.

33. Machin, *Politics*, p.210.

34. Albion, p.101; Chadwick, *Victorian Church*, 1, 294; Norman, *Anti-Catholicism*, pp.57, 60-62 and 69-70; *English Catholic Church*, p.105; Ward, *Wiseman*, 1, 551-553

and 556.

35.   Original letter, 7 Jan. 1851, from Fr Ignatius Spencer to the *Tablet*, *Archivio Segreto Vaticano*, Pius IX, no.605, English and Italian copies in Fr I. Spencer's writing, LISR; *Tablet*, 18 Jan. 1851; Young, *Ignatius*, pp.178 and 180-182; Vanden Bussche, pp.137-138; T. Burke, *Catholic History of Liverpool*, (Liverpool, 1910), p.97.

36.   *Manchester Courier*, 6 and 10 Jan. and 10 Nov. 1849; 30 Apr. and 4 May 1850; and 2 Nov. 1850 to 8 Feb. 1851.

37.   *Protestant Witness*, pp.446-448 and 468. Cf. Lewis, *Evangelical Mission*, p.193.

38.   *Manchester Guardian*, 6 Nov. 1850, MF G23, Microfilm Unit, MCL.

39.   *Manchester Guardian*, 22 Jan. 1851. Cf. Axon, p.255.

40.   *Catholic Directory*, 1849, p.59; D. Glover, 'Roman Catholic Education and the State: A Sociological Analysis', 2 vols, an unpublished Ph.D. thesis, University of Sheffield, 1979, 1, 90 (will be cited as Glover, thesis).

41.   Cf. Chadwick, *Victorian Church*, 1, 509. See Ch.V. p.143.

42.   LGR 31 Jan. 1851, to Fr Croskell.

43.   When the census was taken on 31 Mar. 1851, she was living at 58 Stocks St. See Ch.II, p.33.

44.   Marsden, p.156. Cf. Bembridge, 17 Mar. 1851.

45.   *Manchester Illuminator and General Catholic Record* (Manchester, 1849-50), 16 Feb. 1850 (will be cited as *Manchester Illuminator*). Cf. *Tablet*, 16 Nov. 1850 for a well-attended lecture in St John's Cathedral, explaining the restoration of the hierarchy.

46.   *Manchester Guardian*, 22 Feb. 1851; *Tablet*, 1 Mar. 1851. Cf. *Brit. Parl. Papers, Accounts and Papers*, 29, 1851 (84), LIX.649, *Ecclesiastical Titles: C. Newdegate's Presentation of Anti-Catholic Addresses*, 28 Feb. 1851; and 1851 (236), LIX.741, *Address from Roman Catholics in England*, 15 Apr. 1851.

47.   *Protestant Witness*, pp.510-536 and 543-555.

48.   Bembridge, 17 July 1851.

49.   Marsden, pp.214-215.

50.   Albion, p.105; Chadwick, *Victorian Church*, 1, 303-305; Mathew, p.198; Norman, *Anti-Catholicism*, pp.74-78.

51.   LGR 11 July 1851; Postulants' Agreements; Annals G; Brief Sketch of the Beginning and Progress of the Institute of the Sisters of the Most Holy Cross and Passion, 1879 (Annals B); Notes of the Institute (Annals C); Annals D and F, all GA I/B/3/b-f; *Records of the Foundation and Progress of the Congregation of the Sisters of the Most Holy Cross and Passion 1851-1911* (Dublin, 1911), p.1 (will be cited as *Records*). Cf. Strambi, 2, 204 and 206; Artola, p.11.

52.   Red Bk.

53.   LGR 19 Jan. 1852; Red Bk; Annals A/E, B, C, D and F; *Records*, p.2.

54.   Letters of Robert Croskell [LRC], 31 May and 2 July 1858, GA I/B/2/a.

55.   Red Bk. Cf. Annals A/E, F and *Records*, p.2.

56.   Fr Gaudentius Rossi CP, Rule of the Catholic Sisters of the Holy Family, MS copy in Fr Gaudentius' handwriting, 1852, GA I/B/5/c, ch.5, par.V. He used Arabic numerals to indicate chs 1-19; Roman capital numerals from ch.XX to ch.XXVII. Will be cited as Gaudentian Rule. Cf. Holy Family Rule [1852-5] in E. Prout's writing in a fairly thick, hard-backed, exercise book, GA IV/A/2; Rules and Constitutions of the Sisters of the Holy Family [1855], partly in Fr G. Rossi's writing, partly in E. Prout's and partly in [Sr Clare Wilson's?] with an Italian translation in Fr G. Rossi's writing, in a thick, hard-backed exercise book, GA IV/A/1; and Holy Family Rule [1855-7?] in E. Prout's writing in a fairly big, hard-backed exercise book, GA IV/A/3. See above, Ch.VI. p.153 and note 5. See also Clothing Sermon, 1852, MS copy GA

I/B/1/e; *Records*, p.9; LGR [2 Feb.] 1853; [Burke], *Paul*, p.108; Giorgini and Papa, *Passionists*, p.66.

57. LGR 14 Mar. and 4 Nov. 1850; 27 July 1852 and cf. 20 Apr. 1855. Annals D refers to Fr Croskell as the 'nursing Father of the Infant Institute'.

58. Letter known only from his reply, 24 July 1848.

59. LGR 24 July 1848. Cf. *Words from the Heart*, pp.21 and 55.

60. LGR 24 July 1848. For St Paul of the Cross on a) obedience, b) humility and c) recollection, cf. *Words from the Heart*, a) pp.54, 103, 113, 127 and 145; b) pp.98, 103, 109, 121-124 and 161; Bialas, texts, a) pp.107 and 109-110; b) pp.66 and 82; and c) pp.104 and 142. Cf. also Bialas, *Mysticism*, p.206.

61. LGR 17 Nov. 1849. Cf. Bialas, *Mysticism*, pp.152-159.

62. LGR 30 Nov. 1849. Cf. Bialas, *Mysticism*, p.179.

63. Cf. Davidoff and Hall, p.451; Vicinus, *Independent Women*, pp.5 and 48; C. Willett Cunnington, *Feminine Attitudes in the Nineteenth Century*, 1935 (reprint New York, 1973), p.81 (will be cited as Willett Cunnington).

64. LGR [post 19 July 1850]. Cf. *Words from the Heart*, p.88.

65. LGR [post 19 July 1850].

66. LGR 4 Nov. 1850. For St Paul of the Cross on self-denial and mortification, see *Words from the Heart*, pp.58, 63 and 92.

67. LGR 4 Nov. 1850.

68. LGR 12 Mar. 1851. Cf. *Words from the Heart*, p.64, ftnote 2.

69. See *Regulations To Be Observed by The Sisters of the Most Holy Cross and Passion of Our Lord Jesus Christ*, revised edition (Dublin, 1953), p.32 (will be cited as 1953 *Regulations*); *Manual of Community Prayers* (Dublin, n.d. c.1952), pp.8-9.

70. LGR 11 July 1851, to Fr Croskell.

71. LGR 21 Dec. 1851.

72. *Words from the Heart*, p.30. Cf. Mead, *Sourcebook*, p.123.

73. LGR 21 Dec. 1851; SMR, 4 Dec. 1851. These plaques, said to be seventeenth-century Portuguese or Spanish from the English College, Lisbon, and to have been brought to England during the French revolutionary wars, would certainly have attracted Fr Gaudentius' interest.

74. LGR 21 Dec. 1851, postscript. He did not post the letter until 23 Dec.

75. Bialas, *Mysticism*, p.292.

76. Bialas, *Mysticism*, pp.292 and 312-315.

77. See Bialas, *Mysticism*, pp.287, 291 and 314. Cf. *Words from the Heart*, pp.75-76, 95 and 119; Bialas, texts, pp.69-71 and 153.

78. Strambi, 2, 222; *Words from the Heart*, pp.31 and 133.

79. *Words from the Heart*, pp.79, 100, 104, 150 and 157.

80. *1 Peter*, 1:23. Cf. Bialas, *Mysticism*, pp.128-142.

81. Cf. Fr Dominic Barberi CP to J.H. Newman, 21 Dec. 1845: 'May the Divine Infant find a cradle in our hearts, and fill them with His divine blessings. Amen', original in Birmingham Oratory; copy, LDBPLR, p.103. See also *Letter of Most Revd Leo Kierkels CP, DD, Superior General of the Congregation of the Most Holy Cross and Passion of Our Lord Jesus Christ, to Members of the Congregation* (Rome, 1930), p.19 on traditional Passionist devotions, Community Archives, St Paul's Monastery, Pittsburgh, Pa, USA (will be cited as [P]assionist [P]ittsburgh [A]rchives).

82. Cf. *Orthodox Journal*, 21 (1845), 139-140; 7 (1857), 5; *Tablet*, 29 Apr. 1854; Connolly, thesis, 3/2, 505-510; Davidoff and Hall, pp.31 and 74; Hilton, p.299; A. Briggs, *Victorian People* (Chicago, 1955; paperback, 1972), p.20 (will be cited as Briggs, *Victorian People*); W.L. Burn, *The Age of Equipoise, A Study of the Mid-Victorian Generation*, 1964, pp.246-248 (will be cited as Burn); B. Heeney, *The Women's Movement in the Church of England 1850-1930* (Oxford, 1988), p.10 (will

be cited as Heeney, *Women's Movement*).

83. See above, Ch.VII, pp.204 and 208.

84. LGR 25 June 1852, 2 letters, one to Fr Croskell and one to E. Prout.

85. *Rules and Constitutions for the Congregation of Discalced Clerks of the Most Holy Cross and Passion of Our Lord Jesus Christ*, 1785, English translation 1852 (will be cited as *Passionist Rule*). The *Rules* were written by Paul of the Cross and approved by Benedict XIV in 1741 and in 1746. Shortly before he died, Paul revised them and they were then approved by Pope Pius VI in 1775. Slight amendments were authorised by the Holy See in 1785 and in this form they were translated into English in 1852, probably by Fr Ignatius Spencer. See also *Regulations To Be Observed by the Discalced Clerks of the Congregation of the Most Holy Cross and Passion of Our Lord Jesus Christ*, 1827 (Dublin, 1862), which will be cited as *Passionist Regulations*. The *Regulations*, originally written by Paul of the Cross, were reformulated in 1778, according to the wish he expressed before his death in 1775. Some additional decrees were added by the General Chapter of 1827. The *Regulations* were translated into English by Fr Ignatius Spencer in 1852. The printer used Arabic numbers for Regulations 1-4 and Roman capital numbers for V - X and for the whole of Part II. A Latin copy of the 1775 *Rule* and an Italian copy of the *Regulations*, dated Rome, 1855 are preserved in PPA.

86. *Words from the Heart*, pp.11-14.

87. Paul Francis Spencer CP, Lectures given during a retreat to the Passionist Nuns, Daventry, Northants., 1989, a cassette recording made privately. I am grateful to Fr Paul Francis and the Passionist Nuns for allowing me access to this material.

88. Gaudentian Rule, ch.1, par.1. Italics mine.

89. LGR 19 Mar. 1855. Cf. *Words from the Heart*, p.14, quoting the Paulacrucian Rule of 1720: '... let us *never forget* to have always with us a constant and sorrowful remembrance of Him' and pp.137 and 147, 'The Passion of Jesus and the Sorrows of Mary be ever *in our hearts*'; Mead, *Sourcebook*, p.287, citing the 1741 Rule 'Let them *remember* that the wearing of the black habit means that the brethren of this least Congregation should mourn perpetually in memory of the Most Holy Passion and Death of Jesus Christ'; and p.290 '*promote this holy devotion*'. Italics mine. For a discussion of 'memory' and 'devotion' as synonymous in Paulacrucian terminology and the significance of 'heart', see Artola, pp.12-16.

90. Gaudentian Rule, ch.17, par.XII.

91. Gaudentian Rule, ch.18, par.I.

92. Gaudentian Rule, ch.18, par.II. At Fr Gaudentius' request Elizabeth accepted Margaret Ridge from Oakamoor as an apprentice in 1853. She lived with the sisters at Stocks St until they caught fever later in the year. Elizabeth then sent her home. She returned later to Levenshulme, where she attended school. Fr Gaudentius expected her to be taught needlework and dressmaking 'at least what is more simple for her position in life'. She entered the novitiate on 8 Dec. 1855 but left before receiving the habit. See Postulants' Agreements; LGR 11 Aug., 7 Sept., 3, 14 and 19 Oct. and 14 Nov. 1853; 19 Feb. and 15 Aug. 1854; and 13 July 1855.

93. Gaudentian Rule, ch.18, par.V.

94. Gaudentian Rule, ch.18, par.VI.

95. Gaudentian Rule, ch.18, par.VIII.

96. Cf. M. Hewitt, *Wives and Mothers in Victorian Industry*, 1958, p.3 (will be cited as Hewitt); J. Purvis, *Hard Lessons: The Lives and Education of Working-Class Women in Nineteenth-Century England* (Cornwall, 1989), pp.49-56 (will be cited as Purvis); S. Zlotnick, '"A Thousand Times I'd Be A Factory Girls": Dialect, Domesticity, and Working-Class Women's Poetry in Victorian Britain', *VS*, 35 (1991), 9-10 and 12 (will be cited as Zlotnick).

97. Gaudentian Rule, ch.17, par.X.

98. Gaudentian Rule, chs 2, par.VIII; 4, par.VI. Cf. J. Lown, *Women and Industrialization: Gender at Work in Nineteenth-Century England* (Oxford, 1990), p.29 (will be cited as Lown, *Women and Industrialization)*; C. Stansell, *City of Women: Sex and Class in New York 1789-1860* (New York, 1986), p.121. (will be cited as Stansell).

99. Gaudentian Rule, ch.2, par.IX.

100. LGR 1 May 1852; Gaudentian Rule, ch.3, par.IX.

101. Gaudentian Rule, chs 3, par.XII and 4, par.VI.

102. Cf. Gilley, *Newman*, p.243.

103. Cf. Shelstons, p.32; Stansell, p.124; L. Davidoff, *The Best Circles*, 1973, p.34 (will be cited as Davidoff, *Best Circles*); T.M. McBride, *The Domestic Revolution, The Modernisation of Household Service in England and France 1820-1920*, 1976, p.29 (will be cited as McBride); E.P. Thompson, 'Time, Work-Discipline and Industrial Capitalism', *PP*, no.38 (1967), 90-91.

104. [Burke], *Paul*, p.120.

105. LGR 21 Sept. 1855.

106. Gaudentian Rule, ch.17, par.X. Cf. R.D. Altick, *Victorian People and Ideas* (New York, 1973), p.169.

107. Gaudentian Rule, ch.17, par.X.

108. LGR 21 Dec. 1851; 23 July 1853. Cf. Heeney, *Women's Movement*, p.7; G. Himmelfarb, *The Idea of Poverty, England in the Early Industrial Age*, 1984, p.519; N.N. Feltes, 'To Saunter, To Hurry: Dickens, Time and Industrial Capitalism', *VS*, 20 (1976-7), 253 and 256; A.H. Yarmie, 'British Employers' Resistance to Grandmotherly Government, 1850-1880', *SH*, 9 (1984), 142-143.

109. Cf. P. Horn, *The Rise and Fall of the Victorian Servant* (Gloucester, 1986; reprint 1989), p.12 (will be cited as Horn).

110. For contemporary references to Martha and Mary see Hill, pp.221 and 292; Horn, following the titlepage.

111. Gaudentian Rule, ch.18, par.X; *Passionist Rule*, ch.XIX; *Passionist Regulations*, VII: 4-6.

112. Gaudentian Rule, chs.4, par.VII; 7, par.II; and 11, par.II; LGR 6 Oct. 1852; Bialas, *Mysticism*, pp.110-116. According to the *Catholic Directory*, 1852, A. Rodriguez SJ, *The Practice of Christian and Religious Perfection* (Spain, c.1606), transl. and publ. in 2 vols by a member of the Society of Jesus (Dublin, n.d. but pre-1852), was selling at 5s. at Burns and Lambert, a Catholic bookshop, 17 Portman St, London in 1852. A copy of *The Life of St Teresa*, written by herself and transl. from the Spanish by J. Dalton, 1851, with the inscription inside the front cover 'Elizabeth Prout, Manchester, 1851', is preserved in the General Archives, I/A/3/b. It was handed down from one sister to another from the time of the foundress, until in 1967 Sr Carmelita Morrow CP gave it to Sr Marie Louis McTaggart, Provincial, who put it in the archives, Bolton on 10 Mar. 1967. The condition of the spine indicates it had been very well used. This 1851 edition was on sale in 1858 at 5s., according to the *Catholic Directory*, 1858. Cf. E. Allison Peers (transl. and ed. from the edition of P. Silverio De Santa Teresa, C.D.), *The Complete Works of St Teresa of Jesus*, 3 vols, ninth impression, 1975, vol.1, *The Life of Holy Mother Teresa of Jesus*. For nineteenth-century interest in St Teresa, cf. Eliot, *Middlemarch*, pp.25-26; Houghton, p.292; Vicinus, *Suffer and Be Still*, p.xi. See also LGR 19 Feb. and 11 July 1854, in which latter he also recommended St Alphonsus Liguori's *The Nun Sanctified*, a book to which E. Prout referred in a letter to Fr Gaudentius, 12 Sept. 1855, Letters of Elizabeth Prout (Mother Mary Joseph) [LEP], GA I/B/1/a.

113. See above, Ch.I, p.14. Cf. Annals A/E.

114. Gaudentian Rule, chs 17, par.VIII and 9, pars I and III; *Passionist Rule*, chs XX and XXI; *Passionist Regulations*, 4: 1 and 6.

115. Gaudentian Rule, ch.7, par.I; *Passionist Rule*, ch.XXIX; *Passionist Regulations*, VII: 1-3; Part II, I: 16.

116. Gaudentian Rule, ch.8, par.II; *Passionist Regulations*, 4: 8; Part II, par.III.

117. Gaudentian Rule, chs 2, par.VI; 3, pars III and IX; 4, par.II; 6, par.II; and 17, par.IV. E. Prout's first 2 companions may have been able to read but could not write. In Postulants' Agreements, 9 Aug. 1851, she wrote their names. They signed them with a cross.

118. Gaudentian Rule, ch.3; *Passionist Rule*, ch.XXI.

119. Gaudentian Rule, ch.4. Cf. LGR 1 May 1852, 4 June 1853 and 21 Oct. 1877 (to M. Mary Margaret Chambers).

120. Gaudentian Rule, ch.13, pars I and III.

121. Gaudentian Rule, ch.11, par.V; LEP 25 Sept. 1855.

122. Gaudentian Rule, ch.11, par.V.

123. Gaudentian Rule, chs 2, pars III, VIII and X; 14, pars XI and XIII; 19, par.I; XXV, par.III. Cf. LGR 7 Feb. 1853.

124. Gaudentian Rule, chs 13 and 14; *Passionist Rule*, chs XXVI and XXXVII; *Passionist Regulations*, VIII: 4-15; Part II, VIII: 11, 13 and 17. Cf. Strambi, 2, 136-137.

125. Gaudentian Rule, ch.13, pars II, III and VI.

126. Gaudentian Rule, ch.14, pars I, II, V, VI and XV.

127. See Ch.VII, p.204.

128. Gaudentian Rule, ch.5, pars I, II and IV; *Passionist Rule*, chs XIX and XXI.

129. Gaudentian Rule, ch.20, par.VI.

130. Gaudentian Rule, ch.6, par.I; *Passionist Rule*, chs XIX and XX (for laybrothers); *Passionist Regulations*, 2: 8. According to the *Catholic Directory*, 1852, a new edition of the *Little Office of the Blessed Virgin Mary* was published, in English and Latin, about 1852, at 1s. 6d., 4d. for a miniature edition.

131. Gaudentian Rule, ch.6, pars I and II; *Passionist Rule*, chs XVI and XX. Cf. LGR 2 Aug. 1853: 'When will Sisters Magdalene and Aloysius write to me? Ask them this question.' Sr Magdalene Toler evidently learned to write because she then sent him a letter. See LGR 11 Aug. 1853.

132. Gaudentian Rule, ch.12, pars I, II and III; *Passionist Rule*, ch.XXII; *Passionist Regulations*, VI: 6.

133. Gaudentian Rule, ch.1, pars III and IV; ch.XXIII, par.IX; ch.XXIV, par.VII; *Passionist Regulations*, IX: 4. Cf. LGR 24 Apr. 1855.

134. Gaudentian Rule, chs 3, par.V; 19, par.I; *Passionist Rule*, chs XVII and XXXVII; *Passionist Regulations*, ch. 3: 1-2; LGR 1 and 7 July 1854 and 17 Jan. 1855. The discipline was introduced in July 1854, at the foundress' own request of Jan. 1854, known only from Fr Gaudentius' reply, LGR 9 Feb. 1854. Cf. 1953 *Regulations*, pp.11 and 16.

135. LGR 25 June 1852, to Fr Croskell; Gaudentian Rule, ch.17, pars XII, XIV and XV; [Greenan], pp.11-14. Although he did not specifically mention factory work in his Rule, Fr Gaudentius in LGR 21 July 1852 referred to Sr Magdalene Toler's working in the factory. In his letter 4 Sept. 1852 he mentioned 'three factory Sisters'; in that of 21 Dec. 1852 'two Sisters who have to go to the factory' and in that of 23 July 1853 Sr Magdalene Toler's being in the factory. See also Fr Ignatius Spencer's entry, HMR, 1 Jan. 1854.

136. Cf. Annals D.

137. Otherwise the most northern were Cornelia Connelly's foundation in Derby and Margaret Hallahan's in Coventry. Cf. Vicinus, *Independent Women*, p.55. See above

pp.82-86.

138. B.H. Rosenwein and L.K. Little, 'Social Meaning in the Monastic and Mendicant Spiritualities', *PP*, no.63 (1974), 4-32. Cf. Gilley, *Newman*, p.187; A.M. Allchin, *The Silent Rebellion, Anglican Religious Communities 1845-1900*, 1958, p.43 (will be cited as Allchin); I. Ker, *John Henry Newman, A Biography* (Oxford, 1990), p.193. Will be cited as Ker, *Newman*.

139. Gaudentian Rule, ch.10, pars V and VI; ch.16, par.VIII; LGR 21 Dec. 1852; 17 May 1853; 12 Jan. and 7 July 1855; Annals A/E and B.

140. Cf. Yuhaus, p.225.

141. Cf. Yuhaus, pp.232-234 and see above, Ch.I., p.16.

142. Census, 1851, MF 2904; LGR 11 June 1855. Cf. M.E. Rose, 'The Disappearing Pauper: Victorian Attitudes to the Relief of the Poor' in E. Sigsworth, *In Search of Victorian Values* (Manchester, 1988), pp.56-72 (will be cited as Rose, 'Disappearing Pauper' and Sigsworth respectively).

143. Cf. A.P. Donajgrodzki, *Social Control in Nineteenth-Century Britain*, 1977, pp.9-11 and 15 (will be cited as Donajgrodzki).

144. Gwynn, *Dominic*, p.202; Ker, *Newman*, p.316.

145. Cf. Bembridge, 21 Sept. 1848; 7 and 21 Jan., 9 May, 5 July and 20 Sept. 1849; and 19 July 1851; Best, *Mid-Victorian Britain*, p.211; Gilley, thesis, pp.79-81; Lewis, *Evangelical Mission*, pp.36-37 and 40; and 'Lights in Dark Places': Women Evangelists in Early Victorian Britain, 1838-1857', *Studies in Church History*, 27 (1990), 415-427 (will be cited as Lewis, 'Women Evangelists'); Love, pp.73-74.

146. Gaudentian Rule, ch.17, par.XVI.

147. The Dominican Sisters visited homes in Stone during Lent, 1854 to encourage lapsed Catholics to return to their religious duties. See Records, T 863, p.12, DAS. In general, however, even the active orders concentrated their energies within their institutions.

148. Bebbington, pp.118-119 and 122; Heeney, *Women's Movement*, pp.10, 46-49, 52, 68-69 and 79; Hilton, p.204; Prochaska, *Women and Philanthropy*, pp.37, 97 and 113; Lewis, *Evangelical Mission*, p.221; and 'Women Evangelists', pp.415-427; Shelstons, p.96; Young and Ashton, pp.88 and 119; J.A.V. Chapple, *Elizabeth Gaskell, A Portrait in Letters* (Manchester, 1980), p.36 (will be cited as Chapple); J. Rendall, *The Origins of Modern Feminism: Women in Britain, France and the United States 1780-1860*, 1985, pp.264-265 (will be cited as Rendall, *Origins*); H.D. Rack, 'Domestic Visitation: A Chapter in Early Nineteenth Century Evangelism' *JEH*, 24 (1973), 357-376; J. Seed, 'Unitarianism, Political Economy and the Antinomies of Liberal Culture in Manchester 1830-1850', *SH*, 7 (1982), 14-19 (will be cited as Seed, 'Unitarianism'); G. Stedman Jones, 'Working-Class Culture and Working-Class Politics in London 1870-1900; Notes on the Remaking of a Working Class', *JSH*, 7 (1974), 466 and 469 (will be cited as Stedman Jones, 'Working-Class Culture'); H.M. Wach, 'A "Still, Small Voice" from the Pulpit: Religion and the Creation of Social Morality in Manchester, 1820-1850', *Journal of Modern History*, 63 (1991), 436-438 (will be cited as Wach).

149. M.E. Rose, 'Culture, Philanthropy and the Manchester Middle Classes' in A.J. Kidd and K.W. Roberts (eds), *City, Class and Culture: Studies of Culture Production and Social Policy in Victorian Manchester* (Manchester, 1985), pp.106-108 (will be cited as Rose, 'Culture'). See above, Ch.II, pp.36-37 and 42.

150. *Manchester and Salford District Provident Society Reports*, 1849, p.9. Cf. Ashton, p.4; Donajgrodzki, pp.16-17 and 20; Rose, 'Culture', pp.105-107; A.J. Kidd, 'Charity Organization and the Unemployed in Manchester c.1870-1914', *SH*, 9 (1984), 45-66 (will be cited as Kidd); R.J. Morris (ed.), *Class, Power and Social Structure in British Nineteenth-Century Towns* (Leicester, 1986), p.18 (will be cited as Morris,

Class).

151. Gaudentian Rule, ch.1, par.VII. Cf. Fr Gaudentius' answer to Q.23, Deposition, 1891 for Fr Dominic Barberi's practice in Aston Hall.

152. Annals A/E, citing an article in the *Harvest*, 15 (1902), 276-279.

153. A Statement on the Charitable Works of E. Prout's congregation, GA I/C/1/f, which can be roughly dated 1927 by its reference to the sisters' having done parish visitation 'for over seventy-five years' (will be cited as Charitable Works).

154. Cf. Briggs, *Victorian People*, pp.119, 121 and 129; Hilton, p.16; Kidd, p.47.

155. *St John's Wood Letter*, Nov. 1847.

156. LGR 4 May 1853.

157. Meacham, p.361. Cf. Young and Ashton, pp.227 and 233; M.E. Rose, 'Settlements of University Men in Great Towns: University Settlements in Manchester and Liverpool', *THSLC*, 139 (1989), 143.

158. Cf. Annals A/E; Heeney, *Women's Movement*, pp.47 and 79; Stedman Jones, 'Working-Class Culture', p.469; D.M. Valenze, *Prophetic Sons and Daughters* (Princeton, New Jersey, 1985), p.187; S. Wright, 'Quakerism and Its Implications for Quaker Women: The Women Itinerant Ministers of York Meeting, 1780-1840', *Studies in Church History*, 27 (1990), 403-414.

159. Gaudentian Rule, ch.2, par.VII and ch.3, par.XI. Cf. [Burke], *Paul*, p.215.

160. *Words from the Heart*, pp.85-87.

161. Gaudentian Rule, chs 2, pars I-III; 4, par.V; 12, pars I-III; 17, pars XIII and XV-XVIII; XX, pars II, VI and IX; XXII, par.XVI; XXIV, pars III and XII; XXV, par.IX; *Passionist Rule*, chs III; VIII; XII; XXIV, sections II, III and VI; XXV; XXVII; and XXXIII; *Passionist Regulations*, V: 2; VIII: 1-3; X: 1 and 4; Part II, VIII: 1 and 10.

162. Gaudentian Rule, chs 3, par.VIII; 9, pars IV and XII; 16, par.II; 17, par.IX; 19, par.X; chs XX, par.I; XXIII, passim; *Passionist Rule*, chs II, III, XIII, XIV and XX; *Passionist Regulations*, V: 3; Part II, VIII: 1-6 and 14.

163. Gaudentian Rule, ch. XXIII, par.IV. Cf. LGR 23 July 1853.

164. *Words from the Heart*, p.11; *Passionist Rule*, ch.XIII; Mead, *Sourcebook*, pp.122-123. Cf. Annals F and *Records*, 'Introduction': 'Holy Poverty is also a special mark of the Order. Our Holy Protector, Saint Paul of the Cross, left it as a legacy to his children 'that all should love Poverty as their Mother'.'

165. PRO ED. 7/64/41; Purvis, pp.37-40.

166. Kirk, 'Ethnicity', p.84; O'Tuathaigh, p.155; Scally, p.17.

167. Census, 1851, MF 2899, London Rd District, entry 6, Microfilm Unit, MCL; Rate Books for Relief of the Poor, vol. 2: Districts 3, 4, 6, 7 and 12, 1849, M 10/16, ACCM, Local Studies Unit, MCL.

168. Neff, pp.38-39 and 43; Purvis, pp.34-37; A. Clarke, *The Effects of the Factory System*, 1899, p.43; N. Kirk, *The Growth of Working-Class Reformism in Mid-Victorian England*, 1985, p.36 (will be cited as Kirk, *Reformism*); R. Ritchie, 'Sanitary Arrangements in Factories', 1844 in K.E. Carpenter (ed.), *Conditions of Work and Living: The Reawakening of the English Conscience, Five Pamphlets 1838-1844* (New York, 1972), no.4, p.3 (will be cited as Carpenter, *Conditions*).

169. M. Valverde, '"Giving the Female a Domestic Turn": The Social, Legal and Moral Regulation of Women's Work in British Cotton Mills, 1820-1850', *JSH*, 21 (1988), 624. Will be cited as Valverde.

170. Collins, pp.140 and 144. See also J.J. Monaghan, 'The Rise and Fall of the Belfast Cotton Industry', *IHS*, 3 (1942-3), 81.

171. Cf. Neff, p.31; I. Pinchbeck, *Women Workers and the Industrial Revolution 1750-1850*, 1930, pp.177, 184-185 and 187-188 (will be cited as Pinchbeck); J.T. Ward, *The Factory Movement 1830-1855*, 1962, p.347; H.I. Dutton and J.E. King,

'The Limits of Paternalism: The Cotton Tyrants of North Lancashire 1836-54', *SH*, 7 (1982), 65 and 68; S.O. Rose, '"Gender At Work": Sex, Class and Industrial Capitalism', *History Workshop Journal [HWJ]*, 1986, p.117 (will be cited as Rose, '"Gender At Work"').

172. Gilley, *Newman*, p.263; Holmes, p.79; Hughes, 'The Coming Century', p.19; Kirk, 'Ethnicity', pp.68-69, 72 and 85; Lowe, *Irish in Lancashire*, p.12; Machin, 'Russell', p.293; O'Tuathaigh, p.169; Swift, 'Wolverhampton' p.87; Valverde, p.624; F. Neal, 'Manchester Origins of the English Orange Order', *MRHR*, 4 (1990-91), 23 (will be cited as Neal, 'Orange Order'); J. Skinner, 'The Liberal Nomination Controversy in Manchester 1847', *BIHR*, 55 (1982), 216.

173. Davis, p.124; Redford, *Manchester Merchants*, pp.74-83; Rose, 'Settlement', p.38; Wearmouth, *Working-Class Movements*, p.173; S. Marcus, *Engels, Manchester and the Working Class* (Manchester, 1974), p.11.

174. Noble, p.9. Cf. Frazer, p.40; Lowe, 'Lancashire Irish', pp.139 and 142; and *Irish in Lancashire*, p.35; Pooleys, 'Victorian Manchester', pp.149 and 155; Werly, p.354; Woodham-Smith, p.281.

175. Cf. *Manchester Guardian*, 25 Feb. 1852. See *Brit. Parl. Papers, Accounts and Papers*, 25, 1849[1124], LIV.148-175, *Police Returns, Manchester, 1847*, pp.164-179: In 1847 194 Irishmen and 70 women, but 642 Englishmen and 143 women were taken into custody for being drunk and incapable; 68 Irishmen and 17 women but 457 Englishmen and 101 women had committed breaches of the peace when drunk; 85 Irishmen and 64 women but 305 Englishmen and 130 women had been stealing from shops etc.; 117 Irishwomen but 400 English had been charged with vagrancy and prostitution. See also Faucher, p.30 for Fr T. Mathew's having effected a reformation amongst the Irish labourers in Manchester, when 20,000 of them took the pledge on 22 July 1843, as a result of which there were fewer disturbances. Cf. *Orthodox Journal*, 17 (1843), 170-172 and 182-187; Gilley, 'English Attitudes' p.85; Lowe, *Irish in Lancashire*, pp.38-40; F. Neal, 'A Criminal Profile of the Liverpool Irish', *THSLC*, 140 (1991), 161-199; R. Swift, 'Crime and the Irish in Nineteenth-Century Britain' in Swift and Gilley, *Irish in Britain*, p.177.

176. Cf. Rose, '"Gender At Work"', p.117; Valverde, p.624; Zlotnick, p.10.

177. Cf. Faucher (translator's footnote), p.30; E. Gaskell, *North and South*, p.147 and *Mary Barton*, 1848 (Penguin 1970), pp.43, 61 and 344 (will be cited as Gaskell, *Mary Barton*); P. Gaskell, p.64; Reach, p.19; Corish, p.179; Hewitt, pp.48, 50 and 59; Kennedy, p.52; Neff, p.54; Stansell, p.125; Woodham-Smith, p.30; S.J. Connolly, *Priests and People in Pre-Famine Ireland 1780-1845* (Dublin, 1982), p.186; E.S. Purcell, *Life and Letters of Ambrose Phillipps de Lisle* (ed. and finished by E. de Lisle), 2 vols, 1900, 1, 186; K.H. Connell, 'Land and Population in Ireland 1780-1845', *Econ.HR*, 2 (1950), 279; S. Gilley, 'English Attitudes to the Irish in England, 1789-1900' in C. Holmes (ed.), *Immigrants and Minorities in British Society*, 1978, p.89 (will be cited as Gilley, 'English Attitudes') ; and 'The Roman Catholic Church and the 19-C Irish Diaspora', *JEH*, 35 (1984), 191 (will be cited as Gilley, 'Diaspora'); C. Hall, 'The Home Turned Upside Down? The Working-Class Family in Cotton Textiles 1780-1850' in E. Whitelegg and Others (eds), *The Changing Experience of Women* (Oxford, 1982), p.18 (will be cited as Hall).

178. Neff, pp.55-56.

179. Her religious name was significantly Passionist: Paul of the Cross had had devotion to Mary Magdalene, who was, of course, on Calvary at the Crucifixion. Cf. Strambi, 2, 222.

180. Census, 1851, MF 913, Cheetham, entry 281, Microfilm Unit, MCL; Rate Books for Relief of the Poor, vol.1, Cheetham Overseers, Township of Cheetham 1848-1852, entry 1840, M 10/16, ACCM, Local Studies Unit, MCL. Cf. E. Higgs,

'Domestic Service and Household Production' in A.V. John (ed.), *Unequal Opportunities: Women's Employment in England 1800-1918* (Oxford, 1986), p.130 (will be cited as Higgs, 'Domestic Service').

181. *Brit. Parl. Papers, Accounts and Papers: Population*, 1831-69, *Census of Great Britain*, vol.9, p.633 (will be cited as *Brit. Parl. Papers, Census*). Cf. L. Davidoff, 'Mastered for Life: Servant and Wife in Victorian and Edwardian England', *JSH*, 7 (1973-4), 409. Will be cited as Davidoff, 'Mastered for Life'.

182. *Catholic Luminary and Ecclesiastical Repertory* (Dublin, 1840), pp.226-228 (will be cited as *Catholic Luminary*); *Lamp*, 4 (1852), 71. At that time, the Catholic obligation to do penance on Fridays, in memory of Christ's Passion, was observed by abstinence from meat and from soups made from meat. Cf. also Ker, *Newman*, 344.

183. *Tablet*, 19 Oct. 1850.

184. *Tablet*, 14 Dec. 1850. Cf. *Punch*, 18-19 (1850), 255. Cf. also Gilley, *Newman*, p.263; Holmes, p.79; Norman, *English Catholic Church*, p.105.

185. Cf. D. Chadwick, 'On the Rate of Wages in Manchester and Salford, and the Manufacturing Districts of Lancashire, 1839-1859', *Quarterly Journal of the Statistical Society*, 23 (1860), 7 (will be cited as Chadwick 'Wages'); Gaskell, *Mary Barton*, pp.61-62. See also Burnett, *Useful Toil*, pp.170-171; Hall, p.18; Horn, p.27; Kirk, *Reformism*, p.40; McBride, pp.47 and 51; Murray, pp.330-331; Stansell, pp.157-158; F. Bédarida (transl. A.S. Forster), *A Social History of England 1851-1975*, 1976, p.63 (will be cited as Bédarida); D. Marshall, *The English Domestic Servant in History*, Hist. Assoc. Pamphl., 1949, p.26 (will be cited as Marshall); E. Higgs, 'Domestic Servants and Households in Victorian England', *SH*, 8 (1983), p.208 (will be cited as Higgs, 'Domestic Servants').

186. E. Higgs, *Making Sense of the Census*, HMSO, 1989, p.65.

187. Cf. Burnett, *Useful Toil*, pp.72 and 166-167; Forster, p.178; Hewitt, pp.59 and 200, ftnote 25; Horn, pp.132-135; McBride, pp.102 and 104; Vicinus, *Suffer and Be Still*, p.xiii; L. Mahood, *The Magdalenes, Prostitution in the Nineteenth Century*, 1990, pp.58-59 (will be cited as Mahood); F.K. Prochaska, 'Female Philanthropy and Domestic Service in Victorian England', *BIHR*, 54 (1981), 81 (will be cited as Prochaska, 'Female Philanthropy').

188. LGR 11 July 1851.

189. Branca, 'Image and Reality', p.187; Prochaska, 'Female Philanthropy', pp.79-80 and 82.

190. L. Stanley (ed. and introd.), *The Diaries of Hannah Cullwick, Victorian Maidservant*, 1984, p.4 (will be cited as Cullwick).

191. *Brit. Parl. Papers, Census*, vol.9, p.633: 10-14 yrs: 5,311; 15-19 yrs: 16,259; 20-24 yrs: 16,292; 25-29 yrs: 8,513; and 30-34 yrs: 4,221. Cf. Burnett, *Useful Toil*, p.137; Davidoff, 'Mastered for Life', p.408; Horn, p.32; P. Branca, 'A New Perspective on Women's Work: A Comparative Typology', *JSH*, 9 (1975), 138; D. Vincent, 'Love and Death and the Nineteenth-Century Working Class', *SH*, 5 (1980), 235.

192. McBride, p.48; O'Tuathaigh, p.155; Scally, p.17; Stansell, p.155; L.H. Lees, 'Mid-Victorian Migration and the Irish Family Economy', *VS*, 20 (1976), p.30.

193. Branca, *Silent Sisterhood*, pp.54-55; Davidoff, 'Mastered for Life', pp.410-412; Higgs, 'Domestic Servants', p.201; Horn, pp.13 and 17-18; McBride, pp.12, 14 and 18-19; J. Rendall, *Women in an Industrialising Society: England 1750-1880*, 1990, pp.5-6 and 99.

194. Branca, 'Image and Reality' p.187; Higgs, 'Domestic Service, p.130; and 'Women, Occupations and Work in the Nineteenth-Century Censuses', *HWJ*, 1987, p.69; McBride, p.12.

195. LGR 14 May 1858; Letters of Sr Clare Wilson [LCW], undated, GA I/B/2/c.

Refers to a Miss Gonner's arriving 'tomorrow Thursday'. Miss Gonner arrived on Thursday, 25 Oct. 1855 (Postulants' Agreements). The letter should therefore be dated 24 Oct. 1855.

196. One can only approximate. Chadwick, 'Wages', p.24 gives 9s. to 10s. a week for a woman caring for 2 looms in 1849; Kirk, *Reformism*, p.93 suggests 11s. a week for female powerloom weavers and Hewitt, p.24 gives 10s. Pinchbeck, p.192 suggests 12s. 8d. a week for 2 looms and 19s. 10d. for 4 looms in 1844. Clapham, 1, 551 says that a female powerloom weaver, minding 2 looms, made 10s. 2d. a week in 1849. Branca, 'Image and Reality', p.186 and *Silent Sisterhood*, p.55 suggests between £9 and £14 a year for domestic servants but Higgs, 'Domestic Service', p.138 says the average wage per year for general servants in Rochdale in 1848-52 was £23 4s. Since, as a non-resident servant, C. Toler did not receive food and lodging, she may have been paid this higher sum.

197. Davidoff and Hall, p.23.

198. LGR 19 Nov. 1851.

199. Census, 1851, MF 911, Salford, entry 13, Microfilm Unit, MCL. Cf. Rodgers, p.6. Sarah Lee in the 1851 census was Sarah Ann Lee, and occasionally Ann Lee, according to LGR 1 May and 10 and 25 June 1852. Cf. Postulants' Agreements; Annals C. See also A.E. Musson, *The Life of Sir William Fairbairn, Bart.*, partly written by himself and edit. and completed by W. Pole, 1877 (reprinted Newton Abbot, 1970), p.317. Cf. Branca, *Silent Sisterhood*, p.22; Davidoff and Hall, p.395; Horn, p.19; McBride, pp.23 and 28.

200. Burnett, *Useful Toil*, p.156; Marshall, p.27.

201. LGR 24 Sept. 1855. Cf. McBride, p.23.

202. *Obituary of Sr M. Paul Taylor* [newspaper], GA I/D/1/f and IV/D/7; List of Receptions and Professions, 1852-1892, GA IV/C/1 (will be cited as Receptions and Professions) and List of Professions, GA IV/C/6.

203. Red Bk. Cf. Hurley, p.25.

204. Red Bk. Cf. Annals C; Postulants' Agreements.

205. See above, Ch.VI, pp.156-158.

206. Cf. *Words from the Heart*, p.30.

207. LGR 1 May 1852.

208. LGR Feast of *Corpus Christi* [10 June] 1852. Cf. C.R. Cheney (ed.), *Handbook of Dates for Students of English History*, 1961, p.125 (will be cited as Cheney).

209. Postulants' Agreements; Annals C.

210. P. Gaskell, p.143; Hewitt, pp.64 and 71-72; Neff, p.48; Stansell, p.127.

211. Gaudentian Rule, ch.17, par.XIX.

212. Annals C. Cf. Letters of Fr Ignatius Spencer [LISN], 22 June 1852, to Mrs Canning, GA I/B/1/f-g.

213. Gaudentian Rule, ch.17, par.XII.

214. Cf. Purvis, p.33; S. Alexander, *Women's Work in Nineteenth-Century London: A Study of the Years 1820-50*, 1983, pp.13 and 35 (will be cited as Alexander); D. Bythell, *The Sweated Trades, Outwork in Nineteenth-Century Britain*, 1978, pp.11, 13, 149 and 173 (will be cited as Bythell, *Sweated Trades*); J.A. Schmiechen, *Sweated Industries and Sweated Labour: The London Clothing Trades, 1860-1914* (Kent, 1984), p.3.

215. Golby, pp.7-9; Neff, p.125; Thompson and Yeo, p.24; R.B. Grindrod, 'The Slaves of the Needle', 1844 in Carpenter, *Conditions*, no.5, p.17 (will be cited as Grindrod).

216. Cf. A.B. Reach in J. Ginswick (ed.), *Labour and the Poor in England and Wales 1849-1851*, 8 vols, 1983, vol.2, *Northumberland, Durham, Staffordshire, the Midlands*, p.169, referring to Nottingham (will be cited as Reach (Ginswick). See also

Alexander, p.60; Hellerstein and Others, pp.323-325; J. Burnett, *Plenty and Want, A Social History of Diet in England from 1815 to the Present Day*, third edition 1989, paperback, p.171 (will be cited as Burnett, *Plenty and Want*).
217. Alexander, p.28; Best, *Mid-Victorian Britain*, p.129; Burnett, *Useful Toil*, p.48; Rendall, *Origins*, p.183; Rose, '"Gender at Work"', pp.114-117.
218. *Punch*, 45 (1863), 4-5. See also 12-13 (1847), 117; 16-17 (1849), 241. Cf. Alexander, pp.35-36; M. Hiley, *Victorian Working Women: Portraits from Life*, 1979, pp.24-25.
219. Neff, p.129. Figures can be only approximate. According to Bythell, p.149, fulltimers in a sewing house might receive about 10s. a week; those at home, 2s.-3s. According to Alexander, p.35 seamstresses in London might receive £12-£20 a year. See Grindrod, p.13 for other rates in London.
220. Alexander, p.59; Neff, p.131. Cf. Engels, p.220, referring to conditions in London.
221. Thompson and Yeo, p.122, discussing conditions in London in 1849.
222. Alexander, p.56; Thompson and Yeo, pp.122-123, giving Mayhew's London prices.
223. LGR 14 Oct. 1853; 24 and 27 Jan. 1855.
224. Thompson and Yeo, p.123, London figures. Cf. Best, *Mid-Victorian Britain*, p.42; Burnett, *Useful Toil*, p.144; M.J. Daunton, *House and Home in the Victorian City: Working-Class Housing 1850-1914*, 1983, pp.238 and 244; A. Redford assisted by I.S. Russell, *The History of Local Government in Manchester*, 3 vols, 1939-40, 2, 197 (will be cited as Redford and Russell); D. Vincent, *Bread, Knowledge and Freedom: A Study of Nineteenth-Century Working-Class Autobiography*, 1981, paperback 1982, p.122 (will be cited as Vincent, *Bread*).
225. Engels, p.220; Gaskell, *Mary Barton*, pp.62-64 and 86; Alexander, p.36; Grindrod, pp.15-26; Neff, pp.121-123; Stansell, pp.112-119; F.B. Smith, *The People's Health 1830-1910*, 1979, p.290 (will be cited as Smith, *Health*).
226. Bythell, *Sweated Trades*, p.11.
227. LGR 1 Dec. 1853; 19 Feb. 1854.
228. Annals A/E and C. Cf. LGR 21 Apr. and 14 Nov. 1853 and 22 May 1855.
229. Annals C.
230. Annals C.
231. LGR 22 Mar. 1855. See E. Prout's Exhumation Documents for evidence of her own hardworked hands. Cf. Davidoff, 'Mastered for Life', p.413.
232. Gaudentian Rule, ch.17, pars I and III.
233. Cf. LGR 12 Mar. 1851, 8 July 1853 and 27 Oct. 1854.
234. LGR 6 Oct. 1852.
235. LGR 25 June 1852, to E. Prout.
236. *Lamp*, 5 (1853), 15; *Faithful Companions of Jesus, Salford Diocese, 1852-1973*, a brochure.
237. LGR 19 Aug. 1852.
238. See *Memoirs of the First Companions of St Paul of the Cross*, 'by a priest of the same Congregation' (transl. from Italian, West Hoboken, 1913), p.8, PPAUC. Unless he changed his arrangements, Annals B, C, D, F, G and *Records*, p.3 are inaccurate in saying Fr Gaudentius Rossi preached a retreat from 13 Nov. According to LGR 12 Nov. 1852, he was due to arrive in Manchester at noon on Sat. 20 Nov.
239. LGR 12 Nov. 1852, with service for 21 Nov. appended. In it Fr Gaudentius refers to the sisters' retiring to the dormitory to put on the habit. See also LGR 21 Dec. 1852, 'I should like to give the meditations in the workroom and have the temporary altar removed there as we did for the ceremony of the clothing.' Annals D is therefore inaccurate in saying the ceremony took place in St Chad's church. For 'St

Joseph's' see Postulants' Agreements and cf. Gaudentian Rule, ch.4, par.IV.

240. MS copy GA I/B/1/e; Annals B and C; *Records*, pp.3-13.

241. Devine, *Ignatius*, p.152.

242. Devine, *Ignatius*, pp.212-214 and 348; Vanden Bussche, pp.35-38.

243. Cf. Gilley, thesis, p.329.

244. Allchin, pp.37, 40 and 71-78; Chadwick, *Victorian Church*, 1, 505-506; Gilley, thesis, p.328; Heeney, *Women's Movement*, p.63; Ker, *Newman*, pp.46, 74, 193 and 329; Vicinus, *Independent Women*, p.46; P.F. Anson (revised and ed. A.W. Campbell), *The Call of the Cloister: Religious Communities and Kindred Bodies in the Anglican Communion*, 1964, p.226 (will be cited as Anson and Campbell); B. Aspinwall, 'Changing Images of Roman Catholic Religious Orders in the Nineteenth Century' in *Studies in Church History*, 22 (1985), pp.352 and 355-356 (will be cited as Aspinwall, 'Changing Images'); S.P. Casteras, 'Virgin Vows: The Early Victorian Artists' Portrayal of Nuns and Novices' in G. Malmgreen (ed.), *Religion in the Lives of English Women 1760-1930*, 1986, pp.131 and 133-134 (will be cited as Casteras and Malmgreen respectively); R. Kollar OSB, 'The Oxford Movement and the Heritage of Benedictine Monasticism', *DR*, 101 (1983), 282-284.

245. Allchin, pp.63-64, 66 and 85-113; Anson and Campbell, pp.220-275; Casteras, pp.133-135; Chadwick, *Victorian Church*, 1, 506-507; Hill, pp.143, 221-224 and 292; Vicinus, *Independent Women*, p.49; J.M. Ludlow, *Woman's Work in the Church*, 1865, p.203 (will be cited as Ludlow); K. Philip, *Victorian Wantage* (Wantage, 1968), pp.20 and 67-74; J.F. White, *The Cambridge Movement: The Ecclesiologists and the Gothic Revival* (Cambridge, 1962; 1979 edition), p.211; T.J. Williams, *Priscilla Lydia Sellon*, 1965 (will be cited as Williams, *Sellon*).

246. Anson and Campbell, p.227; Chadwick, *Victorian Church*, 1, 508.

247. Vicinus, *Independent Women*, p.55.

248. Vicinus, *Independent Women*, pp.55 and 77; C.M. Prelinger, 'The Female Diaconate in the Anglican Church: What Kind of Ministry for Women' in Malmgreen, p.165 (will be cited as Prelinger).

249. Holcombe, pp.72-73; Ludlow, pp.202 and 206; Prelinger, pp.162-163; Vicinus, *Independent Women*, p.46.

250. Sisters of the Church, *A Valiant Victorian, The Life and Times of Mother Emily Ayckbowm 1836-1900 of the Community of the Church*, 1964, pp.8, 11, 17, 19, 22 and 42.

251. Heeney, *Women's Movement*, pp.68-69; Vicinus, *Independent Women*, pp.47-48 and 66.

252. Ludlow, p.204; Vicinus, *Independent Women*, p.46.

253. J.P. Marmion, 'Newman and Education', *DR*, 97 (1979), 10.

254. *Tablet*, 22 Apr. 1843 and 23 Dec. 1848 for the Cistercians of Stapehill. See also P.F. Anson, *The Religious Orders and Congregations of Great Britain and Ireland* (Worcester, 1949), pp.163-175, 239-242 and 366-371 (will be cited as Anson); H. Hohn, *Vocations, Conditions of Admission etc. into Convents, Congregations, Societies, Religious Institutes etc.*, 1912, pp.51-52 (will be cited as Hohn); F.M. Steele, *The Convents of Great Britain and Ireland*, 1921, pp.36-39 and 51-56 (will be cited as Steele, *Convents*); B. Whelan OSB, *Historic English Convents of Today*, 1936, pp.39-81, 221, 225, 228 and 246-247.

255. *Tablet*, 30 Jan. 1847 and 24 June 1848.

256. See M.P. Linscott, 'The Educational Work of the Sisters of Notre Dame in Lancashire since 1850', an unpublished M.A. thesis, 1960 (will be cited as Linscott, M.A. thesis); and 'The Educational Experience of the Sisters of Notre Dame de Namur 1804-1964', 2 vols, an unpublished Ph.D. thesis, 1964 (will be cited as Linscott, Ph.D. thesis), both University of Liverpool. Cf. Hohn, pp.181-183; Steele,

Convents, pp.192-193; J.N. Murphy, *Terra Incognita or The Convents of the United Kingdom*, 1873, pp.256-260 and 340-341 (will be cited as Murphy, *Convents*).
257. *Tablet*, 26 Oct. 1844, according to which the Srs of Providence required a dowry of £30 a year during a 3-year novitiate, followed by a sum of £300 at profession; Anson, pp.262-263, 318-321, 346-347, 375-380; Anson and Campbell, p.225; Hohn, pp.93-95, 108-110, 144-147 and 212-214; Murphy, *Convents*, pp.9-16, 28-31, 256-276, 339-345; Steele, *Convents*, pp.116-119, 161-162, 192-193, 217-220 and 275-276; C. Clear, *Nuns in Nineteenth-Century Ireland* (Dublin, 1987), pp.49-50 (will be cited as Clear). For the Loreto Srs see also C. Cross, 'The Religious Life of Women in Sixteenth-Century Yorkshire', *Studies in Church History*, 27 (1990), p.320.
258. LGR 11 Apr. 1866; *Tablet*, 13 Aug. 1842; 18 Nov. 1846; Anson, pp.206-208 and 330-332; Clear, p.51; Hohn, pp.258-261 and 325-327; Murphy, *Convents*, pp.118-138, 153-179 and 359-361; Steele, *Convents*, pp.120-125 and 248-251; Sr M.A. Bolster (ed.), *Catherine McAuley 1778-1978, Bi-Centenary Souvenir Book* (Dublin, 1978); S. O'Brien, *'Terra Incognita*: The Nun in Nineteenth Century England', *PP*, no.121 (1988), 113-114 (will be cited as O'Brien, 'The Nun'); A. Summers, 'Pride and Prejudice: Ladies and Nurses in the Crimean War', *HWJ*, 1983, p.33 (will be cited as Summers).
259. LGR 31 Jan. 1851, to Fr Croskell; *Tablet*, 21 Aug. 1847; Anson, pp.217-219; Murphy, *Convents*, pp.252-255 and 341-342; O'Brien, 'The Nun', p.125, ftnote 46 and p.129; Steele, *Convents* pp.150-152; G.V. Hudson, *Mother Geneviève Dupuis, Foundress of the English Congregation of the Sisters of Charity of St Paul the Apostle, 1813-1903*, 1929.
260. LGR 19 Jan. 1852, to Fr Croskell; Anson, pp.306-308; Murphy, *Convents* pp.277-282 and 364; O'Brien, 'The Nun', p.129; Steele, *Convents* pp.277-280; A. Leroy, *History of the Little Sisters of the Poor*, 1925.
261. Anson, pp.342-343; Murphy, *Convents*, pp.364-365; O'Brien, 'The Nun', p.129; Steele, *Convents*, pp.294-297; Mother M. Owen, *Mother St Basil, Foundress and First Superior-General of the Congregation of the Poor Sisters of Nazareth* (written c.1878; published Aberdeen, 1897). I am grateful to M. Superior, Sisters of Nazareth, Kilmarnock, Ayrshire for lending me a copy of this last.
262. Anson, pp.283-284; Hohn, p.275; Murphy, *Convents*, pp.346-347; O'Brien, 'The Nun', pp.120-123 and 135-136; R. Flaxman SHCJ, *A Woman Styled Bold, The Life of Cornelia Connelly 1809-1879*, 1991 (will be cited as Flaxman); J. Wadham, *The Case of Cornelia Connelly*, 1958; J.P. Marmion, 'Cornelia Connelly's Work in Education 1848-1879', an unpublished Ph.D. thesis, University of Manchester, 1984 (will be cited as Marmion, thesis). See also above, Ch.IV, pp.114-115.
263. Records, 1859-1863, T 865, p.26, DAS.
264. Anson, pp.256-257; Hohn, pp.99-101; S.M.C., *Steward of Souls, A Portrait of Mother Margaret Hallahan*, 1952, p.66. Will be cited as *Steward of Souls*; The Dominican Sisters, *Lines So Truly Parallel* (Hinckley, 1967).
265. See *Steward of Souls*, pp.58-61.
266. Records, T 865, pp.19 and 21. They also received gifts and donations from benefactors, such as £70 from Lady Stafford in 1854 to erect a Rosary Altar in Stone. See Records, T 864, p.56 and cf. *Steward of Souls*, p.62.
267. LISN 13 June 1860. Cf. LGR 2 Apr., 5 Sept., 3 and 17 Oct. 1855; LEP 4 Oct. 1855.
268. *Hallahan*, p.106.
269. S.M.C., *A Short Life of Mother Margaret Hallahan* (a pamphlet), p.11. Cf. Anson and Campbell, p.240.
270. Cf. also Faucher, pp.123-126 for the Pousset brothers' French enterprise, which became an industrial conventual institute although not so intended.

271. Summers, pp. 33-37; F.C. Devas SJ, *Mother Mary Magdalen of the Sacred Heart (Fanny Margaret Taylor), Foundress of the Poor Servants of the Mother of God 1832-1900*, 1927 (will be cited as Devas).
272. See Devas, pp.85, 123, 144 and 149; Gilley, thesis, pp.323, 333 and 357; O'Brien, 'The Nun', pp.129-133; Mathew, 'Old Catholics and Converts' in Beck, p.237; J. Bennett, 'The Care of the Poor' in Beck, p.571.
273. A Sister of the Congregation, *Light After Darkness, Mother Mary Francis (Alice Ingham), Foundress of the Franciscan Missionaries of St Joseph, 1830-1890* (Glasgow, 1963) (will be cited as *Light After Darkness*). Cf. S. O'Brien, 'Lay-Sisters and Good Mothers: Working-Class Women in English Convents, 1840-1910', *Studies in Church History*, 27 (1990), 461-464 (will be cited as O'Brien, 'Lay-Sisters').
274. LGR 27 Oct. and 29 Dec. 1854; *Light After Darkness*, pp.26-30.
275. *Light After Darkness*, pp.20 and 24.
276. Postulants' Agreements, 23 Jan. 1855, name mis-spelt as 'Tynham'. She had left by 12 Apr. 1855.
277. *Light After Darkness*, pp.31-99. See GA V/J/5 for material on M. Mary Paul Taylor and Alice Ingham.
278. Annals A/E.
279. Annals A/E. Cf. Annals D.

NOTES TO CHAPTER IV

1.   The Catholic Poor School Committee, *Catholic Poor School Committee Reports*, 1848-1864 [*CPSC Reports*], 1848 *Report*, p.29, [A]rchives of the [C]atholic [E]ducation [C]ouncil, London. Cf. *Catholic Pulpit*, 1 (n.d.: 1848?), 69-78 for a sermon on education delivered by Bishop Wiseman, 29 Oct. 1848, Catholic Central Library, Westminster. See also *Lamp*, 1 (1850), 130-131; *Manchester Illuminator*, pp.70-71.
2.   *Brit. Parl. Papers, Accounts and Papers*, 13, pt 2, 1849, XLII, pt 2, *Minutes of the Committee of Council on Education, Correspondence 1848-9* (1090), pp.100 and 105.
3.   Everett, p.147; I. Slater, *General and Classified Directory and Street Register of Manchester and Salford and Their Vicinities* (Manchester, 1845), p.36; and 1851, p.1 (will be cited as Slater, *Directory*).
4.   See above, Ch.II, p.35.
5.   Cf. Maltby, pp.v-vi and 49; W.A.C. Stewart and W.P. McCann, *The Educational Innovators 1750-1880*, 1967, p.317 (will be cited as Stewart and McCann); R. Johnson, 'Educating the Educators: 'Experts' and the State, 1833-39' in Donajgrodzki, p.86; D.K. Jones, 'Lancashire, the American Common School and the Religious Problem in British Education in the Nineteenth Century', *British Journal of Educational Studies* [*BJES*], 15 (1967), 293 (will be cited as Jones, 'Religious Problem').
6.   B. Disraeli, 3 Oct. 1844; J. Bright, 23 Oct. 1845, *Manchester Athenaeum Addresses 1843-1848* (Manchester, 1875), pp.20 and 41 respectively. Will be cited as *Athenaeum Addresses*. Cf. Cooke Taylor, p.8.
7.   C. Dickens, 5 Oct. 1843, *Athenaeum Addresses*, p.2.
8.   Bright, *Athenaeum Addresses*, pp.41-42.
9.   Cf. Axon, p.241; Jones, 'Religious Problem', p.296; and 'Socialization and Social Science: Manchester Model Secular School 1854-61', in P. McCann (ed.), *Popular Education and Socialization in the Nineteenth Century*, 1977, p.113 (will be cited as Jones, 'Socialization' and McCann respectively); F. Smith, *A History of*

English Elementary Education 1760-1902, 1931, p.207; D. Fraser, 'Education and Urban Politics c.1832-1885' in D.A. Reeder (ed.), *Urban Education in the Nineteenth Century*, 1977, p.20 (will be cited as Reeder).

10. Maltby, pp.74-75.

11. MUN. A.7.41, Education (39817), Progress of Plan of Manchester and Salford Education Bill, 1848-52, Scrapbook of Printed and Manuscript Material Including Letters, a broadsheet: *The Abandonment of Voluntary Aid in Support of National Education*, 1 Feb. 1848, Chetham's Library, Manchester. Will be cited as MUN. A.7.41.

12. MUN. A.7.41, *A Proposal Sheet of the NPSA*, 1851; C. Richson, 'On the Agencies and Organization Required in a National System of Education', *TMSS*, 1855, p.1 (will be cited as Richson).

13. Cf. D.G. Paz, *The Politics of Working-Class Education 1830-50* (Manchester, 1980), p.146 (will be cited as Paz, *Education*); J.S. Hurt, 'Drill, Discipline and the Elementary School Ethos' in McCann, pp.167-169.

14. Cf. *Rambler*, 6 (1850), 91-109; Carpenter, *Conditions*, no.2(2), pp.24-27; P. Gaskell, p.270. See also J.S. Hurt, *Education in Evolution: Church, State, Society and Popular Education 1800-1870*, 1971, p.113 (will be cited as Hurt, *Education*); B. Simon, *Studies in the History of Education 1780-1870*, 1960, pp.166 and 168 (will be cited as Simon); S. Frith, 'Socialization and Rational Schooling: Elementary Education in Leeds before 1870' in McCann, p.78 (will be cited as Frith); R. Gilmour, 'The Gradgrind School: Political Economy in the Classroom', *VS*, 11 (1967-8), 214-215 and 219; R. Johnson, 'Educational Policy and Social Control in Early Victorian England', *PP*, no.49 (1970), 96-97, 99, 102 and 119; H. Silver, 'Ideology and the Factory Child: Attitudes to Half-Time Education' in McCann, pp.145-146 (will be cited as Silver, 'Ideology').

15. Cf. MUN. A.7.41, *A Notice from an Employer* looking for workers who could read and write; D.I. Allsobrook, *Schools for the Shires, The Reform of Middle-Class Education in Mid-Victorian England* (Manchester, 1986), p.3 (will be cited as Allsobrook); J.S. Maclure, *Educational Documents: England and Wales 1816 to the Present Day*, 1965, fourth edition 1979, p.75 (will be cited as Maclure); M. Sanderson, *Education, Economic Change and Society in England 1780-1870*, 1983, limp, p.18.

16. Cf. Richson, p.2. See also J. Burnett (ed. and introd.), *Destiny Obscure: Autobiographies of Childhood, Education and Family from the 1820s to the 1920s*, 1982, pp.146-147 (will be cited as Burnett, *Destiny Obscure*); I. Sellers, *Nineteenth-Century Nonconformity*, 1977, limp, pp.71-72 (will be cited as Sellers); W.B. Stephens, *Education, Literacy and Society 1830-70* (Manchester, 1987), p.44 (will be cited as Stephens); G.F.A. Best, 'The Religious Difficulties of National Education in England 1800-1870', *Cambridge Historical Journal*, 12 (1956), 155-170.

17. Cf. P.B. Cliff, *The Rise and Development of the Sunday School Movement in England 1780-1980* (Cambridge, 1986), p.143. Will be cited as Cliff.

18. Cf. H. Formby, *The March of Intellect; or The Alleged Hostility of the Catholic Church to the Diffusion of Knowledge Examined; A Lecture Delivered to the Members of the Catholic Literary and Scientific Institute in Birmingham*, 1852, p.15. See also Jones, 'Socialization', p.118.

19. See *A Plan for the Establishment of a General System of Secular Education in the County of Lancaster* (Manchester, 1847), a pamphlet stating the principles of the Association and the plan to be presented to the House of Commons as a bill. Will be cited as LPSA, *Plan*. Cf. *Protestant Witness*, p.324; *Tablet*, 23 Mar. 1850. See also Maltby, p.75; Stewart and McCann, pp.275-276.

20. *National Public Schools Association for Promoting the Establishment of a*

General System of Secular Education in England and Wales (Manchester, 1850), an explanatory pamphlet; *Explanatory Statement of the Objects of the National Public Schools Association* (Manchester, 1850), a pamphlet.

21.   *Punch*, 18-19 (1850), 193.

22.   Cf. *CPSC Report*, 1849, Appendix N, p.142, letter, 22 May 1849, from S.N. Stokes to the Committee of Council asking for 'aid in providing remedies for evils of extraordinary magnitude' in Catholic schools in Lancashire, arising from the 'immigration of destitute Irish families'. S.N. Stokes (1821-91), a barrister-at-law, was educated at St Paul's and Trinity College, Cambridge and was a member of the Camden Society. He became a Catholic about 1847. First secretary of the CPSC, in 1853 he became the second Catholic HMI, serving in that capacity for 38 years. Since he was largely responsible for inspecting Catholic schools in Manchester, he had great influence on the development of Catholic education in the city. He was also later instrumental in promoting teacher training in E. Prout's order (see above, Ch.VII, p.212).

23.   Cf. Kitson Clark, *Churchmen*, p.139.

24.   The Catholic Poor School Committee, *The Catholic School, 1848-1856*, 1848, pp.7-8, ACEC and also in AAW. Will be cited as *Catholic School*. Cf. *Tablet*, 23 Mar. 1850.

25.   *CPSC Reports*, 1848, pp.10-11. Cf. J. Kay Shuttleworth, *Four Periods of Public Education as Reviewed in 1832, 1839, 1846 and 1862*, 1862 (introd. N. Morris, Brighton, 1973), pp.x-xii (will be cited as Kay Shuttleworth, *Four Periods*).

26.   *Catholic Directory*, 1849, p.59.

27.   Slater, *Directory*, 1848, p.1. *CPSC Reports*, 1849, p.63, giving 1845 returns.

28.   PRO ED. 17/14, *General Report for the Year 1850, by Her Majesty's Inspector of Schools, T.W.M. Marshall, Esq., on the Roman Catholic Schools Inspected by him in Great Britain, Reports of the Committee of the Privy Council for Education*, 1850, p.682. Will be cited as PRO ED. 17/14 and Marshall's *Report*. T.W.M. Marshall (1818-77), son of a Governor of New South Wales, was educated at Archdeacon Burney's School and then at Trinity College, Cambridge. He was an Anglican clergyman in Wiltshire from 1841, before becoming a Catholic in 1845. He served as an Inspector of Catholic Schools from 1848-60. See *Brit. Parl. Papers, Accounts and Papers*, 13, pt 1, 1851(103), XLIII, pt 1, *Parliamentary Grants for Education*, p.29 (will be cited as *Brit. Parl. Papers, Grants for Education*, 1851); *CPSC Reports*, 1848, pp.9-10; J.P. Marmion, 'The Beginnings of the Catholic Poor Schools in England', *RH*, 17 (1984-5), 70-71; M.J. Illing, 'An Early H.M.I., Thomas William Marshall, in the Light of New Evidence', *BJES*, 20 (1972), 58-69.

29.   PRO ED. 7/64/41: 20' 2" long; 11' wide; 6' 10" high. Cf. PRO ED. 103/54, p.829. The warehouse belonged to Messrs John Dugdale and Brothers of Irwell Bank near Eccles and of 112 and 116 Market St, Manchester, merchants, spinners, calico printers and manufacturers, whose mill was at Lower House, Padiham near Burnley (Slater, *Directory*, 1850, p.111; Whellan, *Directory*, 1852, pp.391 and 505; *Lowe and Barton's Manchester Exchange Directory* (Manchester, 1847), p.31, Local Studies Library, Salford).

30.   Since Fr Sheehan in Dec. 1849 applied for the apprenticeship of four boys and four girls (PRO ED. 7/64/41) and it was possible, according to the 1847 agreement, to have a pupil teacher for every 25 pupils (*CPSC Reports*, 1848, p.11), Elizabeth must have had a regular roll of at least 100 children. Both she and the master, D.J. Rice agreed to sit the examinations for the certification of teachers. There is no evidence, however, that either of them passed or even took them.

31.   Cf. Silver, 'Ideology', pp.148 and 158; W.C.R. Hicks, 'The Education of the Half-Timer as Shown Particularly in the Case of Messrs McConnell and Co. of

Manchester', *Economic History*, 1939, pp.222-230 (will be cited as Hicks).

32. PRO ED. 17/16, Marshall's *Report*, 1852, p.619.

33. E. and R. Frow, *A Survey of the Half-Time System in Education* (Manchester, 1970), p.19.

34. PRO ED. 17/14, p.670.

35. PRO ED. 17/14, p.682. Cf. *Rambler*, 1 (1848), 317; Purvis, p.39.

36. PRO ED. 17/14, p.682.

37. PRO ED. 17/14, p.660.

38. *CPSC Reports*, 1851, p.88; *Tablet*, 17 and 24 Jan. 1852.

39. PRO ED. 7/64/41; PRO ED. 103/54, p.833; *Catholic School*, Oct., 1848, pp.21 and 31. Cf. Ashton, p.47; Smith, 'Sanitary Economy', pp.66-67.

40. *Catholic School*, Oct. 1848, p.21; *Tablet*, 22 May 1852.

41. PRO ED. 17/16, p.643; *The Foundations of the Sisters of Notre Dame in England and Scotland from 1845-1895* (Anonymous, Liverpool, 1895), p.62, ADS (will be cited as *Notre Dame Foundations*). For a drawing of St Chad's, see M.E.W. Fitzgerald [Sr Agatha IBVM], 'Catholic Elementary Schools in the Manchester Area during the Nineteenth Century', an unpublished M.Ed. thesis, University of Manchester, 1975, between pp.125 and 126 (will be cited as Fitzgerald, thesis). Cf. M. Seaborne, *The English School, Its Architecture and Organization 1370-1870*, 1971, pp.209 and 212-217. Will be cited as Seaborne.

42. *Brit. Parl. Papers, Reports from Committees*, 1852(499), XI.1, *Manchester and Salford Education*, 1852, p.78. Will be cited as *Select Committee Report*.

43. For Notre Dame, see Linscott, M.A. thesis, pp.1-3 and 21 and Ph.D. thesis, 1, iv-13, 25, 35, 40, 56 and 67.

44. PRO ED. 17/14, p.682.

45. *Notre Dame Foundations*, p.62; *Convent of Notre Dame, Manchester 1851-1951*, (Exeter, 1951), p.1. I am grateful to Sr Jean Bunn SND, provincial archivist, Liverpool, for a copy of this brochure. Cf. *Manchester Courier*, 8 Nov. 1851.

46. PRO ED. 103/54, p.841. Cf. Seaborne, p.213.

47. PRO ED. 103/54, pp.833-841.

48. PRO ED. 103/54, pp.837-839. Cf. *CPSC Reports*, 1848, p.10. For other details of the transaction, which was completed on 10 Aug. 1852, see PRO ED. 7/64/41 and ED. 17/20, 1854, p.189; *Lamp*, 3 (1851), 301-302; *Manchester Courier*, 8 Nov. 1851; *Tablet*, 22 May 1852. For John Potter, mayor of Manchester from 1848-1851, see City of Manchester, *Proceedings of the Council, 1857-1858* (Manchester, 1859), pp.330 and 398; Briggs, *Victorian Cities*, pp.130-131 and 136; Jones, 'Socialization', p.115; Wach, p.431.

49. *Catholic School*, Aug. 1852, p.282.

50. PRO ED. 17/22, Stokes' 1856 *Report*, p.797; Battersby, pp.348-349; Marmion, 'Poor Schools', pp.75 and 79; E. Cruise, 'Development of the Religious Orders' in Beck, pp.451-452.

51. Cf. PRO ED. 17/16, Marshall's 1851 *Report*, pp.620-621; Turner, *Pastoral Letter*, 21 Nov. 1856.

52. Cf. *Manchester Guardian*, 16 June 1852; Hempton, p.162; Maltby, p.76.

53. The Catholic Church sees the Bible as part of Tradition and therefore requiring to be read 'in the Church'.

54. Maltby, p.77. For the Irish National System see J.R. Beard, 'The Lancashire School Plan of Secular Education in Relation to the Bible', *Educational Register of the Lancashire Public Schools Association* (Manchester, 1850), pp.1-2; B. Coldrey, *Faith and Fatherland: The Christian Brothers and the Development of Irish Nationalism 1838-1921* (Dublin, 1988), pp.27-28 (will be cited as Coldrey); J.M. Goldstrom, *The Social Content of Education 1808-1870* (Shannon, 1972), p.63 (will be cited as

Goldstrom). For attempts to adopt it in Liverpool from 1836 to 1842 see Murphy, *Religious Problem*, passim; and *Church, State and Schools in Britain 1800-1970*, 1971, pp.15-21. See also J.L. Alexander, 'Lord John Russell and the Origins of the Committee of Council on Education', *Historical Journal [HJ]*, 20 (1977), p.396.

55. Jones, 'Religious Problem', p.304; Maltby, p.81. Cf. *National Public Schools Association: Education in England and in the United States of North America* (Manchester 1850), a pamphlet.

56. Maltby, pp.82-84. Cf. Ashton, p.65.

57. Maltby, p.84.

58. Fitzgerald, thesis, p.68.

59. *Tablet*, 19 Jan. 1850; *Lamp*, 6 (1853), 104-108. Cf. Coldrey, pp.27-30; Yuhaus, p.8.

60. Cf. Gilley, *Newman*, p.267; Mathew, p.198; Thureau-Dangin, 1, 440.

61. *Lamp*, 1 (1850), 4.

62. *Select Committee Report*, p.78. See above pp.92 and 103.

63. Gowland, thesis, pp.144, 179-180 and 197; Hammonds, *Chartists*, pp.185-186 and 206; Hempton, pp.159 and 162-163; Paz, *Education*, p.134.

64. Cf. McClelland, 'Schools', pp.173-175.

65. *Catholic School*, Feb. 1853, 'Manchester and Salford Education: Report of Parliamentary Committee', p.352.

66. Cf. Hempton, pp.30, 38-39, 42-43 and 163; Murphy, *Religious Problem*, p.246.

67. *Catholic School*, Feb. 1853, pp.351-353 and Sept. 1849, pp.167-168 for Catholic Ragged Schools. Cf. Annals-A/E and D. See also M. Carpenter, *Reformatory Schools for the Children of the Perishing and Dangerous Classes and for Juvenile Offenders*, 1851, new impression 1968, p.70 for her comment on the Irish children's 'jealous and blind attachment to their Catholic religion' (will be cited as Carpenter, *Reformatory Schools*); J. Manton, *Mary Carpenter and the Children of the Streets*, 1976, pp.82-83, 87, 102 and 154 (will be cited as Manton).

68. Cf. *Brit. Parl. Papers, Reports of the Inspectors of Factories to Her Majesty's Principal Secretary of State for the Home Department*, 1851[1396], XXIII, pt 2[293], pp.18-20 for L. Horner's approval of the Manchester scheme, although he noted that Catholics and Jews objected. Will be cited as *Factory Reports*.

69. Cf. Maclure, p.76; A.C.F. Beales, 'The Struggle for the Schools' in Beck, p.368.

70. *Catholic School*, Dec. 1851, 'The Manchester Education Scheme, Declaration of the Roman Catholic Clergy of Manchester and Salford on the Proposed Instructions for the Draft of a Bill for Local Education in the Municipal Boroughs of Manchester and Salford', pp.209-211. Cf. *Select Committee Report*, pp.163-164. See also Fitzgerald, thesis, p.70.

71. *Catholic School*, Dec. 1851, 'Minute of the Manchester and Salford (Executive) Committee on Education in Reference to the Declaration of the Roman Catholic Clergy', pp.211-214; *Select Committee Report*, pp.164-166. Cf. W. Whalley, 'An Historical Account of Catholic Education in England with Special Reference to Education Acts in the Salford Diocese', an unpublished M.Ed. thesis, University of Manchester, 1938, p.57 for Russell's objecting to grants' being given to monastic schools. See also PRO ED. 9/12, *Grants under Minutes, 1846: Copies of Letters Selected from Old Letter Books 1847-1858*, pp.171. 179 and 194 for correspondence, July-Nov. 1849, between the Catholic party and the Committee of Council on schools attached to monasteries or convents; and *Brit. Parl. Papers, Grants for Education*, 1851, p.154 for a letter from Stokes to the Committee of Council in 1850 regarding its threatened 'domiciliary visitation' to see if teachers lived in convents. Cf. above, Ch.V, section 4.

72. *Catholic Directory*, 1851, p.59; 1853, pp.63-64; *Select Committee Report*, p.304; *CPSC Reports*, 1852, p.85. For the special position of the Irish Christian Brothers see *Select Committee Report*, pp.129-130; *Tablet*, 5 Jan. 1850; Coldrey, pp.27-30; Goldstrom, p.118; W.L. Gillespie, *The Christian Brothers in England 1825-1880* (Bristol, 1975), p.142 (will be cited as Gillespie); M.C. Normoyle, *A Tree Is Planted: The Life and Times of Edmund Rice, Founder of the Christian Brothers*, 1975, p.458.

73. Strictly, she was not a religious until she took vows. Her order was listed in the *Catholic Directory* for the first time, however, in 1854, p.68, as 'Sisters of the Holy Family, Cheetham Hill', actually before the first professions. In the 1855 *Catholic Directory*, p.68, it was listed as 'Sisters of the Holy Family, Levenshulme'.

74. For the attendance of Protestant children at Catholic schools, see *Select Committee Report*, pp.32 and 72 and Marshall's 1850 *Report* in the *Catholic School*, Oct. 1850, pp.50-51.

75. See G. Richardson, Manchester Catholic Poor School Committee, *CPSC Report*, 1849, Appendix N, p.143: 'The factory population, living principally in the most obscure parts of Manchester, belong to *us*'. Cf. Brotherton, no.37.

76. *Catholic School*, Dec. 1851, pp.211-214; *Select Committee Report*, pp.164-6. For the difficulties Catholic clergy experienced about Catholic children in Poor Law care, see *Tablet*, 5 Jan. 1850. Cf. J. Singleton, 'The Virgin Mary and Religious Conflict in Victorian Britain', *JEH*, 43 (1992), 27 (will be cited as Singleton); Steele, 'Irish Presence', p.228; J.T. Ward and J.H. Treble, 'Religion and Education in 1843: Reaction to the 'Factory Education Bill'', *JEH*, 20 (1969), 95.

77. *Protestant Witness*, p.527.

78. *National Public Schools Association Report of the First Annual Meeting, 22 January 1851* (Manchester, 1851), p.3; Maltby, p.85. For the similar exclusion of Jews see *Select Committee Report*, p.129; *National Public Schools Association Report of the Proceedings, 8 February 1851* (Manchester, 1851), p.6; W.B. Hodgson, *On the Characteristics of the Two Schemes for Public Instruction, Respectively Proposed by the National Public Schools Association and the Manchester and Salford Committee on Education* (Manchester, 1851), p.6 (will be cited as Hodgson). Cf. S. Robinson, 'The Education of the Lower Classes of the People: With Some Remarks on the Measure Proposed for Manchester and Salford in 1851', *TMSS*, 1866, p.61. Will be cited as Robinson. See also Williams, *Jewry*, p.207.

79. Marsden, p.264; *Protestant Witness*, p.660. See *Tablet*, 23 Apr. 1853 for Bp Lee's having shown something of C. Stowell's anti-Catholicism.

80. *Protestant Witness*, p.672. Cf. Marsden, p.214.

81. According to PRO ED. 17/25, Stokes' 1859 *Report*, p.212, verified by PRO ED. 7/64/41, two new infant rooms were added in 1859.

82. LGR 19 Nov. 1851 refers to her 'Christmas holidays' and so he must have expected her to continue teaching somewhere.

83. See above, Ch.II, pp.35-36. Cf. *CPSC Reports*, 1852, p.85; PRO ED. 7/64/12; Deeds Index, pp.187-188; Connolly, thesis, 2, 134; Fitzgerald, thesis, p.278.

84. *CPSC Report*, 1852, p.85.

85. Cf. *Catholic School*, Nov. 1849, pp.198-200; MUN. A.7.41, *NPSA: Types of Schools*, 1851.

86. *Catholic School*, Nov. 1849, pp.198-200.

87. Brotherton, pp.5 and 19. See also Jackson, p.59. According to Hewitt, p.186, 4,000 children were lost in Manchester each year about 1848.

88. *CPSC Reports*, 1852, p.85.

89. LGR 21 and 27 July 1852. E. Prout's letter known only from these.

90. A.P. Wadsworth, 'The First Manchester Sunday Schools', *Bulletin of John*

Rylands Library [*BJRL*], 33 (1950-51), 315. Will be cited as Wadsworth.

91.   Burnett, *Destiny Obscure*, p.141.

92.   Gaskell, *Mary Barton*, pp.75-79; C. Thomson, *The Autobiography of An Artisan*, 1847, pp.169-170. See also Aspin, *Lancashire*, pp.100-102, 105 and 117-124; Frith, p.73; Simon, pp.153, 178, 180-186, 273 and 276; Stephens, pp.48-49, 51 and 93; Thompson, *English Working Class*, pp.163, 322-324, 781-790 and 817-820; Vincent, *Bread*, pp.111-112; G. Sutherland, *Elementary Education in the Nineteenth Century*, Hist. Assoc. Pamphl., 1971, pp.7-9 (will be cited as Sutherland); J. Percy, 'Scientists in Humble Life: The Artisan Naturalists of South Lancashire', *MRHR*, 5 (1991), 3-8.

93.   M. Fitzgerald, 'The Union with Ireland: Its Social Aspect', *TMSS*, 1860, p.31; *Lucas' Penny Library*, Oct. 1842, p.9, Catholic Central Library, Westminster. Cf. *Dublin Penny Journal*, 3-4, 1834-36, passim, SS Library, MCL. See also McGrath, p.517; O'Gráda, p.18.

94.   See above, Ch.VI, pp.156-158.

95.   Cf. Hewitt, pp.27 and 80; Hicks, pp.231-232; Purvis, pp.141-151; Sutherland, pp.3 and 5.

96.   PRO ED. 17/26, Stokes' 1860 *Report*, p.195.

97.   Cf. PRO ED.17/19, Stokes' 1853 *Report*, p.891.

98.   See above, Ch.VI.

99.   Marsden, p.243.

100.   Linscott, M.A. thesis, pp.31-32.

101.   Flaxman, p.116; Marmion, thesis, p.91.

102.   Stephens, p.94.

103.   PRO ED. 17/20, p.109, 1 Mar. 1855, *Draft Circular Explanatory of the Minutes Affecting Night Schools*.

104.   D.A. Reeder, 'Predicaments of City Children: Late Victorian and Edwardian Perspectives on Education and Urban Society' in Reeder, p.76.

105.   Cf. Stephens, pp.18-19.

106.   Cf. Vicinus, *Suffer and Be Still*, p.xi. Cf. *Tablet*, 23 Apr. 1853.

107.   Cf. Rendall, *Origins*, p.143.

108.   Cf. Houghton, p.187.

109.   *Tablet*, 23 Apr. 1853.

110.   Brotherton, p.11.

111.   Maltby, pp.85-86. Cf. *Tablet*, 17 Apr. 1852.

112.   Gaudentian Rule, ch.16, pars I, II, IV, V and VI. For contemporary advice on books, especially those of the Irish National Schools and the Christian Brothers see *Catholic School*, Oct. 1848, pp.27-29; June-July 1849, pp.107-108 and 116-128; Oct. 1850, p.49 (Marshall's 1849 *Report*); Dec. 1850, p.66; Mar. 1851, pp.124-128; Sept. 1851, pp.185-187 (Marshall's 1850 *Report*, also in PRO ED. 17/14, pp.665-667); Dec. 1851, p.224; May 1852, p.260; Oct. 1852, p.313 (Marshall's 1851 *Report*, also in PRO ED. 17/16, p.627); *CPSC Reports*, 1852, pp.89-90. Cf. Goldstrom, p.118.

113.   *Select Committee Report*, pp.28-29.

114.   *Select Committee Report*, pp.41-42.

115.   *CPSC Reports*, 1852, p.85.

116.   *Catholic School*, Feb. 1853, pp.349-350. Cf. *Tablet*, 27 Nov. 1852 for Fr M. Formby's estimate of 90,000 Catholics in Manchester.

117.   *Select Committee Report*, p.101; *Factory Reports*, 1850[1141], XXIII, pt 2.181, *Report of Leonard Horner, Inspector of Factories*, 31 Oct. 1849, p.19; *CPSC Report*, 1849, pp.143-144; *Catholic School*, Sept. 1849, p.170; Manton, p.94; Cf. LPSA, *Plan*, p.2.

118.   *Select Committee Report*, p.53.

119.   *Select Committee Report*, p.56.

120. *Select Committee Report*, p.78.
121. *Select Committee Report*, p.75. Cf. Rendall, *Origins*, p.133; A. Tropp, *The School Teachers*, 1957, p.3 (will be cited as Tropp, *Teachers*).
122. *Select Committee Report*, p.131; *Catholic School*, Feb. 1853, p.351.
123. *Select Committee Report*, p.135.
124. *Select Committee Report*, p.145.
125. See above, Appendix, p.220. Cf. PRO ED. 17/24, Stokes' 1858 *Report*, p.195.
126. *Select Committee Report*, p.407; *Tablet*, 5 Mar. 1853.
127. Turner, *Pastoral Letter*, 24 Sept. 1852.
128. *Select Committee Report*, p.90.
129. *Select Committee Report*, p.129.
130. T. Browning, 'Middle-Class Education', *TMSS*, 1862, pp.93-94 and 104-105. Will be cited as Browning. See also Tropp, *Teachers*, pp.59 and 65-66; and 'The Changing Status of the Teacher in England and Wales' in P.W. Musgrave, *Sociology, History and Education*, 1970, p.200.
131. Cf. *Catholic School*, Nov. 1849, pp.190-195 and Feb. 1850, pp.222-231; C. Dickens, *Hard Times*, 1854 (Penguin 1985), pp.53 and 302-304.
132. PRO ED. 17/22, p.42.
133. *Select Committee Report*, p.129. Cf. Robinson, p.61. See also Williams, *Jewry*, p.207.
134. Cf. Bédarida, p.87; Burnett, *Destiny Obscure*, pp.146-147; Hurt, *Education*, p.25; Ward, 'Establishment', p.279; E.G. West, *Education and the State, A Study in Political Economy*, 1965, pp.157-159 (will be cited as West, *Education and the State*); and *Education and the Industrial Revolution*, 1975, p.103; M.A. Cruickshank, 'The Anglican Revival and Education: A Study of School Expansion in the Cotton Manufacturing Areas of North-West England, 1840-50', *NH*, 15 (1979), 187.
135. Bright, *Athenaeum Addresses*, p.42.
136. Cf. Browning, pp.93-94 and 104-105.
137. Cf. Gowland, thesis, p.81 for the remark that Wesleyans, the co-framers of the scheme, had only marginal influence over [and therefore only marginal interest in] the working classes of Manchester.
138. LPSA, *Plan*, p.2.
139. Joyce, *Work, Society and Politics*, p.32.
140. Hodgson, p.8. Cf. *Rambler*, 6 (1850), 107.
141. Cf. Richson, pp.2-3 and 6. See also West, *Education and the State*, p.153.
142. *CPSC Reports*, 1852, p.85.
143. Annals A/E.
144. *School Inspector Returns*, St Anne's, Sutton, 1858, pp.565-572, Archives of the Diocese of Liverpool deposited in LRO, Preston, RCLv 44. Will be cited as LRO RCLv 44. Cf. ibid., pp.549-556 for similar content in her school in Blackbrook.
145. Cf. Hempton, p.86; Joyce, *Work, Society and Politics*, p.246 and 249-250; Mathias, *First Industrial Nation*, p.207; Purvis, pp.82-84.
146. *Select Committee Report*, p.440.
147. Cf. H.O. Evennett, *The Catholic Schools of England and Wales* (Cambridge, 1944), pp.1-3 (will be cited as Evennett).
148. Cf. McLeod, p.220.
149. Wadsworth, p.311.
150. Cf. *Rambler*, 4 (1855), 90.
151. LRO, RCLv 44, pp.565-572.
152. Cf. Aspin, *Lancashire*, p.109; Burnett, *Destiny Obscure*, p.140; Cliff, p.13; Sellers, pp.36-37; Stephens, pp.27 and 93; T.W. Laqueur, *Religion and Respectability: Sunday Schools and Working-Class Culture 1780-1850*, 1976, pp.80,

98, 101-102, 119, 123 and 148 (will be cited as Laqueur).

153. Gillespie, p.107; A Christian Brother, *Edmund Ignatius Rice and the Christian Brothers* (Dublin, 1926), p.409.

154. Flaxman, p.116; Glover, thesis, 1, 87; Marmion, thesis, 1, 91.

155. Linscott, M.A. thesis, pp.30-31.

156. *CPSC Reports*, 1852, p.85.

157. *Select Committee Report*, p.297.

158. The earliest Catholic Sunday school in Manchester was probably that held about 1734 by Fr Kendal in his chapel near the Apple Market (Connolly, thesis, 1/1, 105). His successors held Sunday schools in St Chad's, Rook St. In 1784 Fr Houghton joined his fellow townsmen in inaugurating the Manchester Sunday School Movement (Cliff, p.38; Connolly, thesis, 1/2, 185; Fitzgerald, thesis, p.36). For the disintegration of the Movement in 1800 see Connolly, thesis, 2, 103; Laqueur, pp.68-69 and 73-74.

159. *Catholic Directory*, 1831, under 'Charitable Institutions'.

160. *Select Committee Report*, p.304.

161. Burnett, *Destiny Obscure*, p.141; Thompson, *English Working Class*, pp.389-390; Wadsworth, p.311; J. McLeish, *Evangelical Religion and Popular Education*, 1969, pp.46-47; R.K. Webb, 'Working-Class Readers in Early Victorian England', *EHR*, 65 (1950), 336. The *Catholic School* published model lessons in arithmetic in Oct., 1850, pp.51-54; Dec. 1850, pp.67-72; Mar. 1851, pp.128-136; May 1851, pp.163-167; Sept. 1851, pp.195-197; May 1852, pp.248-253; and advice on teaching grammar in May 1852, pp.254-259 and Feb. 1853, pp.354-356.

162. Burnett, *Destiny Obscure*, p.141; Laqueur, pp.106, 128 and 132.

163. *CPSC Reports,* 1852, p.85. See also above, Appendix, p.221.

164. Cf. Laqueur, pp.xii, 1 and 8.

165. AMR, entry 29, 8 Mar. 1845, mission given in Derby by Frs Dominic Barberi and Gaudentius Rossi: attendance at sermons and Confessions 'excessive'; 'above a hundred Catholics, who had been out of the church almost their whole life, were now reclaimed.'

166. Cf. Laqueur, pp.148 and 189.

167. Cf. Laqueur, pp.98 and 123; McLeod, p.29; Stephens, p.93.

168. Cf. Frith, pp.83-84.

169. *CPSC Reports,* 1852, p.85. There is no indication of how many, if any, adults attended Catholic Sunday schools, as occurred in others. See Joyce, *Work, Society and Politics*, p.247; Laqueur, p.90; Thompson, 'Religious Census', p.90.

170. Faucher, p.32. Cf. Norman, *English Catholic Church*, p.183.

171. LGR [2 February] 1853.

172. PRO ED. 103/32, pp.895 and 907; *CPSC Reports*, 1855, p.54. The new school was a renovated Wesleyan chapel.

173. *Catholic School*, Oct. 1848, p.21. Cf. Connolly, thesis, 2, 152-153.

174. Turner, *Pastoral Letter*, 24 Sept. 1852. Cf. *Pastorals of Cardinal Wiseman*, 5 June 1851, 17 June 1852, 18 June 1854, 14 June 1855, 26 May 1856 and 16 June 1859, PPAS.

175. *Catholic School*, Oct. 1848, p.21. Cf. Seaborne, pp.209, 212, 223-224.

176. *Catholic Magazine*, 2 (1832), 217-219; *Orthodox Journal*, 19 (1844), 126-128. See also Deeds Index, pp.113-116; PRO ED. 7/64/107 and ED. 7/65.

177. LGR 7 Feb. 1853. Cf. Seaborne, pp.202 and 224.

178. LGR 7 May 1853: 'Munday [*sic*] after Trinity Sunday'. Cf. Cheney, p.94.

179. LGR 4 May 1853.

180. Stokes' *Report*, PRO ED. 17/19, *Minutes of Council, Reports etc.* 1853-4, II, 911, entry 32. For Stokes' favourable comments on nuns as teachers, see his *Report*

for 1853, *Catholic School*, 14 Oct. 1854, pp.89-98, especially pp.91 and 93. Cf. Marshall's 1852 *Report*, PRO ED. 17/17, pp.1049-1051, for his comments on the 'immeasurable superiority of the female schools taken as a whole, over those frequented by boys.... The incomparable excellence of the female schools is to be found in the special character and qualifications of the teachers. They are all under the... members of educational communities....'

181. That this is what he meant by 'instruction... limited' is suggested by his making the same comment on the highly trained Notre Dame Sisters in St Chad's in 1853 (PRO ED. 17/19, p.911, entry 31).

182. *CPSC Reports*, 1853, p.51; 1854, p.43. In 1856, however, St Joseph's received a grant of £10 from the CPSC, so that Fr Stephan more than recouped himself. See *Catholic School*, 1856, p.261.

183. *CPSC Report*, 1852, p.85.

184. Annals C. For Fr Daly and Newton House, see Census, 1851, MF 914, entry 178; H.T. Crofton, *A History of Newton Chapelry in the Ancient Parish of Manchester*, 3 vols, Chetham Society, 1904-5, 2, 14 and 3, 383-385. Fr Daly was born in Newtown Barry, Co. Wexford in 1814. In 1835 he was the first Irishman to join the Oblates of Mary Immaculate, in France. After his ordination in 1841 he was sent to England, arriving in Manchester in 1849. He remained at Newton Heath at Bp Turner's invitation and gathered the funds for the new church of the Immaculate Conception at Failsworth. He died in the Oblates in 1894. See Deeds Index, p.258; *Biographical Notes on Fr W.J. Daly OMI, 1835-94, B32; and St Mary's, Failsworth 1845-1964*, all in ADS; *Harvest*, 7 (1894), 377-378.

185. LGR 19 Apr. 1854. Between 1841 and 1851 Levenshulme's population rose from 1,231 people in 219 houses to 1,902 in 352 houses (*Brit. Parl. Papers, Census*, vol.7, p.138). Levenshulme did not become part of the city of Manchester until 1909 (S.D. Simon, *A Century of City Government: Manchester 1838-1938*, 1938, p.124). For later photographs of the Catholic church, convent and school, see G. Sussex, P. Helm and A. Brown, *Looking Back at Levenshulme and Burnage* (Altrincham, 1987), p.25; Collection of Photographs, St Mary's Roman Catholic Church, Levenshulme, 1904, no.282, Acc. no.51,658, Local Studies Unit, MCL.

186. Annals C; J. Booker, 'Ancient Chapels of Didsbury and Chorlton in Manchester Parish including Sketches of the Townships of Didsbury, Withington, Burnage, Heaton Norris, Reddish, Levenshulme and Chorlton-cum-Hardy', *Remains Historical and Literary Connected with the Palatine Counties of Lancaster and Chester*, Chetham Society, 42 (1857), 230. Will be cited as Booker.

187. Annals C; LGR 21 Apr. 1854, referring to S. Grimshaw and his wife as 'kind and generous benefactors'; Fr Ignatius Spencer CP, Diary, 25 Oct. 1853, PPAS, which records his visit to the new chapel with Grimshaw and the new parish priest, Fr Unsworth (will be cited as Ignatius, Diary). The mission covered Levenshulme, Reddish, Heaton Norris, Heaton Chapel, Withington, Barlow Moor, Fallowfield and Rusholme. See Bolton, p.190; Booker, pp.233 and 235; *Harvest*, 11 (1898), 118-20.

188. According to PRO ED. 7/64/103/G, in 1883 the 1854 poor school building was closed and replaced by the 1854 church. See also Deeds Index, p.40; *Harvest*, 10 (1897), 162-163. The present school is on the site of E. Prout's convent.

189. LGR 27 Jan. 1855.

190. Letters of Rt Reverend William Turner, Bishop of Salford [LWT], 14 Jan. 1857, GA I/B/2/a.

191. Turner, *Pastoral Letter*, 19 Nov. 1853.

192. Noted in Ignatius, Diary, 2 July 1857, although there was still no name or situation of the property on 26 Aug. 1858 in the Rate Book for Relief of the Poor, Parish of Levenshulme, 1858, p.15, entry 204, M10/16, Local Studies Unit, MCL.

193. Annals C.
194. PRO ED. 17/22, p.42, a letter from the Committee of Council, 1857, refusing a grant to middle-class schools.
195. Cf. *Select Committee Report*, p.129. Cf. *Rambler*, 3 (1848), 144.
196. Gaudentian Rule, ch.16, par.III.
197. See 1861 census for Alma Park, Levenshulme, MF 1268, Microfilm Unit, MCL: entry 100: C.G. Richardson, clerk to a cotton merchant; entry 101: C. Marshall, shipping clerk; entry 102: G. Richardson, solicitor. All 3 Catholics, they were friendly with both E. Prout and Fr Ignatius Spencer CP.
198. J. Kay Shuttleworth, 'Middle-Class Education: What Central and Local Bodies are Best Qualified to Take Charge of and Administer Existing Endowments for Education, and What Powers and Facilities should be given to Such Bodies?', *TNAPSS*, 1866, p.340. Cf. *Brit. Parl. Papers, Schools Inquiry Commission*, vol.I: *Report of the Commissioners*, 1868 [Taunton Commission], p.546, 'An educated mother is even more important to the family than an educated father.' Will be cited as *Schools Inquiry Commission Report*.
199. Flaxman, p.115; Marmion, thesis, 1, 81 and 388-389. When she saw the conditions of the poor, however, C. Connelly also opened day, night and Sunday schools for them.
200. Cf. Allsobrook, p.14; Branca, *Silent Sisterhood*, p.45; Evennett, p.45; Linscott, Ph.D. thesis, pp.139-140; E. Jordan, '"Making Good Wives and Mothers"? The Transformation of Middle-Class Girls' Education in Nineteenth-Century Britain', *History of Education Quarterly*, 31 (1991), 449; P. Marks, 'Femininity in the Classroom: An Account of Changing Attitudes' in J. Mitchell and A. Oakley (ed. and introd.), *The Rights and Wrongs of Women*, 1976 (Penguin 1979), p.181 (will be cited as Mitchell and Oakley).
201. *Education Census*, 1851, p.xlv; *Schools Inquiry Commission Report*, p.560; Marmion, thesis, p.390.
202. Cf. Richson, pp.1 and 6.
203. Hodgson, p.8; Richson, p.6.
204. Turner, *Pastoral Letters*, p.2; *Catholic School*, Oct. 1852, p.302.
205. *Notre Dame Foundations*, p.65. Cf. *CPSC Reports*, 1852, p.85; Linscott, M.A. thesis, pp.36 and 127. See also Records, T 862, pp.8, 21 and 37, DAS; *Rambler*, 6 (1850), 107; *Catholic School*, Mar. 1855, p.101; Flaxman, p.237; Marmion, thesis, 1, 111, 360 and 370.
206. When Bp Turner had to tell the Presentation Srs in Salford he could no longer afford to support them in 1851, he told them 'he felt himself obliged to yield to the general wish of the priests in his district, which was that Religious might be procured who... were allowed by their rule to teach... the children of respectable persons and by that means support themselves.' See Presentation Convent Annals, pp.69-70.
207. Fr Gaudentius' question (LGR 19 Sept. 1854), 'What is Sr Magdalene doing?' suggests she had left the factory. In his letter of 19 June 1855 he wanted Srs Magdalene and Aloysius to go into the mills at Ashton. They were therefore both out of them at that time.
208. Laqueur, p.97.
209. SMR, 26 Mar. 1854; LGR 19 and 21 Apr. 1854.
210. LGR 19 Apr. 1854; Salvian Nardocci CP, Diary, 19 vols, 28 Aug. 1867, PPAD (will be cited as Salvian, Diary); F.Bamber, '"Owd Bally" Whittaker' in J.A. Roby (compiled and ed.), *Traditions of Lancashire, Past and Present* (Wigan, 1991), pp.19-24. See also O. Ashmore, *The Industrial Archaeology of North-West England* (Manchester, 1982), pp.168, 170 and 172 (will be cited as Ashmore); T.C. Barker and J.R. Harris, *A Merseyside Town in the Industrial Revolution: St Helens 1750-1900*

(Liverpool, 1954), p.109 (will be cited as Barker and Harris).
211. Cf. B. Heeney, *Mission to the Middle Classes: The Woodard Schools 1848-1891*, 1969, p.119 (will be cited as Heeney, *Woodard Schools*).
212. LGR 10 May 1854.
213. LCW 8 Oct. [1855]. Year indicated by content.
214. Cf. *Schools Inquiry Commission Report*, pp.547 and 560.
215. LCW 8 Oct. [1855]; *Select Committee Report*, pp.430-446. According to PRO ED. 17/22, 1856-7, p.614, in over 80 Catholic schools with a total of 13,986 children 62.27% of the pupils paid 1d. or 1½d. fees; 28.65% 2d.-3d.; 4.98% 3d.-4d.; 2.58% 4d.; only 1.52% more than 4d.
216. LGR 11 June 1855.
217. Heeney, *Woodard Schools*, p.169; Kitson Clark, *Churchmen*, p.111.
218. LCW 24 Oct. 1855. Cf. *Lamp*, 5 (1853), 15 for the opening of a boarding school at Adelphi House, Salford by the FCJ Sisters at £16 a year for girls under 12 and £18 for those above. Cf. also E. Prout, *Prospectus of Parr Hall*, 1855, GA I/B/5/a, for her boarding fees at Parr Hall Seminary: 18 gns for girls over 10; 16 gns for those under. Will be cited as Prout, *Parr Hall Prospectus*. See also Heeney, *Woodard Schools*, p.119.
219. *Schools Inquiry Commission Report*, p.551.
220. LEP 7 Oct. 1855.
221. LGR 10 Oct. 1855, undated other than '10th' but appears to be the continuation of LGR 9 Oct. 1855.
222. Receptions and Professions; Annals C.
223. LGR 15 and 29 Dec. 1854; 12 Jan. 1855; Reach, p.72. Cf. Kirk, 'Ethnicity', pp.73 and 86-87; Ward, 'Factory Movement in Lancashire', pp.194-195; and 'Revolutionary Tory: The Life of Joseph Rayner Stephens of Ashton-under-Lyne (1805-1879)', *TLCAS*, 68 (1958), 94-95, 101 and 114; D. Gadian, 'Class Formation and Class Actions in North-West Industrial Towns' in Morris, *Class*, p.53 (will be cited as Gadian). Fr Quealy, the Irish parish priest and his Irish curate, Fr Lawrence Joseph O'Mara, heard of Elizabeth Prout from Fr Gaudentius when he gave a mission in Ashton from 30 Nov. to 19 Dec. 1854 (SMR, 30 Nov. 1854; HMR, 30 Nov. 1854, pp.78-80). According to W. Glover (compiled) and J. Andrew (ed.), *History of Ashton-under-Lyne and the Surrounding District* (Ashton-under-Lyne, 1884), pp.330-331 (henceforth cited as Glover and Andrew), Fr Quealy took charge of the district in Feb. 1849, saying Mass in a chapel in Wood St. According to PRO HO 129/474, it was an old cotton mill with 2 rooms, one used as a church for a congregation of 500, the other as a school. The site between Burlington St and Newman St was purchased from the earl of Stamford in 1851-2 (Deeds Index, St Ann's, Ashton-under-Lyne, p.241, ADS). See also Bolton, p.165; W.M. Bowman, *England in Ashton-under-Lyne* (Ashton, 1960), pp.390 and 395 (will be cited as Bowman); S.A. Harrop and E.A. Rose, *Victorian Ashton* (Ashton, 1974), p.67; and G.F. Foster (ed.) *Ashton-under-Lyne Centenary 1847-1947* (Ashton, 1947).
224. LGR 17 Jan. 1855.
225. *Brit. Parl. Papers, Census*, vol.6, p.322: 30,676; vol.7, p.42: 29,791. See, however, J.T. Danson, 'On the Area and Population of the Manchester District', *THSLC*, 8 (1855-6), 172, which gives Ashton a population of 40,723 in 1851. Cf. Engels, p.55.
226. SMR, 30 Nov. 1854. Cf. 'Report of a Committee of the Manchester Statistical Society on the Condition of the Working Classes in an Extensive Manufacturing District in 1834, 1835 and 1836', in Carpenter, *Conditions*, no.1, p.xiv for Ashton's then having 399 Catholic heads of families and 290 lodgers. See also J.T. Danson and T.A. Welton, 'On the Population of Lancashire and Cheshire and its Local

Distribution during the Fifty Years 1801-1851', *THSLC*, 11 (1858-9), 47-48.

227. *Ashton Weekly Reporter*, 21 Apr. 1855. Will be cited as *Ashton Reporter*.

228. Annals C and A/E.

229. *Ashton Reporter*, 21 and 28 Apr., 5 May and 28 July 1855. Cf. Engels, p.84.

230. Annals C; LGR 12 Jan. and 7 July 1855.

231. Joyce, *Work, Society and Politics*, pp.241, 249-250 and 257; Kirk, *Reformism*, pp.318-319; Neal, 'Orange Order', p.23; C. Binfield, *So Down To Prayers: Studies in English Nonconformity 1780-1920*, 1977, p.21; M.R. Beames, 'The Ribbon Societies: Lower-Class Nationalism in Pre-Famine Ireland', *PP*, no.97, 1982, pp.128-129 and 143; G.P. Connolly, 'The Catholic Church and the First Manchester and Salford Trade Unions in the Age of the Industrial Revolution', *TLCAS*, 83 (1985), 132, 136-7 and 151; R. O'Higgins, 'The Irish Influence in the Chartist Movement', *PP*, no.20 (1961), 84-89; J.H. Treble, 'The Attitude of the Roman Catholic Church Towards Trade Unionism in the North 1833-1842', *NH*, 5 (1970), 98.

232. Annals A/E.

233. LGR 20 Oct. 1854.

234. *Tablet*, 11 Aug. 1849; LISCAC 7 May 1850 to Mrs Canning; *Platea*, 1851-1883, St Anne's Retreat, Sutton, PPAS (will be cited as Sutton *Platea*); Salvian, Diary, 10 June 1863; *St Helens' Newspaper and Advertiser*, 13 June 1863 (will be cited as *St Helens' Newspaper*). See also Barker and Harris, p.332; L. Woods, 'John Smith:- A Self-Made Man', a typed dissertation, (St Helens, 1986), Local Studies Library, St Helens.

235. Sutton *Platea*. Fr Bernardine Carosi CP arrived in England in Sept. 1849 and lived for a time in Aston Hall. He therefore probably knew of the Prout family. See Salvian, Autobiography, vol.1, pp.168 and 206.

236. Barker and Harris, pp.56 and 109. Cf. Blundell, 2, 34; 3, 111 and 114; Bolton, pp.73, 87-88 and 244; Gillow, 5, 219-221; M.E. Baines, 'Recusancy in St Helens before 1649', *NWCH*, 1971, p.12 (will be cited as Baines); J.F. Giblin, 'The Orrell Family and the Mission of St Mary's, Blackbrook in Parr, St Helens', in *NWCH*, 7 (1980), 8. For a photograph of Parr Hall, see G. Senior and G. Hennin, *St Helens As It Was*, (Nelson, 1973; third impression 1987), n.p.

237. *Catholic Directory*, 1836, p.61. Cf. Ashmore, pp.168 and 170. According to Barker and Harris, p.177, at some time before 1834 a William Grundy and his wife had had a school in Parr Hall.

238. Barker and Harris, pp.177-178.

239. *Catholic Directory*, 1853, p.157. See *CPSC Report*, 1849, pp.144-145 for a description of the industry and increase of population in the St Helens area at that time.

240. LGR 7 July 1855.

241. LGR 29 Dec. 1854; 13 Apr. 1855; LISN, 3 July 1855.

242. *Catholic Directory*, 1836, p.61. See *Punch*, 12-13 (1847), 131 and 18-19 (1850), 193 for comments on 'maps' and 'the use of globes' as contemporary signs of educational distinction.

243. *Catholic Directory*, 1836, p.61.

244. *Catholic Directory*, 1853, p.157. For the fees, cf. *Schools Inquiry Commission Report*, 1, 558, bearing in mind that its figures were those of a decade later. The Parr Hall fees were average to low as compared with other schools in Lancashire, where the dearest in 1864-5 was £112 per year.

245. LISN 3 July 1855. Smith gave her Mt Pleasant in 1861, at a nominal rent. See also Records of the Convent of Holy Cross, 1855-1864, GA I/B/4/d (will be cited as [S]utton [C]onvent [R]ecords); Annals C; LGR 3 Aug. 1860. For the location of Mt Pleasant as the convent, see Ordnance Survey 6" Map CVIII.6, St Helens and Area,

1882, Local Studies Library, St Helens.

246. Letter of Fr Bernardine Carosi CP, 10 July 1855 (GA I/B/2/i) and LGR 13 and 16 July 1855.

247. See Salvian, Diary, 6 Nov. 1855, St Wilfrid's, Cotton: 'Fr Dominic's coffin being opened, we found the flesh dry and every joint flexible and entirely free from any offensive smell.'

248. For Fr C. Houben CP, see Salvian, Diary, 8 July 1857; Paul Francis Spencer CP, *To Heal the Broken Hearted: The Life of Blessed Charles of Mt Argus* (Dublin, 1988), p.22 (will be cited as Spencer, *Blessed Charles*). Canonised 3 June 2007.

249. LGR 14 Aug. 1855.

250. LGR 18 Apr. 1855.

251. Prout, *Parr Hall Prospectus*. Cf. LGR 23 Aug. 1855; Ashmore, p.168; Barker and Harris, pp.346-353; Lowe, *Irish in Lancashire*, p.18; A.E. Dingle, 'The Monster Nuisance of All': Landowners, Alkali Manufacturers and Air Pollution, 1828-1864', *Econ.HR*, 35 (1982), 530-532. See also *St Helens' Newspaper*, 1 Oct.1862 to 18 July 1863 for reports of Lord Derby's Commission on noxious vapours in the area; and G. Kitson Clark, *An Expanding Society: Britain 1830-1900* (Cambridge, 1967), pp.158 and 169.

252. LGR 16 and 19 July and 8 Aug. 1855; Prout, *Parr Hall Prospectus*. Cf. *Lamp*, 5 (1853), 15 for the FCJ Sisters' fees at Adelphi House boarding school, Salford: £16 a year for girls under 12 and £18 for those above.

253. As was recommended 13 years later, in 1868, by the *Schools Inquiry Commission Report*, p.559.

254. LGR 23 Aug. 1855.

255. Annals C. By 5 Sept. 1855 she had Holy Cross convent at Peckershill. It was opened officially on 16 Nov. 1855, feast of Blessed Paul of the Cross. See LGR 5 and 11 Sept. 1855; *SCR*; Annals C; Census, 1861, MF RG9/2754, entry 164, Local Studies Library, St Helens; Barker and Harris, p.366. For the location of Peckershill, see Ordnance Survey 6" Map 108, St Helens and Area, 1846-7, Local Studies Library, St Helens. Cf. Ashmore, pp.170-171. See also *CPSC Report*, 1855, pp.51-52 and 1856, pp.47-48 for grants to the girls' school in Sutton; PRO ED. 17/22, 1856-7, p.125 for £1 16s. 4¼d. granted to St Anne's, Sutton in 1856 for books and apparatus and £5 2s. capitation grant.

256. LEP 25 Sept. 1855. See *Catholic Directory*, 1858, p.79 for E. Prout's order, the Srs of the Holy Family, at St Anne's school in Sutton and St Helen's school in Blackbrook; repeated in 1859, p.81. According to LRO RCLv 44, pp.549-556, there were 20 girls in St Helen's, Blackbrook, all working-class.

257. *St Helens' Newspaper*, 4 Jan. 1862, presentation address to Fr Bernardine Carosi CP. See also LGR 27 July 1858 to Sr Winefride Lynch; Salvian, Small Chronicle, vol.2, 1858-1864, p.14. See *CPSC Report*, 1860, p.xci and PRO ED. 17/26, p.204 for Stokes' 1860 *Report*: 'schools conducted by Sisters of the Holy Family: Sutton, St Anne's:- 1 department, 117 children, 1 certificated teacher, 2 apprentices; Sutton, St Joseph's [Peasley Cross]:- 2 departments, 120 children, 0 certificated teachers, 0 apprentices; and p.627:- Sutton, St Anne's:- Books: £1 16s. 4¼; certificated teacher: £3 6s. 8d.; pupil teacher: £5; capitation grant: £27 8s. 0d. Since E. Prout was 35 yrs old on 2 Sept. 1855, she could have applied for registration as a teacher in 1856. See PRO ED. 8/2, *Annual Grants, Disused Forms*, Jan. 1859 to Dec. 1863, *Form XII*; *CPSC Reports*, 1857, p.lv; *Catholic School*, Mar. 1855, pp.113-124. Cf. Hurt, p.127. See PRO ED. 17/24, 1858-9 for a building grant of £754 to St Joseph's, Peasley Cross. For other grants to St Anne's and St Joseph's, see PRO ED. 17/23, 1857-8, p.126 (St Anne's); 17/24, 1858-9, p.590; 17/25, 1859-60, p.664; 17/27A, 1861-2,

p.181 (St Joseph's); 17/28, 1862-3, pp.115 and 433; 17/29, 1863-4, p.229 (St Joseph's). Note, however, PRO ED. 17/29, 1863-4, p.231 for Stokes' comment, 'withdrawal of grant from Sutton, St Anne, because teacher was uncertificated.' Since this withdrawal coincided with E. Prout's becoming too ill to teach in 1863, it suggests that she was the previous certificated teacher. For the location of Peasley Cross, see Ordnance Survey 6" Map 108, 1846-7. See also *St Joseph's, Peasley Cross 1878-1918*, a brochure, pp.13 and 21, PPAS.

NOTES TO CHAPTER V

1. Gaudentian Rule, as extended in LGR 11 July 1854.
2. LGR 23 Apr. 1855.
3. LGR dated only Dec. 1852, from St Bede's, Masbro', near Rotherham, Yorkshire, where, according to SMR, he gave a mission from 9-26 Dec. Since his previous letter was dated 17 and his next 21 Dec., this letter must have been written 18-20 Dec.
4. LGR [10 June] 1852.
5. LGR 30 Oct. 1852. Cf. Gaudentian Rule, ch.5, par.III.
6. LGR 19 Feb. 1854.
7. LGR 24 July 1854 and cf. 8 Mar. 1855: 'Prayer, prayer, prayer, a thousand times prayer.'
8. Cf. C. J. Colhoun, 'Community: Toward a Variable Conceptualization for Comparative Research', *SH*, 5 (1980), 106-108, 116-117 and 122; L. Davidoff and Others, 'Landscape With Figures: Home and Community in English Society', in Mitchell and Oakley, pp.143-144 (will be cited as Davidoff and Others); A. Russell, 'Local Elites and the Working-Class Response in the North-West, 1870-1895: Paternalism and Deference Reconsidered', *NH*, 23 (1987), 155.
9. LGR 12 Sept. and 14 Oct. 1853.
10. Gaskell, *Mary Barton*, pp.49 and 51. Cf. also p.42 for a mention of blue cotton handkerchieves, which the sisters also used. See Reach p.53 for reference to partitioned cubicles in the Ancoats model lodging house. Cf. *Tablet*, 12 Aug. 1843 for 'cell' in the terminology of the Presentation Sisters, Livesey St.
11. According to Sr E. Bocock's Account, the Sisters of the Infant Jesus each had a 'small deal table with a drawer' and a 'small looking glass'.
12. LGR 24 Jan. 1855. Cf. Cullwick, p.60; M.E. Rose, *The English Poor Law 1780-1930* (Newton Abbot, 1971), p.171 (will be cited as Rose, *English Poor Law*).
13. Gaudentian Rule, ch.3, par. XII; LGR 10 Feb. and 13 Apr. 1855, an enclosure.
14. Sr E. Bocock's Account; Reach, p.15.
15. Gaudentian Rule, ch.19, par.V.
16. J.C. McKenzie, 'The Composition and Nutritional Value of Diets in Manchester and Dukinfield 1841', *TLCAS*, 72 (1962), 135. Will be cited as McKenzie.
17. Burnett, *Plenty and Want*, pp.12-13; McKenzie, pp.127 and 135.
18. Annals C.
19. LGR 24 Jan. 1855. Cf. 19 Feb. 1855.
20. LGR 18 Apr. 1855.
21. LGR 23 Aug. 1855. Cf. above, Ch.IV, pp 117-118 and note 251.
22. LEP 4 Oct. 1855; LGR 9 Oct. 1855.
23. She paid for it in albs, one of the vestments the priests needed for Mass (LGR 12 Feb. 1855).
24. LGR 13 Apr. 1855 enclosure. On serviettes I am arguing from living tradition. Cf. Davidoff and Hall, p.375.

25. LISN 18 Nov. 1863; Receptions and Professions: Sister Mary Ignatia Joseph of Jesus Crucified, Clementina Stuart, Comtesse D'Albanie, daughter of Charles Edward Stuart, Comte d'Albanie and Anne Beresford; date of birth: unknown; entered religion at Sutton: 1 June 1865; clothed: 21 Nov. 1865 (Fr Bernardine CP); professed: 21 Nov. 1867 (Bp Turner); died 9 Jan. 1894. See also Young, *Ignatius*, pp.261-262. She was buried in the Passionist cemetery, Sutton in the grave beside that of E. Prout.
26. Annals A/E.
27. LGR 24 July 1854.
28. Ibid.
29. Cf. McBride, pp.23-25; Prochaska, 'Female Philanthropy', p.415.
30. Cf. Davidoff, *Best Circles*, p.35.
31. Cf. Joyce, *Work, Society and Politics*, p.95 and 101.
32. Cf. *'Perfectae Caritatis'*, Vatican Council II, 'Decree on the Up-to-date Renewal of Religious Life', A. Flannery OP (ed.), *Vatican Council II, The Conciliar and Post-Conciliar Documents*, 1981 edition, paperback, p.619. Will be cited as Flannery.
33. LGR 24 July 1854.
34. LGR 25 Sept. 1854.
35. LGR 24 July 1854.
36. Annals C. Cf. Hill, p.53.
37. LGR 15 Dec. 1854.
38. LGR 22 Nov. 1854, to Bp Turner, answered and returned by the latter to E. Prout; Annals C.
39. At the end of LGR 22 Nov. 1854.
40. LGR 19 Feb. 1854.
41. Gaudentian Rule, ch. XXV, pars II and V.
42. Joyce, *Work, Society and Politics*, p.140.
43. LGR 22 May 1855.
44. LGR 8 July 1853.
45. LGR 22 Nov. 1854.
46. Gaudentian Rule, ch.XXII, pars VI-XI; LGR 30 Aug. 1852; LEP 25 Sept. 1855. A chapter is an official meeting of a religious body to discuss its spiritual and temporal affairs.
47. Cf. Burnett, *Useful Toil*, pp.166-167.
48. LGR 11 May 1855.
49. Cf. G. Eliot, *Felix Holt*, 1866 (Penguin 1987), p.603; Branca, *Silent Sisterhood*, p.7; 'Image and Reality', p.180; Burn, pp.264 and 286; Casteras, p.129; Davidoff and Hall, p.114; Heeney, *Women's Movement*, pp.7-8 and 11; Murray, p.24; Rendall, *Origins*, p.73; Vicinus, *Suffer and Be Still*, pp.ix-xi; G.F.A. Best, 'Popular Protestantism in Victorian Britain' in R. Robson (ed.), *Ideas and Institutions of Victorian Britain* 1967, p.135 (will be cited as Best, 'Popular Protestantism'); R. Billington, 'The Dominant Values of Victorian Feminism' in Sigsworth, p.121.
50. Cf. Hill, p.24.
51. LGR 2 Sept. 1853.
52. Cf. Joyce, *Work, Society and Politics*, p.146.
53. Annals C.
54. AMR, entry 58, 6 Aug. 1846.
55. LGR 4 May 1853.
56. Cf. Eliot, *Middlemarch*, p.792: 'Of course, men know best about everything, except what women know better'; M. Vicinus, *A Widening Sphere, Changing Roles of Victorian Women*, 1977, p.xix (will be cited as Vicinus, *Widening Sphere*).
57. LRC 11 Aug. 1853.
58. LGR 11 Aug. 1853.

59. LISR 13 May 1850, to Fr A. Testa. I am indebted to Fr J.C. Quadri, recently chaplain to Italian immigrants, Salford Diocese, for helping me to translate this letter.
60. LISR 21 Feb. 1851, to Fr A. Testa. I am indebted to Sr Cyprian Connolly CP for her translation of this passage.
61. Cf. Davidoff and Others, pp.141-142; Joyce, *Work, Society and Politics*, p.101.
62. See Joyce, *Work, Society and Politics*, pp.xiii, 175-178 and 241; and 'The Factory Politics of Lancashire in the Later Nineteenth Century', *HJ*, 18 (1975), 525-553.
63. Cf. Davidoff and Others, pp.141-142.
64. Cf. Houghton, p.236; K.D. Brown, *A Social History of the Nonconformist Ministry in England and Wales 1800-1930* (Oxford, 1988), pp.171.
65. LGR 11 May 1855.
66. LGR 29 Aug. 1855.
67. LGR 24 Jan. 1855.
68. LGR 1 Sept. 1855.
69. LGR 29 Aug. 1855.
70. LEP 7 Oct. 1855.
71. LGR 9 Oct. 1855.
72. MS copy GA I/B/1/e; *Records*, p.11. Note the Victorian use of 'industrious' where modern terminology would use 'industrial'. Cf. LGR 14 Nov. 1853 and 16 July 1855; J.A. Bremner, 'Education of the Manual Labour Class', *TNAPSS*, 1866-7, p.308. See above, Ch.III, pp.74, 77 and 79 for the wage rates of the first sisters.
73. LGR 19 Jan. 1852.
74. *Records*, p.12. See above, Ch.III, pp.66-67.
75. Gaudentian Rule, ch.16, pars I-VI. Cf. [Greenan], pp.11-14; Young, *Dominic in England*, p.171; Yuhaus, p.90.
76. Gaudentian Rule, ch.17, par.IX, changed to Part 3, ch.IX in his revision of July 1854.
77. HMR, 1 Jan. 1854; Annals C.
78. Gaudentian Rule, ch.17, par.XII.
79. Annals A/E. Whellan, *Directory*, 1852, p.47. It is therefore very likely that they made the vestments presented by his parishioners to Canon Formby of St Mary's, Mulberry St about Christmas 1856, which were purchased from Browns of Meal St (*Tablet*, 3 Jan. 1857). According to the late Sr Macnissi McKee CP, Sr Frances Wellard, who entered the order in 1854, had overall charge of the sisters' vestment making for T. Brown and Co. An 'excellent needlewoman' she sewed everything by hand by gaslight, until she finally went blind. By 1901, T. Brown and Co. were church furnishers and tailors at 31 Princess St (Slater, *Directory*, 1901, p.654). By then, the sisters, still working for them, were making the University of Manchester's graduation hoods, which in 1901 began to be adorned with rabbit fur. See Parkmount Records, 29 June 1901: 'A new expression is given to the Hoods of the minor degrees by the addition of a band of rabbit fur. So much for the vanity of the XX C.' In 1982 Sr Roberta Moon CP made and embroidered the cloth and frontal for the papal altar and the coverings for the lectern and papal throne when Pope John Paul II celebrated Mass at Heaton Park, Manchester.
80. They also tried to make altar breads until Fr Gaudentius stopped them because he thought it too difficult (LGR Ash Wednesday [21 Feb.] 1855). Cf. Cheney, p.118.
81. Annals C.
82. LGR 12 Nov. 1852; 14 Nov. 1853.
83. Bialas, *Mysticism*, pp.97-101.
84. MS copy, GA I/B/1/e; *Records*, p.12.
85. LGR 1 Dec. 1853.

86.   LGR 9 Dec. 1853.
87.   LGR 11 July 1854.
88.   LGR 3 Oct. 1854.
89.   LGR 19 May 1855.
90.   Manton, p.154.
91.   Cf. Carpenter, *Reformatory Schools*, p.70; Hellerstein and Others, pp.84-85; Manton, pp.12, 74 and 87.
92.   *Tablet*, 5 Aug. 1854, p.485 noted a charity sermon preached the previous Sunday in Manchester for St Joseph's Day and Sunday Schools, 'on the need for the education of the humbler classes of the Catholic community at the present crisis of proselytising, reformatory and educational establishments'. E. Prout was teaching in St Joseph's at that time. Cf. Annals A/E and D.
93.   *Catholic School*, 1856, p.251.
94.   *Catholic School*, 1851, pp.150-151.
95.   *Catholic School*, 1856, pp.229-230.
96.   Expenditure in 1849-50 was £321 3s. 4d., income from sales £261 19s. (*Catholic School*, 1851, pp.150-151). Cf. M. Carpenter, 'On the Nature of the Educational Aid Required for the Destitute and Neglected Portion of the Community', *TNAPSS*, 1866-7, p.353.
97.   PRO ED. 17/19, Stokes' 1853 *Report*, p.891; *Catholic School*, 1854, p.94.
98.   LGR 21 June 1855.
99.   As will be discussed more fully in Ch.VI, pp.162-164 and 168-170.
100.   *Factory Reports*, 1850 [1141], XXIII, pt 2. 181, pp.29 and 32; 1852 [1439], XXI, pt. 1. 353, p.7; 1852 [1500], XXI, pt 1. 377, p.8; 1854 [1712], XIX. 257, p.5; 1854 [1796], XIX. 373; 1854-5 [1881], XV. 275, p.4 and [1947], XV. 367, p.3; 1856 [203], XVIII. 211, p.6; 1856 [2090], XVIII, pt 2. 335; 1857 [2153, Sess.1], III.559, pp.3 and 37-40.
101.   As mentioned in Ch.III, pp.74-77.
102.   *Factory Reports*, 1868[4093-1], XIV.123, pp.193-194; 1867[3794], XVI.327, p.122.
103.   Gaudentian Rule, ch.17, par.XIV.
104.   LGR 19 June 1855.
105.   LGR 19 and 21 June 1855. The *Protestant Witness* made frequent references to Orangemen in Ashton. For references to anti-Catholicism there see Reach, p.72; Joyce, *Work, Society and Politics*, pp.175 and 241; Kirk, *Reformism*, p.83; and 'Ethnicity', pp.73-74; M.A. Lock, 'The Role of Clergymen and Ministers in Ashton, Stalybridge and Dukinfield, 1850-1914', an unpublished M.Phil. thesis, University of Manchester, 1989, pp.187-188 and 276 (will be cited as Lock, thesis).
106.   LGR 16 July 1855.
107.   LGR 8 Aug. 1855.
108.   Cf. LISN 11 Apr. 1863, referring to a remark made by Canon Benoit.
109.   LGR 11 June and 8 Aug. 1855.
110.   LGR 8 Aug. 1855.
111.   LGR 29 Aug. 1855.
112.   LGR 1 Sept. 1855.
113.   LGR 11 Sept. 1855.
114.   LGR 20 Sept. 1856.
115.   LGR 5 Oct. 1856.
116.   For the plight of handloom weavers as a result of steam-powered industrialisation, see D. Bythell, *The Handloom Weavers, A Study in the English Cotton Industry During the Industrial Revolution* (Cambridge, 1969).
117.   Known only from his reply, LGR 3 Feb. 1857.

118. LGR 18 Feb. 1859.
119. LGR 6 Aug. 1862.
120. See above, Ch.VI, section 3, pp.168-172.
121. LGR 25 June 1864.
122. LGR 21 Oct. 1877. For a discussion of the development of the Rule from 1863 to its final approbation by the Holy See in 1887 see Ch.VII, pp.204-209.
123. Davidoff and Hall, p.74.
124. Cf. Branca, *Silent Sisterhood*, p.26; Davidoff and Hall, p.384.
125. LGR 11, 19 and 21 June 1855; LISN 3 July 1855.
126. LCW, undated. From its reference to her writing to the Misses Kinahan on '25 inst.' and from Fr Gaudentius' allusion to the contents of this letter in his own to E. Prout on 3 Oct. 1855, this letter should be dated 26 Sept.-2 Oct. 1855. For the decline in straw-bonnet making, see Rendall, *Origins*, p.158.
127. LGR 19 June 1855. For R. Monteith, see *Tablet*, 4 Apr. 1846 and 15 Apr. 1884; W. Gordon Gorman, *Converts to Rome*, 1910, p.194 (will be cited as Gordon Gorman); B. Aspinwall, 'The Scottish Dimension: Robert Monteith and the Origins of Modern British Catholic Social Thought', *DR*, 97 (1979), 46-68; 'David Urquhart, Robert Monteith and the Catholic Church: A Search for Justice and Peace', *Innes Review*, 31 (1980), 57-70; 'Before Manning: Some Aspects of British Social Concern before 1865', *New Blackfriars*, 1980, pp.113-127.
128. HMR 24 June 1855.
129. LEP 12 Sept. 1855.
130. Cf. C. Dickens, *David Copperfield*, 1850 (Penguin 1985), pp.605 and 667 for Dora's lack of domesticity on account of her 'superior' education. See also J. Roach, *A History of Secondary Education in England 1800-1870*, 1986. pp.151-152.
131. Cf. Horn, p.54; McBride, pp.28 and 30.
132. Branca, *Silent Sisterhood*, pp.22, 26 and 28; Davidoff and Hall, p.384.
133. Gaudentian Rule, ch.XXVI, par.VII and ch.XXVII, par.XVII.
134. Branca, *Silent Sisterhood*, pp.26 and 28-29.
135. Annals C.
136. Ignatius, Diary, 1 and 3-13 July 1857. Cf. Salvian, Diary, 1 July 1857.
137. LGR 24 June 1857.
138. LGR 4 Sept. and 5 Oct. 1856; 5 May 1857. Both came from Pittsburgh. For Irish and German Catholic immigration to North America, see J.P. Dolan, *The American Catholic Experience* (New York, 1985), pp.128-40; F. Grubb, 'Research Note: German Immigration to Pennsylvania 1709-1820', *Journal of Interdisciplinary History*, 20 (1990), 417-436. See also Register of Baptisms and Marriages, St Michael's Parish, West Hoboken, New Jersey, 1861-65 for 11 Irish marriages at which Fr Gaudentius Rossi officiated between 25 May 1862 and 15 Aug. 1864. According to the 1861 Census, Sutton, MF RG9/2754, entry 164, Local Studies Library, St Helens, E. Lang was then 36, making her 31 in 1856. Her name is given variously, in Fr Gaudentius' letters and in the Congregation's records, as 'Louisa', 'Eliza' and 'Lizette'. Bridget Flanagan was 38 in 1861. She was therefore about 34 in 1857.
139. LGR 4 Aug. 1857.
140. Cf. P. Dougherty, *Mother Mary Potter, Foundress of the Little Company of Mary (1847-1913)*, 1961, pp.113-118 for M. Mary Potter's similar experience of begging in 1878 in order to pay off debts run up by her bursar.
141. LWT, 6 Aug. 1857; Annals C. Search in the Lancashire parochial records has failed to indicate where E. Prout went or how much she received.
142. Letter known only from his reply, 2 Oct. 1857.
143. See LGR 1 Sept. 1856 and 2 Oct. 1857. The single fare from Liverpool to the

USA was about £4. See Passenger's Contract Ticket, C263, Liverpool-New York, 20 July 1857, shown in the 'Emigrants to a New World' Exhibition, Maritime Museum, Liverpool, by which 6 adults travelled for £22 10s.

144. LGR 2 Oct. 1857.

145. Ibid. They did not pay rent but they did have to pay the Levenshulme Poor Rate and Highway Rate. See M10/16, Local Studies Unit, MCL for Levenshulme Highway Rate Book 1858, entry 204: rate at 4d in the £; £10 to be paid on 6 May 1858; and Rate Book for Relief of the Poor, Parish of Levenshulme, entry 204: rate at 2/- in the £; rateable value of property: £30; £3 to be paid on 29 Sept. 1858. E. Prout was late in paying the Poor Rate in 1858.

146. LGR 2 Oct. 1857. Cf. LCW dated only Friday (but 21 Sept. 1855, acc. to LGR 21 Sept. 1855 to E. Prout and Cheney, p.119) for Mrs Grimshaw's having given the sisters work to do for St Augustine's bazaar, which necessitated their staying up late at night, a hazard of having lay patrons. See also *Tablet*, 6 Sept. 1842 for a bazaar in Preston for the Cistercians in Leicestershire; 24 June 1848 for one for the Sisters of the Infant Jesus, Northampton; and 9 April 1853 for one in St Chad's, Manchester to raise funds for a purpose-built convent for the Notre Dame Sisters.

147. *Factory Report*, 1857-8[2314], XXIV.66, pp.5 and 10, for the half year ending 31 Oct. 1857 refers to mills on short time and many closed during the previous 3 months. See also 1857-8[2391], XXIV.721, pt 1, p.10. The *Freeman's Journal*, Sat. 19 Dec. 1857, MF 2, National Library of Ireland, Dublin, Eire, noted the short time, unemployment and seeking of poor relief in the cotton towns of Lancashire that had already been going on for some time. Cf. D.A. Farnie, 'The Cotton Famine in Great Britain' in B.M. Ratcliffe (ed.), *Great Britain and Her World 1750-1914* (Manchester, 1975), p.165 (will be cited as Farnie, 'Cotton Famine'); W.T.M. Torrens, *Lancashire's Lesson*, 1864, p.12 (will be cited as Torrens); J.R.T. Hughes, 'The Commercial Crisis of 1857', *Oxford Economic Papers*, 8 (1956), 210-211; H.W. McCready, 'Elizabeth Gaskell and the Cotton Famine in Manchester: Some Unpublished Letters', *THSLC*, 123 (1971), 146 (will be cited as McCready, 'E. Gaskell').

148. Annals C.

149. Known only from LGR 9 Nov. 1857.

150. Annals C, which also says that Sr Aloysius was dismissed on 23 Dec. 1856 but that in 1857 two of the first professed left with Clare. Since three remained, those two must have been Aloysius Gilday and Magdalene Toler. Given the time lag between 1857 and the time of writing, about ten years later, however, the writer's memories may simply have been confused. Since Sr Teresa Hennessy had entered in December 1852, she was one of the earlier sisters, although not one of the first professed.

151. Annals C; SCR.

152. Annals A/E and C.

153. Annals A/E and C. Ignatius, Diary, 25 Nov. 1857 and Annals A/E, F and G record that Sr Catherine Scanlon was E. Prout's companion.

154. Cf. Salvian, Diary, 18 Nov. 1859: after a 'very rough passage from Holyhead to Kingstown', he reached Harold's Cross at 7 a.m. The return fare Liverpool-Dublin was £2, although in 1867 Fr Salvian travelled by steam packet at a night cabin fare of 12s. 6d. (Diary, 28 Oct. 1867). If E. Prout went from Liverpool, she may have sailed on the 'Princess', which arrived at the Pier Head in Dublin, after its 14-hour crossing, on 25 Nov. See *Freeman's Journal*, MF 1, 26 Nov. and 7 Dec. 1857.

155. Ignatius, Diary, 25 Nov. 1857; *Thom's Almanac and Official Directory* (Dublin, 1857 and 1858), p.1058 in each case, in which, however, Miss Nolan's name is spelt as 'Nowlan'. The lodging house, 43 Upper Dorset Street, Dublin, is still inhabited.

156. SCR. Blessed Paul's Retreat, Mt Argus, Harold's Cross, Dublin was founded

on 15 Aug. 1856 with Fr Paul Mary Pakenham as its first rector. He died there on 1 Mar. 1857. See Salvian Nardocci CP, Folio of Newspaper Cuttings, PPAD (will be cited as Salvian, Newspaper Cuttings); Smith, *Pakenham*, pp.85-107.

157. I am grateful to Sr M. Cabrini Delahunty, Archivist the Diocese of Cloyne, Cobh, Co. Cork for a copy of such a letter to the bishop of Cloyne. Srs Cecilia and Ethelreda Reddan from Borrisokane had entered Elizabeth's novitiate in 1855-6.

158. Annals G. Research in conventual, parochial and diocesan archives in Eire, especially in the counties of Kerry, Kildare and Tipperary, has failed to produce evidence of their visits. The South Presentation Convent in Cork City has the tradition that they stayed with them and from them went to the Presentation Convent in Fermoy, Co. Cork. I owe this information to Sr De Sales, South Presentation Convent, Cork. Salvian, Diary, 29 Oct. 1855 records that the Passionist Brother Joseph returned from questing in Ireland with £25.

159. Cf. Gilley, 'Roman Catholic Mission', pp.127-128; Norman, *Roman Catholicism*, p.73. See also Bp Turner's reference in his *Pastoral Letter*, 21 Nov. 1856, to his 'spiritual charge in the midst of a large Catholic population, in which schools, chapels and Priests [were] constantly in demand'.

160. I owe this information to Sr Estelle Izard, Holy Family Provincial House, London; Sr De Sales, South Presentation Convent, Cork and Sr M. Lelia, North Presentation Convent, Cork.

161. Spencer, *Blessed Charles*, p.25.

162. *Freeman's Journal*, MF 2, 15 Jan. 1858; H.K.B., General Index 1852-1902, p.15, PPAUC, Cf. Yuhaus, pp.261 and 264.

163. Fr Osmund Maguire, born John Maguire near Enniskillen, Co. Fermanagh, on 20 June 1831, later moved to Broadway, Worcs. (where his parents taught in the school founded by Fr Bernard O'Loughlin) and received the Passionist habit as a laybrother in Broadway on 29 Sept. 1851. Some time later his novice-master discovered he knew Latin and asked the provincial to apply for a papal dispensation to profess him as a cleric, as happened on 30 Sept. 1852. He was ordained about Dec. 1855. In 1856 he became vice-rector to Fr Paul Mary in Mt Argus and after his death succeeded him as rector. He designed and built the new Blessed Paul's Retreat at Mt Argus from 1857. In 1866 he became rector of St Mungo's, Glasgow, where he built the new Passionist retreat in Stanhope St. In 1868-70 he supplied as parish priest in St Mary's Irvine, Ayrshire, where he opened a school. He moved to England in 1870. In 1877 he returned to Ireland to give a mission, was taken ill and died in Mt Argus on 14 Aug. See Salvian, Diary, 18 May and 14 Aug. 1877; Salvian Nardocci CP, Register of Passionists, 1842-1887, no.48, PPAD; Register of Arrivals and Departures, Mt Argus, Dublin, 1856-1874, 23 Aug. 1856, PPAD; Mt Argus Chronicles, 1856-1876, pp.11, 31, 34 and 93, PPAD. See also Salvian, Diary, 22-23 Apr. 1857, noting he left Ireland at 7.20 p.m. and arrived in Sutton at 7.30 a.m. on 23 Apr.; and 6 Dec. 1858 when he left Kingstown, Dublin about 9 a.m. and arrived in Sutton at 8 p.m.

164. SCR.

165. Annals C; SCR.

166. Annals C. Cf. Ignatius, Diary, 14 Feb. 1858.

167. Letter known only from LGR 6 Apr. 1858.

168. LGR 6 Apr. 1858. Cf. LGR 7 June 1856.

169. LGR 14 May 1858. Sr Philomena (Mary Johnson) entered the Cistercian convent in Stapehill, Dorset in 1858. She left after some months and sought readmission to the Sisters of the Holy Family (LGR 18 Feb. 1859). E. Prout refused to readmit her. She returned to Holy Cross Abbey, Stapehill about 1862-3 but left again after some

months. In 1864 she applied to M. Winefride Lynch for readmission to the Sisters of the Holy Family and was again refused (Letter, Fr Eugene Martorelli CP [LEM] to M. Winefride, 16 Nov. 1864, GA/I/B/2/e). She returned to Stapehill for the third time in Nov. 1873, was clothed as Sr Teresa Bernard on 6 Apr. 1874 and made her profession on 17 June 1875. In 1877 she gave her superiors so much trouble that Bp W. Vaughan of Plymouth had to be called in. See his letter to the abbess, 12 July 1877. Sr Teresa Bernard was dispensed from her vows and left Stapehill on 31 Jan. 1881 (Records, Holy Cross Abbey, Stapehill, Dorset). I am indebted to the archivist, Stapehill for supplying me with this information.

170. Receptions and Professions; Annals C.

171. SCR; Salvian, Diary, 13 May 1858.

172. Annals B and C.

173. LGR 14 May 1858 refers to her having shown Mrs Smith, benefactress in Sutton, at least one of his letters.

174. As relayed back to Elizabeth in LGR 6 Apr. 1858.

175. Letter known only from his reply. See also Annals A/E.

176. LWT 30 May 1858.

177. LRC 31 May 1858.

178. LGR 14 May 1858.

179. Annals B and C.

180. Postulants' Agreements; Receptions and Professions; Salvian, Diary, 7-9 June 1858 and 9 Mar. 1859; Arrivals and Departures, St Saviour's Retreat, Broadway, 1850-1872, 7 June 1858, PPAS (will be cited as Broadway Arrivals and Departures).

181. Annals C; Broadway Arrivals and Departures, 16 June 1858.

182. Letter known only from his reply, 2 July 1858. Fr Bernard (John O'Loughlin) was born on 18 Sept. 1823 in Tunstall, Staffs, of Irish parents. He entered the Passionist novitiate in Aston Hall in 1844, was professed on 2 May 1845 and ordained on 22 Sept. 1849. In 1850 he moved to St Joseph's Retreat, the Hyde, London and on 30 Jan. 1851 to Broadway, where he remained 12 years, mainly as rector. On 8 June 1863 he left Broadway to establish a Passionist house in Paris. See Salvian: Early Novices, pp.68-70; Devine, *Dominic*, p.186; Wilson, p.335. See also *Tablet*, 12 Feb. 1853, for a mission at Gloucester during which his 'manner pleasing and winning; his voice sweet and melodious, [he] inspired his audience with confidence and esteem towards him.'

183. Missions and Retreats, St Saviour's Retreat, Broadway, 1851-61 [BMR], 3 July 1858.

184. LRC 2 July 1858.

185. BMR, 3 July 1858.

186. Blundell, 1, 111.

187. Allchin, p.66; Williams, *Sellon*, p.36.

188. LRC 5 July 1858.

189. See LGR 30 Aug. 1852. See above, Ch.II, pp.40-42 and Ch.IV, pp.107-110.

190. See LGR 27 July, 30 Aug. and 6 Oct. 1852; 17 May 1853.

191. LGR 23 July 1853; 11 Aug. 1853.

192. LGR 6 June 1854; *Harvest*, 5 (1892), 61-63.

193. LGR 27 Oct. 1854.

194. LGR Holy Thursday [5 Apr.] 1855. Cf. Cheney, p.118.

195. LGR 19 June 1855.

196. Letters of Fr Bernard O'Loughlin CP [LBO'L], 27 July 1858, GA I/B/4/a-b.

197. Annals C.

198. Ibid.

199. BMR, 3 July 1858; Salvian, Annals, 1890, pp.315-320; Small Chronicle, vol.2,

1858-64, pp.31-42; Annals A/E.
200. Title of a publication by Bishop Ullathorne in defence of nuns, 1850. See above p.145.
201. J. Black and A. Bellenger OSB, 'The Foreign Education of British Catholics in the Eighteenth Century', *DR*, 105 (1987), 311.
202. *Rambler*, 7 (1851), 450; *Catholic Directory*, 1794, p.16; 1836, p.61; 1853, p.157. Cf. Norman, *Roman Catholicism*, p.74; Roach, pp.180 and 194-207; M.D.R. Leys, *Catholics in England 1559-1829, A Social History*, 1961, pp.163-168.
203. P. Ingram, 'Protestant Patriarchy and the Catholic Priesthood in Nineteenth-Century England', *JSH*, 24 (1991), 786. Will be cited as Ingram. Cf. Casteras, p.129, however, for sentimentalised stereotypes of nuns as the embodiment of the Victorian idealisation of womanhood.
204. See *Brit. Parl. Papers, Accounts and Papers*, 1865[81], XLV.265, *Official Correspondence with Her Majesty's Government Relative to the Abduction of a Nun, Named Mary Ryan*, 25 Feb. 1865. Cf. Arnstein, p.65; Best, 'Popular Protestantism', p.128.
205. *Catholic Luminary*, p.606; *Lamp*, 2 (1850-51), 229. Cf. also *Manchester Guardian*, 1 Jan. 1851 for an 'escape' from Banbury convent.
206. See Best, 'Popular Protestantism', p.132; Chadwick, *Victorian Church*, 1, 509; Yuhaus, pp.7-8; R.A. Billington, 'Maria Monk and her Influence', *Catholic Historical Review*, 22 (1936-7), 283-296.
207. Cf. Best, 'Popular Protestantism', pp.118, 122, 124 and 126; Burn, p.248; Chadwick, *Victorian Church*, 1, 14; Ingram, pp.783-784; Norman, *Anti-Catholicism*, pp.14-15; J.P. Chinnici OFM, *The English Catholic Enlightenment: John Lingard and the Cisalpine Movement 1780-1850* (Shepherdstown, USA, 1980), p.17.
208. Cf. Coleman, p.33; Kirk, 'Ethnicity', pp.73-74.
209. Cf. N. Annan, 'Science, Religion and the Critical Mind' in P. Appleman and Others, *1859: Entering An Age of Crisis* (Indiana, 1959), p.33 (will be cited as Appleman and Others).
210. Vicinus, *Independent Women*, p.31.
211. Cf. *St Helens' Newspaper*, 6 June 1863; Forster, pp.169-170 and 178; Houghton, p.366; Mahood, pp.4-5; J.A. Banks, 'The Challenge of Popular Culture' in Appleman and Others, p.202; A. Briggs, 'Victorian Values' in Sigsworth, p.23.
212. Cf. Ingram, p.789; Wolffe, p.126.
213. Cf. Casteras, p.136; O'Brien, 'Lay-Sisters', p.453.
214. *Punch*, 20-21 (1851), 219. Cf. Davidoff and Hall, p.186.
215. Arnstein, p.212; N. Yates, *The Oxford Movement and Anglican Ritualism*, Hist. Assoc. Pamphl., 1983, p.29.
216. *Punch*, 6-7 (1844), 93; 18-19 (1850), 226-227; 34-35 (1858), 257. Cf. Arnstein, pp.4 and 212; and 'The Murphy Riots: A Victorian Dilemma', *VS*, 19 (1975-6), 59; Best, 'Popular Protestantism', pp.132, 134 and 136; Davidoff and Hall, p.329; Houghton, p.347; Ingram, pp.793-794; Thureau-Dangin, 1, 369-370; Wolffe, pp.123-124.
217. Burn, p.237; Joyce, *Work, Society and Politics*, p.258; Machin, *Politics*, p.253.
218. *Punch*, 6-7 (1844), 93. Cf. Casteras, pp.131-132.
219. *Lamp*, 2 (1850-51), 228-229.
220. Arnstein, pp.62-63; Briggs, *Victorian People*, p.27; Chadwick, *Victorian Church*, 1, 509; Gilley, *Newman*, pp.266 and 269; Ker, *Newman*, p.362; Norman, *Anti-Catholicism*, p.79.
221. *Tablet*, 27 May 1854.
222. Chadwick, *Victorian Church*, 1, 509; Cockshut, 'Newman', p.115; Wolffe, p.125 and cf. p.112 for reprints of Fox's *Book of Martyrs* in 1838 and 1841. See also

Lamp, 2 (1850-1), 309-310 and 401-402; 3 (1851-2), 18-20 and 31-32.

223. See *Rambler*, 10 (1852), 507 for a review of such a book, *The World and The Cloister* by A.M. Stewart. Cf. Casteras, pp.130 and 136.

224. *Brit. Parl. Papers, Bills*, 1851[116], V.511, *A Bill To Prevent the Forcible Detention of Females in Religious Houses*. Cf. Arnstein, pp.14-18 and 62.

225. *Protestant Witness*, p.542.

226. *Punch*, 20-21 (1851), 184.

227. *Rambler*, 8 (1848), 311.

228. *Punch*, 20-21 (1851), 125, 129 and 132-133. Cf. Best, 'Popular Protestantism', p.128.

229. *Punch*, 20-21 (1851), 205, 209 and 219; *Lamp*, 2 (1850-51), 309 and 339-341.

230. *Protestant Witness*, p.666. Cf. *Hansard's Parliamentary Debates*, 3, CXV, 1851, vol.2, p.266; Best, 'Popular Protestantism', pp.124-126; Norman, *Anti-Catholicism*, p.15; Paz, *Connelly*, pp.158, 163, 165 and 177. See Ingram, p.793 for such an Address to Victoria from the women of Liverpool in 1850.

231. Reviewed in *Rambler*, 7 (1851), 440-450. Cf. C. Butler OSB, *The Life and Times of Bishop Ullathorne 1806-1889*, 2 vols, 1926, 1, 169 and 2, 162-163.

232. *Catholic School*, May 1851, pp.142-143, repeated in *Lamp*, 3 (1851-2), 7-9. Cf. Turner, *Pastoral Letter*, 21 Nov. 1856; PRO ED. 17/17, Marshall's 1852 *Report*, pp.1049-1051. See also *Rambler*, 2 (1854), 209-229 for a review of J. Murray, *Hospitals and Sisterhoods*, 1854.

233. *Tablet*, 5 June 1852; and 7 May 1853 for another Catholic lecture, by W. Gillow of Clifton, in defence of nuns. Cf. Casteras, p.138; F.B. Smith, *Florence Nightingale, Reputation and Power*, 1982, p.27 (will be cited as Smith, *Nightingale*).

234. *Catholic Luminary*, 1840-41, pp.300-302 and 606; *Lamp*, 3 (1851-2), 220-221; *Orthodox Journal*, 16 (1842-3), 30-31; and 17 (1843), 123-124; *Tablet*, 13 Aug. 1842; 22 Apr. and 12 Aug. 1843; 26 Oct. 1844; 28 Nov. 1846; 30 Jan., 31 July and 25 Dec. 1847; 24 June, 8 and 22 July and 23 Dec. 1848; 13 Jan. and 3 and 10 Nov. 1849; 1 May and 19 June 1852; and 26 Aug. 1854.

235. Cf. *Words from the Heart*, p.14; Casteras, pp.129-130; L. Billington, 'Revivalism and Popular Religion' in Sigsworth, pp.147-148. Cf. Eliot, *Middlemarch*, p.848 on 'the tradition that fresh garments belonged to all initiation'.

236. See *Words from the Heart*, pp.93-94; '*Lumen Gentium*', 1964, Flannery, p.404.

237. LGR 12 Nov. 1852; *Ceremonies of Vestition and Profession, The Congregation of the Discalced Clerics of the Most Holy Cross and Passion of Our Lord Jesus Christ* (will be cited as *Passionist Rite*), Box: Pittsburgh, St Paul's, PPAUC.

238. LGR 21 Dec. 1852.

239. The Srs of the Infant Jesus probably had bridal dress; the Presentation Srs in Livesey St, Manchester and the Srs of Mercy certainly had. See *Catholic Luminary*, 1841, p.606; *Orthodox Journal*, 17 (1843), 124; *Tablet*, 12 Aug. 1843, 13 Jan. 1849 and 26 Aug. 1854.

240. Ceremonial Rite of Reception and Profession of Novices, GA IV/B/29. Cf. *Passionist Rite*.

241. SMR, 12 Nov. 1854; Annals A/E, B, C, D, F and G; *Records*, p.13.

242. Ceremonial Rite of Profession; *Passionist Rite*; Red Bk; Postulants' Agreements. Cf. *Manchester Courier*, 22 Nov. 1862; Presentation Convent Annals, p.73.

243. Best, 'Popular Protestantism', pp.130-132; Casteras, p.138; Chadwick, *Victorian Church*, 1, 509; Gilley, thesis, p.329.

244. *Tablet*, 24 Apr. 1852.

245. *Tablet*, 14 Aug. 1852. Cf. Chadwick, *Victorian Church*, 1, 509. See Norman, *English Catholic Church*, p.185 and Bennett in Beck, p.560 for these sisters' going to the Crimea in 1854.

246. BMR, 3 July 1858.
247. *Tablet*, 7 May 1853.
248. *Tablet*, 11 June 1853. Cf. Arnstein, p.63.
249. *Tablet*, 21 May 1853.
250. *Rambler*, 12 (1853), 1-11 and 81-82; *Tablet*, 28 May and 4, 11, 18 and 25 June 1853.
251. Reported in *Tablet*, 25 June 1853.
252. *Tablet*, 10 Sept. 1853. See Flaxman, pp.139-153 for P. Connelly's association with H. Drummond MP; and also Paz, *Connelly*, passim, for the case of Connelly v. Connelly, which went on for years until dismissed on 24 June 1858, only a few days before E. Prout's investigation.
253. Annals A/E and C. There is no evidence of what type of fever they had. There was an outbreak of cholera at that time but, according to Ransome and Royston, pp.458-459, 'Manchester entirely escaped'. Other fevers were constant, especially in Angel Meadow. See Aston *Platea*, 1853; *Brit. Parl. Papers, Reports from Commissioners, Public Health*, 1854[1768], XXXV. pt 1, *Report of the General Board of Health on the Administration of the Public Health Act, and the Nuisances Removal and Diseases Prevention Act, from 1848-1854*, 1854 *Report*, pp.6, 9, 17 and 37; *Northampton Herald*, 19 Aug. 1848; *Northampton Mercury*, 12 Aug. 1848; Smith, 'Sanitary Economy', pp.62-63. Cf. Briggs, 'Cholera', p.86; Gauldie, p.112; Kitson Clark, *Churchmen*, pp.204-205; Smith, *Health*, pp.230-241; Wohl, pp.118 and 125-127; S.E. Finer, *The Life and Times of Sir Edwin Chadwick*, 1952, pp.333-336; M. Callcott, 'The Challenge of Cholera: The Last Epidemic at Newcastle-upon-Tyne', *NH*, 20 (1984), pp.167 and 175-176.
254. Annals C and G; LGR 19 and 30 Oct., 3 and 14 Nov. and 1 Dec. 1853. See *Lamp*, 3 (1851), 302 for a reference to Dr J. Walsh as 'a young practitioner of high promise'. According to Branca, *Silent Sisterhood*, p.65, a doctor's fee was about £1 a visit. For Fr Daly and his mother, Martha, whom he left to look after them, see Census, 1851, MF 914, entry 178 and above, Ch.IV, p.112 and note 184. Both Dr Walsh and Fr Daly were Irish. Through Fr Gaudentius, help also came from the Prioress of Mount St Benedict near Rugeley, the Cistercians, the Poor Clares and other convents, monasteries and private individuals outside Manchester.
255. *Brit. Parl. Papers, Bills*, 1854[42], V.531, *A Bill To Secure to Persons Under Religious Vows the Free Exercise of Their Lawful Rights in the Disposal of Their Property*. Cf. Arnstein, p.63.
256. *Tablet*, 1 Apr. 1854.
257. *Tablet*, 27 May 1854.
258. *Tablet*, 27 May 1854; Corish, p.203.
259. See *Tablet*, 22 Mar. 1856 for the death of a Sr of Mercy in the Crimea. Cf. Arnstein, p.63; Chadwick, *Victorian Church*, 1, 509; Devas, pp.19-35; Norman, *English Catholic Church*, p.185; Schiefen, *Wiseman*, p.264; Smith, *Nightingale*, pp.25-27; Summers, pp.33-56.
260. Allchin, p.98.
261. Anson and Campbell, p.264.
262. Ingram, p.784. In 1851 4 of the Srs of the Infant Jesus had died from typhoid fever from bad drains in their new house in Abingdon St. The survivors amalgamated with Notre Dame in 1852 and so the sister who died in 1857 would have been a Notre Dame Sister. See Sr E. Bocock's Account.
263. *Manchester Courier*, 25 Apr. 1857.
264. Cf. Arnstein, p.65; Casteras, p.138; Flaxman, p.224; Norman, *Anti-Catholicism*, p.15.
265. According to LGR 24 June 1857 he had received letters of complaint from Srs

Clare and De Chantal.

266. LGR 21 Jan. 1855 and 24 June 1857.

267. LRC 5 July 1858.

268. BMR, 3 July 1858.

269. Ibid.

270. Anson and Campbell, p.232.

271. See the Victorian Exhibition in the Gallery of English Costume, Platt Hall, Rusholme, Manchester. Cf. Willett Cunnington, p.10.

272. Annals A/E and D.

273. Cf. LGR 13 Jan. 1854. See above, Ch.VI, Section 1.

274. LGR 7 July 1855. There were railway stations at Levenshulme, Ashton and Sutton, although not at Parr. It is clear from LGR 13 Apr. 1855 and Fr Bernardine's letter to E. Prout, 10 July 1855, that she occasionally travelled by train.

275. Eliot, *Middlemarch*, p.597. Cf. A. Briggs, *A Social History of England*, 1984, p.295 (will be cited as Briggs, *Social History*).

276. *Punch*, 18-19 (1850), 252. See AAB, Aston Box for a railway timetable on the back of which Fr Dominic had scribbled a note of some Baptisms he had performed.

277. See Ch.VI.

278. BMR, 3 July 1858. By the kindness of Bp Turner no mention was made of the investigation in the Chapter Minutes. I am indebted for this information to Mgr J. Allen, secretary to Bp T. Holland of Salford, and Canon E. Glynn, secretary to the Chapter of Canons, Salford Diocese.

279. LEP July 1858, to Fr Salvian Nardocci CP, known from his Small Chronicle, vol.2, pp.31-42 and Annals, 1890, pp.315-320 and as copied into Annals A/E and B and printed in *Records*, pp.18-19.

280. Annals C.

281. LBO'L 18 July 1858.

282. Annals C. See Census, 1861, MF 1268, entry 99, Microfilm Unit, MCL for 4 boarders.

NOTES TO CHAPTER VI

1. LGR 25 June 1852, to Fr R. Croskell.

2. LGR 10 Feb. 1855.

3. LGR 12 Sept. 1853; 19 Feb. 1854; 21 Jan., 11 May and 8 Aug. 1855; 24 June 1857.

4. LGR 9 Feb., 1 and 7 July 1854; 5 Sept. 1855.

5. LGR 26 Mar. and 7 and 11 July 1854; Ignatius, Diary, 15 Oct. 1853. A chapter on professions was added in Dec. 1852. See LGR [18-20] Dec. 1852 and Gaudentian Rule, continuation of Chapter XXII. In July 1853 Gaudentius made some changes on the recommendation of his provincial (LGR 23 July 1853). The next year he divided his Rule into three sections (LGR 26 Mar. 1854).

6. LGR 24 July 1854.

7. LGR 21 Jan., 10 Feb., 7 and 16 July 1855; Holy Family Rule [1852-1855], GA IV/A/2. Cf. above, Ch.III, p.265, note 56.

8. LGR 21 Sept. 1855.

9. LEP 25 Sept. 1855; Rules and Constitutions of the Sisters of the Holy Family [1855], GA IV/A/1.

10. LGR 23 Nov. 1855.

11. Holy Family Rule [1855-7?], GA IV/A/3; LWT 14 Jan. 1857; LGR 3 Feb. 1857; LIS 25 Feb. 1857, PPAS; Ignatius, Diary, 2 Jan., 16 Apr., 4, 17, 24 and 28

May, 6, 8, 9 and 12 June 1857; Annals A/E, B, C, F and *Records*, p.14; Letter to Fr
I. Spencer from the Secretary of Bp Goss of Liverpool, 6 Apr. 1857, Bp Goss'
Secretary's Letter Book, p.280, LRO RCLv 15.

12. Cf. Hill, pp.24 and 49.

13. *Rambler*, 7 (1851), 445; *Tablet*, 5 June 1852; Cf. *Rambler*, 1 (1854), 406. See
above, Ch.V, pp.142-145.

14. Cf. Letter to Sr M. Joseph [E. Prout] from the Secretary to Bp Goss of
Liverpool (LRO RCLv 15, p.127), 18 Mar. 1856: 'I am desired by the Bishop to say
that there is no portion of his flock whom he is more anxious to favour than those who
live in Convents because they achieve great good in teaching the Poor and he feels
assured their pious prayers will bring a Blessing on his Diocese...'.

15. SCR; Annals B and C. Cardinal Barnabò was the Prefect of *Propaganda Fide*,
the office of the Holy See that examined the Rules of religious orders.

16. LGR 6 Aug. 1862. LIS known only from this reply.

17. Young, *Ignatius*, p.174.

18. Original letter of Fr I. Spencer CP to the *Tablet*, 7 Jan. 1851, printed 18 Jan.,
Archivio Segreto Vaticano, Pius IX, no.605, English and Italian copies in Fr I.
Spencer's writing, LISR. See also Devine, *Ignatius*, p.398; Vanden Bussche, pp.137-
138; Young, *Ignatius*, p.182.

19. LISN 22 June 1852, to Mrs Canning.

20. Records, T 864, p.32, DAS, referring only to 'Fr Bernard'. Of the 'Fr
Bernards' in England at that time, Fr Bernard Smith of Oscott College seems the
likeliest (*Catholic Directory*, 1852, pp.86-107). See also Thureau-Dangin, 1, 237, 239
and 276.

21. *Tablet*, 26 June 1852.

22. Quoted in the *Lamp*, 4 (1852), 367.

23. Disraeli, *Coningsby*, p.76; *Lamp*, 4 (1852), 367.

24. *Lamp*, 4 (1852), 367.

25. *Illustrated London News*, 10 July 1852; *Lamp*, 4 (1852), 365-367 and 381-382;
Manchester Guardian, 3 July 1852; *Tablet*, 3 July 1852. Cf. Fr Gaudentius' account
of his mission at Rochdale, SMR, 24 June 1852, pp.72-73. See also Steele, 'Irish
Presence', pp.225-226; Wolffe, p.194; E.M. Abbott, *History of the Diocese of
Shrewsbury 1850-1886* (Farnworth, 1986), pp.97-98; W. Astle (ed.), '*Stockport
Advertiser*' *Centenary History of Stockport*, 1922, pp.136-141; H. Heginbotham,
Stockport: Ancient and Modern, 2 vols, 1882, 1, 104-106; P.T. Phillips, *The Sectarian
Spirit: Sectarianism, Society, and Politics in Victorian Cotton Towns* (Toronto, 1982),
pp.72, 89-90, 97, 102 and 105; P. Millward, 'The Stockport Riots of 1852: A Study
of Anti-Catholic and Anti-Irish Sentiment' in Swift and Gilley, *Victorian City*, pp.207-
224; and cf. Swift, 'Wolverhampton', p.87; D.G. Paz, 'Bonfire Night in Mid-
Victorian Northamptonshire: The Politics of a Popular Revolution', *HR*, 63, (1990),
328.

26. *Lamp*, 4 (1852), 381-382. Cf. Singleton, pp.23-26. See above, Ch.I, pp.14-17
and 175 for the centrality of the Eucharist and devotion to Mary in Paulacrucian
spirituality and E. Prout's Rule.

27. *Illustrated London News*, 10 July 1852.

28. *Tablet*, 3 July 1852 and 21 Aug. 1852.

29. *Manchester Guardian*, 14 July 1852.

30. *Lamp*, 4 (1852), 379, 461 and 521.

31. *Tablet*, 21 Aug. 1852.

32. Gaudentian Rule, ch.XXI, par.V.

33. Gaudentian Rule, ch.XXI, par.VI.

34. LGR 27 June 1853. In her notes for her revision of Fr Gaudentius' Rule in

1862-3, E. Prout, in describing the sisters' cape, wrote in brackets, 'We would like the scapular instead of cape'. In fact, she retained the cape, presumably out of deference for Fr Gaudentius' wishes.

35. LGR 27 June 1853. Cf. Willett Cunnington, pp.96 and 131. See above, Ch.V, p.150.

36. LGR 4 May 1853. Cf. Willett Cunnington, pp.60, 95, 130-131 and 165.

37. LGR 27 June 1853.

38. LGR 8 and 23 July 1853.

39. LGR 2 Aug. 1853; LRC 11 Aug. 1853.

40. LGR 27 June and 28 July 1853.

41. Letter known only from LGR 2 Aug. 1853.

42. LGR 2 Aug. 1853.

43. LRC 11 Aug. 1853.

44. LGR 13 Jan. and 9 Feb. 1854. See Sr M.A. McCann, 'Religious Orders of Women in the United States', *Catholic Historical Review*, 1 (1921-2), 317.

45. LGR 10 Feb. 1855.

46. LGR 3 Aug. 1860; Missions and Retreats 1854-1861 and 1861-1888, St Paul's Monastery, Pittsburgh, [PMR], Books 1 and 2 [bound together], 19 July 1859 and 11 July 1860, PPA.

47. LGR 3 Aug. 1860. Cf. LGR 21 July and 17 Dec. 1852; 4 May 1853.

48. See Ch.III, section 2.

49. E. Prout, Notes on the Rule, 1862-3, written on disused copies of her *Parr Hall Prospectus*, GA I/B/5/a (will be cited as E. Prout, 1863 Rule Notes). Cf. *Passionist Rule*, pp.13-15. The novices' white cross was that first envisaged by Paul of the Cross (*Words from the Heart*, p.12 and see above Ch.I, p.14). For underwear she prescribed a flannel tunic, which contemporaries recommended as most healthy. Cf. Willett Cunnington, pp.125-126. See also Williams, *Sellon*, p.24 for her sisters' also having a white cap with black strings and, for out of doors, a cloak and a large, black bonnet and black veil.

50. Holy Family Rule, 1863, rough copy in English and another in Italian, both in Fr Ignatius Spencer's writing, GA I/B/5/f. Will be cited as English 1863 Rule.

51. LGR 19 Jan. 1852.

52. LGR 11 Apr. 1866. Cf. Murray, p.357 for the contemporary idea that shop assistants were more genteel than factory workers.

53. LGR 8 June 1868. M. Mary Margaret Chambers was Superior General from 1867-1885.

54. Young, *Dominic in England*, pp.81-82. See LGR 20 and 27 Oct. 1857 for two examples of his bad memory.

55. See *Brit. Parl. Papers, Reports of Commissioners*, vol.4, pt 2, 1850[1248], XXIII, pt 2, *The Mining Districts*, pp.15-16; *Manchester Guardian*, 14 Jan. 1852; Grindrod, passim.

56. Kay Shuttleworth, *Four Periods*, p.45. Cf. Brotherton, pp.14 and 16; Engels, pp.169-170; P. Gaskell, pp.63-64, 68, 70-71, 103-104 and 133.

57. *Factory Report*, Oct. 1849, pp.3-5, 7 and 22-23.

58. Reach, p.12.

59. *Factory Report*, Oct. 1849, p.5.

60. *Factory Report*, Apr. 1850, 1850[1239], XXIII.261, p.5.

61. Carpenter, *Conditions*, pp.16-17 and 21.

62. Reach, pp.57-62.

63. Annals A/E and D.

64. *Factory Report*, Oct. 1850, 1851[1304], XXIII, pt 2, 217, p.4.

65. *Manchester Guardian*, 21 Jan. 1852.

66. *Factory Report*, Apr. 1853, 1852-3[1642], XL.533, p.21.
67. *Factory Report*, Oct. 1859, 1860[2594], XXXIV.407, pp.48 and 52-53.
68. HMR, 1860, entry 103. Cf. BMR, 1860, entry 52.
69. LGR 18 June 1861; *Factory Report*, Oct. 1861, 1862[2923], XXII.221, pp.12-13; Apr. 1863, 1863[3206], XVIII.587, pp.18-19; *Ashton and Stalybridge Reporter*, 4 Jan. 1862 (will be cited as *Ashton Reporter*); *Manchester Courier*, 16 May 1863, MF MC29, Microfilm Unit, MCL; Bowman, pp.446-455; Farnie, 'Cotton Famine', pp.154-156; and *The English Cotton Industry and the World Market 1815-1896* (Oxford, 1979), pp.135-141 and 156-161; Kirk, *Reformism*, pp.115-116 and 121-124; Mathias, *First Industrial Nation*, p.295; Rose, *English Poor Law*, pp.142-143 and 157-158; 'Disappearing Pauper', p.61; *The Relief of Poverty 1834-1914*, 1972, pp.39-40 (will be cited as Rose, *Relief of Poverty*); 'Rochdale Man and the Stalybridge Riot, The Relief and Control of the Unemployed During the Lancashire Cotton Famine' in Donajgrodzki, pp.185-189 (will be cited as Rose, 'Rochdale Man'); and 'The Crisis of Poor Relief in England 1860-1890' in W.J. Mommsen (in collaboration with W. Mock), *The Emergence of the Welfare State in Britain and Germany 1850-1950*, 1981, p.57; Torrens, pp.16-17 and 38; M. Ellison, *Support for Secession; Lancashire and the American Civil War* (Chicago, 1972), pp.15, 21-25 and 43-44; W.O. Henderson, *The Lancashire Cotton Famine 1861-1865* (Manchester, 1934), pp.1 and 6; N. Longmate, *The Hungry Mills*, 1978, pp.26-27, 71, 74 and 158 (will be cited as Longmate); T. Mackay, *A History of the English Poor Law 1834-Present Day*, 1899, pp.389-390; J. Watts, *The Facts of the Cotton Famine*, 1866, 'Diagram of Fluctuations', front of book, pp.105 and 114 (will be cited as Watts); H.W. McCready, 'The Cotton Famine in Lancashire', *THSLC*, 106 (1954), 130; D.J. Oddy, 'Urban Famine in Nineteenth-Century Britain: The Effect of the Lancashire Cotton Famine on Working-Class Diet and Health', *Econ.HR*, 36 (1983), 72-79 (will be cited as Oddy).
70. Watts, p.153.
71. Cf. Longmate, p.121; Rose, *English Poor Law*, pp.150-152; *Relief of Poverty*, pp.39-40; and 'Rochdale Man', pp.190-192.
72. See C. Evans, 'Unemployment and the Making of the Feminine during the Lancashire Cotton Famine' in P. Hudson and W.R. Lee, *Women's Work and the Family Economy in Historical Perspective* (Manchester, 1990), pp.254 and 258 (will be cited as Evans, 'Unemployment'); and 'The Separation of Work and Home? The Case of the Lancashire Textiles 1825-1865', a Ph.D. thesis, University of Manchester, 1990, pp.293-339 (will be cited as Evans, thesis).
73. *Manchester Courier*, 13 and 20 Sept. 1862, MF MC28, Microfilm Unit, MCL; *Factory Report*, Oct. 1862, 1863[3076], XVIII.437, pp.24-26; Sir J. Kay Shuttleworth, *Thoughts and Suggestions on Certain Social Problems Contained Chiefly in Addresses to Meetings of Workmen in Lancashire*, 1873, pp.121-122 (will be cited as Kay-Shuttleworth, *Thoughts and Suggestions*); Longmate, pp.174-182; Rose, 'Rochdale Man', p.192.
74. *Manchester Courier*, 4 and 25 Oct. 1862.
75. Bp Vaughan's sermon at Fr Cromblehome's Requiem, *Ashton Reporter*, 26 Jan. 1884. Fr William J. Cromblehome, born at Chipping near Preston on 28 Jan. 1825, later entered the novitiate of the De La Salle Brothers and after profession taught in their schools in Liverpool and Bolton. After a time he felt called to the priesthood. Dispensed from his religious vows, he was sent by Bp Turner to study at Roulers and Bruges. Ordained in 1857, he was sent to Ashton in 1858. He built St Ann's church in 1859. See also Glover and Andrew, pp.330-332 and 341. For a photograph of Fr Cromblehome in his later years, see J. Cassidy, *St Ann's Catholic Church, Burlington St, Ashton-under-Lyne* (Ashton, 1978), a pamphlet, centre page.

76.   Ignatius, Diary, 16 Feb. 1858 and 5 Apr. 1861. For his 'little missions', see above, Ch.VII, p.211; Devine, *Ignatius*, pp.464-468; Vanden Bussche, pp.213-240; Young, *Ignatius* pp.238-246.

77.   LISR 26 Oct. 1862; SCR; Annals C.

78.   LISR 7 Nov. 1862. See also Ignatius, Diary, 6 and 7 Nov. 1862.

79.   Annals C. Cf. SCR; Annals B and F; *Records*, p.20.

80.   SCR; Ignatius, Diary, 21 Nov. 1862. Cf. *Lamp, Supplement*, Mar. 1852, pp.9-13 for a Prize Essay on 'How Woman May Best Fulfill Her Religious and Domestic Duties as a Wife and Mother'.

81.   SCR; Ignatius, Diary, 22 Nov. 1862. See above p.173.

82.   Bp Vaughan's sermon, *Ashton Reporter*, 26 Jan. 1884.

83.   SCR. She brought Sr Mary Margaret Chambers, who had been on retreat on 22 Nov., following her profession of vows on the 21st.

84.   SCR; *Ashton Reporter*, 15 and 22 Nov. 1862.

85.   *Manchester Courier*, 15 Nov. 1862.

86.   *Ashton Reporter*, 26 Jan. 1884. For the sewing schools Fr P. Van Meulen (sometimes anglicised as 'Vermeulen') organised in St Mary's, Ashton, see *Harvest*, 12 (1899), 37.

87.   Annals C.

88.   *Factory Report*, Oct. 1863, 1864[3309], XXII.555, p.68.

89.   Longmate, p.179. Cf. Evans, 'Unemployment', p.260.

90.   Clothing was distributed on 6 Dec. 1862 and 13 May 1863. See *Factory Reports*, Oct. 1862, p.25; April 1863, 1863[3206], XVIII.587, p.19; St Ann's Infants' School Logbook (St Ann's primary school, Ashton) for clothing distribution from 17-21 Dec. 1863; and St Ann's Girls' School Logbook (St Ann's presbytery, Ashton), for references to a distribution of clothing in the school on 23 Nov. 1863 and to payment of the sewing girls on 20 Nov. and 4 Dec. 1863.

91.   Annals C.

92.   *Factory Report*, April 1863, p.19; *Harvest*, 12 (1899), 37.

93.   By 29 Dec. 1862, the Borough Relief Committee had paid out £1,368 6s. 8d. to the women and girls in 11 sewing classes (*Ashton Reporter*, 3 Jan. 1863). According to SCR the sisters taught 400 girls and women; according to Annals B and F and *Records* p.20, 500-600. In Jan. 1863 there were 1,941 women and girls in sewing classes; in April 2,348 (*Factory Report*, Apr. 1863, p.18). See also Kay-Shuttleworth, *Thoughts and Suggestions*, pp.121-122; Evans, 'Unemployment', p.258; Hewitt, p.80; Longmate, p.181.

94.   LISR 30 Nov. 1862.

95.   *Ashton Reporter*, 24 and 31 Jan. 1863; Kay Shuttleworth, *Thoughts and Suggestions*, p.117. See also I. Haynes, *Cotton In Ashton* (Tameside, 1987), p.4.

96.   *Ashton Reporter*, 10 Jan. 1863. See Longmate, p.155; Rose, 'Rochdale Man', p.195; Torrens, pp.137-138; R.A. Arnold, *The History of the Cotton Famine*, 1864, p.347.

97.   See Reach, p.72; Joyce, *Work, Society and Politics*, pp.4-5, 175, 177-178, 241, 245-246, 249-250 and 256-257; and also 'Factory Politics', pp.525-553; Lock, thesis, pp.187-188 and 276. Note also *Manchester Courier*, 25 Apr. 1863 for an Orange meeting, at which members spoke 'with great energy' on the objects of their association.

98.   *Manchester Courier*, 28 Mar. 1863; Sharp, p.202. Cf. Rose, 'Rochdale Man', pp.193-194; A. Howe, *The Cotton Masters 1830-1860* (Oxford, 1984), p.175; B. Ellinger, 'The Cotton Famine 1861-1864', *Economic History*, 3 (1934-7), 166.

99.   *Ashton Reporter*, 16 May 1863.

100. *Ashton Reporter*, 7 and 21 Nov. 1863.

101. SCR.

102. Ignatius, Diary, 16 Dec. 1862.

103. Annals C.

104. SCR. Cf. Kay Shuttleworth, *Thoughts and Suggestions*, pp.121-122. See Evans, 'Unemployment', pp.263-264 for a discussion on lady visitors and the social subordination implied in the term 'girls'. See also Chapple, p.121; McCready, 'E. Gaskell', p.147.

105. A. Munro, 'Our Unemployed Females and What May Best Be Done For Them', *TMSS*, 1863, p.29; *Manchester Courier*, 21 Mar. 1863. Cf. P. Gaskell, p.166.

106. Annals C.

107. P. Gaskell, pp.63-64, 68, 73-74 and 93-94. Cf. Gaskell, *Mary Barton*, pp.121 and 344.

108. Gadian, p.53.

109. Brotherton, pp.16-17.

110. Brotherton, pp.4 and 15; P. Gaskell, pp.73-74; *Bolton Weekly Guardian*, 19 Aug. 1876, GA II/A/1/a-m; H.K.B., XII, General Compilation I, p.259, PPAUC.

111. *Brit. Parl. Papers, Reports from Commissioners*, vol.2, pt 1, 1851, XXIII, pt 1. 388, *Report on the Sanitary Condition of Agar Town, St Pancras*; vol. 17, pt 1, 1854[1780], XXXV, pt 1, 115 [but printed in XXXV, part 2], *Common Lodging Houses*, p.16; 1857[2224], XVI, pt 1, 19, *Report on Common Lodging Houses*, pp. 5-6 and 12-13. Cf. *Brit. Parl. Papers, Accounts and Papers*, vol.22, pt 1, 1852-53[237], LXXVIII, pt 1. 525, *The Common Lodging Houses Act*; 1852-53[994], LXVIII, pt 2. 553, *The Operation of the Common Lodging House Act*; 1857, session 2, XLI.119, *Common Lodging Houses*, Part II, pp.4-5 and 9-10; Engels, p.102; P. Gaskell, pp.141-142; Mercer, pp.172-173; Reach, pp.52-53; *Tablet*, 19 Feb. 1853. See also A. Oates, 'A Night in a Common Lodging House', *Harvest*, 1 (1887), 12-16.

112. Hughes, in Beck, p.19. See also Gilley, *Newman*, p.263; Ker, *Newman*, p.344; Lewis, *Evangelical Mission*, p.199.

113. Inglis, p.125.

114. English 1863 Rule; Holy Family Rule, 1865, Ch.1, a handwritten document, dated 2 June 1865, GA I/B/5/e. This unfinished manuscript is a copy of the Rule Ignatius took to Rome in 1863, with some slight alterations later proposed, at his request, by Bp Ullathorne of Birmingham. Will be cited as Holy Family Rule, 1865. Cf. *Rules and Constitutions of the Congregation of the Sisters of the Most Holy Cross and Passion of Our Lord Jesus Christ*, 1887 [final approbation from the Holy See], (reprint Dublin, 1954), pp.14-15.

115. Davidson and Others, p.167; Mahood, pp.54-55, 77-80 and 84; Prochaska, *Women and Philanthropy*, pp.37 and 146; and 'Female Philanthropy', p.81; Young and Ashton, pp.84 and 217-219; O. Anderson, 'The Growth of Christian Militarism in Mid-Victorian Britain', *EHR*, 86 (1971), 59.

116. *Tablet*, 12 Aug. 1843.

117. *Rambler*, 8 (1851), 166-167. Cf. Ashton, p.59; T. Worthington, 'Some Further Remarks on the Homes of the Poor, and the Means of Improving Their Condition', *TMSS*, 1861, pp.101-103.

118. *Manchester Guardian*, 14 Jan. 1852.

119. Burn, p.119; Prochaska, 'Female Philanthropy', pp.79-80.

120. Rose, '"Gender At Work"', p.127; Lown, *Women and Industrialization*, pp.143-144 and 'Not So Much A Factory, More A Form of Patriarchy: Gender and Class During Industrialisation' in E. Gamarnikow and Others (eds), *Gender, Class and Work*, 1983, pp.39-40.

121. SCR, an insertion between pp.16 and 17 possibly in a different hand.

122. SCR; LISR 30 Nov. 1862, to provincial; LISN 18 Dec. 1862, to Ambrose

Phillipps; LISR 23 Dec. 1862, to provincial; Ignatius, Diary, 7 Dec. 1862.

123. At 12 Folds Rd. SCR. Cf. LGR 5 Oct. 1856 for his asking Bp Turner to give them a house nearer than Levenshulme to an industrial area.

124. *Factory Report*, Oct. 1865, 1866[3622], XXIV.251, p.61.

125. SCR.

126. SCR; An undated and unsigned fragment, roughly written, preserved in the General Archives, Northampton but not yet filed. The writing and style suggest the authorship of Fr I. Spencer, the contents about Feb. 1864. Raffles were a popular form of Catholic self-help. See *Lamp*, 1 (1850), 488 for a raffle to build a Catholic church in Chorley; 2 (1851), 225, for a Manchester raffle to build a Catholic church and school at Barnes Green; 3 (1851-2), 253 and 296; 4 (1852), 58, 71 and 435 for a raffle for oil-paintings in Manchester; and *St Helens Newspaper*, 20 Dec. 1862 for a Christmas Raffle at St Anne's Passionist parish, Sutton. The prizes included gold watches, brooches etc.

127. Salvian, Annals, 1890, pp.148-149.

128. Salvian, Diary, 30 May 1868.

129. LISN 15 Jan. 1854.

130. Charitable Works.

131. LISR 21 and 26 Oct. 1862; Annals F; *Records*, p.20.

132. LISR 9 Nov. 1862.

133. See above, Ch.I, p.14.

134. LISR 30 Nov. 1862.

135. See above, Ch.III, pp.62-65. For Fr G. Rossi's having inculcated devotion to Paul of the Cross, see LGR 28 July and 19 Oct. 1853.

136. LISR 7 Nov. 1862.

137. E. Prout, 1863 Rule Notes.

138. In 1860. Cf. LGR 25 Nov. 1859; SCR; Annals C and B.

139. They held the name unofficially, and it was used even in official negotiations with Rome, from 1864. See rough copy of Letter of Fr Alphonsus O'Neill [LAO'N] to the Passionist general, n.d. but 1872-1874, GA I/B/2/g and see above, Ch.VII, p.207.

140. E. Prout, 1863 Rule Notes; Gaudentian Rule, ch.I, par.1; *Passionist Rule*, chs I, XX and XXI.

141. E. Prout, 1863 Rule Notes; *Passionist Rule*, chs XX and XXI. See also above, Ch.I, pp.14-17.

142. Cf. *Passionist Rule*, ch.VI.

143. Cf. *Passionist Rule*, ch. XI.

144. LISR 9 Nov. 1862; Ignatius, Diary, 29 Nov and 1-4 Dec. 1862. See also Register of Baptisms, 1855-1866, St Ann's, Ashton-under-Lyne, entries 27 Nov. 1862 and 15 and 28 Dec. 1862 for 7 Baptisms he performed.

145. LISR 23 Dec. 1862. Cf. Kirk, *Reformism*, pp.123-4; Oddy, p.82.

146. LISR 23 Dec. 1862; Ignatius, Diary, 29 Dec. 1862 and 2 Jan. 1863.

147. Ignatius, Diary, 6 Apr. 1863.

148. LISN 11 Apr. 1863.

149. Holy Family Rule, 1865. Cf. English 1863 Rule.

150. LISN 11 Apr. 1863; Ignatius, Diary, 10-11 Apr. 1863.

151. Ignatius, Diary, 17 Apr. 1863; LISN 14 June 1863; *Records*, pp.20-21; Young, *Ignatius*, pp.258-260.

152. *Prescot Reporter*, 1 Nov. 1862, Local Studies Library, St Helens.

153. *St Helens Newspaper*, 18 Apr. 1863.

154. Fragment of a letter, quoted in a letter of an unknown writer, 20 Nov. 1862. Box: Sutton Locality, PPAS.

155. *Prescot Reporter*, 29 Mar. and 5 Apr. 1862.

156. *Prescot Reporter*, 29 Nov. 1862.

157. *St Helens Weekly News*, 14 May 1862 (on microfilm: *St Helens Newspaper*), Local Studies Library, St Helens. See above, Ch.IV, p.117.

158. *St Helens Weekly News*, 21 May and 8 Nov. 1862.

159. *St Helens Weekly News*, 26 Nov. 1862; Barker and Harris, p.372. For Wigan, cf. Evans, thesis, pp.301-302.

160. LISR 23 Dec. 1862.

161. SCR; Manton, p.63. See also Frazer, p.314; Hellerstein and Others, pp.113-116; Smith, *Health*, p.291; G. Cronjé, 'Tuberculosis and Mortality Decline in England and Wales, 1851-1910' in Woods and Woodward, p.83 (will be cited as Cronjé),

162. SCR. E. Prout could not have paid the expenses herself. For Passionists from England going for health reasons to Bordeaux, where they had a monastery, see Salvian, Diary, 31 Oct. 1859 and 15 Apr. 1864. In Jan. 1864 Brother Joseph Van Riet from Broadway went to the new Passionist house in Paris for his health. See Salvian, Early Novices, no.19; *Origine e primi progressi dell'Ospizio de Parigi Fondazione 1863* [Paris *Platea*, 1863-1924], Box: St Joseph's Province, 2-B-2, PGAR.

163. LISN 11 April 1863.

164. SCR. There is no indication of where she stayed in Paris. The Augustinian convent is a possibility, as it had a connection with Fr I. Spencer, as, according to the *Tablet*, 31 Jan. 1857, the superior there was the sister of E.J. Canning of Foxcote, husband of Ignatius' cousin, Mrs Canning (who had died in 1856). There was an English convent of Carmelites at Rue d'Enfer, Paris in 1863 (R. Addington (ed.), *Faber - Selected Letters*, 1974, pp.340-341). It is possible that E. Prout stayed at the convent of the Assumption, Rue de l'Assumption, Autevil, since Fr S. Nardocci's sister stayed there when she visited Paris with him in 1867 (Salvian, Autobiography, vol.2 and Diary, both June 1867). Research in the archives of these religious orders, however, has failed to show any mention of E. Prout's visit. I am nevertheless indebted for their co-operation to the Mother Prioress, Canonesses of St Augustine, Ealing, London; Mother Abbess, Carmelite Convent, Ware; M. Abbess, Carmelite Monastery, Clamart, France; Little Sisters of the Assumption, Lancaster Rd, London; Sisters of the Assumption, Kensington Sq., London; Convent of the Assumption, Autevil, Paris. The Passionists opened a house in Paris at 39 Rue de Berri in May-June 1863, slightly too late for Elizabeth's visit but she may have stayed with 'Mr and Mrs Blount', who, according to the *Platea*, Paris, pp.1-3, were kind to the Passionists at this time and who were possibly related to Sr Gertrude Blount.

165. SCR.

166. LISN 7 June 1863, a copy.

167. Ignatius, Diary, 28 Apr. and 15 May 1863; LISN 14 June 1863.

168. Petition of M. Mary Joseph (Prout) to Pius IX, 27 May-13 June 1863, English translation in Fr I. Spencer's writing, endorsed by Cardinal Barnabò for the Holy See and signed and sealed by Bishop W. Turner and his secretary, Canon Benoit on 17 Aug. 1863, GA I/B/6/a. The days for gaining the indulgences were: days of clothing and profession; titular feast of the chapel of the convent; Christmas Day; the Circumcision of Our Lord; Sunday within the octave of the Epiphany; the Presentation, Purification and Visitation of the Blessed Virgin; the feast of St Joseph on 19 Mar. and also of his Patronage on the third Sunday after Easter.

169. LISN 14 June 1863. Cf. Annals B and C; *Records*, pp.20-21.

170. SCR.

171. LWT 25 June 1863.

172. LEP 25 Sept.1855; Spencer, *Passionist Spirituality*, p.7.

173. SCR; Annals A/E and C.

174. SCR; Salvian, Diary, 3-12 July 1863; BMR, p.23, entry 9; Broadway Arrivals and Departures, 2 July 1863; *Records*, p.22.

175. SCR.

176. Cronjé, p.79; Neff, p.121; Vicinus, *A Widening Sphere*, p.xv; Willett Cunnington, p.123.

177. Cf. A.O.J. Cockshut, *Truth To Life, The Art of Biography in the Nineteenth Century*, 1974, p.51; E. Jay, *The Religion of the Heart: Anglican Evangelicalism and the Nineteenth-Century Novel* (Oxford, 1979), pp.154-168 and 255; H.D.Rack, 'Evangelical Endings: Death Beds in Evangelical Biography', *BJRULM*, 74 (1992), 39-56.

178. Ignatius, Diary, 2-3 Aug. 1863; LISR 29 July 1863.

179. LISN 13 Oct. 1863; SCR; Annals G; *Records*, p.22. Cf. Ignatius, Diary, 17 Aug. 1863.

180. Ignatius, Diary, 24 Aug. 1863.

181. SCR; Broadway Arrivals and Departures, 27 Aug. 1863; Ignatius, Diary, 27 Aug. 1863.

182. Ignatius, Diary, 6-7 Oct. 1863.

183. LWT 12 Oct. 1863.

184. LISN 13 Oct. 1863.

185. SCR, which do not name the sister. Identified as Sr Catherine Scanlon because her name is missing from the roll of those present.

186. SCR; Ignatius, Diary, 23 Oct. 1863; LISR 26 Oct. 1863; Annals B and C; *Records*, pp.22-23.

187. Bp W. Turner, Certificate of Confirmation of Mother Mary Joseph (Prout) as first Superioress General, 23 Oct. 1863, GA I/B/1/a.

188. Note of Election Results, in Fr I. Spencer's writing, GA II/A/1/a; LISR 26 Oct. 1863; SCR; Annals B and C.

189. LISR 26 Oct. 1863.

190. SCR. Cf. Ignatius, Diary, 21 Nov. 1863 and note also 3 Jan. 1864; Annals F; *Records*, p.23.

191. LISN 18 Nov. 1863. For Mrs Isabella Hutchison, see Gordon Gorman, p.146.

192. LISR 27 Nov. 1863.

193. SCR; *Records*, p.23. Cf. *Words from the Heart*, pp.62, 82, 85, 91, 95, 98, 105, 117, 121, 125, 128, 132 and 141; Bialas, texts, pp.91-92, 124 and 152.

194. Cf. *Words from the Heart*, pp.105 and 117; Bialas, *Mysticism*, pp.284, 289 and 298-299; Strambi, 2, 72 and 77.

195. SCR; *Records*, p.23. Cf. Strambi, 2, 25; [Burke], *Paul*, pp.100-102.

196. SCR.

197. Ignatius, Diary, 9 Jan. 1864. See an envelope in the PPAS, marked: 'A.D. 1863, Fr Ignatius Spencer C.P., Faculties to hear Nuns' Confessions, Sutton Convent, St Helens, Lancs.' Cf. LRO RCLv 15, Bp Goss' Secretary's Letter Bk, p.385 for a letter, 4 Sept. 1863 to Fr I. Spencer, giving him these faculties.

198. SCR; *Records*, pp.23-24. Cf. LISN 18 Nov. 1863; Ignatius, Diary, 30 Dec. 1863; LRO RCLv 44, *School Inspection Returns*, 1864, St Joseph's, Peasley Cross. See also above, Ch.VII, pp.211-212.

199. SCR. Cf. Smith, *Health*, p.290.

200. SCR.

201. *Obituary of Sr Helen James*, 1926 [newspaper], GA IV/D/1.

202. Ignatius, Diary, 11 Jan. 1864.

203. LWT 12 Jan. 1864.

204. SCR. Cf. Bowden, p.444 for a photograph's being taken of Fr Faber's corpse in Sept. 1863.

205. Elizabeth Prout's *Death Certificate*, General Register House, London, taken from Register of Deaths, Prescot, 1864, entry 34.
206. Mass Book, 1855-1882, St Saviour's, Broadway, 12 Jan. 1864, PPAS, in Fr Salvian's writing: 'Five Masses for the repose of the soul of Mother Mary Joseph *defuncta - Charitatis conceda.*'
207. Salvian, Diary, 13 Jan. 1864.
208. Ignatius, Diary, 13 Jan. 1864.
209. SCR; St Anne's Burial Register B, entry 149, St Anne's Retreat, Sutton.

NOTES TO CHAPTER VII

1.   LGR 23 Jan. 1849. Cf. Bialas, *Mysticism*, p.159.
2.   LGR 24 Sept. 1852.
3.   LGR 19 Oct. 1853.
4.   LGR 25 Feb. 1854.
5.   LGR 29 Mar. 1854 and 14 Aug. 1855.
6.   LGR 4 June 1853. According to Annals C, during the fever crisis of 1853-4, on one occasion when she had no money for bread, on invoking St Joseph's help Elizabeth suddenly found 15s. in a bag in which she would never have dreamt of putting money.
7.   Letter known only from his reply, 9 Feb. 1854. Cf. *Words from the Heart*, p.21.
8.   LGR 9 Feb. 1854. Cf. LGR 19 Feb. 1854.
9.   Letter known only from his reply, 19 Feb. 1855.
10.   Letter known only from his reply, 8 Mar. 1855.
11.   *Words from the Heart*, p.46 and cf. p.116.
12.   LGR 8 Mar. 1855.
13.   Annals A/E.
14.   LGR 8 Aug. 1855.
15.   LEP 12 Sept. 1855.
16.   LGR 23 Jan. 1849. On St Paul of the Cross and the will of God see *Words from the Heart*, pp.18, 32, 44, 53, 68, 72, 77, 102, 111, 120, 126-127, 135, 138, 140, 143, 153-154, 156 and 160; Bialas, texts, pp.60-62, 91, 105 and 146. Cf. Bialas, *Mysticism*, p.284 and see also pp.152-162 and 176-177.
17.   LEP 12 Sept. 1855. Cf. *Words from the Heart*, p.124 for Paul's similar concern that those giving even simple catechetical instruction must first 'very, very carefully' study Christian Doctrine. See also Bialas, *Mysticism*, p.98.
18.   LEP 12 Sept. 1855.
19.   LEP 12 Sept. 1855. Cf. *Words from the Heart*, p.124.
20.   LEP 12 Sept. 1855. Cf. *Words from the Heart*, pp.31 and 139 for Paul's consciousness of his own sinfulness and, for his direction on such fears of hell, Bialas, p.99: 'Never worry about hell.... The Lord... will never abandon you, even though... it may seem you are abandoned or, indeed, damned.' Cf. Bradley, pp. 23 and 188; Houghton, p.63; McLeod, pp.217 and 225; Willett Cunnington, p.129; G. Rowell, *Hell and the Victorians* (Oxford, 1974), pp.1, 13 and 171-173.
21.   *Words from the Heart*, p.116. Cf. Bialas, *Mysticism*, p.170.
22.   LEP one of two letters dated 25 Sept. 1855. Its contents refer to LGR 21 Sept., which she received on Saturday 22 Sept. 1855. She had it ready to post when LGR 24 Sept. 1855 arrived. She then enclosed her first letter with her immediate reply to his second. Her first letter is significant in testifying to her habitual meditation on the Passion. Cf. Bialas, *Mysticism*, pp.210-212.

23. LEP 4 Oct. 1855.
24. Ibid.
25. Ibid. Cf. *Words from the Heart*, p.133, 'Every effort should be made to pray in pure and living faith, to seek God alone...'; p.138, 'You must... live only for God and in God'; and pp.140-141.
26. LEP 4 Oct. 1855. Cf. Bialas, texts, pp.62-65 and 125-126.
27. LEP 4 Oct. 1855. For St Paul of the Cross on spiritual desolation and distractions in prayer see *Words from the Heart*, pp.19-21; 24-25, 27-29, 44, 58-59, 82, 85, 105-106, 120, 132 and 141; p.89 for Paul on the presence of God; and cf. p.126 for his direction in 1736, '... even here the devil may intervene to hold the soul conceited. It is better not to hold a high opinion of your own feelings or intentions; instead be watchful and stand in fear....'
28. LEP 4 Oct. 1855.
29. LEP 7 Oct. 1855.
30. SCR; LGR 17 Dec. 1855, to Fr Ignatius Spencer, a copy.
31. SCR.
32. Ignatius, Diary, 23 Nov. 1855; LGR 23 Nov. 1855.
33. LGR 23 Nov. 1855.
34. LGR 17 Dec. 1855, to Fr Ignatius Spencer. As mentioned in the Introduction, the photograph, marked 'St Helens', was discovered by Revd Mother Josephine Murray under the dust sheet of paper at the bottom of her desk about 1950. There is a second, unidentified, sister, standing slightly behind Elizabeth's right shoulder. Elizabeth Prout is clearly the foundress. She is shown seated, the Rule in her hands. A crucifix on a table beside her denotes her Paulacrucian spirituality. Her religious habit, rosary beads and Sign are clearly visible and identical with those described in her notes for her 1862-3 revision of the Rule and also with those exhumed with her bones from St Anne's cemetery, Sutton in 1973. The photo is not dated but the occasion of Fr Gaudentius' departure suggests a reason for its being taken: so that he could show the habit to prospective American postulants. It was not a keepsake. Fr Gaudentius did not give Elizabeth one of himself. Neither the Passionists nor E. Prout's sisters were allowed to have their photos taken without special permission. The earliest extant photograph of Fr Gaudentius Rossi is in a group of capitulars with the Pittsburgh community on 12 July 1866 at the end of the provincial chapter. See H.K. Barr, vol.XI, Records of the Retreat of St Paul's, Pittsburgh 1852-1882, p.36; and Box, Pittsburgh, St Paul's, PPAUC. This photo shows Fr Gaudentius aged 49, of medium build and with an attractive smile. The photograph of him shown in *Records*, opposite the title page and reproduced in this book shows an older man with white hair. It must therefore have been taken in North America, possibly at the sisters' request to have a photograph of their founder and perhaps c.1877.
35. LGR 9 Oct. 1855.
36. Ignatius, Diary, 18-30 Nov. 1855; SCR.
37. Ignatius, Diary, 27 Dec. 1855 - 8 Jan. 1856.
38. SCR; Ignatius, Diary, 1856.
39. Ignatius, Diary, 25 Dec. 1856 - 2 Jan. 1857; LISN 11 Jan. 1857.
40. LISN 11 Jan. 1857.
41. Letter known only from Fr Ignatius' reply, LISN 1 Feb. 1857.
42. LISN 22 June 1852, to Mrs Canning. As did Paul of the Cross. See Bialas, *Mysticism*, p.153.
43. LISN 1 Feb. 1857.
44. LIS 25 Feb. 1857, PPAS.
45. Letter known only from the SCR. Since Fr Pius Devine quoted this passage, *Ignatius*, p.462, it seems likely that the letter was given to the Passionists and has

subsequently been lost.

46. SCR. For Paul's similar experiences see *Words from the Heart*, pp.115, 135-136 and 155.

47. Devine, *Ignatius*, p.489. He heard of the incident from one of the sisters, presumably M. Winefride Lynch or Sr Mary Paul Taylor, when he was collecting materials for his book. His informant had heard of it in confidence from Elizabeth Prout but was willing to divulge it to Fr Pius in the interests of demonstrating Ignatius' holiness. Pius gave her account verbatim. See also Young, *Ignatius*, pp.269-270. He dates the incident 1864 but from late 1863 Elizabeth Prout was too ill to walk and so could not have been 'sent for', as the account describes. Late 1862 or early 1863, when they were working together on the Rule, would appear better dating.

48. Devine, *Ignatius*, p.489.

49. Cf. Bialas, *Mysticism*, p.329.

50. The card, GA I/B/1/h, consists of a red cross, painted on thin, white card, surmounting a square piece of white card. In addition to the verse, Elizabeth wrote, 'A happy feastday to my dearest Sister M. Patrick. Pray for poor M. Joseph. This is your Patrick's Cross. May you never have a more ponderous one. 1862.'

51. LEP 25 Sept. 1855, 2 letters.

52. LGR 19 Mar. 1855. Note also the assertion in Annals A/E that Elizabeth followed Fr Gaudentius' advice 'most faithfully'.

53. Gaudentian Rule, ch. 2, par. VI. Cf. 1953 *Regulations*, p.12; *Community Prayers*, c.1952, pp.8-9.

54. LGR 10 May 1854; 2 June 1859; LEP 25 Sept. 1855.

55. Gaudentian Rule, ch. 3, par. I; LGR 4 Nov. 1850.

56. Letter known only from his reply, LGR 14 May 1858. Cf. LEP 12 and 25 Sept. 1855.

57. LEP early July 1858, to Fr Salvian Nardocci CP, '... St Joseph, Our Blessed Lady, and I don't suppose the Infant was far behind inspired Fr Bernard....' For Paul's devotion to 'the Holy Infant, our dear Mother Mary and also good St Joseph', see *Words from the Heart*, p.133.

58. LGR 11 Apr. 1866. See PPAS for a letter from M. Winefride Lynch, 17 Jan. 1864, to Fr Ignatius Spencer, asking if he was notifying Fr Gaudentius of Elizabeth Prout's death. There is no trace of a reply to either M. Winefride or Fr Ignatius Spencer. Sr Anne Joachim went to N. America in 1864. Her 'misconduct' lay in telling Fr Anthony Calandri CP and others that she had gone to N. America at Fr Gaudentius' wish and that he had paid her fare. See LGR 25 June and 8 Nov. 1864, to M. Winefride.

59. LGR 24 July 1854.

60. LGR 19 July 1855.

61. LGR 8 Aug. 1855.

62. LGR 14 and 23 Aug. 1855.

63. LGR 23 and 25 Aug. 1855.

64. LGR 29 Aug. 1855.

65. LGR 1 Sept. 1855. Cf. LCW, dated only 'Sunday' but from its reference to the arrival of 'Miss Lynch... on Friday' it can be dated Sunday, 9 Sept. 1855, since Anne Lynch, the future M. Winefride, entered on Friday, 7 Sept. 1855, according to Postulants' Agreements.

66. LCW [26 Sept.-2 Oct. 1855].

67. LCW [9 Sept. 1855]; [21 Sept. 1855]; [26 Sept.-2 Oct. 1855]; LGR 3 Oct. 1855.

68. LGR 7 June 1856.

69. LGR 5 Sept. 1855.

70. LGR 7 June 1856.
71. LGR 22 July 1856, to Sr Clare Wilson.
72. LGR 22 July 1856 and 5 Oct. 1856; LCW [24 Oct. 1855].
73. LGR 5 Oct. 1856.
74. Ibid.
75. LWT 14 Jan. 1857.
76. LGR 24 June 1857.
77. LGR 9 Nov. 1857.
78. LGR 14 May 1858.
79. LGR 4 Aug. 1858.
80. LGR 6 Apr. and 14 May 1858; 18 Feb. and 25 Nov. 1859.
81. LGR 6 Apr. and 4 Aug. 1858.
82. LGR 18 Feb. 1859.
83. LGR 2 June and 25 Nov. 1859; 3 Aug. 1860; 18 June 1861.
84. See above, Ch.VI, pp.154-155.
85. LGR 24 Apr. 1863.
86. LGR 28 Aug. 1863.
87. LGR 1 Sept. 1855.
88. LGR 7 June, 1 and 4 Sept. and 5 Oct. 1856; 3 Feb., 5, 15 and 22 May, 24 June, 4 Aug. and 9 Nov. 1857; 18 Feb., 2 June and 25 Nov. 1859.
89. LGR 4 Sept. 1856.
90. LGR 5 and 22 May, 24 June and 4 Aug. 1857.
91. LGR 9 Nov. 1857 and 14 May 1858.
92. LGR 6 Apr. and 14 May 1858.
93. LBO'L 18 July 1858.
94. Yuhaus, pp.107-118.
95. Yuhaus, p.109.
96. LGR 1 and 4 Sept. 1856; 18 Feb., 2 June and 25 Nov. 1859; Letter of Fr John Dominic Tarlattini CP to E. Prout, 5 June 1859.
97. LISR, 13 May 1850 and 21 Feb. 1851; Wilson, pp.330-331, 334, 350-358; Young, *Dominic in England*, pp.98, 103 and 171. See above, Ch.V, p.126.
98. Phrase used by Salvian, Diary, 5 May 1857 and in LISR 7 Nov. 1862.
99. Yuhaus, pp.117 and 241.
100. LGR 25 Nov. 1859.
101. LGR 1 and 4 Sept. 1856; 3 Feb. 1857; 14 May 1858.
102. Vanden Bussche, pp.231-232, ftnote 36. Cf. Yuhaus, pp.110-112.
103. Letter 20 Dec. 1859, Original Letters of Fr Anthony of St James (Testa), concerning the Passionist Foundation in the USA 1852-1862, File VI, III-10, PGAR. See Yuhaus, p.113 for a discussion of it.
104. LGR 3 Aug. 1860.
105. LGR 6 Apr. 1858 and 6 Aug. 1862. Cf. Yuhaus, pp.108-109.
106. Yuhaus, p.109.
107. Yuhaus, p.110.
108. Letter, Fr Anthony Testa to Fr Joseph Pluym, Provincial of St Michael's Province (Belgium, France and Netherlands), 1 Nov. 1860. I am grateful to Fr Paulinus Vanden Bussche CP for this information.
109. Yuhaus, p.111.
110. Yuhaus, p.116.
111. Yuhaus, p.117.
112. LGR 1 Sept. 1856, 2 Oct. and 9 Nov. 1857 and 11 Apr. 1866.
113. SCR; Salvian, Small Chronicle, p.67.
114. Letters of Fr Ignatius Paoli CP [LIP] 21 Mar. 1865, GA I/B/2/f.

115. Having finished a mission at Coatbridge, he was travelling to give another at Leith. When he had to wait for a connecting train at Carstairs, he decided to call at Carstairs House, the home of his friend and godson, Robert Monteith. Fr Ignatius dropped dead as he walked up the drive. See Salvian, Diary, 2 Oct. 1864; Salvian, Annals, 1872, pp.79-82; Salvian, Newspaper Cuttings, 7 Oct. 1864; Mass Book 1862-1874, West Hoboken, 6 Nov. 1864, PPAUC; Devine, *Ignatius*, p.503; Vanden Bussche, p.240; Young, *Ignatius*, pp.276-277. For Monteith, see above, Ch.V, note 127.
116. LIP 21 Mar. 1865.
117. LEM 22 Jan. 1866.
118. LGR 11 Apr. 1866.
119. L'EM 30 May 1866.
120. Letter known only from his reply, LGR 11 Apr. 1866.
121. Red Bk.
122. Annals C.
123. LEM 12 and 25 June and 12 July 1866; LIP 18 Aug. 1866.
124. LIP 7 Feb. and 13 Aug. 1868.
125. Copy of Brief, 1869, Constitutions of the Sisters of the Sacred Cross and Passion of Our Lord Jesus Christ, 1869, GA IV/A/7 [Holy Family Rule, 1869]; LAO'N, [1872-4].
126. LIP 24 Aug. 1869; Fr E. Martorelli, Notes on the Institute, 26 Sept. 1869, GA I/B/4/f; Copy of Petition made by Bp W. Turner, 30 Sept. 1869, GA I/B/2/a.
127. LIP 25 June 1870; Copy of Brief, 1869; LAO'N, [1872-4]. Cf. Acts of the Third Provincial Chapter of the Sisters of the *Holy Cross and Passion of Our Lord Jesus Christ* [italics mine], Bolton, 12 Feb. 1870, 3rd Decree, GA II/A/1/a-m.
128. LGR 12 Apr. 1855; *Records*, pp.59-60.
129. LIP 4 Sept. 1870; H.K.B., XII, General Compilation I, pp.76-77 and 725, PPAUC.
130. LAO'N 11 Jan. 1873.
131. LWT 8 July 1872; Copy of Petition to Rome from the Archbishop of Westminster, H.E. Manning, 8 Sept. 1872, GA I/B/6. Cf. Letter from Provost Croskell to the Clergy of Salford Diocese, 13 July 1872 in Turner, *Pastoral Letters*, ADS.
132. LAO'N [1872-4].
133. Extract from a letter, n.d., to Fr A. O'Neill from Fr Sebastian CP, procurator-general.
134. Letters of M. Mary Margaret Chambers [LMMC] 5 Sept. 1874, GA I/B/2/h; *Records*, pp.36-37.
135. Letter from Passionist General, Fr Dominic of the Name of Mary [Giacchini] CP, 15 Nov. 1874, GA I/B/6/m; *Records*, pp.37-38. See above, Ch.V, pp.140-152.
136. LMMC, n.d. but must be 1874, rough copy in Fr A. O'Neill's writing.
137. Parkmount Records, 9 Apr., 1875; *Records*, p.38; Salvian, Annals, 1890, 9 and 26 Apr. 1875.
138. LAO'N 8 June 1876; LMMC 21 June 1876; Revd Mother General CP, *Official Reports*, 1947-51, GA II/B/5/b.
139. *Bolton Weekly Guardian*, 19 Aug. 1876; H.K.B., XII, p.259; *Records*, pp.39-43.
140. LGR 21 Oct. 1877.
141. Chronicles of St Michael's Monastery, 1861-1937, p.40, Community Archives, Passionist monastery, Union City. Apart from a retreat to his community in Pittsburgh, Fr Gaudentius had begun his public ministry in N. America with a course of sermons on the Passion in Pittsburgh Cathedral, 9 Mar.-8 Apr. 1856. He gave his

first mission, 13-27 Apr. 1856 at Clearfield, Butler Co., Pa. From then his missionary activities took him throughout Pennsylvania, New York State, Erie, Missouri, Illinois, Connecticut, Ohio, Massachusetts, New Jersey, Virginia, Buffalo, Maryland, Rhode Island, Kentucky, Cincinnati, Indiana and into Canada. See LGR 7 June 1856; 2 June 1859; 3 Aug. 1860; PMR, 1854-1888, passim; H.K.B., XII, passim; III, Chronicle of St Michael's, West Hoboken, 1861-1893, passim; VI, Chronicle of the Retreat of the Sacred Heart, Louisville, Kentucky, p.8; Mission Records, St Mary's, Dunkirk, Chautauqua Co., New York, 1863-1897, passim; Mission Records, St Michael's, West Hoboken, 1866-91, passim; Provincial Visitations Consultas 1863-1880, Bk II, 21 Apr. 1870; *Provincial Chapters 1863-1959* (West Hoboken, New Jersey, 1901), pp.2-47, all PPAUC; Arrivals and Departures, St Michael's, 1862-1866, Document 33, Box of Principal Events Files, Community Archives, Union City; Register of Baptisms 1876-1884, St Michael's, West Hoboken, 9 and 23 Apr.; 26 May and 7 July 1878, St Michael's and St Joseph's parish church, Union City; J.M. Flynn, *The Catholic Church in New Jersey* (Morristown, N. J., 1904), pp.241-242; Clement Pavlick CP, *A Passionist Mosaic, Preachers of the Passion, Accounts of Passionist Missionaries of the Passionist Eastern Province of St Paul of the Cross, 1856-1988* (Pittsburgh, 1988), pp.1-2; Cassian Yuhaus CP, 'The Passionists in America 1852-1866', doctoral thesis in Ecclesiastical History, Gregorian University, Rome, 1962; and *Compelled To Speak*, passim. I am grateful to Fr Cassian, Pittsburgh for allowing me to read his thesis. Fr Gaudentius' books were *Meditations on the Passion* (USA, 1876), mentioned in LGR 21 Oct. 1877; *The Voice of Jesus Suffering to the Mind and Heart of Christians, A Book on the Passion* (New York, 1879), (for its good reception see Book of Obits, Pittsburgh, 12 Aug. 1891), all PPA. He also wrote *The Crown of Thorns*, finished in Dec. 1871, according to Provincial Visitation Consultas, 12 Dec. 1871; *The Seven Last Words*, *The Christian Trumpet* and *A Sodality Book* according to H.K.B., IX, Necrology 1863-1893, p.98 and X, Biography CP, p.80, PPAUC.

142. *Provincial Chapters*, pp.2 and 19.

143. Chronicle of St Mary's Retreat, Dunkirk, New York from 1872, 10 July 1878, pp.16-17; St Vincent M. Strambi CP, *A Guide to Sacred Eloquence for the Use of the Students of the Congregation of the Passion by Way of Preparation for the Missions* (transl. and printed Dublin, 1865); *Passionist Centenary in America 1852-1952, A Brief History: St Mary's Monastery, Dunkirk, New York, Second Foundation in the United States 1860-1952* (Dunkirk, New York, 1952), a pamphlet, all PPAUC.

144. Arrivals and Departures, St Paul's Monastery, Pittsburgh, 1869-1883, 5 and 15 Feb. 1877; 22 Apr. and 1 May 1879; Mission Records, St Mary's, Dunkirk, 18 and 26 Aug. 1878; and 23-27 Apr. and 23-31 July 1879, PPA; H.K.B., XI, Records of St Paul's Monastery, Pittsburgh, 1852-1882, p.98, PPAUC.

145. H.K.B., X, p.80; VII, Chronicle of the Retreat of Our Lady of Good Counsel, St Louis, Missouri, 15 Mar. 1885, p.22, PPAUC. See also Chronicle of St Louis, vol.1, pp.8 and 27-28; Mass Book, St Louis, 25 Mar. 1885, p.XIX; Incomes and Expenses, St Louis, 1884-1896, c.1889, [P]assionist [W]est [P]rovincial [A]rchives, Chicago. I am indebted to Fr Roger Mercurio CP, archivist, Passionist West American Province, Chicago, for my references to these archives.

146. DFGR, 1890; H.K.B., X, p.80; LAO'N 26 June 1887; Petition of M. Benedicta Hynes, Superioress General, to the Holy See for Final Approbation, 1 Sept. 1886 [granted by Leo XIII, 12 June 1887], GA I/B/6/g; Salvian, Newspaper Cuttings, 1887; *Records*, pp.67-69.

147. H.K.B., VII, p.25, PPAUC; Chronicle of St Louis, 1, 27-28; Mass Book, St Louis, vol.1, May 1889, PPAC.

148. DFGR, 1890.

149. Arrivals and Departures, St Louis, vol. 1, 1888-1912, 3 July 1890, p.9; Mass

Book, St Louis, 2, 25 Apr. 1890, p.25, PPAC; Arrivals and Departures, St Paul's Monastery, Pittsburgh 1883-1921, 7 and 12 Aug. 1890, pp.34-35, PPA; H.K.B., X, p.80; Local Chapters, St Michael's, West Hoboken, 1866-1894, 15 Sept. 1890, PPAUC.

150. DFGR, 1891.

151. *Liber Defunctorum* 1889-1906, St Paul's Monastery, Pittsburgh, p.37, PPA; Mass Book, St Michael's, W. Hoboken, 1888-1905, pp.3, 6 and 11; Local Chapters, St Michael's, 15 Sept. and 27 Dec. 1890; 23 Jan. and 25 Mar. 1891, PPAUC.

152. See Daily Cash Book, St Michael's Retreat, West Hoboken, New Jersey, 20 Aug. 1890 - Jan. 1893, 12 Aug. 1891: 'Shaving of Fr Gaudentius (dead): 3 dollars.' See also Chronicle of St Michael's Monastery, 1861-1937, p.40; H.K.B., VII, p.28; I, General Index, 1852-1902, pp.61 and 106; Mass Book, St Michael's, West Hoboken, 1888-1905, pp.11 and 14, PPAUC; Book of Suffrages with Biographical Notices, III, 1889-1906, pp.33-37; *Liber Defunctorum*, pp.35-37; Book of Obits, 1890-1900, B, 12 Aug. 1891, all in PPA; *Records*, pp.75-77.

153. LRC 29 Aug. 1891.

154. LGR 15 Oct. 1888.

155. LRC 9 Feb. 1875.

156. LRC 30 Jan. 1878.

157. LRC 4 July 1887.

158. LRC 29 Aug. 1891.

159. LRC 24 May 1893.

160. LRC 3 Apr. 1888; Christmastide 1892-3, 6 Jan., 8 Apr. and 24 Dec. 1899; *Records*, p.96; *Harvest*, 11 (1898), 118 and 120; and 1916, pp.8-9. I owe the information that the sisters visited him each week to the late Sr St Pius Dalton CP.

161. *Harvest*, 28 (1915), 211.

162. Gaudentian Rule, ch.11, par.V. See above, Ch.III, p.68.

163. 26 and 29 Dec. 1720. See *Words From the Heart*, pp.31-32.

164. Cf. Vanden Bussche, pp.197-199 for identical comprehensive expressions Fr Ignatius Spencer was forced to use in documents for which at the same time, 1851-2, he was seeking approval in Rome for his prayer association for the conversion of England. Since he wanted a worldwide campaign, some European bishops had objected that his previous restriction to England's needs was too limited. Hence the inclusion of all 'pagans, infidels and heretics'.

165. See Devine, *Ignatius*, pp.248-257, 400-427, 449-452 and 464-468; Vanden Bussche, passim; Young, *Ignatius*, pp.90-102, 106-8, 178-201, 222-223 and 238-243.

166. Ignatius, Diary, 5 and 8 Jan. 1854. Vanden Bussche, pp.199 and 213-215. See Devine, *Ignatius*, pp.413-427.

167. Vanden Bussche, pp.194-204. Cf. Young, *Ignatius*, p.180.

168. Vanden Bussche, pp.139-140 and 146.

169. Devine, *Ignatius*, pp.464-468; Vanden Bussche, pp.216 and 222-223; Young, *Ignatius*, pp.238-246, 250-252 and 272-276.

170. SCR.

171. PRO ED. 7/64/41, Form VI; ED. 8/1, Forms XIIIa and XXVI; *Catholic School*, Oct. 1850, p.34; Annals G.

172. *Catholic School*, Oct. 1850, p.33.

173. PRO ED. 17/21, 1855-6, pp.530, 539 and 548; PRO ED. 17/22, 1856-7, p.781.

174. Postulants' Agreements; Receptions and Professions; Annals G; *Records*, p.59.

175. SCR.

176. Salvian, Small Chronicle, vol.2, p.430; Annals, 1872, pp.50-51. For Fr Salvian, see Spencer, *Blessed Charles*, p.56.

177. Cf. LGR 17 Oct. 1849 and 6 June 1854.

1.   Mathias, *Brewing Industry*, p.53.
2.   Will of Elizabeth B. Blount, 10th July 1858, Probate, GA II/C/5/b.
3.   Red Bk.
4.   Cf. Gilley, *Newman*, p.236; Ker, *Newman*, p.316.
5.   LGR 23 Nov. 1855; *Passionist Rule*, ch.XXX.
6.   Annals A/E.
7.   LGR 28 Nov. and 15 Dec. 1854 and 4 Jan. 1855; Letter to Sr M. Joseph [E.Prout] from the secretary of Bishop Goss of Liverpool, 18 Mar. 1856, LRO RCLv, 15, p.127; Annals A/E, B, C and D.
8.   Annals A/E.
9.   G. Kitson Clark, *The Making of Victorian England,* 1962, reprinted as a University Paperback 1977, pp.189-190.
10.   Ibid.

PRIMARY SOURCES

GENERAL ARCHIVES OF THE CONGREGATION OF THE SISTERS OF THE CROSS AND PASSION, GREAT BILLING, NORTHAMPTON:

Manuscripts:

An Account of the Exhumation, Recognition and Re-Interment of the Remains of Mother Mary Joseph Prout CP, performed on 20 June 1973 in the graveyard attached to the Monastery, Sutton: Medical Report A, GA I/C/3/ f, h, i and j

Annals A/E - G, GA I/B/3/a-g

An undated and unsigned fragment, roughly written, possibly by Fr Ignatius Spencer CP, c.1864, concerning homes for factory girls [not yet filed]

A Statement on the Charitable Works of E. Prout's congregation, c.1927, GA I/C/1/f

Book of Agreements of Postulants joining the Sisters of the Holy Family, GA IV/C/15

Ceremonial Rite of Reception and Profession of Novices, in E. Prout's handwriting, GA IV/B/29

Certificate of Confirmation, by Bp. W. Turner of Salford, of Mother Mary Joseph (Prout) as first Superioress General, 23 Oct. 1863, GA I/B/1/a

Clothing Sermon, 1852, MS copy, GA I/B/1/e

Copy of Brief, 1869, Constitutions of the Sisters of the Sacred Cross and Passion of Our Lord Jesus Christ, 1869, GA IV/A/7

Copy of Deposition of Father Gaudentius Rossi CP, April 1891, GA I/C/6/b

Copies of Documents pertaining to the Sisters of the Infant Jesus, Northampton, GA I/C/5/a-k

Copy of *Notice* issued by Bp Wareing in Northampton, 4 July 1851, GA I/C/5/a

Copy of Petition made by Bp W. Turner, 30 Sept. 1869, GA I/B/2/a

Copy of Petition of M. Benedicta Hynes, Superioress General, to the Holy See for Final Approbation, 1 Sept. 1886, GA I/B/6/g

Copy of Petition to Rome from H.E. Manning, Archbishop of Westminster, 8 Sept. 1872, GA I/B/6

Extract from Letter, n.d., to Fr Alphonsus O'Neill CP from Fr Sebastian CP, Procurator-General

Feastday Greetings Card given by M. Mary Joseph (Elizabeth Prout) to Sr Mary Patrick O'Neal, 17 Mar. 1862, GA I/B/1/h

Holy Family Rule, 1854-5 in E. Prout's writing, GA IV/A/2

Holy Family Rule, 1855 in E. Prout's writing, GA IV/A/3

Holy Family Rule, 1855-7, Italian in Fr I. Spencer's writing, GA I/B/5/b

Holy Family Rule, 1863, rough copies in English and Italian, both in Fr Ignatius Spencer's writing, GA I/B/5/f

Holy Family Rule, 1863, Italian: copy in Fr Ignatius Spencer's writing; another copy officially made in Rome, GA I/B/5/d

Holy Family Rule, 1863 [Sr M. Paul Taylor's writing?], GA IV/A/4

Holy Family Rule, 1865, a handwritten copy of the Rule Fr I. Spencer took to Rome in 1863, with some slight alterations later proposed, at his request, by Bp Ullathorne of Birmingham, GA I/B/5/e

Letters of:
Carosi CP, Bernardine, 1855, GA I/B/2/i
Chambers CP, Mary Margaret, 1874, GA I/B/2/h
Croskell, Robert, 1853-1902, GA I/B/2/a
Giacchini CP, Dominic, 1874, GA I/B/6/m
Martorelli CP, Eugene, 1864-1872, GA I/B/2/e
O'Loughlin CP, Bernard, 1858-1874, GA I/B/4/a-b
O'Neill CP, Alphonsus, 1869-1899, GA I/B/2/g
Paoli CP, Ignatius, 1865-1870, GA I/B/2/f
Prout, Elizabeth (M. Mary Joseph), 1855-1863, GA I/B/1/a
Rossi CP, Gaudentius, 1848-1888, GA I/B/1/b-d
Spencer CP, Ignatius, 1850-1864, GA I/B/1/f-g
Taylor CP, Mary Paul (A. Ingham Correspondence), GA V/J/5
Turner, Rt Revd William, Bp of Salford, 1857-1872, GA I/B/2/a
Wilson, Sr Clare, 1855, GA I/B/2/c
List of Receptions and Professions, 1852-1892, GA IV/C/1
List of Professions, GA IV/C/6
Note of Election Results, 1863, in Fr I. Spencer's writing, GA II/A/1/a
Note on the 1858 Investigation in Fr B. O'Loughlin's writing, GA I/B/4/b
Notes on the Institute signed by Fr Eugene Martorelli CP, 26 Sept. 1869, GA I/B/4/f
Notes on the Rule, 1862-3, written by E. Prout on disused copies of the *Parr Hall Prospectus*, GA I/B/5/a
Petition of M. Mary Joseph (Prout) to Pius IX, 27 May-13 June 1863, English translation in Fr I. Spencer's writing, endorsed by Cardinal Barnabò for the Holy See and signed and sealed by Bishop W. Turner and his secretary, Canon Benoit on 17 Aug. 1863, GA I/B/6/a
Photograph of Elizabeth Prout, St Helens [1855?], GA I/B/1/h
Photograph of the corpse of Elizabeth Prout, 1864, GA I/A/4/a
Records of the Convent of Holy Cross, Sutton, 1855-64, GA I/B/4/d
Records of the Institute of the Holy Family, 1849-1852, GA I/B/4/c
Rule of the Catholic Sisters of the Holy Family, written by Fr Gaudentius Rossi CP, 1852, GA I/B/5/c
Rules and Constitutions of the Sisters of the Holy Family, 1855, partly in Fr G. Rossi's writing, partly in E. Prout's, partly in another hand [Sr Clare Wilson's?] and an Italian transl. in Fr G. Rossi's writing, GA IV/A/1
Printed:
Bolton Weekly Guardian, 19 Aug. 1876 [a cutting], GA II/A/1/a-m
Manual of Community Prayers (Dublin, c. 1952)
Obituary [newspaper] of Sr Helen James, 1926, GA IV/D/1
Obituary [newspaper] of Sr M. Paul Taylor, 1903, GA I/D/1/f and IV/D/7
Office of the Blessed Virgin Mary, used by E. Prout, GA I/A/3/a
Records of the Foundation and Progress of the Congregation of the Sisters of the Most Holy Cross and Passion 1851-1911 (Dublin, 1911)
Regulations To Be Observed by The Sisters of the Most Holy Cross and Passion of Our Lord Jesus Christ, revised edition (Dublin, 1953)
Rules and Constitutions of the Congregation of the Sisters of the Most Holy Cross

and Passion of Our Lord Jesus Christ, 1887 (reprint Dublin, 1954)
Solemn Beatification of Blessed Dominic of the Mother of God, Passionist, GA
1/C/7/d
The Life of St Teresa, written by herself and transl. from the Spanish by J. Dalton,
1851, used by E. Prout, GA I/A/3/b

Community Archives, Cross and Passion Convent, Parkmount, Salford:
Records of St Mary's Convent, Manchester, vol. 1, 1873-1900

*GENERAL, POSTULATION, PROVINCIAL, COMMUNITY AND PARISH
ARCHIVES OF THE CONGREGATION OF THE PASSION:*

General and Postulation Archives, Passionist Retreat of SS John and Paul, Rome:
B. Domenico d. Madre de Dio Testimonanze, Lettere ... File: A Testa a P.
Domenico
Letters of Fr A. Testa, File: St Joseph's Province
Letters of Fr Dominic Barberi CP: Ven. Domenico della Madre di Dio Passionista:
Lettere Postulazione dei PP. Passionisti
Original Letters of Fr Anthony of St James, General, concerning the Passionist
Foundation in the USA 1852-1862, File VI 1862
Original letter of Fr Ignatius Spencer CP to the *Tablet*, 7 Jan. 1851, printed
18 Jan., *Archivio Segreto Vaticano*, Pius IX, no.605; Copies in English and Italian
in Fr I. Spencer's writing, Letters of Fr Ignatius Spencer, 1839-1864, File: St
Joseph's Province
Origine e primi progressi dell'Ospizio de Parigi Fondazione 1863 [Paris *Platea*,
1863-1924], Box: St Joseph's Province, 2-B-2
Recollections Left to Our Young Missionaries in England, written by Fr Dominic
Barberi CP, 1849 (transl. Fr Conrad Charles CP), Barberi MSS, VII

Passionist Provincial Archives, St Anne's Retreat, Sutton, St Helens:
Arrivals and Departures: St Michael's Retreat, Aston, 1842-1851; St Saviour's,
Broadway, 1850-1872
Diary of Fr Ignatius Spencer CP
Envelope marked: 'A.D. 1863, Fr Ignatius Spencer C.P., Faculties to hear Nuns'
Confessions, Sutton Convent, St Helens, Lancs.'
Fragment of a letter quoted in a letter of an unknown writer, 20 Nov. 1862, Box:
Sutton Locality
Letter of M. Winefride Lynch, 1864
Letters of Fr Ignatius Spencer CP, 1857-1863
Mass Book, 1855-1882, St Saviour's, Broadway
Missions and Retreats: St Michael's, Aston, 1842-1852; St Saviour's, Broadway,
1851-1949; St Joseph's Retreat, The Hyde; St Anne's Retreat, Sutton, 1851-55 and
1861-1880
Platea, St Michael's Retreat, Aston, 1842-1853; St Saviour's Retreat, Broadway,
1850-57; St Anne's Retreat, Sutton, 1851-1883
Suffrages for Our Benefactors and Religious Dead, 1848-1850, Woodchester
Typescript of English translation by B. O'Brien CP of F. Menegazzo CP, *Life of*

Ven. Dominic of the Mother of God (Rome, 1962)
Printed:
Spencer CP, I. (transl.), *The Life of Blessed Paul of the Cross, Founder of the Congregation of Discalced Clerks of the Most Holy Cross and Passion of Jesus Christ*, 1860
Pastorals of Cardinal Wiseman, 1851-9
St Joseph's, Peasley Cross 1878-1918, a brochure

St Anne's Parish, Sutton, St Helens:
Declaration by Very Revd Fr E. Kennan CP, Rector of St Anne's, Sutton, by virtue of the Declarations Act, 1835 concerning the Exhumation of the Remains of Mother Mary Joseph Prout at St Anne's Monastery, Sutton, St Helens, on Wed., 20 June 1973
St Anne's Burial Register B, Sutton

Passionist Provincial Archives, St Paul's Retreat, Mt Argus, Dublin, Eire:
Arrivals and Departures, Mt Argus, Dublin, 1856-1874
Mt Argus Chronicles, 1856-1876
Nardocci CP, Salvian:
Annals of the Anglo-Hibernian Province, 1842-1890, 9 vols
Autobiography, 1822-1865, 2 vols
Diary, 1855-1896, 19 vols
Early Novices, 1842-1859
Folio of Newspaper Cuttings, 1856-1895
List of Missions and Retreats given by the Passionists of the Anglo-Hibernian Province, 1842-1883
Register of Passionists, 1842-1887

Archives of Passionist Eastern Province, Community and Parish, Union City, USA:
Manuscripts:
Arrivals and Departures, St Michael's, 1862-1866, Document 33, Box of Principal Events Files
Barr CP, Hugh K. (H.K.B.):
I, General Index, 1852-1902
II, St Mary's Retreat, Dunkirk
III, Chronicle of St Michael's, West Hoboken, 1861-1893
VI, Chronicle of the Retreat of the Sacred Heart, Louisville, Kentucky
VII, Chronicle of the Retreat of Our Lady of Good Counsel, St Louis, Mo.
IX, Necrology 1863-1893
X, Biography CP: Biographical Sketches of the Passionist Priests, Students and Brothers in the Province of St Paul of the Cross in America, 1893
XI, Records of the Retreat of St Paul of the Cross, Pittsburgh, Pennsylvania 1852-1882
XII, General Compilation I: Newspaper Cuttings
XIII, World CP Foundations 1733-1897
Chronicle of St Mary's Retreat, Dunkirk, New York from 1872
Chronicles of St Michael's Monastery, 1861-1937

Daily Cash Book, St Michael's Retreat, West Hoboken, New Jersey, 1890-1893
Historical Records of St Mary's Church and of the Passionist Monastery attached to it in Dunkirk, New York, 1860-1904
Local Chapters held in St Mary's Monastery, Dunkirk from 1864
Local Chapters, St Michael's, West Hoboken, 1866-1894
Mass Books, St Michael's, West Hoboken, 1862-1874; 1875-1888; 1888-1905
Minutes of St Michael's Passionist Monastery Corporation 1866-1934
Mission Records, St Mary's, Dunkirk, Chautauqua Co., New York, 1863-97
Mission Records, St Michael's, West Hoboken, 1866-91
Photograph of the Pittsburgh Community and Capitulars, 1866, Box: Pittsburgh, St Paul's
Provincial Visitations Consultas 1863-1880
Register of Baptised Protestants 1856-1862 kept by Fr Gaudentius Rossi CP

Printed:
Cenni Necrologici Dei Nostri Religiosi Che Son Passati A Migliar Vita Nel Carso Dell' Anno 1891 (Rome, 1892)
Ceremonies of Vestition and Profession, The Congregation of the Discalced Clerics of the Most Holy Cross and Passion of Our Lord Jesus Christ, Box: Pittsburgh, St Paul's
Memoirs of the First Companions of St Paul of the Cross, by a priest of the same Congregation (transl, from Italian, West Hoboken, 1913)
Passionist Centenary in America 1852-1952, A Brief History: St Mary's Monastery, Dunkirk, New York, Second Foundation in the United States 1860-1952 (Dunkirk, N. York, 1952), a pamphlet
Pavlick CP, Clement (compiled and ed.), *Preachers of the Passion, Accounts of Passionist Missionaries 1856-1988* (Pittsburgh, 1988), limp
Provincial Chapters 1863-1890 (West Hoboken, New Jersey, 1901)
Regolamenti da Osservarsi Dai Cheirici Scalzi della Congregazione Della Passione Di Gesu Cristo (Rome, 1855)
Regulae et Constitutiones Congregationis Clericorum Excalceatorum SS. Crucis et Passionis Domini Nostri Jesu Christi (Rome, 1775)
St Vincent M. Strambi CP, A Guide to Sacred Eloquence for the Use of the Students of the Congregation of the Passion by Way of Preparation for the Missions (transl. and printed Dublin, 1865)
The Passionists in New Jersey 1861-1936, pamphlet (Union City, 1936)

Parish Records, St Michael's, West Hoboken, St Michael's and St Joseph's Parish Church, Union City:
Register of Baptisms and Marriages 1861-1865
Registers of Baptisms 1865-1875; 1876-1884; 1884-1891
Register of Marriages 1862-1864; 1865-1877

Archives of the Passionist Western Province, Chicago:
Arrivals and Departures, St Louis, vol. 1, 1888-1912
Chronicle of St Louis
Incomes and Expenses, St Louis, 1884-1896

Mass Book, St Louis, vols 1 and 2

Community Archives, St Paul's Monastery, Pittsburgh:
Arrivals and Departures, St Paul's Monastery, Pittsburgh, 1869-1921
A Written Statement of the Virtue and Holiness of Life of the Deceased Father
Dominic of the Mother of God ... Made in the City of St Louis, by Fr Gaudentius
Rossi CP, 25 Jan. 1890 [c/o Fr C. Yuhaus]
Book of Obits, 1890-1900, B, St Paul's Monastery, Pittsburgh
Book of Suffrages with Biographical Notices, I (1856-71); III (1889-1906)
Chronicles of St Paul's Monastery, Pittsburgh, 1852-1920
Liber Defunctorum 1889-1906, St Paul's Monastery, Pittsburgh
Missions and Retreats 1854-1888, St Paul's Monastery, Pittsburgh
Mission Records, St Mary's Monastery, Dunkirk, Chautauqua Co. New York,
1863-1897 [c/o Fr C. Yuhaus]
Local Chapters, 1857-1900, St Paul's, Pittsburgh
Special Mass Book 1858-1881, St Paul's Monastery, Pittsburgh
Printed:
*Letter of Most Revd Leo Kierkels CP, DD, Superior General of the Congregation of
the Most Holy Cross and Passion of Our Lord Jesus Christ, to Members of the
Congregation* (Rome, 1930)
Rossi CP, Gaudentius, *The Voice of Jesus Suffering to the Mind and Heart of
Christians, a Book on the Passion* (New York, 1879)

ARCHIVES OF HOLY CROSS CISTERCIAN ABBEY, STAPEHILL, DORSET:
Records of Holy Cross Abbey, Stapehill

ARCHIVES OF ST MARY'S BENEDICTINE ABBEY, COLWICH, STAFFS.:
Letter of Fr Gaudentius Rossi CP, 1849
Letters of Fr Dominic Barberi CP, 1842-1846
Letters of Fr G. (Ignatius) Spencer CP, 1841-1856

ARCHIVES OF THE PRESENTATION CONVENT, LIVESEY ST, MANCHESTER:
Annals of the Presentation Convent, Livesey St, 1836-1957

GENERAL DOMINICAN ARCHIVES, STONE:
Necrology of the Congregation of St Catherine of Siena, Stone, G.1
Records of Bristol Convent, T 862
Records of St Dominic's Priory, Stone, 1853-1855 (T 863);
1850-1859 (T 864); 1859-1863 (T 865)
Register of the English Congregation of St Catherine of Siena, G.1
Printed:
Life of Mother M. Margaret Hallahan, 'written by her religious children'

ARCHIVES OF THE CATHOLIC EDUCATION COUNCIL, LONDON:
Catholic Poor School Committee, *Catholic Poor School Committee Reports*, 1847-
1864
Catholic Poor School Committee, *The Catholic School, 1848-1856*

DIOCESAN ARCHIVES:
Archdiocese of Westminster:
Letter of the St John's Wood Catholic Ladies' Association, 18 Nov. 1847, 2/4/42b
Catholic Poor School Committee, *The Catholic School, 1848-1856*

Archdiocese of Birmingham:
Letters, Bp Walsh to Dr Errington, 1844-1845, B.797 and B.817
Register of Confirmations, Aston-by-Stone, Aston Box, vol. 4
Register of Confirmations, St Chad's, Birmingham, vol.1, 1850-1863

Diocese of Northampton:
Letter of Rt Revd W. Wareing, Vic. Ap. of the E. Dist, to the Clergy, 4 Nov 1845

Diocese of Salford:
Acta Primi Episcopi Salfordensis, Printed Documents of Bishop W. Turner 1851-1872 [*Pastoral Letters* and *Ad Clerums*]
Biographical Notes on Fr W. Daly OMI, 1835-94, B 32
Catholic Almanac, 1880
Faithful Companions of Jesus, Salford Diocese, 1852-1973, P53
Letter from Provost Croskell to the Clergy of Salford Diocese, 13 July 1872
Manchester Guardian 5 May 1821
Notes on the Levenshulme Catholic Mission, Box B
Salford Diocesan Deeds Index
St Mary's, Failsworth 1845-1964, P23, a brochure
The Foundations of the Sisters of Notre Dame in England and Scotland from 1845-1895 (Anonymous, Liverpool, 1895)

LIBRARIES:
Chetham's Library, Manchester:
MUN. A.7.41, Education (39817): Progress of Plan of Manchester and Salford Education Bill, 1848-52, Scrapbook of Printed and Manuscript Material Including Letters

Manchester Central Library, Local Studies Unit:
Archives of the Corporation of the City of Manchester:
Letter of complaint, 7 June 1848, from the occupier of 53 Stocks St to the Lamp and Scavenging Committee (M9/62/1/20)
Letter, 18 Sept. 1853 for a direction from the Town Council to the nuisance officers (M9/62/1/20)
Letter, 30 Jan. 1854, from the ratepayers of St Michael's Ward to the Manchester Improvements Committee (M9/63/3/16)
Letter, 1 July 1854, from the clergyman, churchwardens and others of St Michael's church (Letter Book M9/62/1/21)
Memorandum submitted by the Chief Constable to the Watch Committee on 2 Aug. 1849 (M9/62/1/20)
Resolution, 24 Jan. 1849, of the Building and Sanitary Regulations Committee (M9/62/1/20)

Rate Books (M 10/16): Highway Rate Book, Levenshulme, 1858 Rate Book for Relief of the Poor, Parish of Levenshulme, 1858
Rate Books for Relief of the Poor, vol. 1: Cheetham Overseers, Township of Cheetham 1848-1852
Rate Books for Relief of the Poor, vol. 2: Districts 3, 4, 6, 7 and 12, 1849
Canon L. Toole, *Catholic Tradition of Manchester and Salford*, a newspaper account of a lecture he gave in St John's, Salford, May 1867, Owen MSS, MF 572, ff.95-96
Census, 1851, MF 911, 913, 914, 2891, 2897, 2899, 2900, 2904, 2905
Census, 1861, MF 1268
Journal of J. Bembridge, 1841-1853, 13 vols (B. R. MS 259 B1, Nineteenth Century Diaries)
Manchester and Salford Education Aid Society: Folio of Newspaper Cuttings collected by E. Brotherton; *Reports*, 1865-1872
Manchester and Salford Provident Society Reports 1833-1858 (361 M20)
Manchester and Salford Sanitary Association Reports (M126/2/3/1-26)
Manchester Statistical Society Papers, 3 vols (MS F 310.6 M5)
Ordnance Survey 6" Map of Central Manchester, 1848, Sheet 104

Shrewsbury Local Studies Library: Bowdler's Trustees Minute Book

St Helens Local Studies Library: Census, 1861, MF RG9/2754
Ordnance Survey 6" Map 108, St Helens and Area, 1846-7
Ordnance Survey 6" Map CVIII.6, St Helens and Area, 1882

MARITIME MUSEUM, LIVERPOOL:
Passenger's Contract Ticket, C263, Liverpool-New York, 20 July 1857, 'Emigrants to a New World' Exhibition

PARISH RECORDS:
All Saints, Wellington, Shropshire: Registers of Baptisms and Marriages

St Ann's, Ashton-under-Lyne: Register of Baptisms, 1855-1866
St Ann's Girls' and Infants' School Logbooks, 1863

St Dominic's Church, Stone: Register of Deaths and Burials, 1856-1957

St Michael's Church, Stone: Register of Burials, 1862-3

PRIVATE PAPERS: Mr and Mrs P. Rowlands: Coleham Brewery Deeds

RECORD OFFICES:
Public Record Office, London:
PRO ED 7:   *Public Elementary Schools: Preliminary Statements*
PRO ED 8:   *Annual Grants, Disused Forms*
PRO ED 9/12:   *Grants under Minutes, 1846: Copies of Letters Selected from Old Letter Books 1847-1858*

PRO ED 17:   *Committee of the Privy Council on Education: Minutes and*
                  Reports
PRO ED 103:   *Treasury and Committee of Council on Education: Building*
                  Grant Applications
PRO HO 129:   *Census of Great Britain 1851: Ecclesiastical Returns,*
                  Manchester: 129/473-1-1 (St Ann's);
                  /473-3-12 (St Augustine's); /473-4-19 (St Chad's);
                  /473-4-18 (St Mary's); /473-5-13 (St Patrick's)
PRO HO 129:   /472-3-1-7 (St John's, Salford)
PRO HO 129:   /474 (Catholic chapel, Wood St, Ashton-under-Lyne)

Lancashire Record Office, Preston:
Archives of the Diocese of Liverpool: Bishop Goss' Papers, RCLv 13; 15; 43/25;
and 44
Manchester Parochial Archives: Miscellaneous Nineteenth Century Papers
(RCMc/ 45); St Mary's Building Fund Account Book, 1835-61 (RCLy/7/4);
Registers of St Augustine's, 1820-1855 (RCMa/); St Chad's, 1810-1850 (RCMc);
St Mary's, 1794-1855 (RCMm); St Patrick's, 1832-1856 (RCMp); St Wilfrid's,
1842-1855 (RCMw)

Shropshire Record Office, Shrewsbury:
Noted Breweries of Great Britain, Wellington Papers, Shropshire Brewery, 3022/2
Old Brewery, Coleham, Sale Catalogue, 16 July 1959, 2118/115
Register of Baptisms, 1813-33, St Julian's, Shrewsbury, 2711/Rg/6
Sale of William Hazledine's Property, Coleham, 1841, Shrewsbury Papers, 901/1,
1709/16/II 4

Staffordshire Record Office, Stafford:
Archdeacon's Visitation Report, St Michael's, Stone, 1830
Census, 1841, MF 41/9
Census, 1851, MF 51/3
Census, 1861, MF CEN 61/4

REGISTRY OFFICES:
General Register Office, London:
Certificate of the Death of Elizabeth Prout, 11 Jan. 1864

Registry Office, Prescot: Register of Deaths, 1864

Registry Office, Stafford:
Certified Copy of the Entry of Death of Ann Prout 1862, entry 489, HB 955359
Certified Copy of the Entry of Death of Edward Prout 1863, entry 88, HB 955360

PRIMARY SOURCES: PUBLISHED

BRITISH PARLIAMENTARY PAPERS:
HOUSE OF LORDS PAPERS:
Report to Her Majesty's Principal Secretary of State for the Home Department from the Poor Law Commissioners on an Inquiry into the Sanitary Condition of the Labouring Population of Great Britain, 1842
Local Reports on the Sanitary Condition of the Labouring Population of England, 1842, Report 20: Dr R.B. Howard, *Report on the Prevalence of Diseases Arising from Contagion and Certain Other Physical Causes Amongst the Labouring Classes in Manchester*

REPORTS FROM COMMISSIONERS:
Vol.13, XXXIV (40), *Report on the State of the Irish Poor in Great Britain*, 1836
Vol.4, pt 2, 1850[1248], XXIII, part 2, *The Mining Districts*
Vol.2, part 1, 1851, XXIII, pt 1, 388, *Sanitary Condition of Agar Town, St Pancras*
Vol.17, part 1, 1854[1768], XXXV, part 1, *Report of the General Board of Health on the Administration of the Public Health Act, and the Nuisances Removal and Diseases Prevention Act, from 1848-1854*, 1854 Report
Vol.17, part 1, 1854[1780], XXXV, part 2.115, *Common Lodging Houses*
Vol.1, session 2, 1857[2224], XVI, pt 1, 19, *Common Lodging Houses*
Schools Inquiry Commission, vol.1: *Report*, 1868

REPORTS FROM SELECT COMMITTEES:
1852(499) XI.1, *Manchester and Salford Education*
Vol.7, part 1, 1854-55[308], XIII, pt 1, *Poor Removal*
Vol.7, part 2, 1854-5[244], XIII, pt 2, 43, *Public Health Bill and Nuisances Removal Amendment Bill, Select Committee Report on Public Health: Manchester*

REPORTS OF THE INSPECTORS OF FACTORIES TO HER MAJESTY'S PRINCIPAL SECRETARY OF STATE FOR THE HOME DEPARTMENT:
Oct. 1849, 1850[1141], XXIII, pt 2.181 to Oct. 1868, 1868[4093 - I], XIV.123

ACCOUNTS AND PAPERS:
21, 1847 (193) LIV.5, *Relief of Distress, Public Works (Ireland)*
25, 1849[1124], LIV.148-175, *Police Returns, Manchester, 1847*
13, pt 2, 1849, XLII, pt 2, *Minutes of the Committee of Council on Education, Correspondence 1848-9* (1090)
13 pt.1, 1851(103), XLIII, pt.1, *Parliamentary Grants for Education*
29, 1851 (84), LIX.649, *Ecclesiastical Titles: C. Newdegate's Presentation of Anti-Catholic Addresses*
29, 1851 (236) LIX.741, *Address from Roman Catholics in England*
Population, 1831-1869, *Census of Great Britain*: vols.3 and 4: *1841 Census of Great Britain*; vol.5: *1851 Religious Census of Great Britain*: vol.6, *1851 Education*; vols 6, 7 and 9: *1851 Population Census*
22, part 1, 1852-53[237], LXXVIII, pt 1, 525, *The Common Lodging Houses Act*

1852-53[994], LXXVIII, pt 2, *The Operation of the Common Lodging House Act*
1857, session 2, XLI.119, *Common Lodging Houses*
24, 1863, LII. 288, *Letter from Mr Baker, Inspector of Factories, to the Home Secretary, on the Present State of the Cotton Districts*, May 1863; and also *Report of R. Rawlinson on the Public Works required in the Cotton Manufacturing Districts and the Employment of the Operatives thereon*, May 1863
16, 1865[81], XLV.265, *Official Correspondence with Her Majesty's Government Relative to the Abduction of a Nun, Named Mary Ryan*, 25 Feb. 1865

BILLS
1851[116], V.511, *A Bill To Prevent the Forcible Detention of Females in Religious Houses*
1854[42], V.531, *A Bill To Secure to Persons Under Religious Vows the Free Exercise of Their Lawful Rights in the Disposal of Their Property*
Hansard's Parliamentary Debates, 3, CXV, 1851, vol.2

CITY OF MANCHESTER:
Proceedings of the Council, 1857-1858 (Manchester, 1859)

CONTEMPORARY AND NEAR-CONTEMPORARY WRITINGS:
Aikin, J.,   *A Description of the Country from Thirty to Forty Miles Round Manchester*, 1795
Arnold, R.A.,   *The History of the Cotton Famine*, 1864
Bamford, S. (ed.Hilton,T.), *Passages in the Life of a Radical*, 1844, 1967 edition
Butterworth, J.,   *History and Description of the Town and Parish of Ashton-Under-Lyne in the County of Lancaster and the Village of Dukinfield* (Ashton, 1823)
Carpenter, K.E.(ed.) *Conditions of Work and Living: The Reawakening of the English Conscience, Five Pamphlets 1838-1844* (New York, 1972)
Carpenter, M.,   *Reformatory Schools For the Children of the Perishing and Dangerous Classes and for Juvenile Offenders*, 1851, new impression 1968
Church, R.W. (ed. & introd. Best, G.) *The Oxford Movement: Twelve Years 1833-1845*,c. 1890 (Chicago, 1970)
Cooke Taylor, W., *Notes of a Tour in the Manufacturing Districts of Lancashire*, 1842
Darwin, C.R.,   *The Origin of Species*, 1859
Dickens, C.,   *David Copperfield*, 1849-50, Penguin 1985
--   *Hard Times*, 1854, Penguin 1985
Disraeli, B.,   *Coningsby or The New Generation*, 1844, World's Classics paperback (Oxford, 1982)
--   *Sybil or the Two Nations*, 1845, Penguin 1985
Eliot, G.,   *Felix Holt*, 1866, Penguin 1987
--   *Middlemarch*, 1871-2, Penguin 1985
Engels, F.,   *The Condition of the Working Class in England* (Germany, 1845; Penguin 1987)

Faber, F.W.,   *The Precious Blood*, 1863

Faucher, L.   *Manchester in 1844*, 1844; 1969 edition

Fielden, J.,(introd. Ward, J.T.), *The Curse of the Factory System*, 1836; 1969

Formby, H.,   *The Catholic Christian's Guide to the Right Use of the Christian Psalmody and of the Psalter*, 1846

--   *The March of Intellect; or The Alleged Hostility of the Catholic Church to the Diffusion of Knowledge Examined; A Lecture Delivered to the Members of the Catholic Literary and Scientific Institute in Birmingham*, 1852

Gaskell, E.   *Mary Barton*, 1848, Penguin 1985

--   *North and South*, 1854-5, Penguin 1988

--   *Wives and Daughters*, 1864-6, Penguin 1986

Gaskell, P.   *The Manufacturing Population of England, Its Moral, Social and Physical Conditions, and the Changes which have Arisen from the Use of Steam Machinery*, 1833

Hodgson, W.B.,   *On the Characteristics of the Two Schemes for Public Instruction, Respectively Proposed by the National Public Schools Association and the Manchester and Salford Committee on Education* (Manchester, 1851)

Hulbert, C.,   *The History and Antiquities of Shrewsbury by Thomas Phillips, the Second Edition with a Continuation of the History including the History and Description of the County of Salop*, 2 vols (Shrewsbury, 1837)

--   *Memoirs of Seventy Years of an Eventful Life* (Shrewsbury, 1852)

Kay Shuttleworth, J.P. (ed. Chaloner, W.H.) *The Moral and Physical Condition of the Working Classes Employed in the Cotton Manufacture of Manchester*, 1832; 1970

Four Periods of Public Education as Reviewed in 1832; 1839; 1846 and 1862, 1862 (Brighton, 1973)

--   *Thoughts and Suggestions on Social Problems Contained Chiefly in Addresses to Meetings of Workmen in Lancashire*, 1873

Love, B.,   *Manchester As It Is* (Manchester, 1839; second edition 1842; reprint Manchester, 1971)

LPSA   *A Plan for the Establishment of a General System of Secular Education in the County of Lancaster* (Manchester, 1847).

Ludlow, J.M.,   *Woman's Work in the Church*, 1865

Marsden, J.B.,   *Memoirs of the Life and Labours of the Reverend Hugh Stowell, M.A.*, 1868

Newman, J.H.(introd. Ward, M.),*Apologia Pro Vita Sua* 1864; 1946 edition

Newman, J.H.,   *Sermons Preached on Various Occasions*, 1887

NPSA,   *Education in England and in the United States of North America* (Manchester, 1850)

--   *Explanatory Statement of the Objects of the National Public Schools Association* (Manchester, 1850), a pamphlet

--   *National Public Schools Association for Promoting the*

	Establishment of a General System of Secular Education in England and Wales (Manchester, 1850), a pamphlet
--	*Report of First Annual Meeting* (Manchester, 1851)
--	*Report of the Proceedings* (Manchester, 1851)
Owen, H.,	*Some Account of the Ancient and Present State of Shrewsbury* (Shrewsbury, 1808)

Owen, H. & Blakeway, J.B. *A History of Shrewsbury*, 2 vols (Shrewsbury, 1825)

Phillips, T.,	*The History and Antiquities of Shrewsbury* (Shrewsbury, 1779)
Pidgeon, H.,	*Memorials of Shrewsbury*, n.d.: c.1854?
Pitt, W.	*A Topographical History of Staffordshire* (Newcastle-under-Lyme, 1817)
Prentice, A.,	*Historical Sketches and Personal Recollections of Manchester*, second edition, 1851
Procter, R.W.,	*Memorials of Manchester Streets* (Manchester, 1874)

Ralston, J. & Others, *Old Manchester, A Series of Views* (Manchester, 1875)

Reach, A.B. (ed. Aspin, C.), *Manchester and the Textile Districts in 1849* (Helmshore, 1972)

-- (ed. Ginswick, J.), *Labour and the Poor in England and Wales 1849-1851: The Letters to 'The Morning Chronicle' from the Correspondents in the Manufacturing and Mining Districts, the Towns of Liverpool and Birmingham and the Rural Districts*, 8 vols, 1983: vol.1, *Lancashire, Cheshire and Yorkshire*; vol.2, *Northumberland and Durham, Staffordshire — The Midlands*

Reilly, J.,	*History of Manchester* (Manchester, 1861)
Rodriguez SJ, A.,	*The Practice of Christian and Religious Perfection* (Spain, c. 1606), transl. and publ. in 2 vols by a member of the Society of Jesus (Dublin, n.d. but pre-1852)
Thomson, C.,	*The Autobiography of an Artisan*, 1847
Torrens, W.T.M.,	*Lancashire's Lesson*, 1864
Watts, J.,	*The Facts of the Cotton Famine*, 1866
Waugh, E.,	*Home-Life of the Lancashire Factory Folk during the Cotton Famine*, 1867
Whately, R.,	*Essays on the Errors of Romanism*, 1850
Wiseman, N.,	*Lectures on the Principal Doctrines and Practices of the Catholic Church*, 2 vols, 1836

Worrall, E.S. (transcribed), *Returns of Papists, 1767, Diocese of Chester* (Catholic Record Society, 1980)

ADDRESSES AND ARTICLES:

Beard, J.R.,	'The Lancashire School Plan of Secular Education in Relation to the Bible', *Educational Register of the Lancashire Public Schools Association*, March, 1850
Booker, J.,	'Ancient Chapels of Didsbury and Chorlton in Manchester Parish including Sketches of the Townships of Didsbury, Withington, Burnage, Heaton Norris, Reddish, Levenshulme and Chorlton-cum-Hardy' in *Remains Historical and Literary Connected with the Palatine Counties of Lancaster and Chester,*

Chetham Society, vol.42, 1857

Bremner, J.A., 'Education of the Manual Labour Class', TNAPSS, 1866-7, pp.307-317

Bright, J., 'Address', 23 Oct. 1845, Manchester Athenaeum Addresses 1843-1848 (Manchester, 1875), pp.38-44

Browning, T., 'Middle-Class Education', TMSS, 1862, pp.93-107

Carpenter, C., 'On the Nature of the Educational Aid Required for the Destitute and Neglected Portion of the Community', TNAPSS, 1866-7, pp.348-354

Chadwick, D., 'On the Rate of Wages in Manchester and Salford, and the Manufacturing Districts of Lancashire 1839-1859', Journal of the Royal Statistical Society, 23 (1860), 1-36

-- 'On the Social and Educational Statistics of Manchester and Salford', TMSS, 1861, pp.1-48

Dalton, A., 'Bishop Challoner and Education', Catholic School, 1850, pp.234-236

Danson, J.T., 'On The Area and Population of the Manchester District', THSLC, 8 (1855-6), 165-180

Danson, J.T. & Welton, V.P. & T.A., 'On the Population of Lancashire and Cheshire and Its Local Distribution during the Fifty Years 1801-1851', THSLC, 9 (1856-7), 195-212; 10 (1857-8), 1-36; 11 (1858-9), 31-70; 12 (1859-60), 35-74

Dickens, C., 'Address', 5 Oct. 1843, Athenaeum Addresses, pp.1-8

Disraeli, B., 'Address', 3 Oct. 1844, Athenaeum Addresses, pp.9-24

Fitzgerald, M., The Union with Ireland: Its Social Aspects, TMSS, 1860, pp.30-41

Gallway, S.J., 'A letter on the Proceedings of certain Westminster Magistrates' from 'A Lover of Celt and Saxon', Month, 8 (1868), pp.28-32

Greaves, G., 'Homes for the Working Classes', TMSS, 1861, pp.81-91

Hume, A., 'Remarks on the Census of Religious Worship for England and Wales', THSLC, 12 (1859-60), 1-34

Kay Shuttleworth, J.P., 'Middle Class Education: What Central and Local Bodies are best qualified to take charge of and administer Existing Endowments for Education, and What Powers and Facilities should be given to Such Bodies?', TNAPSS, 1866, pp.330-348

Mercer, J.E., 'The Conditions of Life in Angel Meadow', TMSS, 1897, pp.159-180

Munro, A., 'Our Unemployed Females and What May Best Be Done For Them', TMSS, 1863, pp.25-38

Noble, D., 'Popular Fallacies Concerning the Production of Epidemic Disease', TMSS, 1859, pp.1-22

Oats, H.C., 'Report of the Committee set up by the Manchester Statistical Society to Inquire into the Educational and Other Conditions of a District in Deansgate', TMSS, 1864, pp.1-13

A. Ransome & W. Royston, 'Report upon the Health of Manchester and Salford during the Last Fifteen Years', TNAPSS, 1866-7, pp.454-472

Richson, C., 'On the Agencies and Organization Required in a National

System of Education', *TMSS*, 1855, pp.1-20

Robertson, J.,   'The Duty of England to Provide a Gratuitous Compulsory
                    Education for the Children of Her Poorer Classes', *TMSS*,
                    1865, pp.83-96

Robinson, S.,   'The Education of the Lower Classes of the People: With Some
                    Remarks on the Measure Proposed for Manchester and Salford
                    in 1851', *TMSS*, 1866, pp.52-69

[Anon.]   'Sanitary State of the Cotton Districts', *The Builder*, 20
                    (1862), 840 and 856-860

Simpson, R.,   'The Catholic Church in England in 1859', printed in *DR*, 84
                    (1966), 171-192

Smith, R.A.,   'Some Ancient and Modern Ideas of Sanitary Economy',
                    *Memoirs of the Literary and Philosophical Society of
                    Manchester*, 11 (1854), pp.39-89

Worthington, T.,   'Some Further Remarks on the Homes of the Poor,
                    and the Means of Improving Their Condition', *TMSS*, 1861,
                    pp.92-114

DIRECTORIES:

Duffield, H.G.,   *The Stranger's Guide to Manchester*, 1850 (reprint 1984)
Everett's,   *Manchester Guide* (Manchester, 1840)
Hickman, W. & Burgess, J.T., *The Directory and Guide of Northampton* (1847)
Kelly, W.,   *Directory of Northamptonshire* (Northampton, 1847)
Lowe and Barton's *Manchester Exchange Directory* (Manchester, 1847)
Pigot and Co.,   *National Commercial Directory, Midland*, 1835
Pigot & Slater's,   *Directory of Manchester, Salford and Their Vicinities* 1843
Slater, I.,   *General and Classified Directory and Street Register
                    of Manchester and Salford and Their Vicinities* (Manchester,
                    1845-52 and 1901)
Thom, A.,   *Thom's Almanac and Official Directory* (Dublin, 1857-8)
Wetton, G.N.,   *Visitor's Guidebook to Northampton* (Northampton, 1847)
W. Whellan and Co. Ltd, *Directory of Manchester and Salford* (Manchester, 1852)
White, W.,   *History, Gazetteer and Directory of Staffordshire*
                    (Sheffield, 1834)

MAPS:

Godfrey, G.,   *Old Ordnance Survey Maps* (Gateshead, 1987-8)
Sheet 23,   *Manchester Victoria 1849*
Sheet 24,   *Manchester (New Cross) 1849*
Sheet 28,   *Manchester City Centre 1849*
Sheet 29,   *Manchester (Piccadilly) 1849*
Sheet 33,   *Manchester (Oxford Street and Gaythorn) 1849*
Green, W.,   *A Plan of Manchester and Salford 1787-1794* (M'chester, 1794)
Heywood, J.,   *New Map of Greater Manchester* (Manchester, 1884-5)
Richmond, G.,   *Ordnance Survey Around Manchester Map* (Birmingham, 1883)
Ordnance Survey Map of Manchester, 1849, sheet 104/6, Geography Department,
University of Manchester

NEWSPAPERS/PERIODICALS:

Ashton [and Stalybridge] [Weekly] Reporter
Bolton Weekly Guardian
Catholic Luminary and Ecclesiastical Repertory
Catholic Magazine
Catholic Pulpit
Catholic Times and Catholic Opinion
Dolman's Magazine
Dublin Penny Journal
Freeman's Journal
Harvest
Illustrated London News
Lamp
London and Dublin Orthodox Journal of Useful Knowledge
Lucas' Penny Library
Manchester Courier
Manchester Guardian
Manchester Illuminator and General Catholic Record
Northampton Herald
Northampton Mercury
Prescot Reporter
Protestant Witness
Punch
Rambler
Salopian Shreds and Patches
Shrewsbury Chronicle and North Wales Advertiser
Staffordshire Advertiser
St Helens' Intelligencer [News][paper] and Advertiser]
Tablet

PASSIONIST SOURCES:
Bialas CP, M., (ed. and transl. O'Leary CP, A. and Others), *In this Sign: The Spirituality of St Paul of the Cross* (Dublin, 1984)
Burke CP, E., Mercurio CP, R. and Rouse CP, S. (eds), *Words From The Heart, A Selection from the Personal Letters of St Paul of the Cross* (Dublin, 1976)
Devine CP, P., *Life of Father Ignatius of St Paul, Passionist (The Hon. and Rev. George Spencer) Compiled Chiefly From His Autobiography, Journal and Letters* (Dublin, 1866)
Mead CP, J. (ed.), *St Paul of the Cross: A Source/Workbook for Paulacrucian Studies* (New York 1983)
Regulations to be observed by the Discalced Clerks of the Congregation of the Most Holy Cross and Passion of Our Lord Jesus Christ newly compiled in the fifteenth General Chapter, held in the Retreat of SS John and Paul, A.D. 1827 (Dublin, 1862)
Rules and Constitutions for the Congregation of Discalced Clerks of the Most Holy Cross and Passion of Our Lord Jesus Christ, 1785 (English translation 1852)

Strambi CP, Rt Revd, later St Vincent, *The Life of Blessed Paul of the Cross,
Founder of the Congregation of the Barefooted Clerks of the Most Holy Cross and
Passion of Jesus Christ*, 3 vols, transl. Oratorian Series, 1853
Young CP, U. (transl. and ed.), *Life and Letters of the Venerable Father Dominic
(Barberi) CP, Founder of the Passionists in Belgium and England*, 1926
Young CP, U. (transl. and ed.), *Dominic Barberi in England — A New Series of
Letters*, 1935

SECONDARY SOURCES: BOOKS

A Christian Brother, *Edmund Ignatius Rice and the Christian Brothers*
    (Dublin, 1926)
A Sister of the Congregation, *Light After Darkness: Mother Mary Francis
    (Alice Ingham), Foundress of the Franciscan Missionaries of St
    Joseph, 1830-1890* (Glasgow, 1963)
Addington, R. (ed.), *Faber - Selected Letters*, 1974
Alexander, S., *Women's Work in Nineteenth-Century London: A Study of the
    Years 1820-1850*, 1983
Allchin, A.M., *The Silent Rebellion: Anglican Religious Communities
    1845-1900*, 1958
Allison Peers, E. (transl. & ed.), *The Complete Works of St Teresa of Jesus*,
    3 vols, ninth impression, 1975
Allsobrook, D.I., *Schools for the Shires: The Reform of Middle-Class Education in
    Mid-Victorian England* (Manchester, 1986)
Altholz, J.L., *The Liberal Catholic Movement in England: The "Rambler" and
    its Contributors 1848-1864*, 1962
--   *The Religious Press in Britain, 1760-1900* (Westport,
    Connecticut, 1989)
Altick, R.D., *Victorian People and Ideas* (New York, 1973)
Anderson, M., *Family Structure in Nineteenth-Century Lancashire* (Cambridge,
    1971)
Anson, P.F., *The Religious Orders and Congregations of Great Britain and
    Ireland* (Worcester, 1949)
Anson, P.F. (revised & ed. Campbell, A.W.), *The Call of the Cloister: Religious
    Communities and Kindred Bodies in the Anglican Communion*,
    1964
Appleman, P. & Others (eds), *1859: Entering An Age of Crisis*
    (Indiana,1959)
Archer, J.H.G., *Art and Architecture in Victorian Manchester* (Manchester,
    1985)
Arnstein, W.L., *Protestant versus Catholic in Mid-Victorian England: Mr
    Newdegate and the Nuns*, 1982
Artola CP, A.M., *The Presence of the Passion of Jesus in the Structure and
    Apostolate of the Passionist Congregation*, SPHS, 3 (Rome,
    1982)
Ashmore, O., *The Industrial Archaeology of North-West England* (Manchester,

1982)

Ashton, T.S.,   *Economic and Social Investigations in Manchester 1833-1933:*
                    A Centenary History of the Manchester Statistical Society, 1934
Aspin, C.,   *Lancashire: The First Industrial Society* (Helmshore, 1969)
--   *The Cotton Industry* (Haverfordwest, 1981), limp
Astle, W. (ed.),   *'Stockport Advertiser' Centenary History of Stockport*, 1922
Avery, G.,   *The Best Type of Girl: A History of Girls' Independent Schools*,
                    1991
Axon, W.E.A.,   *The Annals of Manchester*, 1886
Bailey, P.,   *Leisure and Class in Victorian England*, 1978
Barker, T.C.,   *The Glassmakers: Pilkington: 1826-1976*, 1977
Barker, T.C. & Harris, J.R., *A Merseyside Town in the Industrial Revolution:*
                    St Helens 1750-1900 (Liverpool, 1954)
Barnes, A.S.,   *The Catholic Schools of England*, 1926
Barsotti, D.,   *The Eucharist in St Paul of the Cross*, SPHS, 21 (Rome, 1988)
Bebbington, D.W.,   *The Nonconformist Conscience: Chapel and Politics,*
                    1870-1914, 1982
--   *Evangelicalism in Modern Britain: A History from the 1730s to*
                    the 1980s, 1989
Beck AA, Rt Revd G.A. (ed.), *The English Catholics 1850-1950*, 1950
Bédarida, F.(transl. Forster, A.S.), *A Social History of England 1851-1975*, 1976
Best, G.,   *Mid-Victorian Britain 1851-1875*, 1971, Fontana 1979
Bialas CP, M.,   *The Mysticism of the Passion in St Paul of the Cross*
                    (1694-1775): An Investigation of Passioncentrism in the Spiritual
                    Doctrine of the Founder of the Passionist Congregation
                    (San Francisco, 1990)
Binfield, C.,   *George Williams and the Y.M.C.A.: A Study in Victorian Social*
                    Attitudes, 1973
--   *So Down To Prayers: Studies in English Nonconformity*
                    1780-1920, 1977
Black, E.C. (ed.), *Victorian Culture and Society*, 1973
Blundell OSB, F.O., *Old Catholic Lancashire*, 3 vols, 1925-38
Bolster, Sr M.A. (ed.), *Catherine McAuley 1778-1978, Bi-Centenary*
                    Souvenir Book (Dublin, 1978)
Bolton, C.A.,   *Salford Diocese and its Catholic Past: A Survey,*
                    1950 (Manchester, 1950)
Bossy, J.,   *The English Catholic Community 1570-1850*, 1975
Bowden, J.E.,   *The Life and Letters of Frederick William Faber, D.D.*, 1869
Bowers, W.H. & Clough, J.W.(comp.), *Researches into the History of the Parish*
                    and the Parish Church of Stone (Birmingham, 1929)
Bowman, W.M.,   *England in Ashton-under-Lyne* (Ashton, 1960)
Bracken, R.,   *Irish-Born Secular Priests in the Diocese of Salford,*
                    (Manchester, 1984), a pamphlet
Bradley, I.,   *The Call To Seriousness: The Evangelical Impact on the*
                    Victorians, 1976
Branca, P.,   *Silent Sisterhood: Middle-Class Women in the Victorian*
                    Home, 1977

Briggs, A.,   *Victorian People* (Chicago, 1955; paperback 1972)
--   *Victorian Cities*, 1963, Penguin 1968
--   *A Social History of England*, 1984
Brindley, W.H. (ed.), *The Soul of Manchester* (Manchester, 1929;
                      reprint Yorkshire, 1974)
Brovetto CP, C.,   *The Spirituality of St Paul of the Cross and Our Passionist
                      Spirituality as Symbolized in the Fourth Vow*, SPHS, 7 (Rome,
                      1982)
Brown, C.,   *Northampton 1835-1985, Shoe Town, New Town* (Rochester,
                      1990)
Brown, K.D.,   *A Social History of the Nonconformist Ministry in England
                      and Wales 1800-1930* (Oxford, 1988)
Brumhead, D. & Wyke, T., *A Walk Round Manchester Statues*, 1990, limp
Bruton, F.A.,   *A Short History of Manchester and Salford* (Manchester, 1924)
[Burke] CP, E.,   *Hunter of Souls: A Study of the Life and Spirit of St Paul
                      of the Cross* (Dublin, 1946)
Burke, T.,   *Catholic History of Liverpool* (Liverpool, 1910)
Burn, W.L.,   *The Age of Equipoise: A Study of the Mid-Victorian Generation*,
                      1964
Burnett, J. (ed.),   *Useful Toil: Autobiographies of Working People from the 1820s
                      to the 1920s*, 1974
--   *Destiny Obscure: Autobiographies of Childhood, Education and
                      Family from the 1820s to the 1920s*, 1982
--   *Plenty and Want, A Social History of Diet in England from
                      1815 to the Present Day*, third edition 1989, paperback
Butler OSB, C.,   *The Life and Times of Bishop Ullathorne 1806-1889*, 2 vols,
                      1926
Bythell, D.,   *The Handloom Weavers, A Study of the English Cotton Industry
                      During the Industrial Revolution* (Cambridge, 1969)
--   *The Sweated Trades: Outwork in Nineteenth-Century Britain*,
                      1978
Cannadine, D.,   *Lords and Landlords: The Aristocracy and the Towns 1774-1967*
                      (Leicester, 1980)
Cassidy, J.,   *St Ann's Catholic Church, Burlington St, Ashton-under-Lyne
                      1846-1978* (Ashton, 1978), a pamphlet
Chadwick, O.,   *The Victorian Church*, 2 vols, 1966
Chancellor, V.E. (ed. & introd.), *Master and Artisan in Victorian England*, 1969
Chapman, R.,   *Father Faber*, 1961
Chapple, J.A.V.,   *Elizabeth Gaskell: A Portrait in Letters* (Manchester, 1980)
Charles CP, C.,   *Il B. Domenico della Madre di Dio*, (Rome, 1963)̛,
                      a pamphlet in five languages
Cheney, C.R.,   *Handbook of Dates For Students of English History*, 1961
Chinnici OFM, J.P.,   *The English Catholic Enlightenment: John Lingard and the
                      Cisalpine Movement 1780-1850* (Shepherdstown, USA, 1980)
Clapham, J.H.,   *An Economic History of Modern Britain*, 2 vols
                      (Cambridge, 1926-32)
Clarke, A.,   *The Effects of the Factory System*, 1899

Clay, H. & Brady, K.R., *Manchester at Work* (Manchester, 1929)

Clear, C., *Nuns in Nineteenth-Century Ireland* (Dublin, 1987)

Cliff, P.B., *The Rise and Development of the Sunday School Movement in England 1780-1980* (Cambridge, 1986)

Clinch, D., *Manchester's Hidden Gem* (Manchester, 1992)

Cockshut, A.O.J (ed.), *Truth To Life: The Art of Biography in the Nineteenth Century*, 1974

Cohen, S. & Skull, A. (eds), *Social Control and the State* (Oxford, 1983)

Coldrey, B., *Faith and Fatherland: The Christian Brothers and the Development of Irish Nationalism 1838-1921* (Dublin, 1988)

Coleman, B.I., *The Church of England in the Mid-Nineteenth Century*, Hist. Assoc. Pamphlet, 1980

Connell, J., *The Roman Catholic Church in England 1780-1850: A Study in Internal Politics* (Philadelphia, 1984)

Connolly, S.J., *Priests and People in Pre-Famine Ireland 1780-1845* (Dublin, 1982)

[Anon.] *Convent of Notre Dame, Manchester 1851-1951* (Exeter, 1951), a brochure

[Anon.] *Convent of Notre Dame, Northampton 1852-1952* (Exeter, 1952), a brochure

Cook, E.T., *Life of Florence Nightingale*, 1913

Cope, N.A., *Stone in Staffordshire: The History of a Market Town* (Hanley, 1972)

Corish, P., *The Irish Catholic Experience: A Historical Survey* (Dublin, 1985)

Crofton, H.T., *A History of Newton Chapelry in the Ancient Parish of Manchester*, 3 vols, Chetham Society, 1904-5

Crossick, G., *An Artisan Elite in Victorian Society: Kentish London 1840-1880*, 1978

Cruickshank, M., *Children and Industry: Child Health and Welfare in North-West Textile Towns during the Nineteenth Century* (Manchester, 1981)

Cullen, M.J., *The Statistical Movement in Early Victorian Britain* (New York, 1975)

[Curran CP, Sr O.], *Sisters of the Cross and Passion* [publ. anonymously], (Dublin, 1960)

Curran CP, Sr O., *Unless the Grain of Wheat Die ...: Life of Mother Mary Joseph, Foundress of the Sisters of the Cross and Passion*, a pamphlet (Bolton, 1973)

Curtis, L.P., *Anglo-Saxons and Celts* (Connecticut, 1968)

Daly CP, Sr W., *Compassion, A Biographical Sketch of Mother Mary Joseph Prout, Foundress of the Sisters of the Cross and Passion* (privately printed, Ballycastle, Co. Antrim, N. Ireland, 1963)

Daunton, M.J., *House and Home in the Victorian City: Working-Class Housing 1850-1914*, 1983

Davidoff, L., *The Best Circles*, 1973

Davidoff, L. & Hall, C., *Family Fortunes: Men and Women of the English Middle Class 1780-1850*, 1987

Davies, R.E.,   *Methodism*, 1963

Dennis, R.,   *English Industrial Cities of the Nineteenth Century: A Social Geography* (Cambridge, 1984)

Devas SJ, F.C.,   *Mother Mary Magdalen of the Sacred Heart (Fanny Margaret Taylor) Foundress of the Poor Servants of the Mother of God 1832-1900*, 1927

Devine CP, P.,   *The Life of St Paul of the Cross*, 1867; revised 1924

--   *Life of the Very Rev. Father Dominic of the Mother of God (Barberi), Passionist, Founder of the Congregation of the Passion, or Passionists, in Belgium and England*, 1898

Di Bernardo CP, F., *The Mystique of the Passion*, SPHS, 5 (Rome, 1984)

Dolan, J.P.,   *Catholic Revivalism: The American Experience* (Notre Dame, Indiana, USA, 1978)

--   *The American Catholic Experience* (New York, 1985)

Donajgrodzki, A.P. (ed.), *Social Control in Nineteenth-Century Britain*, 1977

Dougherty, P.,   *Mother Mary Potter, Foundress of the Little Company of Mary (1847-1913)*, 1961

Doyle, F.J.,   *The Society of St Vincent de Paul in Manchester: The First Hundred Years 1845-1945* (Manchester, 1945)

Duffy, E. (ed.),   *Challoner and His Church: A Catholic Bishop in Georgian England*, 1981

Dunn, A.J.,   *Frederic Ozanam and the Establishment of the Society of St. Vincent De Paul*, 1913

Dyos, H.J. & Wolff, M. (eds), *The Victorian City: Images and Reality*, 2 vols, 1973, paperback 1976-8

Elkington, G.,   *The Coopers: Company and Craft*, 1933

Elliott-Binns, L.E., *Religion in the Victorian Era*, 1936

Ellison, M.,   *Support for Secession: Lancashire and the American Civil War* (Chicago, 1972)

Evennett, H.O.,   *The Catholic Schools of England and Wales* (Cambridge, 1944)

[Anon.]   *Faithful Companions of Jesus, Salford Diocese, 1852-1973*, 1973, a brochure

Farnie, D.A.,   *The English Cotton Industry and the World Market 1815-1896* (Oxford, 1979)

Fielding, S.,   *Class and Ethnicity: Irish Catholics in England, 1880-1939* (Buckingham, 1993)

Finer, S.E.,   *The Life and Times of Sir Edwin Chadwick*, 1952

Fitzgerald-Lombard OSB, C., *English & Welsh Priests 1801-1914* (Bath, 1993)

Flannery OP, A. (ed.), *Vatican Council II, The Conciliar and Post-Conciliar Documents*, 1981 edition, paperback

Flaxman SHCJ, R., *A Woman Styled Bold, The Life of Cornelia Connelly 1809-1879*, 1991

Flynn, J.M.,   *The Catholic Church in New Jersey* (Morristown, N.J., 1904)

Forrest, H.E.,   *The Old Churches of Shrewsbury* (Shrewsbury, 1922)

Forrestall, J.P.,   *Catholic Bi-Centenary Exhibition Souvenir 1773-1973*, a brochure (Worsley, 1973)

Forster, M.,   *Significant Sisters: The Grassroots of Active Feminism*

1839-1939, 1984

Foster, G.F. (ed.), *Ashton-under-Lyne Centenary 1847-1947* (Ashton, 1947)

Foster, J.,   *Class Struggle and the Industrial Revolution*, 1974

Fothergill, B.,   *Nicholas Wiseman*, 1963

Frangopulo, N.J. (ed.), *Rich Inheritance: A Guide to the History of Manchester*
(Manchester, 1962)

Frazer, W.M.,   *A History of English Public Health 1834-1939*, 1950

Free, F.W.,   *Our Heritage in Parr* (St Helens, 1975), a pamphlet

--   *Our Heritage in Sutton and Bold* (St Helens, 1979), a pamphlet

Frow, E. & R.,   *A Survey of the Half-Time System in Education*
(Manchester 1970)

--   *Chartism in Manchester 1838-1858* (Manchester, 1980)

Gauldie, E.,   *Cruel Habitations: A History of Working-Class Housing
1780-1918*, 1974

Gilbert, A.D.,   *Religion and Society in Industrial England: Church, Chapel
and Social Change 1740-1914*, 1976

Gilding, B.,   *The Journeymen Coopers of East London* (Oxford, 1971)

Gillespie CFC, W.L., *The Christian Brothers in England 1825-1880* (Bristol, 1975)

Gilley, S.,   *Newman and His Age*, 1990

Gillow, J.,   *A Bibliographical Dictionary of the English Catholics from
1534 - The Present Time*, 5 vols, 1885

Giorgini CP, F.,   *St Paul of the Cross, Founder of the Passionists,
1694-1775*, SPHS 4 (Rome, 1984)

-- (ed. & introd.), *St Paul of the Cross: Guide for the Spiritual Animation of
Passionist Life: "The Common Regulations of 1775"*,
SPHS, 2 (Rome, 1984)

Giorgini CP, F. & Others, *History of the Passionists*, 2 vols (Rome, 1987)

Giorgini CP, F. (ed. Papa CP, D.), *The Congregation of the Passion of Jesus*
(Rome, 1988)

Giorgini CP, F. (ed. & introd.) *St Paul of the Cross: The Congregation of the
Passion of Jesus — What It Is and What It Wants To Do,
1747-1768*, SPHS, 1 (Rome, 1982 transl. Rouse CP, S.)

Glover, W. (comp.) & Andrew, J. (ed.), *History of Ashton-under-Lyne and The
Surrounding District* (Ashton-under-Lyne, 1884)

Golby, J.M. (ed.), *Culture and Society in Britain 1850-90* (Oxford, 1986)

Goldstrom, J.M.,   *The Social Content of Education 1808-1870* (Shannon, 1972)

--   *Education: Elementary Education 1780-1900*
(Newton Abbot 1972)

Gordon Gorman, W., *Converts to Rome*, 1910

Graham, F. (comp.),*Lancashire One Hundred Years Ago*
(Newcastle-upon-Tyne,1968)

Gray, R.Q.,   *The Labour Aristocracy in Victorian Edinburgh* (Oxford, 1976)

--   *The Aristocracy of Labour in Nineteenth-Century Britain
c.1850-1914*, 1981

[Greenan] CP, H., *The Preachers of the Passion; or, The Passionists of the
Anglo-Hibernian Province*, 1924

Gwynn, D.,   *The Second Spring 1818-52: A Study of the Catholic Revival in*

England, 1942
--   *Bishop Challoner*, 1946
--   *Lord Shrewsbury, Pugin and the Catholic Revival*, 1946
--   *Father Dominic Barberi*, 1947
--   *Father Luigi Gentili and His Mission 1801-1848* (Dublin, 1951)
Haig, A.,   *The Victorian Clergy*, 1984
Halévy, E., (transl. Watkin, E.I.), *A History of the English People in 1815*, 1924, paperback 1987
Hammond, J.L. and B., *The Age of the Chartists 1832-1854, A Study of Discontent*, 1930
--   *The Bleak Age*, 1934
Hanoteau IEJ, Sr M.E., *Mère Gertrude (Justine Desbille), Fondatrice des Soeurs de l'Enfant-Jèsus De Nivelles 1801-1866* (Nivelles, Belgium, 1985)
Hanson, E.O., *The Catholic Church in World Politics* (Princeton, N.J., 1987)
Harrison, B., *Drink and the Victorians*, 1971
Harrop, S.A. & Rose, E.A., *Victorian Ashton* (Ashton, 1974)
Hartwell, R.M., *The Industrial Revolution and Economic Growth*, 1971
Hatley, V.A., *Shoemakers in Northamptonshire 1762-1911* (N'hampton, 1971)
Hawkins, K.H. and Pass, C.L., *The Brewing Industry*, 1979
Haynes, I., *Cotton in Ashton* (Tameside, 1987)
Heeney, B., *Mission to the Middle Classes: The Woodard Schools 1848-1891*, 1969
--   *The Women's Movement in the Church of England 1850-1930* (Oxford, 1988)
Heginbotham, H., *Stockport: Ancient and Modern*, 2 vols, 1882
Hellerstein, E.O. & Others (eds), *Victorian Women* (Brighton, 1981)
Hempton, D., *Methodism and Politics in British Society 1750-1850*, 1984
Henderson, W.O., *The Lancashire Cotton Famine 1861-1865* (Manchester, 1934)
Hewitt, M., *Wives and Mothers in Victorian Industry*, 1958
Hickey, J., *Urban Catholics: Urban Catholicism in England and Wales from 1829 to the Present Day*, 1967
Higgs, E., *Making Sense of the Census*, HMSO, 1989
Hiley, M., *Victorian Working Women: Portraits from Life*, 1979
Hill, M., *The Religious Order: A Study of Virtuoso Religion and its Legitimation in the Nineteenth-Century Church of England*, 1973
Hilton, B., *The Age of Atonement: The Influence of Evangelicalism on Social and Economic Thought 1795-1865* (Oxford, 1988)
Himmelfarb, G., *The Idea of Poverty: England in the Early Industrial Age*, 1984
Hobsbawm, E.J., *Labouring Men: Studies in the History of Labour*, reprint of second edition 1968
--   *Industry and Empire: The Pelican Economic History of Britain*, vol.3, *From 1750 to the Present Day*, Penguin 1968; 1972 edn.
Hohn, H., *Vocations, Conditions of Admission etc. into Convents, Congregations, Societies, Religious Institutes etc.*, 1912
Holcombe, L., *Victorian Ladies At Work* (Newton Abbot, 1973)
Hollis, P., *Women in Public 1850-1900: Documents of the Victorian Women's Movement*, 1979

Holmes, J.D.,   *More Roman than Rome: English Catholicism in the Nineteenth Century*, 1978

Hopkins, E.,   *A Social History of the English Working Classes 1815-1945*, 1975

Horn, P.,   *The Rise and Fall of the Victorian Servant* (Gloucester, 1986; reprint 1989)

Houghton, W.E.,   *The Victorian Frame of Mind 1830-1870*, 1957

Howe, A.,   *The Cotton Masters 1830-1860* (Oxford, 1984)

Hudson, G.V.,   *Mother Geneviève Dupuis, Foundress of the English Congregation of the Sisters of Charity of St Paul the Apostle, 1813-1903*, 1929

Hughes, P.,   *A Historical Record of St Chad's Parish 1773-1966* (Manchester, 1966), a brochure

Hurdy, P.,   *The Diocese and Cathedral of Northampton* (N'hampton, 1984)

Hurley SJ, M. (ed.) *John Wesley's Letter to a Roman Catholic*, 1968

Hurt, J.S.,   *Education in Evolution: Church, State, Society and Popular Education 1800-1870*, 1971

Hylson-Smith, K.,   *Evangelicals in the Church of England 1734-1984* (Edinburgh, 1988)

Inglis, K.S.,   *Churches and the Working Classes in Victorian England*, 1963; reprint 1964

Irvine, H.C.,   *The Old D.P.S. 1833-1933* (Manchester, 1933)

Jackson, J.A.,   *The Irish in Britain*, 1963

Jay, E.,   *The Religion of the Heart: Anglican Evangelicalism and the Nineteenth-Century Novel* (Oxford, 1979)

--   *The Evangelical and Oxford Movements* (Cambridge, 1983)

--   *Faith and Doubt in Victorian Britain*, 1986

Jay, E. and R.,   *Critics of Capitalism: Victorian Reactions to 'Political Economy'* (Cambridge, 1986)

Jones, D.K.,   *The Making of the Education System 1851-1881*, 1977

Joyce, P. (ed.),   *Work, Society and Politics: The Culture of the Factory in Later Victorian England* (Brighton, 1980)

--   *The Historical Meanings of Work* (Cambridge, 1987)

--   *Visions of the People: Industrial England and the Question of Class 1848-1914* (Cambridge, 1991)

Keenan, D.J.,   *The Catholic Church in Nineteenth-Century Ireland* (Dublin, 1983)

Kelly CP, B.,   *Listen To His Love: A Life of St Paul of the Cross* (Union City, New Jersey, 1985)

Kennedy, M.,   *Portrait of Manchester*, 1970

Ker, I.,   *John Henry Newman, A Biography* (Oxford, 1990)

Kidd, A.,   *Manchester* (Keele, 1993)

Kidd, A.J. & Roberts, K.W. (eds), *City, Class and Culture: Studies of Cultural Production and Social Policy in Victorian Manchester* (Manchester, 1985)

Kidd, A., Roberts, K. and Wyke, T. (eds), *Ancoats: the first industrial suburb*, a special issue of *MRHR*, 7 (1993)

Kilby, K.,   *The Cooper and His Trade*, 1971
--   *The Village Cooper* (Aylesbury, 1977)
Kirby, R.G. & Musson A.E., *The Voice of the People: John Docherty, 1798-1854,*
                      Trade Unionist, Radical and Factory Reformer
                      (Manchester, 1975)
Kirk, N.,   *The Growth of Working-Class Reformism in Mid-Victorian*
                      England, 1985
Kitson Clark, G., *The Making of Victorian England*, 1962, reprinted as
                      a University Paperback 1977
--   *An Expanding Society, Britain 1830-1900* (Cambridge, 1967)
--   *Churchmen and the Condition of England 1832-1885*, 1973
Lacqueur, T.W., *Religion and Respectability: Sunday Schools*
                      and Working-Class Culture 1780-1850, 1976
Larkin, E.,   *The Historical Dimensions of Irish Catholicism*, paperback
                      (New York, 1976; 1984 edition)
Lawton, R. (ed.), *The Census and Social Structure*, 1978
Lee, C.H.,   *A Cotton Enterprise 1795-1840: A History of McConnel and*
                      Kennedy, Fine Cotton Spinners (Manchester, 1972)
Lees, L.H.,   *Exiles of Erin: Irish Migrants in Victorian London*
                      (Manchester, 1979)
Leetham, C.R., *Luigi Gentili, A Sower for the Second Spring*, 1965
Leroy, A.,   *History of the Little Sisters of the Poor*, 1925
Lewis, D.M.,   *Lighten Their Darkness: The Evangelical Mission to Working-*
                      Class London, 1828-1860 (Westport, Connecticut, 1986)
Leys, M.D.R.,   *Catholics in England 1559-1829, A Social History*, 1961
Lloyd-Jones, R. & Lewis, M.J., *Manchester and the Age of the Factory*, 1988
Lockhart, W. (ed.), *Life of Antonio Rosmini Serbati, Founder of the Institute*
                      of Charity, 2 vols, 1886
Longmate, N., *The Hungry Mills*, 1978
Lowe, W.J.,   *The Irish in Mid-Victorian Lancashire: The Shaping of*
                      a Working-Class Community (New York, 1989)
Lown, J.,   *Women and Industrialization: Gender at Work in Nineteenth-*
                      Century England (Oxford, 1990)
McBride, T.M.,   *The Domestic Revolution: The Modernisation of Household*
                      Service in England and France 1820-1920, 1976
McCann, P. (ed.), *Popular Education and Socialization in the Nineteenth*
                      Century, 1977
McClelland, V.A., *Cardinal Manning, His Public Life & Influence 1865-92*, 1962
Machin, G.I.T.,   *Politics and the Churches in Great Britain 1832-1868*
                      (Oxford, 1977)
McIntire, C.T.,   *England Against The Papacy 1858-1861* (Cambridge, 1983)
Mackay, T.,   *History of the English Poor Law 1834 - Present Day*, 1899
McLeish, J.,   *Evangelical Religion and Popular Education*, 1969
McLeod, H.,   *Class and Religion in the Late Victorian City*, 1974
Maclure, J.S.,   *Educational Documents, England and Wales, 1816 to*
                      the Present Day, 1965, fourth edition 1979
Mahood, L.,   *The Magdalenes: Prostitution in the Nineteenth Century*, 1990

Makepeace, C., *Manchester As It Was*, 3 vols (Manchester, 1973)

Malcolmson, P.E., *English Laundresses: A Social History, 1850-1930* (Illinois, 1986)

Malmgreen, G. (ed.), *Religion in the Lives of English Women 1760-1930*, 1986

Maltby, S.E., *Manchester and the Movement for National Elementary Education 1800-1870* (Manchester, 1918)

[Anon.] *Manchester St Vincent de Paul Society Manual, 1854-1929* (Manchester, 1929)

Manton, J., *Mary Carpenter and the Children of the Streets*, 1976

Marcus, S., *Engels, Manchester, and the Working Class*, 1974

Marshall, D., *The English Domestic Servant in History*, Hist. Assoc. Pamphlet, 1949

Marshall, J., *The Lancashire and Yorkshire Railway*, 3 vols (Newton Abbot, 1969-72)

Martin, B., *John Henry Newman: His Life and Work*, 1982; second edition 1990

Masefield, C., *Staffordshire*, 1910, third edition 1923

Mathew, D., *Catholicism in England 1535-1935, Portrait of a Minority: Its Culture and Tradition*, 1936

Mathews, H.F., *Methodism and the Education of the People 1791-1851*, 1949

Mathias, P., *The Brewing Industry in England 1700-1830* (Cambridge, 1959)

-- *The First Industrial Nation, An Economic History of Britain 1700-1914*, 1969

Mead CP, J., *Shepherd of the Second Spring, The Life of Blessed Dominic Barberi CP, 1792-1849*, (Paterson, New Jersey, 1968)

Meara, D., *A.W.N. Pugin and the Revival of Memorial Brasses*, 1991

Menegazzo CP, F. (transl. O'Brien CP, B.), *Il B. Domenico Della Madre Di Dio, Passionista 1792-1849* (Rome, 1962-3)

Messinger, G.S., *Manchester in the Victorian Age, The Half-Known City* (Manchester, 1985, reprint paperback 1986)

Mitchell, J. & Oakley, A. (ed. & introd.), *The Rights and Wrongs of Women*, 1976, Penguin 1979

Moody, T.W. & Martin, F.X. (eds), *The Course of Irish History* (Cork, 1967)

More, C., *The Industrial Age: Economy and Society in Britain 1750-1985*, 1989

Morris, R.J. (ed.), *Class, Power and Social Structure in British Nineteenth-Century Towns* (Leicester, 1986)

Mould, G., *Manchester Memories* (Lavenham, Suffolk, 1972)

Murphy, J., *The Religious Problem in English Education: The Crucial Experiment* (Liverpool, 1959)

-- *Church, State and Schools in Britain 1800-1970*, 1971

Murphy, J.N., *Terra Incognita or The Convents of the United Kingdom*, 1873

Murray, J.H., *Strong-Minded Women*, 1982, Penguin 1984

Musgrave, P.W., *Society and Education in England since 1800*, 1968, 1976 edn.

Musson, A.E. *The Life of Sir William Fairbairn, Bart.*, (reprinted), partly written by himself, ed. and completed by W. Pole, 1877 (Newton Abbot, 1970)

Musson, A.E.,   *The Growth of British Industry*, 1978
Musson, A.E. & Robinson, E., *Science and Technology in the
                    Industrial Revolution*, 1969
Myerscough SJ, J.A., *A Procession of Lancashire Martyrs and Confessors*
                    (Glasgow, 1958)
Neal, F.,   *Sectarian Violence: The Liverpool Experience, 1819-1914, An
                    Aspect of Anglo-Irish History* (Manchester, 1988)
Neff, W.F.,   *Victorian Working Women* (Holland, 1966)
Newsome, D.,   *Godliness and Good Learning*, 1961
Norman, E.R.,   *Anti-Catholicism in Victorian England*, 1968
--   *Church and Society in England 1770-1970* (Oxford, 1976)
--   *The English Catholic Church in the Nineteenth Century*
                    (Oxford, 1984)
--   *Roman Catholicism in England* (Oxford, 1985)
Normoyle, M.C.,   *A Tree Is Planted: The Life and Times of Edmund Rice,
                    Founder of the Christian Brothers*, 1975
O'Dea, J.,   *The Story of the Old Faith in Manchester*, 1909
O'Gráda, C.,   *Ireland Before And After The Famine: Explorations in Economic
                    History, 1800-1925* (Manchester, 1988)
Owen, Mother M., *Mother St Basil, Foundress and First Superior-General
                    of the Congregation of the Poor Sisters of Nazareth*
                    (c.1878; publ. Aberdeen, 1897)
Page, W. (ed.),   *The Victoria History of the County of Stafford*, vol.1, 1908
Pawley, M.,   *Faith and Family — The Life and Circle of Ambrose Phillipps
                    de Lisle* (Norwich, 1994)
Paz, D.G.,   *The Politics of Working-Class Education 1830-50* (Manchester,
                    1980)
--   *The Priesthoods and Apostasies of Pierce Connelly* (New York,
                    1986)
Philip, K.,   *Victorian Wantage* (Wantage, 1968)
Phillips, P.T. (ed. & introd.), *The View From The Pulpit: Victorian Ministers and
                    Society* (Canada, 1978)
Phillips, P.T.,   *The Sectarian Spirit: Sectarianism, Society and Politics
                    in Victorian Cotton Towns* (Toronto, 1982)
Pickstone, J.V.,   *Medicine and Industrial Society* (Manchester, 1985)
Pinchbeck, I.,   *Women Workers and the Industrial Revolution 1750-1850*, 1930
Prochaska, F.K.,   *Women and Philanthropy in Nineteenth-Century England*
                    (Oxford, 1980)
Prothero, I.,   *Artisans and Politics in Early Nineteenth-Century London: John
                    Gast and His Times* (Chatham, 1979)
Purcell, E.S. (ed. & finished De Lisle, E.), *Life and Letters of Ambrose Phillipps
                    de Lisle*, 2 vols, 1900
Purvis, J.,   *Hard Lessons: The Lives and Education of Working-Class
                    Women in Nineteenth-Century England* (Cornwall, 1989)
Reaney, P.H.,   *A Dictionary of British Surnames*, second edition 1976
Reardon, B.M.G.,   *Religious Thought in the Victorian Age*, 1971, paperback 1980
Redford, A.,   *Manchester Merchants and Foreign Trade 1794-1858*

                     (Manchester, 1934)
--   (assisted by Russell, I.S.), *The History of Local Government in Manchester*, 3 vols, 1939-40
Redford, A.,   *Labour Migration in England 1800-1850*, 1926 (revised Manchester, 1964)
Reeder, D.A. (ed.), *Urban Education in the Nineteenth Century*, 1977
Rendall, J.,   *The Origins of Modern Feminism: Women In Britain, France and the United States 1780-1860*, 1985
--   *Women in an Industrializing Society: England 1750-1880*, 1990
Reynders CP, C.,   *St Paul of the Cross: His Spirit and Virtues* (New York, 1960)
Rhodes. J. & Ecclestone, C., *And By Joule's It's Good — Joule's Brewery Bi-Centenary 1780-1980* (Stafford, 1980), a pamphlet
Richter, D.C.,   *Riotous Victorians* (Ohio, 1981)
Roach, J.,   *A History of Secondary Education in England 1800-1870*, 1986
Robbins, K.,   *Nineteenth-Century Britain: Integration and Diversity* (Oxford, 1988)
--   *Protestant Evangelicalism: Britain, Ireland, Germany and America c.1750-c.1950* (Oxford, 1990)
Roberts, J.,   *Working-Class Housing in Nineteenth-Century Manchester: The Example of John St, Irk Town 1826-1936* (Swinton, 1982)
Rose, M.,   *Re-Working the Work Ethic*, 1985
Rose, M.E.,   *The English Poor Law 1780-1930* (Newton Abbot, 1971)
--   *The Relief of Poverty 1834-1914*, 1972
-- (ed.),   *The Poor and the City: The English Poor Law in its Urban Context, 1834-1914* (Leicester, 1985)
Rowell, G.,   *Hell and the Victorians* (Oxford, 1974)
Royle, E.,   *Victorian Infidels: The Origins of the British Secularist Movement 1791-1866* (Manchester, 1974)
Sanderson, M.,   *Education, Economic Change and Society in England 1780-1870*, 1983
Schiefen, R.J.,   *Nicholas Wiseman and the Transformation of English Catholicism* (Shepherdstown, USA, 1984)
Schmiechen, J.A.,   *Sweated Industries and Sweated Labour: The London Clothing Trades, 1860-1914* (Kent, 1984)
Scola, R.,   *Feeding the Victorian City: The Food Supply of Manchester 1770-1870* (Manchester, 1991)
Scott OSB, G.   *Gothic Rage Undone: English Monks in the Age of Enlightenment* (Bath, 1992)
Seaborne, M.,   *The English School, Its Architecture and Organization 1370-1870*, 1971
Sellers, I.,   *Nineteenth-Century Nonconformity*, 1977
Senior, G. & Hennin, G., *St Helens As It Was* (Nelson, 1973; 3rd impr. 1987)
Shapiro, S.,   *Capital and the Cotton Industry in the Industrial Revolution* (New York, 1967)
Sharp, J.,   *Reapers of the Harvest: The Redemptorists in Great Britain and Ireland 1843-1898* (Dublin, 1989)
Shaw, W.A.,   *Manchester Old and New*, 3 vols, 1894

Shelston, D. and A., *The Industrial City 1820-1870*, 1990

Sherlock, R., *The Industrial Archaeology of Staffordshire* (N'ton Abbot, 1976)

Sigsworth, E.M. (ed.), *In Search of Victorian Values* (Manchester, 1988)

Silver, P. and H., *The Education of the Poor: The History of a National School 1824-1974*, 1974

Simon, B., *Studies in the History of Education 1780-1870*, 1960

Simon, S.D., *A Century of City Government: Manchester 1838-1938*, 1938

Sisters of the Church, *A Valiant Victorian: The Life and Times of Mother Emily Ayckbowm 1836-1900 of the Community of the Sisters of the Church*, 1964

Slugg, J.T., *Reminiscences of Manchester Fifty Years Ago* (Manchester, 1881)

S.M.C., *Steward of Souls: A Portrait of Mother Margaret Hallahan*, 1952

Smith, F., *A History of English Elementary Education, 1760-1902*, 1931

Smith, F.B., *The People's Health 1830-1910*, 1979

-- *Florence Nightingale: Reputation and Power*, 1982

Smith CP, J., *Paul Mary Pakenham, Passionist* (Dublin, 1930)

Spencer CP, P.F., *To Heal the Broken Hearted: The Life of Blessed Charles of Mt Argus* (Dublin, 1988)

-- *Elements of Passionist Spirituality, SPHS 29 (Rome, 1992)*

-- *The Role of Symbol in Passionist Spirituality, SPHS*, 30 (ibid.)

-- *As a Seal upon your Heart — The Life of St Paul of the Cross, Founder of the Passionists* (Slough 1994)

Stanley, L. (ed. & introd.), *The Diaries of Hannah Cullwick, Victorian Maidservant*, 1984

Stansell, C., *City of Women: Sex and Class in New York 1789-1860* (New York, 1986)

Steele, F.M., *The Convents of Great Britain and Ireland*, 1921

Stephens, W.B., *Education, Literacy and Society 1830-70* (Manchester, 1987)

Stevens, T.H.G., *Manchester of Yesterday* (Altrincham, 1958)

Stewart, C., *The Stones of Manchester*, 1956

Stewart, W.A.C. & McCann, W.P., *The Educational Innovators 1750-1880*, 1967

Stocks, J.L., *The Victorians* (Manchester, 1941)

Strachey, L., *Eminent Victorians*, 1922

Stuhlmueller CP, C., *Remembrance in the Old Testament, SPHS*, 21 (Rome, 1988)

Sussex, G., Helm, P. & Brown, A., *Looking Back at Levenshulme and Burnage* (Altrincham, 1987)

Sutherland, G., *Elementary Education in the Nineteenth Century*, Hist. Assoc. Pamphlet, 1971

Swift, R. & Gilley, S. (eds), *The Irish in the Victorian City*, 1985

-- *The Irish in Britain 1815-1939*, 1989

Swindells, T., *Manchester Streets and Manchester Men*, fourth series (Manchester, 1908)

Tarn, J.N., *Five Per Cent Philanthropy: An Account of Housing in Urban Areas between 1840 and 1914* (Cambridge, 1973)

[Anon.] *The Cathedral Church of St John the Evangelist, Salford*

1890-1990 (Salford, 1990)

The Dominican Srs, *Stone and the Catholic Revival*, 1949

—   *Lines So Truly Parallel* (Hinckley), 1967

Thernstrom, S. & Sennett, R. (eds), *Nineteenth Century Cities*, 4th printing (Yale, 1974)

Thompson, E.P., *The Making of the English Working Class*, 1963, Pelican 1980

Thompson, E.P. & Yeo, E.(ed. & introd.), *The Unknown Mayhew: Selections from the 'Morning Chronicle' 1849-1850*, 1971

Thompson, W.J., *Industrial Archaeology of North Staffordshire* (Buxton, 1978)

Thomson, W.H., *History of Manchester to 1852* (Altrincham, 1966)

Thureau-Dangin, P. (revised and re-ed.), *The English Catholic Revival in the Nineteenth Century*, 2 vols, 1914

Thurston SJ, H., *No Popery*, 1930

Trevor, M., *The Pillar of the Cloud*, 1962

Tropp, A., *The School Teachers*, 1957

Turner, H.A., *Trade Union Growth, Structure and Policy: A Comparative Study of the Cotton Unions*, 1962

Vanden Bussche CP, J., *Ignatius (George) Spencer, Passionist (1799-1864), Crusader of Prayer for England and Pioneer of Ecumenical Prayer* (Louvain, 1991)

Valenze, D.M., *Prophetic Sons and Daughters* (Princeton, New Jersey, 1985)

Vereb CP, J., *Ignatius Spencer, Passionist, Apostle of Christian Unity*, a pamphlet, n.d.: 1973; reprint 1992

Vicinus, M. (ed.), *A Widening Sphere: Changing Roles of Victorian Women*, 1977

— (ed.),   *Suffer and Be Still: Women in the Victorian Age*, 1980

—   *Independent Women: Work and Community for Single Women, 1850-1920*, 1985

Vidler, A.R., *The Orb and the Cross: A Normative Study in the Relations of Church and State with reference to Gladstone's Early Writings*, 1945

—   *A Century of Social Catholicism 1820-1920*, 1964, paperback 1969

Villers SJ, M., *The Will of God in the Spiritual Doctrine of St Paul of the Cross*, SPHS, 25 (Rome, 1990)

Vincent, D., *Bread, Knowledge and Freedom: A Study of Nineteenth-Century Working-Class Autobiography*, 1981, paperback 1982

Wadham, J., *The Case of Cornelia Connelly*, 1958

Wall, A.G., *The Glory of Aston Hall*, 1963, limp

Walsh, B., *Father Spencer*, a pamphlet, 1981

Walsh, M., *The Tablet, 1840-1990, A Commemorative History*, 1990

Walter, E.V., *The Sense of Ruins: Urban Mythology in Manchester*, 1976

Ward, B., *The Sequel to Catholic Emancipation*, 2 vols, 1915

Ward CP, F., *The Passionists* (New York, 1923)

Ward, J.T., *The Factory Movement 1830-1855*, 1962

—   *The Factory System*, 2 vols (Newton Abbot, 1970)

— (ed.),   *Popular Movements c.1830-1850*, 1970, paperback 1983

Ward, W., *William George Ward and the Catholic Revival*, 1893

Ward, W.,   *The Life and Times of Cardinal Wiseman*, 2 vols, 1897

Ward, W.R.,   *Religion and Society in England 1790-1850*, 1972

Watkin, E.I.,   *Roman Catholicism in England from the Reformation to 1950*, 1957

Wearmouth, R.F., *Methodism and the Common People of the Eighteenth Century*, 1945

--   *Methodism and the Working-Class Movements of England 1800-1850*, 1937

West, E.G.,   *Education and the State: A Study in Political Economy*, 1965

--   *Education and the Industrial Revolution*, 1975

Whelan OSB, B.,   *Historic English Convents of Today*, 1936

White, J.F.,   *The Cambridge Movement, The Ecclesiologists and the Gothic Revival* (Cambridge, 1962, 1979 edition)

Widdowson, F.,   *Going Up Into The Next Class: Women and Elementary Teacher Training 1840-1914*, 1980, paperback 1983

Wigley, J.,   *The Rise and Fall of the Victorian Sunday* (Manchester, 1980)

Willett Cunnington, C., *Feminine Attitudes in the Nineteenth Century*, 1935 (reprint New York, 1973)

Williams, B.,   *The Making of Manchester Jewry 1740-1875* (Manchester, 1976)

Williams, M. with Farnie, D.A., *Cotton Mills in Greater Manchester* (Preston, 1992), limp

Williams, T.J.,   *Priscilla Lydia Sellon*, 1965

Wilson CP, A.,   *Blessed Dominic Barberi*, 1967

--   *Blessed Dominic Barberi CP, Apostle of Unity*, a pamphlet (St Helens, n.d.)

--   *St Paul of the Cross, Passionist*, a pamphlet (Consett, n.d.)

Wilson, J.F.,   *Lighting The Town: A Study of Management in the North West Gas Industry 1805-1880*, 1991

Winter, J. (ed.),   *The Working Class in Modern British History* (Cambridge, 1983)

Wohl, A.S.,   *Endangered Lives: Public Health in Victorian Britain*, 1983

Wolffe, J.,   *The Protestant Crusade in Great Britain 1829-1860* (Oxford, 1991)

Wood., J.F.,   *The Story of Manchester*, 1915

Woodham-Smith, C., *The Great Hunger: Ireland 1845-1849*, 1962

Woods, R., & Woodward, J. (eds), *Urban Disease and Mortality in Nineteenth-Century England*, 1984

Wrigley, E.A. (ed.), *Nineteenth-Century Society* (Cambridge, 1972)

Yates, N.,   *The Oxford Movement and Anglican Ritualism*, Hist. Assoc. Pamphlet, 1983

Young, A.F. & Ashton, E.T., *British Social Work in the Nineteenth Century*, 1956

Young CP, U.,   *Life of Father Ignatius Spencer CP*, 1933

Yuhaus CP, C.J.,   *Compelled To Speak: The Passionists in America, Origin and Apostolate* (New York, 1967)

Zimmern, A.,   *The Renaissance of Girls' Education in England, A Record of Fifty Years' Progress*, 1898

Zubizarreta CP, J.R. *Passionists and the Present-Day Theology of the Cross*,

SPHS 11 (Rome, 1982)

SECONDARY SOURCES: ARTICLES

Ahern CP, B.,   'Remembering the Passion of Christ' in *The 'Memoria*
                     Passionis' in the Constitutions, SPHS, 20 (Rome, 1986), 1-9
Albramson, H.J.,   'Ethnic Diversity Within Catholicism: A Comparative Analysis
                     of Contemporary and Historical Religion', *JSH*, 3 (1971),
                     359-388
Alexander, J.L.,   'Lord John Russell and the Origins of the Committee of Council
                     on Education', *HJ*, 20 (1977), 395-415
Alger, B.,   'Sources for a Life of Alexander Goss, Second Bishop of
                     Liverpool', *NWCH*, 2 (1970), 66-73
Allbut, M.,   'The Directories of Trade', pp.4-6;
Allbut, M. & Broadbridge, S.R., 'The Origins of Stone', pp.1-6 both in *The Stone*
                     Survey, JSIAS, 4 (1973), 1-23
Allen, L.,   'Ambrose Phillipps De Lisle 1809-1878', *Catholic Historical*
                     Review, 40 (1954), 1-14
Ambler, R.W.,   'The 1851 Census for Religious Worship', *LH*, 11 (1975),
                     375-381
Anderson, O.,   'The Political Uses of History in Mid Nineteenth-Century
                     England', *PP*, no.36 (1967), 87-105
--   'Women Preachers in Mid-Victorian Britain: Some Reflexions
                     on Feminism, Popular Religion and Social Change', *HJ*, 12
                     (1969), 467-484
--   'The Growth of Christian Militarism in Mid-Victorian Britain',
                     EHR, 86 (1971), 46-72
Arnstein, W.L.,   'The Murphy Riots: A Victorian Dilemma', *VS*, 19 (1975-6),
                     51-71.
Artola CP, A.M.,   'The Memory of the Passion in the Constitutions' in *The*
                     'Memoria Passionis', SPHS, 20 (Rome, 1986), 11-30
Aspinwall, B.,   'The Scottish Dimension: Robert Monteith and the Origins of
                     Modern British Catholic Social Thought', *DR*, 97 (1979), 46-68
--   'David Urquhart, Robert Monteith and the Catholic Church: A
                     Search for Justice and Peace', *Innes Review*, 31 (1980), 57-70
--   'Before Manning: Some Aspects of British Social Concern
                     Before 1865', *New Blackfriars*, 1980, pp.113-127
--   'Changing Images of Roman Catholic Religious Orders in the
                     Nineteenth Century, *Studies in Church History*, 22 (1985),
                     351-363
Altholz, J.L.,   'Newman and History', *VS*, 7 (1964-5), 285-294
Atkins, P.J.,   'Sophistication Detected: Or, The Adulteration of the Milk
                     Supply 1850-1914', *SH*, 16 (1991), 317-339
Atwood, R.S.,   'The Localisation of the Cotton Industry in Lancashire,
                     England', *Economic Geography*, 4 (1928), 187-195
Bailey, P.,   '"Will The Real Bill Banks Please Stand Up?" Towards a Role

                Analysis of Mid-Victorian Working-Class Respectability', *JSH*, 12 (1979), 336-353

Baines, M.E.,   'Recusancy in St Helens before 1649', *NWCH* 3 (1971), 1-30

Bamber, F.,   '"Owd Bally" Whittaker' in J.A.Roby (compiled and ed.), *Traditions of Lancashire, Past and Present* (Wigan, 1991), pp.19-24

Barker, W.H. & Fitzgerald, W., 'The City and Port of Manchester', *JMGS*, 41 (1925), 11-31

Barnsby, G.,   'The Standard of Living in the Black Country during the Nineteenth Century', *Econ.HR*, 24 (1971), 220-39

Baugh, G.C., Greenslade, M.W. & Johnson, D.A., 'West Bromwich', *VCH Staffs*, XVII (Oxford, 1976), 1-86

Beames, M.R.,   'The Ribbon Societies: Lower-Class Nationalism in Pre-Famine Ireland', *PP*, no.97 (1982), 128-143

Bellenger OSB, A., 'The King's House, Winchester 1792-6', *DR*, 100 (1982), 101-109

Berridge, V.,   'Victorian Opium Eating: Responses to Opiate Use in Nineteenth-Century England', *VS*, 21 (1978), 433-461

Best, G.F.A.,   'The Religious Difficulties of National Education in England, 1800-70', *Cambridge Historical Journal*, 12 (1956), 155-173

--   'Popular Protestantism in Victorian Britain' in R. Robson (ed.), *Ideas and Institutions of Victorian Britain*, 1967, pp.115-142

Bialas CP, M.,   'Fundamentals of our Life' in *Commentaries on the General Constitutions C.P., SPHS*, 16 (Rome, 1987)

Billington, R.A., 'Maria Monk and her Influence', *Catholic Historical Review*, 22 (1936-7), 283-296

Black, J. & Bellenger OSB, A., 'The Foreign Education of British Catholics in the Eighteenth Century', *DR*, 105 (1987), 310-316

Blackwood, B.G., 'Plebeian Catholics in Later Stuart Lancashire', *NH*, 25 (1989), 153-173

Bliss, S.,   'Ecclesiastical Buildings in Staffordshire by A.W.N. Pugin', *SCH*, 22 (1984), 28-44

Bossy, J.,   'Catholic Lancashire in the Eighteenth Century' in J. Bossy and P. Jump (eds), *Essays Presented to Michael Roberts* (Belfast, 1976), pp.54-69

Branca, P.,   'Image and Reality: The Myth of the Idle Victorian Woman' in M.S. Hartmann and L. Banner (eds), *Clio's Consciousness Raised: New Perspectives on the History of Woman*, 1974, pp.179-191

--   'A New Perspective on Women's Work: A Comparative Typology', *JSH*, 9 (1975), 129-153.

Briggs, A.,   'Middle-Class Consciousness in English Politics, 1780-1846', *PP*, no.9 (1956), 65-74

--   'Cholera and Society in the Nineteenth Century', *PP*, no.19 (1961), 76-96

Broadbridge, S.R., 'Occupations in Stone from the Census of 1851', pp.7-8;

--   'The Trent and Mersey Canal', pp.15-17;

--	'The Boot and Shoe Industry', pp.21-22, all *JSIAS*, 4 (1973)
Brook, F.,	'The Trunk Roads', *JSIAS*, 4 (1973), 11-15
Budd, S.,	'The Loss of Faith: Reasons For Unbelief Among Members of the Secular Movement in England, 1850-1950', *PP*, no.36 (1967), 106-125
Callcott, M.,	'The Challenge of Cholera: The Last Epidemic at Newcastle-upon-Tyne', *NH*, 20 (1984), 167-186
Cecily OP & Barbara OP, Srs,	'M. Margaret Hallahan in Staffordshire', *SCH*, 10 (1968), 1-42
Champ, J.F.,	'The Demographic Impact of Irish Immigration on Birmingham Catholicism 1800-1850', *Studies in Church History*, 25 (1989), 233-242
Chapman, S.D.,	'The Cotton Industry in the Industrial Revolution', 1972, second edition in L. Clarkson (ed.), *The Industrial Revolution: A Compendium*, 1990, pp.1-64
--	'Financial Restraints on the Growth of Firms in the Cotton Industry 1790-1850', *Econ.HR*, 32 (1979), 50-69
Charles CP, C.,	'The Origins of the Parish Mission in England and the Early Passionist Apostolate, 1840-1850', *JEH*, 15 (1964), 60-75
Chiswell, A.,	'The Nature of Urban Overcrowding', *LH*, 16 (1984), 156-160
Cockshut, A.O.J.,	'The Literary and Historical Significance of the *Present Position of Catholics*' in I. Ker and A.G. Hill (eds), *Newman After A Hundred Years* (Oxford, 1990), pp.111-127
Colhoun, C.J.,	'Community: Toward A Variable Conceptualization For Comparative Research', *SH*, 5 (1980), 105-29
Collins, B.,	'Proto-Industrialisation, a Pre-Famine Emigration', *SH*, 7 (1982), 127-146
Connell, K.H.,	'Land and Population in Ireland 1780-1845', *Econ.HR*, 2 (1950), 278-289
Connolly, G.P.,	'Little Brother Be At Peace: The Priest as the Holy Man in the Nineteenth-Century Ghetto', *Studies in Church History*, 19 (1982), 191-206
--	'"With More Than Ordinary Devotion To God" - The Secular Missioner of the North in the Evangelical Age of the English Mission', *NWCH*, 10 (1983), 8-31
--	'The Transubstantiation of Myth: Towards a New Popular History of Nineteenth-Century Catholicism in England', *JEH*, 35 (1984), 78-104
--	'The Catholic Church and the First Manchester and Salford Trade Unions in the Age of the Industrial Revolution', *TLCAS*, 83 (1985), 125-160
--	'Shifting Congregations: Catholic Rural Migration in Late Eighteenth-Century Lancashire' in J.A. Hilton (ed.), *Catholic Englishmen* (Wigan, 1984), pp.13-20
Cross, C.,	'The Religious Life of Women in Sixteenth-Century Yorkshire', *Studies in Church History*, 27 (1990), 307-324
Crossick, G.,	'The Labour Aristocracy and Its Values: A Study of

Mid-Victorian Kentish Town', *VS*, 19 (1975-6), 301-328

Cruickshank, M.A., 'The Anglican Revival and Education: A Study of School Expansion in the Cotton Manufacturing Areas of North-West England, 1840-50', *NH*, 15 (1979), 176-190

Currie, C.R.J. & Others, 'Walsall', *VCH Staffs.*, XVII (Oxford, 1976), 143-284

Daniels, G.W., 'The Early Records of a Great Manchester Cotton-Spinning Firm', *Economic Journal*, 25 (1915), 175-188

Davidoff, L., 'Mastered for Life: Servant and Wife in Victorian and Edwardian England', *JSH*, 7 (1973-4), 406-428

Davies, A., 'Saturday Night Markets in Manchester and Salford 1840-1939', *MRHR*, 1 (1987-8), 3-12

Denholm, A.F., 'The Impact of the Canal System on Three Staffordshire Market Towns 1760-1850', *MH*, 13, (1988), 59-76

Dingle, A.E., '"The Monster Nuisance of All": Landowners, Alkali Manufacturers and Air Pollution, 1828-64', *Econ.HR*, 35 (1982), 529-548

Doyle, P., 'A Victorian Bishop on Visitation', *NWCH*, 3 (1971), 87-98

-- 'Bishop Goss of Liverpool (1856-1872) and the Importance of Being English', *Studies in Church History*, 18 (1982), 433-447

Duffy, E., '"Over The Wall": Converts From Popery in Eighteenth-Century England', *DR*, 94 (1976), 1-25

Dutton, H.I. & King, J.E., 'The Limits of Paternalism: The Cotton Tyrants of North Lancashire 1836-54', *SH*, 7 (1982), 59-74

Dyos, H.J., 'The Growth of Cities in the Nineteenth Century: A Review of Some Recent Writing', *VS*, 9 (1966), 225-237

-- 'The Slums of Victorian London', *VS*, 11 (1967), 5-40

Ellinger, B., 'The Cotton Famine of 1861-4', *Economic History*, 3 (1934-7), 152-167

Ellis, A.C.O., 'Influences on School Attendance in Victorian England', *BJES*, 12 (1973), 313-326

Evans, C., 'Unemployment and the Making of the Feminine during the Lancashire Cotton Famine' in P. Hudson and W.R. Lee, *Women's Work and the Family Economy in Historical Perspective* (Manchester, 1990), pp.248-270

Farnie, D.A., 'The Commercial Development of Manchester in the Later Nineteenth Century', *Manchester Review*, 7 (1956), 327-337

-- 'The Cotton Famine in Great Britain' in B.M. Ratcliffe (ed.), *Great Britain and Her World 1750-1914* (Manchester, 1975), pp.153-178

Feltes, N.N., 'To Saunter, To Hurry: Dickens, Time and Industrial Capitalism', *VS*, 20 (1976-7), 245-267

Fielding, S., 'The Catholic Whit Walks in Manchester and Salford, 1890-1939', *MRHR*, 1 (1987), 3-10

Figlio, K., 'Chlorosis and Chronic Disease in Nineteenth-Century Britain: The Social Constitution of Somatic Illness in a Capitalist Society', *SH*, 3 (1978), 167-197

Foster, J.,   'Some Comments on "Class Struggle and the Labour
                   Aristocracy 1830-60"', *SH*, 1-2 (1976-7), 357-366
Frangopulo, N.J., 'Foreign Communities in Victorian Manchester', *Manchester
                   Review*, 10 (1965), 189-206
Freifield, M.,   'Technological Change and the 'Self-Acting' Mule: A Study of
                   Skill and the Sexual Division of Labour', *SH*, 11 (1986),
                   319-343
Gansden, T.,   'Manchester Early Dwellings Research Group', *MRHR*, 2
                   (1988), 37-41
Gatrell, V.A.C.,   'Labour, Power and the Size of Firms in Lancashire Cotton in
                   the Second Quarter of the Nineteenth Century', *Econ.HR*, 30
                   (1977), 95-139
George, A.D. & Clark, S.C., 'A Note on "Little Ireland", Manchester', *Industrial
                   Archaeology*, 14 (1979), 36-40
Giblin, J.F.,   'The Orrell Family and the Mission of St Mary's, Blackbrook in
                   Parr, St Helens', *NWCH*, 7 (1980), 6-19
Gielen CP, H.,   'Solitude: In Search of a Value' in *Reflections on Some
                   Traditional Characteristics of Passionist Christian Spirituality -
                   Part II, SPHS*, 9 (Rome, 1982), 23-36
Gilley, S.,   'The Roman Catholic Mission to the Irish in London 1840-60',
                   RH, 10 (1969-70), 123-145
--   'Protestant London, No Popery and the Irish Poor 1830-60, Part
                   I', *RH*, 10 (1969-70), 210-230
--   'Heretic London, Holy Poverty and the Irish Poor 1830-1870',
                   DR, 89 (1971), 64-89
--   'Protestant London, No Popery and the Irish Poor: II
                   (1850-1860)', *RH*, 11 (1971-2), 21-46
--   'English Catholic Charity and the Irish Poor in London, Part I,
                   1700-1840'; 'Part II, 1840-1870', *RH*, 11 (1971-2), 179-195
                   and 253-269
--   'Papists, Protestants and the Irish in London, 1835-70', *Studies
                   in Church History*, 8 (1972), 259-266
--   'The Garibaldi Riots of 1862', *HJ*, 16 (1973), 697-732
--   'Supernaturalised Culture: Catholic Attitudes and Latin Lands
                   1840-60', *Studies in Church History*, 11 (1975), 309-323
--   'English Attitudes to the Irish in England, 1789-1900' in C.
                   Holmes (ed.), *Immigrants and Minorities in British Society*,
                   1978, pp.81-110
--   'Christianity and Enlightenment: An Historical Survey', *History
                   of European Ideas*, 1 (1981), 103-121
--   'Nationality and Liberty, Protestant and Catholic: Robert
                   Southey's Book of the Church', *Studies in Church History*, 18
                   (1982), 409-432
--   'The Roman Catholic Church and the 19-C Irish Diaspora',
                   JEH, 35 (1984), 188-207
Gilmour, R.,   'The Gradgrind School: Political Economy in the Classroom',
                   VS, 11 (1967-8), 207-224

Gooch, L.,   'Priests and Patrons in the Eighteenth Century', *RH*, 20 (1990), 207-222

Greenall, R.L.,   Popular Conservatism in Salford 1868-1886', *NH*, 9 (1974), 123-138

Greville, M.D. & Holt, G.O., 'Railway Development in Manchester - 1, 2 & 3', *Railway Magazine*, 103 (1957), 613-620, 720-726, 731, 764-769, 804

Grubb, F.,   'Research Note: German Immigration to Pennsylvania 1709-1820', *Journal of Interdisciplinary History*, 20 (1990), 417-436

Hall, B.,   'Alessandro Gavazzi: A Barnabite Friar and the Risorgimento', *Studies in Church History*, 12 (1975), 303-356

Hall, C.,   'The Home Turned Upside Down? The Working-Class Family in Cotton Textiles 1780-1850' in E. Whitelegg and Others (eds), *The Changing Experience of Women* (Oxford, 1982), pp.17-29

Hatley, V.A.,   'Some Aspects of Northampton's History, 1815-1851', *Northamptonshire Past and Present*, 3 (1965-6), 243-253

Haydon, C.,   'The Gordon Riots in the English Provinces', *[BI]HR*, 63 (1990), 354-359

Hennock, E.P.,   'Urban Sanitary Reform A Generation Before Chadwick?', *Econ.HR*, 10 (1957-8), 113-119

Hicks, W.C.R.,   'The Education of the Half-Timer as Shown Particularly in the Case of Messrs McConnel and Co. of Manchester', *Economic History*, 4 (1939), 222-239

Higgs, E.,   'Domestic Service and Household Production' in A.V. John, *Unequal Opportunities: Women's Employment in England 1800-1918* (Oxford, 1986), pp.125-150

--   'Domestic Servants and Households in Victorian England', *SH*, 8 (1983), 201-210

--   'Women, Occupations and Work in Nineteenth-Century Censuses, *HWJ*, (1987), pp.59-80

Hillsman, W.,   'Women in Victorian Church Music: Their Social, Liturgical, and Performing Roles in Anglicanism', *Studies in Church History*, 27 (1990), 443-452

Hilton, B.,   'The Role of Providence in Evangelical Social Thought' in D. Beales and G. Best (eds), *History, Society and the Churches* (Cambridge, 1985), pp.215-233

Hobsbawm, E.J.,   'Artisan or Labour Aristocrat?', *Econ.HR*, 37 (1984), 355-372

Hopkins, E.,   'Working Hours and Conditions during the Industrial Revolution: A Re-Appraisal', *Econ.HR*, 35 (1982), 52-66

--   'Religious Dissent in Black Country Industrial Villages in the First Half of the Nineteenth Century', *JEH*, 34 (1983), 411-424

Horn, P.,   'Mid-Victorian Elementary School Teachers', *LH*, 12 (1976-7), 161-166

Hughes, J.R.T.,   'The Commercial Crisis of 1857', *Oxford Economic Papers*, 8 (1956), 194-222

Illing, M.J.,   'An Early H.M.I., Thomas William Marshall in the Light of

New Evidence', *BJES*, 20 (1972), 58-69

Inglis, K.S., 'Patterns of Religious Worship in 1851', *JEH*, 11 (1960), 74-86

Ingram, P., 'Protestant Patriarchy and the Catholic Priesthood in Nineteenth-Century England', *JSH*, 24 (1991), 783-97

Irvine, H.S., 'Some Aspects of Passenger Traffic Between Britain and Ireland, 1820-50', *JTH*, 4 (1960), 224-241

Jenkins, J.G., 'Footwear', *VCH Staffs.*, II (Oxford, 1967), 230-235

Jewkes, J., 'The Localisation of the Cotton Industry', *Economic History*, 2 (1930), 91-106

Johnson, J.H., 'Harvest Migration from Nineteenth-Century Ireland', *Transactions of the Institute of British Geographers*, 41 (1967), 97-112

Johnson, R., 'Educational Policy and Social Control in Early Victorian England', *PP*, no.49 (1970), 96-119

Johnson, W.J., 'Piety Among 'The Society of the People': The Witness of Primitive Methodist Local Preachers in the North Midlands 1812-1862', *Studies in Church History*, 26 (1989), 343-356

Jones, D.K., 'Lancashire, the American Common School, and the Religious Problem in British Education in the he Nineteenth Century', *BJES*, 15 (1967), 292-306

Jordan, E., '"Making Good Wives and Mothers"? The Transformation of Middle-Class Girls' Education in Nineteenth-Century Britain', *History of Education Quarterly*, 31 (1991), 439-462

Joyce, P., 'The Factory Politics of Lancashire in the Later Nineteenth Century', *HJ*, 18 (1975), 525-553

Keith-Lucas, B., 'Some Influences Affecting the Development of Sanitary Legislation in England', *Econ.HR*, 6 (1953-4), 290-296

Kerr, B.M., 'Irish Seasonal Migration to Great Britain 1800-1838', *IHS*, 3 (1942-3), 365-380

Kerr, D.A., 'England, Ireland, and Rome 1847-1848', *Studies in Church History*, 25 (1989), 259-277

Kidd, A.J., 'Charity Organisation and the Unemployed in Manchester c.1870-1914', *SH*, 9 (1984), 45-66

Kirk, N., 'Ethnicity, Class and Popular Toryism 1850-1870' in K. Lunn (ed.) *Hosts, Immigrants and Minorities: Historical Responses to Newcomers in British Society 1870-1914* (Folkstone, 1980), pp.64-106

Kitching, J., 'The Catholic Poor Schools 1800 to 1845, Part I, The Catholic Poor: Relief, Welfare and Schools; Part II, The Schools: Development and Distribution', *Journal of Educational Administration and History*, June and Dec. 1969, pp.1-8 and 1-12 respectively

Kitson Clark, G.S.R., 'The Romantic Element - 1830 to 1850' in J.H. Plumb (ed.), *Studies in Social History*, 1955, pp.211-239

Kollar OSB, R., 'The Oxford Movement and the Heritage of Benedictine Monasticism', *DR*, 101 (1983), 281-290

Lacqueur, T.W., 'Literacy and Social Mobility in the Industrial Revolution in

England', *PP*, no.64, (1974), 96-107

Lannon, D., 'Rook St Chapel, Manchester', *NWCH*, 16 (1989), 10-17

Larkin, E., 'The Devotional Revolution in Ireland 1850-1875', *American Historical Review*, 77 (1972), 625-652

Lawton, R., 'Irish Immigration to England and Wales in the Mid-Nineteenth Century', *Irish Geography*, 4 (1959), 35-54

-- 'Population Trends in Lancashire and Cheshire from 1801', *THSLC*, 114 (1962), 189-213

Lees, L.H., 'Mid-Victorian Migration and the Irish Family Economy', *VS*, 20 (1976), 25-44

Levine, D., 'Illiteracy and Family Life during the First Industrial Revolution', *JSH*, 14 (1980), 25-44

Lewis, D.M., '"Lights in Dark Places": Women Evangelists in Early Victorian Britain, 1838-1857', *Studies in Church History*, 27 (1990), 415-427

Lister, A., 'The Althorp Library of Second Earl Spencer, now in the John Rylands University Library of Manchester: Its Formation and Growth', *BJRULM*, 71 (1989), 67-86

Lloyd-Jones, R. & Le Roux, A.A., 'The Size of Firms in the Cotton Industry: Manchester 1815-41', *Econ. HR*, 33 (1980), 72-82

Lowe CP, B., 'St Paul of the Cross and Prayer as a Characteristic of our Congregation' in *Reflections on Some Traditional Characteristics of Passionist Christian Spirituality - Part I*, *SPHS*, 8 (Rome, 1982), 3-11

-- 'Poverty as a Characteristic of our Congregation' in *Reflections ... Spirituality - Part II*, *SPHS*, 9 (Rome, 1982), 5-18

Lowe, W.J., 'The Lancashire Irish and the Catholic Church 1846-71: The Social Dimension', *IHS*, 20 (1976), 129-155

Lown, J., 'Not So Much A Factory, More A Form of Patriarchy: Gender and Class During Industrialisation' in E. Gamarnikow and Others (eds), *Gender, Class and Work*, 1983, pp.28-45

McCann, M.A. Sr, 'Religious Orders of Women in the United States', *Catholic Historical Review*, 1 (1921-2), 316-331

McClelland, V.A., The Protestant Alliance and Roman Catholic Schools, 1872-74', *VS*, 8 (1964-5), 173-182

McCready, H.W., 'The Cotton Famine in Lancashire', *THSLC*, 106 (1954), 127-133

-- 'Elizabeth Gaskell and the Cotton Famine in Manchester: Some Unpublished Letters', *THSLC*, 123 (1971), 144-150

McElligot CP, I., 'Blessed Dominic Barberi and the Tractarians: An Exercise in Tractarian Diologue', *RH*, 21 (1992), pp.51-85

McGrath, T.G., 'The Tridentine Evolution of Modern Irish Catholicism, 1563-1962: A Re-examination of the 'Devotional Revolution' Thesis', *RH*, 20 (1991), 512-523

Machin, G.I.T., 'Lord John Russell and the Prelude to the Ecclesiastical Titles Bill, 1846-1851', *JEH*, 25 (1974), 277-295

McKenzie, J.C., 'The Composition and Nutritional Value of Diets in Manchester

	and Dukinfield, 1841', *TLCAS*, 72 (1962), 123-40
McLennan, G.,	'The 'Labour Aristocracy' and 'Incorporation': Notes on Some Terms in the Social History of the Working Class', *SH*, 6 (1981), 71-81
Markus, J.,	'Bishop Blougram and the Literary Men', *VS*, 21 (1977-8), 171-195
Marmion, J.P.,	'Newman and Education', *DR*, 97 (1979), 10-29
--	'The Beginnings of the Catholic Poor Schools in England', *RH*, 17 (1984-5), 67-83
Meacham, S.,	'The Church in the Victorian City', *VS*, 11 (1968), 359-378
Middleton, R.D.,	'Tract Ninety', *JEH*, 2 (1951), 81-101
Miller, D.W.,	'Irish Catholicism and the Great Famine', *JSH*, 9 (1975), 81-98
Monaghan, J.J.,	'The Rise and Fall of the Belfast Cotton Industry', *IHS*, 3 (1942-3), 1-17
Moorhouse, H.F.,	'The Significance of the Labour Aristocracy', *SH*, 6 (1981), 229-233
Moorhouse, H.M.,	'The Marxist Theory of the Labour Aristocracy', *SH*, 3 (1978), 61-82
Morris, K.L.,	'The Cambridge Converts and the Oxford Movement', *RH*, 17 (1985), 386-398
Mounfield, P.R.,	'The Footwear Industry of the East Midlands', *East Midland Geographer*, 3 (1965), 434-453
Neal, F.,	'Liverpool, the Irish Steamship Companies and the Famine Irish', *Immigrants and Minorities*, 5 (1986), 28-61
--	'Manchester Origins of the English Orange Order', *MRHS*, 4 (1990-91), 12-24
--	'A Criminal Profile of the Liverpool Irish', *THSLC*, 140 (1991), 161-199
Neale, R.S.,	'Class and Class-Consciousness in Early Nineteenth-Century England: Three Classes or Five?', *VS*, 12 (1968-9), 5-32
O'Brien, S.,	'*Terra Incognita*: The Nun in Nineteenth Century England', *PP*, no.121 (1988), 110-140
--	'Lay-Sisters and Good Mothers: Working-Class Women in English Convents, 1840-1910', *Studies in Church History*, 27 (1990), 453-465
Oddy, D.J.,	'Urban Famine in Nineteenth-Century Britain: The Effect of the Lancashire Cotton Famine on Working-Class Diet and Health', *Econ.HR*, 36 (1983), 68-86
Ogden, H.W.,	'The Geographical Basis of the Lancashire Cotton Industry', *JMGS*, 43 (1927-8), 8-30
O'Gráda, C.,	'Technical Change in the Mid-Nineteenth Century British Cotton Industry: A Note', *Journal of European Economic History*, 13 (1984), 345-52
O'Higgins, R.,	'The Irish Influence in the Chartist Movement' *PP*, no.20 (1961), 83-96
O'Neill, J.E.,	'Finding a Policy for the Sick Poor', *VS*, 7 (1964), 265-284
O'Rourke, K.,	'Did the Great Irish Famine Matter?', *Journal of Economic*

History, 51 (1991), 1-22

O'Sullivan CP, D., 'Passionist Missions and Retreats in Staffordshire 1842-1850', *SCH*, 18 (1978), 19-22

O'Tuathaigh, M.A.G., 'The Irish in Nineteenth-Century Britain: Problems of Integration', *TRHS*, 31 (1981), 149-175

Patmore, J.A., 'The Railway Network of the Manchester Conurbation', *Transactions and Papers of the Institute of British Geographers*, 34 (1964), 159-173

Paxton, N., 'M.E. Hadfield and the Rebuilding of St Mary's, Manchester, 1844', *NWCH*, 17 (1990), 29-36

Paz, D.G., 'Popular Anti-Catholicism in England, 1850-1851', *Albion*, 11 (1979), 331-359

-- 'Bonfire Night in Mid-Victorian Northamptonshire: The Politics of a Popular Revolution', *[BI]HR*, 63 (1990), 316-328

Percy, J., 'Scientists in Humble Life: The Artisan Naturalists of South Lancashire', *MRHR*, 5 (1991), 3-10

Perkin, H.J., 'The 'Social Tone' of Victorian Seaside Resorts in the North-West', *NH*, 11 (1975), 180-194

Phillips, A.D.M. & Turton, B.J., 'Staffordshire Turnpike Trusts and Traffic in the Early Nineteenth Century', *JTH*, 8 (1987), 126-46

Phillips, P., 'A Catholic Community: Shrewsbury Part I: 1750-1850'; 'Part II: 1850-1920', *RH*, 20 (1990-91), 239-262 and 380-402

Pickering, W.S.F., 'The 1851 Religious Census - A Useless Experiment?', *British Journal of Sociology*, 18 (1967), 382-407

Prochaska, F.K., 'Female Philanthropy and Domestic Service in Victorian England', *BIHR*, 54 (1981), 79-85

Rack, H.D., 'Domestic Visitation: A Chapter in Early Nineteenth-Century Evangelism', *JEH*, 24 (1973), 357-376

-- 'Evangelical Endings: Death-Beds in Evangelical Biography', *BJRULM*, 74 (1992), 39-56

Rainbow, B., 'The Rise of Popular Music Education in Nineteenth-Century England', *VS*, 30 (1986-7), 25-49

Ralls, W., 'The Papal Aggression of 1850: A Study in Victorian Anti-Catholicism' in G. Parsons, *Religion in Victorian Britain*, 4 vols (Manchester, 1988), 4, 115-134

Ravetz, A., 'The Victorian Coal Kitchen and Its Reformers', *VS*, 11 (1967-8), 460-435

Redford, A., 'The Emergence of Manchester', *History*, 24 (1939-40), 32-49

Reynolds CP, Sr A.M., 'Born out of Love', *The Cross*, 67 (1976), 19-20

-- 'Loss and Gain: A Tale of Two Converts', *Clergy Review*, 62 (1977), 308-317

Richards, P., 'R.A. Slaney, The Industrial Town, and Early Victorian Social Policy', *SH*, 4 (1979), 85-101

Rodgers, H.B., 'The Suburban Growth of Victorian Manchester', *JMGS*, 58 (1961-2), 1-12

Rose, A.G., 'The Plug Riots of 1842 in Lancashire and Cheshire', *TLCAS*, 67 (1957), 75-113

Rose, M. & Others, 'Debate: The Economic Origins of Paternalism: Some
        Objections', *SH*, 14 (1989), 89-98

Rose, M.E.,   'Settlement, Removal and the New Poor Law' in D. Fraser
        (ed.), *The New Poor Law in the Nineteenth Century*, 1976,
        pp.25-44

--   'The Crisis of Poor Relief in England 1860-1890' in W.J.
        Mommsen (in collaboration with W. Mock), *The Emergence of
        the Welfare State in Britain and Germany 1850-1950*, 1981,
        pp.50-70

--   'The Anti-Poor Law Movement in the North of England', *NH*, 1
        (1966), 70-91

--   'Settlements of University Men in Great Towns: University
        Settlements in Manchester and Liverpool', *THSLC*, 139 (1989),
        137-160

Rose, S.O.,   '"Gender at Work", Sex, Class and Industrial Capitalism',
        HWJ, 1986, pp.113-131

Rosenweim, B.H. & Little, L.K., 'Social Meaning in the Monastic and Mendicant
        Spiritualities', *PP*, no.63, (1974), 4-32

Rouse CP, S.,   'Solitude in the Christian Mystery and in St Paul of the Cross',
        Reflections ... Spirituality - Part III, SPHS, 10 (Rome, 1982)

Rowlands, M.,   'The Education and Piety of Catholics in Staffordshire in the
        Eighteenth Century, *RH*, 10 (1969-70), 67-78

Rushton, P.,   'Anomalies as Evidence in Nineteenth-Century Censuses', *LH*,
        13 (1979), 481-487

Russell, A.,   'Local Elites and the Working-Class Response in the
        North-West, 1870-1895: Paternalism and Deference
        Reconsidered', *NH*, 23 (1987), 153-173

Scally, R.,   'Liverpool Ships and Irish Emigrants in the Age of Sail', *JSH*,
        17 (1983), 5-30

Scott OSB, G.,   'Fighting Old Battles: The English Benedictine Mission
        1689-1715', *DR*, 98 (1980), 9-24

Seed, J.,   'Unitarianism, Political Economy and the Antinomies of Liberal
        Culture in Manchester 1830-50', *SH*, 7 (1982), 1-25

Sharp, J.,   'Juvenile Holiness: Catholic Revivalism Among Children in
        Victorian Britain', *JEH*, 35 (1984), 220-238

Sharrat, A. & Farrar, K.R., 'Sanitation and Public Health in Nineteenth-
        Century Manchester', *Memoirs and Proceedings of Manchester
        Literary and Philosophical Society*, 114 (1971-2), 1-20

Singleton, J.,   'The Virgin Mary and Religious Conflict in Victorian Britain',
        JEH, 43 (1992), 16-34

Skinner, J.,   'The Liberal Nomination Controversy in Manchester 1847',
        BIHR, 55 (1982), 215-218

Smelser, N.J.,   'Sociological History: The Industrial Revolution and the British
        Working-Class Family', *JSH*, 1 (1967), 17-36

Smith, J.H.,   'Ten Acres of Deansgate in 1851', *TLCAS*, 80 (1979), 43-59

Southall, H.R.,   'The Tramping Artisan Revisits: Labour Mobility and Economic
                     Distress in Early Victorian England', *Econ.HR*, 44 (1991),
                     272-296

Spencer, K.M.,   'Census Enumeration Schedules', *LH*, 11 (1974-5), 155-161

Spencer CP, P.F.,   'Retreat Lecture given to the Passionist Nuns, Daventry,
                     Northants.', 1989, a cassette recording made privately

Stanhope, J.,   'Noticeboard', *MRHR*, 4 (1990-91), 60

Stedman Jones, G.,   'Working-Class Culture and Working-Class Politics in London,
                     1870-1900; Notes on the Remaking of a Working-Class', *JSH*, 7
                     (1974), 460-508

--   'Class Expression versus Social Control', *HWJ*, 1977,
                     pp.163-170

Steele, E.D.,   'The Irish Presence in the North of England 1850-1914', *NH*,
                     12 (1976), 220-241

Stoker, G.J.,   'The Oldest Railway Station in the World: Liverpool Rd
                     Station, Manchester', *Railway Magazine*, 11 (1902), 385-392

Storch, R.D.,   'The Plague of the Blue Locusts, Police Reform and Popular
                     Resistance in Northern England 1840-57', *International Review
                     of Social History*, 20 (1975), 61-90

Stuart, E.B.,   'Bishop Baines and His 1840 Lenten Pastoral', *DR*, 105 (1987),
                     40-59

Summers, A.,   'Pride and Prejudice: Ladies and Nurses in the Crimean War',
                     HWJ, 1983, pp.33-56

Supple, J.,   'The Catholic Clergy of Yorkshire, 1850-1900: A Profile', *NH*,
                     21 (1985), 212-235

Swift, R.,   'Anti-Catholicism and Irish Disturbances: Public Order in
                     Mid-Victorian Woverhampton', *MH*, 9 (1984), 87-108

Taylor, A.J.,   'Concentration and Specialization in the Lancashire Cotton
                     Industry 1825-1850', *Econ,HR*, 1 (1949), 114-122

Taylor, A.J.P.,   'The World's Cities (1): Manchester', *Encounter*, 8 (1957),
                     3-13

Thane, P.,   'Women and the Poor Law in Victorian and Edwardian
                     England', *HWJ*, 1978, pp.29-51

Thompson, D.M.,   'The 1851 Religious Census: Problems and Possibilities', *VS*, 11
                     (1967-8), 87-97

Thompson, E.P.,   'Time, Work-Discipline and Industrial Capitalism', *PP*, no.38
                     (1967), 56-97

Thompson, F.M.L.,   'Social Control in Victorian Britain', *Econ.HR*, 34 (1981),
                     189-208

Tomes, N.,   'A Torrent of Abuse: Crimes of Violence Between
                     Working-Class Men and Women in London 1840-75', *JSH*, 11
                     (1978), 328-345

Trainor, R.H.,   'Anti-Catholicism and the Priesthood in the Nineteenth-Century
                     Black Country', *SCH*, 16 (1976), 19-41

Treble, J.H.,   'The Attitude of the Roman Catholic Church towards Trade
                     Unionism in the North, 1833-42', *NH*, 5 (1970), 93-113

Tropp, A.,   'The Changing Status of the Teacher in England and Wales' in
                     P.W. Musgrave, *Sociology, History and Education*, 1970,
                     pp.193-214

Turner, M.,   'Drink and Illicit Distillation in Nineteenth-Century
                     Manchester', *MRHR*, 4 (1990), 12-16

Underhill, C.H. & Jenkins, J.G., 'Beer', *VCH Staffs.*, II (Oxford, 1967), 242-246

Valverde, M.,   '"Giving the Female a Domestic Turn": The Social, Legal and
                     Moral Regulation of Women's Work in British Cotton Mills,
                     1820-1850', *JSH*, 21 (1988), 619-634

Vincent, D.,   'Love and Death and the Nineteenth-Century Working Class',
                     SH, 5 (1980), 223-247

Vorspan, R.,   'Vagrancy and the New Poor Law in Late-Victorian and
                     Edwardian England', *EHR*, 92 (1977), 59-81

Wach, H.M.,   'A "Still, Small Voice" from the Pulpit: Religion and the
                     Creation of Social Morality in Manchester, 1820-1850', *Journal
                     of Modern History*, 63 (1991), 425-455

Wadsworth, A.P.,   'The First Manchester Sunday Schools', *BJRL*, 33 (1950-1),
                     299-326

Walker, R.B.,   'Religious Changes in Liverpool in the Nineteenth Century',
                     JEH, 19 (1968), 195-211

Walkowitz, J.R.,   'Male Vice and Feminist Virtue: Feminism and the Politics of
                     Prostitution in 19-C Britain', *HWJ*, 1982, pp.79-93

Walton, J.K.,   'The Demand for Working-Class Seaside Holidays in Victorian
                     England', *Econ.HR*, 34 (1981), 249-265

--   '"The Seaside Resort" and Its Rise in Victorian and Edwardian
                     England', *The Historian*, 7 (1985), 16-22

Ward, J.T.,   'Revolutionary Tory: The Life of Joseph Rayner Stephens of
                     Ashton-Under-Lyne (1805-1879)', *TLCAS*, 68 (1958), 93-116

--   'The Factory Movement in Lancashire 1830-1855', *TLCAS*,
                     75-6 (1965-6), 186-210

Ward, J.T. & Treble, J.H. 'Religion and Education in 1843: Reaction to the
                     "Factory Education Bill"', *JEH*, 20 (1969), 79-110

Ward, W.R.,   'The Cost of Establishment: Some Reflections on Church
                     Building in Manchester', *Studies in Church History*, 3 (1966),
                     277-289

Webb, R.K.,   'Working-Class Readers in Early Victorian England', *EHR*, 65
                     (1950), 333-351

Werly, J.,   'The Irish in Manchester 1832-49', *IHS*, 18 (1973), 345-358

Williamson, J.G.,   'The Impact of the Irish on British Labor Markets During the
                     Industrial Revolution', *Journal of Economic History*, 46 (1986),
                     693-720

Wolff, M.,   'Victorian Study: An Interdisciplinary Essay', *VS*, 8 (1964-5),
                     59-70

Wood CP, S.P.,   'The Liturgical Spirit of St Paul of the Cross' in Mead,
                     Sourcebook, pp.246-250

Wright, S.,   'Quakerism and Its Implications for Quaker Women: The

Women Itinerant Ministers of York Meeting, 1780-1840',
Studies in Church History, 27 (1990), 403-414

Yarmie, A.H.,   'British Employers' Resistance to Grandmotherly Government
1850-1880', *SH*, 9 (1984), 141-169

Young, B. & Others, 'Longton', *VCH* Staffs., VIII (Oxford, 1963), 224-246

Zlotnick, S.,   '"A Thousand Times I'd Be A Factory Girl": Dialect,
Domesticity, and Working-Class Women's Poetry in Victorian
Britain', *VS*, 35 (1991), 7-27

UNPUBLISHED THESES

Allan, K.,   'The Recreations and Amusements of the Industrial Working
Class, in the Second Quarter of the Nineteenth Century with
Special Reference to Lancashire', M.A., University of
Manchester, 1947

Charles CP, C.,   'The Foundation of the Passionists in England 1840-1851', 2
vols, a Doctoral Thesis in Ecclesiastical History, Gregorian
University, Rome, 1961

Connolly, G.P.,   'Catholicism in Manchester and Salford 1770-1850: The Quest
for 'Le Chrétien Quelconque'', 3 vols, Ph.D., University of
Manchester, 1980

Doyle, P.J.,   'The Giffards of Chillington, a Catholic Landed Family
1642-1861', M.A., University of Durham, 1968

Evans, C.,   'The Separation of Work and Home? The Case of the
Lancashire Textiles 1825-1865', Ph.D., University of
Manchester, 1990

Fitzgerald, M.E.W., 'Catholic Elementary Schools in the Manchester Area during
the Nineteenth Century', M.Ed., Univ. of Manchester, 1975

Gilley, S.,   'Evangelical and Roman Catholic Missions to the Irish in
London 1830-1870', Ph.D., University of Cambridge, 1970

Glover, D.,   'Roman Catholic Education and the State: A Sociological
Analysis', 2 vols, Ph.D., University of Sheffield, 1979

Gowland, D.A.,   'Methodist Secessions and Social Conflict in South Lancashire
1830-1857', Ph.D., University of Manchester, 1966

Kennedy, S.,   'An Examination of Catholic Education and the Work of the
Catholic Poor School Committee 1800-1888', M.Ed., University
of Bristol, 1977

Linscott, M.P.,   'The Educational Work of the Sisters of Notre Dame in
Lancashire since 1850', M.A., University of Liverpool, 1960

--   'The Educational Experience of the Sisters of Notre Dame de
Namur 1804-1964', 2 vols, Ph.D., Univ. of Liverpool, 1964

Lock, M.A.,   'The Role of Clergymen and Ministers in Ashton, Stalybridge &
Dukinfield, 1850-1914', M.Phil., Univ. of Manchester, 1989

Marmion, J.P.,   'The Educational Principles of Eight Catholic Teaching Orders
from 1550 to Vatican II', M.Ed., Univ. of Manchester, 1978

--   'Cornelia Connelly's Work in Education 1848-1879', 2 vols,

Ph.D., University of Manchester, 1984

Rushton, P.,   'Housing Conditions and the Family Economy in the Victorian
                  Slum: A Study of a Manchester District, 1790-1871', Ph.D.,
                  University of Manchester, 1977
Ryan, P.A.,   'Public Health and Voluntary Effort in Nineteenth-Century
                  Manchester, with Particular Reference to the Manchester and
                  Salford Sanitary Association', M.A., Univ. of Manchester, 1973
Whalley, W.   'An Historical Account of Catholic Education in England with
                  Special Reference to Educational Activities in the Salford
                  Diocese', M.Ed., University of Manchester, 1938
Wilcox, P.J.,   'Problems facing the Catholic Church in trying to provide an
                  elementary education for the Irish in Manchester in the
                  mid-nineteenth century; The provision of elementary education
                  for Roman Catholics in Manchester from about 1840-1900; The
                  contribution of the Catholic Hierarchy to the development of
                  educational facilities for Catholics in the nineteenth century; The
                  maintenance of educational facilities for Catholics from the
                  Elizabethan Settlement of 1559 to the Catholic Emancipation
                  Act of 1829', Four Essays, M.Ed., Univ. of Manchester, 1987
Wilson, F.L.,   'The Irish in Great Britain During the First Half of the
                  Nineteenth Century', 2 vols, M.A., Univ. of Manchester, 1946
Woods, L.,   'John Smith:- A Self-Made Man', St Helens, 1986 (a typed
                  dissertation, St Helens Local Studies Library)
Yuhaus CP, C.J., 'The Passionists in America 1852-1866', Doctoral Thesis in
                  Ecclesiastical History, Gregorian University, Rome, 1962

INDEX